The PRIMORDIA of Bishop White Kennett, the First English Bibliography on America

THE *PRIMORDIA* OF BISHOP WHITE KENNETT, THE FIRST ENGLISH BIBLIOGRAPHY ON AMERICA

Introductory study by Frederick R. GOFF

Pan American Union   Washington, D. C.   Mcmlix

FOREWORD

The discovery of the New World is doubtless, as Gómara so aptly put it, "the greatest thing after Creation . . ."—a fact which seems to be borne out by the great literary output it produced. It was the object of all sorts of writings at the time and immediately afterwards, of which only a fraction have seen the light of day through the printing presses, as continually demonstrated by the discovery of new manuscripts, many of which are being published for the first time.

It is therefore not surprising that Antonio de León Pinelo should feel the urge to compile a catalogue of books about the New World a century after its discovery; and that in England, Bishop White Kennett should undertake a similar project barely a century after the first British settlement in this Hemisphere. To draw a parallel, Bishop Kennett is, in a sense, the Pinelo of the English language.

The Inter-American Committee on Bibliography of the Organization of American States tries to select the person who can best evaluate the documents and works it considers for publication. For this reason, the Committee turned to Mr. Frederick R. Goff, Chief of the Rare Book Division of The Library of Congress, to write the introductory study to this volume. Despite the fact that Mr. Goff is young as bibliographers go, he has already earned a safe place in English-language bibliography of the XVth through the XIXth centuries, with a wide range of publications in the field.

With the appearance of the Bibliothecæ Americanæ Primordia, we have taken a step forward in our efforts to make available to the public certain "bibliographic gems" of difficult access, which to many are known only at second or third hand.

Our purpose, also, is to bring back to life, as it were, some bibliographical works which are forgotten or simply not known today. The continuous flow of current books and periodicals tends to make the old or rare book a thing to be consulted only by bibliophiles, depriving many of first-hand information. The synthesis of a historical period may be magnificently presented in a work which is considered a classic on that period; but, nevertheless, the documents on which such a study is based must be constantly consulted and revaluated if history is to be interpreted in the proper perspective. It is in this connection that original bibliographic guides are indispensable work tools.

The Bibliothecæ Americanæ Primordia is the second volume in a series which began with Pinelo's Epítome. Others will follow gradually, until we have published the complete cycle of the first bibliographies relating to the four main cultural areas in this Hemisphere.

v

We are grateful to Dr. Lawrence C. Wroth, former librarian of The John Carter Brown Library, for determining the first English bibliography on the New World; to Mr. Goff, for his invaluable introductory study to this volume; and, as always, to Dr. Howard F. Cline, Director of the Hispanic Foundation of The Library of Congress, for providing the microfilm of the Primordia *for reproduction purposes.*

Javier MALAGÓN.

Washington, D. C., 1958

Bishop White Kennett and his
Bibliothecæ Americanæ Primordia

by Frederick R. Goff

Engraved by James Fittler A.R.A.

WHITE   KENNETT, S.T.P.

Episcopus   *Petroburgensis*

A.D. MDCCXVIII.

$\mathcal{W}$HITE KENNETT, BISHOP OF PETERBOROUGH (1660-1728)

Bishop White Kennett, churchman, writer, antiquarian and book collector, was born in Dover the year that Charles II was restored to the English throne. After the usual schooling, he was entered in 1678 at St. Edmund Hall, Oxford, from which he was graduated with the degree of B.A. in 1682. He later secured his M.A., and having taken holy orders soon began his career as a churchman, serving as curate and assistant to Samuel Blackwell, vicar and schoolmaster of Buester in Oxfordshire. For a time he was tutor and vice-principal of his former school, St. Edmund Hall. At the age of 40, he was created D.D. on July 19, 1700, the same year that he was presented to the rectory of St. Botolph, Aldgate. He was installed in the deanery of Peterborough on February 21, 1708 and was later consecrated Bishop of Peterborough at Lambeth on November 9, 1718. Ten years later, at the age of 68, he died. He was buried in Peterborough Cathedral, where a marble monument was erected to his memory.

Briefly, in fact too briefly stated, these are the salient dates in the Bishop's chronology. But he cannot be dismissed in such a cavalier manner, for his distinguished life was a record of accomplishment. From the time he was a young student at Oxford his pen was seldom idle. His first work, written when he was 20, was published anonymously in 1681 with the title *A Letter from a Student at Oxford to a Friend in the Country, concerning the approaching Parliament, in vindication of His Majesty, the Church of England, and the University* (Wing K 301). This pamphlet "gave grave Distaste to the factious Party of the House of Commons, who wou'd have endeavour'd to find out the Author, and have him punish'd, had not they been suddenly dissolv'd." This incident provoked Kennett's second piece, a broadside poem entitled *To Mr. E. L. on his Majestie's dissolving the late Parliament at Oxon, March 28, 1681.* (Wing K 305). In 1683, at the age of 23, he published a translation of Erasmus' *Moriae Encomium,* entitled *Witt against Wisdom, or a Panegyrick upon Folly* (Wing E 3215). Actually, this had been undertaken by "Way of Exercise" at the instigation of his tutor, Mr. Allam, who arranged for the publication through a bookseller in Oxford. A similar exercise was Kennett's translation of a panegyric by Pliny with the title *An Address of Thanks to a good Prince, presented in the Panegyrick of Pliny, upon Trajan, the best of Roman Emperors* (Wing P 2573); this was published at Oxford in 1685, also at the instigation of his tutor, and enjoyed three printings. Kennett prepared his translation with a "highflown" preface in which he expressed his loyalty to the throne at that time occupied, but not for long, by James II. He quickly modified his views regarding the Jacobites and commenced a series of sermons against "popery." He first opposed and later supported the Revolution of 1688, thereby exposing himself to much calumny from former friends who called him "Weathercock Kennett."

He was to expose himself to renewed attacks from his Jacobite enemies in 1706, at the time the third volume of the *Compleat History of England* appeared; Bishop Kennett had been induced by the booksellers to write this third continuation volume covering the years from the death of Charles II to the time of Queen Anne. The published denunciations which this evoked led, however, to his being appointed chaplain in ordinary to Her Majesty.

During the intervening years, Kennett's historical and antiquarian researches had won him some reputation among English scholars. He had undertaken the study of Anglo-Saxon and other northern tongues; he had published certain topographical studies, of which the most important was the *Parochial Antiquities, attempted in the History of Ambrosden, Burcester, and other adjacent Parts, in the Counties of Oxford and Bucks,* printed at Oxford in 1695 (Wing K 302).

The first of his innumerable sermons to be published appeared in the same year. Called *The Righteous taken away from the Evil to come, apply'd to the Death of Queen Mary* (Wing K 303), this sermon had been preached in St. Martin's Church in Oxford on January 20, 1694.

In this present study of Bishop Kennett, interesting as his career was as an ecclesiastic, we are primarily interested in his works as an antiquarian and as a book collector. As an original member of the Society for the Propagation of the Gospel, Bishop Kennett assembled an extraordinary collection of original source materials with the ultimate purpose in mind of composing a history of the propagation of Christianity in the American colonies. The project never materialized, and he decided to present the collection to the Society. Since the body of this paper will describe this collection in detail, we need only mention it here. It should be recalled, however, that he also formed another collection of books and manuscripts which he presented to a library he founded at Peterborough. Comprising about fifteen hundred books and tracts, this library is now maintained in the chapel over the west porch of the Cathedral.

Unlike his American library, no printed catalogue was prepared, but there apparently still exists a manuscript catalogue subscribed: *Index librorum aliquot vetustorum quos in commune bonum congessit W. K., Decan. Petriburg. 1712.* "Brought together for the common good"—what an appropriate motto for the learned and distinguished Bishop. Before taking leave of our subject in this précis of his life and writings, we cannot forbear from quoting a paragraph from the Rev. William Newton's biography which in a few words epitomizes Bishop Kennett's humanity, his understanding, and his generosity:

> "His good Will and Charity to Mankind in general, was conspicuous in the indefatigable Labours he sustain'd to promote the Interest of Religion and Learning, and every good Design. Far from engrossing any Sort of Knowledge to himself, he was exceedingly free and communicative and improving, to all he convers'd with, or that, far or near, desir'd his Assistance and Advice."

II

BISHOP KENNETT'S LIBRARY OF AMERICANA

The Society for the Propagation of the Gospel in Foreign Parts was established in 1701 through the Charter executed by William III on June 16 of that year. This Charter incorporated the Archbishop of Canterbury and 93 others as "one Body Politick and Corporate, in Deed and in Name, by the Name of, The Society for the Propagation of the Gospel in Foreign Parts." Among the 93 others who were nominated original members of this society the name of White Kennett appears as one of 12 Doctors in Divinity. Bishop Kennett refers to this honor in his dedicatory letter addressed to the Society and prefixed to his *Bibliothecæ Americanæ Primordia. An Attempt Towards laying the Foundation of an American Library, In several Books, Papers, and Writings, Humbly given to the Society for Propagation of the Gospel in Foreign Parts, For the Perpetual Use and Benefit of their Members, their Missionaries, Friends, Correspondents, and Others concern'd in the Good Design of Planting and Promoting Christianity within Her Majesties Colonies and Plantations in the West-Indies* (London: Printed for J. Churchill, at the Black Swan in Pater-Noster-Row, 1713). As this rather lengthy transcription of the title page indicates, Bishop Kennett was presenting his library for the perpetual use of the Society. In his dedicatory letter alluded to above he tells us in more detail the circumstances which led to its formation. He wrote:

> "The better to discharge my Trust, I had occasion to pick up several Tracts and Papers relating to the General Subject of the Propagation of the Gospel, Conversion of Infidels, Institution of the College at Rome *de propaganda Fide,* Missions of the Monks and Jesuites, Methods of the Inquisition, etc. But more especially to the particular Affairs of *AMERICA,* the first Discovery of those Regions sufficient to be called a NEW WORLD, the several Expeditions and Voyages made to every Coast and Port and River, the Advances and Settlements there made, the Tyranny and Cruelty of the *Spaniards* in *MEXICO* and *PERU* . . . Above All, I sought for the Rélations and Journalls of our own Countrymen upon those Seas and Coasts, their Discoveries and Observations, their Settlement of Plantations and Colonies, their Improvements in Trade and Strength, their Conversation with the Natives, and their Endeavours to bring them to Civility and Religion."

We have intentionally allowed Bishop Kennett to describe the circumstances which led to the formation of his library since this text will be evaluated in some detail later on in this presentation.

Before proceeding further it should be stated, as it has previously been pointed out by earlier bibliographers, that this catalogue is in fact the earliest ever made devoted exclusively to the subject of Americana, with the exception of Antonio Rodríguez de León Pinelo's *Epítome de la biblioteca Oriental i Occidental, Náutica i Geográfica* (Madrid, Juan González, 1629).[1] The *Epítome,* on the one hand, in the section devoted to "Biblioteca Occidental," is confined essentially to Spanish and Portuguese Americana, whereas the Kennett catalogue is devoted largely to publications of his "own Countrymen." Thus, the two works complement one another. León Pinelo's *Epítome* should be regarded as a *catalogue raisonné,* for it attempted to include American source materials wherever found and did not represent, as did Bishop Kennett's catalogue, the contents of a single specialized collection.

The five or six English works mentioned by Pinelo include, however, certain outstanding rarities such as Thomas Harriot's *A Brief and True Report of the New Found Land of Virginia* (London, 1588), Ralph Hamor's *A True Discourse of the Present State of Virginia* (London, 1615), Thomas Ashley's translation of Lucas J. Wagenaer's *The Mariners Mirrour* (London, 1588), Thomas Hood's *The Mariners Guide* (London, 1596), and accounts of Sir Francis Drake's voyage during the year 1577, and the later voyages of 1586 and 1596. Pinelo very likely is referring here to Richard Hakluyt's *The Principal Navigations, Voiages, Traffiques and Discoveries of the English Nation* (London, 1598-1600), which devoted considerable attention to these Drake voyages.

Bishop Kennett's library, which with several gifts from other individuals comprised some 1216 books, broadsides and manuscripts, did not possess copies of any of these, although a later edition of Hood's *The Mariners Guide,* printed in 1620 with William Bourne's *A Regiment for the Sea,* is present. Also, there is recorded a copy of the 1589 edition of Hakluyt's *The Principall Navigations, Voiages and Discoveries of the English Nation;* one of the analytical entries in the catalogue extracted from this edition of Hakluyt appears on page 28 and refers to Harriot's *A Brief and True Report of the New Found Land of Virginia,* which, as the catalogue indicates, commences on page 748 of the volume.

One of the chief interests in Kennett's bibliography is the presence of literally hundreds of such analytical entries. In addition to the analysis of Hakluyt, similar treatment has been given to Samuel Purchas' *His Pilgrimes in Five Bookes* (London, 1626), the gift of Col. Francis Nicholson, "Governour

[1] See *El "Epítome" de Pinelo, Primera Bibliografía del Nuevo Mundo.* Estudio preliminar de Agustín Millares Carlo. Washington, D. C., Unión Panamericana, 1958.

of Nova Scotia, and her Majesties General in the *West-Indies*"; John Smith's *Generall Historie of Virginia, New England, and the Summer Isles* (London, 1627); Baron Lahontan's *New Voyages to North America* (London, 1703); a 1704 London edition of *A Collection of Voyages and Travels,* which incidentally was also the gift of Col. Francis Nicholson; and several other collected works.

To return for a moment to oustanding early English books, the Kennett Library contained two editions of John Frampton's translation of Dr. Nicolas Monardes' famous work entitled, in the London edition of 1577, *Of the thynges that are brought from the occidental Indies,*[2] and in the later London edition of 1596, *Joyfull Newes out of the Newe-Found-World.* The earliest of the 114 titles, however, which belong to the period of early English printing prior to 1641, covered by the *Short Title Catalogue,* is the 1549 edition of *The Historye of Italye* by William Thomas, which possesses no American interest whatsoever. But there is more than sufficient compensation in the numerous early titles of English Americana represented by such works as *Virginia richly valued* (1609), written by a "Portugal Gentleman of Elvas"; *A treatyse of the Newe India* (London, 1553), a translation by Richard Eden of a portion of Sebastian Münster's *Cosmographia universalis,* represented in only three American collections, namely the John Carter Brown Library, the New York Public Library, and the William L. Clements Library; and Eden's later translation of Martín Cortés' *The Arte of Navigation* (London, 1572). Other important early works on the subject of navigation include William Cunningham's *The Cosmographical Glasse* (London, 1559); Pedro de Medina's *L'Art de Naviguer* in two editions, Lyon, 1554 and Rouen, 1633; William Barlow's *The Navigators Supply* (London, 1597); *The true Honor of Navigation and Navigators* (London, 1618); and *A Regiment for the Sea* (London, 1620), by William Bourne, which has already been mentioned.

In a more strictly chronological presentation, we record André Thevet's *The New found Worlde or Antarticke* (London, 1568); Lopes de Castanheda's *The first Booke of the Historie of the Discoverie of the East Indias* (London, 1582), a translation from the original Portuguese by Nicholas Lichefield; *The Observations of Sir Richard Hawkins in his Voiage into the South Seas, 1593* (London, 1622); Delgadillo de Avellaneda's *A Libell of Spanish Lies* (London, 1596), an English account of the naval battle between the Spanish and English in the West Indies and the subsequent death there of Sir Francis Drake. Other equally interesting and important titles relating to this dis-

---

[2] This appears to be a made-up title which suggests that the copy described probably lacked its title page.

tinguished English circumnavigator are Philip Nichols' *Sir Francis Drake Revived* (London, 1626) "set forth by . . . his Nephew" and namesake, who was responsible for the writing of a related book entitled *The World Encompassed by Sir Francis Drake* (London, 1628). An important English book in the early history of French America is *Nova Francia: Or the Description of that Part of New France, which is one Continent with Virginia* (London, 1609), a translation undertaken by Pierre Erondelle, acting at the suggestion of Hakluyt, of a portion of Lescarbot's *Histoire de la Nouvelle France.* A choice group of these early English books not previously mentioned relates more specifically to English-speaking North America, *e.g.* John Smith's *A Map of Virginia* (Oxford, 1612) and his later more extensive work *The Generall Historie of Virginia, New England, and the Summer Isles* (London, 1627), a later issue of the first edition of 1624 which, as previously indicated, was carefully analyzed; *An Historicall Discoverie and Relation of the English Plantations in New England* (London, 1627), a possibly unique copy now in the British Museum of one of the earliest accounts of the settlement of Plymouth; Richard Whitbourne's *A Discourse and Discovery of New-found-land* (London, 1622); the two earliest editions of the first detailed account of Massachusetts, William Wood's *New England's Prospect* (London, 1634 *and* 1635), and Luke Fox's *North-West Foxe, or Foxe from the North-West Passage* (London, 1635), "one of the most important documents in the history of Arctic explorations." There were few manuscripts in the learned Bishop's collection, but one of more than usual interest was a holograph letter written at *"James Citie in Virginia* the 27th *May, Anno* 1634," by Sir John Harvey, Colonial Governor of that colony. Addressed to the Board of Treasurers of the Virginia Company in London, the text relates to the "noble Undertakings of the Lord *Baltimore,* in seating himself and his Associates upon that Tract of Ground, now called *Mary-Land.*"

The Kennett Library possessed the two earliest editions of Thomas Morton's satirical writing on the early settlers of Plymouth and Massachusetts entitled *New English Canaan; or New Canaan;* one was printed at Amsterdam by Jacob Frederick Stam in 1637, and the other, an undated English edition most probably unique, was printed for Charles Greene about the same time. Virtually all of the foregoing titles belong to the period of early English printing covered by A. W. Pollard and G. R. Redgrave's *A Short-Title Catalogue of Books Printed in England . . . 1475-1640* (London, 1926). With the chronological arrangement of the 1713 catalogue, it is relatively easy to spot them, and this selection is made even easier by the fact that the printer had set the majority of these titles in English black-letter.

There are, of course, important English titles for the latter decades of the seventeenth century, but there are not quite so many of these, although several appear to be of equal if not greater importance than those that have been described. Among these, mention should be made of Thomas Lechford's *New England's First Fruits* (London, 1643); Roger Williams' *A Key into the Language of America* (London, 1643), not one of the Bishop's books but the gift of the Rev. Robert Watts, who prepared the 224-page index to the 1713 catalogue; and John Cotton's *The Bloudy Tenent Washed and made White in the Bloud of the Lamb* (London, 1647), written in reply to an earlier pamphlet of Roger Williams of similar title but not in the Kennett Library. Cotton's outpouring provoked another reply from Williams' facile pen and a copy was in Kennett's collection; entitled *The Bloody Tenent yet more Bloody,* this further discussion of Roger Williams' views on liberty of conscience was published at London in 1652. Not unrelated to these expressions pro and con on the doctrine of toleration is Nathaniel Ward's *The Simple Cobler of Aggawam in America,* written while the author was residing in New England in 1645, but not printed until after he returned to London in 1647. The beginning pages of this book, described by Lawrence C. Wroth in his introduction to a facsimile edition published in 1937 as "the pleasantest . . . ever written by a Puritan," are strongly anti-toleration in tone, for Ward "detested . . . Tolerations of divers Religions." In this prose satire which occupies such an important place in early American literature, Mr. Wroth has pointed out that the anti-toleration section falls into a relatively unimportant position when considered in conjunction with its plea to Presbyterians and Independents to compromise, and its plea to King and people to come together once more in love and mutual confidence.

Nathaniel Ward is the author of the address "To the Reader" in Thomas Shepard's *The Day-Breaking, if not the Sun-Rising of the Gospel with the Indians in New-England,* also printed at London in 1647. This short pamphlet of 26 pages is a valued source for information relating to the Indians of New England; as such, it is the second of the so-called "Eliot's Indian Tracts," a series of eleven narratives in all, published by the Corporation for the Promoting and Propagating the Gospel of Jesus Christ in New England and the Company which succeeded it. It is not at all surprising that the learned Bishop had secured for his library no less than ten of the eleven Eliot Indian Tracts, namely:

1. *New England's First Fruits.* London, 1643.
2. *The Day-Breaking; if not the Sun-Rising of the Gospel with the Indians in New-England,* by Thomas Shepard *or* John Wilson. London, 1647.

3. *The clear Sunshine of the Gospel breaking forth upon the Indians in New England,* by Thomas Shepard. London, 1648.
4. *The Glorious Progress of the Gospel amongst the Indians in New England,* published by Edward Winslow. London, 1649.
5. *The Light appearing more and more towards the perfect day,* published by Henry Whitfield. London, 1651.
6. *Strength out of Weakness; or a glorious Manifestation of the farther progress of the Gospel among the Indians in New-England,* published by Henry Whitfield. London, 1652.
7. *Tears of Repentance: Or a further Narrative of the Progress of the Gospel amongst the Indians in New-England,* related by Mr. Eliot and Mr. Mayhew. London, 1653.
8. *A late and further Manifestation of the Progress of the Gospel amongst the Indians in New-England,* related by Mr. John Eliot. London, 1655.
9. [*A further account of the progress*] *Of the Gospel amongst the Indians in New-England, being a Relation of the Confessions made by several Indians . . . in order to their Admission into Church-Fellowship,* by Mr. John Eliot. London, 1660.
10. *A Brief Narrative of the Progress of the Gospel amongst the Indians in New-England in the Year 1670,* given in by the Reverend Mr. John Eliot. London, 1671.

Another of the significant books of this period relating to the same locale is a copy of *New England's Jonas cast up at London* by John Child, a work printed in 1647, to which we are indebted for the earliest contemporary reprint of "The Freeman's Oath," the first issue of the press established at Cambridge, Massachusetts, in 1639; unhappily, no copy of the original printed broadside text has ever been located.

We are not unmindful of the fact that thus far no mention has been made of *A Letter from William Penn Proprietary and Governour of Pensylvania in America to the Committee of the Free Society of Traders of that Province residing in London* (London, 1683); *A Brief Account of the Province of East-Jersey in America. Pulished* (sic) *by the present propriators* (London, 1682), one of three surviving copies of the third of the series of "Scottish Proprietors' Tracts"; the fourth pamphlet in the same series, equally rare, entitled *Proposals by the Proprietors of East-Jersey in America, for the Building of a Town on Ambo-Point* (London, 1682); and *The Fundamental Constitutions of Carolina,* in two editions (London, 1669 and 1689). Nor, for that matter, has any mention been made of the seven pamphlets of George Keith relating to his differences with the Quakers in Pennsylvania. In spite of many omissions, however, this seems a logical point to digress, for an interval, to a discussion of the early books printed in America that found their way eastward across the Atlantic Ocean to the Bishop's library. Earliest in point of time is a copy of the 1649 edition of *A Plat-Form of Church Discipline gathered out of the word of God,* printed by Samuel Green at Cambridge. The earliest known book from the press of Samuel Green, this is also the first edition of Richard

Mather's celebrated Cambridge Platform which embodies the ecclesiastical policy of New England Congregationalism. But six copies appear to have survived of this rather scarce production of the New England press, which is known in two issues. The White Kennett copy carrying in the imprint the statement "Printed by *S. G.* at *Cambridge*" rather than "Printed at *Cambridge* by *S.G.*" now reposes on one of the shelves at the Henry E. Huntington Library in San Marino, California.

On page 109 of the *Bibliothecæ Americanæ Primordia,* a somewhat baffling entry appears under the year 1657. The full title reads: *The Life and Death of that deservedly Famous Mr. John Cotton, the late Reverend Teacher of the Church of Christ at Boston in New England. Collected out of the Writings and Information of the Reverend Mr. John Davenport, Pastor of the Church at Newhaven, the Reverend Mr. Samuel Whiting, Pastor of the Church at Lynne, the pious Widow of the Deceased, and others; And compiled by his unworthy Successor. Boston, Novemb. 6, 1657. 4to. p. 51.* Is this the edition described but not located by Joseph Sabin's *A Dictionary of Books relating to America,* Volume XIII, number 55885? Sabin gives the imprint as *"Cambridge: Printed by S. Green. 1657"* and supplies the pagination of 56 pages. Since Charles Evans in his bibliography of early books printed in the United States contains no entry for any such biographical work under 1657, it seems not unlikely that Sabin, following the entry in the Kennett catalogue, created a ghost. But if this is so, why did the Kennett catalogue distinguish this entry from the subsequent entry of similar content also described as a quarto of 51 pages: *Abel being dead yet speaketh; Or, The Life and Death of that deservedly Famous Man of God Mr. John Cotton, late Teacher of the Church of Christ at BOSTON in New-England. By John Norton, Teacher of the same Church. London, Printed by Tho. Newcomb, 1658. [Ex dono Reverendi viri Gershomi Rawlins.]* (*Cf.* Sabin, *op. cit.,* 55881)? It is our conviction after an examination of this last, that the entries actually duplicate each other; the former seems to have been an imperfect copy lacking the title page or a major portion of it and the supplementary 5 unnumbered pages of the publisher's advertisements at the end. The evidence which seems most incontrovertible in laying the ghost is the text found on page 51 which parallels so closely the entry in the catalogue:

Collected out of the writings and information

OF {
The Reverend Mr. John Davenport, Pastor of the Church at New-Haven.
The Reverend Mr. Samuel Whiting, Pastor of the Church at Lynne.
The Pious Widow of the Deceased and others.

And compiled by his unworthy Successor,
Qui ——————— ———————
A longè sequitur vestigia semper adorans.
Boston, Novemb. 6, 1657.

No problem of identification exists regarding the other early American imprints, for they are well documented. Next in point of time to the Platform of 1649 is a copy of Richard Mather's and Jonathan Mitchel's *A Defense of the Answer and Arguments of the Synod met at Boston in the Year 1662* (Cambridge: S. Green and M. Johnson, 1664; Evans 89), followed by John Eliot's *Indian Grammar Begun* (Cambridge: Marmaduke Johnson, 1666; Evans 106), and Increase Mather's *The first Principles of New-England, concerning the Subject of Baptisme and Communion of Churches* (Cambridge: Samuel Green, 1675; Evans 208). Increase Mather is also represented by another work of his printed by Samuel Green the same year entitled *A Discourse concerning the Subject of Baptisme* (Evans 207), and a later publication, *A Relation of the Troubles which have hapned in New-England by reason of the Indians there, from the Year 1614 to the Year 1675* (Boston: John Foster, 1677; Evans 238), the gift incidentally of the Rev. Philipp Stubbs, whom Sir Richard Steele "eulogized" in *The Spectator* as an example to all for his reading of the service. The original copies of both of these editions of Increase Mather are now owned by the British Museum.

The entry for Increase Mather's *A Relation* is followed in the Kennett catalogue by a dual entry for the London and Boston editions, both dated 1677, of William Hubbard's related work; the Boston edition is entitled *A Narrative of the Troubles with the Indians in New-England* (Boston: John Foster, 1677; Evans 231), which contained the earliest map to be engraved in America, whereas the London edition is known under a slightly different title, *The present State of New-England, being a Narrative of the Troubles with the Indians in New England* (London, for Thomas Parkhurst). William Hubbard was also represented in the Kennett Library through a copy of an election sermon, called *The Happiness of a People in the Wisdome of their Rulers Directing* (Boston: John Foster, 1676; Evans 214).

With some regret it is reported that the Kennett collection presented to the S. P. G. in 1713 did not possess a copy of the first edition of John Eliot's Indian Bible printed in 1663,[3] but it did include a copy of the second corrected and amended edition, dated 1680 and 1685, and printed by Samuel Green "for the Right Honourable Corporation in London, for the propogation (*sic*) of the Gospel among the Indians in New-England" (Evans 385). One can scarcely consider any other work more appropriate than this one

---

[3] Actually Bishop Kennett owned a copy of this first edition, but apparently he retained it for his personal library. In 1869, Mr. George Brinley of Hartford, Connecticut, purchased this copy from Mr. Bernard Quaritch, who wrote: "I believe it *must* be the finest copy in the world." At the Brinley sale in 1879, this copy, described by number 787 in the sale catalogue, sold for $1000. The Pierpont Morgan Library in New York is the present owner. (PML 5441)

for the library formed and donated by Bishop Kennett, with the possible exception of the London broadside edition, dated 1649, of *An Act for the Promoting and Propagating the Gospel of Jesus Christ in New England, by Erecting a Corporation in England,* printed for Edward Husband.

Several later American books not previously alluded to include Matthew Mayhew's *A Brief Narrative of the Success which the Gospel hath had, among the Indians, of Martha's Vineyard* (Boston: Bartholomew Green, 1694; Evans 701), of which Evans located only the copy in the Massachusetts Historical Society; *The Charter granted by their Majesties King William and Queen Mary, to the Inhabitants of the Province of the Massachusetts-Bay in New-England* (Boston: Bartholomew Green and John Allen, 1699; Evans 868), and the related *Acts and Laws of his Majesties Province of the Massachusetts-Bay in New-England,* printed at Boston the same year by the same printers (Evans 867); a very rare early New York imprint, Daniel Leed's *A Trumpet Sounded out of the Wilderness of America,* printed by William Bradford in 1699 (Sabin 39821; Church 764 *note*); a later imprint of Bradford's New York press, *An Account of the Illegal Prosecution and Tryal of Coll. Nicholas Bayard, in the Province of New-York* (1702; Evans 1038); four pamphlets of 1706, printed in Boston by Bartholomew Green: John Rogers' *A Sermon Preached before his Excellency, the Governour, the Honourable Council and Representatives of the Province of Massachusetts-Bay* (Evans 1279), Eliphalet Adams' *A Discourse putting Christians in mind to be ready for every Good Work* (Evans 1238), Increase Mather's *A Discourse concerning the Maintenance due to those that Preach the Gospel* (Evans 1269), and Cotton Mather's *Wussukwhonk . . . An Epistle to the Christian Indians, giving them a short Account, of what the English desire them to know and to do, in order to their Happiness* (Evans 1266); two works of Cotton Mather both printed by Bartholomew Green in 1707, *Another tongue brought in, to confess the Great Saviour of the World* (Evans 1307), and *Ne Kesukod Jehovah Kessehtunkup . . . The Day which the Lord hath made* (Evans 1313), printed in both the Indian language and in English; and finally a sermon of Ebenezer Pemberton's, *The Divine Original and Dignity of Government Asserted; and an Advantageous Prospect of the Rulers Mortality recommended* (Boston: Bartholomew Green, 1710; Evans 1484), the gift of "Mr. Jeremy Dummer, Agent to Her Majesty at London for the said Province" [*i.e.* Massachusetts Bay.]

It would perhaps not be correct to say that the American books in this present collection represented in 1713 the most important and sizable aggregation assembled in a public library in England, and no assertion to this effect is made. Regardless of this fact, however, Bishop Kennett must be considered one of the earliest collectors abroad to have collected them with a purpose.

Since the Kennett Library essentially was composed of Americana written in the English language, emphasis has naturally been placed on the important titles falling within this category, but one must not gather the impression that this was the exclusive content of the collection. The oldest book recorded in the 1713 catalogue, for example, is the Aldine edition of Pomponius Mela's *De situ orbis* (Venice, 1518) in which other related works have been included. Now owned by the British Museum, this copy is bound in a nearly contemporary stamped binding with stamps of St. George, signed I. R., and of the Baptism of Christ.[4] A later work of geographical interest is Henricus Glareanus' *Geographia* (Freiburg im Breisgau, 1543), a volume which contains a brief reference to the Western Hemisphere. Of greater significance is a copy of Peter Martyr's *Opus epistolarum* (Amsterdam, 1670). Since this is one of the works analyzed by the compiler of the 1713 catalogue, numerous entries extracted from this appear among the earliest entries ranging from 1493 through 1525. Another work that has been analyzed is the Bishop's copy of the 1555 edition—which is the most complete one—of the *Novus orbis regionum ac insularum veteribus incognitarum, una cum tabula cosmographica,* printed at Basel by Johann Hervagius.

As it has been said earlier, there are few titles which fall within the field of Spanish Americana, but an important work in this category is Antonio de Herrera's *An Account of the Spanish Historie of the West-Indies, entitled, Historia General de los Hechos de los Castellanos en las Islas, y Tierra Firme del mar Oceano;* a work in four volumes, it was printed at Madrid during the years 1601 to 1615. Of all the Spanish historians Herrera furnishes the most accurate information concerning the conquest of Mexico as well as the general history of the New World, and his decades "may be considered amongst the most judicious and useful collections." Another title of Spanish American interest is Gaspar Ens' *Indiae occidentalis historia* (Cologne, 1612), a rare little volume containing the accounts of the Columbus voyages, the expeditions of Cortes, Pizarro,. and other conquistadores, and descriptive as well of certain well-known sections of South and Central America. This book had been given to the library by the Rev. Joseph Sparke of Peterborough, who became the custodian of Bishop Kennett's valuable collection of historical and theological documents which were presented to the cathedral library of Peterborough. This well-respected antiquary is also recorded in the 1713

---

[4] Identical with the panel stamps described and attributed to John Reynes by the late E. P. Goldschmidt in his *Gothic & Renaissance Bookbindings* (London, 1928), p. 233, and Plate LIII.

catalogue as the donor of at least four important early works of astronomical interest. The first of these is a copy of *De mundi ætherij recentioribus phoenomenis liber secundus* (Prague, 1603), an important contribution of the Danish astronomer Tycho Brahe. An uncommon later book on astronomical observations is Philippe van Lansberg's *Commentationes in motum terrae diurnum & annuum, & in verum adspectabilis cœli typum* (Middelburg, 1630). Of greater prominence are the *Systema cosmicum* of Galileo Galilei (Lyons, 1641), and the writings of one of his disciples, Pierre Gassend, entitled *Institutio astronomica* (Paris, 1647).

A much later volume of scientific interest is a botanical work of unusual content relating to America, and still esteemed by botanists; this is a copy of Hans Sloane's *Catalogus plantarum quae in insulâ Jamaica sponte proveniunt* (London, 1696), presented by its author, which has been entered in the catalogue both in the main part, on pages 168 and 169, and also in the postscript on page 275.[5] Sir Hans, the author, is perhaps best known to posterity for a later benefaction which led ultimately to the establishment of the British Museum. Who can say what influence the gift of Bishop Kennett's library to the Society for the Propagation of the Gospel might have had upon the important decision which Sir Hans was to reach several years later? Happily, the notable Sloane collection is still intact, but Bishop Kennett's collection was not destined to enjoy such a happy fate, as we shall learn later.

In the preface to the catalogue, the learned Bishop expressed several hopes. One of these, stated in his own words in well-chosen phrases, is quoted in full:

> "The Truth is, for any single Person to undertake the founding a complete Library, requires a Genius, as well as a Fortune, above the common sort of Mankind, a *BODLEY,* a *TENISON,* or some such superiour Spirit of Piety, Learning, and Liberality.
>
> However, as the drawing of one Furrow was formerly the Designation of a City, so I hope this rude Draught may direct a little to the raising, furnishing, and endowing a full and perfect AMERICAN LIBRARY, to contain all sorts of Books, Charts, Maps, Globes, Instruments, and other Utensils, that can possibly tend to the more exact Survey and Knowledge of the Earth and Seas, and Heavenly Bodies; and to be more especially stock'd with such Discourses, Letters, Journals, and other Instructions, as may best serve for the Conduct of our Missionaries, the Help of Mariners and Merchants, the Information of Strangers, and the Entertainment of all Persons, who wish well to the Propagation of our Faith, and to the Trade and Commerce of our Country, among ALL NATIONS."

[5] This gift as well as Dr. Sloane's gift of another of his writings, *A Voyage to the Islands Madera, Barbados, Nieves, St. Christophers and Jamaica* (London, 1707), are chronicled in the Society's annual report for 1713-14, appended to Dean George Stanhope's sermon, *The early conversion of Islanders . . .* (London, 1714).

In the dedication, Bishop Kennett went on to state to what purposes his library might be put. First, it was intended to serve the purposes of the membership of the Society enabling them "to satisfie their Curiosity and improve their Knowledge in the Affairs intrusted to them." Other bodies of men, including ministers of state, and the English companies whose interests are related to commerce, naval affairs and history should also be given access to the Library. Bishop Kennett felt especially that the Colonial Governors through this library might "better qualifie themselves" before they left to assume their posts overseas, but in the final analysis it was to serve as a place of orientation of the Society's missionaries. The perspicacious churchman wrote:

> "they must be let into the particular Disposition of the Country and Nation wherein they are to exercise their Mission, they must understand somewhat of the Constitution of that Government they are to live under, of the first Rise and following Advances of that Colony or Plantation that is to receive them, the Temper and Infirmities of the People, the present State of Letters and Religion among 'em, the most prevailing Errours and Divisions, and whatever else is most necessary to be known for their better discharge of the Care of those Souls. And as that Care is to extend toward the Negro Slaves and the *Indian* Natives, they might here examine the various Accounts that have been given by Eye witnesses of their Genius and Capacity, their Notions and Manners, their Prejudices and their Obstinacy in them. And to enable themselves to converse a little with those ignorant Natives, they might here dip into the *Indian* Languages, or the chief Dialects of the Borderers on us, by turning over the several Essays of Grammar and Dictionary, that are here to be met with in one or more of those Tongues, and especially by examining THE INDIAN GRAMMAR, and THE INDIAN BIBLE prepared and publish'd by the industrious and pious Mr. *ELLIOT*; with the Lord's Prayer, Creed, Commandments, short Catechisms, and other familiar Expositions of our common Articles of Faith, which have been printed in *New-England* under the Encouragement of Mr. *Boyle* and the Corporation for the Propagation of the Gospel unto the *Indians* there adjoyning, and are most of them to be found in this Collection. Or if they have not time to run over the Books themselves, the very Catalogue however will supply them with the full Titles of Such, as they may procure to carry with them, or may leave or send a Commission for them."

Later he went on to express another hope that his library was capable of becoming the "common Fund and Treasury of all the Remains of that Country"; could it not become, he asked, the future depository of unpublished journals, papers, and letters of the missionaries themselves as well as of mariners and other travellers. If such a Bank or Treasury of Papers were established, he wrote in noble terms which all custodians of manuscripts and archives must roundly applaud:

> "I doubt not but many worthy Persons would be casting into it some or other valuable Remains, that would not otherwise outlive the present Possessor of them. Heirs and Executors are very apt to think Manuscripts and loose Papers to be a sort of Refuse not worth the keeping; and therefore, if they could hear of any proper Office to receive them, they would transmit them thither for Acknowledgment and Thanks, or at least for some other small Consideration. There be now living many industrious Collectors of Voyages and Travels, Navigation, Commerce, *etc.* who probably after their Decease would not trust them to the custody of a careless

Heir, or mercenary Administrator; but will be glad to hear of such a Publick Place as this, wherein they may be safely disposed and preserved with the Memory of their Donour. If such a curious and judicious Collector as Mr. *PEPYS* had known of any such Design, it is very probable that He would have given all his laborious Effects that way, and they would in such manner have made a National Treasure to Posterity."

Another hope he expressed, bless him, related to the founding of a "Librarian's Place" with a "competent Salary or Support to it." Whether or not the excellent advice was followed has not been established as a fact, but it is known for a fact that the library did not grow and expand as its auspicious establishment might have led one to expect. That it was used there is no doubt, for the books from the original collection that have survived show evidence of hard usage.

The Kennett Library in the main appears to have remained as a unit, although obviously substantially smaller than its original size, until 1917, when the remaining portion was offered for sale at auction by Sotheby, Wilkinson & Hodge on Monday, the 30th of July. The title page of the auction catalogue of 36 pages, describing 226 lots, of which 176 related almost exclusively to the Bishop's books, stated that it was sold by order of the Society "under a Scheme authorised by the Charity Commissioners of England" and the proceeds were to be used to establish a perpetual Trust, the income of which was to be "applied by the Society in the purchase of books for the General Library of the Society." The sale of the Bishop's books fetched 4,890 pounds; thus, while the purposes of the original library had been radically altered, the money realized from this sale continues, one trusts, to add books to the Society's library for much the same basic purpose that the library was intended to serve.[6] Prior to the sale, the British Museum as a condition of the Scheme was permitted to select those volumes which were deemed appropriate for its collections; its representatives made a selection of 81 titles, of which number 50 have been identified in the 1713 catalogue. With but one exception, lot 110—the unique undated edition of Thomas Morton's *New English Canaan,* printed for Charles Greene, that was withdrawn prior to the sale—none of these is recorded in the auction catalogue. The 175 distinct lots in the sale represented at least 321 titles, since in most cases several titles comprised each lot. Of these 321 distinct works, 200 have been identified in the original catalogue of 1713, which comprised 1216 pieces, or roughly speaking 16 per cent; the 50 titles now in the British Museum account for an additional 4 per cent. Thus, 20 per cent of the original library could be accounted for in 1917. As a result of the auction sale at least 74 volumes have crossed the Atlantic.

[6] Miss Holland, the present librarian of the Society, informed me during a visit to their headquarters in London on September 19, 1956, that this is the case. The income last year from this fund amounted to 178 pounds.

Since it will never be possible to reassemble the Kennett Library in one place, it seemed desirable to record in this paper the 100 or more titles from the original library which can now be identified.[7] As undoubtedly the outstanding volumes in the original collection are included among these survivors, the recording here will serve as further indication of the importance and significance of the collecting tastes and acumen of their collector. In each instance, references are given to the 1713 Catalogue, the sale catalogue, the sale price, and obvious bibliographical references.

ORIGINAL WORKS AND THEIR PRESENT LOCATION*

1.—*The Allegations of the Turkey Company, and others, against the East-India Company, relating to the management of that trade.* [London, 1681.]
　　　Catalogue (1713) p. 135. Wing A 954.
　　　New York Public Library.

2.—ANGHIERA, Pietro Martire d'.—*De novo orbe, or the historie of the West Indies . . . comprised in eight decades . . . three . . . formerly translated into English by R. Eden . . . the other five . . . by . . . M. Lok.* London: for Thomas Adams, 1612.
　　　Catalogue (1713) p. 54. STC 650. JCB II p. 86. Church 358.
　　　British Museum.

3.—*An Answer to the case of the old East-India Company; as represented by themselves to the Lord's spiritual and temporal in Parliament assembled.* London: K. Astwood, 1700.
　　　Catalogue (1713) p. 181. Wing A 3395.
　　　British Museum.

[7] In the preparation of the listing of the volumes identified as having come from Bishop Kennett's library of Americana, I am indebted to the following individuals for furnishing the record of the titles owned by the libraries with which they are affiliated: F. C. Francis, British Museum; Thomas R. Adams, Chapin Library; Lewis M. Stark, New York Public Library; Howard H. Peckham, William L. Clements Library; James G. McManaway, Folger Shakespeare Library; Marjorie G. Wynne, Yale University Library; Elizabeth Baer, The John Work Garrett Library; Lawrence C. Wroth, The John Carter Brown Library; Lyle H. Wright, Henry E. Huntington Library; John Cook Wyllie, Alderman Library; William H. McCarthy, Jr., the Rosenbach Foundation; Howell J. Heaney, Free Library of Philadelphia; Thompson R. Harlow, Connecticut Historical Society; Alexander D. Wainwright, Princeton University Library; and John Fleming. I am also obliged to Douglas G. Parsonage for several helpful suggestions and to Curt F. Bühler for information concerning the Eliot Indian Bible in the Pierpont Morgan Library.

* REFERENCES:

　　Baer. *Seventeenth century Maryland. A bibliography compiled by Elizabeth Baer, librarian of The John Work Garrett Library.* Introduction by Lawrence C. Wroth. Baltimore, 1949.
　　Chapin. *The Chapin Library, Williams College. A short-title list,* compiled by Lucy Eugenia Osborne. Portland, Maine, 1939.
　　Church. *A catalogue of books relating to the discovery and early history of North and South America forming a part of the library of E. D. Church,* compiled and annotated by George Watson Cole. New York, 1907. 5v.
　　De Puy. *A bibliography of the English colonial treaties with the American Indians, including a synopsis of each treaty,* by Henry F. De Puy. New York, 1917.
　　Evans. *American bibliography by Charles Evans. A chronological dictionary of all books, pamphlets, and periodical publications printed in the United States of America.* Volume I, 1639-1720. Chicago, 1903.
　　Holmes. *Increase Mather, his works; being a short-title catalogue of the published writings that can be ascribed to him,* compiled by Thomas J. Holmes. Cleveland, 1930.

4.—AVITY, Pierre d'.—*Les estats, et principautez du monde.* Rouen: Adrian Ovyn, 1644.
> Catalogue (1713) p. 91. *cf.* Sabin 2498.
> British Museum.

5.—B., G.—*A fig for the Spaniard, or Spanish spirits.* London: John Woolfe, 1591.
> Catalogue (1713) p. 32. STC 1026.
> Folger Shakespeare Library, Washington, D. C.

6.—Barbary.—*Late newes out of Barbary in a letter written of late from a merchant there, to a gentleman not long since employed into that countrie from his Majestie.* London: Arthur Johnson, 1613.
> Catalogue (1713) p. 55. STC 1377.
> Folger Shakespeare Library, Washington, D. C.

7.—BAYARD, Nicholas *and* LODOWICK, Charles.—*A journal of the late actions of the French at Canada, with the manner of their being repuls'd by his Excellency Benjamin Fletcher, their Majesties Governour of New-York.* London: for Richard Baldwin, 1693.
> Catalogue (1713) p. 160. Sale catalogue 17 (£127). Wing B 1458. Sabin 4035. Church 727.
> Chapin Library, Williamstown, Mass.

8.—BERKELEY, *Sir* William.—*A discourse and view of Virginia.* [London, 1663].
> Catalogue (1713) p. 114. Sale catalogue 16 (£255). Wing B 1975.
> Princeton University Library.

9.—[BIDDULPH, William].—*The travels of foure Englishmen and a preacher.* London: Felix Kyngston, 1612.
> Catalogue (1713) p. 233. Sale catalogue 92 (£25). STC 3052. Chapin p. 57.
> Chapin Library, Williamstown, Mass.

10.—[BOEMUS, Johann].—*The fardle of facions, conteining the auncient manners, customes, and lawes of the people enhabiting the two partes of the earths, called Affrike and Asie. Translated into English by William Watreman.* London: John Kingstone, 1555.
> Catalogue (1713) p. 15. Sale catalogue 165. STC 3197. Chapin p. 58.
> Chapin Library, Williamstown, Mass.

11.—BOEMUS, Johann.—*The manners, lawes, and customs of all nations.* London: G. Eld, 1611.
> Catalogue (1713) p. 53. Sale catalogue 19. STC 3198. Chapin p. 58.
> Chapin Library, Williamstown, Mass.

JCB. *Bibliotheca Americana. Catalogue of the John Carter Brown Library in Brown University, Providence, Rhode Island.* Providence, 1919-1931. 3v.

Jones. *Adventures in Americana 1492-1897. The Romance of Voyage and Discovery from Spain to the Indies, the Spanish Main and North America . . . Being a Selection of Books from the Library of Herschel V. Jones, Minneapolis, Minnesota.* New York, 1928.

Kimber. *Cambridge Press Title-pages, 1640-1665. A pictorial representation of the work done in the first printing office in British North America,* by Sidney A. Kimber. Takoma Park, Md. [c. 1954].

Sabin. *A dictionary of books relating to America, from its discovery to the present time.* By Joseph Sabin. New York, 1868-1936. 29v.

STC. *A short-title catalogue of books printed in England, Scotland, & Ireland, and of English books printed abroad, 1475-1640.* Compiled by A. W. Pollard & G. R. Redgrave. London, 1926.

Wing. *Short-title catalogue of books printed in England, Scotland, Ireland, Wales and British America, and of English books printed in other countries, 1641-1700.* Compiled by Donald Wing of the Yale University Library. New York, 1945-1951. 3v.

12.—BOND, Henry.—*The boat swaines art, or the compleat boat swaine. Wherein is shewed a true proportion for the masting, yarding and rigging of any ship.* London: R. Cotes for W. Lugger, 1642.

> Catalogue (1713) p. 87. Wing B 3560.
> British Museum.

13.—BOND, Henry.—*The longitude found: or, a treatise shewing an easie and speedy way ... to find the longitude.* London: William Godbid, 1676.

> Catalogue (1713) p. 132 *bis.* Wing B 3564.
> British Museum.

14.—BOURNE, William.—*A regiment for the sea ... whereunto is added a new regiment ... by Thomas Hoode.* London: W. I. for Edmund Weaver, 1620.

> Catalogue (1713) p. 64. STC 3430.
> British Museum.

15.—BRAHE, Tycho.—*De mundi aetherei recentioribus phaenomenis.* Prague: Typis Schumanianis, 1603.

> Catalogue (1713) p. 44. Sale catalogue 21 (£2 4s). Chapin p. 525.
> Chapin Library, Williamstown, Mass.

16.—BRAY, Thomas.—[Caption title.] *A letter from Dr. Bray, to such as have contributed towards the propagating Christian knowledge in the plantations.* [London, 1700].

> Catalogue (1713) p. 181. Baer 197. Evans 903.
> John Work Garrett Library, Baltimore, Md.

17.—BRINSLEY, John.—*A consolation for our grammar schooles of a faithful incouragement, for laying of a sure foundation of all good learning in our schooles.* London: Richard Field for Thomas Man, 1622.

> Catalogue (1713) p. 66. Sale catalogue 24 (£50). STC 3767. JCB I p. 162.
> Chapin Library, Williamstown, Mass.

18.—BROKESBY, Francis.—*Some proposals towards promoting the propagation of the Gospel in our American plantations.* London: G. Sawbridge, 1708.

> Catalogue (1713) p. 202. Sabin 8190.
> British Museum.

19.—Cambridge. *Synod. 1648. A platform of church discipline gathered out of the work of God: and agreed upon by the elders and messengers of the churches assembled in the synod at Cambridge in England.* Cambridge: S[amuel] G[reen] 1649.

> Catalogue (1713) p. 97. Evans 25. Kimber p. 29.
> Huntington Library, San Marino, California.

20.—CAMPANELLA, Tommaso.—*A discourse.* London: Philemon Stephens, 1654.

> Catalogue (1713) p. 105. Sale catalogue 25. Wing C 401.
> Yale University Library, New Haven, Conn.

21.—CASTELL, William.—*A petition of W. C. exhibited to the high court of Parliament, now assembled, for the propagating of the Gospel in America and the West-Indies, and for the setling of our plantations there.* [London] 1641.

> Catalogue (1713) p. 84. Sale catalogue 28 (£44). Wing C 1230 JCB II p. 287. Church 449.
> Chapin Library, Williamstown, Mass.

22.—CELLARIUS, Christophorus.—*Geographia antiqua.* Cizae: Sumtu Io. Bielkii, 1686.
> Catalogue (1713) p. 146.
> British Museum.

23.—CHILD, John.—*New England's Jonas cast up at London; or a relation of the proceedings of the Court at Boston in New England, against divers honest and godly persons,
for petitioning for government in the commonwealth according to the laws of England,
&c.* London: for T. R. and E. M., 1647.
> Catalogue (1713) p. 94. Sale catalogue 29 (£ 22). Wing C 3851. JCB II p. 353. Church
> 478.
> Chapin Library, Williamstown, Mass.

24.—*The Clothiers complaint: or, reasons for passing the bill against the Blackwell-Hall
factors, &c. . . . humbly offer'd to the Parliament.* London: Randal Taylor, 1692.
> Catalogue (1713) p. 156. Wing C 4734.
> British Museum.

25.—COOK, Ebenezer.—*The sot-weed factor: or a voyage to Maryland: a satyr. In which
is described the laws, government, courts and constitutions of the country.* London:
B. Bragg, 1708.
> Catalogue (1713) p. 200.
> New York Public Library.

26.—COOPER, Thomas.—*The blessing of Japheth, proving the gathering in of the
Gentiles, and finall conversion of the Jewes.* London: T. C. for R. Redmer, 1615.
> Catalogue (1713) p. 58. STC 5693.
> British Museum.

27.—CORTES, Martin.—*The arte of navigation, conteyning a compendious description of
the sphere . . . translated out of Spanyshe into Englyshe by Richarde Eden.* London:
R. I., 1572.
> Catalogue (1713) p. 19. STC 5799.
> British Museum.

28.—COTTON, John.—*A censure of that reverend and learned man of God Mr. John
Cotton, lately of New England.* London: for John Stafford, 1656.
> Catalogue (1713) p. 108-109. Sale catalogue 37 (3rd title) £ 8 (entire lot). Wing C
> 6415. JCB II p. 460.
> Folger Shakespeare Library, Washington, D. C.

29.—COTTON, John.—*The controversie concerning liberty of conscience, in matters of
religion.* London: Thomas Bankes, 1646.
> Catalogue (1713) p. 93. Sale catalogue 41 (£ 3 10s). Wing C 6420. JCB II p. 339.
> Chapin Library, Williamstown, Mass.

30.—COTTON, John.—*The controversie concerning liberty of conscience in matters of
religion truly stated, and distinctly handled.* London: Robert Austin for Thomas Banks,
1649.
> Catalogue (1713) p. 97. Sale catalogue 42 (£ 3 3s). Wing C 6421. Chapin p. 316.
> Chapin Library, Williamstown, Mass.

31.—COTTON, John.—*The covenant of God's free grace most sweetly unfolded and comfortably applied to a disquieted soul . . . Whereunto is added a profession of faith, made
by Mr. John Davenport in New England.* London: for Matthew Simmons, 1645.
> Catalogue (1713) p. 92. Sale catalogue 37 (1st title) £ 8 (entire lot). Wing C 6423.
> JCB II p. 329.
> Folger Shakespeare Library, Washington, D. C.

32.—COTTON, John.—*A modest and cleare answer to Mr. Ball's discourse of set forms of prayer.* London: Henry Overton, 1642.

        Catalogue (1713) p. 86. Sale catalogue 36 (1st title) £12 (entire lot). Wing C 6445. JCB II p. 296.

           William L. Clements Library, Ann Arbor, Michigan.

33.—[CROUCH, Nathaniel].—*The English acquisition in Guinea and East-India; containing first, the several forts and castles of the Royal African Company . . .* London: Nathaniel Crouch, 1708.

        Catalogue (1713) p. 201-202. *cf.* Wing C 7318 (ed. of 1700).

           British Museum.

34.—DAVENPORT, John.—*The power of Congregational Churches asserted and vindicated, in answer to a treatise of Mr. J. Paget.* London: for Richard Chiswell, 1672.

        Catalogue (1713) p. 129. Wing D 362.

           British Museum.

35.—DESBOROW, Charles.—*The humble address of the Lords Spiritual and Temporal to His Majesty, in relation to the petition of C. Desborow, late Captain of His Majesty's ship Mary-Gally.* [London], 1699.

        Catalogue (1713) p. 176. Wing E 2801.

           British Museum.

36.—ECHARD, Lawrence.—*A most compleat compendium of geography.* The second edition, corrected. London: for T. Salusbury, 1691.

        Catalogue (1713) p. 154. Wing E 149.

           British Museum.

37.—ELIOT, John.—*A brief narrative of the progress of the gospel amongst the Indians in New-England in the year 1670.* London: John Allen, 1671.

        Catalogue (1713) p. 27. Sale catalogue 63 (£90). Wing E 503. JCB III p. 217.

           Chapin Library, Williamstown, Mass.

        .... [another copy] Sale catalogue 65 (£70).

           William L. Clements Library, Ann Arbor, Mich.

        .... [another copy] Sale catalogue 64 (£72).

           The Connecticut Historical Society, Hartford, Conn.

38.—ELIOT, John.—*A late and further manifestation of the progress of the gospel amongst the Indians of New-England.* London: M.S., 1655.

        Catalogue (1713) p. 107. Sale catalogue 61 (£70). Wing E 517. JCB II p. 447. Church 536.

           Chapin Library, Williamstown, Mass.

39.—ELIOT, John *and* MAYHEW, Thomas.—*Tears of repentance; or a further narrative of the progress of the gospel amongst the Indians in New-England.* London: Peter Cole, 1653.

        Catalogue (1713) p. 104. Sale catalogue 60 (£20). Wing E 522. JCB 429. Church 527.

           Chapin Library, Williamstown, Mass.

        .... [another copy] Sale catalogue 59 (£20).

           The Connecticut Historical Society, Hartford, Conn.

40.—England. *Treaties* (Charles II).—*Articles of peace between the most serene and mighty Prince Charles II by the grace of God King of England . . . And several Indian*

Kings and Queens &c. ·Concluded the 29th day of May, 1677. London: John Bill, Christopher Barker, &c., 1677.

> Catalogue (1713) p. 129 *bis.* Sale catalogue 80 (£160). Wing C 2909. De Puy p. 1. Church 657. Jones 133.
> Free Library of Philadelphia (Elkins Collection).
> . . . . [another copy] Sale catalogue 81 (£70).
> Chapin Library, Williamstown, Massachusetts.

41.—England. *Treaties* (James II).—*Treaty of peace, good correspondence & neutrality in America, between . . . James II . . . and . . . Lewis XIV . . . concluded the 6/16 day of November 1686.* [London:] T. Newcomb, 1686.

> Catalogue (1713) p. 145. Wing J 393.
> British Museum.

42.—ENS, Gaspar.—*Indiæ occidentalis historia: In qua prima regionum istarum detectio, situs, incolarum mores, aliaq; eo pertinentia, breviter explicantur.* Cologne: Gulielmus Lutzen-kirchen, 1612.

> Catalogue (1713) p. 55. JCB II p. 83.
> William L. Clements Library, Ann Arbor, Mich.

43.—FEATLEY, John.—*A sermon preached to the nobly-deserving gentleman, Sir Thomas Warner, and the rest of his companie bound to the West Indies.* London: for Nicholas Bourne, 1629.

> Catalogue (1713) p. 74. Sale catalogue 66 (£1 12s). STC 10743.
> Folger Shakespeare Library, Washington, D. C.

44.—Friesland.—*Resolutie vande Ed. Mo. Heeren Staten van-Vriesland vanden 23 Mey* . . . Leyden: C. Vander Linden, 1663.

> Catalogue (1713) p. 114.
> British Museum.

45.—*A Full and impartial history of the expedition into Spain in the year 1702. Extracted from the journals and memoirs of the generals . . .* London: W. Davis, 1704.

> Catalogue (1713) p. 191.
> British Museum.

46.—GASSEND, Pierre.—*Institutio astronomica iuxta hypotheses tam veterum, quam Copernici, et Tychonis.* Paris, apud L. de Henqueville, 1647.

> Catalogue (1713) p. 95.
> British Museum.

47.—*The Great loss and damage to England by the transportation of wool to foreign parts.* [London, 1677].

> Catalogue (1713) p. 131 *bis.* Wing G 1708 [London? 1662].
> British Museum.

48.—*The Glorious progress of the gospel amongst the Indians in New England, manifested by three letters under the hand of . . . Mr. John Eliot, and another from Thomas Mayhew, jun . . .* London: for Hannah Allen, 1649.

> Catalogue (1713) p. 97. Sale catalogue 53 (£46). Wing W 3036 (under Edward Winslow). JCB II p. 385. Church 497.
> The Connecticut Historical Society, Hartford, Conn.

49.—HAMMOND, John.—*Leah and Rachel, or the two fruitful sisters Virginia and Maryland their present condition, impartially stated and related.* London: T. Mabb, 1656.
> Catalogue (1713) p. 109. Sale catalogue 73 (£181). Wing H 620. JCB II p. 463.
> Chapin Library, Williamstown, Mass.

50.—*The History and progress of the four Indian kings, to the kingdom of England, &c.* London: A. Hinde, 1710.
> Catalogue (1713) p. 206. Sabin 32113.
> British Museum.

51.—HOOD, Thomas.—*The use of the two mathematicall instruments, the crosse staffe (differing from that in common use with the mariners) and the Jacob's staffe.* London: Richard Field, 1596.
> Catalogue (1713) p. 35. Sale catalogue 77 (dated 1595; £15). STC 13701.
> Folger Shakespeare Library, Washington, D. C.

52.—HUBBARD, William.—*The present state of New-England.* London: for Tho. Parkhurst, 1677.
> Catalogue (1713) p. 130 *bis.* Sale catalogue 78 (£86). Wing H 3212. Sabin 33446. Church 651.
> Princeton University Library.

53.—HUGHES, William.—*The American physitian, or a treatise of the roots, plants, trees, shrubs, fruit, herbs, etc. growing in the English plantations in America.* London: for William Crook, 1672.
> Catalogue (1713) p. 130. Sale catalogue 79 (£6 12s 6d). Wing H 3332. JCB III p. 240.
> Chapin Library, Williamstown, Mass.

54.—JOHNSON, Robert.—*Nova Britannia. Offering most excellent fruites by planting in Virginia. Exciting all such as be well affected to further the same.* London, printed for Samuel Macham, 1609.
> Catalogue (1713) p. 50. Sale catalogue 82 (£134). STC 14699. JCB II p. 60. Church 338. Jones 59.
> John Fleming, Inc., New York City.

55.—[Item cancelled.]

56.—*The Judgment given forth by twenty eight Quakers against George Keith and his friends; with answers to the said judgment, declaring those twenty eight Quakers to be no Christians.* Printed at Pennsylvania; reprinted at London: for Richard Baldwin, 1694.
> Catalogue (1713) p. 162. Sale catalogue 86 (£4). Wing J 1173.
> Chapin Library, Williamstown, Mass.

57.—KEITH, George.—*An account of the great divisions amongst the Quakers in Pensilvania &c.* London: John Guillim, 1692.
> Catalogue (1713) p. 157. Sale catalogue 127 (1st title) £26 (entire lot). Wing K 136. Church 724.
> William L. Clements Library, Ann Arbor, Mich.

58.—KEITH, George.—*The causeless ground of surmises, jealousies and unjust offences remov'd, in a full clearing of faithfull friends, and a sober vindication of my innocency.* London: for R. Levis, 1694.
> Catalogue (1713) p. 262. Sale catalogue 85 (£4 4s). Wing K 149. Sabin [37182].
> Chapin Library, Williamstown, Mass.

59.—KEITH, George.—*The Christian Quaker; or, George Keith's eyes opened . . . Good news from Pensilvania.* Printed in Pensilvania, and reprinted in London, for Benjamin Keach, 1693.
> Catalogue (1713) p. 161. Sale catalogue 84 (£4 4s). Wing K 153. Sabin 37186.
> Chapin Library, Williamstown, Mass.

60.—KEITH, George.—*A farther account of the great divisions among the Quakers in Pensilvania, &c.* London: J. Dunton, 1693.
> Catalogue (1713) p. 161. Sale catalogue 127 (2nd title) £26 (entire lot). Wing K 166. Sabin [23894].
> William L. Clements Library, Ann Arbor, Mich.

61.—KEITH, George.—*More divisions amongst the Quakers as appears by the following books of their own writing* . . . Reprinted [London]: R. Baldwin, 1693.
> Catalogue (1713) p. 161. Sale catalogue 128 (£8). Wing K 182. Sabin 37202.
> Chapin Library, Williamstown, Mass.

62.—LANGFORD, John.—*A just and cleere refutation of a false and scandalous Pamphlet, Entituled, Babylons fall in Maryland &c. And, a true discovery of certaine strange and inhumane proceedings of some ungratefull people in Maryland.* London, 1655.

> Catalogue (1713) p. 107. Sale catalogue 89 (£182). Baer 42. Wing L 387.
> John Work Garrett Library, Baltimore, Md.
> . . . . [another copy] Sale catalogue 90 (£158).
> John Carter Brown Library, Providence, R. I.

63.—LECHFORD, Thomas.—*Plain-dealing, or news from New England. A short view of New-England's present government, both ecclesiastical and civil.* London: for Nathaniel Butter, 1642.
> Catalogue (1713) p. 86. Sale catalogue 93 (£95). Wing L 810. Church 454. JCB II p. 298.
> Chapin Library, Williamstown, Mass.

64.—LEDERER, John.—*The discoveries of John Lederer in three several marches from Virginia to the west of Carolina and other parts of the continent; begun in March, 1669, and ended in September, 1670.* London: J. C. for Samuel Heyrick, 1672.
> Catalogue (1713) p. 130. Sale catalogue 95 (£182). Wing L 835. JCB III p. 242. Church 619.
> Chapin Library, Williamstown, Mass.

65.—LEEDS, Daniel.—*A trumpet sounded out of the wilderness of America which may serve as a warning to the government and people of England to beware of Quakerism.* New York: William Bradford, 1699.
> Catalogue (1713) p. 179. Church 764 (*note*). Sabin 39821.
> British Museum.

66.—LOPEZ, Duarte.—*A reporte of the kingdom of Congo, a region of Africa, and of the countries that border round about the same.* London: John Wolfe, 1597.
> Catalogue (1713) p. 37. STC 16805.
> New York Public Library.

67.—LOPEZ DE GOMARA, Francisco.—*The Pleasant Historie of the Conquest of the Weast India.* London: Henry Bynneman, 1578.
> Catalogue (1713) p. 23. STC 16807. JCB I p. 271. Church 123.
> Massachusetts Historical Society, Boston, Mass.

68.—LUDOLPH, Hiob.—*A new history of Ethiopia; being a full and accurate description of the kingdom of Abyssinia, vulgarly, though erroneously, called the Empire of Prester John.* Made English by J. P. London: for Samuel Smith, 1682.

> Catalogue (1713) p. 138. Wing L 3468.
> British Museum.

69.—MAGNUS, Olaus.—*Historia Olai Magni . . . de gentibus septentrionalibus, earumque diversis statibus . . .* Franckfurt: I. Schmidlinus, 1622.

> Catalogue (1713) p. 67.
> British Museum.

70.—MARSHALL, William.—*Philosophy delineated, containing a resolution of divers knotty questions upon sundry philosophical notions.* London: Obadiah Blagrave, 1678.

> Catalogue (1713) p. 133 *bis.*
> British Museum.

71.—MARSTON, Edward.—*To the most noble Prince Henry Duke of Beaufort, Marquis and Earl of Worcester, Baron Herbert, Lord of Ragland, Chepstow, and Gower, Palatine of the Province of South Carolina in America.* [signed at end: "From my Study, against Trinity Church, in the Minores, Novemb. 15th, 1712."] [London, 1712.]

> Catalogue (1713) p. 213 (first entry where it is described under a made-up title).
> John Carter Brown Library, Providence, R. I.

72.—Massachusetts (Colony).—*Acts and laws of his majestie's province of the Massachusetts-Bay in New-England.* Boston: Bartholomew Green and John Allen, 1699.

> Catalogue (1713) p. 174. Evans 867.
> British Museum.

73.—Massachusetts (Colony).—*The charter granted by their Majesties King William and Queen Mary to the inhabitants of Massachusetts-Bay in New England.* Boston: Bartholomew Green and John Allen, 1699.

> Catalogue (1713) p. 174. Evans 868.
> British Museum.

74.—MATHER, Increase.—*A brief history of the war with the Indians in New-England.* London: for Richard Chiswell, 1676.

> Catalogue (1713) p. 126 *bis.* Sale catalogue 102 (£66). Wing M 1188. Sabin [46641]. Church 643. Holmes 16-B.
> Princeton University Library.

75.—MATHER, Increase.—*A discourse concerning the subject of baptisme, wherein the present controversies that are agitated in the New English churches are from scripture and reason modestly enquired into.* Cambridge: Samuel Green, 1675.

> Catalogue (1713) p. 125 *bis.* Evans 207. Holmes 37.
> British Museum.

76.—MATHER, Increase.—*A relation of the troubles which have hapned in New-England by reason of the Indians there: from the year 1614 to the year 1675.* Boston: John Foster, 1677.

> Catalogue (1713) p. 130 *bis.* Evans 238. Holmes 110-A.
> British Museum.

77.—MEDINA, Pedro de.—*L'art de naviguer . . . traduict de Castillan en Françoys, avec augmentation & illustration de plusieurs figures & annotations, par Nicolas de Nicolai.*

Lyons: Guillaume Roville, 1554.
>Catalogue (1713) p. 14. JCB I p. 182.
>British Museum.

78.—MELA, Pomponius.—*Pomponius Mela. Julius Solinus. Itinerarium Antonini Aug. Vibus Sequester, P. Victor. Dionysius Afer de situ orbis.* Venetiis, in aedibus Aldi, Mense Octobri, MDXVIII.
>In a nearly contemporary stamped binding, with stamps of St. George and of the Baptism of Christ, the former signed I. R.
>Catalogue (1713) p. 8.
>British Museum.

79.—MORTON, Thomas, *of Clifford's Inn.*—*New English Canaan, or New Canaan. Containing an abstract of New England composed in three books.* [London] for Charles Green [1637?]
>Catalogue (1713) p. 77. Sale catalogue 110 (with reproduction of title-page). STC 18203. This lot was withdrawn from the sale.
>British Museum.

80.—MUNSTER, Sebastian.—*A treatyse of the newe India . . . Translated out of Latine into Englishe by Rycharde Eden.* London: Edward Sutton, 1553.
>Catalogue (1713) p. 14. STC 18244. JCB I p. 177.
>New York Public Library.

81.—[NAIRNE, Thomas].—*A letter from South Carolina, giving an account of the soil, air, product, trade, government, laws, religion, people, military strength &c. of that province.* London: for A. Baldwin, 1710.
>Catalogue (1713) p. 205. Sale catalogue 26 (£7 10s). Sabin 87859.
>Princeton University Library.

82.—New England.—*The deplorable state of New-England by reason of a covetous and treacherous governour and pusillanimous counsellors.* London, 1708.
>Catalogue (1713) p. 200. Sale catalogue 117 (£7 5s). Sabin [196392].
>University of Virginia Library, Charlottesville, Virginia.
>In the sale catalogue the statement is made that "a note in a contemporary hand assigns the authorship to Sir Henry Atkins." *Book-Prices Current* for 1917 enters this under the name of A. Holmes. Sabin quotes the *North American Review,* where it is attributed to Alex. Holmes although the name of the Rev. John Higginson, of Salem, as author, is also mentioned. Mr. John C. Wyllie, on the other hand, states that the contemporary attribution appearing on the title page is to Sir Henry Ashurst.

83.—New England.—*An historical discoverie and relation of the English plantations in America, containing their adventurous passage, their happy arrival, and comfortable planting, manifesting the goodness of God in their preservations from many apparent dangers.* London: for John Bellamie, 1627.
>Only the title-leaf is new. The rest of the pamphlet is made up of leaves from *A relation or journall of the beginning of the English plantation at New Plimouth* (1622), and *A briefe relation of the discovery and plantation of New England* (1622). On the title page is a note followed by the name A. Mourt, perhaps an autograph signature.
>Catalogue (1713) p. 73. STC 18484.
>British Museum.

84.—New England.—*A modest enquiry into the grounds and occasions of a late pamphlet, intituled, A memorial of the present deplorable state of New-England. By a disinterested hand.* London, 1707.
>Catalogue (1713) p. 197. Sabin 49822.
>British Museum.

85.—New England.—*News from New-England; being a true and just account of the present bloody wars carried on betwixt the infidels, natives, and the English Christians and converted Indians.* London: for J. Coniers, 1676.

    Catalogue (1713) p. 127 *bis*. Sale catalogue 115 (£110). Wing N 983. Church 647. Chapin Library, Williamstown, Mass.

86.—*New England's first fruits; in respect, first, of the conversion of some, conviction of divers, preparation of sundry of the Indians; secondly, of the progresse of learning in the colledge at Cambridge in Massachuset's Bay.* London: R. O. and G. D. for Henry Overton, 1643.

    Catalogue (1713) p. 88. Sale catalogue 50 (£42). Wing E 519 (under John Eliot). JCB II p. 308. Church 458. Chapin Library, Williamstown, Mass.

87.—New Jersey.—*A brief account of the province of East-Jersey in America.* Pulished *(sic)* by the present propriators. London: for Benjamin Clark, 1682.

    Catalogue (1713) p. 137. Wing B 4517. Church 674A (variant). British Museum.

88.—New Jersey.—*Proposals by the proprietors of East-Jersey in America, for the building of a town on Ambo-Point, and for the disposition of lands in that Province.* London: for Benjamin Clark, 1682.

    Catalogue (1713) p. 137. Wing P 3717. Sabin 1000. British Museum.

89.—NORTON, John.—*Abel being dead yet speaketh; or, the life & death of that deservedly famous man of God, Mr. John Cotton.* London: Tho. Newcomb for Lodowick Lloyd, 1658.

    Catalogue (1713) p. 109. Wing N 1313. Sabin 55881. JCB II p. 483. Princeton University Library.

90.—O., S.—*An adioynder of sundry other particular wicked plots . . . of the Spaniards . . . gathered and translated out of severall Dutch writers.* [London] 1624.

    Catalogue (1713) p. 69. STC 18756. British Museum.

91.—*An Oration or Speech appropriated unto the . . . Princes of Christendom. Wherein the right and lawfulnesse of the Netherlandish warre, against Phillip King of Spain is approved and demonstrated . . .* Englished by Thomas Wood. [London] 1624.

    Catalogue (1713) p. 69. STC 18837. British Museum.

92.—OSORIO DA FONSECA, Jeronimo.— *. . . De rebus Emmanuelis, Luisitaniae regis invictissimi . . . Item: Jo. Matalii Metelii . . . in eosdem libros praefatio, & commentarius: de reperta ab Hispanis & Lusitanis, in Occidentis & Orientis Indiam.* Coloniae: In officina Birckmannica, 1597.

    Catalogue (1713) p. 230 *cf.* Sabin 57804. British Museum.

93.—PARKER, Thomas.—*The true copy of a letter written by Mr. Thomas Parker, a learned and godly Minister in New-England unto a member of the assembly of divines now at Westminister.* London: Richard Cotes, 1644.

    Catalogue (1713) p. 89. Sale catalogue 121 (£7). Wing P 482. JCB II p. 320. William L. Clements Library, Ann Arbor, Mich.

94.—P[ERROT], J[OHN].—*Glorious glimmerings of the life of love, unity, and pure joy. Written in Rome . . . but conserved . . . until my arrival at Barbados in the year 1662.* London: Robert Wilson, 1663.
> Catalogue (1713) p. 114. Wing P 1618.
> British Museum.

95.—POINTIS, Jean Bernard Louis Desjeans, *baron de.*—*An account of the taking of Carthagena by the French in the year 1697.* Illustrated with a large copper plate. London: for Samuel Buckley, 1698.
> Catalogue (1713) p. 173. Wing P 2742.
> British Museum (plate wanting).

96.—PRICE, Daniel.—*Sauls prohibition staide; or the apprehension and examination of Saule . . . with a reproofe of those that traduce the honourable Plantation of Virginia.* London: M. Law, 1609.
> Catalogue (1713) p. 232. STC 20302.
> British Museum.

97.—[SANDYS, *Sir* Edwin].—*Europae speculum: or a view or survey of the state of religion in the western parts of the world.* Hagae Comtis, 1629.
> Catalogue (1713) p. 74. Sale catalogue 137 (£2). STC 21718. Chapin p. 113.
> Chapin Library, Williamstown, Mass.

98.—SAVILE, *Sir* Henry.—*Praelectiones tresdecim in principium elementorum Euclidis, Oxonii habitae. M.DC.XX.* Oxonii: Johannes Litchfield & Jacobus Short, 1621.
> Catalogue (1713) p. 65. STC 21782.
> British Museum.

99.—SELDEN, John.—*Mare clausum seu de domino maris, libri duo.* London: William Stansby, 1635.
> Catalogue (1713) p. 240. Sale catalogue 142. STC 22175. Chapin p. 114.
> Chapin Library, Williamstown, Mass.

100.—SELLER, John.—*A description of New-England in general; with a description of the town of Boston in particular.* London: John Seller, 1682.
> Catalogue (1713) p. 139. Wing S 2470.
> British Museum.

101.—SHEPARD, Thomas.—*The clear sun-shine of the gospel breaking forth upon the Indians in New England.* London: R. Cotes for J. Bellamy, 1648.
> Catalogue (1713) p. 96. Sale catalogue 52 (£35). Wing S 3109. JCB II p. 378. Church 489.
> The Connecticut Historical Society, Hartford, Conn.

102.—[SHEPARD, Thomas].—*The day-breaking if not the sun-rising of the gospell with the Indians in New-England.* London: R. Cotes for F. Clifton, 1647.
> Catalogue (1713) p. 95. Sale catalogue 51 (£50). Wing S 3110. JCB II p. 359. Church 482.
> The Connecticut Historical Society, Hartford, Conn.

103.—SMITH, John.—*Advertisements for the unexperienced Planters of New England or anywhere. Or the Path way to Experience to erect a Plantation.* London: John Haviland, 1631.

Catalogue (1713) p. 76. Sale catalogue 145 (£40). STC 23787. JCB II p. 238. Church 419.

Folger Shakespeare Library, Washington, D. C.

104.—SMITH, John.—*A map of Virginia, with a description of the Countrey, the commodities, people, government, and religion.* Oxford, Joseph Barnes, 1612.

Catalogue (1713) p. 54. STC 22791. Church 359.

New York Public Library.

105.—*Some observations upon discourses lately publish'd on the publick revenues, and on the trade of England.* London, 1698.

Catalogue (1713) p. 172.

British Museum.

106.—STAFFORDE, Robert.—*A geographical and anthological description of all the empires and kingdoms.* London: N.O. for John Parker, 1618.

Catalogue (1713) p. 61. STC 23136a.

British Museum. (To this copy a new title page is prefixed with the above imprint, and the imprint of the other title page it torn away.)

107.—STEVENS, *Capt.* John.—*The present and ancient state of Portugal.* London: J. King, 1711.

Catalogue (1713) p. 212.

British Museum.

108.—STOFFLER, Johann.—*Elucidatio fabricae ususque astrolabii.* Paris: for H. de Marnef, 1585.

Catalogue (1713) p. 227. Sale catalogue 142. Chapin p. 524.

Chapin Library, Williamstown, Mass.

109.—*Strength out of weakness, or a glorious manifestation of the farther progress of the gospel among the Indians in New-England.* London: M. Simmons, for John Blague and Samuel Howes, 1652.

Catalogue (1713) p. 102. Sale catalogue 58 (£30). Wing W 2002 (under Henry Whitfield). JCB II p. 424.

William L. Clements Library, Ann Arbor, Mich.

.... [another issue] Sale catalogue 57 (£44).

Chapin Library, Williamstown, Mass.

.... [another issue] Sale catalogue 56 (£42 10s).

The Connecticut Historical Society, Hartford, Conn.

110.—TERRY, Edward.—*The merchants and mariners preservation, and thanksgiving: or thankfulness returned for mercies received.* London: Thomas Harper, 1649.

Catalogue (1713) p. 98. Wing T 780.

New York Public Library.

111.—*A Treatise touching the East-Indian trade: or, a discourse (turned out of French into English) concerning the establishment of a French company for the commerce of the East Indies.* London: for H. B., 1676.

Catalogue (1713) p. 128 *bis.* Wing C 3715 (under François Charpentier).

British Museum.

112.—*The Tryals of Peter Boss, George Keith, Thomas Budd, and William Bradford, Quakers, for several great misdemeanours.* London: for R. Baldwin, 1693.

Catalogue (1713) p. 162. Sale catalogue 129 or 130 (£6 6s). Sabin [37226]. Wing T 2254.
    Princeton University Library.

113.—VINCENT, Philip.—*A true relation of the late battell fought in New England, between the English and the salvagès.* London: M. P. for Nathaniel Butter and John Bellamie, 1637.
    Catalogue (1713) p. 82. Sale catalogue 159 (£650). STC 24758. JCB II p. 267.
    The Connecticut Historical Society, Hartford, Conn.

114.—Virginia.—*Strange newes from Virginia, being a true relation of a great tempest.* London: for W. Thackery, 1667.
    Catalogue (1713) p. 119. Wing S 5910. JCB III p. 164.
    British Museum.

115.—W., J.—*The merchants hand-maide; or, a booke containing verie necessarie and compendious tables, for speedie casting up . . . of any commoditie whatsoever.* London: William Jones, 1622.
    Catalogue (1713) p. 68. STC 24908.
    British Museum.

116.—[WELDE, Thomas].—*A brief narration of the practices of the churches in New England.* London: M. Simmons for J. Rothwell, 1645.
    Catalogue (1713) p. 93. Sale catalogue 114 (£50). Wing W 1263. *cf.* Sabin 102552. JCB II p. 334.
    Chapin Library, Williamstown, Mass.

117.—WITTENHORST, W. von.—*Propositions made by Monsieur Vander-Hurst, at the assembly of the general states of the United Provinces, upon the 13th of January 1608.* London: Philip Harison, 1609.
    Catalogue (1713) p. 51. STC 25934.
    Yale University Library, New Haven, Conn.

118.—[WODENOTH, Arthur].—*A short collection of the most remarkable passages from the originall to the dissolution of the Virginia Company.* London: Richard Cotes for Edward Husband, 1651.
    Catalogue (1713) p. 100. Sale catalogue 176 (£43). JCB II p. 413. Church 515. Wing W 3243. Jones 118.
    The Philip H. & A. S. W. Rosenbach Foundation, Philadelphia, Pa.

A study of the foregoing record of surviving volumes from the original Kennett collection, presented to the Society for the Propagation of the Gospel in 1713, reveals that the major cache is now in the British Museum. At the time that the collection was broken up, that fortunate institution was permitted to select from the residue prior to the issuance of the auction catalogue those volumes of pertinence which the Museum desired for addition to its collections. In all, 81 titles were selected, of which number 50 have been identified through their listing in the 1713 catalogue. It should be pointed out that Bishop Kennett apparently continued to add books to this American library during the fifteen remaining years of his life.

In this present roundup of books which were at one time in his possession —and he collected books in many fields of interest as well as Americana— we have located some 16 other titles with this interesting provenance. Thus, with a total of 124 in the foregoing list, including duplicates, plus 31 titles in the British Museum, and the 16 odd others, we have traced 171 volumes which were at one time in the Bishop's library. They are usually readily identified since he customarily wrote his name, "White Kennett," or more usually in abbreviated form as "Wh. Kennett," at least once and occasionally twice on the title page. One of the books in the Folger Shakespeare Library is signed "Peterborough," which of course was the Bishop's diocese. He is also known to have used a bookplate, but this is not as commonly encountered as the autograph signature, although some of his books contain both.

In this summary of the present whereabouts of Bishop Kennett's American books, institutions other than the British Museum in which they have been located are: Chapin Library of Williams College, 29 titles; New York Public Library, 7; William L. Clements Library of the University of Michigan, 7; Connecticut Historical Society, 7; Folger Shakespeare Library, 7; Princeton University Library, 6; John Work Garrett Library, 2; Yale University Library, 2; John Carter Brown Library, 2; and one each in the Henry E. Huntington Library, the Free Library of Philadelphia, the Massachusetts Historical Society, the University of Virginia, and the Philip H. and A. S. W. Rosenbach Foundation.

The seven titles in the Connecticut Historical Society were purchased originally by the late Morgan Bulkeley, of Hartford, Connecticut, who acquired them through the good offices of our late friend, Lathrop C. Harper. He seems to have been the agent responsible for bringing to America so many of the Kennett books which were placed on sale in 1917. Among the seven titles acquired by Mr. Bulkeley was a copy of Philip Vincent's *A true relation of the late battell fought in New England, between the English and the Salvages* (London: M. P., for Nathaniel Butter, and John Bellamie, 1637), described by number 159 in the sale catalogue. At the sale, it brought the considerable sum of 650 pounds, probably the high point in the auction. The three volumes which were formerly owned by the late Herschel V. Jones, of Minneapolis, have been dispersed, but they remain in American ownership.

There are evidences that certain books from the Kennett Library found their way to America, presumably before the 1917 sale. In what fashion the Society for the Propagation of the Gospel released them for sale has not been determined; presumably, this was arranged through private negotiation. The learned Bishop, while he might lament the dispersal of his original library, would undoubtedly be happy that these books are being cared for and used by several of the great research libraries in this country. As inanimate missionaries, they still serve a purpose which Bishop Kennett himself would heartily approve.

III

SELECTED BIBLIOGRAPHY

BIBLIOTHECÆ AMERICANÆ PRIMORDIA

[KENNETT, White] *bp. of Peterborough, 1660-1728.*

Bibliothecæ americanæ primordia. An attempt towards laying the foundation of an American library, in several books, papers, and writings, humbly given to the Society for the propagation of the gospel in foreign parts, for the perpetual use and benefit of their members, their missionaries, friends, correspondents, and others concern'd in the good design of planting and promoting Christianity within Her Majesties colonies and plantations in the West-Indies. By a member of the said society. London, Printed for J. Churchill, at the Black Swan in Pater-Noster-Row, 1713. 1 p. l., iii, xvi, 3-275 (*i.e.* 283) p. 112 l. 21.5 cm.

Paging irregular; no. 125-132 (sig. L1-Mm) repeated. Index (pages not numbered) sig. Cccc-Mmmmmm in twos.

Only 250 copies printed.

"Advertisement," "Auctarium Bibliothecæ americanæ. An addition of some other books and papers humbly given to the Society ..." and "Index," by Robert Watts.

The dedication is dated Oct. 20, 1713, but the Advertisement has date Nov. 1, 1714, and the "addition" contains entries of books published in 1714.

The entries are arranged chronologically by date of publication; "extracts" from Purchas and Hakluyt are entered under the date of the voyage described.

The copy formerly owned by President Thomas Jefferson is now in the possession of the Library of Congress. (*cf.* Sowerby 472). The copy in the John Carter Brown Library may possibly have been used by Leman Thomas Rede in the preparation of the *Bibliotheca Americana* in 1789. According to Stuart C. Sherman: "This copy is interleaved, many of its titles have been crossed out, and many new ones inserted on the blank leaves. Beginning with the year 1714 and continuing to the year 1788 all titles have been added in longhand. From 1716 onward these titles, with few exceptions, form the content of the *Bibliotheca Americana* for 1716-1788. Many peculiarities of handwriting found in the manuscript title page reproduced on page 337 of this article are repeated in headings and interleaved titles of the John Carter Brown copy of White Kennett. The correspondence is not exact between the contents of this book and the contents of the printed *Bibliotheca Americana,* but it is close enough to make legitimate the foregoing suggestion that the John Carter Brown interleaved White Kennett catalogue was a working copy used by Rede at one stage in his preparation of the *Bibliotheca Americana.*" (*William and Mary Quarterly,* July 1947). In the Stetson sale, February 25, 1953, a copy sold for $35; in 1951 a copy sold at Hodgson's brought £15. The copy owned by Charles Deane and included in the sale of his library in 1898 brought $16.

Bibliothecæ americanæ primordia. Catalogue of the remaining portion of the famous collection of early Americana formed by the Right Rev. White Kennett, D.D. (1660-1728) bishop of Peterborough, and given by him in 1712 to the Society for the propagation of the gospel in foreign parts. Sold by order of the society under a scheme authorized by the Charity commissioners of England ... Also of certain other books bequeathed at different times to the society ... Which will be sold by auction by Messrs. Sotheby,

Wilkinson & Hodge . . . auctioneers . . . the 30th of July, 1917 . . . [London] Dryden press, J. Davy & sons [1917]. iv, 36 p. facsims. 25.5 cm.

226 lots (lot 110 was withdrawn from the sale).

"Described as 'the remaining portion' of the collection . . . because . . . so many of the books of the original collection had been lost or mislaid, and a certain proportion . . . sent to the British Museum."—Letter from Sotheby & co.

a) *THE KENNETT LIBRARY*

ASHE, St. George.

A sermon preach'd before the incorporated Society for the propagation of the gospel in foreign parts; at their anniversary meeting in the parish-church of St. Mary-le-Bow, on Friday the 18th of February, 1714. London, printed and sold by J. Downing, 1715. 62 (2) p. 19.5 cm.

"An abstract of the most material proceedings and occurrences within the last year's endeavours of the Society for the propagation of the gospel in foreign parts, from Friday the 19th of February 1713, to Friday the 18th of February 1714." (p. 25-62).

On page 32 of the following resolution is printed: "Agreed, That the Thanks of the Society be given to the Dean of Peterborough, for such his great and useful Benefaction; and for his great pains in drawing a Catalogue, with the chief Contents of the said Books, and causing the same to be Printed: Ordering, at the same time a considerable Number of them to be work'd off at their own Charge, and 50 copies to be put into his Hands, to be distributed as he, the said Dean should think fit."

BARTLETT, John Russell.

Bibliotheca americana. A catalogue of books relating to North and South America in the library of John Carter Brown of Providence, R. I. Part III—1701 to 1800. Vol. 1. With notes by John Russell Bartlett. Providence, 1870. iv, 446 p. 26.5 cm.

The entry describing the Kennett catalogue is numbered 178 on page 52.

BRITISH MUSEUM.

Return. British Museum. 1917. Ordered, by the House of Commons, to be printed, 1 May 1917. London, Published by His Majesty's stationery office, 1917. 98 p. 24.5 cm.

On page 19 there is a reference to the gift of 79 books and pamphlets "bequeathed" to the Society for the Propagation of the Gospel by Bishop White Kennett.

DEANE, Charles.

An account of the White Kennett Library of the Society for the propagation of the gospel in foreign parts. Cambridge, J. Wilson and Son, 1883. 8 p.

HARRISSE, Henry.

Bibliotheca americana vetustissima. A description of works relating to America, published between the years 1492 and 1551. New York, G. P. Philes, 1866. 4 p.l., liv p., 1 l., 519 [1] p. 25 cm.

References to Bishop Kennett appear on pages xv-xvi of the introduction.

MOORE, John.

Of the truth & excellency of the gospel. A sermon preach'd before the Society for propagation of the gospel in foreign parts, at their anniversary meeting, in the parish-church of St. Mary-le-Bow, on Friday the 20th of February 1712/13. By the right reverend father in God, John, Lord Bishop of Ely. London, printed by Joseph Downing, 1713. 56 p. 19.5 cm.

"An abstract of the most remarkable proceedings and occurrences of the Society for the propagation of the gospel in foreign parts, from February 15, 1711/12 to Feb. 20, 1712/13." (p. 37-56).

On page 52 there is a reference to the intention of one of their members to present for the perpetual use of the Society between "2 and 300 Tracts relating to the Country and Affairs of America."

REDE, Leman Thomas, *comp.*

Bibliotheca americana; or a chronological catalogue of the most curious and interesting books, pamphlets, state papers, &c. upon the subject of North and South America, from the earliest period to the present, in print and manuscript; for which research has been made in the British Musæum, and the most celebrated public and private libraries, reviews, catalogues, &c. with an introductory discourse on the present state of literature in those countries. London: Printed for J. Debrett, J. Sewell, R. Baldwin, J. Bew, and E. Harlowe, 1789. 2 p. l., 271 p. 26.5 cm.

> Although the compiler makes no mention of his obligation to the *Bibliothecæ americanæ primordia*, the entries in this catalogue for the years 1170-1712 are readily identified as having been transcribed from Bishop Kennett's catalogue. That this is probably certain is borne out by the fact that an annotated copy of the Kennett catalogue in the John Carter Brown Library was owned by Rede. (*cf.* Stuart C. Sherman's *Leman Thomas Rede*). Further corroboration is the fact that the compiler is known to have consulted material in the Library of the Society for the Propagation of the Gospel in America.

RICH, Obadiah.

Bibliotheca americana nova; or, a catalogue of books in various languages, relating to America, printed since the year 1700. Compiled principally from the works themselves by O. Rich . . . London. O. Rich . . . New York: Harper and Brothers, 1835. 3 v. 23 cm.

> Mr. Rich appraises the Kennett catalogue in these terms:
> "This, as far as it goes, is the best catalogue of books relating to America extant; the titles being copied at full length with the greatest exactness together with the name of the printer, and the number of pages in each volume, *etc.*"—Vol. 1, p. 21.

SHERMAN, Stuart C.

"Leman Thomas Rede's *Bibliotheca Americana.*" (In: *The William and Mary Quarterly,* 3rd series, Vol. IV, no. 3, July 1947, pp. 332-349).

SOWERBY, E. Millicent, *comp.*

Catalogue of the Library of Thomas Jefferson, Volume I, Washington, Library of Congress, 1952. xv, 562 p. 29.5 cm.

> (See particularly entries 377 on page 160, and 472 on pages 217-218.)

STANHOPE, George.

The early conversion of Islanders a wise expedient for propagating Christianity. A sermon, preached before the incorporated Society for the propagation of the gospel in foreign parts; at their anniversary meeting in the parish-church of St. Mary-le-Bow, on Friday the 19th of Feb. 1713-14. London, printed and sold by J. Downing, 1714. 36 p. 2 plans. 20 cm.

> "An abstract of the most material proceedings and occurrences within the last year's endeavours of the Society for the propagation of the gospel in foreign parts from Friday the 20th of February, 1712 [1713] to Friday the 19th of February, 1713 [1714]. (p. 23-26).
>
> On pages 25-26 there is a detailed reference to the receipt of the catalogue of the Kennett Library on April 17, 1713, and the order that it be printed in an edition of 250 copies.

WINSHIP, George Parker.

The Cambridge press 1638-1692. A reexamination of the evidence concerning the Bay Psalm Book and the Eliot Indian Bible as well as other contemporary books and people. Philadelphia, University of Pennsylvania Press, 1945. ix, (1) 385 p. 24 cm.

> On page 288 there is a reference to Bishop Kennett's copy of Henry Neville's *The Isle of Pines* (London, printed by S. G. for Allen Banks and Charles Harper, 1668), which sold in 1917 for 12 shillings (1713 Catalogue, p. 121-2; sale catalogue, 113). Later that year it was re-sold at auction in New York for $400 on the strength of a spurious claim that it was "one of the lost books of the Colonial Press at Cambridge in New England."

WROTH, Lawrence C.

"Early Americana." (In: *Standards of bibliographical description,* Philadelphia, University of Pennsylvania Press, 1949. pp. 93-120).

b) *BISHOP KENNETT*

BENNETT, Gareth V.

White Kennett, 1660-1728, bishop of Peterborough. A study in the political and ecclesiastical history of the early eighteenth century. The Thirlwall prize essay in the University of Cambridge, 1955. London: S.P.C.K., 1957. xii, 290 p. front. 22cm. Bibliography, pp. 276-286.

The dictionary of national biography founded in 1882 by George Smith, Edited by Sir Leslie Stephen and Sir Sidney Lee. From the earliest times to 1900. Volume XI. Kennett-Lluelyn. Published since 1917 by the Oxford University Press, London, Humphrey Milford. xx, 1335 p. 24 cm.

The article devoted to Bishop Kennett found on pages 2-6 was composed by Thompson Cooper.

NEWTON, William.

The life of the right reverend Dr. White Kennett, late lord Bishop of Peterborough. With several original letters of the late Archbishop of Canterbury, Dr. Tennison, the late Earl of Sunderland, Bishop Kennett, &c. And some curious original papers and records, never before published. London, Printed for S. Billingsley, 1730. xi, (ix), 288 (2) p. 20 cm.

References to the Americana library are found on pages 147-8, 209. A catalogue of his works, tracts, and sermons, some 57 in number, is found on pages 195-213.

Bibliothecæ Americanæ Primordia

by Bishop White Kennett

Bibliothecæ Americanæ Primordia.

An Attempt

Towards laying the Foundation of an

American Library,

In several

BOOKS, PAPERS, and WRITINGS,

Humbly given to the

SOCIETY

FOR

Propagation of the GOSPEL in

FOREIGN PARTS,

For the Perpetual Use and Benefit of their MEMBERS, their MISSIONARIES, FRIENDS, CORRESPONDENTS, and Others concern'd in the Good Design of Planting and Promoting CHRISTIANITY within Her MAJESTIES Colonies and Plantations in the *WEST-INDIES.*

By a MEMBER *of the* said SOCIETY.

LONDON:

Printed for *J. CHURCHILL,* at the *Black Swan* in *Pater-Noster-Row.* 1713.

ADVERTISEMENT.

THIS Catalogue had been publiſhed ſome time ago, had not the Multiplicity of *Matters*, *Perſons* and *Places*, made the compiling the *INDEX*, a Work of a Tedious, as well as a Laborious Nature.

The Reader is deſired to correct with his Pen the Literal Miſtakes he ſhall obſerve therein, and to add a * to the 125, 126, 127, 128, 129, 130, 131 and 132 Pages, under the Signatures of (L l) and (M m) which by Miſtake happen to be repeated, that the References thereto in the *INDEX* may be more eaſily found.

He is deſired likewiſe to take Notice, That the *Hiſtoire des Indes Occidentales.* A. D. 1622. And the *Bullarium Romanum.* A. D. 1638. out of which ſeveral Extracts are mentioned in the *CATALOGUE*, which were through Haſte omitted to be inſerted therein, are to be found in the *AUCTARIUM*, wherein are likewiſe inſerted in a fuller Manner, the *Sixth Article* of Page 62. and the *Seventh Article* of pag. 185. And that in the *POSTSCRIPT* there are inſerted the Titles of *Seven* Books, which are already in the *Societies* Poſſeſſion.

(*)   There

There are likewife in the *Auctarium*, feveral Extracts of a Treatife, the Title of which is not inferted there, but is as follows :

Strange News from the *Indies* or *Eaft-India* Paffages further difcovered *Auguft* in *Jubilee*. 1650. as partly difcovering the Manner and Tenour of our *Eaft-India* Trade hither-to ; together with Part of the woful and fad Sufferings of *William Coorten*, Efq; written for *Information*, *Confir-mation*, and *Confutation* ; by a conftant Well-willer, and continual Sufferer for Truth, and Publick Good. *J. D.* [*viz. John Darell*,] therein imploring and intimating to all in Authority, and others for fpeedy Juftice, and right Underftanding in Judgment and Practice, and by Prin-ciples, and grounded Reafons, pointing at a Foundation and Regulation of that hitherto much abufed *Eaft-India Trade*, fo vaft, fpacious, neceffary, and of extraordinary high Concernment, to enrich and advance Kingdoms and Common Wealths being the Trade of Trades, the Ma-gazeen of Merchandizers, the Honour of Nations, and the Glory of this World. *London* for *Stephen Bowtel.* 1652, 4*to*. *pag*. 39. [Ex Dono, *Roberti Watts*, L. L. B.]

I humbly prefume to fuggeft, That this *Catalogue* may ferve for feveral good Purpofes, befides thofe mentioned by the ge-nerous Donor in the *Dedication* : As,

Firft, That either the Government in general, or private Proprietors in particular, may find therein *Inftructions* for en-couraging People to tranfplant themfelves to their Colonies and Plantations.

Secondly,

Secondly, That the Accounts of *Companies* inserted herein, may be a means of either reviving some *old* ones, or of forming *new* ones.

Thirdly, The Government may hence form Instructions to be given to such as they employ in Expeditions, and Merchants to such as they shall employ in *Voyages* at their Charge.

Fourthly, Merchants may learn from thence to meet together, and give God Thanks in a Publick Manner, on the News of the Arrival of any of their Ships, by having Sermons preach'd to them suitable to such Occasions, according to the Example of Mr. *Terry*'s. A. D. 1649.

Fifthly, Travellers may from the Examples mentioned in this *Catalogue*, learn to take God's Blessing along with them, by hearing from some Godly Minister or other a *Farewell Sermon* of which Sort are Mr. *Featly*'s to Sir *Tho. Warner* and his Company bound to the *West-Indies*, for their Farewell on *Sept.* 6. 1629. and Mr. *Hardy*'s, occasion'd by the Voyage of *Nathan. Wych*, Esq; President to the *East-Indies*. A. D. 1658.

Sixthly, This *Catalogue* may induce publick-spirited Persons, to pick up such Tracts as are mentioned herein, and throw them into the *Society's* Store, that thereby the *Society* may henceforward be able to furnish their *Missionaries* with Accounts of the Places they are sent to.

All I shall add, is, my hearty Wishes of Success to this, and all other good Designs, which tend to the Advancement of the Glory of God, and the Honour of our Church and Nation.

London Nov. 1.   *Robert Watts.*
1714.

To the WORTHY

SOCIETY

ESTABLISHED

For Propagation of the Gospel

IN

FOREIGN PARTS.

HAving had the Honour to be nominated among Others a Member of your Society, in the Royal CHARTER for Inſtitution of it in the Year 1701. I have from that Time thought my ſelf obliged (as far as my private mean Abilities could ſerve) to labour and aſſiſt in promoting your great Deſigns of DOING GOOD. For we muſt acknowledge this to be a CHRISTIAN DUTY and DEBT, That in our ſeveral Stations We All owe unto God and our Neighbour, and muſt one day give Account of our Diſcharge or Neglect of it, according to the Powers and Opportunities we had in this Life. A daily DUTY, that when honeſtly and willingly perform'd, brings along with it ſo much Comfort and Satisfaction in our Mortal State, as to give a Pledge and Foretaſte of its greater Reward Above.

I had the farther Honour of receiving your Commands for drawing up ſome *ACCOUNT of this Society, with their Pro-*

a   *Proceedings*

ceedings and Success in 1706. which you have since thought fit to be enlarged, and brought down to the present time. In a pursuit of those Orders, the better to discharge my Trust, I had occasion to pick up several Tracts and Papers relating to the General Subject of the Propagation of the Gospel, Conversion of Infidels. Institution of the College at Rome *de propaganda Fide,* Missions of the Monks and Jesuites, Methods of the Inquisition, &c. But more especially to the particular Affairs of *A M E R I C A,* the first Discovery of those Regions sufficient to be called A N ɪ w Wᴏ ʀ ʟ ᴅ, the several Expeditions and Voyages made to every Coast and Port and River, the Advances and Settlements there made, the Tyranny and Cruelty of the *Spaniards* in *M E X I C O* and *P E R V,* their Baptizing in Blood, and then teaching a Religion of such outward Pomp and Ceremony, as was very little different from the Pagan Idolatry. Above All, I sought for the Relations and Journalls of our own Countrymen upon those Seas and Coasts, their Discoveries and Observations, their Settlement of Plantations and Colonies, their Improvements in Trade and Strength, their Conversation with the Natives, and their Endeavours to bring them over to Civility and Religion.

Upon this View, my Curiosity by degrees encreas'd the little Stock, and brought me in a tolerable Connexion of Books and Papers, relating to those Arguments. And because I saw an Affinity of other Matters, and a sort of necessary Dependence of Things and Places upon one another; I proceeded to gather up some of the chief Tracts, of antient and modern Geography, of Astronomical Observations, of Experiments in Hydrography, of Shipping, and the progress of Navigation, of Commerce and Exchange, of War, Peace, and Embassies, of Voyages and Travels to all Parts of the World, especially to *A F ʀ I C A* and the *E A S T - I N D I E S,* that chiefly supply our Traffick to *A M E R I C A.*

I found some Difficulty in making a small Collection of this Kind, especially in getting up the lesser Tracts and single Papers; which I thought therefore, if once dispers'd and carry'd back into various Hands, would be harder to recollect and put

together

together again. For this Reason I preserv'd them, and within my own Intentions all along devoted them to your publick Use and Service. I now humbly offer them to your Acceptance and Custody, to be reposited in such a Place, and under such Directions, as the PRESIDENT and SOCIETY shall think fit to appoint by any standing Rules and Orders: Which I submit to their Judgment, and would not seem to prescribe my own Opinion in the Disposal of them. Only I wish the Place to be allotted for them, may be capable of containing a much larger Accession of Volumes, Globes, Maps, &c. that no doubt will be soon brought in by other Hands. However, I do hereby engage for the Delivery of my little Store (according to this printed Catalogue) upon demand made on me or my Assigns, as soon as there is set apart any such convenient Room or Place for the Reception and safe Custody of the said Books and Papers, for the continual Use and Benefit of this Corporation and their Successors for ever.

I have often thought with some Regret, on the want of proper Evidences and Memoirs for us to have recourse to, as the Nature and Occasions of our Foreign Business may require. I hope the World will so interpret this Omission and Defect in us, as to believe that we took more care of others abroad, than of our selves at home; and had sent over several little Libraries for the Use of our Missionaries, and their People in those distant Parts, before we thought of providing for our own nearer Accommodation: And let it be consider'd, that the constant Demands of our Aid and Assistance for Churches, Missionaries, Schools, Books, and other Exigencies, have been so great and pressing, that they have for several Years taken up more than our ordinary Income, and before this time we must have contracted our Expences and Designs, if Her MAJESTY in Her Pious Disposition had not extended Her Royal Favours to us. Nor have we been hitherto able to afford our selves a common Place to meet in, but have ow'd that Conveniency to the generous Care and Kindness of the PRESIDENT, our continual Friend and Benefactor.

Hence

Hence the providing of a Select LIBRARY for the Propagation of the Gospel, seems of necessity to be assign'd over to another Age, unless some unexpected Friend and Patron shall arise up to our present Relief, and by charitable Gift or Legacy, supply us with a Stock sufficient for the Establishment and Maintenance of it. To keep up the Hopes of finding such a pious Founder and Benefactor, and to excite some worthy Man of Wealth and publick Spirit, I have here form'd a rude Scheme of what may be done, and offer a little toward the Beginning of it.

Where any publick Work is visibly wanting, it is an honest Labour to bring in some Materials towards laying the Foundation ; and so to leave the raising and finishing Part to longer Time, and more able Workmen. The Truth is, for any single Person to undertake the founding a complete Library, requires a Genius, as well as a Fortune, above the common sort of Mankind, a *BODLEY*, a *TENISON*, or some such superiour Spirit of Piety, Learning, and Liberality.

However, as the drawing of one Furrow was formerly the Designation of a City, so I hope this rude Draught may direct a little to the raising, furnishing, and endowing a full and perfect *AMERICAN* LIBRARY, to contain all sorts of Books, Charts, Maps, Globes, Instruments, and other Utensils, that can possibly tend to the more exact Survey and Knowledge of the Earth and Seas, and Heavenly Bodies ; and to be more especially stock'd with such Discourses, Letters, Journals, and other Instructions, as may best serve for the Conduct of our Missionaries, the Help of Mariners and Merchants, the Information of Strangers, and the Entertainment of all Persons, who wish well to the Propagation of our Faith, and to the Trade and Commerce of our Country, among ALL NATIONS.

I might easily suggest, that the LIBRARY here projected would serve to many excellent Purposes. Our own Members would be all glad to be better inform'd of the Air and Soil, the Manners and Customs, the Product and Trade, the Government and Religion of those Provinces, committed in Charity to our peculiar Charge. And when the special Books and

                                                                Papers

Papers are near at hand, they will often make it their bufinefs and pleafure, to fatisfie their Curiofity and improve their Knowledge in the Affairs intrufted to them. And the confequence would be, that the more perfectly they underftood the State of thofe Countries and People, they would be the better affected to do them good, and more able to advife and refolve on the beft methods of fo doing. Such a conveniency of Books and Writings with an eafie Accefs to them would be our School and General Study, would inftruct and improve us in our noble Profeffion of feeking and labouring to propagate the GOSPEL of *CHRIST.*

In many of our Meetings and Committees, there arife in courfe fuch Queftions and Debates, as are beft decided by an Appeal to the authority of particular Tracts or Maps or Writings; and if they are within our Search and View upon any fuch emergent occafion, it will fave trouble and needlefs Altercation and bring the Matters in queftion to an eafie and effectual Iffue. We can direct our Confultations, govern our Refolves, and anfwer all the Addreffes and Propofals made to us with more certainty and expedition, when we have our Evidences open, and as it were the proper ORACLES before us

A Refort to this variety of Books and Papers would be of fome confiderable ufe and fervice to other BODIES of Men. The Honourable *Commiffioners for Trade and Plantations* might here upon occafion command a Tranfcript of fome valuable Notices of things that come immediately before them. Articles and Agreements made for Commerce and Exchange of Goods, Petitions for Equity and Right, Anfwers of Decifion and Redrefs, Orders, Inftructions, Reports, and many other Acts of mutual Correfpondence between our Government here, and our *Englifh* Colonies in thofe Parts. Of which uncommon kind, great numbers are to be found even in this poor Collection, and a more abundant Stock will I hope be foon added to it.

The Honourable *Lords of the ADMIRALTY* will pleafe to obferve, that they may have Searches here made for Com-

b

miffions,

miffions, Sailing Orders, Secret Inftructions, Relations of Sea-
fights, Defcents, Retreats, &c. Proceedings in Courts Mar-
tial, and other Maritime Affairs, of which nature Many are
here preferv'd and Many may be daily recover'd, which would
perhaps otherwife be loft for ever. So likewife the Judges;
the Advocates, and Proctors concern'd in the *Court of AD-*
MIRALTY might here find fome of the oldeft Precedents
for Letters of Marque and Reprizal, Trials for Piracy and
Depredation; Compacts for Freight and Paffage; Allowances
for Demorage, Averidge, and other Contributions; Policies
of Affurance, Bills of Exchange; Complaints, Proceedings,
Sentences, Appeals, and like Forms and Methods in Maritime
Caufes under the cognizance of that High and Ancient
Court.

Nay *the Hiftorian, the Herald,* and other Remembrancers of
worthy Names and Families, may here find a *Foundation,* as
it were, *eftablifhed upon the Floods,* to many noble Houfes, that
have fprung from brave Adventurers and Commanders at Sea,
who loved their Nation and did Honour to it, by fpreading the
Terrour of our Arms, and bringing home Spoils and Trophies
in Wealth and Glory to the Publick and themfelves. Such
were the immortal Names of Patriots, *HAWKINS, DRAKE,*
FROBISHER, RALEGH, CAVENDISH, SOMERS, &c.

And the greateft *Minifters of State* might pleafe to think,
that fuch a Repofitory of Books and Papers of Navigation and
Commerce might at one time or other be of fome advantage
in the moft arduous Affairs of thefe Kingdoms: Particularly in
afferting our Dominion of the Seas, in keeping up the wonted
Superiority of *Englifh* Fleets and Navies, in fecuring and encouraging our Fifhery and our Manufactures, in forming and
maintaining our Treaties and Alliances; there being already
put into this imperfect Collection the greateft part of the A R-
T I C L E S of Peace and Amity, Alliance and Commerce, that
have been made between this Crown and other States and
Princes from the Beginning of K. *James* I. to the prefent Times:
All in their firft Editions publifh'd by Authority, more correct
than the later Recapitulations of them. To thefe are added

many

many private Papers of Negotiations and Intrigues, Cautions and Recoveries, Secret Articles, and other Political Mysteries, that may be turn'd and applied to some Use and Service at one time or other.

And in a narrower Sphere, all our *English* COMPANIES establish'd for Trade and Commerce, to the *East-Indies*, to the *Levant* Seas, to *Africa*, to *Russia*, to *Hudson*'s-Bay, *&c.* might here find a great many Treatises and Memorials relating to their peculiar Affairs ; and perhaps of such Weight and Importance to them as may encourage each Company to lay the like Foundation of a Singular LIBRARY for all Books and Writings and Remains whatever, that more immediately concern their own BODY.

But especially the GOVERNOURS and other Administrators of Justice in her Majesty's Plantations before they go from hence to take possession of their Charge, may the better qualifie themselves, if they please to see what has been written about their peculiar Province : When the Discovery and Settlement was made, what the Laws and particular Constitutions are, what Good Names and sufficient Estates have been gotten by Justice and Moderation, what Examples of Ruin and Infamy to Tyrants and Oppressors, what Credit and Comfort in Governing always and every where ACCORDING TO LAW.

However (what is our greatest Concern) the Benefit of Access to this *AMERICAN* LIBRARY will be very convenient to our MISSIONARIES, when first approved and retained by Us. For it is well known, that upon their Entrance into this Service of God and his Church in Foreign Parts, they are so uncertain of their transportation by the Stay of Ships, Change of Winds, and other casualties, that they have generally a void Space of time upon their hands, which they cannot better spend, than in such a sober studious Place, where they may enquire after the Country and People they are going to, and may in effect converse with them before they see them. They may at least pick up such intelligence and notices of the Seas and Coasts and Rivers, of the Planters and Merchants, of the Soil and Air, of the Latitude and Situation, as may not at

their

their Landing there expose them to a perfectly New and Un-known World, and drop them altogether Strangers and Pil-grims in it. The better acquainted they are with that Sphere wherein they are to act, the better Figure they will make in it; All the odd appearances of Mankind are commonly owing to Ignorance and Surprize.

It might indeed take up their whole Time to study the One Necessary Thing, the Obligations of their Mission and the Du-ties and Difficulties of it; they will find here a good Collection of Discourses and Advices to that End and Purpose of recom-mending the wisest and most successful Methods of Propaga-ting and Promoting the Gospel of Christ. But besides their knowledge of the General Duty, they must be let into the par-ticular Disposition of the Country and Nation wherein they are to exercise their Mission, they must understand somewhat of the Constitution of that Government they are to live under, of the first Rise and following Advances of that Colony or Plan-tation that is to receive them, the Temper and Infirmities of the People, the present State of Letters and Religion among 'em, the most prevailing Errours and Divisions, and whatever else is most necessary to be known for their better discharge of the Care of those Souls. And as that Care is to extend to-ward the Negro Slaves and the *Indian* Natives, they might here examine the various Accounts that have been given by Eye-witnesses of their Genius and Capacity, their Notions and Manners, their Prejudices and their Obstinacy in them. And to enable themselves to converse a little with those ignorant Natives, they might here dip into the *Indian* Languages, or the chief Dialects of the Borderers on us, by turning over the several Essays of Grammar and Dictionary, that are here to be met with in one or more of those Tongues, and especially by examining THE INDIAN GRAMMAR, and THE INDIAN BIBLE prepared and publish'd by the industrious and pious Mr. *ELLIOT*; with the Lord's Prayer, Creed, Commandments, short Catechisms, and other familiar Expo-sitions of our common Articles of Faith, which have been printed in *New-England* under the Encouragement of Mr. *Boyle*

and

and the Corporation for the Propagation of the Gospel unto the *Indians* there adjoyning, and are most of them to be found in this Collection. Or if they have not time to run over the Books themselves, the very Catalogue however will supply them with the full Titles of Such, as they may procure to carry with them, or may leave or send a Commission for them.

They ought all to furnish themselves with such Tracts and Dissertations as recommend and explain the Great Duty of Planting the Gospel in All Nations, and direct the most effectual ways and means of bringing over the poor Pagan Souls to Christian Knowledge and Salvation. Of which excellent kind there be many here collected: *Josephus Acosta de Promulgatione Evangelij apud Indos.* 1596. *De Legatione Evangelica ad Indos capessenda Admonitio Justi Heurnij, cum Censura ac Judicio Joannis Polyandri.* 1618. *Georgi Horni de Originibus Americanis.* 1652. *De Successu Evangelij apud Indos in Nova Anglia Epistola Crescentij Matheri ad D. Jo. Leusdenum, &c.* A *Sermon of Mr. Symond's before the Adventurers and Planters in* Virginia *for the Advancement of their Christian purpose.* 1609. *Mr.* Price's *Sermon with a Reproof of those that traduce the Honourable Plantation of* Virginia. 1609. *Sermons of Mr.* Cowper, *Of the Gathering in of the* Gentiles, *with his Epistle to the Commissioners for Plantations.* 1615. *The Planters Plea or Grounds of Plantations examined.* 1620. *God's Promise made to his Plantation by Mr.* Cotton. 1625. *Mr.* Featly's *Sermon to Sir* Thomas Warner *and Company bound to the* West-Indies. 1629. *Mr.* Castel's *Petition to the Parliament for the Propagating of the Gospel in* America. 1641. *The Pagans Debt and Dowry by Mr.* John Goodwyn. 1642. *Dr.* Hardy's *Pious Votary and Prudent Traveller.* 1658. *Mr.* Thoroughgood's Jews *in* America. 1660. *Dr.* Fletcher's Israel Redux. 1677. *The* Negroes *and* Indians *Advocate, by Mr.* Godwyn. 1680. 8vo. *The same Mr.* Godwyn's *Trade preferr'd before Religion.* 1685. *Dr.* Bray's *Apostolick Charity.* 1699. And the several *Sermons Preached at the Anniversary Meetings of the Society.* All which are so directly useful to every Missionary, that I wish they could be made a Part of the Library allowed to Him by the Society. To supply the want of that Accommodation, it feems the more neceffary, that every intended Miffionary fhould know where and how to look into them, and to draw out fuch Notes and Obfervations, as may efpecially remind 'em and affift 'em when they come Abroad. It is certain, that a Man of Confcience with his Thoughts upon the *Indies* may here profecute his preparatory Studies with fo much advantage and delight, that it would not be amifs, if all our Miffionaries were oblig'd hereafter by a Standing Order to take a previous Courfe of Studies in this Library for fome Weeks before their Expedition.

For their fuller Information, I have caft in a good number of thofe Narratives and controverfial Letters which the Jefuites and other Orders call'd Religious in the Church of *Rome* have publifh'd to the World concerning their Labours and Succeffes (as they reprefent them) in fpreading their New Gofpel throughout the *Eaft-Indies, Ethiopia, Congo, Tartary,* and other Infidel Parts ; and efpecially of the Diffimulation and Bigotry of the Jefuites in *China* ; where they have made themfelves Idolaters, inftead of turning Men from Idols to ferve the Living God. Together with all the Accounts I could gather up of the Society *De propaganda Fide* eftablifh'd at *Rome,* firft inftituted and all along employed rather to convert Hereticks than Pagan Unbelievers, and therefore a ftanding Part of the I N Q U I S I T I O N, that Court which they call H O L Y, and think the Proceedings M O S T C H R I S T I A N, when Nothing upon Earth can be more oppofite to Chrift and his holy Religion. I have added the Accounts of the Propagation of the Gofpel in the Eaft by the *Danifh* Miffionaries and fome Relations of the Care of the States and Companies of the United Provinces in fettling Minifters of the Reformed Religion within their Colonies and Factories in the *E A S T - I N D I E S :* And laftly, the Progrefs in fome good Defigns of promoting Chriftian Knowledge and true Devotion among the Papifts in *I R E L A N D,* the Ignorant Sort in the High-Lands of *S C O T - L A N D,* in *W A L E S, &c.* becaufe thefe Matters are all in a connexion and dependance upon our Office of Propagating the Gofpel.

Among

Among the Uses to be made of this *AMERICAN LI-BRARY*, I ought not to forget that it is capable of becoming the common Fund and Treasury of all the Remains of that Country, and of all the following Discoveries and Remarks that shall be hereafter made upon it. In such a fix'd Repository, some modest Mariners and Travellers may lay up their own Notes and Observations, who being diffident of their own Performance, and afraid of a critical World, would not suffer those Essays to appear in Publick. And even the most exact and perfect Writers would perhaps be equally pleased to deposite here their Journals and Itineraries, that for want of due encouragement, they could not get printed in their life-time, and yet would not have Posterity deprived of the knowledge and intelligence to be received from them. This however would be a convenient Place to preserve and dispose in order the several Letters and loose Papers that come so frequently from our Friends and Correspondents in those Parts; and all the Descriptions and Accounts that every Missionary might be desired or enjoined to give of the particular District committed to him, relating not only to the State of Religion, but to the Natural History of those Ends of the Earth, of the Climates, Soils, Seasons, Winds, Tides, Waters, &c. of the Animals, Vegetables, Minerals, Fossiles, &c. of the Manufactures, Inventions, Commodities, and whatever may conduce to the better Cultivation and Improvement of those vast Regions, and the Trade with them.

To direct a Missionary in the Method of doing this Service to the World, there be very good Advices and Instructions given by Dr. *Robert Hooke* in his Preface to the *Historical Relation of CEYLON by Mr. Robert Knox. 1681.* Fol. and by Mr. *Boulton* in his *General Heads for the Natural History of a Country, for the sake of those who go beyond Seas. 1700. 8vo.* and in other Tracts dispers'd in this Collection.

I only hint at these things in my Affection to our common Cause of serving God and our Country. The Improvement of any Suggestion here made, and the offer of maturer Thoughts I leave to the Judgment of the Society, and the Discretion of

every

every Member. In the mean time I doubt not, but that this imperfect Foundation will by degrees arise up into a confummate Building. Some Royal Bounty, or some other Noble Beneficence will provide a convenient Site and Structure for Us; Some pious Gifts and Legacies will be daily encreafing our Store of Books, Papers, Charts, Maps, and other Literary Merchandize. Then some one or other Publick Spirit will found a Librarian's Place, and affign a competent Salary or Support to it. Some other Endowments and Conditions will be settled for Agents and itinerant Correfpondents to procure and tranfmit hither all manner of Draughts, Figures and other Reprefentations of the things of Nature and Art : And efpecially to pick up all the written Journals of Voyages, Travels, and Adventures; all the Defcriptions of Coaftings, Bearings, Soundings, Sands, Shelves, Rocks, Tides, and all manner of Obfervations and Experiments now lying in a thoufand private Hands of Mariners, Merchants, Strangers, and perhaps Widows, Orphans, and Executors, who underftand nothing of them, and would take but little care to preferve them from Fire or other Confumption.

It was a Glory done to this Nation by Mr. *HAKLUYT* and Mr. *PURCHAS* (both Clergymen of the Church of *England*) that they fpared no Pains or Coft, to hunt after and gather up a great variety and plenty of fuch Journals and Maritime Papers, which had otherwife long before this time been wreckt and loft for ever. Mr. *Robert Afbley*, in his Dedication of the Extracts of *COCHIN CHINA* to Sir *Maurice Abbot* Governour of the Honourable Company of Merchants trading to the *Eaft-Indies.* 1633. concludes thus. " I could wifh, " that as the remote Navigation publifhed by the *Venetian* " *Rhamufius* awakened the Induftry of Mr. *HAKLUYT* and " happely of Mr. *PURCHAS* after him, to their diligent " Gatherings of the moft remarkable Voyages of our Nation : " So fome other able Perfon (of which our Country hath " good Store) were encouraged and ftirred up to continue " fuch Collections. Yet not only to the recording the Ex- " ploits of our own Nation ; but alfo to collect and publifh
" what

" what they find worth the regarding amongst Foreigners, that
" may any way be serviceable for the instruction of Ours.

Now if such a common Bank or Treasury of Papers were once fix'd and establish'd in this Great City, I doubt not but many worthy Persons would be casting into it some or other valuable Remains, that would not otherwise outlive the present Possessor of them. Heirs and Executors are very apt to think Manuscripts and loose Papers to be a sort of Refuse not worth the keeping ; and therefore if they could hear of any proper Office to receive them, they would transmit them thither for Acknowledgment and Thanks, or at least for some other small Consideration. There be now living many industrious Collectors of Voyages and Travels, Navigation, Commerce, &c. who probably after their Decease would not trust them to the custody of a careless Heir, or mercenary Administrator; but will be glad to hear of such a Publick Place as this, wherein they may be safely disposed and preserved with the Memory of their Donour. If such a curious and judicious Collector as Mr. PEPYS had known of any such Design, it is very probable that He would have given all his laborious Effects that way, and they would in such manner have made a National Treasure to Posterity.

To raise and fill by degrees such a LITERARY BANK I willingly subscribe and am ready to pay in this little Stock of mine, to begin with. And to prevent all Deceit or Mistake, I think it proper to present you with this *Printed Catalogue* of the few several Books and Papers I have thus thrown together for your Use, that you may have the surer title to them, and that you may see what great room is left for more ample Benefactions of the like kind. In drawing the Catalogue, I have not only recited the general Titles of the distinct Volumes ; but I have pointed at the particular Discourses, Letters, Instruments, and other eminent Acts contain'd in them ; which I have likewise cast into a Chronological Series and Order of Succession, that so the bare Catalogue may be in Itself a sort of History of NAVIGATION and COMMERCE from the first Discovery of the New World to the present State of Things.

d   And

And I did this with another View and Defire, that the future Publifhers of any Volumes of VOYAGES and TRAVELS may obferve fuch an orderly Method in the Connexion of their feveral Tracts according to Age and Time of Writing, which by fuch fucceffive dependance and reference would give Light and Strength to One Another, and the Bookfellers and Readers would be trading in a Chain of Pearls inftead of a Rope of Sand. I intimate this with the more willing mind, becaufe few Books are more entertaining and inftructive to the World, than fuch various Collections, and becaufe the moft accurate Defcriptions of Remote Parts are ftill confined to fmall fingle Tracts, or perhaps to fhort and loofe Papers, written upon the Spot, as Things and Thoughts offer'd themfelves to the Senfes of the Writer : If thefe were digefted and put together in their native Simplicity, they would make a better figure and ferve to better purpofe, than the elaborate Work of any one Author.

We might apply this to our immediate Province of *AMERICA*, of which the Coafts and Navigable Rivers, and All that relates to the Geography and Natural Hiftory of it, have been beft defcribed and accounted for by Eye-witneffes, who have fent or brought over the plain Narratives and Obfervations under their own hands. Now if a Collection of thefe feparate Sheets were digefted according to Time and Place, and fo publifh'd in a Set of larger Volumes, this would be of good Ufe and Service, and I hope therefore this CATALOGUE will lend fome encouragement and help to it. For example, in this fhort Catalogue may be found about twenty original Tracts relating to *Newfoundland* ; above fifty concerning *Virginia* ; a hundred or more of *New-England* ; and fo on in proportion to our other Colonies and Plantations. Now if thefe were connected in due order of Place and Time, and fairly put into one or more Volumes, it would prevent the fcattering and lofing of many valuable Pieces, and tend much to encourage the reading and remembring of things of the neareft and moft natural Importance to us.

If the flower Sale of such large Volumes would not encourage a common Undertaker; the Work might be the better done by some Publick Spirit. Suppofing a Governour or Sea-Commander returning Rich from those foreign Parts, will be so generous and grateful as to bear the Charge of an Impreffion, with the moft exact and beautiful Maps and Sculptures. A diftinct Volume or two of *NEW-ENGLAND*, another of *VIRGINIA*, of *CAROLINA, MARYLAND*, or other Province according to the particular Relation that the noble Editor bears to it, who by this means may obtain Arms and Infcriptions of the trueft honour, and may prefent his Books, as Princes do their Medals, to be had in perpetual remembrance by them.

I have only this in Juftice and Charity to add, if I could have ask'd freely for a Contribution of Books or Money to this Defign, I prefume the Catalogue would have been much larger, and I might have raifed this Attempt into fome appearance of a LIBRARY. But my Intention was not fo much to Beg, as to fet a little Example of Giving. Only upon an occafional mention of this Defign fome Friends and Promoters of good Works readily caft in fome Books, to the Titles whereof I have thought it honeft to add the Donors Names. While the Prefs was working, I continued to gather up all the Reliques I could meet with of the like kind, and refolv'd not to be too much difcouraged by thofe terrible Lets and Impediments of Doing Good, Trouble and Expence; and thefe additional Books and Papers I have caft into an *Appendix* or *Auctarium* at the end of the other; which in a following Impreffion may be inferted in the fame View and Order. There is an INDEX of Perfons and Matters drawn out by the care and pains of the Rev. Mr. *Robert Watts*, which may be of great ufe to the diligent Searcher after thefe things; as it brings the variety of Matters into one view, and directs the fingular Ufe and Application of 'em.

But undoubtedly the beft Ufe of the Catalogue will be this, if any Perfons in running it over will pleafe to remember, that they have any Books or Papers of this kind not herein after

specified,.

specified, or better Editions of those Books and Maps that are here inserted, and will then willingly transmit them to the Secretary or Treasurer, or other Member of the Society, to enrich and enlarge the common Stock.

I might possibly have improved this Collection by the purchase of a greater number of Memorials of the same nature, but that I was oblig'd to make it consistent with my Circumstances, and with another little Design of gathering together an ANTIQUARIAN and HISTORICAL LIBRARY for the use of a Cathedral Church, wherein some Progress is already made, and I hope in few years to finish and settle it for ever. There is something in Humane Nature that incites to DOING GOOD, and that noble Instinct is highly improv'd and promoted by the Powers of our Christian Religion. Every Minister of Christ is more especially obliged to follow the Great Master who *went about Doing Good*, and made it his usual Saying unto others, *It is more blessed to Give than to Receive*. If we thus chiefly employ our Time and other Talents, and unite and correspond in all manner of Beneficence, it will most effectually divert us from all the idle and the busie Humours that disturb the World, from Impertinence and Pragmaticalness, from Envy and Censure, Strife and Faction: It will by the Grace and Blessing of God make us by degrees of one Heart and of one Mind, in whatsoever Things are True, and make for Peace and Publick Good.

I am with all Duty and Respect

Octob. 20. 1713.　　　　*Your Affectionate Fellow Member,
and Faithful Humble Servant*

WHITE KENNETT.

AMERICAN LIBRARY.

THE Voyage of *MADOC* ap *OWEN GUYNETH*, Prince of   1170. *North Wales*, to the Continent now call'd *America*, or the *West-Indies*, 16 *Hen. 2.* in the Year 1170. as taken chiefly out of the History of *Wales*, publish'd by Master *David Powell*, D. D. [Printed in *Hakluyt's* Voyages. Fol. 1589. p. 506.]

The Voyage of *Alonso Sanchez*, a *Spaniard*, trading to the *Canaries* and   1484. *Madera*, thence driven by a Tempest to a remote Island, suppos'd to be *Hi-* 1 *Ric. 3.* *spaniola*; who returning to *Tercera*, after great Toils and Losses, lodg'd in the House of *Christopher Colon*, or *Columbus*, and gave him the first Hints of discovering a New World. [In the Commentar. of the *Inca* of *Cages*, abridg'd. in *Purchas* Pilgrim. Vol. IV. p. 1454.]

The Offer of the Discovery of the *West-Indies*, by *Christopher Columbus*, to   1488. King *HENRY* the Seventh, in the Year 1488. the thirteenth of *February*; 3 *Hen. 7.* with the King's Acceptation of the Offer, and the Cause whereupon he was depriv'd of the same; as taken out of the Life and Deeds of *Christopher Co-lumbus*; with another Testimony concerning the said Offer. [Relation of Mr. *Hakluyt*, in his Collect. of Voyages. Vol. I. Fol. p. 407.]

A Map of the World made by *Bartholomew Columbus*, then at *London*, and there publish'd with this Inscription.

> *Janua cui patria est, nomen cui Bartholomeus*
> *Columbus, de terra rubra, opus edidit istud*
> *Londonijs, Ann. Domini* 1480. *atque insuper anno*
> *Octavo, decimaq; die cum tertia mensis*
> *Februarij, Laudes Christo cantentur abunde.*

And so presented to K. *Hen*. VII. [*Purchas* Pilgrim. Vol. III. p. 807.]

Navigatio Christopheri COLUMBI *inchoata prima Septembris luce Anno*   1492. MCCCCXCII. *quâ multas regiones hactenus orbi incognitas invenit, inventasq;* 7 *Hen. 7.* Hispaniæ

4

Hispaniæ Rex coli jussit & frequentari, capitibus CIX. comprehensa. [Novus Orbis, Basileæ 1555. Fol. a. p. 64. ad p. 84.]

The History of the Life and Actions of Admiral *CHRISTOPHER COLUMBUS*, and of his Discovery of the *West-Indies*, call'd the *NEW WORLD*, written by his own Son D. *Ferdinand Columbus*. Translated from the *Italian*. [Publish'd in the Collection of Voyages, Printed for Mr. *Churchill*. Fol. 1704. Vol. II. a. p. 557. ad p. 688.]

Sir. *William Monson*'s Account of the Discovery of *AMERICA* by *Columbus*, in the Year 1492. [*Naval Tracts* in the said Collect. Vol. III. p. 403.

A Relation of *Columbus* his first Voyage and Improvement therein of the Mariners Art ; in *Aug.* 1492. [In *Purchas* Pilgrim. Vol. I. B. 2. p. 10.]

1493.
8 Hen. 7. Petri Martyris Anglerij *Epistola Comiti* Tendillæ & *Archiepiscopo* Granatensi *de Novis Terris & nudis Gentibus inventis per* Colonum Ligurem *inter Occiduos Antipodes. Dat.* Barchinonæ. *Idus Septembris, anno* MCCCCXCIII. *cum alijs Literis de terris & hominibus in Occiduo nuperrimè inventis.* [Pet. Martyris Angler. Epistolæ, Amstelodami. 1670. *Fol. p.* 73. &c.]

Exemplar Bullæ sive Donationis, authoritate cujus, Episcopus Romanus Alexander *ejus nominis sextus concessit & donavit Ferdinando &* Elizabethæ *Regi & Reginæ* Castellæ, Legionis, &c. & *suis Successoribus Regiones & Insulas Novi Orbis. Dat.* Romæ. *apud* S. Petrum. *Anno Incarnationis Dominicæ* 1493. *IV. Non. Maij. Pont. nostri anno primo.* [Printed in Lat. and Engl. in *Purchas* Pilgrim. Vol. I. B. II. Ch. 1. p. 14.] With Animadversions on the said Bull.

1494.
9. Hen. 7. P. Martyris Anglerij *Epistola Archiepiscopo* Granatensi *de Indicis rebus & Admiraldo* Columbo, *qui magna pollicetur se detecturum ad occiduos Antarcticosq; Antipodes. Dat. ex* Valleoleto, *prid. Cal. Februarij, anno* MCCCCXCIV. *cum alijs ejusdem argumenti Literis de* Hispaniola ; *de secunda Navigatione ad Indos. De Canibalibus ; De Antipodum orbe latente hactenus, &c. Sub eodem anno.* [Pet. Mart. Epistolæ, Fol. *p.* 69. Ep. CXL.]

1495.
10 Hen. 7. *Epistola ejusdem* Petri Martyris *Amico suo* Pomponio Læto, *de Longitudinis & Latitud. gradibus in* Hispaniola ; *de illarum terrarum & cœli naturâ ; de modo vivendi ; de Regulis & domibus, & nudo Incolarum incessu, &c. Dat. IV. Idus Januar.* MCCCCXCV. [Ib. P. Mart. Epistolæ. *p.* 88. &c.]

Exemplar

Exemplar Literarum HENRICI *Regis Angliæ VII. Johanni* CABOTTO   1496.
civi Venetiarum *ac Ludovico Sebastiano & Sancto filijs dicti Johannis ad in-*   11 *Hen. 7.*
veniendum, disccoöperiendum, & investigandum, quascunq; Insulas, Patrias, Re-
giones, sive Provincias Gentilium & Infidelium in quacunq; Parte Mundi positas,
quæ Christianis omnibus ante hæc tempora fuerunt incognitæ, teste Rege apud
Westmon. *quinto die Martij An. reg. XI.* 1496. [Printed in Latin and English
in Mr. *Hakluyt's* Voyages. . *Fol.* 1589. *p.* 509.]

Petri Martyris Anglerij *Epistola* Bernardino Caravaialo, *Cardinali de ijs*
quæ ex Orbe Novo attulit Admirantus noster Colonus. *Dat. Burgis III. Nonas*
Octob. MCCCCXCVI. [Pet. Mart. Angler. Epist. *Fol.* 1670. *Lib. IX. Ep.*
CLXVIII.]

Petri Martyris Anglerij *Epistola missa* Pomponio *suo de Superstitionibus &*   1497.
Cæremonijs Insularium Novi Orbis in Hispaniola. *Dat.* Methinnæ *campi, Idibus*   12 *Hen. 7.*
Junij, anno MCCCCXCVII. *cum alijs ejusdem argumenti Literis sub eodem anno.*
[Pet. Mart. Epist. *Lib. X. Ep. CLXXVII.*]

An Account of the Discovery of *Newfoundland*, by *John Cabot*, a *Venetian*,
and *Sebastian* his Son, on the 24th of *June* 1497. in *English* Ships, with a
Commission of *Hen. VII.* With the Account given by *Sebastian Cabot* of
coming home along the Coasts of *America* to *Florida*. [Purchas *Pilgrim.*
Vol. III. p. 807.]

Petri Martyris Anglerij *Epistola* Bracharensi & Pompelonensi *Præsulibus*   1498.
de novo Latriæ genere apud Insulares in Novo Orbe, de Simulacris quæ Zemes *ap-*   13 *Hen. 7.*
pellant, aliisq; Monstris cornutis, dentatis, caudatisq;. Dat. Compluti, *Nonas*
Aprilis MCCCCXCVIII. [Ib. Pet. Mart. Epist. 1670. *Fol. Lib. XI. Ep. CXC.*]

AMERICI VESPUTII *Navigatio prima à Calicio portu, Anno*
Domini MCCCCXCVII. *die xx mensis Maij, usq; ad Reditum in eundem Calicium*
portum cum CCXXII. *captivatis personis decimo quinto Octobris* MCCCCXCVIII.
[Novus Orbis. Basileæ. 1555. *Fol. à p.* 210. *ad* 221.]

A Discourse of *Sebastian Cabot*, touching his Discovery of Part of the
West-India, out of *England, Anno* 1497. at the Charge of K. *Henry* VII.
used to *Galeacius Butrigarius*, the Pope's Legate in *Spain*, and reported by the
said Legate in this sort. With several other Testimonies concerning the
said Discovery. [*Hakluyt's Voyages. Fol. p.* 512. Purchas *Pilgrim. Fol.*
Vol. II. p. 809. Ibid. *Vol. III. p.* 461.]

1499.
14 Hen. 7. Petri Martyris Anglerij *Epistola* Pomponio Laeto *de Novis rebus in utriſq; Antipodibus occiduis ſcilicet & Antarcticis. Dat.* Oceaniæ *prid. Nonas Febr.* MCCCCXCIX. [Pet. Mart. Epiſtolæ, Lib. XII. Ep. CCII.]

A Note of *Sebaſtian Cabot's* firſt Diſcovery of Part of the *INDIES*, taken out of the latter part of *Robert Fabian's* Chronicle; with an Account of the three Savages brought home by him, and preſented unto the King in the fourteenth Year of his Reign. [In Mr. *Hakluyt's* Voyages. *Fol.* p. 515.]

An Extract taken out of the Mapp of *Sebaſtian Cabot,* cut by *Clement Adams,* concerning his Diſcovery of the *Weſt-Indies,* which was to be ſeen in her Majeſty Queen *Elizabeth's* private Gallery at *Weſtminſter,* and in many other ancient Merchant's Houſes. [*Ib. Hakluyt,* p. 511.]

AMERICI VESPUTII *Navigatio ſecunda à* Calicio *portu ad novum Orbem anno Domini* MCCCCXCIX. *undecima Maij die.* [Novus Orbis. *Fol.* p. 221.]

De Navigatione VINCENTIANI *dicti* PINZONI *necnon* ARIETIS *Germani Socij olim* COLUMBI, *& de terris & rebus per eum repertis, ſub anno* MCCCCXCIX. [*Ib.* Novus Orbis, Baſileæ. 1555. *Fol.* p. 85.]

1500.
15 Hen. 7. *Narratio de Gentibus varijs lociſq; innumeris ab* ALONSO NIGRO, *in longa ſua Navigatione repertis anno.* M. D. [Novus Orbis Baſil. *Fol.* p. 84.]

An Account of the firſt Diſcovery of *Braſil,* on the Coaſts of *America,* by *Peter Alvarez Capralis,* in a Fleet ſet out by *Emanuel* King of *Portugal,* being driven thither in their way to the *Eaſt Indies* 23. *Apr.* 1500. [*Purchas Pilgrim.* Vol. I. p. 30.]

1501.
16 Hen. 7. AMERICI VESPUTII *Navigatio tertia à* Lisbonæ *portu cum tribus conſervantiæ navibus ad Novum Orbem ulteriùs detegendum die Maij decima anno* M. D. I. [Novus Orbis, *Fol.* p. 125.]

Epitome Navigationum ALBERICI VESPUTII, *ab Ulisbonæ portu X. Maij* M. D. I. *verſus Novum Orbem;* à lingua Hiſpanica *in* Italicam *traducta.* [*Ib.* Novus Orbis, p. 87.

Exemplar.

Exemplar Literarum cujusdam CRETICI *Dominorum Venetorum Legati apud Regem Lusitanorum die vigesima septima Junij anno M. D. I. de Rebus memorabilibus in Urbe* CALECHUT *apud Indos : cum alijs ejusdem argumenti Literis.* [Ib. Novus Orbis, *p.* 94.]

AMERICI VESPUTII *Navigatio quarta ex* Lisbonæ *portu cum sex conservantiæ navibus ad Novum Orbem decimo Maij die M. D. III.* [Novus Orbis, Basileæ. *Fol. p.* 230.]   1503. 18 *Hen.* 7.

Navigatio ALOYSII CADAMUSTI Veneti, *ab anno à partu Virginis M. D. IIII. ad terras ignotas investigandum: Capitibus* LXXXIII. *comprehensa.* [Novus Orbis, Basil. *p.* 64.]   1504. 19 *Hen.* 7.

Sir *William Monson's* Account of the first Discovery of the *South Sea,* by VASCO NUNEZ de BALBOA, which was the first Step to the Discovery and Conquest of *Peru,* in the Year 1513. [*His Naval Tracts in the Collection of Voyages, printed for Mr.* Churchill. *Fol.* 1704. Vol. III. *p.* 405.]   1513. 4 *Hen.* 8.

Epistola Potentissimi ac Invictissimi Principis EMANUELIS *Regis* Portugalliæ & Algarbiorum *de victorijs habitis in* India & Malacha, *ad S. in Christo Patrem & Dominum nostrum Dominum* Leonem X. *Pont. Max. Dat. in Urbe nostra* Olispone, *octavo Idus Junias, anno* MDXIII. [Novus Orbis, Basil. 1555. *Fol. p.* 232.]

Petri Martyris Anglerij *Epistola* Ludovico Furtato Mendocio *de Rebus* DARIENIS, *in Novo Orbe, & quàm iniquè* VASCHUS NUNNEZ BALBOA, *imperium sibi usurpaverat in Darienenses Hispanos, ejecto Gubernatore* NICUESSA, *&c. Dat. ex* Valleoleto X. *Cal. Aug.* MDXIV. [Petri Mart. Epistolæ. Amstelodami. *Fol. Lib.* XXVII. *Ep.* DXI.]   1514. 5 *Hen.* 8.

Petri Martyris Anglerij *Epistola* Ludovico Furtato Mendocio, *de ijs quæ ab Orbe Novo scribuntur de Insula quadam Fortunatissima unionibus abundante nuper reperta ad Australe pelagus. Dat. ex* Aranda Dariana III. *Non. Aprilis,* Anno MDXV. *Cum alia Epistola ad Amicum de Lectura Libelli de Orbe Novo per ipsummet Papam coram Cardinalibus & Sorore invitatis. Dat.* VII. *Cal. Jan.* MDXV. [Pet. Mart. Epist. *Fol. Lib.* XXVIII. *Ep.* DXLVII.]   1515. 6 *Hen.* 8.

The Voyage of Sir *Thomas Pert* Knight, and *Sebastian Cabot,* about the eighth Year of King *Henry* the 8th, toward the end of the Year 1516. to *Brasil, S. Domingo,* and *S. John de Porto Rico,* as extracted from an Epistle of *Richard Eden.* [Printed in Mr. *Hackluyt's* Voyages. *Fol.* 1598. *p.* 515.]   1516. 7 *Hen.* 8.

Petri.

1517.   Petri Martyris Anglerij *Liber de Insulis nuper repertis in Novo Orbe, & de*
8 *Hen.* 8. *Moribus Incolarum earundem.* [Novus Orbis. Fol. 1555. *p.* 497.]

1518.   *Pomponius Mela. Julius Solinus. Itinerarium Antonini Aug. Vibius Sequester.*
9 *Hen.* 8. *P. Victor. Dionysius Afer de Situ Orbis. Impreff.* Venetijs *in Ædibus* ALDI,
menfe Octobri. MDXVIII. 8vo.

1519.   FERDINANDI CORTESII *de Nova Maris Oceani* Hilpania,
10 *Hen.* 8. *Narratio fecunda de Navigatione fuscepta, die* XVI. *Julij, Anno* M. D. XIX. *per
Seipfum fcripta ; cum Præfatione ad* Carolum V. *Imperatorem.* [Novus Or-
bis, Bafil. 1555. *Fol.* p. 537.]

An Account of the Voyage of *FARNANDUS MAGELLANES*,
when he difcover'd the Streights leading to the South Sea, and gave Name
to them, fetting out in a Fleet prepar'd by the Emperour, from *Sevill.* 10.
Aug. 1519. [In *Purchas* Pilgrim. *Vol.* 1. *B.* 2. *Ch.* 2. *p.* 34.]

Petri Martyris Anglerij *Epiftola de Orbe Novo, ac præfertim de* Ferdinando
Cortefio *coloniam fibi fuifq; exigente. Dat.* IV. *Non. Decemb.* MDXIX. [Pet.
Mart. Epift. *Fol. Lib.* XXXII. *Ep.* DCL.]

1521.   *Epiftola* Petri Martyris Anglerij *de Novis ab India allatis, de Infula* Fer-
12 *Hen.* 8. nandina, *de Civitate* Tenuftila, *alias* Mexico, *de Rege* Muteczuma, *alijfq;
rebus. Dat. ex Valleoleto. Non. Martij.* MDXXI. [Pet. Mart. Epift. *Lib.*
XXXIV. *Ep.* DCCXVII.]

1522.   *Du Voyage de* Ferdinand Magellaens *vers le Deftroit de* Magellanes, *avec* L'
13 *Hen.* 8. *Armade que partit de* Seville *le dixiefme d' Aöuft, l' An.* 1519. *& retourna l'
an.* 1522. [Defcription des Indes Occidentales, &c. Amfterdam 1622. *Fol.*]

The famous Exploit of *Ferdinand Magellanes,* who. firft fail'd round the
World ; fetting out from S. *Lucar* in 1519. and arriving there again in
September 1522. [In Sir *William Monfon's Naval Tracts. Collect. of Voyages,*
Printed for Mr. Churchill, *Vol.* 3. *p.* 396.]

De MOLUCCIS *Infulis atq; pluribus mirandis quæ noviffima* Caftel-
lanorum *Navigatio Sereniff. Imperatoris* Caroli V. *aufpicio fufcepta nuper invenit.* Maximiliani *Tranfylvani ad Reverendiff. Cardinalem* Saltzburgenfem,
Epiftola lectu perquam jucunda. Dat. Valliisoleti. *die* XXVI. Octobris. MDXXII.
[Novus Orbis, Bafileæ. 1555. Fol. à p. 524. ad p. 535.]

Tertia

Tertia FERDINANDI CORTESII *Narratio de rebus à se gestis* 1524.
inter Indos occiduos. *Cum Præfatione Doctoris* Petri Savorgnani *ad* Clementem 15 *Hen.*8.
VII. *P. P. Dat. ex* Norimberga *die ultima Martij* MDXXIV. [Novus Orbis.
Fol. à p' 599. ad. p. 655.]

Sir *William Monson's* Account of the Actions of *Francis Pizarro,* Conque- 1525.
rour of *Peru,* in the Year 1525. [*Naval Tracts in Collect. of Voyages, Prin-* 16 *Hen.* 8.
ted for *Mr.* Churchill. *Fol.* 1704. *Vol.* 3. *p.* 406.]

La Voyage de Don Frere Garcia de Loaysa, *qu' envoya l' Empereur* Charles
avec six Naviers à la Recherche du Destroit de Magellanes *en l' an.* 1525. [De-
scription des Indes Occidentales. Amsterdam 1622. *Fol. en Recueil au fin.*]

Epistola Petri Martyris Anglerij *de duabus navibus ex* India *redeuntibus cum*
thesauro & tigre, &c. anno M. D. XXV. *de magna classe ad* Indos *parata: de*
discessu Cortesij *ad delendum* Christopherum Olitum : *De* Jamaica *Insula, &c.*
Dat. Toleti. Id. Junij M. D. XXV. [Pet. Mart. Angler. Epist. *Lib.* XXXVIII.
Ep. DCCCIX.]

A Declaration of the *Indies* and Lands discovered and subdued unto the 1527.
Emperour and King of *Portugal* ; and also of other Parts of the *Indies,* and 18 *Hen.* 8.
rich Countries to be discover'd ; which the worshipful Mr. *Robert Thorne,*
Merchant of *London,* exhorted King *Henry* the Eighth to take in Hand. [In
Hackluyt's Voyages. Fol. p. 250.]

The Book made by the right worshipful Mr. *Robert Thorne,* in the Year
1527. in *Sivill,* to Dr. *Ley,* Lord Embassadour for King *Henry* the Eighth,
to *Charles* the Emperour ; being an Information of the Parts of the World
discover'd by him, and the King of *Portugal* ; and also of the Way to the
Molucco's, by the North. [*Hakluyt. ib. p.* 252.]

An Account of the Voyage of two Ships, whereof the one was call'd the
Dominus Vobiscum, set out the 20th Day of *May,* in the Year of our Lord
1527. for the Discovery of the North Parts of *Newfoundland,* and *Cape Brit-*
ton. [*Hakluyt's Voyages. Fol. p.* 517.]

A Letter written to King *Henry,* in the Haven of St. *John* in *Newfound-*
land, by *John Rut,* Master of a Ship sent thither, and employ'd in Fishing.
3. *Aug.* 1527. [*Purchas* Pilgrim. *Vol.* 3. *p.* 809.]

1530.
21 Hen. 8. A Relation of a Voyage to Brasil, made by the Worshipful Mr. William Hawkins of Plimouth, Father to Sir John Hawkins, in the Year 1530. and of his bringing one of the Savage Kings of that Brasilian Country home with him, and presenting him to King Henry the Eight. [In Hakluyt's Voyages. Vol. p. 520.]

Extracts out of Gonçalo Ferdinando de Oviedo his Summary and general History of the Indies, translated from Ramusio's Italian Edition. The Summary being written to CHARLES V. Emperour, An. 1525. The General History about 1530. [Purchas Pilgrim. Vol. 3. p. 970.]

The Relation of NUNNO DI GUZMAN, written to CHARLES the fifth Emperour, concerning divers Expeditions of the Spaniards from Mexico, to the more Northerly Parts of America, Dat. VIII. Julij 1530. [Purchas Pilgrim. Vol. IV. p. 1556.]

Exemplar Literarum Pat. Henrici Regis octavi de concedendo dilecto suo Subdito Dionysio Harrys, de civitate Londoniæ Mercatori, officium sive locum Magistri, Gubernatoris, Protectoris, sive Consulis infra insulam sive civitatem de Candye. Test. Rege apud Chelschich vicesimo sexto die Aprilis. Reg. XXII.

1531.
22 Hen. 8. A Narrative of the Conquest of PERU and CUSCO, call'd NEW CASTILE, directed to the Emperour by Francisco de Xeres, Secretary to Captain Francis Pizarro; who conquer'd the said Places in the Year 1531. [Purchas Pilgrim. Vol. 4. p. 1491.]

Other brief Notes of Francis Pizarro his Conquest of PERU, in the Year 1531. written by a Spanish Captain therein employ'd. [Purchas ib. p. 1489.]

Exemplar Literarum Pat. Henrici Regis octavi, in quibus concessit Benedicto Justiniano Mercatori Genuensi officium sive locum Magistri, Protectoris, sive Consulis infra Insulam sive Civitatem de Syo. Teste Rege apud Chelschith quinto die Octobris Reg. XXIII.

De Fratrum Minorum Regularis observantiæ profectâ & animarum lucro in Huketan sive Nova Hispania, Epistola venerandi Patris fratris Martini de Valentia custodis Sancti Evangelij in terra premissâ ad Revendum P. F. Matthiam Vuenissein generalem Commissarium Cismontanum eorundem Fratrum. Dat. ex Conventu nostro Thalmanaco prope magnam Civitatem Messicanan. die XII. Junij MDXXXI.

Copia

Copia Litterarum sub vadim dato missarum Reverendo Patri Electo cæterisq; 1532.
Patribus Capituli generalis Tholosani *in Festo Pentecostes* Tholosæ *celebrati.* 23 *Hen.* 8.
Anno Domini M. D. XXXII. *per Reverendum Patrem Dominum Episcopum illius*
civitatis magna, qua dicitur Temixtitan Mexico, *in* Huketan, *& alios Patres*
ibi commorantes; de Laboribus suis assiduis in Infidelium Conversione. [Novus
Orbis, 1555. *p.* 665. *&c.*]

Relations of Occurrents in the Conquest of *Peru*, after *Fernand Pizarro's* 1534.
Departure, written at *Xauxa July* 15. 1534. by *Pedro Sancho*, Notary Ge- 25 *Hen.* 8.
neral in the Kingdoms of *New Castile*, and Secretary to the Governour *Fr.*
Pizarro, subscrib'd by the said Governour himself and others, and sent to
his Majesty. [*Purchas* Pilgrim. *Vol. IV. p.* 1494.]

The Voyage of Master *Hore*, and divers other Gentlemen to *Newfoundland*,   1536.
and *Cape Breton*, in the Year 1536. and in the 28th Year of King *Henry* 27 *Hen.* 8.
the Eighth. [In *Hakluyt's* Voyages.   *Fol. p.* 517.]

De Indis convertendis: *Epitome convertendi Gentes Indiarum ad fidem Christi,*
adeoq; ad Ecclesiam Sacro-sanctam Catholicam & Apostolicam. Autore R. P. T.
Nicolao Herborn *regularis observantiæ ordinis Minorum Generali Commissario*
Cismontano. [Novus Orbis, Basileæ. 1555. *à p.* 667. *ad* 677.]

A Relation of *Alvaro Nunez*, concerning that which happen'd to the Fleet
in *India*, whereof *Pamphilo Narvaez* was Governour, from the Year 1527.
until the Year 1536. who return'd unto *Sevill* with three of his Companions
only; translated out of *Ramusis*, and abbreviated. [*Purchas* Pilgrim. *Vol. IV.*
p. 1499.]

A Relation of *Ferdinando de Soto*, his Voyage to *Florida*, and Discovery
of the Regions in that Continent: With the Travels of the *Spaniards* four 1539.
Years together therein, and the Accidents which befel them: Written by a 30 *Hen.* 8.
Portugal of the Company in that Expedition, in the Year 1539. [*Purchas*
Pilgrim. *Vol. IV. p.* 1532.]

Joannis Joviani Pontani ad Lucium Franciscum Filium Meteororum liber
cum Expositione. Argentorati *apud* Cratonem Mylium *mense Septembri.*
M. D. XXXIX. 8*vo.*

A. Rutter of *Don John* of *Castro* of the Voyage which the *Portugals* made 1540.
from *India* to *Zoez*, dedicated to the most Illustrious Prince, the Infant *Don* 31 *Hen.* 8.
Luys, and here abbreviated. Shewing the State of *Socatora*, and the Parts on
both sides the Red Sea, in 1540. The Original of which is reported to have
been

been bought by Sir *Walter Raleigh* at sixty Pounds, and by him caused to be done into *English* out of the *Portugal.* [*Purchas* Pilgrim. *Vol. II. p.* 1122. *Lib. VII.*]

1541.
32 *Hen.* 8.
Brief Extracts out of *Jerom Benzo*'s three Books of the *New World,* touching the *Spaniard*'s cruel handling of the *Indians,* and the Effects thereof, from his first going to *America,* in the Year 1541. [*Purchas* Pilgrim. *Vol. IV. p.* 1448.]

1542.
33 *Hen.* 8.
The several Propositions made by the Lord *Bartholomew de Las Casas,* in the Assembly of Prelates and Learned Men, whom the King of *Spain* call'd together at *Valledolid,* to reform the Affairs of the *Indies* in the Year 1542. With Arguments for the King to take the *Indians* under his Protection, and save them from the Tyranny and Insolence of the *Spaniards.* [Printed in *A Relation of the* Spanish *Cruelties in the* West Indies. *By* Barth. de Las Casas. 8*vo.* 1699. *p.* 114. &*c.*] With a Dispute between Don *Bartholomew de Las Casas,* Bishop of *Chiapa,* and Dr. *Sepulveda,* on that Subject, *Ibid. p.* 150. With another Proposal by the said Bishop, for the Re-establishment of Peace and Tranquillity in *America. Ib. p.* 184.

A brief Narration of the Destruction of the *Indies* by the *Spaniards,* written by a Dominican Frier, *Bartholomew de Las Casas,* a *Spaniard,* and Bishop of *Chiapa* in *America;* from the first Discovery till the Year 1542. in which this was written. [*Purchas* Pilgrim. *Vol. IV. p.* 1567.]

1543.
24 *Hen.* 8.
HENRICI GLAREANI Helvetij *Poetæ Laureati de* GEOGRA-PHIA *Liber unus, ab ipso Authore jam novissime recognitus.* Friburgi Brisgoiæ. Stephanus Melechus Gravius *Excudebat.* Anno M. D. XLIII. 4*to. folijs* 35.

1545.
36 *Hen.* 8.
Divi Alphonsi Romanorum & Hispaniarum Regis Astronomicæ Tabulæ in propriam integritatem restitutæ, ad calcem adjectis tabulis quæ in postrema editione deerant, cum plurimorum locorum correctione & accessione variarum tabellarum, ex diversis autoribus huic operi insertarum, cum in usus ubertatem, tum difficultatis subsidium. Qua in re Paschasius Hamellius *Mathematicus insignis idemq; Regius Professor sedulam operam suam præstitit.* Parisijs. *Ex officina* Christiani Wecheli. Anno 1545. 4*to.* [*Ex dono Rev. viri* Josephi Sparke Petriburgensis.]

1548.
2 *Ed.* 6.
An Act against the Exaction of Money, or any other thing, by any Officer, for License to Traffique in *Ireland* and *Newfoundland,* made in *An.* 2. *Edwardi sexti.* [Printed in *Hakluyt. p.* 521.]

A

A Copie of the Letters Pat. of King *Edward* VI. to *Sebastian Calota*, con-
stituting him Grand Pilot of *England*, and graunting him an Annuitie cr
yeerly Revenue of One Hundred Threescore and Six Pounds Thirteen
Shillings and Four Pence. Witnefs the King at *Westminster* 6. *Januar*.
Second Yeere of our Reign. 1548. [Printed in *Hakluyt's* Voyages, *p.* 519]

1548.
2 *Ed.* 6.

𝕿𝖍𝖊 𝕳𝖎𝖘𝖙𝖔𝖗𝖞𝖊 of ITALYE, 𝖆 𝖇𝖔𝖐𝖊 𝖊𝖝𝖈𝖊𝖇𝖎𝖓𝖌 𝖕𝖗𝖔𝖋𝖎𝖙𝖆𝖇𝖑𝖊 𝖙𝖔 𝖇𝖊
𝖗𝖊𝖇 : 𝖇𝖊𝖈𝖆𝖚𝖘𝖊 𝖎𝖙 𝖎𝖓𝖙𝖗𝖊𝖆𝖙𝖊𝖙𝖍 𝖔𝖋 𝖙𝖍𝖊 𝖊𝖘𝖙𝖆𝖙𝖊 𝖔𝖋 𝖒𝖆𝖓𝖞 𝖆𝖓𝖇 𝖔𝖞𝖇𝖊𝖗𝖘
𝖈𝖔𝖒𝖒𝖔𝖓𝖜𝖊𝖆𝖑𝖊𝖘 ; 𝖍𝖔𝖜 𝖙𝖍𝖊𝖞 𝖍𝖆𝖇𝖊 𝖇𝖊𝖓𝖊 𝖆𝖓𝖇 𝖓𝖔𝖜 𝖇𝖊 𝖌𝖔𝖇𝖊𝖗𝖓𝖊𝖇.
𝕭𝖞 William Thomas. Imprinted at *London* in *Fleteftrete* by *Thomas Marsh*.
1549. 4.ᵗᵒ

1549.
3 *Ed.* 6.

Plurimæ Epiftolæ Francisci Xaverij *è Societate Jesu inter Indos peregrinantis ad
Socios in* Europa *commorantes. Dat.* Ma!aca. X. Cal. Jul. MDXLIX, *&c.
Cum Literis* Johis Fernandi, Pauli Japonij, Edvardi Sylvij: *Aliorumq; de re-
bus Indicis & Evangelio ibidem promovendo. Selectarum ex India Epiftolarum
Libri* IV. *in* Petri Maffei Hiftor. Indic. Coloniæ. 1593. *p.* 335. &c.

An Account of the feventeen Years Travels of *Peter de Cieza*, through
the mighty Kingdom of *Peru*, and the large Provinces of *Cartagena* and *Popayan* in *South America*, begun to be written by him in the City *Cartago*, of
the Province of *Popayan*, in the Year 1541. and ended in the City of *Lima* in
Peru in 1550. [Tranflated into *English*, and publifh'd in *Stevens's* Collection
of Voyages. 1711. 4.ᵗᵒ *Vol.* I.]

1550.
4 *Ed.* 6.

*Le Sphere du Monde proprement ditte Cofmographie compofée nouvellement en
Francois par* ORONCE FIN *du Daulphine, lecteur Mathematicien du
tres Chreftien Roy de France en L'Univerfité de* Paris. M.D.L.I. 4to.

1551.
5 *Ed.* 6.

Sphaera JOANNIS *de* SACRO BOSCO. *Antverpiæ apud Joannem
Richardum.* 1551. 8vo.

Ordinances, Inftructions and Advertifements of and for the Direction of
the intended Voyage for *Cathaye*, compiled, made, and delivered by the
Right Worfhipful M. *Sebaftian Cabota*, Efquire, Governour of the Myftery
and Company of the Merchants Adventurers for the Difcovery of Regions,
Dominions, Iflands and Places unknown the 9th Day of *May*, in the Year
of our Lord God 1553. 7 *Ed.* VI. [Printed at large in *Hakluyt's* Voyages.
Fol. 1589, *p.* 1259.]

1553.

Exemplar Epiftolæ feu Litterarum Miffivarum quas illuftriffimus Princeps Ed-
vardus *ejus nominis fextus, &c. mifit ad Principes Septentrionalemac Orientalem*

D
mundi

grandi plagam inhabitantes juxta mare glaciale, necnon Indiam Orientalem. Anno Domini 1553. regni sui anno septimo & ultimo. [ib. Hakluyt, p. 263.]

1553. 1 Mar.
The true Copy of a Note found written in one of the two Ships, to wit, the Speranza, which wintred in Lappia, where Sir *Hugh Willoughbie* and all his Company died, being frozen to Death. Anno 1553. [Ib. Hakluyt. p. 265.]

La Cosmographie de Pierre Apian Docteur & Mathematicien tres excellent. A Paris, par vivant Gualtherot. 1553. 4'o.

A treatyse of the Newe India, withe other newe founde landes and Islandes, as well Eastwarde as Westwarde, as they are knowen and founde in these oure dayes, after the descriptyon of Sebastian Munster, in his boke of Universal Cosmographie. Translated out of Latine into Englyshe by Richarde Eden. 1553. Imprinted at *London* in *Lombarde strete*, by *Edw. Sutton*. 8vo.

1554. 2 Phi. Mar.
L' Art de Naviguer de Maistre PIERRE de MEDINE *Espaignol, contenant toutes les Reigles Secrets, & enseignemens necessaries à la bonne* NAVIGATION. *Traduit de* CASTILLAN *en Francoys avec augmentation & illustration de plusieurs figures & annotations par Nicholas de Nicholas du Dauphiné Geographe du tres Chrestien Roy Henri II. A Lyon chez Guillaume Rouille.* 1554. Fol.

Cosmographia universalis. Libri VI. *in quibus, juxta certioris fidei Scripturum traditionem describuntur Omnium habitabilis Orbis partium Situs, propriaeq; dotes, Regionum topographica effigies, terra ingenia,* &c. *Item omnium Gentium mores, leges, religio, mutationes, atq; memorabilium in hunc usq; annum 1554. gestarum rerum Historia.* Autore SEBASTIANO MUNSTERO *Basileæ.* 1554. *mense Martio.* Fol.

The Travels of *Huldericke Schmirdel,* in Twenty Years Space, from 1534 to 1554. abbreviated; relating his Voyage up the River of Plate, *Parana, Parabol,* &c. [*Purchas Pilgrim. Vol. IV. p.* 1347.]

A Letter of *Richard Chanceller,* written to his Uncle Master *Christopher Frothingham,* touching his Discovery of *Moscovia,* and his Travels therein, &c. [*Purchas* Pilgrim. *Fol. Vol. III. p.* 213.] With some Additions for better Knowledge of this Voyage, taken by *Clement Adams,* Schoolmaster to the Queen's Henshmen, from the Mouth of Captain *Chancellour.* [*Purchas, Ib. p.* 218.]

A General Prognoſtication for ever. By Leonard Digges, with Rules to judge Weather. Tables for Movable Feaſts. For Sun and Moon. For Tides, &c. With a Preface againſt the Reprovers of Aſtronomy and Sciences Mathematical. 1555. 4to.

1555. 3 Phil Ma.

The Fardle of Factions, conteining the auncient manners, cuſtomes, and lawes of the people enhabiting the two partes of the earthe, called Affrike and Aſie. Gathered long ſence by one Joannes Boëmus. Tranſlated into Englyſhe by William Watreman. Printed at London by John Kingſtone, the xxii Day of December. 1555. 8vo.

A Relation of the Voyage of Robert Tomſon, Merchant, into Nova Hiſpania, in the Year 1555. With divers Obſervations concerning the State of the Countrey ; and certain Accidents touching himſelf. His Sufferings in the Inquiſition, &c. [Printed at large in Hakluyt's Voyages, Fol. p. 580.]

NOVUS ORBIS Regionum ac Inſularum veteribus incognitarum, una cum Tabula Coſmographica & aliquot alijs conſimilis argumenti libellis, nunc novis Navigationibus auctus, quorum omnium catalogus ſequenti patebit pagina. Adjecta eſt huic poſtrema Editioni Navigatio Caroli Cæſaris Auſpicio in Comitijs Auguſtanis inſtituta. Baſileæ. Apud Joh. Hervagium Anno M. D. LV. Menſe Septembri. Fol. p. 677.

The Caſtle of knowledge, contayninge the Explication of the SPHERE, bothe celeſtial and material, and diverſe other thinges incident thereto; with ſundrye pleaſaunt proofes and certaine newe demonſtrations not written before in any vulgare worke. Ded. to Quene Marye, and Cardinal Pole. By Robert Recorde Phyſicion. Imprinted at London, by Reginalde Wolfe. 1556. p. 286.

1556. 4 Phil. Ma.

L' Eſtat de l' Egliſe avec le Diſcourſe des Temps, depuis les Apoſtres ſous Neron juſques à preſent, ſous Charles V. Contenant en bref les Hiſtoires tant anciennes que nouvelles, celles ſpecialement qui concernent l' Empire & le ſiege Romain, entre autres : Affaires des Indies occidentales. L' an M. D. LVI. 8vo. [Ex dono Rev. Viri Johis Mapletoft. S. T. P.]

Ignatij Loyolæ vita à Johanne Petro Maſſeio ſcripta & Claudio Aquavivæ, Præpoſito Generali Societatis Jeſu dicata, ab Ortu ejus anno poſt Virginis partum MCDXCI.

MCDXCI. *ad Obitum feria sexta pridie Kalendas Augusti, anno MDLVI.* [Ad calcem Petri Maffei, Lib. de Histor. Indic. Fol. 1593. *a p.* 455. *ad p.* 517.]

1557.
5 Mar.

Plurimæ Epistolæ Cosini Turriani, Gasparis Vilelæ, Melchioris Nonnij, *aliorumq; Societate Jesu inter Indos Missionariorum ad Socios suos in Lusitania aliisq; Europæ partibus de Rebus suis in Japonia & Insula Firando, Anno MDLVII, &c.* [*Selectæ ex India Epistolæ : in* Petri Maffei *Histor. Indic.* Fol. Colon. 1593. p. 349. *&c.*]

A Relation of the first Voyage made by Mr. *Anthony Jenkinson* from the City of *London,* toward the Land of *Russia* ; begun the 12th of *May* 1557. With his Voyage from *Mosco* in *Russia* to the City of *Bozhar* in *Bactria,* in the Yeere 1558. [*Purchas* Pilgrim. *Vol. III. p.* 222.]

Ad A S T R O R V M Judicia facilis Introductio Claudio Dariato Pomarcensi *Medico ac Mathematico autore, &c. Quibus accessit Fragmentum de morbis & diebus criticis ex Astrorum motu cognoscendis.* Lugduni. *Apud* Mauricium Roy & Ludovicum Pemot. 1557. 4to. p. 120.

1558.
6 Mar.

Annuli Astronomici Instrumenti cùm certissimi tum commodissimi usus, ex varijs Authoribus, Petro Beausardo, Gemma Frisio, Johanne Dryandro, Boneto Hebræo, Burchardo Mythobio, Orontio Finæo, *una cum Meteoroscopio, per* Johannem Regiomontanum. Luteciæ. *Apud* Gulielmum Carillat. 1558. 8vo.

1559.
1 Eliz.

𝕿𝖍𝖊 𝕮𝖔𝖘𝖒𝖔𝖌𝖗𝖆𝖕𝖍𝖎𝖈𝖆𝖑 𝕲𝖑𝖆𝖘𝖘𝖊, 𝖈𝖔𝖓𝖙𝖊𝖎𝖓𝖞𝖓𝖌 𝖙𝖍𝖊 𝖕𝖑𝖊𝖆𝖘𝖆𝖓𝖙 𝕻𝖗𝖎𝖓𝖈𝖎𝖕𝖑𝖊𝖘 𝖔𝖋 𝕮𝖔𝖘𝖒𝖔𝖌𝖗𝖆𝖕𝖍𝖎𝖊, 𝕲𝖊𝖔𝖌𝖗𝖆𝖕𝖍𝖎𝖊, 𝕳𝖞𝖉𝖗𝖔𝖌𝖗𝖆𝖕𝖍𝖎𝖊, 𝖔𝖗 𝕹𝖆𝖛𝖎𝖌𝖆𝖙𝖎𝖔𝖓. 𝕮𝖔𝖒𝖕𝖎𝖑𝖊𝖉 𝖇𝖞 William Cunningham, 𝕯𝖔𝖈𝖙𝖔𝖗 𝖎𝖓 𝕻𝖍𝖞𝖘𝖎𝖈𝖐𝖊. Excusum Londini in officina Joan. Dän Typographi Anno 1559. *Fol.* [*The fourth Part treateth of* America, *taking its Name of* Americus Vesputius, *who by the Commandment of* Ferdinando *King of* Castell, *found it out in the Year* 1497. *about the end of* June, *&c.*]

1562.
4 Eliz.

A Relation of the first Voyage of the Right Worshipful and Valiant Knight Sir *John Haukins,* afterward Treasurer of Her Majesty's Navy Royal, made to the *West Indies* 1562. and particularly to the Island *Hispaniola.* [Printed in M. *Hakluyt's* Voyages. Fol. 1589. *p.* 521.]

1563.
5 Eliz.

Regimen Omnium Iter agentium, postremò Editum. Authore Guilhelmo Gratarolo Bergomate *Philosopho & Medico. Argentorati per* Vuendelinum Rihelium. MDLXIII. 8vo. p. 190.

A printed Copy of 𝕬𝕟 𝕬𝕔𝕥 𝕥𝕠𝕦𝕔𝕙𝕚𝕟𝕘 𝕔𝕖𝕣𝕥𝕒𝕚𝕟 𝕡𝕠𝕝𝕚𝕥𝕚𝕜𝕖 𝕮𝕠𝕟𝕤𝕥𝕚𝕥𝕦𝕥𝕚𝕠𝕟𝕤, 𝕞𝕒𝕕𝕖 𝕗𝕠𝕫 𝕥𝕙𝕖 𝕓𝕖𝕥𝕥𝕖𝕣 𝕞𝕒𝕚𝕟𝕥𝕖𝕟𝕒𝕟𝕔𝕖 𝕒𝕟𝕕 𝕖𝕟𝕔𝕣𝕖𝕒𝕤𝕖 𝕠𝕗 𝕥𝕙𝕖 𝕹𝕒𝕧𝕚𝕖 𝕠𝕗 𝕥𝕙𝕚𝕤 𝕽𝕖𝕒𝕝𝕞𝕖 𝕠𝕗 England. *An. V. Eliz. Cap. V.* — 1563.

Relation of a Voyage made by M. *Roger Bodenham* to S. *John de Ullua*, in the Bay of *Mexico*, in the Yeere 1564. [In M. *Hakluyt's* Voyages. *Fol.* 1589. *p.* 522.] — 1564. 6 *Eliz.*

Notes of Voyages and Plantations of the *French* in the Northern *America*, both in *Florida* and *Canada*; and especially of the second Colony sent to *Florida* in three Ships, under the Command of *Rene Laudonniere*, in *April* 1564. [*Purchas* Pilgrim. *Vol. IV. p.* 1603.]

An Account of the Voyage made by the Worshipful M. *John Haukins*, Esquire, Captain of the *Jesus* of *Lubek*, one of Her Majesty's Ships, and General of the *Salomon*, and other two Barkes going in his Company to the Coast of *Guinea*, and the *Indies* of *Nova Spania*, being in *Africa* and *America*: Begun in *An. Dom.* 1564. [In M. *Hakluyt. ib. p.* 524.]

De Gallorum Expeditione in FLORIDAM *& clade ab Hispanis non minus injuste quam immaniter Ipsis illata, Anno* 1565. *Brevis Historia. Cui adjunctum est Supplicis Libelli & Querelæ à Viduis, liberis, cognatis & amicis Gallorum, ab Hispanis in* Florida *contra fas ac fidem casorum, ad* Carolum IX. *Galliæ Regem delatæ exemplum.*—— [*Ad finem Libri* Urbani Calvetonis *de rebus ab Hispanis in India Occidentali gestis.* 8vo. 1581.] — 1565. 7 *Eliz.*

An Account of the Arrival and Courtesie of M. *Hawkins* to the distressed *French* Men in *Florida* 1565. as in the Register of the Voyage of Mr. *Hawkins*; and as is elsewhere also recorded both in *French* and *English*, in the History of *Laudonier*, written by himself, and printed in *Paris Anno* 1586. And translated into *English* by me *Richard Hakluyt*, *Anno* 1587. [Publisht in M. *Hakluyt's* Voyages. *p.* 543.]

The printed Copy of an 𝕬𝕔𝕥 𝕔𝕠𝕟𝕔𝕖𝕣𝕟𝕚𝕟𝕘 𝕾𝕖𝕒 𝕸𝕒𝕣𝕜𝕤 𝕒𝕟𝕕 𝕸𝕒𝕣𝕚𝕟𝕖𝕣𝕤, 𝕖𝕟𝕒𝕓𝕝𝕚𝕟𝕘 𝕥𝕙𝕖 𝕸𝕒𝕤𝕥𝕖𝕣, 𝕎𝕒𝕣𝕕𝕖𝕟𝕤, 𝕒𝕟𝕕 𝕬𝕤𝕤𝕚𝕤𝕥𝕒𝕟𝕥𝕤 𝕠𝕗 𝕥𝕙𝕖 Trinity 𝕳𝕠𝕦𝕤𝕖 𝕠𝕗 Deptford Strond, 𝕥𝕠 𝕤𝕖𝕥 𝕦𝕡 𝕭𝕖𝕒𝕔𝕠𝕟𝕤, 𝕸𝕒𝕣𝕜𝕤 𝕒𝕟𝕕 𝕾𝕚𝕘𝕟𝕤 𝕗𝕠𝕫 𝕥𝕙𝕖 𝕾𝕖𝕒. An. VIII. Eliz. Cap. XIII. — 1566. 8 *Eliz.*

𝕿𝕙𝕖 𝕷𝕖𝕒𝕘𝕖𝕣, 𝕠𝕫 𝕲𝕣𝕖𝕒𝕥 𝕭𝕠𝕠𝕜 𝕠𝕗 𝕷𝕖𝕥𝕥𝕖𝕣 𝕬. 𝕱𝕠𝕫 𝕥𝕙𝕖 𝕒𝕔𝕔𝕠𝕞𝕡𝕥𝕖𝕤 𝕚𝕟 𝕥𝕣𝕒𝕗𝕚𝕢𝕦𝕖 𝕠𝕗 𝕸𝕒𝕣𝕔𝕙𝕒𝕦𝕟𝕕𝕚𝕤𝕖, 𝕒𝕡𝕡𝕖𝕣𝕥𝕒𝕪𝕟𝕚𝕟𝕘𝕖 𝕥𝕠 𝕞𝕪 𝕸𝕒𝕤𝕥𝕖𝕣 Fraunces Twyforde, 𝕮𝕚𝕥𝕚𝕫𝕖𝕟 𝕒𝕟𝕕 𝕸𝕖𝕣𝕔𝕖𝕣 𝕠𝕗 London, 𝕜𝕖𝕡𝕥𝕖 𝕒𝕟𝕕 𝕨𝕣𝕚𝕥𝕥𝕠𝕟 𝕓𝕪 𝕞𝕖 Anthonie Rice, 𝕙𝕚𝕤 𝕤𝕖𝕣𝕧𝕒𝕦𝕟𝕥𝕖. Decemb. **xxxi.** 1566. Fol.

E   𝕬𝕟

An Act for the Corporation of Merchants, Adventurers for the discovering of Lands, Territories, Iles, Dominions, and Seignories unknown, made in the eight yere of Queen Elizabeth. Anno 1566. [Printed at large in *Haklnyt*'s Voyages. *Fol.* 1589. *p.* 394.]

1568.
10 Eliz.   An Account of the third unfortunate Voyage made with the *Jesus*, the *Minion*, and four other Shippes, to the partes of *Guinea* and the *West Indias*, in the yeeres 1567 and 1568. By Mr. *John Hawkins*. [Ib. *Hakluyt*. p. 553. *Purchas* Pilgrim. *Vol. IV. p.* 1177.]

The New found Worlde, or Antarticke, wherein is contained wonderful and strange things, as well of humaine Creatures, as Beastes, Fishes, Foules, and Serpents, Trees, Plants, Mines of Gold and Silver: garnished with many learned authorities, travailed and written in the French Tongue, by that excellent learned Man Master AN-DREWE THEVET. And now newly translated into Englishe, wherein is reformed the errours of the auncient Cosmographers. Imprinted at *London* by *Henry Bynneman* for *Thomas Hacket*. 1568. 4to. *Folijs* 138.

A Discovery and playne Declaration of sundry subtill practises of the HOLY INQUISITION of Spayne. Certain special Examples set apart by themselves, besides other that are here and there dispersed in their most convenient places, wherein a Man may see the foresaid practises of the Inquisition, as they be practised and exercised, very lively described. Set forth in Latine by Reginaldus Gonsalvius Montanus, and newly translated. Imprinted at *London* by *John Day*, dwelling over *Aldersgate*, beneath *Saint Martines*. 1568. 4to. *Folijs* 99.

The Relation of *David Ingram* of *Barking*, in the Countie of *Essex*, *Sailer*, of sundry things which he with others did see, in traveiling by Land from the most Northerly partes of the *Baie* of *Mexico*, (where he with many others were set on Shoare by Master *Hawkins*) through a great part of *America*, untill he came within fifty Leagues or thereabouts of *Cape Britton*, in the latter end of the yeere 1568. [Printed at large in M. *Hakluyt*'s Voyages. *Fol.* 1589. *p.* 557.]

1571.
12 Eliz.   *De quinquaginta duobus à Societate Jesu dum in Brasiliam navigant, pro Catholica fide interfectis, Epistolæ duæ, Petri Diaz:j ad Leonem Henricium Provinciæ Lusitanæ pro Societate Jesu Præpositum dat. ex Insula Materca XV. Kal. Sept. MDLXX. & Francisci Henrici Præpositi domus Olisiponensis ad Socios Roman. dat. Olisipone V. Idus Decembris MD. LXXI.* [*Ad calcem Libri Petri Maffei* Histor. Indic. *Fol.* 1593. p. 448, &c.]

The

The whole Worke of MUNSTER abridged into a little Manuell in Englishe, being a briefe Abstract of straunge Novelties out of the Cosmographye of Sebastian Munster. With an Epist. to the Reader. Dat. 13. Apr. 1572. 8vo, [The Title wanting.]

A Relation of the Commodities of *Nova Hispania*, and the Manners of the Inhabitants, written by *Henry Hawkes* Merchant, which lived five yeeres in the said Countrey, and drew the same at the request of M. *Richard Hakluyt* Esquire, of *Eiton* in the Countie of *Hereford.* 1572. [Publisht in *Hakluyt*'s Voyages, *p.* 545.]

The Arte of NAVIGATION, contayning a compendious Description of the SPHERE, with the makyng of certaine instruments and rules for Navigations: and exemplified by many Demonstrations. Written in the Spanishe Tonge by Martin Curtes, and directed to the Emperour Charles the fyst. Translated out of Spanyshe into Englyshe by Richard Eden, and now newly corrected and amended in dyvers places. 1572. 4to. Folijs LXXXIII. With an Epistle Ded. to the ryght worshipful Syr William Garerd Knyght, and Maister Thomas Lodge, Aldermen of the Citye of London, and Governours of the honourable Fellowship or Societie, as well of certaine of the Nobilitie, as of Marchants, Adventurers, for the discoverye of Lands, Territories, Islands, and Seigniories unknowen. By Richard Eden.

A Relation of the first Voyage, attempted and set forth by the expert and valiant Captaine M. *Francis Drake* himself, with a Ship called the *Dragon*, and another Ship and a Pinnesse, to *Nombre-de Dios* and *Dariene*, about the yeare 1572. Written and recorded by one *Lopez* a *Spaniard*, who with the Discourse about him, was taken at the River of *Plate*, by the Ships set forth by the right Honourable the Earl of *Cumberland*, in the yeere 1586. [Printed in M. *Hakluyt*'s Voyages. *Fol.* 1589. *p.* 594.]

Plurimæ Epistolæ Melchioris Nonnij, Joannis Fernandi, Laurentij Japonij. *Aliorumq; à Societate Jesu inter Indos Orientales ad Socios suos in Europa. de Periculis suis & Laboribus in Evangelio promovendo ab anno* M.D.LVII. *ad An.* MDLXXIII. [Selectarum ex India Epistolarum. Libri IV. in Pet. Maffei Histor. Indic. 1593. *Fol.* à p. 356. ad 447.]

Extracts out of Sir *Jerome Horsey*'s Observations in seventeen Yeares Travells and Experience in *Russia*, and other Countries adjoining: Having before seen *France* and the Low Countries by Sir *Edward Horsey*'s Means, and in the Company and Charge of Master *William Mericke*, Agent for the Company; arriving in *Muscovia* 1573. [*Purchas* Pilgrim. *Vol. II. Append.*]

Alæ seu Scalæ Mathematicæ, quibus visibilium remotissima Cælorum theatra conscendi, & Planetarum omnium itinera novis & inauditis methodis explorari, tum hujus portentosi syderis in Mundi Boreali plaga insolito fulgore coruscantis, Distantia & Magnitudo immensa, Situsq; protinus tremendus indagari possit. THOMA DIGGESIO *Cantiensi Authore.* Londini. *Anno* 1573. 4to. ⅜

𝕾ir FRANCIS DRAKE 𝕽e𝔳i𝔳e𝔡, calling upon this 𝔡ull o𝔷 effeminate 𝖆ge, to follo𝔴 his noble 𝕾teps fo𝔷 𝔊ol𝔡e an𝔡 𝕾il𝔳er. 𝕭𝔶 this memo𝔷able 𝕽elation of the rare 𝔒ccurrences (ne𝔳er 𝔶et 𝔡eclare𝔡 to the 𝖂o𝔷l𝔡) in a thir𝔡e 𝖁o𝔶age ma𝔡e b𝔶 him into the West-Indies, in the 𝔶eares 72 an𝔡 73, 𝔴hen Nombre de Dios 𝔴as b𝔶 him an𝔡 52 others onl𝔶 in his 𝕮ompan𝔶 su𝔷p𝔷ise𝔡. 𝕱aithfull𝔶 taken out of the 𝕽epo𝔷tes of 𝕸r. Christopher Ceely, El's Hixon, an𝔡 others, 𝔴ho 𝔴ere in the same 𝖁o𝔶age 𝔴ith him. 𝕭𝔶 Philip Nichols 𝕻𝔷eacher. 𝖆n𝔡 also b𝔶 𝕾ir Francis Drake himself befo𝔷e his 𝕯eath, much holpen an𝔡 enlarge𝔡 b𝔶 𝔡i𝔳ers 𝕹otes 𝔴ith his o𝔴n han𝔡 here an𝔡 there inserte𝔡. 𝕾et fo𝔷th b𝔶 𝕾ir Francis Drake 𝕭aronet, his 𝕹ephe𝔴. London. 4to. pag 94. [Ex dono Rev. Viri *Samuelis Blackwell,* S. T. B. Rectoris de *Brampton* in agro *Northams.*]

An Account of the first Establishment of the Court of Inquisition at *Mexico* in the *West-Indies,* beginning in the yeere 1574. And also of the Chief Inquisitor and other Officers, with their bloody and cruel Proceedings against some *English* Prisoners. [*Hakluyt's* Voyages. *Fol. p.* 572.]
1574.
16 *Eliz.*

Cosmographia PETRI APIANI *per* GEMMAM FRISIUM *apud Lovanienses Medicum & Mathematicum insignem, jam demum ab omnibus vindicata mendis, &c. Additis ejusdem argumenti libellis ipsius Gemmæ Frisij.* Antverpiæ. MDLXXIV. *apud* Johannem Bellerum. 4to.

A Discourse written by Sir *Humfrey Gilbert* Knight, to prove a Passage to be on the Northside of *America,* to go to *Cataia, China,* and the *East Indies.* With certain Reasons alleaged for the proving of such Passage before the Queen's Majestie. and certaine Lords of the Counsel, by Master *Anthonie Jenkinson. Hakluyt., Ib. p.* 597. &c. Certaine other Reasons or Arguments to proove a Passage by the North West; learnedly written by M. *Richard Wilkes,* Gentleman. *Ib. p.* 610.
1575.
17 *Eliz.*

A Relation of the Voyage of *John* Oxnam of *Plymouth,* to the *West India,* and over the Straight of *Dariene* into the South Sea, *Anno* 1575. as written by one *Lopez* a *Spaniard.* [Publisht in *Hakluyt's* Voyages. *p.* 594.]

A Notable Historie of the Saracens, briefly and faithfully describing the Originall, Beginnyng, Continuance and Succeße, as well of the Saracens, Aſſaſſines, as alſo of the Turks, Souldans, Mamalukes, Tartarians, and Sophians, with a Diſcourſe of their Affayres and Actes, till this preſent yeare of grace 1575. Drawn out of ſundrye Authours by Thomas Newton. Imprinted at *London* by *William How.* 1575. *4to. Folijs* 144. 1575.

Notes framed by M. *Richard Hakluyt* of the *Middle Temple*, Eſquire, given to certaine Gentlemen that went with M. *Frobiſher*, in his North Weſt Diſcoverie for their Directions. [Printed in M. *Hakluyt's* Voyages. *Fol.* 1589. *p.* 636. 1576. 17 *Eliz.*

A Relation of the firſt Voyage of M. *Martine Frobiſher* to the North Weſt, for the ſearch of the Straight or Paſſage to *China*, written by *Chriſtopher Hall*, and made in the yeere of our Lord 1576. [Printed in M. *Hakluyt's* Voyages. *p.* 615.]

The ſecond Voyage of Maſter *Martin Frobiſher*, made to the Weſt and North Weſt Regions in the yeere 1577. With a Deſcription of the Country and People. Written by *Dioniſe Settle.* [*Hakluyt, Ib. p.* 622.] 1577. 18 *Eliz.*

Of the thynges that are brought from the occidental Indies, in three Books, wherein are diſcovered great ſecretes of Nature, and great Experiences, made and compiled by Doctor Monardus, Phiſitian of Sevill. Tranſlated by John Frampton, with his Epiſtle Ded. to Maiſter Edwarde Dier Eſquire. Dat. from London the firſt of October 1577. *4to. folijs* 109.

Sir *Francis Drake's* Voyage round the World, departing from *Plymouth* 13. *Dec.* 1577, with an Introduction to the ſaid Voyage, writ by Sir *William Monſon*, and inſerted in his Naval Tracts, publiſh'd in the Collection of Voyages printed for Mr. *Churchill* 1704. Fol. Vol. III. p. 399. *Purchas Pilgrim*, Vol. IV. p. 1180.

Voyage de Sieur Francois Draque vers le deſtroit de Magallanes l'an 1577. [Recueil & Abregé de tous les Voyages, qui ont eſté faicts devers le deſtroit de Magellanes. *En la Deſcription des Indes Occidentales.* Amſterdam, 1622. *Fol.*]

The ſecond Circumnavigation of the Earth, in the Renowned Voyage of Sir *Francis Drake*, the firſt Generall which ever ſailed round the whole Globe, begun in the Year 1577. heretofore publiſht by Mr. *Richard Hakluyt*, now Review'd and Corrected. [*Purchas Pilgrim*, p. 46.]

F

A Set

A Sermon of the true and gladsome Olivetree mentioned in the epistle of Saint Paul to the Romans, chap. xi. concerning the Conversion of the Jews, and the Calling of the Gentiles. Preached at London by a faithful Minister of God John Foxe, at the Christening of a certaine Jewe, translated out of Latine into Englishe. Together with the Confession of faith which Nathanael a Jewe borne made before the Congregation in the Parish Church of Allhallows in Lombarde street at London, when baptized the first of April 1577. Imprinted at London by Christopher Barker. Anno 1578. 8vo.

1578.
19 Eliz.

A Discourse of the valiant Voyage to Meta Incognita, by Maister Forboysher in his last setting foorth the xxv of Maye, from Blackwall, for the discovery of Cattaye, and other frozen land or seas, from 67. ℣. towards the North, and from thence towards the South along the coast of America. With an Epistle Ded. dated from the Courte the last of April, Thomas Churchyard. Printed the tenth of May 1578. [Ex dono Reverendi viri Samuelis Blackwell. S. T. B.]

The third and last Voyage into *Meta Incognita*, made by Mr. *Martin Frobisher* in the Year 1578, written by *Thomas Ellis*. [Publisht in *Hakluyt's* Voyages, *Fol.* 1589. p. 630.]

The Report of *Thomas Wiars* Passenger in the *Emanuel*, otherwise called the *Busse* of *Bridgwater*, wherein *James Leeche* was Master, one of the Shippes in the last Voyage of Master *Martin Frobisher* 1578. concerning the discoverie of a great Island in their way homeward the 12th of *September*. [*Ib. Hakluyt, p.* 635.]

A Letter written to M. *Richard Stapers* by *John Whithall*, from *Brasill* in *Santus*, the 26th of *June*, 1578. concerning the Mines of Gold and Silver newly discovered at St. *Vincent*, &c. [*Ib. Hakluyt*, p. 638.]

A Letter written to M. *Richard Hakluyt* of the *Middle Temple*, conteining a Report of the true State and Commodi ies of *Newfoundland*, by M. *Anthonie Parkhurst*, Gentleman, 1578. [*Ib. Hakluyt's* Voyages, *p.* 674.]

The Letters Patents graunted by her Majestie to Sir *Humfrey Gilbert* of *Compton*, in the Countie of *Devon* Knight, for the inhabiting and planting of our People in *America*. Witness Ourself at *Westminster* the xi day of *June*, the 20th yeare of our Reigne. [Printed at large in *Hakluyt's* Voyages, *p.* 679.]

The

The Pleasant Historie of the Conquest of the Weast India, now called New Spayne, Atchieved by the worthy Prince Hernando Cortez, Marques of the valley of Huaxacac, most delectable to read: translated out of the Spanishe tounge by T. N. [*i. e.* Thomas Nicholas] *Anno* 1578. Imprinted at London by Henry Bynneham. 4to. pp. 405.

Novæ Novi Orbis Historiæ, id est, *Rerum ab Hispanis in India Occidentali hactenus gestarum, & acerbo illorum in eas gentes dominatu, Libri tres, URBANI CALVETONIS opera industriaq; ex Italicis* Hieronymi Benzonis Mediolanensis, *qui eas terras* XIII. *annorum peregrinatione obijt. Commentariis descripti, Latini facti, ac perpetuis notis, argumentis & locupleti memorabilium rerum accessione illustrati. His ab eodem adjuncta est, De Gallorum in Floridam expeditione, & insigni Hispanorum in eos sævitiæ exemplo, Brevis Historia.* Genevæ. *Apud Eustathium Vignon*, M.D.LXXVIII. 8vo. pp. 480.

Advertisements and Reportes of the sixt Voyage into the parts of *Persia* and *Media*, gathered out of sundry Letters, written by *Christopher Burrough*, and more especially a Voyage over the *Caspian* Sea, departing from *Gravesend* 19 *June* 1579. [*Purchas* Pilgrim. Vol. III. p. 243.]

Voyage de Pedro Sarmiento, qui partie de Lima *l' an* 1579. *en intention de recognoistre & visiter le Destroit de Magellanes de la part du Sud.* [Recueil & Abbregé de tout les Voyages devers le destroit de Magellanes. *En la Description des Indes Occidentales. Amsterdam* 1622. Fol.]

A Copie of the Letters of the Adventurers for *Brasill*, sent to *John Whithall* dwelling in *Santos*, by the Minion of *London*, with the Commodities demanded, dat. *London* 1580. 24. *October*. [Printed in *Hakluyt*'s Voyages, *p.* 640.]

Certain Notes of the Voyage to *Brasill* with the *Minion* of *London* aforesaid, in the yeere 1580. Written by *Thomas Gregges* Purser of the said Shippe. *Ib. p.* 641.

Commission given by Sir *Rowland Hayward* Kt. and *George Barne*, Aldermen and Governours of the Company of *English* Merchants, for discovery of New Trades unto *Arthur Pet* and *Charles Jackson*, for a Voyage by them to be made for discoverie of *Cathay* 1580. With Instructions to be observed in the said Voyage; and certain briefe Advises, and other Notes in Writing. [Printed at large in *Hakluyt*'s Voyages. Fol. 1589. *p.* 455. &c.]

An.

1581.
22 Eliz.

An Act for the Increase of Mariners, and for Maintenance of the Navigation, towards repairing the late decay of the number of two hundred Sayle and more of good and serviceable Ships, which yearly traded to Iland, for taking of Fishe. Anno XXII. Eliz. Cap. VII. [Printed Copy.]

The Relation of *Alexandro Ursino* concerning the Coast of *Terra Firma*, and the Secrets of *Peru* and *Chili*, where he had lived four and thirty yeeres. Written in 1581. [*Purchas Pilgrim. Vol. IV. p.* 1418.]

A compendious or brief Examination of certaine ordinarye complaints of divers of our Countrymen in these our dayes: (relating to Merchandise and Trade) which although they are in some part unjust and frivolous, yet they are all by way of dialogues throughly discussed and debated By W. S. Gentleman. Imprinted at *London* in *Fleetstreet* neere unto Sainte *Dunstones* Church, by *Thomas Marshe*, 1581. *Cum Privilegio. Folijs* 55.

1582.
23 Eliz.

A Muster of Ships and Mariners throughout *England*, taken in the year 1582. two years before the Death of the Earl of *Lincoln* Lord Admiral. [Sir *Will. Monson's Naval Tracts, publisht in Collect. of Voyages.* Printed for Mr. *Churchill*, 1704. *Vol. III. p.* 279.]

The first Booke of the Historie of the Discoverie of the East Indias, enterprised by the Portingales in their daungerous Navigations, in the time of King Don John, the second of that Name. Set foorth in the Portingall Language by Hernan Lopez de Castaneda. And now translated into Englishe by N. L. Gentleman. Imprinted at *London* by *Thomas East*, 1582. 4to. pag. *Folijs* 164.

A Discourse written by one *Miles Phillips* an Englishman, one of the Company put a shore in the *West-Indies* by M. *John Hawkins*, in the yeere 1568. containing many special Thinges of that Countrie, and of the *Spanish* Government, but especially of their Cruelties used to our *English* Men, and amongst the rest to himself for the space of 15 or 16 yeeres together, untill by good and happy meanes he was delivered from their bloudy hands, and returned to his own Countrie *Anno* 1582. [Printed at large in M. *Hakluyt's* Voyages. *Fol.* 1589. *p.* 562.]

1583.
24 Eliz.

A Report of the Voyage and Successe thereof, attempted in the yeere of our Lord 1583. by Sir *Humfrey Gilbert* Knight, with other Gentlemen assisting him in that Action, intended to discover, and to plant Christian Inhabitants

habitants in place convenient, upon those large and ample Countries extended Northward from the Cape of *Florida*, not in the actual possession of any Christian Prince, written by Mr. *Edward Haies*, Gentleman, and principal Actor in the same Voyage, who alone continued unto the end, and by God's special assistance returned home with his Retinue safe and entire. [*Hakluyt's* Voyages, *p.* 679.]

Instructions given by the honourable the Lords of the Counsell to *Edward Fenton* Esquire for the Order to be observed in the Voyage recommended to him for the *East Indies* and *Cathay*, *Apr.* 9. 1582. [Printed in M. *Hakluyt's* Voyages, *p.* 644.]   1582. 24 *Eliz.*

A Relation of the Voyage intended towards *China*, but made on the Coast of *Brasill* in *America*. Written by Master *Luke Ward* his Vice Admiral, and Captain of the *Edward Bonaventure*, begun *Anno Dom.* 1582. [*Ib. Hakluyt. p.* 647.]

An Extract out of the Discourse of one *Lopez* a *Spaniard*, touching the Sea-Fight between M. *Fenton* with two *English* Ships, and three *Spanish* Shippes, in the Port of St. *Vincent* in *Brasill*; together with a Report of the Proceeding of M. *John Drake*, after his departing from him. *Ib. p.* 673.

The first Booke of the History of the Discovering and Conquest of the *East Indias*, enterprised by the *Portingales* in their daungerous Navigations, in the time of their King *Don John*, the second of that Name. Which Historie conteineth much varietie of Matter, very profitable for all Navigators, and not unpleasaunt to the Reader. Set forth in the *Portingale* language, by *Hernan Lopes de Casteneda*. And now translated into *English* by N. L. [*i. e. Nicholas Lichfield*] Gentleman. Imprinted at *London* by *Thomas East*, 1582. *4to. Folijs* 163. [*Ex dono* Roberti Watts, *LL. B.*]

A true Report of the late discoveries, and possession taken in the right of the Crowne of *England* of the *New-found-lands*, by that valiant and worthy Gentleman Sir *Humfrey Gilbert*, Kt. wherein is also briefly set downe her Highness a lawful Title thereunto, and the great and manifold Commodities, &c. Written by Sir *George Pecham*, Kt. the chief Adventurer and Furtherer of the said Voyage to *Newfoundland*. [*Hakluyt's* Voyages, *p.* 718.]   1583. 25 *Eliz.*

A Letter written from M. *Thomas Aldworth*, Marchant, and Major of the Citie of *Bristow*, to the right honourable Sir *Francis Walsingham*, principal Secretarie to her Majestie, concerning a Western Voiage, intended for Dis-

G   coveries

coveries in *America*, dat. *Bristow March* 27. 1583. [*Hakluyt's* Voyages, p. 718.]

A brief and summarie Discourse upon the intended Voyage to the hithermost parts of *America*. Written by Captain *Carlill* in *Aprill* 1583. for the better inducement to satisfie the Merchants of the *Moscovian* Companie and others. [*Ib. Hakluyt.* p. 718.]

A Copie of the Letters in *Latine* and *English* to the worshipfull Master *Richard Hakluyt*, at Oxford in *Christ Churche*, Master of Arts, dated in *Newfoundlande*, at St. *John's* Port the sixt of *August* 1583. giving an account of that Island. [Printed in *Hackluyt's* Voyages. Fol. 1589. p. 698.]

A Relation of *Richard Clarke* of *Weymouth*, Master of the Shippe called, *The Delight*, going for the Discoverie of *Norumbege*, with Sir *Humfrey Gilbert*, 1583. Ib. p. 700.

Articles set down by the Committees appointed in the behalf of the Companie of *Moscovian* Merchants, to conferr with Master *Carleil*, upon his intended discoveries and attempt into the hithermost partes of *America*. Ib. p. 724.

The Letters Patents graunted by the Queenes Majestie to M. *Walter Raleigh*, for the discovering and planting of new Lands and Countries, to continue the space of six yeares and no more. Witnes, &c. at *Westm.* the 25th of *March*, in the 26th yeare of our Reigne. [Printed at large in *Hakluyt's* Voyages, Fol. p. 728.]

The first Voyage made to the Coasts of *America* with two Barkes, wherein were Captaines Master *Philip Amadas*, and Master *Arthur Barlowe*, who discovered part of the countrey now called *Virginia*, *Anno* 1584. written by one of the said Captains, and sent to Sir *Walter Ralegh*, Kt. at whose charge and direction the said Voyage was set foorth. [*Hakluyt.* p. 728. *Purchas*, Vol. IV. p. 1645.]

The Letters Patents of the Queens Majestie, graunted to Master *Adrian Gylbert* and others, for the search and discoverie of the North West Passage to *China*. Witnesse ourself at *Westminster* the sixt day of *Februarie* in the six and twentieth yeere of our Reigne. [*Hakluyt's* Voyages, p. 774.]

Notes concerning the Discoverie of the River *Ob*, taken out of a Roll, written in the *Russian* tongue, which was attempted by the means of *Anthonie Marshe*,

Marſhe, a chief Factor for the *Moſcovie* Company of *England* 1584. With other Notes of the North Eaſt. [*Purchas* Pilgrim. *Vol. III, p. 804.*]

‾ The Diſcovery of *Virginia*, made in purſuance of the Queen's Letters Patents granted to Sir *Walter Raleigh*, in two ſmall Barks under the command of Captain *Philip Amidas*, and Captain *Barlow*, who ſailed from the *Thames* in *April* 1584. [Publiſhed in Capt. *Smith's* Hiſtorie. *Fol.* 1627. *Cap. I.*]

The firſt Voyage of Maſter *John Davis*, undertaken in *June* 1585. for the Diſcoverie of the North Weſt Paſſage. Written by *John Janes* Merchant, Servant to the worſhipful M. *William Sanderſon*. [In *Hakluyt's* Voyages, *p.* 776.]

1585.
27 Eliz.

An Extract of Mr. *Lane's* Letter to M. *Richard Hakluyt*, and another Gentleman of the *Middle Temple*, dated from the *New Fort* in *Virginia*, 3 *Sept.* 1585. [*Hakluyt's* Voyages, *p.* 793.]

Sir *Francis Drake's* Voyage to the *Weſt Indies*, *Anno Dom.* 1585. as related by Sir *Will. Monſon*, in his Navall Tracts. [Publiſht in the Collection of Voyages. Printed for Mr. *Churchill. Fol. Vol. III. p.* 169.]

A Relation of the Voyage made by Sir *Richard Greenvile*, for Sir *Walter Raleigh* to *Virginia*, in the yeere 1585. With the Names of all thoſe, as well Gentlemen as others, that remained one whole Yeer in *Virginia*, under the Government of Maſter *Ralfe Lane*. [*Hakluyt's* Voyages, *p.* 734, &c.]

Sir *Richard Greenvil's* Voyage to *Virginia* for Sir *Walter Raleigh*, Knight, in *April* 1585. With the Obſervations of Mr. *Thomas Heriot* in that Voyage. [Publiſhed in Capt. *Smith's* Hiſtorie. *Fol.* 1626. *p.* 5.]

A Relation of the Voyage ſet out by the right Honourable the Earl of *Cumberland*, in the yeere 1586. intended for the South Sea, but performed no farther than the Latitude of 44 Degrees to the South of the Equinoctial, written by *John Sarracole*, Merchant in the ſame Voyage. [Mr. *Hakluyt's* Voyages *Fol. p.* 793. *Purchas* Pilgrim. *Vol. II. p.* 1141.]

1586.
28 Eliz.

A Notable Diſcourſe of Maſter *JOHN CHILTON*, touching the People, Manners, Mynes, Cities, Riches, Forces, and other memorable thinges of the *WEST-INDIAS*, ſeen and noted by himſelfe in the time of his travailes, continued in thoſe partes the ſpace of 17 or 18 yeeres from 1551. to his arrival at *London* in *July* 1568. [Mr. *Hakluyt's* Voyages, *Vol. I. Fol. p.* 587.]

A

A Relation of the second Voyage attempted by Master *John Davis,* with others, for the discoverie of the Northwest Passage in *Anno* 1586. With a Letter of Maister *Davis* to M. *William Sanderson* of *London,* concerning his said Voyage. [Mr. *Hakluyt's* Voyages. *Fol. p.* 781.]

The Relation of the course which the *Sunshine,* a barke of fifty Tunnes, and the *Northstarre,* a small Pinnesse, being two Vessels of the Fleet of Mr. *John Davis,* held after he had sent them from him to discover the Passage between *Groenland* and *Iseland* in 1586. Written by *Henry Morgan,* Servant to M. *William Sanderson* of *London.* [In Mr. *Hakluyt's* Voyages, *p.* 787.]

A short Account of Mr. *Cavendishes* Voyage round the World, in the year 1586. [In Sir *Will. Monson's* Naval Tracts, published in the Collect. of Voyages, Printed for Mr. *Churchill* 1704. *Vol. III. p.* 401.]

La Premiere Navigation de CANDISS *allant devers l' Estroit de Magellan avec deux Navires de Pleymude le* 21. *de Juillet* 1586. [Recueil & Abregé de tous le Voyages devers le Destroit de Magellanes. *En la Description des Indes Occidentales* 1622. Fol.]

An Account of the Particularities of the Employments of the *Englishmen* left in *Virginia* by Sir *Richard Greenville,* under the Charge of Master *Ralfe Lane,* General of the same, from the 17th of *August* 1585, untill the 18th of *June* 1586. at which time they departed the Countries : Sent and directed to Sir *Walter Raleigh.* [*Hakluyt's* Voyages. Fol. 1589. *p.* 737.]

A Relation of the third Voyage made by a Ship sent in the yeere 1586. to the reliefe of the Colonie planted in *Virginia,* at the sole charges of Sir *Walter Raleigh. Ib. Hakluyt, p.* 747.

A briefe and true Report of the *Newfoundland* of *Virginia :* Of the Commodities there found and to be raised, as well merchantable as others. Written by *Thomas Harriot,* Servant to Sir *Walter Raleigh,* a Member of the Colonie, and there employed in discovering a full twelvemonth. With an Epistle to the Reader by *Ralphe Lane,* Governour. [*Hakluyt's* Voyages, *p.* 748.]

The Historie of *Lopez Vaz,* a *Portugall,* (taken by Captain *Withrington* at the River of *Plate, Anno* 1586. With this Discourse about him) touching *American* Places, Discoveries, and Occurrents, abridged. [*Purchas* Pilgrim. *Vol. IV. p.* 1432.]

Historia Navigationis in BRASILIAM *qua & * AMERICA *dicitur. Qua describitur Autoris navigatio, quaq; in mari vidit memoriæ prodenda. Villagagnonis in America gesta: Brasiliensium victus & mores à nostris admodum alieni, cum eorum linguæ dialecto: animalia etiam, arbores atq, herbæ, reinquaq, singularia & nobis penitus incognita.* A JOANNE LERIO *Burgundio Gallicè Scripta. Nunc vero primum Latinitate donata & varijs figuris illustrata. Excudebat* Eustathius Vignon. *Anno M. D. LXXXVI, 8ve. p. 341.*

1586. 28 Eliz.

A Relation of the third Voyage Northwestward, made by *John Davis*, Gentleman, as chief Captain and Pilott Generall, for the discoverie of a Passage to the Isles of the *Molucca*, or the Coast of *China*, in the yeere 1587. Written by *John Janis*, Servant to the aforesaid M. *William Sanderson*. [*Hakluyt*'s Voyages, *p.* 789.]

1587. 29 Eliz.

A Relation of the fourth Voyage made to *Virginia* with three Shippes, in the yeare 1587. wherein was transported the second Colonie. With the Names of all the Men, Women and Children, which safely arrived in *Virginia*, and remained to inhabite there 1587. [*Hakluyt*'s Voyages, *p.* 764.]

Sir *Francis Drake*'s second Voyage to the Road of *Cadiz*, and towards the *Tercera* Islands, as related by Sir *Will. Monson*, in his Naval Tracts, publisht in the Collection of Voyages. Printed for Mr. *Churchill*. *Fol. Vol. III. p.* 170.

An Account of the fifth Voyage intended for the supply of the Colonie planted in *Virginia*, by *John White*, which being undertaken in the yeere 1588. by casualtie took no effect. [*Hakluyt*'s Voyages, *p.* 771.]

1588. 30 Eliz.

The Copie of a Letter sent out of England to Don Bernardin Mendoza, **Ambassadour in** France for the **King of** Spaine, **declaring the State of** England, **contrary to the opinion of Don** Bernardin, **and of all his Partizans,** Spaniards **and others. This Letter, although it was sent to Don** Bernardin Mendoza, **yet by good hap the copies thereof, as well in** English **as in** French, **were found in the chamber of one** Richard Leigh **a Seminary Priest, who was lately executed for High Treason, committed in the time that the** Spanish **Armada was on the Seas. Whereunto are adioyned certain late Advertisements concerning the losses and distresses happened to the** Spanish **Navie,** &c. Imprinted at *London* by *J. Vautrollier* 1588. 4to. H. 11

The first Action undertaken by the *Spaniards* in 1588. the Duke of *Medina Sidonia*, General, encountred by our Fleet, &c. as in Sir *Will. Monson's* Navall Tracts, publisht in the Collect. of Voyages, printed for Mr. *Churchill*. 1704. *Fol. Vol. III. p.* 171.

A Letter of Master *Thomas Candish* to the right Honorable the Lord Chamberlaine, one of her Majesties most honourable Privie Counsell, touching the Success of his Voyage about the World: Dated at *Plimouth* this 1xth of *September*, 1588. [*Hakluyt's* Voyages. *Fol. p.* 808.]

A full Relation of the worthy and famous Voyage of Master *Thomas Candishe*, made round about the Globe of the Earth, in the space of two yeeres and less than two Months, setting out from *Plimouth* the 21st of *July* 1586. and returning to the same place the 9th of *September* 1588. [In M. *Hakluyt's* Voyages, *p.* 809.]

Certaine Notes or References taken out of the large Mappe of *China*, brought home by Master *Thomas Cavendishe* 1588. [*Ib. Hakluyt. p.* 813.]

The third Circumnavigation of the Globe; or the admirable and prosperous Voyage of Master *Thomas Candish* of *Trimley*, in the County of *Suffolk*, Esquire, into the South Sea, and from thence round about the Circumference of the whole Earth. Begun in the Yeare of our Lord 1586. and finished 1588. Written by Mr. *Francis Pretty*, lately of *Eye* in *Suffolk*, Gentleman, employed in the same Action. Published by Master *Hakluyt*, and now corrected and abbreviated. [*Purchas* Pilgrim. *Fol. Vol. I. B. II. Ch.* 4. *p.* 57.]

A Treatise of *Russia*, and the adjoining Regions, written by Doctor *Giles Fletcher*, Lord Ambassadour from Queen *Elizabeth* to *Theodore*, Emperour of *Russia*. A.D. 1588. [*Purchas Pilgrim Vol. III. p.* 413.]

The second Voyage of the Earl of *Cumberland*, toward the Coasts of *Spain*, in the latter end of *Octob.* 1588. and his third Voyage toward the *West Indies* in 1589. [*Purchas* Pilgrim. *Vol. IV. p.* 1142.]

The Historie of the greate and mightie Kingdome of CHINA, **and the Situation thereof. Togither with the great riches, huge Cities, politike Government, and rare Inventions in the same. Translated out of** Spanishe by R. Parke. *London* Printed by *J. Wolfe*, 1588. *4to. p.* 410.

A

A Relation of the fifth Voyage to *Virginia*, undertaken by Mr. *John White*, 1589. in *March* 1589. Written by the said Master *John White*. [Published in 31 *Eliz.* Capt. *Smith*'s Gen. Historie. *Fol.* 1626. *p.* 15.]

The Expedition to *Portugal An.* 1589. under *Sir Francis Drake* and *Sir John Norris*, for restoring Don *Antonio* to the Crown of *Portugal*, and setting a Trade of the *English* to the *West-Indies*. [In Sir *Will. Monson's* Naval Tracts, publisht in the Collect. of Voyages, printed for Mr. *Churchill. Fol.* 1704. *Vol. III. p.* 174.]

A Discourse of the said Voyage, written as it is thought by Colonel *Anthonie Wingfield*, imployed therein, to a Friend of his, and here abbreviated. [*Purchas* Pilgrim. *Vol. IV. p.* 1914.]

An Assignment from Sir *Walter Raleigh* to divers Gentlemen and Merchants of *London*, for the inhabiting and planting of our People in *Virginia*, by Indenture made the 7th of *March*, in the 31st Yeere of our Sovereign Lady *Elizabeth*, &c. [Printed at large in *Hakluyt*'s Voyages, *p.* 815.]

A briefe Remembrance of a Voyage made in the Year 1589. by *William Michelson* Captain, and *William Mace* of *Retcliffe* Master of a Ship called the *Dogge*, to the Bay of *Mexico* in the *West India*. [*Hakluyt, p.* 817.]

The Principall Navigations, Voiages and Discoveries of the English Nation, made by Sea, or over Land, to the most remote and farthest distant Quarters of the Earth, at any time, within the compass of these 1500 Yeares: Devided into three several parts, according to the Positions of the Regions whereunto they were directed; &c. Whereunto is added the last most renowned English Navigation round about the whole Globe of the Earth. By Richard *Hakluyt*, Master of Arts, and Student some time of Christ Church in Oxford. Imprinted at *London* by *George Bishop* and *Ralph Newberrie*, Deputies to *Christopher Barker*, Printer to the Queen's most Excellent Majestie. 1589. *Fol. p.* 825.

A Voyage undertaken by the Earl of *Cumberland*, with one Ship Royal of her Majesties, and six of his own and other Adventurers, *Anno Dom.* 1589. [In Sir *Will. Monson's* Naval Tracts. *Ib. p.* 176.]

A true Coppie of a Discourse written by a Gentleman employed in the late Voyage of Spaine and Portugalle, sent to his particular friende, and by him published for the better Satisfaction.

faction of all such, as having been seduced by particular report, have entred into conceits, tending to the discredit of the Enterprise, and Actors of the same. *London* Printed for *Thomas Woodcock*, 1589. 4to. p. 58. [*Ex dono Rev. Viri Johannis Mapletoft*, S. T. P.]

1590.
32 Eliz.
  Sir *John Hawkins* and Sir *Martin Forbusher*, their Voyage to the Coast of *Spain* and Islands, *Anno* 1590. [In Sir *Will. Monson's* Naval Tracts, publisht in Collect. of Voyages, printed for Mr. *Churchill*. Fol. *Vol. III. p.* 177.]

1591.
33 Eliz.
  Relacion Summaria de las Prisiones y Persecusiones de ANTONIO PEREZ *Secretario d' Estado, que fue del Rey Catholico Don Phelippe* II, *d' este nombre, con particularidades, y copia de papeles nunca vistos, dignos defer visto* : 1590. [*Las Obras y Relaciones de* Ant. *Perez* Geneva 1631. 8vo. à p.* 1. *ad* 215.]

  La Deuxieme & derniere Navigation de Candiss *allant avec trois grands Navires & deux Barcques, devers l' Estroit de Magellan, de Pleymude le* 26. *d' Aoust,* 1591. [Recueil & Abbrege de tous les Voyages devers le destroit de Magelhanes. *En la Description des Indes Occidentales.* Fol. 1622.]

  Relacion de la Succedido en Caragoca de Aragon à 24. *de Septembre del año de* 1591. *por la libertad da Antonio Perez, y de sus Fueros, y Justicia.* [Ib. à p. 216. ad p. 260.]

A Fig for the Spaniard, or Spanish Spirits ; wherein are lively pourtraied the damnable Deeds, miserable Murders, and monstrous Massacres of that cursed Spaniard ; with a true rehearsall of the late Nobles, and noblesome estate of Aragon, Catalonia, Valencia and Portingall, with other Matters of much marveile. *London*, Printed by *John Woolfe*, 1591. 4to.

  Master *Thomas Candish*, his Discourse of his fatal and disastrous Voyage towards the South Sea ; with his many Disadventures in the *Magellan* Straits, and other places ; written with his own Hand to Sir *Tristram Gorges* his Executor, concluding that he *was scant able to hold a Pen in his Hand*. [*Purchas* Pilgrim. *Vol. IV. p.* 1182.]

  An Account of the admirable Adventures and strange Fortunes of Master *Anthonie Knivet*, which went with Master *Thomas Candish*, in his Second Voyage to the South Sea, 1591. [Written by himself. *Purchas* Pilgrim. *Vol. IV. p.* 1201.]

Account

Account of the two Fleets at Sea, the *English* under the Lord *Thomas Howard*, and the *Spanish* commanded by Don *Alonfon Baffon*, expecting the *Indian* Fleets wintering in the *Havana, Anno* 1591. [In Sir *Will. Monfon's* Naval Tracts in Collect. of Voyages printed for Mr. *Churchill*, 1704. Fol. *Vol. III. p.* 178.]

The Voyage of the Earl of *Cumberland* to the Coast of *Spain*, in her Majesties Ship the *Garland*, and seven other Ships of his and his Friends, *Anno* 1591. [Sir *Will. Monfon, Ib. p.* 179. And *Purchas* Pilgrim. *Vol. IV. p.* 1144.]

A Voyage undertaken by Sir *Walter Raleigh*, toward attempting some Place in the *West Indies*, but he returning, left the charge of it to Sir *Martin Forbusher, Anno* 1592. [Sir *Will. Monfon's* Naval Tracts, *Ib. p.* 180.] *1592. 34 Eliz.*

A Voyage of the Earl of *Cumberland* to the Coast of *Spain* with Captain *Monfon*, and Sir *Edward Yorke, Anno* 1593. [Sir *Will. Monfon's* Naval Tracts, *Ib. p.* 181. *Purchas* Pilgrim. *Vol. IV. p.* 1144.] *1593. 35 Eliz.*

A brief Relation of the Shipwrack of *Henry May*, on the North West of the *Bermudas*, in *December* 1593. as written by himself after his arrival at *Falmouth*. [Publisht in Capt. *Smith's* Gen. Hist. 1626. Fol. *p.* 172.]

The Observations of Sir *Richard Hawkins*, Knight, in his Voyage into the South Sea, *An. Dom.* 1593. once before publish'd, now reviewed and corrected by a written Copie, illuftrated with Notes, and in divers places abbreviated. [*Purchas* Pilgrim. *Vol. IV. p.* 1367.]

A briefe Note written by Master *John Ellis*, one of the Captains with Sir *Richard Hawkins*, in his Voyage through the Strait of *Magellan*, begunne the ninth of *April* 1593. concerning the said Straite, and certaine places on the Coast and Island of *Peru*. [*Purchas* Pilgrim. *Vol. IV. p.* 1435.]

JOAN. PETRI MAFFEI *Burgomatis è Societate Jefu Hiftoriarum Indicarum Libri XVI. Salectarum item ex India Epiftolarum eodem Interprete Libri IV. Acceffit* Ignatij Loiolæ *Vita. Omnia ab Autore recognita, & nunc primum in Germania excufa. His nunc recens adjecta eft Charta Geographica, ære nitidiffimè expreffa, qua Lectori utriufq; Indiæ fitus, & longinqua ad eas Navigatio accurate ob oculos fpectanda proponitur, non minus adfpectu quam hiftoria ipfa lectu jucunda.* Coloniæ *Agrippinæ. In Officina Birckmannica fumptibus* Arnoldi Mylij. *Anno* MDXCIII. Fol. *p.* 541.

The Obſervations of Sir Richard Hawkins, Knight, in his Voiage into the South Sea, Anno Domini 1593. Written by himſelf, and put to the Preſſe in his own Life time, though not publiſhed till the Year 1622. London, Printed by J. D. for John Jaggard, 1622. Fol. p. 169.

The Seventh Voyage of the Earl of Cumberland toward the Spaniſh Weſt-Indies, his Deſcent on Hiſpaniola, Jamaica, &c. in the Yeere 1593. [Purchas Pilgrim. Vol. IV. p. 1146.]

1594.
35 Eliz.
The Expedition of Sir Martin Forbuſher, with a Fleet to Breſt in Britany, then taken from the Spaniards. [Sir Will Monſon's Naval Tracts. Ibid. p. 182.]

The Eighth Voyage of the Earl of Cumberland, toward the Coaſts of America, and engaging with Spaniſh Carricks, and doing great harm to the Enemy, without bringing home any Prize, in 1594. [Purchas Pilgrim. Vol. IV. p. 1148.]

Of the Interchangeable Courſe or Variety of things in the whole World, and the concurrence of Armes and Learning, thorough the firſt and famouſeſt Nations: from the beginning of Civility and Memory of Man to this Preſent, &c. Written in French by Loys le Roy, called Regius: and tranſlated into Engliſh by R. A. [i. e. Robert Aſhley.] At London Printed by Charles Yetſweirt, Eſquire, 1594. Cum Privilegio Regiæ Majeſtatis. Folijs 126.

The firſt North Voyage of the Hollanders and Zelanders, along the Coaſts of Norway, Muſcovy, and Tartary, in Queſt of a Paſſage to the Kingdoms of Cathai and China, in three Ships under Balthaza Moucheran, who began his Voyage in 1594. [Collection of Voyages by the Dutch Eaſt India Company. 1703. 8vo. p. 1.]

The firſt Navigation of William Barents, alias Bernards, into the North Seas, in the Year 1594. Written by Gerat de Veer. [Purchas, Vol. III. p. 473.]

1595.
37 Eliz.
The Ninth Voyage of the Earl of Cumberland, in a Ship built at his own Charge, which the Queen at lanching called the Scourge of Malice; in 1595. when he was commanded back, &c. [Purchas Pilgrim. Vol. IV. p. 1148.]

A

A Voyage to the *West Indies* by an *English* Fleet, under the Command of Sir *Francis Drake* and Sir *John Hawkins*, Generals, wherein they ventur'd deeply, and dy'd in the Voyage, *Anno* 1594. [Sir *William Monson's* Naval Tracts, *Ib. p.* 182. *Purchas Pilgrim,* Vol. IV. *p.* 1183.]

A briefe Declaration of *Barents* his second Navigation made in *Anno* 1595. behinde *Norway, Muscovia* and *Tartaria.* Written by *Gerat de Veer.* [*Ib. p.* 478.]

The Second North Voynge of the *Hollanders* and *Zelanders,* along the Coast of *Norway, Muscovy* and *Tartary,* in Quest of a Passage to *Cathai* and *China*; in seven Ships setting out in the Year 1595. [*Collection of Voyages by the* Dutch East-India *Company.* 8vo. 1703. *p.* 8.]

A Relation of the first Voyage of the *Dutch* into the *East-Indies* in four Ships from *Amsterdam,* sailing from the *Texel, Apr.* 2. 1595. With an Account of all that hapned in the Voyage, the Condition, Religion, and Manners of the *Indians*: With their way of Living, the Nature, Fertility, and Product of that Country; the Beasts and other Creatures which are to be seen there; and generally what is most remarkable and fit to be observed in those Regions. [*Collection of Voyages by the* Dutch East-India *Company.* 8vo. 1703. *p.* 94.]

The Estate of *ENGLISH FUGITIVES* under the King of *Spaine* and his Ministers. Containing, besides a Discourse of the said King's manner of Government, and the injustice of many late dishonourable Practises by him contrived. *London,* Printed for *John Drawater, &c.* 1595. 4to.

1596.
38 *Eliz.*

The Expedition of the Earl of *Essex,* and the Lord Admiral of *England,* Generals, equally both by Sea and Land, against the *Spaniards, Anno* 1596. [Sir *Will. Monson's* Naval Tracts publisht in the Collect. of Voyages, printed for Mr. *Churchill.* 1704. *Fol. p.* 184.]

The Use of the two Mathematicall Instruments, the crosse Staffe, (differing from that in common use with the mariners) and the Jacob's Staffe. Set foorth Dialogue wise in two briefe and plaine treatises. Set forth by Th. Hood, Mathematicall Lecturer in the Citie of London. Newly reviewed, and the second time imprinted at London by Richard Field. 1596. 4to.

A Libell

⁵ 𝕬 𝕷𝖎𝖇𝖊𝖑𝖑 𝖔𝖋 Spanish 𝕷𝖎𝖊𝖘 : 𝕱𝖔𝖚𝖓𝖉 at the Sacke of Cales, 𝖉𝖎𝖘𝖈𝖔𝖚𝖗𝖘𝖎𝖓𝖌 𝖙𝖍𝖊 𝕱𝖎𝖌𝖍𝖙 𝖎𝖓 𝖙𝖍𝖊 West-Indies, 𝖙𝖜𝖎𝖝𝖙 𝖙𝖍𝖊 English 𝕹𝖆𝖛𝖎𝖊, 𝖇𝖊𝖎𝖓𝖌 𝖋𝖔𝖚𝖗𝖙𝖊𝖊𝖓 𝕾𝖍𝖎𝖕𝖘 𝖆𝖓𝖉 𝕻𝖎𝖓𝖓𝖆𝖘𝖘𝖊𝖘, 𝖆𝖓𝖉 𝖆 𝕱𝖑𝖊𝖊𝖙𝖊 𝖔𝖋 𝖙𝖜𝖊𝖓𝖙𝖞 𝕾𝖆𝖎𝖑𝖊 𝖔𝖋 𝖙𝖍𝖊 𝕶𝖎𝖓𝖌 𝖔𝖋 Spaines, 𝖆𝖓𝖉 𝖔𝖋 𝖙𝖍𝖊 𝖉𝖊𝖆𝖙𝖍 𝖔𝖋 𝕾𝖎𝖗 Francis Drake. 𝖂𝖎𝖙𝖍 𝖆𝖓 𝕬𝖓𝖘𝖜𝖊𝖗𝖊 𝖇𝖗𝖎𝖊𝖘𝖊- 𝖑𝖞 𝖈𝖔𝖓𝖋𝖚𝖙𝖎𝖓𝖌 𝖙𝖍𝖊 Spanish 𝕷𝖎𝖊𝖘 ; 𝖆𝖓𝖉 𝖆 𝖘𝖍𝖔𝖗𝖙 𝕽𝖊𝖑𝖆𝖙𝖎𝖔𝖓 𝖔𝖋 𝖙𝖍𝖊 𝕱𝖎𝖌𝖍𝖙, 𝖆𝖈𝖈𝖔𝖗𝖉- 𝖎𝖚𝖌 𝖙𝖔 𝖙𝖗𝖚𝖙𝖍, 𝖜𝖗𝖎𝖙𝖙𝖊𝖓 𝖇𝖞 Henrie Savile 𝕰𝖘𝖖𝖚𝖎𝖗𝖊, 𝖊𝖒𝖕𝖑𝖔𝖞𝖊𝖉 𝕮𝖆𝖕𝖙𝖆𝖎𝖓𝖊 𝖎𝖓 one of her 𝕸𝖆𝖏𝖊𝖘𝖙𝖎𝖈𝖘 𝕾𝖍𝖎𝖕𝖕𝖊𝖘 𝖎𝖓 𝖙𝖍𝖊 𝖘𝖆𝖒𝖊 𝕾𝖊𝖗𝖛𝖎𝖈𝖊 𝖆𝖌𝖆𝖎𝖓𝖘𝖙 the Spaniards. 𝕬𝖓𝖉 𝖆𝖑𝖘𝖔 𝖆𝖓 𝕬𝖕𝖕𝖗𝖔𝖇𝖆𝖙𝖎𝖔𝖓 𝖔𝖋 𝖙𝖍𝖎𝖘 𝕯𝖎𝖘𝖈𝖔𝖚𝖗𝖘𝖊, 𝖇𝖞 𝕾𝖎𝖗 Thomas Baskervile, 𝖙𝖍𝖊𝖓 𝕲𝖊𝖓𝖊𝖗𝖆𝖑 𝖔𝖋 𝖙𝖍𝖊 English 𝕱𝖑𝖊𝖊𝖙. London, 𝕻𝖗𝖎𝖓𝖙𝖊𝖉 𝖇𝖞 John Winder. 1596. 4to. p. 47.

Othonis Casmanni Marinarum Quæstionum Tractatio Philosophica Bipartita, Disceptans Quæstiones parte Priore ad Maris naturam pertinentes interiorem: Posteriore de motu Maris agitatas, præcipue verò de eo qui dicitur Affluxus & Refluxus Marinus. Cum Cæs. Majest. privilegio decennali. Francofurti. Ex Officina M. Zachariæ Palthenij. Anno M. D. XCVI. p. 244.

A Relation of the third Voyage Northward to the Kingdoms of *Cathaia* and *China* in *Anno* 1596. Written by *Gerat de Veer*. [*Purchas* Pilgrim. *Vol. III. p.* 482.]

Josephi Acosta *Societatis Jesu de Natura Novi Orbis Libri duo. Et de Promulgatione Evangelij apud Barbaros, sive de procuranda Indorum Salute Libri sex. Coloniæ Agrippinæ, in officina Birckmannica, sumptibus Arnoldi Mylij.* M. D. XCVI. 8vo. p. 581. *Epist. Ded. Philippo secundo Hispaniarum atq; Indiarum Regi Catholico. Dat. Cal. Febr.* 1588.

𝕵𝖔𝖞𝖋𝖚𝖑 𝕹𝖊𝖜𝖊𝖘 out of the New-found-World, 𝖜𝖍𝖊𝖗𝖊𝖎𝖓 𝖆𝖗𝖊 𝖉𝖊𝖈𝖑𝖆𝖗𝖊𝖉 𝖙𝖍𝖊 𝖗𝖆𝖗𝖊 𝖆𝖓𝖉 𝖘𝖎𝖓𝖌𝖚𝖑𝖆𝖗 𝖁𝖊𝖗𝖙𝖚𝖊𝖘 𝖔𝖋 𝖉𝖎𝖛𝖊𝖗𝖘 𝕳𝖊𝖗𝖇𝖘, 𝕿𝖗𝖊𝖊𝖘, 𝕻𝖑𝖆𝖓𝖙𝖘, 𝕺𝖞𝖑𝖊𝖘, 𝖆𝖓𝖉 𝕾𝖙𝖔𝖓𝖊𝖘, 𝖜𝖎𝖙𝖍 𝖙𝖍𝖊𝖎𝖗 𝕬𝖕𝖕𝖑𝖎𝖈𝖆𝖙𝖎𝖔𝖓𝖘, as well to the use of 𝕻𝖍𝖎𝖘𝖎𝖈𝖐𝖊, 𝖆𝖘 𝖔𝖋 𝕮𝖍𝖎𝖗𝖚𝖗𝖌𝖊𝖗𝖞, &c. 𝕬𝖑𝖘𝖔 𝖙𝖍𝖊 𝖕𝖔𝖗𝖙𝖗𝖆𝖙𝖚𝖗𝖊 𝖔𝖋 𝖙𝖍𝖊 𝖘𝖆𝖎𝖉 𝕳𝖊𝖆𝖗𝖇𝖘, 𝖛𝖊𝖗𝖎𝖊 𝖆𝖕𝖙𝖑𝖞 𝖉𝖊𝖘𝖈𝖗𝖎𝖇𝖊𝖉. Englished 𝖇𝖞 John Frampton, 𝕸𝖊𝖗𝖈𝖍𝖆𝖓𝖙; 𝖜𝖍𝖊𝖗𝖊𝖚𝖓𝖙𝖔 𝖆𝖗𝖊 𝖆𝖉𝖉𝖊𝖉 𝖙𝖍𝖗𝖊𝖊 𝖔𝖙𝖍𝖊𝖗 𝖇𝖔𝖔𝖐𝖊𝖘, 𝖙𝖗𝖊𝖆𝖙𝖎𝖓𝖌 𝖔𝖋 𝖙𝖍𝖊 Bezaar 𝕾𝖙𝖔𝖓𝖊, 𝖙𝖍𝖊 𝖍𝖊𝖗𝖇 Escuerconera, 𝖙𝖍𝖊 𝖕𝖗𝖔𝖕𝖊𝖗𝖙𝖎𝖊𝖘 𝖔𝖋 𝕴𝖗𝖔𝖓 𝖆𝖓𝖉 𝕾𝖙𝖊𝖊𝖑𝖊 𝖎𝖓 𝕸𝖊𝖉𝖎𝖈𝖎𝖓𝖊, 𝖆𝖓𝖉 𝖙𝖍𝖊 𝖇𝖊𝖓𝖊𝖋𝖎𝖙 𝖔𝖋 𝕾𝖓𝖔𝖜. London, 𝕻𝖗𝖎𝖓𝖙𝖊𝖉 𝖇𝖞 E. Allde. 1596. 4to. folijs 197. 𝕯𝖊𝖉. to 𝕸𝖆𝖘𝖙𝖊𝖗 Edward Dier, 𝕰𝖘𝖖𝖚𝖎𝖗𝖊.

𝕿𝖍𝖊 𝕯𝖎𝖘𝖈𝖔𝖛𝖊𝖗𝖎𝖊 of the 𝕷𝖆𝖗𝖌𝖊, 𝕽𝖎𝖈𝖍 and 𝕭𝖊𝖜𝖙𝖎𝖋𝖚𝖑 𝕰𝖒𝖕𝖎𝖗𝖊 of GUIANA, 𝖜𝖎𝖙𝖍 a relation of the 𝖌𝖗𝖊𝖆𝖙 𝖆𝖓𝖉 𝖌𝖔𝖑𝖉𝖊𝖓 𝕮𝖎𝖙𝖎𝖊 of Manoa, (𝖜𝖍𝖎𝖈𝖍 the Spanyards call El. Dorado) 𝖆𝖓𝖉 𝖔𝖋 𝖙𝖍𝖊 𝕻𝖗𝖔𝖛𝖎𝖓𝖈𝖊 𝖔𝖋 Emeria, Arromaia, Amapaia, 𝖆𝖓𝖉 𝖔𝖙𝖍𝖊𝖗 𝕮𝖔𝖚𝖓𝖙𝖗𝖎𝖊𝖘, 𝖜𝖎𝖙𝖍 𝖙𝖍𝖊𝖎𝖗 𝕽𝖎𝖛𝖊𝖗𝖘 𝖆𝖉𝖏𝖔𝖞𝖓𝖎𝖓𝖌. 𝕻𝖊𝖗𝖋𝖔𝖗𝖒𝖊𝖉 𝖎𝖓 the yeare 1595. 𝖇𝖞 𝕾𝖎𝖗 W. Ralegh, 𝕶𝖓𝖎𝖌𝖍𝖙, 𝕮𝖆𝖕𝖙𝖆𝖎𝖓𝖊 of her 𝕸𝖆𝖏𝖊𝖘𝖙𝖎𝖊𝖘 𝕲𝖚𝖆𝖗𝖉, 𝕷𝖔. 𝖂𝖆𝖗𝖉𝖊𝖓 of the 𝕾𝖙𝖆𝖓𝖓𝖆𝖗𝖎𝖊𝖘, 𝖆𝖓𝖉 her 𝕳𝖎𝖌𝖍𝖓𝖊𝖘𝖘𝖊 𝕷𝖎𝖊𝖚𝖙𝖊𝖓𝖆𝖓𝖙 𝕲𝖊𝖓𝖊𝖗𝖆𝖑𝖑 of the 𝕮𝖔𝖚𝖓𝖙𝖎𝖊 of Cornwall. 𝕴𝖒𝖕𝖗𝖎𝖓𝖙𝖊𝖉 at London 𝖇𝖞 Robert Robinson. 1596. 4to. p. 112. 𝕰𝖕. 𝕯𝖊𝖉. to the right 𝕳𝖔𝖓. my 𝖘𝖎𝖓𝖌𝖚𝖑𝖆𝖗
𝖌𝖔𝖔𝖉

good Lord and Kinsman, Charles Howard, Knight of the Garter, Baron, and Counseller, and of the Admirals of England most renowned, and to the right hon. Sir Robert Cecill, Knight.

The third North Voyage of the *Dutch* through the Seas of *Muscovy* and *Tartary*, to find a Passage that Way to the Kingdoms of *Cathai* and *China*, by the permission of the Town and Council of *Amsterdam*, in the Year 1596. [*Collection of the* Dutch East-India *Company*, 8vo. 1703. *p.* 16.]

The Voyage to Saint *John de Porto Rico*, made by the right honourable *George* Earl of *Cumberland*, and written by himself in a Letter to the Queen, in 1596. [*Purchas* Pilgrim. *Vol. IV. p.* 1150.]

A briefe and true Report of the Honourable Voyage unto *Cadiz*, 1596. Of the overthrow of the King *Spain*'s Fleet; and of the winning of the Citie, with other Accidents gather'd out of *Meteranus*, Master *Hakluyt*, and others. [Publisht by Mr. *Purchas* in his *Pilgrim. Vol. IV. p.* 1927.]

The Path-Way to Knowledge. Conteining certaine briefe Tables of English weights and measures, with the proportions, kindes and numbers belonging properly unto the same. Whereunto is annexed a most excellent Invention of Julius Cæsar Patavinus, for the buying and selling of all kind of Merchandise. And lastly, the Order of keeping of a Merchants booke, after the Italian manner, by Debitor and Creditor; with an Instruction to lead you to the same. Written in Dutch, and translated into English by W. P. Printed at London for William Barley. 1596. 4to.

The Voyage of the Earl of *Cumberland* to the Island of *Puerto Rico*, to intercept the *Carreck* going to the *East-Indies*, as taken out of the printed Copy publisht by Dr. *Layfield*, Chaplain to my Lord in that Expedition. 1596. [Sir *William* Monson's *Naval Tracts. Ib. p.* 209. And *Purchas Pilgrim. Vol. IV. p.* 1155.]

A Reporte of the Kingdom of Congo, a Region of Africa, and of the Countries that border round about the same, &c. Drawn out of the Writinges and Discourses of Odoardo Lopez, a Portugal, by Philippo Pigafetta. Translated out of Italian by Abraham Hartwell. London, Printed by John Wolfe, 1597, 4to. p. 217,

1597.
39 *Eliz.*

K   The

The Hiſtorie of the Weſt-Indies, containing the Acts and Adventures of the Spaniards, which have conquered and peopled thoſe Countries, inriched with varietie of pleaſant relation of the Manners, Ceremonies, Lawes, Governments, and Warres of the Indians. Publiſhed in Latin by Mr. Hakluyt, and tranſlated into Engliſh by M. Lok, Gent. London, Printed for Andrew Hebb. 4to. folijs 318.— A Preface to the Reader by M. Lok. And certaine Preambles gathered by R. Eden heretofore, of the firſt diſcovering of the Weſt-Indies, &c.

A Relation of the Voyage to the Iſles of *Azores*, under the Conduct of the right Honourable *Robert* Earl of *Eſſex*, given by the ſaid Earl and other Commiſſioners. With a larger Relation of the ſaid Voyage, written by Sir *Arthur Gorges*, Knight. [*Purchas* Pilgrim. Vol. IV. p. 1935.]

An Expedition deſigned to aſſault the King of *Spain*'s Shipping in the Harbour of *Ferrol*, and afterwards to take the *Tercera* Iſlands, and there to expect the coming home of the *Indian* Fleet, *Anno* 1597. under the Earl of *Eſſex*, General, and the Lord *Thomas Howard*. [Sir *Will. Monſon*'s *Naval Tracts*, in the *Collection of Voyages* printed for Mr. *Churchill. Fol. Vol.* III. p. 189.]

A Project in the Days of Queen *Elizabeth*, for the ſettling her Subjects in *Guinea*, ſhewing of what conveniency it would be, and to be preferr'd before our Planting in *Gaiana*, on the Continent of *America*. Writ in the Year 1597. [*Naval Tracts, Ib. p.* 471.]

The Inſtructions given by Don *Martin de Padilla*, Mayor of *Caſtile*, Earl of *Buendia*, Captain General of the Gallies of *Spain*, and of the Navy Royal of the Ocean Sea, and of the Catholick King's Army, in their Expedition for *England*, *Anno* 1597. [*Naval Tracts, Ib. p.* 353.]

A Project how to make War upon *Spain*; written in the Queen's time, and preſented to Sir *Robert Cecil*, by her Majeſties Appointment. *Ibid. p.* 400.

The Navigators Supply. Conteining many thinges of principal importance belonging to Navigation, with the deſcription and uſe of divers Inſtruments framed chiefly for that purpoſe; but ſerving alſo for ſundry other of Coſmographie in generall: The Inſtruments made by Charles Whitwell: Inſtructions to be given by John Goodwin. Imprinted at London by G. Biſhop, 1597. 4to. L. 2.

An

An Account of the Voyage of five *Roterdam* Ships, which sailed *June* 27. 1598. 40 Eliz. 1598. to the Streight of *Magellan*, from whence *Sebald de Veert*, Captain of the Ship the *Faith* sailed the 21st of *January*, to return into *Holland*, and arrived in the *Maese July* 13. 1600. [*Collection of* Dutch East-India *Voyages.* 1703. 8vo. p. 297.]

𝕬 𝕸𝖊𝖙𝖍𝖔𝖉 𝖋𝖔𝖗 𝕿𝖗𝖆𝖛𝖊𝖑𝖑. 𝕾𝖍𝖊𝖜𝖊𝖉 𝖇𝖞 𝖙𝖆𝖐𝖎𝖓𝖌 𝖙𝖍𝖊 𝖛𝖎𝖊𝖜 𝖔𝖋 France, 𝖆𝖘 𝖎𝖙 𝖘𝖙𝖔𝖔𝖉𝖊 𝖎𝖓 𝖙𝖍𝖊 𝕻𝖊𝖆𝖗𝖊 𝖔𝖋 𝖔𝖚𝖗 𝕷𝖔𝖗𝖉 1598. London, Printed by *Thomas Creede*, 4to. p. 2.

𝕬 𝖙𝖗𝖚𝖊 𝕮𝖔𝖕𝖕𝖞 𝖔𝖋 𝖙𝖍𝖊 𝕬𝖉𝖒𝖔𝖓𝖎𝖙𝖎𝖔𝖓𝖘 𝖘𝖊𝖓𝖙 𝖇𝖞 𝖙𝖍𝖊 𝖘𝖚𝖇𝖉𝖚𝖊𝖉 𝕻𝖗𝖔𝖛𝖎𝖓𝖈𝖊𝖘 𝖙𝖔 𝖙𝖍𝖊 𝕾𝖙𝖆𝖙𝖊𝖘 𝖔𝖋 Hollande, 𝖆𝖓𝖉 𝖙𝖍𝖊 Hollanders 𝕬𝖓𝖘𝖜𝖊𝖗𝖊 𝖙𝖔 𝖙𝖍𝖊 𝖘𝖆𝖒𝖊. 𝕿𝖔𝖌𝖊𝖙𝖍𝖊𝖗 𝖜𝖎𝖙𝖍 𝖙𝖍𝖊 𝕬𝖗𝖙𝖎𝖈𝖑𝖊𝖘 𝖔𝖋 𝕻𝖊𝖆𝖈𝖊 𝖈𝖔𝖓𝖈𝖑𝖚𝖉𝖊𝖉 𝖇𝖊𝖙𝖜𝖊𝖓𝖊 𝖙𝖍𝖊 𝖍𝖎𝖌𝖍 𝖆𝖓𝖉 𝖒𝖎𝖌𝖍𝖙𝖞 𝕻𝖗𝖎𝖓𝖈𝖊𝖘 Philip, 𝖇𝖞 𝖙𝖍𝖊 𝖌𝖗𝖆𝖈𝖊 𝖔𝖋 𝕲𝖔𝖉 𝕶𝖎𝖓𝖌 𝖔𝖋 Spaine, &c. 𝖆𝖓𝖉 Henry 𝖙𝖍𝖊 𝖋𝖔𝖚𝖗𝖙𝖍 𝖙𝖍𝖊 𝖒𝖔𝖘𝖙 𝕮𝖍𝖗𝖎𝖘𝖙𝖎𝖆𝖓 𝕶𝖎𝖓𝖌 𝖔𝖋 France, 𝖎𝖓 𝖙𝖍𝖊 𝕻𝖊𝖆𝖗𝖊 1598. 𝕿𝖗𝖆𝖓𝖘𝖑𝖆𝖙𝖊𝖉 𝖎𝖓𝖙𝖔 English 𝖇𝖞 H. W. 𝕴𝖒𝖕𝖗𝖎𝖓𝖙𝖊𝖉 at London 𝖇𝖞 John Wolfe. 1598. 4to.

Voyage de cinq Basteaux de JAQUES MAHU & SIMON de COR-DES *Qui partirent de Rotterdam l' an.* 1598. *pour l' Estroit de Magellanes.* [Recueil & Abregé de tous le Voyages devers le Destroit de Magellanes *En la Description des Indes Occidentales.* 1622. Fol.]

Navigation de M. Olivier du Nort *Laquelle il fit en l' an.* 1598. *avec quatre Navires &* 248 *Persones, partis de* Goree *le* 13 *Septembre* 1598. *Ib: p.* 193.

The Voyage of *Oliver Noort* round about the Globe, being the fourth Circumnavigation of the same by a *Dutch Fleet*, the chief Pilot being Captain *Melis*, an *English* Man ; setting Sail from *Roterdam* 2d *July* 1598. [*Purchas. Vol. I. Lib. II. Cb. V.*]

Another Voyage of *Sebald de Wert* in five Ships of *Amsterdam*, to the South Sea ; their Miserie in the Streights, wherein *William Adams*, *Englishman*, was chief Pilot, in the yeere 1598. [*Purchas* Pilgrim. *Vol. I. p.* 8.]

A briefe Relation of Master *John Davis*, chiefe Pilot to the *Zealanders*, in their *East-India* Voyage, departing from *Middleborough*, the fifteenth of *March*, *Anno* 1598. [*Purchas. Vol. I. Lib. III. p.* 116.]

A Relation of the Second Voyage of the *Dutch* into the *East-Indies*, made by a Fleet of eight Ships, in the yeere 1598. under the Command of *James Corneliz*

Cornelis Van Neck, Admiral, and *Wybrant Van Warwick*, Vice-Admiral, taken out of the Printed Journals, and other Manuscripts. [*Collection of* Dutch East-India *Voyages.* 1703. 8vo. p. 250.]

1599.
41 Eliz.
Account of an intended Expedition against the *Spaniards*, under the Lord *Thomas Howard*, Admiral in the Downs, from whence he return'd in a Month, *Anno* 1599. [Sir *Will. Monson's Naval Tracts. Ib. p.* 195.]

An Answer to a Project of the *Hollanders*, for surprizing the Island of *Canaria*, and that of St. *Thomas*, under the Equinoctial, *An.* 1599. in reproof of some of my Countrymen, who seek to prefer their Actions before ours. By Sir *Will. Monson*, in his *Naval Tracts*, publisht in [*Collect. of Voyages. Vol. III. p.* 483.]

The Travailles of *John Mildenhall* into the *Indies*, and in the Countries of *Persia*, and of the great *Mogor* or *Mogull*, wherein he is reported afterward to have died of poison. Written by himself in two Letters. Setting out 12 *Febr.* 1599. [*Purchas* Pilgrim. *Vol. I. Lib. III. p.* 114]

The Voyage of *William Adams*, chief Pilot of a Fleet of five Saile of *Dutch* Ships through the *Magellane* Streights, where they winter'd in the Yeere 1599. and so through the South Sea to *Japan*. Written in two Letters by himselfe. [*Purchas* Pilgrim. *Vol. I. Lib. III. p.* 125.]

1600.
42 Eliz.
The Expedition of Sir *Richard Lewson*, in three of her Majesties Ships, to the Islands, there to expect the *Carrecks* and *Mexico* Fleet, *Anno Dom.* 1600. [Sir *Will. Monson's Naval Tracts. Ib. p.* 196.]

The Voyage of Captain *John Davies* to the Eastern *India*, Pilot in a *Dutch* Ship; written by himself to *Robert* Earl of *Essex*. Dat. 1. *Aug.* 1600. [*Purchas* Pilgrim. *Vol. I. Lib. III. p.* 116.]

A Copy of the Letters Patents of Queen *Elizabeth*, granting several Priviledges for fourteen years, to certaine Adventurers, for the discoverie of the Trade to the *East-Indies*. *Westminster* 31. *Decemb. reg.* 43. [*Purchas* Pilgrim. *Vol. I. Lib. III. p.* 144.]

A Geographical Historie of *AFRICA*; written in *Arabicke* and *Italian*, by *JOHN LEO*, a *More*, borne in *Granada*, and brought up in *Barbarie*. Wherein he hath at large described, not only the Qualities, Situations, and true Distances of the Regions, Cities, Towns, Mountains, Rivers, and other places throughout all the Northe and Principall Partes of *Africa*,

but

but also the Descents and Families of their Kinges, the Caufes and Events of their Warres, with their Manners, Cuftoms, Religions, and civile Government, and many other memorable Matters. gathered out of his own diligent Obfervations, and partly out of the ancient Records and Chronicles of the *Arabians* and *Mores*. Before which, out of the beft ancient and modern Writers, is prefixed a general Defcription of *Africa*; and alfo a particular Treatife of all the main Lands and Ifles, undefcribed by *John Leo*. And after the fame is annexed a relation of the great Princes, and the manifold Religions in that part of the World. Tranflated and collected by *JOHN PORT*, lately of *Gonevill* and *Caius* College in *Cambridge*. *Londini; Impenfis Georgij Bifhop*. 1600. Fol. p. 420.

Bulla Clementis *Papæ VIII. Quod in partibus* INDIARUM, *in ordine Fratrum Minorum Ordinû S. Francifci de Obfervantiâ, non pofint affumi ad munus Provincialatus, & aliorum Officiorum, nifi Filij, aut Incorporati in illis Provincijs. Dat. Romæ apud S. Petrum, fub annulo Pifcatoris die quarta Martij, millefimo fexcentefimo, Pont. noftri anno nono.* [*Bullarium Romanum. Tom. III.* 1638. Fol.]

Ordinationes Clementis Papæ VIII. circa acceffum Regularium in JAPONICAS *& adjacentes* CHINÆ, *&* INDIÆ *Orientalis Infulas, prædicandi aut docendi causâ. Dat. Romæ. apud S. Petrum, fub Annulo Pifcatoris, die* 12. *Decembris* 1600. *Pont. noftri anno nono.* [*Bullarium Romanum. Tom. III. Romæ* 1638. Fol.]

The firft Voyage made to *Eaft-India*, by Mafter *James Lancafter*, for the Merchants of *London*, with four tall Shippes, fetting out from *Wolwich* 13 *Febr.* 1660. [*Purchas* Pilgrim. *Vol. I. Lib. III. p.* 148.]

Guilielmi Gilberti Colceftrenfis Medici Londinenfis de MAGNETE, *Magneticifq; Corporibus, & de Magno Magnete tellure, Phyfiologia nova, plurimis & argumentis & experimentis demonftrata.* Londini, *Excudebat Petrus Short, Anno MDC.* Fol. p. 240. [Ex dono *Awnfhami Churchill Armig.*]

The Expedition and great Succefs of Sir *Richard Lewfon*, with five of her 1601. Majefties Ships againft the *Spanifh* Fleet invading *Ireland. Anno* 1601. 43 *Eliz.* [Sir *Will. Monfon's Naval Tracts. Ib. p.* 197.]

A Difcourfe writ by Sir *Will. Monfon*, at the Requeft of Sir *Robert Cecil*, Principal Secretary to her Majefty, concerning the Abufes of our Seamen, and the beft courfe for a Reformation of them. [*Naval Tracts. Ib. p.* 215.]

L   A Re-

A Relation of the taking of Saint *Vincent* and *Puerto Bello*, by Captain *William Parker* of *Plimouth*, the seventh of *Febr.* 1601. as given by himself [*Purchas* Pilgrim. *Vol.* IV. *p.* 1243.]

Certaine Notes of a Voyage made by me *David Middleton* into the *West-Indies*, with Captain *Michael Geare*, *An. Dom.* 1601. [*Purchas* Pilgrim. *Vol.* IV. *p.* 1246]

A Description of the *West-Indies*, by *Antonio de Herrera*, Chief Chronicler of the *Indies*, and of *Castile*, taken out of the *Spanish* Original, and compared with the *Latine* Translation, and so abbreviated in *English*. With the Ep. Ded. dated from *Valledolid* 15. *Octob.* 1601. [*Purchas* Pilgrim. *Vol.* III. *Descriptio*, &c. *p.* 856.]

Descriptio INDIÆ OCCIDENTALIS per Antonius de Herrera *Regium Indiarum & Castella Historiographum.*—*Epistre à Monsieur* Paul de Leguna *Licentie President au Royal & Souverain Conseil des* Indes *de Valledolid le* 15 *d' Octobre* 1601. [*Description des Indes Occidentales.* 1622. *Fol.*]

A Treatise of *Brasil* in *America*, written by a *Portugal*, which had long lived there; from whom this written Book was taken by one *Francis Cooke* of *Dartmouth*, in a Voyage outward bound for *Brasill*, *An.* 1601. who sold it to Master *Hacket*, for 20 s. by whose procurement it was translated out of *Portugall* into *English*, which Translation is now compared and corrected. [*Purchas* Pilgrim. *Vol.* IV. *p.* 1289.]

Particulier Description de l' INDE OCCIDENTALE *touchant la Situation de ses terres & Provinces, le chemin qu'il faut tenir à les passer, & quelles Riches d' or & argent se trouvent en chascune d' icelles. Par le Prestre* Pedro Ordonnez de Cevallos, *Qui les a recerché Fort curieusement.* [Ib. à p. 203. ad p. 227.]

1602.   A Letter of Father *Diego de Pantoia*, one of the Company of *Jesus*, to Fa-
44 *Eliz.* ther *Luys de Guzman*, Provincial in the Province of *Toledo*, written in *Paquin*, which is the Court of the King of *China*, the ninth of *March*, in the Yeere 1602. concerning the Success of their Mission. [*Purchas* Pilgrim. *Vol.* III. *p.* 350.]

The Voyage of Captain *George Weymouth*, intended for the discoverie of the North West Passage toward *China*, in two Flyeboats, in *May* 1602. [*Purchas* Pilgrim. *ib. Vol.* III. *p.* 809]

The

The Description of the Isle of *Trinidad*, the rich Countrie of *Guiana*, and the mightie River of *Orenoco*, written by *Francis Sparrey*, left there by Sir *Walter Raleigh*, 1595. and in the end taken by the *Spaniards*, and sent Prisoner into *Spaine*, and after long Captivity got into *England* by great sute in 1602. [*Purchas* Pilgrim. *Vol. IV. p.* 1247]

Master *Bartholomew Gosnold*'s Letter to his Father, touching his first Voyage to *Virginia*; dat. 7. *Sept.* 1602. With a Relation of the said Captain *Gosnold*'s Voyage to the North Part of *Virginia*, begunne the 26 of *March*, 44 *Eliz.* 1602. and delivered by *Gabriel Archer*, a Gentleman in the said Voyage. [*Purchas* Pilgrim. *Vol. IV. p.* 1647.]

A brief Relation of the Description of *Elizabeth's Isle*; and some others towards the North Part of *Virginia*, and what else they discovered in the Yeare 1602. by Captain *Bartholomew Gosnell*, and Captain *Bartholomew Gilbert*, and divers other Gentlemen, their Associates. Written by *John Brierton*, one of the Voyage. [Published in Capt. *Smith's* Gen. Historie. *Fol.* 1626. *p.* 17.]

The Expedition of Sir *Richard Lewson* Admiral, and Sir *William Monson* Vice-Admiral, to the Coasts of *Spain*, to wait for the Silver Ships that were arrived at the *Terceras, Anno* 1602. [Sir *William Monson's* Naval Tracts, publisht in the *Collect. of Voyages*, printed for Mr. *Churchill*. 1704. *Fol. Vol. III. p.* 198.]

A second Expedition of Sir *William Monson*, to the Coast of *Spain*, to divert the *Spanish* Fleet from their Design upon the *Ireland*, toward the latter end of the same Year 1602. [Sir *William Monson's* Naval Tracts, *Ib. p.* 204.]

An Account of sundry the Personal Voyages, performed by *John Sanderson* of *London*, Merchant, begun in *October* 1584. ended in *October* 1602. With an Historical Description of *Constantinople*. [*Purchas* Pilgrim. *Vol. II. p.* 1614.]

Patrum quorundam Societatis Jesu. Iter susceptum Anno MDCII. Ex oppido Baiano ad Brasilios & *praesertim* Carigios *Brasiliae gentem, religionis causa, & quis inde fructus secutus est.* [Petri Jarrici *Thesaurus* Indicus. *Tom. III. p.* 632. &c. 8vo.]

A Voyage of Captain *Martin Pring*, with two Barks from *Bristow*, for for the North Part of *Virginia*; in *June* 1603. Written by *Robert Salterne*. [Published in Capt. *Smith's* Gen. Historie. *Fol.* 1626. p. 18. *Purchas* Pilgrim. *Vol. IV. p.* 1654.]

1603.
1 *Jam.* 1.

The

The Expedition of Sir *Richard Lawson* and Sir *William Monson*, into the Narrow Seas, to keep a continual Force upon the *Spanish* Coast, from *February* to *November* 1603. [*Sir Will. Monson's* Naval Tracts. *Ibid. p.* 206.]

An Act to encourage the Seamen of *England* to take Fish, for the better Increase of Seamen, to be ready at all times to serve in the King's Majesties Navie, and the Navy of *England. Anno* 1 *Jac. Cap. XXIX.* [Printed Copie.]

A Project how to ruine *Spain*, with the assistance of *Holland*, if his Majesty enter into a new War with that Crown. Writ by Sir *Will. Monson*, and publisht in his [Naval Tracts Printed for Mr. *Churchill.* 1704. *Fol. Vol. III. p.* 487.]

A Voyage performed to the Northwards *Anno* 1603. in a Ship called the *Grace*, set forth at the cost and charges of the worshipfull *Francis Cherie*; being the first Voyage to *Cherie Island.* Written by *William Gorden.* [*Purchas* Pilgrim. *Vol.* III. *p.* 566.]

A Relation of the Voyage made to *Virginia*, in the *Elizabeth* of *London*, of fifty Tunnes, by Captain *Bartholomew Gilbert*, in the Yeere 1603. Written by *Thomas Canner*, a Gentleman of *Bernardes Inne*, his Companion in the same Voyage. [*Purchas*, Vol. IV. *p.* 1656.]

A Relation of the Voyage of *Samuel Chaplaine* of *Brovage*, made unto *Canada*, in the Yeere 1603. Dedicated to *Charles de Montmorencie*, High Admiral of *France.* [*Purchas* Pilgrim. Vol. IV. *p.* 1605.]

A briefe Relation of an *English* Man, which had been thirteen Yeares Captive to the *Spaniards* in *Peru*, and returned into *England* 7 *Dec.* 1603. [*Purchas* Pilgrim. Vol. IV. *p.* 1418.]

TYCHONIS BRAHE *De Mundi Ætherij Recentioribus Phænomernis Liber Secundus. Typis incoatus Uraniburgi Daniæ, absolutus Pragæ Bohemiæ* M.DC.III. *Cum Cæsaris & Regum Complurium Privilegijs.* 4to. p. 465. [*Ex dono Reverendi Viri Josephi Sparke, Petriburgensis.*]

Bulla Clementis Papæ VIII. *de Approbatione Confraternitatum sub invocatione Sanctissimi nominis* JESU, *in Provincijs regni* PERU *institutarum & instituendarum, cum Indulgentiarum elargitione. Dat. Romæ apud Sanctum Marcum, sub annulo Piscatoris, die trigesima Junij. Millesimo Sexcentesimo tertio, Pont. nostri anno duodecimo.* [*Bullarium Romanorum.* Tom. III. *Romæ* 1638. *Fol.*]

The

The Voyage of Monſieur *De Monts* into *New France*, in purſuance of his Letters Pat. of the *French* King, for the inhabiting of the Countries of *La Cadia*, *Canada*, and other Places, from the 40th degree to the 46th. Written by *Mark Lescarbot*. [*Purchas* Pilgrim. Vol. IV. *p.* 1620.]

The ſecond Voyage ſet forth by the Companie into the *East-Indies*, Sir *Henry Middleton*, being General, in four Shippes, in *April* 1604. Written by *Thomas Clayborne*, in a larger Diſcourſe, of which the Extract is here delivered. [*Purchas* Pilgrim. Vol. I. Lib. III. *p.* 185.]   1604. 2 *Jac.* 1.

A Relation of Captaine *Charles Leigh*, his Voyage to *Guiana*, in 1604. and of his Plantation there; and a Copy of his Letter to Sir *Olave Leigh*, his Brother, for ſupply of Men, and for ſober Preachers, dar. from *Mount Howard* 2 *July* 1604. [*Purchas* Pilgrim. Vol. IV. p. 1251.]

The Naturall and Morall Hiſtorie of the *East* and *West-Indies*, intreating of the remarkable thinges of Heaven, of the Elements, Metalls, Plants and Beaſts, which are proper to that Country; Together with the Manners, Ceremonies, Laws, Goverments, and Warres of the *Indians*. Written in *Spaniſh* by *Joſeph Acoſta*, and tranſlated into *Engliſh* by E. G.   *London*, Printed for *Edward Blount* and *William Aſpley*. 1604. 4to. *p.* 590.

The Travels of *Peter Teixera* from *India* to *Italy* by Land, departing from *Goa*, the Metropolis of the *Portugueſe* Dominions in *India*, on the 9th of *February* 1604. [Tranſlated and publiſht in *Stevens*'s Collect. of Voyages. 1711. 4to. Vol. II.]

The ſecond Voyage of *John Davis* with Sir *Edward Michelborne* Knight, into the *East-Indies*, in the *Tigre*, with a Pinnaſſe called the *Tiger's Whelp*, ſetting Sail from *Cowes* in the *Iſle of Wight*. 5 *Decemb.* 1604. [*Purchas* Pilgrim. Vol. I. Lib. III. *p.* 132.]

Extracts out of certain Letters of Father *Martin Perez* of the Societie of *Jeſus*, from the new Miſſion of the Province of *Cinoloa* to the Fathers of *Mexico*, dated in the Month of *Decemb.* 1591. With a Letter added, written 1605. of later Diſcoveries. [*Purchas* Pilgrim. Vol. IV. *p.* 1562.]   1605. 3 *Jac.* 1.

A true Relation of the traiterous Maſſacre of the moſt part of threeſcore and ſeven *Engliſh* Men, ſet on Land out of a Ship of Sir *Oliph Leagh*, bound for *Guiana*, 1650. in *Sancta Lucia*, an Iſland of the *West-Indie*, the 23d of *August*. Written by *John Nicol*. [*Purchas* Pilgrim. Vol. IV. *p.* 1255.]

A Relation of a Difcovery towards the Northward of *Virginia*, by Captain *George Waymouth* 1605. employed thither by the right Honourable *Thomas Arundell*, Baron of *Warder*, in the Reigne of our Royal King *James*. Written by *James Rofier*, one of the Voyage. [Publifh'd in Captain *Smith's* Gen. Hiftorie. *Fol.* 1626. *p.* 19]

A Difcourfe of *Java*, and of the firft *Englifh* Factorie there, with divers *Englifh* and *Dutch* Occurrents, written by Mafter *Edmund Scot*, containing a Hiftorie of things done, from the eleventh of *Februarie* 1602. till the fixt of *Octob.* 1605. [*Purchas* Pilgrim. Vol. I. Lib. III. *p.* 164.]

Articles of Peace, Entercourfe and Commerce, concluded in the Names of the moft high and mighty Kings and Princes *James* by the Grace of God, King of *Great Britain*, &c. And *Philip* the thirde King of *Spain*, &c. And *Albertus* and *Ifabella Clara Eugenia*, Archdukes of *Auftrice*, &c. In a Treatie at *London* the 18th Day of *Auguft* 1604. Tranflated out of *Latine* into *Englifh*. Imprinted at *London* by *Robert Barker*, Printer to the King's moft Excellent Majeftie. *Anno* 1605. 4to.

1606.
4 *Jac.* 1.
The Voyage of Mafter *John Knight*, for the Difcovery of the North-Weft Paffage, begun the 18th of *April* 1606. [*Purchas* Pilgrim. Vol. III. *p.* 827.]

The Letters of the Great *Turke*, lately fent unto the Holy Father the Pope, and to *Rodulphus*, naming himfelf King of *Hungarie*, and to all the Kinges and Princes of *Chriftendome*. Tranflated out of the *Hebrew* Tongue into *Italian*, and out of the *Italian* into *French*, and now into *Englifh* out of the *French* Copie. Imprinted at *London* by *John Windet*, &c. 1606. 4to.

The fixt Voyage made to *Virginia* 1606. and that Part of it now planted by our *Englifh* Colonies, whom God increafe and preferve. Difcovered and defcribed by Captain *John Smith*. Written with his own Hand. [Publifhed in Cap^r. *Smith's* Gen. Hiftorie 1626. *Fol. p.* 21.] Whereunto are added fome few Words of their Language.

An Effay of the Means, how to make our Travailes into Foreign Countries, the more profitable and honourable. By *Tho. Palmer* of *Wingham* in *Kent*. At *London* for *Matthew Lownes*. 1606. 4to. *p.* 131.

The Voyage of Mr. *David Middleton* in the *Confent*, fetting forth from *Tilburie Hope* on 12th *March* 1606. to the *Moluccan* Iflands. [*Purchas* Pilgrim. Vol. I. Lib. III. *p.* 226.]

The

The Sea Fight in the Road of *Gibraltar* the 25th of *April* laſt, betwixt 1607.
the K. of *Spaines* Carackts and Gallions, and the *Hollandiſh* Men of Warre, 5 *Jan.* 1.
reported by a Letter written aboard the *Hollands* Fleete, by a Commaunder
in the ſame, and faithfully tranſlated into *Engliſhe.* *London,* Printed for
John Hardie, &c. 1607. 4to.

The Proceedings and Accidents of the *Engliſh* Colony in *Virginia,* till
their firſt ſupply in 1607. with the Names of the Planters. Written by
Thomas Studley, the firſt Cape Merchant in *Virginia, Robert Fenton, Edward
Harrington,* and *J. S.* [Publiſhed in Capt. *Smith's* Gen. Hiſtorie, 1626.
Fol. p. 47.]

An Account of the Arrival of that Supply, with their Proceedings, and
the Ships returne. The Arrival of the *Phœnix, &c.* 1607. From the Writings of *Thomas Studley* and *Anas Todkill.* [Publiſht in Capt. *Smith's* Gen.
Hiſt. 1626. *Fol. p.* 51.]

A Journal of the third Voyage to the *Eaſt-India,* ſet out by the Company
of Merchants, trading in thoſe Parts, in three Ships falling to the *Downes,*
April 1. 1607. Written by *William Keeling,* chief Commander thereof.
[*Purchas* Pilgrim. *Vol.* I. *Lib.* III. *p.* 188.]

Divers Voyages, and Northern Diſcoveries of that worthy irrecoverable
Diſcoverer Maſter *Henry Hudſon,* his Diſcoverie toward the North Pole, ſet
forth at the charge of certain worſhipful Merchants of *London,* in *May* 1507.
Written partly by *John Playſe,* one of the Company, and partly by *H. Hudſon.* [*Purchas* Pilgrim. *Vol.* III. *p.* 567.]

L' INDIEN *ou Portrait Au Naturel des Indiens, Preſentè au Roy d'
Eſpagne, Par D. Juan de Palafox Eveſque de la Puebla de les Angeles, en la
nouvelle Eſpagne.* [*En la Relation de divers Voyages.* IV. *Partie.* A *Paris,*
1672. Fol.]

*Ordinatio ſive Decretum Pauli Papæ V. Quod Rectores Eccleſiarum Parochiá-
lium* INDIARUM OCCIDENTALIUM, *ab ijs qui in Eccleſijs &
Domibus Ordinis Fratrum Eremitarum S. Auguſtini ſepeliuntur, majorem non exi-
gant eleemoſynam, quàm à Concilio Tridentino præſcriptam, & à Pio quarto ex-
plicatam. Dat. Romæ apud S. Petrum die* 16 *Febr.* 1607. *Pont. noſtri anno
ſecundo.* [*Bullarium Romanum.* Tom. III. *Romæ* 1638. *Fol.*]

The

1608.
6 Jac. 1. The Miferies of *B A R B A R Y*, Plague, Famine, Civil Warre. With a Relation of the Death of *Mahamet*, the late Emperour, and a briefe Report of the now prefent Warres between the three Brothers. Printed by *W. J.* for *Henry Goffon*, &c. 4to.

A briefe Narration of the fourth Voyage to the *Eaft-Indies*, with the *Afcenfion* and *Union*, under the command of *Alexander Sharpey*, Generall, weighing Anchor at *Woolwich*, 14th *March* 1608. Written by *Thomas Jones*. *Purchas* Pilgrim. [*Vol. I. Lib. III. p.* 228.]

A Relation of the Accidents that hapned in the Difcovery of the Bay of *Chifapeack* by Captain *John Smith*, in *June*, 1608. Written by *Walter Ruffel*, *Anas Todkill*, and *Thomas Momford*. [Publifhed in Capt. *Smith's* Gen. Hiftorie. 1626. *Fol. p.* 57]

Captain *William Hawkins*, his Relations of the Occurrents, which happened in the time of his refidence in *India*, in the Country of the Great *Mogoll*, arriving at *Surat* 24 *Aug.* 1608. and of his departure from thence, written to the Company by himfelfe. [*Purchas* Pilgrim. *Vol.* I. *Lib.* III. *p.* 206.]

A Treatife of *Juer Boty*, a *Groenlander*, tranflated out of the *North* Language into *High Dutch*, in the yeere 1560. and after out of *High Dutch* into *Low Dutch*, by *William Barentfon* of *Amfterdam* : And out of *Low Dutch* into *Englifh*, by Mafter *William Steere* Merchant, in the yeere 1608, for the ufe of Mr. *Henry Hudfon*. Concerning *Ifeland* and *Groenland*. [*Purchas* Pilgrim. *Vol.* IV. *p.* 518.]

A fecond Voyage or Employment of Mafter *Henry Hudfon*, for finding a Paffage to the *Eaft-Indies* by the North Eaft, in *April* 1608. Written by himfelf. [*Purchas* Pilgrim. *Vol.* III. *p.* 574]

A Relation of a Voyage to *Guiana*, begun *March* 23. 1608. and performed by *Robert Harcourt* of *Stanton Harcourt* in the Countie of *Oxford* Efquire to Prince *Charles*. [*Purchas* Pilgrim. Vol. *IV.* p. 1267.]

1609.
7 Jac. 1. *Nova Francia* : Or the Defcription of that Part of *New France*, which is one Continent with *Virginia*. Defcribed in the three late Voyages and Plantations made by Monfieur *de Monts*, Monfieur *du Pont Grave*, and Monfieur *de Poutrincourt*, into the Countries called by the *French*, *La Cadie*, lying to the South-Weft of *Cape Breton*. Together, with an excellent feveral Treatie of all the Commodities of the faid Countries, and Maners of the naturall Inhabitants of the fame. Tranflated out of *French* into *Englifh* by
P. E.

P. E. *Londini*; *Inipenfis Georgij Bifbop* 1609. 4*to. p.* 307. Ep. Ded. to the Bright Starre of the North *Henry*, Prince of *Great Britain.* — *P. Erondelle.*

A Relation of the New Difcoverie in the South Sea, made by *Pedro Fernandez Giros Portuguez,* with his Petitions to the King, touching the Difcoverie of the fourth part of the World called *Terra Auftralis incognita* ; and of the great Riches, and Fertilitie of the fame. Printed with licenfe in *Sivill, An.* 1610. And tranflated into *Englifh.* [*Purchas* Pilgrim. *Vol. IV. p.* 1422.]

A Letter of Mr. *Gabriel Archer,* touching the Voyage of the Fleet of Ships, which arrived at *Virginia,* without Sir *Thomas Gates* and Sir *George Summers* in 1609. [*Purchas* Pilgrim. *Vol. IV. p.* 1733.]

Copies of the Letters from their High and Mightyneffes, and from his Highnefs the Prince of *Orange,* to the Emperour of *CEYLON,* and the Proceedings of the *Dutch Eaft India* Companie in that Ifland, in the Year 1609. [In the Collection of Voyages, Printed for Mr. *Churchill.* Fol. *Vol.* III. *p.* 683.]

Virginia richly valued, by the Defcription of the maine land of *Florida,* her next Neighbour : Out of the foure yeeres continuall travell and difcoverie, for above one thoufand Miles Eaft and Weft, of *Don Ferdinando de Soto,* and fixe hundred able Men in his companie. Wherein are truly obferved the riches and fertilitie of thofe parts abounding with things neceffary, pleafant and profitable for the Life of Man : With the Natures and Difpofitions of the Inhabitants. Written by a *Portugal* Gentleman of *Elvas,* emploied in all the action, and tranflated out of *Portuguefe* by *Richard Hakluyt.* At *London,* Printed by *Felix Kyngfton.* 1609. 4*to. p.* 180. — Ep. Ded. to the right Honourable, the right Worfhipfull Counfellors, and others the cheerfull Adventurors for the advancement of that Chriftian and Noble Plantation in *VIRGINIA.* — Dat. from my Lodging in the Colledge of *Weftminfter,* 15 *Apr.* 1609. *Richard Hakluyt.*

VIRGINIA. A Sermon Preach'd at *White Chappel,* in the Prefence of many Honourable and Worfhipfull the Adventurers and Planters for *Virginia,* 25 *April* 1609. Publifhed for the benefit and ufe of the Colony, planted and to be planted there, and for the advancement of their Chriftian purpofe. By *William Symondes,* Preacher at Saint *Saviours* in *Southwarke.* London, Printed by *J. Windet* for *Eleazar Edgar.* 1609. 4*to.* Ep. Ded. to right noble and worthie Advancers of the Standard of Chrift among the *Gentiles,* the Adventurers for the Plantation of *Virginia.*

N   NOVA

NOVA BRITANNIA, Offering most excellent Fruites, by Planting in *VIRGINIA*. Exciting all such as be well affected to further the same. *London*, Printed for *Samuel Macham*, 1609. 4*to*. E. 2.

A true Historicall Discourse of *Muley Hamets* rising to the three Kingdomes of *Morocos*, *Fes* and *Sus*; the Dis-union of the three Kingdoms by Civil Warre, kindled amongst his three ambitious Sons, *Muley Sheek*, *Muley Boferes*, and *Muley Sidan*. The Religion and Policie of the *More* or *Barbarian*. The Adventures of Sir *Anthony Sherley*, and divers other *English* Gentlemen in those Countries. With other Novelties. At *London*, Printed by *Thomas Purfoot* for *Clement Knight*, &c. 1609. 4*to*.

The true Proceedings in *Virginia*, for the Year 1609. according to the Examinations of Doctor *Simons*, and two learned Orations published by the Companie; with the Relation of the Right Honourable the Lord *De la Ware*. [Published in Capt. *Smith's* Gen. Historie. 1626. *Fol. p.* 105.]

A Relation of the Shipwrack of Sir *George Somers*, upon the Island of *Bermudas*, in the Year 1609. as given by Mr. *Jordan*, Master *John Evans*, Master *Henry Shelley*, and divers others. With a Description of the Land, by Mr. *Norwood*. [Published in Capt. *Smith's* Gen. Historie. 1626. *Fol. p.* 174.]

The Voyage of Mr. *Joseph Salbancke* through *India*, *Persia*, part of *Turkie*, the *Persia Gulfe*, and *Arabia*, 1609. Written unto Sir *Thomas Smith*. [*Purchas* Pilgrim. *Vol. I. Lib. III. p.* 234.]

The Voyage of M. *David Middleton* to *Java* and *Banda*, extracted out of a Letter written by himself to the Company, this being the fifth Voyage set forth by them. [*Purchas, ib. p.* 239.]

Observations of Captain *John Saris*, of Occurrents which happened in the *East-Indies*, during his Abode at *Bantam*, from *Octob.* 1605. till *Octob.* 1609. With an Account of the Marts and Marchandises of those parts. [*Ib. Purchas, Vol. I. Lib. IV. p.* 384.]

The third Voyage of Master *Henrie Hudson* toward *Nova Zembla*, and at his Returne, his passing from *Farre* Islands to *Newfoundland*, and along to fourty four degrees ten minutes; and thence to *Cape Cod*, and so to 33 degr. &c. in 1609. Written by *Robert Ivet* of *Limehouse*. [*Purchas, Vol. III. p.* 581.]

Extracts

Extracts out of *Amgrim Jonas*, an *Iselander*, his *Chrymægaa*, or Historie of *Iseland*, published *Anno Dom.* 1609. [*Purchas* Pilgrim. *Vol.* III. *p.* 654.]

The Voyage of *Henry Hudson*, an *English* Mariner, set out by the Directors of the *Dutch East-India* Companye, to discover a Passage to *China*, by the North or North-West; in *March* 1609. [*Collection of Voyages by* Dutch East-India *Companie. 8vo.* 1703. *p.* 68.]

Propositions made by Monsieur *Vander-Hurst*, at the Assembly of the General States of the United Provinces, upon the 13th of *January* 1608. With the Answer of the said General States, given unto the said Monsieur *Vander-Hurst*, touching the said Propositions. And also a Declaration touching Peace to be made with *Spain*. And the final Answer made by the said General States of the United Provinces unto the Commissioners for the King of *Spaine*, and the Arch-Duke, assembled in the *Hagne*, concerning Peace to be made, 1608- *London*, Printed for *Philip Harison*, 1609. *4to. p.* 18.

The Voyage of Captaine *Samuel Argal*, from *James Town* in *Virginia*, to seek the Isle of *Bermuda*, and missing the same, his putting over toward *Sagadahoc* and Cape *Cod*, and so back againe to *James Town*, begun the 19th of *June* 1610. [In *Purchas* Pilgrim, *Vol.* IV. *p.* 1785.] 1610. 8 *Jac.* 1.

The Beginning of the Patent for *Newfoundland*, and the Plantation there, made by the *English*, 1610. delivered in a Latter dated thence from M. *Guy* to M. *Slany*: Also of the Weather the three first Winters, and of Captain *Weston*, with other remarkable Occurrents. [*Purchas* Pilgrim. *Vol.* II. *p.* 1876.]

Fidei Christianæ in Provincia Goana progressus ab anno MDC. *ad usque* MDCX. *Enarratio.* [*Petri Jarrici Thesaurus Indicus.* Tom. III. *p.* 15. *8vo.*]

A Voyage set forth by the right worshipfull Sir *Thomas Smith*, and the rest of the *Muscovie* Companie, to *Cherry Island*, and for a further Discoverie to be made towards the North Pole, for the likelyhood of a Trade or Passage that way; in a Ship called the *Amitie* of 70 Tuns, of which I *Jonas Poole* was Master, in the yeere 1610. [*Purchas* Pilgrim. *Vol.* III. *p.* 699.]

The Proceedings of the *English* Colonie in *Virginia*, taken faithfully out of the Writings of *Thomas Studly*, Cape Merchant, *Anas Todkill*, Doctor *Russell*, *Nathaniel Powell*, *William Phetiplace*, and *Richard Pot*, *Richard W.ffin*, *Tho. Abbay*, *Tho. Hope*, and since enlarged out of the Writings of Capt. *John Sm.* . . . Agent and Patient in these *Virginian* Occurrents, from the

the beginning of the Plantation 1606. till *An.* 1610.   Somewhat abridged.
[*Purchas* Pilgrim. *IV. IV. p.* 1705.]

A true Report of the Wracke and Redemption of Sir *Thomas Gates,* Knight, upon and from the Iſlands of *Bermudas,* his coming to *Virginia,* and the Eſtare of that Colonie then, and after, under the Government of the Lord *La Warre, July* 15. 1610. Written by *William Strachy,* Eſquire. [*Purchas* Pilgrim. *Vol. IV. p.* 1734.]

The Copie of a Letter that Signeur *Arenetten Grottenhuyſe,* a *Dutch* Merchant and Partner, wrote unto Mr. N. N. from *Amſterdam,* dat. 29. *July* 1710. concerning the late Voyage made by two *Dutch* Ships to the Iſland of *Japan,* there to obtain licence of the Emperour freely to trade, and to make a Contract with him touching the ſame, according to the Letters by the Prince of *Orange* written unto the ſaid King. 4*to. p.* 4.

Sir *William Monſon's* Diſcourſe, concerning the North-Weſt Paſſage, upon the Attempt to be made for the Diſcovery of it, in the Year 1610. [*Naval Tracts in Colleĉt. of Voyages,* printed for Mr. *Churchill.* 1704. Fol. *Vol. III. p.* 246.]

The unhappy Voyage of the Vice-Admiral, the *Union,* outward bound to the *Eaſt-Indies,* till ſhe arrived at *Priaman,* reported by a Letter which Maſter *Samuel Bradſhaw* ſent from *Priaman* by *Humphry Biddulphe,* 11 *March,* 1609.   Written by the ſaid *Henry Moris* at *Bantam, Sept.* 14. 1610. [*Purchas* Pilgrim. *Vol. I. Lib. III. p.* 232.]

The ſixth Voyage ſet forth by the *Eaſt-Indian* Company in three Shippes, under the Command of Sir *Henry Middleton,* Admirall, in 1610.   Written by Sir *H. Middleton* himſelf. [*Purchas* Pilgrim. *Vol. I. Lib. III. p.* 247.]

An Abſtract of the Journal of Maſter *Henry Hudſon,* for the Diſcoverie of the North-Weſt Paſſage, begunne the 17th of *April* 1610. and ended with his End, being treacherouſly expoſed by ſome of the Companie.   With a larger Diſcourſe of the ſame Voyage, written by *Abacuc Pricket.* [*Purchas* Pilgrim, *Vol. III. p.* 596]

1611.   A Voyage made to *Pechora,* for diſcoverie of *Obi Teriſſe,* and the River 9 *Jac.* 1. *Geta,* unto the Frontiers of *Cataia.* Written by *William Gourdon* of *Hull,* appointed chief Pilot for the ſaid Diſcoverie, in *April* 1611. With many other Letters and Tracts, relating to *Pechora,* and thoſe Northern Parts. [*Purchas* Pilgrim. *Vol. III. p.* 530.]

The

The Character of the famous Odcombian, or rather Ployropian, Thomas the Coryate, Traveller and Gentleman, Author of the Quinquemeftrial Crudities. Being Panegyrick Verfes upon the Author and his Book. 1611. 4to. imperfect.

The feventh Voyage to the *Eaft-India*, made in the *Globe*, fet out under the Command of Captain *Anthony Hippon* in 1611. obferved and written by *Nathaniel Marten*, Mafters Mate in the faid Shippe. [*Purchas* Pilgrim. *Vol. I. Lib.* III. *p.* 314.]

Extracts of *Peter Williamfon Floris*, his Journal in that feventh Voyage to the *Eaft-Indies*, tranflated out of *Dutch*. [*Purchas* Pilgrim. *Vol. I. p.* 318.]

The Manners, Lawes and Cuftoms of all Nations. Collected out of the beft Writers by *JOANNES BOEMUS AUBANUS*, a *Dutch* Man. With many other things of the fame Argument, gather'd out of the Hiftorie of *Nicholas Damafcene*. The like alfo out of the Hiftorie of *America* or *Brafill*, written by *John Lerius*. The Faith, Religion and Manners of the *Æthiopians*, and the Deploration of the people of *Lappia*, compiled by *Damianus a Goes*. With a fhort Difcourfe of the *Æthiopians*, taken out of *Jofeph Scaliger*, his feventh Booke, *De Emendatione Temporum*. Written in *Latine*, and now newly tranflated into *Englifh*. By *Ed Afton*. At *London*, Printed by *G. Eld, &c.* 1611. 4to. *p.* 589.

A fhort Relation made by the Lord *De la Warre* to the Lords and others of the Counfell of *Virginia*, touching his unexpected Returne home; and afterwards delivered to the General Affemblie of the faid Company, at a Court holden the 25th of *June* 1611. Publifhed by authoritie of the faid Counfell. [*Purchas* Pilgrim. *Vol. IV. p.* 1762.]

A true and allmoft incredible Report of an *Englifh* Man, that being caft   1612. away in the good Ship called the *Afcenfion* in *Cambaya*, the fartheft part of 10 *Jac.* 1. *Eaft-Indies*, travelled by Land through many unknowne Kingdoms and great Cities. With a particular Defcription of all thofe Cities, Kingdoms and People. With a Difcovery of a Great Emperour call'd the Great *Mogoll*, a Prince not till now knowne to our *Englifh* Nation. By Captaine *Robert Coverte*. *London*, Printed by *William Hall*. 1612. 4to. *p.* 68.

The Report of *William Nicols*, a Mariner in the *Afcenfion*, which travelled from *Bramport* by Land to *Mafulipatan*; written from his Mouth at *Bantam*

sam by *Henry Moris*, Sept. 12. 1612. [*Purchas* Pilgrim. *Vol. I. Lib. III.*
p. 232.]

A Relation of the ninth Voyage of the *Indian* Companie to the *East-Indies*,
in the *James*, whereof was Captaine Mr. *Edmund Marlowe* of *Bristoll*, and the
Maſter *John Davy*, who wrote this Journall. *An.* 1612. [*Purchas*, *Ib. Lib. IV.*
p. 440.]

A Relation of ſome *Engliſh* Voyages to the *Summer* Iſlands, of *Henry May's*
Shipwracke there 1593. Of the firſt Colonie ſent thither 1612. [*Purchas*
Pilgrim, *Vol. IV p.* 1793] With a Copy of the Articles which Maſter
R. More, Governour Deputie of the Summer Iſlands, propounded to the
Company there with him, and ſubſcribed 2 *Aug.* 1612.

A Map of *VIRGINIA*, with a Deſcription of the Countrey, the Commodities, People, Government, and Religion. Written by Captaine *Smith*,
ſometimes Governour of the Countrey. Whereunto is annexed the Proceedings of thoſe Colonies, ſince their firſt departure from *England.* With
the Diſcourſes, Orations, and Relations of the Salvages, and the Accidents
that befell them in all their Journies and Diſcoveries. Taken faithfully as
they were written out of the Writings of Doctor *Ruſſel*, *Tho. Studley*, &c.
And the Relations of divers other diligent Obſervers there preſent then, and
now many of them in *England.* By *W. S.* At *Oxford*, Printed by *Joſeph
Barnes* 1612. 4ᵗᵒ. *p.* 39.

The Proceedings of the *Engliſh* Colonie in *Virginia*, ſince their firſt beginning from *England* in the yeare of our Lord 1606. till this preſent 1612.
With all their Accidents that befell them in their Journies and Diſcoveries, &c.
Unfolding even the fundamental Cauſes, from whence have ſprang ſo many
Miſeries to the Undertakers, and Scandals to the Buſineſſe. And peruſed and
confirmed by diverſe now reſident in *England*, that were Actors in this Bu-
ſineſs. By *W. S.* At *Oxford*, printed by *Joſeph Barnes.* 1612. *p.* 109.

The firſt beginning of a Colonie in the *SOMER ISLES*, under the
Command of Maſter *Richard More*, extracted out of a Plot of Maſter *Richard
Norwood*, Surveior, and the Relation of divers others, in 1612. [Inſerted
in the Gen. Hiſtorie of Capt. *John Smith.* 1626. Fol. *p.* 177.]

De Novo Orbe, or the Hiſtorie of the *Weſt-Indies.* Contayning the actes
and adventures of the *Spanyardes*, which have conquered and peopled thoſe
Countries, inriched with varietie of pleaſant Relation of the Manners, Ceremonies,

monies, Lawes, Governments and Warres of the *Indians.* Comprised in eight Decades. Written by *Peter Martyr a Millanoise* of *Angleria,* Chief Secretary to the Emperour *Charles* the Fifth, and of his Privie Counsell, whereof three have been formerly translated into *Englishe,* by *R. Elen,* whereunto the other five are newly added by the Industrie, and painefull Travaille of Mr. *Lok,* Gent. *London,* printed for *Thomas Adams.* 1612. 4to. *folijs* 318. [*Ex dono Reverendi Viri R. Mayo.*]

A Relation written by *Jonas Poole,* of a Voyage to *Greenland,* in the year 1612. with two Ships, the one called the *Whale,* the other the *Sea Horse,* set out by the right worshipfull the *Muscovie* Merchants, in *Apr.* 1612. [*Purchas* Pilgrim. *Vol. III. p.* 713.]

The fourth Voyage of *James Hall* to *Groenland,* wherein he was set forth by *English* Adventurers, *Anno* 1612. and slaine by a *Greenlander.* Written by *William Baffin.* [*Purchas* Pilgrim. *Vol. III. p.* 831.]

INDIÆ OCCIDENTALIS HISTORIA: *In quâ Prima Regionum istarum Detectio, Situs, Incolarum Mores, aliaq; eo pertinentia, breviter explicantur. Ex varijs Autoribus collecta. Opera & Studio* GASPARIS ENSL. *Coloniæ. Apud Guilielmum Lutzen-kirchen. Anno* MDCXII. 8vo. *p.* 370. [*Ex dono Rev. Josephi Sparke Petriburgensis.*]

1613.
11 Jac. 1.

Late News out of *Barbary,* in a Letter written of late from a Merchant there, to a Gentleman not long since employed into that Countrie from his Majestie. Containing some strange Particulars of this new Saintish King's Proceedings, as they have been very credibly related from such as were Eye-Witnesses. Imprinted at *London* for *Arthur Johnson,* 1613. 4to. [*Ex dono Rev. Viri Joannis Mapletoft,* S. T. P.]

The newe Prophetical King of *BARBARY;* or the last Newes from thence. In a Letter written of late from a Merchant there, to a Gentleman not long since employed into that Countrie from his Majestie. Containing some strange particulars, how the new King hath overthrowne *Mulley Sidan,* the former King many times in Battell, &c. *London,* Printed by *Tho. Creede,* &c. 1613. 4to. [*Ex dono ejusdem Joannis Mapletoft.* S. T. P.]

A Journal of the Voyage made to *Greenland* with sixe *English* Ships and a Pinnasse, in the Yeare 1613. Written by Master *William Baffin.* [*Purchas.* Pilgrim. *Vol. III. p.* 716.]

A Let-

A Letter of Sir *Samuell Argoll*, touching his Voyage to *Virginia*, and Actions there: Written to Master *Nicholas Hawes* in *June* 1613. [*Purchas Pilgrim. Vol. IV. p.* 1764]

Part of a Tractate written at *Henrico* in *Virginia*, by Master *Alex. Whitaker*, Minister to the Colony there governed by Sir *Tho. Dale*. 1613. [*Purchas* Pilgrim. *Vol. IV. p.* 1771.]

Bulla Pauli Papæ V. pro Erectione Seminarij sub invocatione S. Pauli in Urbe, Fratrum Carmelitarum Discalceatorum Congregationis Italiæ, pro Missione ad conversionem Infidelium instituenda, ad Christianæ fidei Propagationem. Dat. Romæ apud S. Petrum die 7. Martis 1613. *Pont. nostri anno octavo.* [*Bullarium Romanum. Tom. III. Romæ.* 1638. *Fol.*]

An Account of the laborious Work, entitled, *Delle Navigationi & Viaggi, Raccolse da M. Gio. Battista Ramusio. Venice.* 3 Vol. Fol. 1613. Ramusio's Collection of Voyages and Travels, the most perfect Work of that Nature, extant in any Language whatsoever? Containing all the Discoveries made to the East, West, North, and South; with full Descriptions of all the Countries discover'd; with many learned Discourses and Observations of the Author. [Introductory Discourse to the Collection of Voyages, printed for Mr. Churchill. 1704. p. lxxviii.]

1614.
2 Jan. 1.　The State of *Virginia*, under the Government of Sir *Thomas Dale*, in a Letter from thence dated *June* 18. 1614. [Published in Capt. *Smith*'s Gen. Historie. 1626. Fol. p. 116.]

The first Voyage to *New England*, and Plantation made upon it, with the old Names of the most remarkable places, and the new Names given by Prince *Charles*. The Description of the Country, &c. By Captain *John Smith*, Anno 1614. [Inserted in his Gen. Historie. 1626. Fol. p. 218.]

A Voyage by Sir *William Monson*, during the time he serv'd as Admiral in the Narrow Seas, about *England*, *Scotland* and *Ireland*, *Anno Dom.* 1614. [Sir *Will. Monson*'s Naval Tracts, publisht in Collect. of Voyages, printed for Mr. Churchill. Fol. Vol. III. p. 246.]

The fifth Circumnavigation, in the Voyage of GEORGE SPILBERGEN, General of a *Dutch* Fleet of sixe Shippes, which passed by the *Magellane* Streights, and South Sea unto the *East-Indies*, and thence having encompassed the whole Circumference of the Earth, returned home; gathered out of the *Latine* Journal, beginning 8 *Aug.* 1614. [*Purchas* Pil. Vol. I. Lib. II. p. 80.]

Notes

Notes of *Virginian* Affaires in the Government of Sir *Thomas Dale*, and of Sir *Thomas Gates*, till *Anno* 1614. Taken out of Mr. *Ralph Hamor* (Secretary to the Colonie) his Booke. [*Purchas* Pilgrim. *Vol. IV. p.* 1766.

A Letter of Sir *Thomas Dale*, and another of Master *Whitaker's*, from *James Towne* in *Virginia*, *June* 18. 1614. and a piece of a Tractate written by the said Master *Whitakers*, from *Virginia* the Yeere before. [*Purchas* Pilgrim. *Vol. IV. p.* 1768.]

A Voyage of Discoverie to *Greenland*, &c. *Anno* 1614. Written by *Ro. Fotherbye*. [*Purchas* Pilgrim. Vol. III. *p.* 720]

The Contents of the Declaration of the Lottery, published by the Counsell of *Virginia*, Sir *Thomas Smith* being Treasurer in 1615. With an Account of the *Wellcome's*, *Prizes*, and *Rewards*. [Published in Capt. *Smith's* Gen. Historie. 1626. Fol. *p.* 117.]   1615. 13 *Jac.* 1.

A Relation of the second Voyage made to *New England* by Capt. *John Smith*, employed by Sir *Ferdinando Gorges*, Dr. *Sutcliffe*, Dean of *Exeter*, and other Friends, *Anno* 1615. writ with his own Hand. [Published in his Gen. Historie. 1626. Fol. *p.* 225.]

'A true Report of a Voyage *Anno* 1615. for Discoverie of Seas, Lands, and Islands to the Northwards, as it was performed by *Robert Fotherbie*, in a Pinnace of 20 Tuns, called the *Richard of London*, set forth at the charge of the right worshipfull Sir *Tho. Smith*, Kt. and Master *Richard Wiche*, Governours, and the rest of the Companie of the Merchants of new Trades and Discoveries. [*Purchas* Pilgrim. Vol. III. *p.* 728.]

De ABASSINORUM *Rebus, deq; Æthiopiæ Patriarchis* Joanne Nonio Barreto, *&* Andrea Oviedo, *Libri tres.* P. NICOLAO GODIGNO *Societatis Jesu Auctore: Nunc primum in lucem emissi. Lugduni. Sumptibus Horatij Cardon.* MDCXV. 8vo. *p.* 414.

Decouver de quelques Pays qui sont entre l' Empire l·s Abyssines *& la côte de* Melindes *par le Pere* Antonio Fernandez *qui retourna a la Cour de l' Empereur au mois de Septembre de l' annee* 1614. [*Relation de divers Voyages, &c. A Paris IV. Partie.* 1672. Fol.]

An Account of the *Spanish* Historie of the *West-Indies*, entitled, *Historia General de los Hechos de los Castellanos en las Islas, y Tierra Firma del mar Oceano, Escrita por* Antonio de Herrera. Madrid 1615. 4 Vol. Folio. A most excellent

P   cellent

cellent and complete History of the Discovery and Conquest of *America*, by the *Spaniards* ; reaching from *Columbus*'s first Discovery *An.* 1492. to 1554. Divided into four Volumes, and those into eight Decads. [Preface to the Collection of Voyages, Printed for Mr. *Churchill.* 1704. *p.* lxxxvii.]

Epistola R.P.M. PAULI ANTONII FOSCARINI *Carmelitani circa* Pythagoricorum *&* Copernici *opinionem de Mobilitate Terræ, & Stabilitate Solis : Et de Novo Systemate seu Constitutione Mundi. In qua Sacra Scriptura autoritates & Theologica Propositiones, communiter adversus hanc opinionem adductæ, concilientur. Ad Reverendissimum P. M. Sebastianum Fantonum Generalem Ordinis Carmelitani. Ex Italica in Latinam Linguam perspicue & fideliter nunc conversa. Juxta editionem Neapoli typis excusam apud Lazarum Scorigium Anno 1615.* [*Appendix ad Galilei Dialogum de Systemate Mundi. Londini* 1663. *8vo.*]

R.P. PETRI JARRICI *Tholosani Societ.* JESU *Thesaurus Rerum Indicarum. In qua Christianæ ac Catholicæ Religionis tam in India Orientali quam alijs Regionibus Lusitanorum opera nuper detectis Ortus, Progressus, Incrementa, & maxime quæ à P.P. Soc. Jesu ibidem in dicta Fidei plantatione ac propagatione ad Annum usq; MDC. gesta atq; exantlata sunt, non minus vere quàm eleganter recensentur. Additæ sunt passim Earundem Regionum & eorum quæ ad eas pertinent tam Chorographicæ quàm Historicæ Descriptiones. Opus nunc primum à M. Matthia Martinez e gallico in latinum sermonem translatum. Permissu Superiorum. Coloniæ Agrippinæ. Sumptibus Petri Henningij. Anno MDCXV. tribus tomis. Tom. I. p.* 794. *Tom. II. p.* 808. *Tom. III. p.* 653 *&* 621.

The Blessing of *JAPHETH* ; Proving the Gathering in of the *GEN-TILES*, and final Conversion of the *JEWS.* Expressed in divers profitable Sermons. By *Thomas Cowper.* Dedicated to the Lord Mayor, Aldermen, and Sheriffs of *London* ; together with the worthie Commissioners for the Plantations in *Ireland* and *Virginia. London,* Printed for *Richard Redmer. 4to.* 1615. *p.* 62.

A true Relation of such things as happened in the fourth Voyage for the Discoverie of the North-West Passage, performed in the yeare 1615. Written by *William Baffin.* [*Purchas* Pilgrim. *Vol. III. p.* 836.]

Journal & Miroir de la Navigation Australe du vaillant & bien renommeé Seigneur Jaques le Maire *Chef & Conducteur de deux Navires Concorde & Horne ; avec les quelles il partit de la ville de* Horne *en l' An.* 1615. [*Au fin de la Description des Indes Occidentales.* 1622. Fol.]

The

The Sixth Circum-Navigation, by *William Cornelison Schouten of Horne*, who Southwards from the Straights of *Magelan* in *Terra del Fuego*, found and discovered a new Paſſage through the great South Sea, and that way ſayled round about the World, ſetting out of the *Teſſell* 14 *June* 1615. [*Purchas* Pilgrim. *Vol. I. Lib. II. p.* 88.]

Obſervations collected out of the Journall of Sir *Thomas Roe*, Knight, Lord Embaſſadour from his Majeſtie of *Great Britaine* to the Great *Mogol*, in 1615. of Matters occurring worthy Memory in the way, and in the *Mogol's* Court. His Cuſtoms, Cities, Countries, Subjects, and other *Indian* Affaires. [*Ib. Purchas. Vol. I. Lib. III. p.* 535. And more Full and Correct in the Collect. of Voyages, by Mr. *Churchill. Vol. I. p.* 767.]

A Relation of a Voyage to the Eaſtern *India*, obſerved by *Edward Terry*, Maſter of Arts, and Student of *Chriſt Church* in *Oxford*, *Anno* 1515. in his attendance on the Embaſſador Sir *Tho. Roe*. [*Purchas* Pilgrim. *Vol. II. p.* 1464.]

An Abſtract of a Relation given in Writing to the moſt high and vertu- 1616. ous Princeſſe Queen *Anne* of *Great Britain*, by the Lady *Rebecca*, Daughter 14 *Jac.* 1. to *Powhatan*, King of the Salvages in *Virginia*, Wife of Maſter *John Rolfe*, now in *England*, 1616. where ſhe died. [Inſerted in Capt. *Smith's* Ger. Hiſtorie. 1626. *Fol. p.* 121.]

To the right Honourable the Lord *Elſmore*, Lord Chancellour of *England*, and Sir *Francis Bacon*, Attorney and Councellor: A Diſcourſe of Sir *William Monſon*, after his Impriſonment in the *Tower*, *Anno Dom.* 1616. concerning the Inſolencies of the *Dutch*. And a Juſtification of Sir *William Monſon*, and his Services at Sea, from *July* 1604. [In his Naval Tracts publiſht in the Collect. of Voyages, printed for Mr. *Churchill:* 1704. *Fol. Vol. III. p.* 239.]

A Journall of the Journey of *Richard Steel* and *John Crowther*, from *Azmere* in *India*, the place of the Great *Mogul's* Reſidence, to *Spahan*, the Royal Seat of the King of *Perſia*, in the Affaires of the *Eaſt Indian* Society, in the yeares 1615 and 1616. [*Purchas Pilgrim, Vol. I. Lib. IV. p.* 519.]

Some Letters of Mr. *Thomas Coryat*, who travailled by land from *Jeruſalem* to the Court of the Great *Mogol*, written to Mr. *L. Whitaker*, from *Aſmere* in the Oriental *India*, *Anno* 1615. and from *Agra* in *October*. 1616, &c. [*Purchas* Pilgrim. *Vol. I. Lib. IV. p.* 597.]

A brief

A brief and true Relation or Journal, contayning such Accidents as happend in the fifth Voyage, for the discoverie of a Passage to the North-West. Set forth at the charges of the right Worshipfull Sir *Thomas Smith*, Kt, *Dudley Digges*, &c. performed in the yeere 1616. [*Purchas* Pilgrim. *Vol. III. p.* 844.]

1617.
15 *Jac.* I.
A Consultation before the Lords of the Council in 1617. and a Proposition made, how the Pyrates of *Argiers* might be suppress'd, and the Town attempted, with the Advice given by Sir *William Monson* thereupon. [Sir *Will. Monson's* Naval Tracts, *Ib. p.* 252.]

Observations of things most remarkable, collected out of the first Part of the Commentaries Royal, written by the *Inca Garcillasso de la Vega*, Native of *Cozco*, in nine Books : Of the Original, Lives, Conquests, Lawes and Idolatries of the *Incas*, or antient Kings of *Peru*, &c. Which first Part was set forth *Anno* 1608. and the other *An.* 1617. [*Purchas* Pilgrim. *Vol. IV. p.* 1489.]

Disceptatio DE SECRETIS SOCIETATIS JESU *Inter* D. JOANNEM *Canonicum Vratislaviensem*, D. LUDOVICUM *Juris consultum Brandeburgicum*, P. ADAMUM CONTZEN *Societat. Jesu Habita. Lugduni, apud Claudium Cayne. M. DCXVII. Cum Permissu Superiorum. 8vo.* p. 189.

1618.
16 *Jac.* I.
The true Honor of Navigation and Navigators : Or Meditations for Seamen. Written upon our Saviour Christ his Voyage by Sea, *Matth.* 8. 23. &c. Whereunto are added certain Formes of Prayers for Sea-Travellers, suited to the former Meditations upon the several Occasions that fall at Sea. By *John Wood*, Doctor in Divinitie. *London*, Imprinted by *Felix Kingston.* 1618. 4to. p. 128.

De Legatione Evangelica Ad INDOS *capessenda Admonitio* JUSTI HEURNII *Joan. Fil. Lugduni Batavorum. Ex Officina Elzeviriana. Anno* CIƆIC.C.XVIII. *8vo. Cui præmittitur Epistola Johannis Polyandri in Acad. Leydensi S. S. Theologiæ Professoris Ordinarij, & Magnifici Rectoris ad suum Collegam* Otthonem Heurnium *Joan. Fil. Ordinarium Professorem Medicinæ, Anatomiæ, & Chirurgiæ, Continens ipsius Censuram ac Judicium, super hac exhortatione de Legatione Evangelica ad Indos capessenda. Dat. VII. Julij* MDCXVIII. *8vo. paginis* 300. [*Ex dono Rev.* P. JOANNIS *Episcopi* ELIENSIS.]

An Account of the Voyage of two Cannoes set out by the King of Spaine, commanded by Don Juan de More, in October 1618. who made the first Circle clean round the *Tierra del Fuego*, and proved it demonstratively to be an Island separate from all other Land. [In the Collect. of Voyages printed for Mr. *Churchill. Vol.* III. *p.* 53.]

A Geographical and Anthological Description of all the Empires and Kingdoms, both of Continent and Islands in this Terrestrial Globe. Relating their Scituations, Manners, Customs, Provinces, and Governments. *London,* 1618. 4to. *p.* 27.

Newes from *Turkie*; Or a true and perfect Relation sent from *Constantinople*, touching the Death of *Achmet*, the last Emperour of the *Turkes*. As also the miraculous Deliverances of *Mustapha* (Brother to the said *Achmet*, then Emperour) and his strange Escapes from his purposed Death. Together with the memorable accesse of the said *M U S T A P H A* into the *Turkish* Empire, and a Narration of such things as have since hapned. *London,* Printed by *William Jones;* &c. 4to. 1618.

An Account of the Division of the *Somer Isles* into Tribes, by Master *Richard Norwood,* Surveyor : With the Names of the Adventurers, and their Shares, &c. in 1618. Collected out of their Records by *N. B.* And the Relations of Mr. *Pollard* and divers others. [Inserted in the Gen. Historie of Capt. *Smith,* 1626. Fol. *p.* 190.]

The Journall of Master *Nathaniel Courthop* his Voyage from *Bantam* to the Islands of *Banda,* being chiefe Commander of the two Shippes, the *Swanne,* and the *Defence* ; with the Cruelties of the *Dutch* at *Amboyna* in 1618. [*Purchas* Pilgrim. Vol. I. Lib. V. *p.* 664.] With a Continuation of the said Journal, and several Letters sent out of those Parts.

A Note of the Shipping, Men, and Provisions sent to *Virginia* by the Treasurer and Company, in the yeere 1619. With the Orders and Constitutions, partly collected out of his Majesties Letters Patents, and partly ordained upon mature Deliberation, by the Treasurer, Counsail, and Company of *Virginia,* for the better governing of the Actions and Affaires of the said Company, here in *England* residing. 4to. 1619.

1619.
17 *Jac.* 1.

Another Note of the Shipping, Men and Provisions, sent to *VIRGINIA,* by the Treasurer and Company, in the yeere 1619. Published by his Majesties Counsell for *Virginia.* 4to. *p.* 16. With the Names of the Adventurers, with their several Summs adventured, paid in to Sir *Thomas Smith,*

Q

Knight

Knight, late Treafurer of the Company for *Virginia.* 4*o.* p. 30. And ano
ther Lift of the Names of fome other Adventurers. With the Summs paid
by Order to Sir *Baptift Hicks*, Knight, and to Sir *Edwin Sandys*, Knight.

Relation des deux Caravelles, que le Roy d' Espagne envoya de Lisbonne le an' 1618. au mois d' Octobre, foubs la conduite du Capitaine Don Jean de Maire *pour vifiter & defcouvir le Paffage de Le Maire de vers le Sud: Lefquelles re- tournerent en Scoille au mois d' Aouft 1619. & firent le rapport au Roy de tout ce qui leur eftoit advenu.* [*En la Defcription des Indés Occidentales.* 1622. Fol.]

An Account of the Voyage made by two Caravals, fent forth by the King of *Spain*, 1619 to fearch the Streight of St. *Vincent*; lately difcover'd by *James le Maire*, and their eafy Paffage through it into the South Sea, made the King of *Spain* refolve on this way of fending Reliefe to the *Philippine* Iflands. [In the Collection of Voyages printed for Mr. *Churchill.* 1704. Vol. III. p. 56.]

An Account of the Letters for *Virginia* : Of Sir *Thomas Dale*'s Return : Of the *Spaniards* in *Virginia* : Of *Pocahuntas* and *Jomocoma* : Of Captain *Yerd- ley*, and Captain *Argoll* (both fince Knighted) their Government ; the Lord *La Ware*'s Death, and other Occurrents till *Anno* 1619. [*Purchas* Pilgrim. Vol. IV. p. 1773.]

A Letter of Mafter *Tho. Dormer* to his worfhipfull Friend Mafter *Samuel Purchas*, Preacher of the Word within *Ludgate*, dated from *Cap. Martyn* his Plantation in *Virginia* 27 *Decemb.* 1619. touching his Voyage for the South Sea With a Note of the Shipping, Men and Provifions fent to *Virginia* by the Treafurer and Company in the yeere 1619. [*Purchas* Pilgrim. Vol. IV. p. 1776.]

1620.
18 *Jac.* 1.
A Declaration of the State of the Colonie and Affaires in *VIRGINIA*, with the Names of the Adventurors, and Summes adventured in that Action. By his Majefties Counfell for *Virginia*, 22 *Junij* 1620. *London*, Printed by T. S. 1620. 4*o.*

The Planters Plea, or the Grounds of Plantations examined, and ufual Objections anfwer'd. Together with a manifeftation of the Caufes, moving fuch as have lately undertaken a Plantation in *NEW ENGLAND*: For the Satisfaction of thofe that queftion the lawfulneffe of the Action. *London*, Printed by *William Jones* 1620. 4*o.* p. 84.

Ano-

Another Declaration by his Majesties Councell for *VIRGINIA*, touching the present Estate of their Colony in that Country. dat. 20. *Sept.* 1620. 4*to.* *p.* 11.

Orders and Constitutions, partly collected out of his Majesties Letters Patents, and partly ordained upon mature Deliberation, by the Treasuror, Counsell, and Company of *VIRGINIA*, for the better governing of the Actions and Affaires of the said Company here in *England* residing, *Anno* 1619 and 1620. 4*to.* *p.* 37.

A Relation of a desperate Sea-Fight betwixt two *Spanish* Men of Warre, and a small *English* Ship, at the Isle of *Dominica*, going to *Virginia*, in 1620. by Captain *Anthony Chester*. [Published in Capt. *Smith's* Gen. Historie, 1626. *Fol. p.* 128.]

A brief Discourse of the Trials of *New-England*, with certain Observations of the *Hollanders* Use and Gain by Fishing ; and the present Estate of that happy Plantation, begun but by sixtie weak Men, in the yeere of our Lord 1620. by the Report of Mr. *Dee*. [Publisht in Capt. *Smith's* Gen. Historie. 1626. *Fol. p.* 227.]

Description D' Amerique qui est Le Nouveau Monde, tirée des Tableaux Geographiques de Petrus Brentius. *De Nouveau Monde en general, &c.* [*En la Description des Indes Occidentales. Fol.* 1622.]

Vox Populi : Or Newes from *Spain.* Translated according to the *Spanish* Copie, which may serve to forewarn both *England* and the United Provinces how farre to trust to *Spanish* Pretences. Imprinted in the Year 1620. 4*to.*

Extracts of a Journall of a Voyage to *Surat*, and to *Jasques* in the *Persian* Gulfe, set forth by the *East-India* Societie of Merchants, in the beginning of. the year 1620. [*Purchas* Pilgrim. *Vol.* 1. *Lib.* V. *p.* 723.]

A Discourse of Trade from *England* unto the *East-Indies*, answering to divers Objections, which are usually made against the same, particularly as to the exporting of Gold and Silver, for unnecessary Wares. Written by *T. Mun.* 1620, [*Purchas, Ib. p.* 732.]

A true

A true Relation of a Sea-Fight between two great and well-appointed Spanish Ships, or Men of Warre, and an English Ship, called the Margaret and John, or the Black Hegge going for Virginia in 1620. [Purchas Pilgrim. Vol. IV. p. 1780.]

A Regiment for the Sea ; Containing very necessary Matters for all sorts of Men and Travaillers : Whereunto is added an Hydrographical Discourse, touching the five several Passages into Cattay, written by William Borne. Whereunto is added a new Regiment. A Table of Declination. The Mariners Guide, with a perfect Sea Card thereunto belonging. By Thomas Hoode, Doctor in Physicke, newly corrected this yeare 1620. At London, Printed for Edward Weaver, 1620. 4to. folijs 96.

An Account of COCHIN CHINA, in two Parts. The first treats of the Temporal State of that Kingdom. The second of what concerns the Spiritual. Written in Italian by the R. F. Christopher Boni a Milaneze, of the Society of Jesus, who was one of the first Millioners in that Kingdom, in the Year 1620. [Collect. of Voyages for Mr. Churchill. Vol. II. p. 787.]

1621.
19 Jac. 1. More excellent Observations of the Estate and Affaires of Holland; In a Discourse, shewing, how necessarie and convenient it is, for their neig bouring Countries, as well as the Netherland Provinces, to trade into the West-Indies, &c. Written in hast the first of September 1621. 4to p. 33.

A Paradoxe ; Proving that the Inhabitants of the Island, called MADA-GASCAR, or St. Laurence (in temporal Things) are the happiest People in the World. By Walter Hammond. 4to.

Relations of the Kingdom of Golchonda, and other neighbouring Nations, within the Gulfe of BENGALA, Arreccan, Pegu, Tannassery, &c. And the English Trade in those Parts, by Master William Methold. [Purchas Pilgrim. Vol. II. Append. p. 993.]

A Note of the Shipping, Men, and Provisions, sent and provided for Virginia, by the right Honourable Henry Earl of Southampton, and the Company, and other private Adventurers in the yeere 1621. With other Occurrents then published by the Companie. [Purchas Pilgrim. Vol. IV. p. 1783]

A Copie of the King's Patent to Sir William Alexander, Knight, for the Plantation of New Scotland in America, dat. 10 September 1621. and his Proceedings therein; with a Description of Mawooshen, for better Knowledge of those Parts. [Purchas Pilgrim. Vol. IV. p. 187.]

Newes

Newes from *Virginia*, in Letters sent thence 1621. partly published by the Companie, partly tranfcribed from the Originals, with Letters of his Majeftie, and of the Companie, touching Silke workes. [*Purcha* Pilgrim. *Vol. IV. p.* 1787.]

A Copie of the Kings Patent to Sir *William Alexander*, Knight, for the Plantation of *New Scotland* in *America*, dat. 10. *September* 1621. and his Proceedings therein ; with a Defcription of *Mawooshen*, for better knowledge of thofe Parts. [*Purchas* Pilgrim. *Vol. IV. p.* 1871.]

A Relation of fome fpecial Points, concerning the State of *HOLLAND.* By many Reafons, fhewing why for the good and fecurity of the *Netherland United Provinces*, WARRE is much better than PEACE. Printed at the *Hage* by *Aert Muris*, Bookfeller. 1621. 4*to. p.* 19.

Prælectiones Trefdecim in Principium Elementorum Euclidis, Habitæ Oxonij M.DC.XX. *ab* HENRICO SAVILIO. *Oxonij.* Excudebant *Johannes Lichfield & Jacobus Short.*1621. 4*to. p.* 260.

Bulla Gregorij Papæ XV. *pro Erectione Sacræ Congregationis* S. R. E. *Cardinalium, necnon Prælatorum, ac Regularium virorum, de Fide Catholica propaganda, una cum Proventuum affignatione, Privilegiorumq; conceffione, & præcipuè quòd omnes Scripturæ ejus ftatum aut res concernentes gratis ipfius Miniftris tradantur. Dat. Romæ. apud S. Mariam majorem, anno Incar. Dom, 1621. decimo Kalendas Julij, Pont. noftri anno fecundo.* [*Bullarium Romanun. Tom. II. Romæ.* 1638. *Fol.*]

1622. 20 Jac. 1.

Order of the King in Council at *Theobalds* the 12th of *April* 1622. With the Copy of a Reference from the Kings moft excellent Majeftie, for recommending Captain *Whitbournes* Difcourfe, concerning *Newfoundland*, fo as the fame may be diftributed to the feveral Parifhes of this Kingdom, for the incouragement of Adventurers unto the Plantation there. As alfo a Letter from the right Honourable the Lords of the Council, to the moft Reverend Fathers in God the Lords Archbifhops of *Canterbury* and *Yorke.* Dat. *Whitehall* the laft Day of *June* 1621. With a Lift of the Names of fome who have undertaken to helpe and advance his Majefties Plantation in the *New-foundland.* 4*to.* 1622.

Newes from *Turkie* and *Poland :* Or a true and compendious Declaration of the Proceedings between the Great *Turke* and his Majeftie of *Poland,* from the beginning of the Warres untill the latter end. With a Relation of their daily militarye Actions, *&c.* Printed at the *Hage* 1622. 4*to.*

R The

The Obfervations of Mr. *John Pory*, Secretarie of *Virginia*, in his Travels; with an Account of the lamentable Maffacre of the *Englifh* by the *Indians* in 1622. [Inferted in Capt. *Smith*'s Gen. Hiftorie 1626. *Fol. p.* 143.]

An Abftract of divers Relations fent from the Colony in *New England, July* 16. 1622. [Publifht in Capt. *Smith*'s Gen. Hiftorie. *Fol.* 1626. *p.* 236]

A Confolation for our Grammer Schooles : Or a faithfull and moft comfortable Incouragement, for laying of a fure Foundation of all good Learning in our Schooles, and for profperous building thereupon. More efpecially for all thofe of the inferiour fort, and all ruder Countries and Places : Namely for *Ireland, Wales, Virginia,* with the *Sommer Iflands,* and for their more fpeedy attaining of our *Englifh* Tongue by the fame labour, that all may fpeak one and the fame Language, for the perpetual benefit of thefe our Nations, and of the Churches of Chrift. *London,* Printed by *Richard Field, &c.* 1622. 4to. *p* 84. With an Epiftle to the right Honourable and right worfhipful the Governour, Councell, and Companie for *Virginia,* and of the *Sommer* Iflands, that *beginning with the Lord, and carefully planting and watering of his facred Religion, they may find a more happy Growth and Increafe, and overmore found and lafting Joy to their own Souls.*——*Especially for drawing the poor Natives in* Virginia, *and all other of the reft of the Rude and Barbarous from Sathan to God.*——*John Brinfley.*——With the Judgment and Approbation of Dr. *James Ufher* and Dr. *Daniel Featly, March* 16. 1620.

Relations of the *Summer Iflands,* taken out of Mr. *Richard Norwood*'s Map and Notes added thereto. Printed 1622. The Hiftory of the Creatures growing or living therein, being inlarged out of Captain *Smith*'s written Relations. [*Purchas* Pilgrim. *Vol. IV. p.* 1796.]

The Names of divers honourable Perfons, and others, who have undertaken to helpe advance his Majefties Plantation in the *New-found-Land*; with Extracts of certain Letters written from the Governour, Capt. *Edward Winne* to Sir *George Calvert,* his Majefties Secretary of State, and others in this Year 1622. [*Purchas* Pilgrim. *Vol. IV. p.* 1189.]

A briefe Relation of the Difcoverie and Plantation of *New England*; and of fundry Accidents therein occurring, from the yeere of our Lord 1607. to this prefent 1622. Publifhed by the Prefident and Councell, and dedicated to the Princes Highnefs here abbreviated. [*Purchas* Pilgrim. *Vol. IV. p.* 1827.]

Extracts

Extracts of a Booke of Captain *John-Smith*, printed 1622, entitled *New England's Trialls*, and continuing the Storie thereof, with Motives to the Business of fishing there: And the Benefit of fishing reported by *Master Dee*. [*Purchas* Pilgrim. Vol. IV. p. 1837.]

A Discourse and Discovery of *New-found-land*, with many Reasons to prove how worthy and beneficial a Plantation may there be made, after a far better manner than now it is. Together, with the laying open of certaine Enormities and Abuses committed by some that trade to that Countrey, and the Meanes laid down for the Reformation thereof. Written by Captaine *Richard Whitbourne* of *Exmouth*, in the County of *Devon*, and published by Authority. As also an Invitation: and likewise certaine Letters sent from that Countrey; which are printed in the latter part of this Booke. Imprinted at *London* by *Felix Kingston*. 1622. 4to. p. 107, &c.

A Declaration of the State of the Colony and Affaires in *VIRGINIA*; with a Relation of the barbarous Massacre in the time of Peace, and League, treacherously executed by the native Infidels upon the *English*, the 22 of *March* last. Together with the Names of those that were then massacred, that their lawfull heirs by this notice given may take order for the inheriting of their Lands and Estates in *Virginia*. And a Treatise annexed, written by that learned Mathematician Mr. *Henry Briggs*, of the North-West Passage to the South Sea through the Continent of *Virginia*, and by *Fretum Hudson*. Also a Commemoration of such worthy Benefactors as have contributed their Christian Charitie towards the advancement of the Colony. And a Note of the Charges of necessarie Provisions fit for every Man that intends to go to *Virginia*. Published by Authoritie. *London*, for *Robert Mylbourne*. 1622. 4to. p. 54.

OLAI MAGNI GOTHI *Archiepiscopi* Upsalensis Sueciæ & Gothiæ *Primatis de Gentibus Septentrionalibus, Earumq; diversis Statibus, conditionibus, moribus, superstitionibus, ritibus, disciplinis, exercitiis, regimine, victu, bellis, structuris, instrumentis, mineris, metallicis, & rebus mineralibus. Necnon universis penè Animalibus in Septentrione degentibus eorumq; naturâ.* 1622. Francofurti. *Typis* Johannis Friderici Weissij. 8vo. p. 461.

The Maintenance of FREE TRADE, according to the three essential Parts of Traffique; namely Commodities, Moneys, and Exchanges of Moneys, by Bills of Exchanges for other Countries. Or an Answer to a *Treatise of Free Trade; or the Meanes to make Trade flourish,* lately published. By GERARD MALYNES, Merchant. *London*, Printed for *William Sheffard*. 1622. 8vo. p. 105. Ep. Ded. to King *JAMES*.——*Your Majesties*

jesties

jesties vigilant Princely Care hath been pleased to referr the consideration of this important business of State to the Learned Lord Viscount Maundevile, *Lord President of your Majesties most Honourable Privy Council, and other Persons of Knowledge and Experience, (amongst whom (although unworthy) my self was called, and our Opinions were certified unto your Highness.*

A Report made to the King's Majestie by the Lord Viscount Maundevile, Lord President of the Councel, Sir *Robert Cotton*, Kt. and Baronet, Sir *Ralph Maddison*, Kt. Mr. *John Williams*, his Majesties Goldsmith, Mr. *William Sanderson*, and Mr. *Gerard Malynes*, Merchants, concerning the Nature of Exchange of Moneys by Bills, how it went in elder times, and how it is now carried to the prejudice of the Realme, and what will be the best Means to reduce it to the former Equity and Parity: Delivered in the moneth of *April* 1622. [Center of the Circle of Commerce by *Gerard Malynes*, Merchant. 1623. 4to. p. 76.]

A briefe Discoverie of the Northern Discoveries of Seas, Coasts, and Countries, deliver'd in order as they were hopefully begun, and have ever since happily been continued by the singular industrie and charge of the worshipful Company of *Muscovia* Merchants of *London*, with the ten several Voyages of Captain *Thomas Edge*, the Author. 1622. [*Purchas Pilgrim.* Vol. III. p. 462.]

The MERCHANTS HAND MAIDE: Or a Book containing very necessarie and compendious Tables, for the speedy casting up, and true valuing of any Commoditie whatsoever. Very behoovefull for Merchants, Gentlemen, Tradesmen, and all such as buy, sell, or deale in any manner of Accounts. By *J. W.* Gent. *London*, Printed by *William Jones*. 1622. 4to. p. 28.

1623.
21 Jan. 1.   HISPANUS *conversus, qui narrat causas quibus impulsus fuit ad deserendam Ecclesiam Romanam.* Per Ferdinandam Texeda *Hispanum dei gratia conversum.* V. D. M. *Londini. Excudebat* T. S. *pro* Roberto Mylbourne. 1623. 4to. p. 22.

The Project and Offer of Captain *John Smith*, to the right Honourable and right Worshipfull Company of *VIRGINIA*: With their Answer in 1623. [Published in Capt. *Smith's* Gen. Historie 1626. Fol. p. 152.]

Sir *Benjamin Rudyer's* Speech concerning a *West-India* Association, at the Committee of the whole House in the Parliament 21 *Jacobi*. Sir *Dudley Diggs* in the Chair.

                                                                    Extracts

Extracts out of Captaine *John Smith's* Historie of *Bermuda, or Summer Islands*, touching the *English* Acts and Occurrents there, from the beginning of the Plantation till the yeare 1623. [*Purchas* Pilgrim. Vol. *IV. p.* 1802.]

The CENTER of the CIRCLE of COMMERCE: Or a Refutation of a Treatife, intituled *The Circle of Commerce; or the Ballance of Trade*, lately published by E. M. By *GERARD MALINES*, Merchant. *London*, Sold by *Nicholas Bourne* at the *Royal Exchange.* 1623. 4to. p. 139. Ep. Ded. to *CHARLES* Prince of *Wales*, complaining of the false Notions of *Edward Misselden*, in propofing to inhaunce the Moneys of the Realme, and make the Foreigne Coyne currant.

An Account of the Work entitled, *Theodori & Joannis de Brye Indiæ Orientalis & Occidentalis.* 6 Vol. Fol. *Francofurti.* 1624. Containing three Volumes of the *East*, and three of the *West-Indies.* A Collection, which of itself is a fmall Library, including all the Voyages and Difcoveries of any Note to this time, illuftrated and adorned with Maps and Cuts. [Introductory Difcourfe to the Collection of Voyages printed for Mr. *Churchill,* p. lxxvii.]

An Adjoynder of fundry other particular wicked Plots, and cruel, inhumane, perfidious, yea unnatural Practices of the *Spaniards*; Chiefly againft the feventeen Provinces of the *Netherlands*, yea, before they took up Arms. Gathered and tranflated out of feveral *Dutch* Writers, as that Reverend Divine *Gulielmus Baudaitius*, in his *Morgan Weeker*, and *Emanuel de Mister*, by *S. O.* a Lover of Truth and Equity, and an unfeigned hater of Oppreffion and Tyrannie, the Bane of Commonwealths. Printed *Anno* 1624. p. 14.

An Oration or Speech appropriated unto the moft Mighty and Illuftrious Princes of *Chriftendom*, wherein the Right and Lawfullnefs of the *Netherlandifh* Warre againft *Philip* King of *Spaine*, is approved and demonftrated. Compofed by a *Netherlandifh* Gentleman, and faithfully tranflated out of divers Languages into *Dutch.* And now *Englifhed* by *Thomas Wood.* According to the Printed Copie at *Amfterdam. Anno* 1608. Printed *Anno* 1624. 4to. p. 70.

A true Relation of the unjuft, cruel, and barbarous Proceedings againft the *English* at *AMBOYNA* in the *East-Indies*, by the *Netherlandifh* Governour and Councel there. Alfo the Copy of a Pamphlet, fet forth firft in *Dutch*, and then in *English*, by fome *Netherlander*, falfely intituled, *A true Declaration of the Newes that came out of the East-Indies, with the Pinace called Hare, which arrived at Texel in June 1624.* Together, with an Anfwer to the fame Pamphlet. By the *Englifh Eaft-India* Company. Publifhed by Authoritie. *London*, Printed for *Nathaniel Newberry*, 1624. 4to. p. 38. & 20. & 34.

A brief Relation written by Captain *John Smith* to his Majefties Commiffioners for the Reformation of *VIRGINIA*, concerning fome Afperfions against it. With his Anfwer to the feven Queftions propounded to him by the faid Commiffioners, *Anno* 1624. [Publifhed in his Gen. Hiftorie. 1626. Fol. p. 104, &c.]

The General Hiftorie of the *BERMUDAS*, now called the *Summer Ifles*, from their Beginning in the Year of our Lord 1593. to this prefent 1624. With their Proceedings, Accidents, and prefent State. [Publifhed in Capt. *Smith's* Gen. Hiftorie. 1626. *Fol. p.* 169.]

The Saracenical Hiftorie ; containing the Actes of the *Muflims*, from *Muhammed* to the reigne of *Atabaceus*, in the Succeffion of nine and fourtie Emperours. Written in *Arabick* by *George Elmacin*, &c. and tranflated into *Latine* by *Thomas Erpenius*, &c. Englifhed by *Samuel Purchas*. [Publifht at the end of the fecond Vol. of his *Pilgrims, p.* 1011.]

A true Defcription of the Bay *Todos los Santos* in *Brafill*, and taking the Town *Salvador* by the Admiral Mafter *Jacob Wilkins*, 1624. [*Purchas Pilgrim, Vol. II. p.* 1858.]

Brief Intelligence from *Virginia* by Letters ; a Supplement of *French Virginian* Occurrents, and their Supplantation, by Sir *Samuel Argal*, in right of the *Englifh* Plantation. [*Purchas* Pilgrim. *Vol. IV.* 1805.]

Virginia's Verger : Or a Difcourfe fhewing the Benefits which may grow to this Kingdom from *American Englifh* Plantations, and fpecially thofe of *Virginia* and *Summer Iflands*. [Written by Mr. *Samuel Purchas*, and abridged in his Pilgrim. *Vol. IV. p.* 1809.]

1625.   A Refolution of War with *Spain*, and what followed upon the fecond Ex-
1 Car. 1. pedition to *Cadiz* in 1625. With the Opinion of Sir *William Monfon* concerning that Expedition, which he writ to a noble Friend of his before the Fleet fail'd : As alfo what he conceived of the firft News brought of the taking of the Fort of *Cadiz* ; with a Book of the Proceedings of that Expedition, and the Anfwer made to it. [Sir *Will. Monfon's* Naval Tracts, publifht in the Collect. of Voyages, printed by Mr. *Churchill*. Fol. 1704. *Vol. III. p.* 258.]

God's

God's Promise to his Plantation : As it was delivered in a Sermon by *John Cotton*, B. D. and Preacher of God's Word in *Boston*. *London*, Printed by *William Jones*. 4to. *p.* 26.

HAKLUYTUS POSTHUMUS; or *PURCHAS* his *PILGRIMS* : Contayning a History of the World in Sea-Voyages, and Land Travels, by *Englishmen* and others ; wherein God's Wonders in Nature and Providence, the Actes, Arts, Varieties and Vanities of Men ; with a World of the Worlds Rarities, are by a Worlde of Eye-Witnesse Authors, related to the World. Some left written by Mr. *Hakluyt* at his Death. More since added : His also perused and perfected. All examined, abbreviated, illustrated with Notes, enlarged with Discourses, adorned with Pictures, and expressed in Mapps. In foure Partes. Each containing five Bookes. By *SAMUEL PURCHAS*, B. D. Imprinted at *London* for *Henry Fetherston*. 1625. Fol. *p.* 748.

PURCHAS his *PILGRIMES*, in five Books, the sixth containing Navigations, Voyages, and Land Discoveries, with other Historical Relations of *Africa*. The Seventh, Navigations, Voyages, and Discoveries of the Sea-Coasts and Inland Regions of *Africa*, called *Æthiopia*. The Eighth, Peregrinations and Travels by Land in *Asia*. The Ninth, Peregrinations and Discoveries by Land of *Assyria*, *Armenia*, *&c.* The Tenth, *Præteritorum*, or Discoveries of the World, specially such as in the other Bookes are omitted. The Second Part. *London*, for *Henry Fetherstone*. 1625. Fol. p. 1112

PURCHAS his *PILGRIMES*, in Five Books. The First, containing Peregrinations and Discoveries in the remotest North and East Parts of *Asia*, called *Tartaria* and *China*. The Second, Peregrinations, Voyages and Discoveries of *China*, *Tartaria*, *Russia*, and other the North and East Parts of the World, by *Englishmen* and others. The Third, Voyages and Discoveries of the North Parts of the World, *&c.* and in the North West of *America*. The Fourth, *English* Northerne Navigations and Discoveries of *Greenland*, *&c.* The Fifth, Voyages and Travels to, and in, the New World called *America*, *&c.* The Third Part. *London*, for *Henry Fetherstone*. 1625. Fol. p. 1140.

PURCHAS his *PILGRIMES*, in Five Bookes. The Sixth, containing *English* Voyages to the East, West, and South Parts of *America*, *&c.* The Seventh, Voyages to and about the Southern *America*, with many Marine Observations and Discourses, *&c.* The Eighth, Voyages to, and Land Travels in *Florida*, *Virginia*, and other Partes of the Northern *America*, *&c.* The Ninth, *English* Plantations, Discoveries, Acts and Occurrents in *Virginia*

ginia and *Summer Islands*, &c. The Tenth, *English* Discoveries and Plantations in *New England*, *New-foundland*, with the Patent and Voyages to *New Scotland*, &c. The Fourth Part. *London*, for *Henry Fetherstone*. 1625. Fol. p. 833

Some Advertisements touching his Majesties Care for *Virginia*; delivered by Mr. *Samuel Purchas*, and added to the *Conclusion* of his *Worke*, Ib. p. 198

1626.
2 *Car.* 1.
PURCHAS his *PILGRIMAGE*; or Relations of the World, and the Religions observed in all Ages and Places, discovered from the Creation unto this present. Containing a Theological and Geographical Historie of *Asia, Africa,* and *America,* with the Islands adjacent. Declaring the ancient Religions before the Floud, the Heathenish, Jewish and Saracenicall in all Ages since, &c. With briefe Descriptions of the Countries, Nations, States, Discoveries, &c. The Fourth Edition, much enlarged with Additions, and illustrated with Mappes through the whole Worke. And three whole Treatises annexed, &c. By *SAMUEL PURCHAS,* Parson of St. *Martins* by *Ludgate, London.* Printed for *Henry Fetherstone.* 1626. p. 1047. Fol. [These Five Volumes of Mr. *Purchase* are the Gift of the Hon. Col. *Francis Nicholson,* Governour of *Nova Scotia,* and her Majesties General in the *West-Indies.*]

The New Rates for Sea-Men's Wages, confirmed by the Commissioners of his Majesties Navy, according to his Majesty's several Rates of Ships, and Degrees of Officers Monthly, *An. Dom.* 1626. [Sir *William Monson's* Naval Tracts in Collect. of Voyages, printed for Mr. *Churchill.* 1704. *Vol.* III. p. 278.]

1627.
3 *Car.* 1.
The Generall Historie of *VIRGINIA, NEW ENGLAND,* and the *SUMMER ISLES,* with the Names of the Adventurers, Planters and Governours, from their first Beginning, *Anno* 1584. to this present 1626. With the Procedings of those several Colonies, and the Accidents that befell them in all their Journys and Discoveries. Also the Maps and Descriptions of all those Countrys, their Commodities, People, Government, Customs and Religion not yet knowne. Divided into Six Bookes, by Captain *John Smith,* sometimes Governour in those Countries, and Admiral of *New England. London,* Printed by *J. D.* and *J. H.* for *Michael Sparkes.* 1627. Fol. p. 248.

An

An Historicall Discoverie and Relation of the English Plantations in New England. Containing their Adventurous Passage, their happy Arrival, and comfortable Planting, manifesting the Goodness of God in their Preservations from many apparent Dangers. With a Relation of such Religious and Civil Laws and Customs as are in practise amongst the Indians, with their Natures and Habits. As also a Narration of the Ayre, Earth, Water, Fish, and Fowles of that Countrie. Continued from the first Beginning in the Year of our Lord 1607. and so handling all Passages of Moment successively from time to time. By G. Mourt. London, Printed for John Bellamie. 1627. 4to. [Ex dono Rev. viri Philippi Stubs.]

New England in America; or a Relation of the Beginning and Proceedings of the English Plantation in the North Parts of America, called New England, now in his Majesties Dominions, from Wednesday 6. Sept. 1620. With a Letter sent from New England to a Friend in these Parts; setting forth a briefe and true Declaration of the worth of that Plantation: As also certain usefull Directions for such as intend a Voyage into those Parts; Dated Plimouth in New England this 11th of December, 1621. E. W. With Reasons and Considerations touching the lawfullnesse of removing out of England into the Parts of America. [Signed] R. C. London, 1627. 4to p. 72. 4° [Ex dono Rev. viri Philippi Stubs.]

An Examination of the Errors committed in the Expedition to the Isle of Ree, collected by Sir William Monson, Anno 1627. [Sir Will. Monson's Naval Tracts, publisht in Collect. of Voyages printed for Mr. Churchill. Fol. Vol. III. p. 276.]

Exemplar Bullæ Urbani P. P. VIII. de celebrando Missam, & recitando Officium die 15. Febr. pro viginti tribus Martyribus ex Ord. Min. S. Francisci de Observantiæ, Provinciæ Discalceatorum S. Gregorij, Philippinarum & Japoniæ, qui pro Christi nomine in civitate nuncupata Nangasaqui in regno Japoniæ cruce affixi & transverberati fuerunt. Dat. Romæ apud S. Mariam Majorem, die 14. Septembris, 1627. Pont. nostri anno quinto.

The World encompassed by Sir FRANCIS DRAKE; Being his next Voyage to that to Nombre de Dios, formerly imprinted; carefully collected out of the Notes of Master FRANCIS FLETCHER, Preacher in this Imployment, and divers other his Followers in the same. Offered now at last to publick View, both for the Honour of the Actor, but especially for the stirring up of Heroisk Spirits to benefit their Country, and
T. J. eternize

1628. 4 Car.

eternize their Names by like noble Attempts. *London*, Printed for *Nicholas Bourne*, 1628. 4*to*. *p*. 108.

A Sermon Preached to the nobly-deserving Gentleman, Sir *THOMAS WARNER*, and the rest of his Companie bound to the *WEST-INDIES*, for their Farewell. At St. *Buttolph's Aldersgate London. Septemb*. 6. 1629. By *John Featly*, Preacher of the Word of God. *London*, for *Nicholas Bourne*, 1629. 4*to*. *p*. 34. [The first Preacher upon Saint *Christopher*'s Islands.]

Considerations touching a Warre with *Spaine*, written about five Years since, and inscribed to his Majestie, at that time Prince of *Wales*; by *Francis* Lord *Verulam*, Viscount of St. *Albans*. *London*, Printed by *John Haviland*, 1629. 4*to*. *p*. 76. With an Advertisement touching an Holy Warre, written in the Yeare 1622. Whereunto the Author prefixed an Epistle to the Bishop of *Winchester* last deceased.

Exemplar Bullæ Urbani Papæ VIII. de Uniqne quarundam Domorum Regularium Provinciarum novi Regni Granatensis sive Quitensis in IN DIIS OC-CIDEN TALIBUS, *Fratrum Discalceatorum Ordinis Eremitarum Sancti Augustini sub gubernio Fratrum Discalceatorum ejusdem Ordinis existentium, &c. Dat. Romæ. Apud S. Mariam majorem die 16 Julij* 1629. *Pont. nostri anno sexto.*

EUROPÆ SPECULUM: Or a View or Survey of the State of Religion in the *Westerne* Parts of the World. Wherein the Romane Religion, and the pregnant Policies of the Church of *Rome*, to support the same, are notably displayed: With some other memorable Discoveries and Memorations. Never before till now published according to the Authours originall Copie. *Hagæ. Comitis*. 1629. 4*to*. *p*. 248. From *Paris* 1x° *April*. 1599. Copied out by the Authours Originall, and finished 2 *Octob. An.* M. DC. XVIII.

God's Power and Providence shewed in the miraculous Preservation and Deliverance of eight *English* Men, left by Mischance in *Greenland, Anno* 1630. nine Months and twelve Days. With a true Relation of all their Miseries, their Shifts and Hardships they were put to, their Food, *&c.* such as neither Heathen nor Christian ever before endur'd. With a Description of the chief Places and Rarities of that barren and cold Country. Faithfully reported by *Edward Pelham*, one of the eight Men aforesaid. As also

alſo a Map of *Greenland.* [Reprinted in Collect. of Voyages for Mr. *Churchill. Fol. Vol. IV. p.* 868.]

Articles of Peace, Entercourſe and Commerce, concluded in the Names of the High and Mighty Kings, *CHARLES*, by the Grace of God King of *Great Britaine, France* and *Ireland,* Defender of the Faith, *&c.* And *PHILIP* the fourth King of *Spain, &c.* In a Treaty at *Madrid,* the fifth Day of *November,* after the Old Stile, in the Yeere of our Lord God M.DC.XXX. Tranſlated out of *Latine* into *Engliſh.* Imprinted at *London* by *Robert Barker, &c.* 1630. 4to. With a Declaration of Peace with *Spain.* Given at his Majeſties Palace of *Weſtminſter* the fifth Day of December, in the ſixth Yeere of his Majeſties Reign.

The *Engliſh Spaniſh* Pilgrim; Or a New Diſcoverie of *Spaniſh* Popery, and Jeſuitical Stratagems. With the Eſtate of the *Engliſh* Penſioners and Fugitives, under the King of *Spain*'s Dominions, and elſewhere at this preſent. Alſo laying open the New Order of the *Jeſuitrices* and preaching *Nunnes.* Compoſed by *James Wadeſworth,* Gentleman, newly converted into his true Mother's boſome, the *Church of England,* with the Motives why he left the See of *Rome,* a late Penſioner to his Majeſtie of *Spaine,* and nominated his Captaine in *Flanders,* Sonne to Mr. *James Wadſworth,* Batchelor of Divinity. Sometime of *Emanuell Colledge* in the Univerſity of *Cambridge,* who was perverted in the Yeere 1604. and late Tutor to *Donna Maria Infanta* of *Spaine.* Publiſhed by Authority. Printed for *Michael Sparke.* 1630. 4to. *p.* 95.

PHILIPPI LANSBERGII, *Commentationes in Motum Terræ Diurnum & Annuum, & in verum Adſpectabilis Cæli Typum. In quibus ἐπιστημονικῶς oſtenditur, Diurnum Annuumq; Motum qui apparet in Sole & Cælo non deberi* Soli *aut* Cœlo, *ſed ſoli Terræ; ſimulq; adſpectabilis Primi Cæli Typus ad vivum exprimitur. Ex Belgico Sermone in Latinum verſa a* MARTINO HORTENSIO *Delfenſi: Una cum Ipſius Præfatione in quâ Aſtronomiæ Braheanæ Fundamenta examinantur ; & cum Lansbergianâ Aſtronomiæ Reſtitutione conferuntur.* MIDDELBURGI. *Apud Zachariam Romanum* M.DC.XXX. *Cum Privilegio.* 4to. *p.* 65. [*Ex dono Rev. viri Joſephi Sparke, Petribuɟgenſis.*]

The true Travells, Adventures and Obſervations of Captain *JOHN SMITH,* in *Europe, Aſia, Africa* and *America,* from *Anno Domini* 1593. to 1629. His Accidents and Sea Fights in the Straights. His Service and Stratagems of Warre in *Hungaria, Tranſylvania, Walachia* and *Moldavia,* againſt the *Turkes* and *Tartar's:* His three ſingle Combats betwixt the Chriſtian Armie and the *Turkes.* How after he was taken Priſoner by the *Turkes.* ſold fold for a Slave, and fent into *Tartaria*; his Defcription of the *Tartars*; their ftrange Manners and Cuftomes of Religions, Diets, Buildinges, Warres, Feafts, Ceremonies, and Living; how he flew the *Bafha* of *Nalbrit's* in *Cambia*, and efcaped from the *Turks* and *Tartars*. Together with a Continuation of his General Hiftorie of *VIRGINIA*, *Summer Ifles*, *New-England*, and their Proceedings fince 1624. to this prefent 1629. As alfo of the New Plantations of the great River of the *Amazons*, the Ifles of St *Chriftopher*, *Mevis*, and *Barbados* in the *Weft-Indies*. All written by actual Authors, whofe Names you fhall find all along the Hiftory. *London*, Printed for *Thomas Slater*. 1630. Fol. *p.* 60. [Reprinted in the Collection of Voyages for Mr. *Churchill*. Vol. II. *p.* 373.]

The Mapp and Defcription of *New England*, together with a Difcourfe of Plantation and Colonies. Alfo a Relation of the Nature of the Climate, and how it agrees with our own Country, *England*, How neere it lyes to *Newfoundland*, *Virginia*, *Nova Francia*, *Canada*, and other Parts of the *Weft-Indies*. Written by Sir *William Alexander*, Knight. *London*, Printed for *Nathaniel Baker*, 1630. 4to. *p.* 47. [*Ex dono Rev. viri Philippi Stubbs.*]

631.
Car. 1.

Advertifements for the unexperienced Planters of *New England* or any where. Or the Path way to Experience to erect a Plantation. With the yearly Proceedings of this Country in Fifhing and Planting fince the year 1614. to the year 1630. and their prefent Eftate. Alfo how to prevent the greateft inconveniences by their Proceedings in *Virginia*, and other Plantations by approved Examples. With the Countries Arms, a Defcription of the Coaft, Harbours, Habitations, Land-marks, Latitude and Longitude. With the Mapp allowed by our Royal King *Charles*. By Captain *JOHN SMITH*, fometime Governour of *Virginia*, and Admirall of *New England*. *London* Printed by *John Haviland* for *Robert Milbourne* 1631. 4to. pag. 40.

ΜΙΚΡΟΚΟΣΜΟΣ A Little Defcription of the Great World. The fifth Edition. By *PETER HEYLIN*. *Oxford* Printed for *William Turner* and *Robert Allot*. 1631. 4to. *p.* 807.——The fourth and laft Part is of *America* or the *New World*. With the Longitude and Latitude of the chief *American* Cities.

Las Obras Y Relaciones de ANT. PEREZ *Secretario de Eftado que fue del Rey de Efpana Don* PHELIPPE II. *defte nombre. Illuftrat: dum vexat. En Geneva. Por. Juan de la Planche* M, DC. XXXI. 8vo. *p.* 1126.

E1

El *Memorial que* ANTONIO PEREZ *presento del Hecho de su* causa *en el juyzio del tribunal del Justicia de Arragon,* &c. Ib.

Cartas de ANTONIO PEREZ *Secretario de estado que fue del Rey* Catholico Don Philippe II. de este nombre Para diversas Personas des pues de su salida de Espanna.

ANTONII PEREZII *ad Comitem Essexium Singularem Angliæ* Magnatem & ad Alios Epistolarum Centuria una. Ib.

New *English Canaan*; or *New Canaan*. Containing an Abstract of New England. Composed in three Bookes. The First setting forth the originall of the Natives, their Manners and Customs. II. Together, with their tractable Nature and Love towards the *English*. The Natural Indowments of the Countrie, and what Staple Commodities it yeeldeth. III. What People are planted there, their Prosperity, what remarkable Accidents have happened since the first planting of it; together with their Tenents and Practise of their Church. Written by *Thomas Morton* of *Cliffords Inne*, Gent. upon ten Yeers Knowledge and Experiment of the Country. [Having arrived there in *June* 1622.] Printed for *Charles Green*. 4to. p. 188. Dedicated to the right Honourable the Lord, and others of his Majesties most Honourable Privy Councill, Commissioners for the Government of all his Majesties foraigne Provinces. 1632. 8 Cer. 1

A Publication of *GUIANA*'s Plantation, newly undertaken by the Right Honourable the Earl of *Barkshire* (Knight of the most Noble Order of the Garter) and Company, for that most famous River of the *Amazones* in *America*. Wherein is briefly shewed the Lawfulness of Plantations in Foreign Countries; Hope of the Natives Conversion; Nature of the River; Qualitie of the Land, Climate, and People of *GUIANA*: With the Provisions for Man's Sustenance; and Commodities therein growing for the Trade of Merchandise, and manner of the Adventure. With an Answer to some Objections touching feare of the Enemy. *London*, Printed by *William Jones*. 1632. 4to. p. 24.

Captain *Thomas James*'s strange and dangerous Voyage, in his intended Discoverie of the North-West Passage into the South Sea, in the Years 1631 and 1632. Wherein the Miseries indured both going, wintering, and returning, and the Rarities observed, both Philosophical and Mathematical are related at large. Published by his Majesties Command. To which are added a Plat, or Card for the Sailing in those Seas. Also divers little Tables

U   of

of the Author's. Of the Variation of the Compass, &c. With an *Appendix* concerning *Longitude*, by Mr. *Henry Gellibrand*, Aftronomy Reader of *Grefham* Colledge, *London*. And an Advice concerning the Philofophie of thefe late Difcoveries, by *W. W.* [Reprinted in Colle&. of Voyages by Mr. *Churchill. Vol. II. p.* 481.]

1633.
9 *Car. 1.*

An *Eaft-India* Collation; or a Difcourfe of Travells, fet forth in fundry Obfervations, briefe and delightfull; Colle&ed by the Author in a Voyage he made unto the *Eaft-Indies*, of allmoft four Years continuance. Written by *C. F. London*, Printed by *B. A.* and *J. F.* 1633. 8*vo. p.* 69. [Subfcribed *Chr. Farewell.*]

COCHINCHINA: Containing many admirable Rarities and Singularities of that Countrey: Extra&ed out of an *Italian* Relation, lately prefented to the Pope by *Chriftopher Barri*, that lived certaine Yeeres there; and publifhed by *ROBERT ASHLEY*. Ded. to the right worthy Knight Sir *Maurice Abbot*, Governour of the Honourable Company of Merchants trading to the *Eaft-Indies*, and the reft of that renowned Society. *London*, by *Robert Raworth*, &c. 1633. 4*to.*

A fhort Account of the Voyages of Mr. *Zachaery Wagener*, performed in 35 Years, through *Europe*, *Afia*, *Africa* and *America*; taken out of his own Journal, beginning 3 *June*, 1633. [In Colle&. of Voyages for Mr. *Churchill. Vol. II. p.* 552.]

HISTORIA NAVALIS Antiqua, *Libris quatuor Autore* THO. RIVIO *Regis in Anglia Advocato. Londini. Apud Robertum Barker, Typographum Regium. Anno* 1633. 8*vo. p.* 491. [*Ex dono* Awnfhami Churchill, *Armig.*]

Bulla Urbani *Papæ VIII. D. Miffionibus Religioforum cujufcunq; Ordinis ad* Japonicas *& alia Indiarum Orientalium Regiones, de Impedientium pænis, & aliis ad eas pertinentibus. Dat. Romæ apud S. Petrum fub annulo Pifcatoris die* 22 *Februarij* 1633. *Pont. noftri anno decimo.* [*Bullarium Romanum. Romæ.* MDCXXXVIII. *Append. Urbanus Octavus. Num. XVI.*]

Bulla ejufdem Urbani P. P. Quod Fratres S. Auguftini Difcalceati Hifpaniarum, in PHILIPPINIS *&* Occidentalibus INDIIS *degentes, à quovis Catholico Epifcopo communionem Sedis Apoftolicæ habente Minores & Sacros Ordines, etiam non fervatis interftitiis, fufcipere poffint. Dat. Romæ apud S. Mariam Majorem die* 9 *Julij* 1633. *Pont. noftri anno decimo.* [*Ib. num. XVIII.*]

Hugo

Hugo Grotius *de* MARI LIBERO *five de Jure quod Batavis competit ad Indicana commercia Differtatio.* Pauli Merulæ *Differtatio* DE MARI-BUS. *Marci Zuerij Boxhornij Apologia pro* NAVIGATIONIBUS *Hollandorum adverfus Pontum Heutcrum Tractatus Pacu, Mutui Commercij five Intercurfus Navigationum confirmatus Londini anno MCCCCXCV. inter Henricum Septimum Angliæ Regem & Philippum Archiducem Auftriæ, Burgundiæ, &c. Lugd. Batavorum.* Ex officina Elzeviriana. *Anno* 1633. 12° *p.* 308.

Two Journals. The firft kept by feven Sailers in the Ifle of Sr. *Maurice* in *Greenland,* in the yeare 1633, 1634. The fecond by feven other Sailers, who in the yeare 1633. and 1634. winter'd at *Spitzbergen.* Done out of *Low Dutch.* [In the Firft Vol. of Voyages printed by Mr. *Churchill.* 1704. *Fol. p.* 415.]   1634. 10 *Car.* 1.

New England's Profpect: A true, lively, and experimental Defcription of that part of *America,* commonly called *New-England:* Difcovering the State of that Countrie, both as it ftands to our new-come *Englifh* Planters, and to the old native Inhabitants. Laying down that which may both enriche the Knowledge of the Mind-travelling Reader, or benefit the future Voyager. By *William Wood.* Printed at *London* for *John Bellamie.* 1634. 4to. *p.* 89.

A briefe Defcription of the whole World; wherein is particularly defcribed all the Monarchies, Empires, and Kingdoms of the fame, with their Academies. As alfo their feveral Titles and Situations thereunto adjoyning. Written by the Right Reverend Father in God, *George,* late Archbifhop of *Canterburie. London,* Printed for *William Sheares.* 1634. 8vo. *p.* 329. [At *p.* 240. begins the Account of *AMERICA,* or the *New World.*]

A Letter of Sir *John Harvey,* Governour of *Virginia;* written with his own Hand, and dated *James Citie* in *Virginia* the 27th of *May, Anno* 1634. to the Board of Treafurer, and Company in *London,* for the Affaires of *Virginia,* upon occafion of his Majefties Letters of Privy Seal, directed to himfelf and Council, requiring all lawfull help and affiftance to the noble Undertakings of the Lord *Baltimore,* in feating himfelf and his Affociates upon that Tract of Ground, now called *Mary-Land;* giving an Account of the Sufpicions and Treacherie of the *Indians,* upon the firft arrival of the *Englifh,* and of the Means to be ufed by the *Englifh* for their Defence and Prefervation; and of the happinefs of that Colony in the abundance of Corne and Cattel, &c. 1 Sheet *Fol. MS.*

North-

1635.   North-Weſt *Foxe*, or *Foxe* from the North-Weſt Paſſage.   Beginning with
11 Car. 1. King *Arthur*, *Malga*, *Octhur*, the two *Zeni* of *Iſeland*, *Eſtotiland*, and *Dor-*
gia: Following with briefe Abſtracts of the Voyages of *Cabot*, *Frobiſher*,
Davis, *Waymouth*, *Knight*, *Hudſon*, *Button*, *Gibbons*, *Bylot*, *Baffin*, *Hawkridge*.
Mr. *James Hall*'s three Voyages to *Groynland*; with a Topographical Deſcription of the Countries, the Salvages, &c.   With the Author his own
Voyage, being the XVIth: With the Opinions and Collections of the moſt
famous Mathematicians and Coſmographers, &c.   By Captain *Luke Foxe* of
Kingſton upon *Hull*, Captain and Pylot for the Voyage, in his Majeſties Pin-
nace the *Charles*.

The Reaſons given by Sir *William Monſon*, why the King did not ſooner
reſent the Wrongs offered him by the *Dutch*, and for his ſetting out the Fleet
in 1635. With an Account of it.   [Sir *Will. Monſon*'s Naval Tracts publiſht
in Collect. of Voyages printed for Mr. *Churchill*. 1704. *Fol. Vol. III.*
p. 290.]

Inſtructions given under 34 Heads in the Voyage of 1635. by the right
Honourable *Robert* Earl of *Lindſey*, dated on Board the *Mere-Honour*, riding
in the *Downs* 30 *May*, 1635.   [Sir *Will. Monſon, Ib. p.* 333.]

The Hiſtory of the Imperial Eſtate of the Grand Seigneurs : Their Habitations, Lives, Titles, Qualities, Exerciſes, Workes, Revenues, Habit,
Diſcent, Ceremonies, Magnificence, Judgments, Officers, Favourites, Religion, Power, Government and Tyranny.   Tranſlated out of *French* by
E. G. S. A. [*i. e. Edward Grimeſton*, Serjeant at Armes.]   *London*, Printed
by *William Stansby*. 1635. 4to. *p.* 191.

The Hiſtory of the Court of the King of C H I N A, written in *French*
by the Seigneur *Michael Baudier* of *Languedoc*.   Tranſlated by *E. G.* [*i. e.*
Edward Grimeſton.]   *London*, Printed by *William Stansby*. 4to. 1635.

Foure SEA SERMONS, Preached at the Annual Meeting of the
TRINITY COMPANY, in the Pariſh Church of *Deptford*, by
HENRY VALENTINE, Vicar.   *London*, Printed by M. *Fleſher* for
John Marriott, &c. MDCXXXV. 4to.   With Forms of Prayer to be uſed
by the Mariner before he go to Sea, at Sea, and after his return from Sea.

A ſhort Journal of ſeven Sea-Men, who being left in 1634. at *Spitz-*
bergen, to paſs the Winter, died there of Cold and Hunger in 1635.
[Collection of Voyages for Mr. *Churchill. Fol. Vol. II. p.* 427.]

N E W

NEW ENGLANDS PROSPECT. A true, lively, and experimental Defcription of that part of *America*, commonly called *NEW ENGLAND*, difcovering the State of that Countrie, both as it ftands to our new-come *Englifh* Planters, and to the old Native Inhabitants. Laying downe that which may both enrich the Knowledge of the Mind-travelling Reader, or benefit the future Voyager. By *WILLIAM WOOD.* Printed at *London* by *Tho. Cotes*, &c. 1635. 4to. p. 83. To which is added a Nomenclator of the Natives Language.

An Hiftorical Relation of the moft memorable Paffages in *Germany*, and elfewhere, fince the Beginning of this prefent Yeere 1635. Wherein is a Manifefto or Declaration of the *French* King for a Warre with *Spain*. And a Manifefto of the Cardinal Infant of *Spain*, for a Warre with *France*, both by Sea and Land. *London*, 1635. 4to. p. 73.

The Copy of the Treaty of Peace between the Emperour and the Elector of *Saxony*, concluded at *Prague* the 20-30. Day of *May*, *Anno* 1635. *Ib.*

P. MERULÆ *Cofmographiæ Partis II. Lib. I. & II. quibus univerfim* EUROPA *& fpeciatim* HISPANIA *defcribitur. Editio ultima. Novis Additamentis & Regnorum regimine aucta. Tabulifq; Geographicis illuftrata. Amfterdami. Apud Guilielmum Blaeu. MDCXXXV. 8vo. p. 350.*

An Introduction to the Earl of *Northumberland's* Voyage in the Year 1636. Written by Sir *William Monfon*; with an Account of the Voyage itfelf; and the Errours committed in it. [Sir *Will. Monfon's* Naval Tracts in Collect. of Voyages, printed for Mr. *Churchill*. 1704. Vol. III. p. 300.] *1636. 12 Car. 1.*

Hiftoire de la Haut Ethiopie *ecrite fur les lieux par le* R. P. MANOEL D' ALMEIDA *Jefuite, qui paffa a* Angola *l' annee* 1636 *d'* Angola *au* Brezil *du* Brezil *a* Cartagene, *& de la en* Efpagne *pour y foliciter le fecours pour la Miffion d' Ethiopie. Extraite & traduite de la copie Portugaife du* R. P. BALTAZAR TELLEZ.——*Remarques fur les Relations d'* Ethiopie *des* R. R. Jeronimo Lobo *& de* Balthafar Tellez *Jefuites, &c.* [*Relation de divers Voyages, &c. a Paris* 1672. IV. *Partié.*]

The Copie of a Letter written by the King of *Siam* to *Frederick Henry*, Prince of *Orange* in 1636. With Obfervations on it. [In Collect. of Voyages for Mr. *Churchill*. Fol. Vol. III. p. 579]

X   *Joan*

1637.
13 Car. 1.
Joan. Petri MAFFEII *Bergomatis è Societate Jesu Historiarum Indicarum Libri XII. Omnia ab Auctore recognita & emendata. In singula copiosus Index. Lugduni. Apud Joannem Champion* MDCXXXVII. 8vo. *p.* 718.

A bewayling of the Peace of *Germany* ; or a Discourse touching the Peace of *PRAGUE,* unhappily and unjustly concluded at *PRAGUE* in *BOHEMIA,* the 30th of *May* 1635. Wherein the Subtilities and Practises of the *Austrians,* the Weakness of the *Saxons,* the Dangers of the *Protestants,* and the Justness of the Warre deservedly set on foot by the *French* and *Swedes,* are most evidently declared. 4to. 1637.

JOH. ISACII PONTANI *Discussionum Historicarum Libri duo. Quibus præcipuè quatenus & quodnam in mare liberum vel non liberum clausumq; accipiendum difficitur expenditurq; Accedit præter alia* CASPARIS VAR-RERII *Lusitani de* Ophyra *Regione, & ad eam Navigatione Commentarius.* Item BART. KECKERMANNI *Problemata Nautica, & Commonitio ad Lectorem Spectans* VARRERIUM & KECKERMANNUM *Quod ad* OPHYRÆ *Regionem.* Hardevici Golrorum M. DC. XXXVII. 8vo. *p.* 431.

A true Relation of the late Battell fought in *New England,* between the *English* and the Salvages : With the present State of things there. *London,* Printed for *Nathaniel Butter* and *John Bellamie.* 1637. 4to. *p.* 23.

New English Canaan ; or *New Canaan.* Containing an Abstract of *New England.* Composed in three Books. The first Booke setting forth the Original of the Natives, their Manners and Customs. Together with their tractable Nature and Love towards the *English.* The second Book setting forth the natural Indowments of the Country, and what Staple Commodities it yieldeth. The third Booke setting forth, what People are planted there, what remarkable Accidents have happened since the first planting of it ; together, with their Tenents and Practise of their Church. Written by *Thomas Morton* of *Clifford's Inne,* Gent. upon ten Yeares Knowledge and Experiment of the Countrey. Printed at *Amsterdam* by *Jacob Frederick Stam,* in the Yeare 1637. 4to. *p.* 188.

Compassion towards Captives ; chiefly towards our Brethren and Countrey Men, who are in miserable Bondage in *BARBARIE.* Urged and pressed in three Sermons, on *Hebr.* 13. 3. Preached in *Plymouth* in *October* 1636. By *Charles Fitz-Geffry.* Whereunto are annexed an Epistle of St. *Cyprian,* concerning the Redemption of the Brethren from the Bondage of *Barbarians.*

bariani. And a Paſſage concerning the Benefits of Compaſſion, extracted out of St. *Ambroſe* his ſecond Book of Offices. *Oxford*, Printed by *Leonard Litchfield*, 1637. 4to. p. 50.

The Diſcovery of a Worlde in the Moon : Or a Diſcourſe tending to prove, that 'tis probable there may be another habitable World in that Planet. *London*, for *Michael Sparke*. 1638. 8vo. p. 209.

1638.
14 Car. 1.

A Voyage into the *LEVANT*. A briefe Relation of a Journey lately performed by Maſter *Henry Blunt*, Gentleman, from *England*, by the way of *Venice* into *Dalmatia, Sclavonia, Boſrah, Hungary, Macedonia, Theſſaly, Thrace, Rhodes* and *Egypt* unto *Grand Cairo*. With particular Obſervations concerning the modern Condition of the *Turkes*, and other People under that Empire. The third Edition. *London*. 1638. 4to. p. 126.

The Marchants Mapp of Commerce, neceſſarie for all ſuch as ſhall be employed in the publique Affaires of Princes in foraigne Parts. For all Gentlemen and others that travell abroad for Delight and Pleaſure. And for all Marchants, or their Factors, that exerciſe the Art of Marchandiſeing in any Parte of the habitable World. By *Lewes Robarts*, Marchant. Printed for *Ralfe Mabb*. 1638. Fol. [Chap. XI. Of *AMERICA*, and the Provinces thereof.]

Relation de ce qui s' eſt Paſſé en la NOUVELLE FRANCE *en L' Annee* 1638. *Envoyee au R. Pere Provincial de la Compagnie de* Jeſus *en la Province de* France. *Par le P.* PAUL LE JEUNE *de la meſme Compagnie Superieur de la Reſidence de* KEBEC. *A Paris chez* Sebaſtian Cramoiſy, MDCCXXXVIII. *Avec Privilege du Roy*, 8vo. p. 78.

Relation de le qui s' eſt Paſſé en la Miſſion de là Compagnie de Jeſus *dans le Pays dès* HURONS *en l' Annees* 1637 & 38. *Envoyes a* Kebec *au R. P.* Paul le Jeune *Superieur des Miſſions de la Compagnie de* Jeſus *en la* Nouvelle France p.r *Joſeph le Mercier. De la Reſidence de la Conception au pays des Hurons. Au bourg d' Oſſoſarie ce* 9 *Juin* 1638. 8vo. p. 67.

Some Yeares TRAVELS into divers Parts of *ASIA* and *AFRIKE*, deſcribing eſpecially the two famous Empires, the *Perſian* and great *Mogull*, weaved with the Hiſtory of theſe latter times. As alſo many rich and ſpacious Kingdoms in the Oriental *India*, and other Partes of *Aſia*; together, with the adjacent Iſles. Severally relating the Religion, Language, Qualities, Cuſtoms, Habit, Deſcent, Faſhions, and other Obſervations touching them. With a Revival of the firſt Diſcoverer of *AMERICA*. [Or a
Diſſertation

Diſſertation to prove that *Madoc ap Owen Gwyneth* diſcovered *America* above three hundred Yeares before *COLUMBUS*.] Reviſed and Enlarged by the Author. *London*, Printed for *Jacob Blome* and *Richard Biſhop*. 1638. Fol. *p.* 364.

1640.
16 Car. 1.   Mr. St. *John*'s Speech to the Lords in the Upper Houſe of Parliament, *January* 7. 1640. concerning SHIP MONEY. Printed *Anno Domini*. 1640. 4*to. p.* 45.

A Deſcription of *UKRAINE*: Containing ſeveral Provinces of *POLAND*, lying between the Confines of *Muſcovy*, and the Borders of *Tranſylvania*. Together with their Cuſtoms, Manner of Life, and how they manage their Wars. Written in *French* by the *Sieur de Beauphan* in 1640. [Collect. of Voyages for Mr. *Churchill*, *Vol.* I. *p.* 573.]

A brave and valiant Sea-Fight upon the Coaſt of *Cornwall*, the 17*th* of *June* laſt paſt, betwixt three *Turkiſh* Pyrates, Men of Warre, and only one *Engliſh* Merchants Shippe of *Plymouth*, called the *Elizabeth*, not above 200 Tun. Wherein they quit their Ship out of the Hands of the cruel *Turke*, with the loſs only of three Men, but ſlue many of the *Turkes*, to their everlaſting Honour. *London*, for *Nathaniel Butter*, *Jul.* 14. 1640. 4*to.*

Sir *Thomas Roe* his Speech in Parliament, wherein he ſheweth the Cauſe of the Decay in Coyne and Trade in this Land, eſpeciall of Merchants in Trade : And alſo propoundeth a way to the Houſe, how they may be increaſed. Printed in the Yeare 1640. 4*to. p.* 10.

1641.
17 Car. 1.   A Copy of a Letter of Mr. *Cotton* of *Boſton* in *New England*, ſent in anſwer of certaine Objections made againſt their Diſcipline and Orders there, directed to a Friend. With the Queſtions propounded to ſuch as are admitted to the Church-Fellowſhip, and the Government itſelf. Printed in the Yeare 1641. 8*vo. p.* 6.

A Petition of *W. C.* [*William Caſtell*, Parſon of *Courtenhall* in *Northamptonſhire*] Exhibited to the High Court of Parliament, now aſſembled, for the propagating of the Goſpel in *AMERICA* and the *WEST-INDIES*, and for the ſetling of our Plantations there ; which Petition is approved by 70 able *Engliſh* Divines. Alſo by Maſter *Alexander Henderſon*, and ſome other worthy Miniſters of *Scotland*. Printend in the Year 1641. 4*to. p.* 19.

                                            England's

Decay of Trade. A Treatise against the abating of INTEREST: Or Reasons shewing the inconveniences which will insue, by the bringing down of Interest-Money to six or five in the Hundred, and raising the price of Land in this Kingdome. By a Well-wisher of the Common-wealth. Printed at *London* for *John Sweeting*, 1641. 4*to*. *p*. 9.

England's Safety, in Trade's Encrease ; most humbly presented to the High Court of Parliament. By *HENRY ROBINSON*, Gent. *London*, Printed for *Nicholas Bourne*, 1641. 4*to*. *p*. 62.

Considerations touching TRADE, with the Advance of the King's Revenue, and present Reparation of his MAJESTIE. Containing these four Heads, *viz*. 1. From the Customes. 2. From Fines and Confiscations. 3. From Acts of Resumptions. 4. And from Subsidies. Humbly represented to the View of the Right Honourable High Court of Parliament. Printed in the Year 1641. 4*to*. *p*. 16.

A short Account of the Island of *FORMOSA* in the *Indies*, situate near the Coast of *China* ; and of the Manners, Customs and Religions of its Inhabitants. By *George Candidius*, Minister of the Word of God to the *Dutch* in that Island. [In the Collection of Voyages printed for Mr. *Churchill*, *Vol. I. p.* 526.]

Pyramidographia ; or a Description of the Pyramids of *Ægypt*. By *John Greaves*, Professor of Astronomy in the University of *Oxford*. With his Discourse of the *Roman* Foot and *Denarius* ; and his Epistle to the famous Mathematician *Claudius Hardy*, giving an Account of his Travels in the East, and the Observations there made. Dated *London*, *May* 14. 1641. [Reprinted in the Collection of Voyages, *Vol. II. p.* 685. Printed for Mr. *Churchill*.]

GALILÆI GALILÆI *Lyncei*, *Academiæ Pisanæ Mathematici*, *Serenissimi Magni Ducis Hetruriæ Philosophi & Mathematici primarii* SYSTEMA COSMICUM: *In quo Dialogis IV. de duobus maximis Mundi Systematibus Ptolemaico & Copernicano Rationibus utrinque propositis indefinitè disseritur. Accessit locorum S. Scripturæ cum terræ mobilitate conciliatio.* LUGDUNI *Sumptibus* Joan. Antonij Huguetan, MDCXLI. 4*to*. *p*. 377. [*Ex dono Reverendi viri* Josephi Sparke *Petriburgensis*.]

A Relation of a Voyage made towards the South *Terra Incognita*, extract-ed from the Journal of Captain *Abel Janson Tasman*, beginning 1642. *Aug. 14.* by which not only a new Paſſage by Sea to the Southward of *Nova Hollandia*, *Vandemen's Land*, &c. is diſcovered, and a vaſt ſpace of Land and Sea, incompaſſed and ſailed round, but many conſiderable and inſtructive Obſervations concerning the Variation of the Magnetical Needle in Parts of the World, allmoſt Antipodes to us; and ſeveral other curious Remarks, concerning thoſe Places and People, are ſet forth. Not long ſince publiſhed in the *Low Dutch* by *Dirk Rembrantſe*, and now in *Engliſh* from Dr. *Hook's* Collections. [In the Account of Voyages. 1. Sir *John Narborough*. 2. Capt. *J. Aaſman*, &c. 1711. 8vo.

The Churches Reſurrection; or the Opening of the fifth and ſixth Verſes of the 20th Chapter of the *Revelation*. By that Learned and Reverend *John Cotton*, Teacher to the Church of *Boſton* in *New-England*, and there corrected by his own Hand. *London*, for *Henry Overton*, 1642. 4to. *p.* 30.

A modeſt and cleare Anſwer to Mr. *Bal's* Diſcourſe of ſet Forms of Prayer. Set forth in a moſt ſeaſonable time, when this Kingdom is now in Conſultation about Matters of that Nature, and ſo many Godly, long after the Reſolution in that Point. Written by the Reverend and Learned *John Cotton*, B. D. and Teacher of the Church of Chriſt at *Boſton* in *New-England*. *London*, for *Henry Overton*, 1642. 4to. *p.* 49. [*Ex dono Reverendi viri* Gerſhomi Rawlins.]

Plain-Dealing, or News from *New-England*. A ſhort View of *New-England's* preſent Government, both Eccleſiaſtical and Civil. Compared with the antiently received and eſtabliſhed Government of *England*, in ſome material Points; fit for the graveſt Conſideration in theſe Times. By *Thomas Lechford* of *Clements Inne*, in the County of *Middleſex*, Gent. *London*, for *Nath. Butter*, 1642. 4to.

The Pagan's Debt and Dowry; or a brief Diſcuſſion of theſe Queſtions, *Whether, how far*, and in *what ſence* ſuch Perſons of Mankinde, amongſt whom the Letter of the Goſpel never came, are notwithſtanding bound to believe on Jeſus Chriſt. (With ſome other Particulars relating hereunto, &c.) By *John Goodwin*, Miniſter of the Goſpel. *London*, Printed. for *H. Cripps*. 4to. *p.* 1642.

The

The true Conftitution of a particular vifible Church, proved by Scripture; wherein is briefly demonftrated by Queftions and Anfwers, what Officers, Worfhip, and Government Chrift hath ordained in his Church. By that Reverend and Learned Divine Mr. *John Cotton*, B. D. and Paftor of *Bofton* in *New-England*, 1643, 4to. p. 13.

The Tyranny of Satan, difcovered by the Teares of a Converted Sinner. In a Sermon preached in St. *Paule's* Church, on the 28th of *Auguft* 1642. By *THOMAS GAGE*, formerly a Romifh Prieft for the fpace of 38 Years, and now reconciled to the Church of *England*. [The fame Perfon who had lived fo long in the *Weft-Indies*, and foon after publifht a Survey of thofe Parts.] *London*, Printed for *Humphrey Mofley*, 1642. 4to. p. 27.

Inftructions for Forreigne Travell: Shewing by what Courfe, and in what Compaffe of Time, one may take an exact Survey of the Kingdoms and States of *Chriftendome*, and arrive to the practical Knowledge of the Languages to good Purpofe. [Ded. to Prince *Charles* by Mr. *James Howell*.] *London*, for *Humphry Mofye*, 1642. 12° p. 236.

Articles of Peace and Commerce, between the High and Mighty Kings *Charles*, by the grace of God King of *Great Britain*, &c. and *John* the IVth King of *Portugal*, &c. Concluded at *London* the nine and twentieth day of *January*, in the Yeere of our Lord 1642. *Stilo novo*. Tranflated out of *Latine* into *Englifh*. *London*, 1642. 4to.

The Boate Swaine's Art: Or the Compleat Boat Swaine. Wherein is fhewed a true proportion for the Mafting, Yarding, and Rigging of any Ship, whofe Length, Bredth and Depth is knowne. With Rules for the Sizes and Lengths of all forts of Rigging that belongs to any Ship. By *Henry Bond*, Teacher of Navigation, Surveying, and other Partes of the Mathematicks in the Bulwarke neere the *Tower*. Printed at *London* by *Richard Cotes*, 1642. 4to. p. 22.

Hydrographie, *Contenant La theorie & la Practique de Toutes Parties de la* 1643 *Navigation*. *Compofé par le Pere* George Tournier *de la Compagnie de Jefus* 19 Car. 1 *A Paris* M. DC. XLIII. *Fol. p.* 922. *Livre vingtiefme* De la Devotion des Gens de Mer.

An Account of a Voyage to the Coaft of *CHILI* in *America*, performed by Order from the *Dutch Eaft-India* Company, in the Years 1642 and 1643, under the Command of Mr. *Henry Brawern*, and *Elias Herckermann*. With a Defcription of the Ifland of *Caftro*, lying off the South Coaft of *Chili*; as alfo

of

of the River of *Baldivia* in that Kingdom. [In Collect. of Voyages printed for Mr. *Churchill.* 1704. *Fol. Vol. I. p.* 507.]

A Speech, or Complaint lately made by the *Spanish* Embassadour to his Majestie at *Oxford*, upon occasion of the taking of a Ship called *Sancta Clara*, in the Port of *Sancto Domingo*, richly laden with Plate, Cocheneale, and other Commodities of great Value, by one Captaine *Bennet Strafford*, and by him brought to *Southampton*. Being a Matter of high Concernment betwixt the two Kinges of *Spain* and *England*. Also a Proclamation prohibiting the buying or disposing of any of the Lading of the Ship called the *Sancta Clara*, lately brought into *Southampton*. Translated out of the *Spanish* in *Oxford* by the *Sieur Torriano*, an *Italian. London*, printed for *Nathaniel Butter, Jan.* 17. 1643. 4*to. p.* 8.

New England's First Fruits; in respect, *first*, Of the Conversion of some, Conviction of divers, Preparation of sundry of the *Indians*; *secondly*, Of the progresse of Learning in the Colledge at *Cambridge* in *Massachuset's* Bay. With divers other special Matters relating to that Country. Published at the instant request of sundry Friends, who desire to be satisfied in those Points, by many *New-England* Men, who are here present, and were Eye or Eare-witnesses of the same. *London*, for *Henry Overton*. 1643, 4*to. p.* 46.

Church-Government and Church-Covenant discussed, in an Answer of the Elders of the several Churches in NEW ENGLAND, to two and thirty Questions sent over to them by divers Ministers in *England*, to declare their Judgments therein. Together with an Apologie of the said Elders in *New-England* for Church-Covenant, sent over in Answer to Master *Bernard*, in the Year 1639. As also in an Answer to nine Positions about Church-Government. And now published for the Satisfaction of all who desire Resolution in those Points. *London*, for *Benjamin Allen*. 1603. 4*to. p.* 46.

An Answer of the Elders of the several Churches in *New-England*, unto Nine Positions sent over to them by divers Reverend and Godly Ministers in *England*, to declare their Judgments therein. Written in the Year 1639. And now published for the Satisfaction of all who desire Resolution in those Points. *London*, for *Benjamin Allen*. 1643. 4*to. p.* 78.

1644.   A short Story of the Rise, Reign, and Ruine of the Antinomians, Fa-
20 *Car.* 1. milists, and Libertines that infected the Churches of *New-England*, and how they were confuted by the Assembly of Ministers there: As also of the Magistrates

giftrates proceedings in Court against them. Together with God's strange and remarkable Judgments from Heaven, upon some of the chief Fomenters of these Opinions; and the lamentable Death of Mr. Hutchison, a Vote ft for these Times; here being the same Errours amongst us, and acted by the same Spirit. Publifhed at the inftant Requeft of fundry, by One that was an Eye and Ear Witneffe of the Carriage of Matters there. *London*, Printed for *Ralph Smith*. 1644. 4to. *p*. 66.

A briefe Relation of fome Church Courfes, held in Opinion and Practife in the Churches lately erected in *New-England*. Collected out of fundry of their own printed Papers and Manuscripts, with other good Intelligence. Together with fome fhort Hints (given by the way) of their Correfpondence with the like Tenets and Practifes of the Separatifts Churches; and fome fhort Animadverfions upon fome principal Paffages for the benefit of the vulgar Reader. Prefented to publike View, for the good of the Church of God, by *W. R. London*, for *Edward Brewfter*. 4to. 1644. *p*. 55.

An Anfwer to *W. R.* his Narration of the Opinions and Practifes of the Churches, lately erected in *New-England*, vindicating thofe godly and Orthodoxal Churches from more than an hundred Imputations fathered on them and their Church way, by the faid *W. R.* in his Booke. By *Thomas Welde*, Paftor of the Church of *Roxborough* in *New-England*. *London*, for *H. Overton*. 1644. 4to. *p*. 68.

A modeft and brotherly Anfwer to Mr. *Charles Herle* his Book againft the Independency of Churches. Wherein his foure Arguments for the Government of Synods over particular Congregations are friendly Examined, and clearly Anfwered. Together with Chriftian and Loving Animadverfions upon fundry other obfervable Paffages in the faid Booke. All tending to declare the true ufe of Synods, and the Power of Congregational Churches in the Points of electing and ordaining their own Officers, and cenfuring their Offenders. By *Richard Mather*, Teacher of the Church at *Dorchefter*; and *William Thompfon*, Paftor of the Church at *Braintree* in *New-England*. Sent from thence after the Affembly of Elders were diffolved that laft met to debate Matters about Church-Government. *London*, Printed for *H. Overton*, 1644. 4to. *p*. 58.

The true Copy of a Letter written by Mr. *Thomas Parker*, a learned and godly Minifter in *New-England* unto a Member of the Affembly of Divines now at *Weftminfter*; declaring his Judgment touching the Government ufed in the Churches of *England*. *Imprimatur Ja. Cranford. London*, Printed by *Richard Cotes*, 1644. 4to. *p*. 4.

Z   The

The Keyes of the Kingdom of Heaven, and Power thereof, according to the Word of God, by that Learned and Judicious Divine Mr. John Cotton, Teacher of the Church at Boston in New-England, tending to reconcile some present Differences about Discipline. Published by Tho. Goodwin and Philip Nye. London, for Henry Overton, 1644. 4to. p. 59.

The Doctrine of the Church, to which is committed the Keyes of the Kingdome of Heaven. Wherein is demonstrated by way of Question and Answer, What a visible Church is, according to the Order of the Gospel; and what Officers, Members, Worship, and Government Christ hath ordained in the New Testament. By that Reverend and Learned Divine Mr. John Cotton, B. D. and Teacher of the Church at Boston in New-England. The 3d Edit. more exactly corrected, the Marginal Proofes in the former Edition misplaced, being herein placed more directly, &c. London, 1644. 4to. p. 14.

Mr. Cotton's Letter lately printed, examined and answered by Roger Williams of Providence in New-England. London, Imprinted in the Yeere 1644. 4to. p. 47.

The New Church-Way in New-England, and in Old: Wherein are handled these Questions following. 1. Whether a stinted Form of Prayer and set Liturgie be unlawfull, &c. By that learned and godly Minister of Christ John Ball of Whitmore. Penned a little before his Death, and sent over to the New England Ministers, Anno 1637, as a Reply to an Answer of theirs in Justification of the said Positions. Now published (by occasion mentioned in the Epistle to the Reader following) upon the desire of many faithfull and godly Ministers, in and about the Citie of London, who love and seek the Truth. By William Rathband and Simeon Ashe. London, for Thomas Underhill. 1644. 4to. p. 90.

An Ordinance of the Lords and Commons assembled in Parliament, for exempting from Custom and Imposition all Commodities exported for, or imported from NEW-ENGLAND, which has been very prosperous, and without any publick Charge to this State, and is likely to prove very happy for the Propagation of the Gospel in those Parts. Printed half Sheet.

A short Discoverie of the Coasts and Continent of America, from the Equinoctiall Northward, and of the adjacent Isles. By William Castell, Minister of the Gospell at Courtenhall in Northamptonshire. Whereunto is prefixed the Author's Petition to this present Parliament, for the Propagation of the Gospel in America, attested by many eminent English and Scottish Divines. And a late Ordinance of Parliament for that Purpose, and for the
better

better Government of the English Plantations there. Together with Sir *Benjamin Rudyer's* Speech in Parliament, 21*st January*, concerning *America*. *London*, Printed in the Year 1644. 4*to. p.* 54.

The Path-Way to Perfect Sailing; shewing briefly the six principal Points of NAVIGATION, written by *Mr. RICHARD POLTER*, one of the late principal Masters of the Navie Royall. And now published for the common Good of all Masters, Pilots, and other Sea-Men whatsoever. Whereunto is added A NATURAL DISCOURSE, necessary to be *NAVTICAL* knowen of all Sea Men, to prove the way of a Ship (upon the Superficies of the Sea) outward and homeward, to be both one, returning by the opposite Point of the Meridian Compasse. And also to prove the East and West, directed by the Meridian Compasse to lead in a Magnetical Parallel. First penned by *JOHN BASSET*, deceased, a Teacher of Navigation at *Chattam* in *Kent*. And now put forth to publike View, with some Addition by *Henry Bond*. *London*, Printed for *George Hurlock*. 1644. 4*to. p.* 58.

A Voyage to *Madagascar*, the Adjacent Islands, and Coast of *Africk*, By *Francis Cauche* of *Roan* : Setting out from *Diep* in *January* 1638. and returning thither on the 21*st* of *July* 1644. With an Account of the Religion, Customs and Manners of the People of *Madagascar*. As also of the Birds, Beasts, Fishes and Plants there, and in the neighbouring Islands. [Printed in *Stevens's* Collection of Voyages, 1711. 4*to. Vol. II.*]

An Account of ISELAND, opposite to *Greenland*, sent to Monsieur *de la Mothe le Vayer*, in a Letter from Monf. *Le Peyrere*, dated at *Copenbagen*, *Decemb.* 18. 1644. [Collect. of Voyages for Mr. *Churchill*, *Vol. II. p.* 440.]

Les Estats, Empires & Principautez du Monde representes par la Description des Pays, Moeurs des Habitans, Richesses des Provinces, les Forces, le Gouvernement, la Religion & les Princes qui ont gouverné chacun Estat, avec l' Origine de toutes les Religions, & de tous les Chevaliers & Ordres Militaires. Par le Sieur D T. V. Y. *Gentilhomme Ordinaire de la Chambre du Roy.* A Roven M. DC. XLIV. 4*to. p.* 1469 & 75. [*Ex Dono Rev.* Josephi Sparke *Petriburgensi.*]

Questions propos'd to the Holy Congregation, *De Propagandâ Fide*, by the Missioners of *China*. With the Answers to them, given by the Fathers Qualificators of the said Inquisition, approved by Decree of the said Holy Congregation, held the 12th of *September*, 1645. Printed at *Rome* in the Printing-House of the Holy Congregation, *de Propagandâ Fide*, 1645. *Permissu*

1645.
21 *Car.* 1.

missu Superiorum. [Reprinted in the Collection of Voyages for Mr. Churchill, Vol. I. p. 374.]

The Covenant of God's Free Grace most sweetly unfolded, &c. By that Reverend and Faithfull Minister of God's Word, Mr. JOHN COTTON, Teacher of the Church at *Boston* in *New England.* Whereunto is added a Profession of Faith, made by the Reverend Divine Mr. *John Davenport* in *New-England,* at his Admission into one of the Churches there. *London,* Printed for *Matthew Simmons.* 1645. 4to. p. 40.

A fresh Discovery of some prodigious new wandring Blazing-Stars, and Fire-Brands, stiling themselves New-Lights; firing our Church and State into new Combustions, &c. Wherein some *Letters* and *Papers* lately sent from the *Summer Islands* are subjoined, relating the *Schismatical, Illegal, Tyrannical* Proceedings of some *Independents* there, in gathering their new Churches, to the great Distraction and Prejudice of that *Plantation.* Published for the common Good. By *William Prynne* of *Lincoln's-Inne,* Esquire. *London,* Printed by *John Macock* for *Michael Sparke,* &c. 1645. 4to. p. 48. & 28.

Truth gloriously appearing from under the sad and sable Cloud of Obloquie: Or a Vindication of the Practise of the Church of Christ in the *Summer Islands,* in an Apologetical Answer unto some Letters and Papers lately sent from the *Summer Islands,* by *Richard Beake* and Mr. *Norwood,* lately published by Master *Prynne,* in his *Fresh Discourie of some prodigious New wandring Blazing-Stars,* 4to. 1645, &c. For Satisfaction concerning the Model of that Church-way, at this time much controverted, touching the way of Worship, very commonly misunderstood, very falsly interpreted, but very truly called *Independent.* Published not for Offence but Defence, by *Nath. White,* Batchelor of Divinity and Pastor of the Church of Christ at *Summer Islands.* To which is added a Postscript, as an Antidote against the Poison of ill-affected Persons, that have publickly here reproached the Church of Christ there. *London,* for G. *Calvert,* 1645. 4to. p. 168.

The History of the Provinces of *Paraguay Incumiore, Rio de la Plata, Parana, Guaira,* and *Uraica,* and something of the Kingdom of *Chili* in *South America.* Written in *Latin* by F. *Nicholas del Techo,* Priest of the Society of *Jesus.* [The *English* Translation publisht in the Collect. of Voyages printed for Mr. *Churchill,* 1704. Fol. Vol. IV. p. 681.]

The Way of the Churches of Christ in N Hengland, or the Way of Churches walking in brotherly Equalitie, or Co-ordination, without Subjection

jection of one Church to another. Measured and Examined by the Golden Reed of the Sanctuary. Containing a full Declaration of the Church-way in all Particulars. By Mr. *J. Cotton*, Teacher of the Church at *Boston* in *New England*. Published according to Order. *London, Printed by Matthew Simmons*, 1645. 4*to. p.* 116.

Vindiciæ Clavium; Or a Vindication of the Keyes of the Kingdom of Heaven into the Hands of the right Owners. Being some Animadversions upon a Tract of Mr. *J. C.* [*viz. J. Cotton*,] called *The Keys of the Kingdom of Heaven.* Printed 1644. As also upon another Tract of his called *The Way of the Churches of New England.* Manifesting 1. The Weakness of his Proofes. 2. The Contradictions to himselfe and others. 3. The middle Way (so called) of Independents, to be the Extreme or By-way of the *Brownists.* By an earnest Well-wisher to the Truth. *London,* Printed for *Peter Whaley*, 1645. 4*to. p.* 90.

A brief Narrative of the Practises of the Churches in *New England.* Written in private to one that desired Information therein; by an Inhabitant there, a Friend to Truth and Peace. Published according to Order. *London,* for *John Rothwell*, 1645. 4*to.*

A Reply to a Confutation of some Grounds for Infant's Baptisme : As also concerning the Form of a Church put forth against me by one *Thomas Lamb.* Hereunto is added a Discourse of the Verity and Validity of Infants Baptisme, &c. By *George Philips* of *Watertown* in *New-England. London,* Printed by *Matthew Simmons*, 4*to.* 1645. *p.* 154.

A full Account of the Warrs in *Brasil*, between the *Portugueses* and the *Dutch*, with the several Letters and Declarations thereupon, in the Year 1645. [In the Collect. of Voyages, printed for Mr. *Churchill.* Fol. Vol. II. *p.* 80, &c.]

An Account of the Voyage of *Feodor Iskowitz Backhoff*, the *Muscovite* Envoy into *China*, describing the Way from *Moskow* to *Peking*, in the Year 1645. [Collect. of Voyages for Mr. *Churchill*, Vol. II. *p.* 547.]

The Controversie concerning Liberty of Conscience, in Matters of Religion, truly stated, and distinctly and plainly handled, by Mr. *John Cotton* of *Boston* in *New England.* By way of Answer to some Arguments to the contrary sent unto him, &c. *London,* Printed for *Thomas Bankes*, 1646. 4*to. p.* 14.

1646. 22 *Car.* 1.

To the Parliament of the Common-wealth of *England*; A Declaration of the Sufferings of feveral of the People of God, (our Friends and Brethren, who work out their Salvation in Fear and Trembling) in *New England*, and amongft the *Dutch* inhabiting in that Land, the Sum of which Sufferings are as followeth, the moft part of which Sufferings have been fuftained in twelve Months, 1646. 4to. p. 18.

An Account of *Greenland* to Monfieur de *la Mothe le Vayer*, in a Letter from Monf. *La Peyrere* dated from the *Hague*, *Jan.* 18. 1646. [Collection of Voyages, for Mr. *Churchill*, *Vol. II. p.* 449.]

1647. Singing of Pfalms, a Gofpel Ordinance, or a Treatife wherein are handled
23 *Car.* 1. thefe four Particulars. 1. Touching the Duty itfelf. 2. Touching the Matter to be Sung. 3. Touching the Singers. 4. Touching the manner of Singing. By *John Cotton*, Teacher of the Church at *Bofton* in *New-England*. *London*, Printed by *M. S.* [*viz. Matthew Simmons*] for *Hannah Allen* and *John Rothwell*, 1647. 4to. p. 72.

The Grounds and Ends of the Baptifme of the Children of the Faithfull, opened in a familiar Difcourfe by way of a Dialogue, or Brotherly Conference. By the Learned and Faithful Minifter of Chrift, *John Cotton*, Teacher of the Church of *Bofton* in *New England*. With a fhort Preface by *Thomas Goodwin*. *London*, Printed by *R. C.* for *And. Crooks*, 1647. 4to. p. 196.

The Bloudy Tenent wafhed and made White in the Bloud of the Lamb: Being difcuffed and difcharged of Bloud Guiltynefs by juft Defence. Wherein the great Queftions of this prefent time are handled, *viz.* How farre Liberty of Confcience ought to be given to thofe that truly feare God? And how farre reftrained to turbulent and peftilent Perfons, &c. Whereunto is added a Reply to Mr. *William's* Anfwer to Mr. *Cotton's* Letter. By *John Cotton*, Batchelour in Divinity, and Teacher of the Church of Chrift at *Bofton* in *New England*. *London*, Printed by *Matthew Simmons*, 1647. 4to. p. 144, & 195.

New England's Jonas caft up at *London*; Or a Relation of the Proceedings of the Court at *Bofton* in *New England*, againft divers honeft and godly Perfons, for petitioning for Government in the Commonwealth, according to the Laws of *England*, &c. Together with a Confutation of fome Reports of a fained Miracle upon the forefaid Petitions, being thrown over-board at Sea; As alfo a brief Anfwer to fome Paffages in a late Book (entituled *Hypocrify Unmask'd*.) Set out by Mr. *Winflowe*, concerning the Independent

Churches

Churches holding Communion with the Reformed Churches. By Major John Child. London, 1647. 4to. p. 15.

The Simple Cobler of *Aggawam* in *America*, willing to help mende his native Countrey, lamentably tattered, both in the Upper-leather and Sole, with all the honest Stiches he can take, and as willing never to be paid for his Work, by old *English* pay, &c. By *Theodore de la Guarde*. 1647. 4to. p. 18.

The Day-Breaking, if not the Sun-Rising of the Gospel with the *Indians* in *New England*. London, for *Fulk Clifton*, 1647. 4to. p. 25.

The Temple measured; Or a brief Survey of the Temple Mystical, which is instituted in the Church of Christ. Wherein are solidly and modestly discussed most of the material Questions, touching the Constitution and Government of the visibleChurch-Militant here on Earth, &c. By *James Noyes*, Teacher of the Church of *Newbery* in *New England*. London, 4to. 1647. p. 95.

INSTITUTIO ASTRONOMICA *juxta Hypotheses tam veterum quam Copernici & Tychonis. Dictata à* PETRO GASSENDO *Regio Matheseos Professore. Ejusdem Oratio Inauguralis, iterató edita. Parisijs apud Ludovicum de Heuqueville.* M.DC.XLVII. *Cum Privilegio,* 4to. p. 251. [*Ex Dono Reverendi Viri* Josephi Sparke *Petriburgensis.*]

The Merchant's Remonstrance, published in the time of the late Warre, Revived and Enlarged. Wherein is set forth the inevitable Miseries which may suddenly befall this Kingdom by want of Trade and Decay of Manufactures. With a Copy of a Letter to the King's Majestie, presented unto him at *Hampton-Court*, *Octob.* 30, 1647, &c. Whereunto is annexed *A Discourse of the Excellency of Wool*, manifested by the Improvement in its Manufactures, and the great Good thence arising before the late Warre. By *JOHN BATTIE* of *London*, Merchant. Published by Authority. *London*, Printed for *William Hope*, 1648. 4to. p. 38.

The *English American* his Travail by Sea and Land: Or a new Survey of the *West-Indies*, containing a Journall of three thousand and three hundred Miles within the main Land of *America*. Wherein is set forth his Voyage from *Spain* to St. *John de Ulhua*, and from thence to *Xalappa* to *Flaxcalla*, the City of *Angeles*, and forward to *Mexico*; With a Description of that great City, as it was in former times, and also at this present. Likewise his journey from *Mexico* through the Provinces of *Guaxaca*, *Chiapa*, *Guatemala*, *Vera Paz*, *Truxillo Comayagua*; with his abode twelve Yeares about *Guatemala*, and especially in the *Indian* Towns of *Mexico*, *Pinola*, *Petapa*, *Amatitlan*. As also his strange and wonderful Conversion and Calling from those remote

Parts

Parts to his Native Countrey. With his Return through the Province of
Nicaragua and Costa Rica, to Nicoya, Panama, Porto Belo, Cartagena, and Havana; with divers Occurrents and Dangers, that did befal him in the said
Journey. Also a new and exact Discovery of the Spanish Navigation to those
Parts; And of their Dominions, Government, Religion, Forts, Castles,
Ports, Havens, Commodities, Factions, Behaviour of Spaniards, Priests and
Friers, Blackmores, Mulattoes, Mestisoes, Indians, and of their Feasts and
Solemnities. With a Grammar, or some few Rudiments, of the Indian
Tongue, called Pochonci, or Pocoman. By the true and painful Endeavours
of Thomas Gage, now Preacher of the Word of God at Acris in the County of
Kent. Ann. Dom. 1648. London; Printed by R. Cotes, &c. 1648. Fol. p. 220.

Certain select Cases resolved, specially tending to the right ordering of
the Heart, that we may comfortably walke with God in our general and
particular Callings, sent over from New-England, in a Letter to a precious
Friend here. By Thomas Shepheard, sometimes of Emanuel College in Cambridge, now Preacher of God's Word in New-England. With a Preface by
William Adderley. Dated from the Charter-house in London, Feb. 1. 1647. As
also another Tract, entituled, The first Principles of the Oracles of God.
Collected by Thomas Shepheard, &c. London, Printed by M. Simmons for
John Rothwell, 1648. 12°. p. 247.

The Way of Congregational Churches cleared in two Treatises. In the former from the Historical Aspersions of Mr. Robert Baylie, in his Book called,
A Dissuasive from the Errors of the Time. In the latter from some Contradictions
of Vindiciæ Clavium. And from some Misconstructions of Learned Mr. Rutherford, in his Book intituled, The due Right of Presbyteries. By Mr. John
Cotton, sometime Preacher at Boston in Lincolnshire, and now Teacher of the
Church at Boston in New England. To which is prefixed an Epistle Pacificatory to the Brethren dissenting from this Way, by Nathaniel Homes. Imprimatur, John Bachiler, January 1. 1647. London, Printed by Matthew
Simmons, for John Bellamie, 4to. 1648.

1641.
24 Car. 1.
The clear Sunshine of the Gospel breaking forth upon the Indians in New
England: Or an Historical Narration of God's Wonderful Workings upon
sundry of the Indians, both chief Governors and common People, in bringing them to a willing and desired Submission to the Ordinances of the Gospel
and framing their Hearts to an easie inquirie after the Knowledge of God
the Father, and of Jesus Christ the Saviour of the Worlde. By Mr. Thomas
Shephard, Minister of the Gospel of Jesus Christ at Cambridge in New England.
London, for John Bellamy, 1648. 4to. p. 38.

The

The Glorious Progress of the Gospel amongst the Indians in New-England Manifested by three Letters, under the hand of that famous Instrument of the Lord, Mr. *John Eliot*: And another from Mr. *Thomas Mayhew* jun. both Preachers of the word as well to the *English* as *Indians* in *New England*. Wherein the Riches of God's Grace in the effectual calling of many of them is cleared up: As also a Manifestation of the hungring desire of many People in sundry parts of that Country, after the most full Revelation of *Jesus Christ*, to the exceeding confolation of every Christian Reader; together with an Appendix to the foregoing Letters; holding forth Conjectures, Observations, and Applications. By *J. D.* Minister of the Gospel. Published by *Edward Winslow*. *London*, Printed for *Hannah Allen*, 1649. 4to, p. 28.

A Plat-Form of Church Discipline gathered out of the word of God, and Agreed upon by the Elders and Messengers of the Churches Assembled in the Synod at *Cambridge* in *New-England*, to be Presented to the Churches and General Court for their Consideration and Acceptance in the Lord, the Eighth Moneth. *Anno* 1645. Printed by *S. G.* at *Cambridge* in *New-England*, 1649. 4to. p. 29.

The Controversie concerning Liberty of Conscience in Matters of Religion truly Stated, and distinctly Handled. By Mr. *John Cotton* of *Boston* in *New-England*. By way of Answer to some Arguments to the contrary sent unto him. Wherein you have, against all Cavils of turbulent Spirits, clearly manifested; wherein Liberty of Conscience in Matters of Religion ought to be permitted, and in what Cases it ought not; by the said Mr. *Cotton*. *London*, Printed for *Thomas Banks*, 1649. 4to. p. 24.

An Act for the Promoting and Propagating the Gospel of Jesus Christ in *New-England*, by Erecting a Corporation in *England*, consisting of Sixteen Persons, viz. a President, Treasurer, and fourteen Assistants, to be called by the Name of the *President and Society for Propagation of the Gospel in New-England*; and that a General Collection be made for the Purpose aforesaid, throughout *England* and *Wales*. Ordered to be published, *Die Veneris*, 27 *Jul.* 1649. *Lond.* Printed for *Edward Husband*, Feb. half sheet.

VIRGINIA impartially Examined, and left to publick View, to be considered by all Judicious and Honest Men. Under which Title is comprehended the Degrees from 34 to 39, wherein like the rich and healthful Countries of *Roanock*, the now Plantations of *Virginia* and *Maryland* — being the Adventurer's or Planter's faithful Steward, disposing the Adventure for the best Advantage; advising People of all degrees, from the highest Ma-

ster,

ther, as the meanest Servant, how suddenly to raise their Fortunes. By William Bullock Gent. Imprimatur, 29 Sept. 1649. London, Printed by John Hammond. 1649. 4to. p. 66.

A Voyage to the Kingdom of *Chili* in *America*, Performed by Mr. *Henry Brower*, and Mr. *Elias Herckman* in the Year 1642, and 1643. with a Description of the Isles of *Formosa* and *Japan*. Translated from the High-Dutch Original, Printed at *Frankford* upon the *Maine*, 1649. [Inserted in the 1st Vol. of Collect. of Voyages, Printed by Mr. *Churchill*, Fol. p. 505.]

An Historical Relation of the Kingdom of *CHILE*, by *Alonso de Ovalle* of the *Company of Jesus*: A Native of *St. Jago of Chile*, and *Procurator* at *Rome* for that Place. Printed at *Rome* by *Francisco Cavallo*, 1649. with Licence of his Superiors. Translated out of *Spanish* into *English*. [in Collect. of Voyages by Mr. *Churchill*, 1704. Fol. Vol. III. p. 1.]

Voyages and Travels into *Brasil* and the *East-Indies*; containing an exact Description of the *Dutch Brasil*; with an Account of all Passages that happened in it during the Author's stay, especially in relation to the Revolt of the *Portugueses*, and the War there; from 1640, to 1649. By Mr. *John Nieuhoff*, Translated from the *Dutch*. [Collect. of Voyages, Printed by Mr. *Churchill*. Fol. Vol. 13. p. 17.]

A Transcript of several Letters, Secret Orders, and express Covenants and Treaties between the Dutch Factory at *Suratte* in the *East-Indies*, and the Great *Mogul*, in the Year 1649. [In Collect. of Voyages by Mr. *Churchil*. Fol. Vol. III. p. 568. &c.]

The Merchants and Mariners Preservation, and Thanksgiving: or Thankfulness returned for Mercies received. Set forth in a Sermon of Thanksgiving, Preached at St. *Andrews Undershaft*, Sept. 6. 1649. to the R. Worshipful Committee of Merchants Trading for *Eastern India*, upon a late Return of seven of their Ships together. By *EDWARD TERRY* Minister of the Word, (who was sometime in their Service there) now Rector of the Church at *Great Greenford* in the County of *Middlesex*. *London*, Printed by *Thomas Harper*, 1649. 4to.

Compendium Geographicum succinctâ methodo adornatum. Opera & Studio Abrah. Golnitz. Amstelodami *Apud* Ludovicum Elzevirium. 1649. 12°. p. 278.

Georgii

Georgii Fournier è Societate Jesu, Geographica Orbis Notitia per Litorae & Ripas Fluviorum. Parisiis apud Jo. Henault, &c. 1649. 12°. p. 651.

Descriptio Regni Japoniæ cum quibusdam affinis materia, ex varijs auctoribus collecta & in ordinem redacta per Berphardum Varenium Med. D. Amstelodami apud Lud. Elzevirium. Anno 1649. 12°. p. 267.

Descriptio Regni Siam, per Jodocum Schoutenium è Belgico Sermone translata in Latinum per B. Varenium. ibid.

Tractatus, in quo agitur De Japoniorum religione; De Christiana religionis introductione in ea loca; De ejusdem extirpatione. Adjuncta est de diversa diversarum gentium totius telluris Religione brevis informatio Auctore Bernhardo Varenio, Med. D. Amstelodami, apud Lud. Elzevirium; 1649, 12°. p. 320.

Jodoci Sinceri Itinerarium Galliæ, ita accommodatum, ut ejus ductu Mediocri Tempore tota Gallia obiri, Angliæ & Belgium adiri possint: nec bis terve ad eadem loca rediri oporteat: notatis cujuscunque loci, quas vocant, delicijs; Cum Appendice de Burdigala: ac Iconibus Urbium præcipuarum illustratum. Amstelodami apud Jodocum Janssonium. 1649. 12°. p. 340.

The Copy of a Letter written by Mr. *Thomas Parker* Pastor of the Church of *Newbury* in *New-England*, to his Sister Mrs. *Elizabeth Avery*, sometimes of *Newbury* in the County of *Berks*, touching sundry Opinions by her Professed and Maintained. *Imprimatur Nov. 22. 1649. John Downame.* London, Printed by *John Field.* 1650. 4to. p. 20.

Of the Holiness of Church Members. By *John Cotton* Teacher of the Church of Christ in *Boston* in *New-England*. London, Printed for *Hannah Allen.* 1650. 4to. p. 95.

An Act for charging of *Tobacco* brought from *New-England* with Custom and Excise. *Die Jovis 20 Junii.* 1650. Printed half sheet.

An Act for the Advancing and Regulating the *Trade* of this Commonwealth. *Die Jovis 1° Aug* 1650. Fol. 2 sheets.

An Act Prohibiting *Trade* with the *Barbada's, Virginia, Bermudas,* and *Antego.* Ordered to be Printed, and Published *die Jovis.* 3 Octob. 1650. Fol. a half sheet.

An

An Account of the most dangerous Voyage Performed by the famous Captain John Monck, in the Years 1619, and 1620. by the special Command of *Christian* IV. King of *Denmark*, to *Hudson's Straits*, in order to discover a Passage on that side betwixt *Groenland* and *America* to the *West-Indies*. With a Description of the Old and New *Groenland*: Translated from the *High Dutch* Original; Printed at *Frankford* upon the *Maine*, 1650. [In Collect. of Voyages Printed by Mr. *Churchill*. 1704. *Vol.* I *Fol. p.* 545.]

Singing of Psalms a Gospel Ordinance; or a Treatise wherein are handled these Particulars. 1. Touching the Duty it self. 2. Touching the Matter to be Sung. 3. Touching the Singers. 4. Touching the manner of Singing. By *John Cotton* Teacher of the Church at *Boston* in *New-England*. *London*, Printed for *J. R.* 1650. 4to. *p.* 72.

1652
3 *Car.* 2.   A brief Discourse touching *New-England*, and particularly *Rode-Island*, with many Providential Occurrences in them. As also a Faithful and True Relation of the Prosecution of *Obadiah Holmes*, *John Cradnall*, and *John Clark*, meerly for Conscience toward God, by the Principal Members of the Church or Commonwealth of the *Massachusets* in *New-England*, which Rules over that part of the World; wherein is shewed their discourteous Entertainment of Strangers, &c. in the Year 1651. [Printed at large in The Narrative of *New-Englands* Persecution, 1652. 4to.]

The Light appearing more and more towards the perfect day. Or a Farther Discovery of the present State of the *Indians* in *New-England*, concerning the Progress of the Gospel amongst them. Manifested by Letters from such as Preach'd to them there. Published by *Henry Whitfield*, late Pastor to the Church of Christ in *New-England*, who came lately thence. *London*, Printed for *John Bartlet*, 1651. 4to. *p.* 46.

A Short Collection of the most Remarkable Passages from the Original to the dissolution of the *VIRGINIA COMPANY*. *London*, for *Edward Husband*. 1651. 4to. *p.* 20.

The Original Articles Agreed on this xxiiith day of *May*, 1651, by and between Admiral *Blake*, and Colonel *Clerke*, Commanders in Chief of all the Forces by Sea or Land, in or about the Islands of *Friscoe* and *Briar*, of the one part, and Sir *John Greenvile* Kt. Governour of the Islands of St. *Marys* and *Agnes* in *Scilley* on the behalf of his Majesty on the other part; touching the rendition of the said Islands of *St. Marys* and *Agnes*; together with all the Castles, Forts, Fortresses, Sconces and Fortifications unto them belonging,

belonging to the use and behoof of the *Parliament* of *England*, 1651.
2 sheets Fol. *Manuscript.*

A Description of the New World, or *America*; Islands and Continent;
and by what People those Regions are now Inhabited: And what Places are
there desolate, and without Inhabitants; and the Bays, Rivers, Capes,
Forts, Cities, and their Latitudes, the Seas on their Coasts; the Trade
Winds, the *North-West-Passage*, and the Commerce of the English Nation,
as they were all in the Year 1649. Faithfully described for information
of such of his Country as desire Intelligence of these Particulars. By *George*
Gardyner of *Peckham* in the County of *Surrey* Esq; *London*, for *Robert Ley-*
bourn. 1651. 8vo. p. 186.

Dissertationum Marinarum Decas. In quâ Præter Marina Problemata,
varia passim fundamentalia, & solidioris Philosophiæ Principiis deducta
Dogmata discutiuntur. Autore NICOLAO ab AMAMA, Cum
Indice Capitum & Articulorum. *Franekeræ* Excudit *Idzardus Alberti.* 1651.
8vo. p. 596.

GEORGI HORNII De Originibus Americanis Libri quatuor. 1652.
Hagæ Comitis. Sumptibus *Adriani Ulacq.* CIƆICCLII. 8vo. p. 282. Typis 4 *Car.* 2.
Philippi de Croy Arnhemo-Geldri, 1652. [Ex dono Rev. JOANNIS
Episcopi ELIENSIS.]

Dominium Maris, or the Dominion of the Sea; expressing the Title
which the *Venetians* pretend unto the sole Dominion and absolute Sovereignty of the *Adriatick Sea*, commonly called the *Gulph of Venice*; manifested in a *Pleading* or *Argument* betwixt the Republick of *Venice*, and the
Emperor *Ferdinand*. Whereby is sufficiently proved, that *the Sea as well as*
the Land is liable to the Laws of Property, and may be brought under the
Jurisdiction and Protection of particular Princes and States, contrary to the
Assertion of those who affirm the Sea to be free, and under the Dominion
of no Man. Translated out of Italian from the publick Registers of *Venice*,
and publish'd with a Preface by CLAREAMONTOS [viz. Thomas
Chaloner] *London*, Printed by *William Duguard*. 1652. 4to. p. 22.

A Declaration of the *Parliament* of the *Commonwealth of England*, Rela-
ting to the Affairs and Proceedings between this *Commonwealth*, and the
States General of the *United Provinces* of the *Low Countries*, and the present
Differences occasioned on the S.T.A.T.E.S Part. And the Answer of the
Parliament to three Papers from the Ambassadors Extraordinary of the

States General, upon occasion of the late Fight between the Fleets. Wkh a Narrative of the late Engagement between the English and Holland FLEET. As also a Collection of the Proceedings in the Treaty between the *States General* of the *United Provinces*, and the *Parliament* of the *Common-wealth* of *England*. *London*, Printed by *John Field* Printer to the Parliament of *England*, 1652. 4*to*. p. 70.

A *Declaration* or *Manifest* of the High and Mighty Lords the *States General* of the *United Netherland Provinces*. Comprehending a true Relation of their sincere Intention, and lawful Proceedings in the Treaty with the Extraordinary Embassadors and the Commissioners of the present *Government* of *England*, so as the same hath been held here in the *Hague*, as also at *London*. At *Amsterdam*. Translated out of the Original Copy. 1652. 4*to*.

The PSALMES Hymns and Spiritual Songs of the *Old* and *New* Testament, faithfully Translated into *English* Metre. For the Use, Edification and Comfort of the Saints in Publick and Private, especially in *NEW-ENGLAND*. With a Preface concerning the Duty of Singing Psalms. *London*, for *John Blague*, &c. 1652. 12°.

Strength out of Weakness; or a glorious Manifestation of the farther Progress of the Gospel among the *Indians* in *New-England*. Held forth in sundry Letters from divers Ministers and others to the *Corporation* established by Parliament for promoting the Gospel among the Heathen in *New-England*; and to particular Members thereof since the last Treatise to that effect, Published by *Mr. Henry Whitfield* late Pastor of *Gilford* in *New-England*. *London*, for *John Blague*. 1652. 4*to*.

The *Fourth* Paper presented by *Major Butler* to the Honourable *Committee* of Parliament, for the Propagating the Gospel of Jesus Christ. Which Paper was humbly owned, and was, and is attended to be made good, by *Major Butler*, *Mr. Charles Vane*, *Col. Danvers*, *Mr. Jackson*, *Mr. Wall*, and *Mr. Turner*. Also a Letter from Mr. *Goad* to Major *Butler* upon occasion of the said Paper and Proposals. Together with a Testimony to the said *fourth* Paper by way of Explanation upon the four Proposals of it. By *R. W.* Unto which is subjoyned the *Fifteen Proposals* of the Ministers. *London*, for *Giles Calvert*, 1652. 4*to*. p. 23.

Several Queries now Published, and Propounded to be considered of by All, especially of those which assume a Power of Propagating the Gospel, &c. *London*, Printed for the publick Good. 1652. 4*to*. p. 20.

An

An Act Prohibiting the Planting of *Tobacco* in *England*, to the prejudice and hindrance of the *English* Plantations. Ordered to be Printed and Published, 1 *April.* 1652. half Sheet. by *John Field*, Printer to the Parliament.

The Bloody Tenent yet more Bloody, by *Mr. Cotton*'s endeavour to wash it white in the Blood of the Lamb; of whose precious Blood spilt in the Blood of his Servants, and of the Blood of Millions spilt in for-former and later Wars for Conscience-sake, that most bloody Tenent of PERSECUTION, for cause of Conscience, upon a second tryal, is found now more apparently and more notoriously guilty, &c. Also as a Testimony to Mr. *Clarke*'s Narrative is added a Letter to Mr. *Endicot*, Governour of the *Massachusets* in *NewEngland*. By *R. Williams* of *Providence* in *New-England. London*, for *Giles Calvert*. 1652. 4to. *p.* 320.

Ill News from *NEW-ENGLAND*; or a Narrative of *New-England*'s Persecution. Wherein is declared that while *Old England* is becoming *New*, *New-England* is become *Old*. Also four Proposals to the Honoured Parliament and Council of State, touching the way to *propagate the Gospel of Christ*, (with small Charge and great Safety) both in *Old England* and *New*. Also four Conclusions touching the Faith and Order of the Gospel of Christ out of his last Will and Testament, confirmed and justified. By *JOHN CLARK*, Physitian of *Rode-Island* in *America. London*, Printed by *Henry Hills*, &c. 1652. 4to. *p.* 76. [*Ex dono Reverendi viri* Gershomi Rawlins.]

The Civil Magistrates Power in Matters of Religion modestly debated, impartially stated according to the Bounds and Grounds of Scripture; and an Answer return'd to those Objections against the same, which seem to have any Weight in them. Together with a brief Answer to a certain slanderous Pamphlet, call'd *Ill News from New-England*; or a Narrative of *New-England*'s Persecution, by *John Clark* of *Road-Island*, Physitian. By *Thomas Cobbet*, Teacher of the Church of *Lynne* in *New-England. London*, Printed for *Philemon Stephens*, 1653. 4to. *p.* 108. 52.

*1653.
5 Car. 2.*

A Plat-Form of Church-Discipline: Gathered out of the Word of God, and agreed upon by the Elders and Messengers of the Churches assembled in the Synod at *Cambridge* in *New-England*: To be presented to the Churches and General Court for their Consideration and Acceptance in the Lord. Reprinted in *London* for *Peter Cole*, 1653. 4to. *p.* 29.

A

A Treatife of *Liturgies, Power of the Keys*, and of *Matter of the vifible Church*. In Anfwer to the Reverend Servant of Chrift, Mr. *John Balk*. By *Thomas Shephard*, fometimes Fellow of *Emanuel Colledge* in *Cambridge*, and late Paftour of *Cambridge* in *New-England*. *London*, Printed for *Andrew Crook*, &c. 1653. 4to. f. 211.

The remarkable Voyages and Travels of Mr. *John Nieuhoff*, a *Dutch* Man, in the *Eaft Indies*, defcribing *Amboyna*, the *Molucco* Iflands, *Formofa*, *Batavia*, the *Indian* Coaft, &c. in the Year 1653. [Collection of Voyages Printed for Mr. *Churchill*. Fol. Vol. II. p. 1181.]

Tears of Repentance : Or a further Narrative of the Progrefs of the Gofpel amongft the *Indians* in *New-England*: Setting forth not only their prefent State and Condition, but fundry Confeffions of Sin, by diverfe of the faid *Indians*, wrought upon by the faving Power of the Gofpel ; together with the Manifeftation of their Faith, and Hope in *Jefus Chrift*, and the Work of Grace upon their Hearts. Related by Mr. *Eliot* and Mr. *Mayhew*, two faithful Labourers in that Work of the Lord. Publifhed by the Corporation for propagating the Gofpel there, for the Satisfaction and Comfort of fuch as wifh well thereunto. *London*, Printed by *Peter Cole*, 1653. 4to. p. 47.

England's Command on the SEAS; or *the Englifh* Seas guarded. Wherein is proved, that as the *Venetians, Portugals, Spaniards, French, Danes, Polands, Turks*, the Duke of *Tufcany*, and the Popes of *Rome*, have Domion on their *Seas* ; fo the Common-wealth of *England* hath on our *Seas*. Wherein the *Dutch* unjuft Procuration and Profecution of War againft *England* is alfo defcribed. *London*, Printed for *Jof. Blaik Cock*, &c. 1653. 12°. p. 106. Dedicated to the Right Honourable the Council of State, by *Donald Lupton*.

A true Relation of the late great Sea Fight, as it was fent in a Letter to his Excellency the Lord General *Cromwell*, from Gen. *Blake* and Gen. *Monck*. [Dated from on Board the *Refolution* at Sea off of *Oftend*, North Eaft, *July* 4. 1653.] Wherein is a Lift of what *Dutch* Ships were taken and funk, with the Number of Prifoners likewife, the number of what Men were flain and wounded on our fide. *London*, Printed for *Henry Hills*, and fold by him and *Tho. Brewfter*, 1653. 4to. p. 6.

Joannis Seldeni *Vindiciæ feeundum integritatem Exiftimationis fuæ per Convitium de Scriptione* Maris Claufi *Petulantiffimum, Mendaciffimumq; infolentius Læfæ in Vindicijs.*—Maris Liberi *adverfus*, Petrum Baptiftam Burgum *Liguftici Maritimi*

Maritimi Dominij assertorem Hagæ Comitum *jam nunc emissis.* Londini 1653. *ap.* Cornelium Bee, *4to. p.* 64. *Dat. ex Ædibus Londini* Carmeliticis. *Cal. Maij. Juliani* 1653.

Tho. Campanella *de Monarchia* Hispanicâ, *Edit. novissima aucta & emendata ut præfatio ad Lectorem indicat.* Amsterodami *ap.* Ludovic. Elzevir 1653. 24°. *p.* 376.

A brief Exposition, with Practical Observations upon the whole Book of *Ecclesiastes,* by that late pious and worthy Divine Mr. *John Cotton,* Pastor of *Boston* in *New England.* Published by *Anthony Tuckney,* D. D. Master of St. *John's College* in *Cambridge,* [formerly Fellow-Pastor with Mr. *Cotton* at *Boston* in *Lincolnshire.*] *London,* for *Ralph Smith,* 1654. 8vo. *p.* 277.

1654. 6 Car. 2.

A History of *New-England,* from the *English* Planting in the Yeere 1628. untill the Yeere 1652. Declaring the Form of their Government, Civil, Military, and Ecclesiastique. Their Wars with the *Indians,* their Troubles with the *Gortonists,* and other Heretiques. Their manner of gathering Churches; the Commodities of the Country, and Description of the principal Towns and Havens, with the great Encouragements to increase Trade betwixt them and *Old England.* With the Names of all their Governours, Magistrates, and eminent Ministers. *London,* Printed for *Nath. Brooke,* 1654. 4to. *p.* 236. [*Ex dono Reverendi* ——— *Thomas.*

A Discourse touching the *Spanish* Monarchy: Wherein we have a Political Glasse, representing each particular Country, Province, Kingdome, and Empire of the World; with Wayes of Government by which they may be kept in Obedience. As also the Causes of the Rise and Fall of each Kingdom and Empire. Written by *Tho. Campanelia.* Newly translated into *English* according to the third Edition of this Book in *Latine. London,* for *Philemon Stephens,* 1654. 4to. *p.* 232, [the latter Part treating of the *Spanish* Dominions in the *New-World,* and recommending it as necessary. First to institute some certain Order of *Preachers of the New World,* to be expresly known by that Name.———and that there ought to be strong Castles and Block-Houses erected upon all Havens and Mouths of Rivers, least the *English* breaking into these Parts, should bring in Heresy.]

Articles of *Peace* made between this *Common-wealth* of England, and that of the *United Provinces* of the *Netherlands,* with a Proclamation of it by his Highness the *Lord Protector.* Given at *Whitehall* 26. April, 1654. 4to. The same translated from the *Dutch,* and published at *London* May 2. 1654. 4to. *p.* 17.

Articles of Peace, Union and Confederation, concluded and agreed between his Highness *Oliver*, Lord Protector of the Common-wealth of *England*, *Scotland*, and *Ireland*, and the Dominions thereto belonging, and the Lords the *States General* of the *United Provinces* of the *Netherlands*, in a Treaty at *Westminster*, bearing Date the 5th of *April*, Old Style, in the Year of our Lord God 1654. Printed and published by his Highness special Command. *London*, by *William Du-Gard* and *Henry Hills*. Fol.

Articles of Peace, Friendship and Entercourse, concluded and agreed between the *Protector* and *Common-wealth* of *England*, and the Queen and Kingdom of *Sweden* ; with reference had to a peculiar Treaty, or Contract, for what concerns Commerce to be exercised in *America*. Date May 19. 1654.

1655.
7 *Car.* 2.   The Substance of divers Letters from the Generals and Commissioners in the *West-Indies* to his Highness, bearing Date *Aug.* 8. 1655. 4to. *Ib.*

AMERICA; Or an exact Description of the *WEST-INDIES*, more especially of those Provinces, which are under the Dominion of the King of *Spain*. Faithfully represented by *N. N.* Gent. *London*, for *Edw. Dod.* 1655. 8vo. p. 484.

Articles of the Treaty of Peace betwixt *England* and *France*, and a particular Reference of the Controversie betwixt both Parties, touching the Forts of *Pentacoet*, St. *John*, and *Port-Royal*, lately taken in *America*. With a Proclamation of the said Peace, by *Oliver*, Lord Protector. Given at *Whitehall* 20th of *November* 1655. 4to.

A brief Description of the Island of *JAMAICA*; and a Relation of possessing the Town of St. *Jago de la Viga*, with the Routing of the Enemies from their Forts and Ordinance, and taking the said Island, *May* 10. 1655. 4to.

God's Mercy shewed to his People, in giving them a faithfull Ministry and Schooles of Learning, for the continual Supplyes thereof. Delivered in a Sermon Preached at *Cambridge* the Day after the Commencement, by *Charles Chauncy*, B. D. President of *Harward* Colledge in *New England*. Published with some Additions thereunto, at the Request of divers Honoured and much Respected Friends, for publick Benefit, as they judged. Printed by *Samuel Green* at *Cambridge* in *New England*, 1655. 12o. p. 56. [*Ex dono Reverendi viri Gershomi Rawlins.*]

A late

A late and further Manifestation of the Progress of the Gospel amongst the *Indians* in *New-England*: Declaring their constant Love and Zeal to the Truth: With a readinesse to give accompt of their Faith and Hope; as of their Desires in Church-Communion, to be Partakers of the Ordinances of Christ. Being a Narrative of the Examinations of the *Indians*, about their Knowledge in Religion, by the Elders of the Churches. Related by Mr. *John Eliot*. Published by the *Corporation* established by Act of Parliament for *Propagating the Gospel* there. *London*, Printed by *M. S.* 1655. 4*to*. *p.* 23.

A brief and perfect Journal of the late Proceedings and Successe of the *English* Army in the *West-Indies*. Continued untill *June* 24*th*, 1655. Together with some Queries inserted and answered. Published for Satisfaction of all such who desire truly to be informed in these Particulars. By *J. S.* an Eye-witnesse. *London*, Printed 1655. 4*to*. *p.* 27.

A just and cleere Refutation of a false and scandalous Pamphlet, entituled *Babylon's Fall in Maryland*. And a true Discovery of certaine strange and inhumane Proceedings of some ungratefull People in *Maryland*, towards those who formerly preserved them in time of their greatest distresse. To which is added a Law in *Maryland* concerning Religion, and a Declaration concerning the same. By *John Langford*, Gentleman Servant to the Lord *Baltemore*. *London*, Printed for the Author, 1655. *p.* 35.

A Survey of the Estate of FRANCE, and some of the adjoyning Islands: Taken in the Description of the principal Cities, and chief Provinces; with the *Temper*, *Humour* and *Affections* of the People generally; And an exact accompt of the publick Government, in reference to the *Court*, the *Church*, and the *Civil State*. By *PETER HEYLYN*. Published according to the Author's own Copy, and with his Consent for preventing of all false, imperfect, and surreptitious Impressions of it. *London*, Printed by *E. Cotes*. MDCLVI. 4*to*. *p.* 276.

1656.
Car. 2.

The second Journey, containing a Survey of the Estate of the two Islands GUERNSEY and JARSEY, with the Isles appending, according to their Politie, and Formes of Government, both Ecclesiastical and Civill. *London*, by *E. Cotes*, &c. 1656. 4*to*.

De vero TELESCOPII Inventore, cum brevi omnium CONSPICILIORUM Historia, Ubi de Eorum Confectione, ac Usu, seu de Effectibus agitur, novaqz quadam circa ea proponuntur. Accessit etiam Centuria OBSERVATIONUM MICROSCOPICARUM Authore PETRO BORELLO

RELLO *Regis Christianissimi Consiliario, & Medico Ordinario. Hagæ Co-*
mitum. Ex Typographiâ Adriani Ulacq. M.DC.LVI. 4to.

Answers of the Holy Congregation of the Universal Inquisition, approv'd
by our most Holy Father *Alexander* the Seventh, to the Questions propos'd,
by the Missioners of the Society of *Jesus* in CHINA, concerning the best
ways of propagating the Christian Faith in that Kingdom. *Ann.* 1656. [In
the Collection of Voyages Printed for Mr. *Churchill. Fol. Vol. I. p.* 377.]

Reflexions on the Propositions made at *Rome* by F. *Martin Martinez, Anno*
Dom. 1656. for recalling and annulling what had been decreed upon the
abovesaid Questions. [*Ib. p,* 381.]

Clamor Sanguinis Martyrum: Or the Bloody Inquisition of *Spain.* Wherein is unfolded the prodigious and unparallel'd Cruelties of the Bloody-minded
Spaniard against the Protestants. Humbly presented to the serious Consideration of all Protestant Princes and States. By a Friend to the Protestant
Interest. *London, &c.* 1656. *8vo. p.* 223.

Proposals humbly presented to his Highness O L I V E R, Lord Protector
of *England, &c.* for the calling to Accompt all Persons entrusted with the
publick Revenue ; — for the passing an Act against transporting Gold and
Silver ; and against melting down the currant Silver Monies of the Nation.
Likewise a Narrative of the Proceedings in the Court of *Admiraltie,* against
the Silver Ships, *Sampson, Salvador,* and *George.* By *Tho. Violet* of *London,*
Goldsmith. *London,* Printed *Anno Dom.* M.DC.LVI. *Fol. p.* 112. *&* 79.

A true Narrative of the late Successe which it hath pleased God to give to
some part of the Fleet of this Common-wealth, upon the *Spanish* Coast,
against the King of *Spain's West-India* Fleet, in its return to *Cadiz,* being the
Substance of several Letters writ, and sent by the Generals of the Fleet.
Octob. 4. 1656.

Orthodoxal Navigation, or the Admirable and Excellent Art of the Arithmetical Great Circle, Sailing, *&c.* By *Benjamin Hubbard,* late Student of
the Mathematicks in *Charles Town* in *New England. London ;* Printed for
William Weekly, 1656. *8vo. p.* 90.

A Censure of that Reverend and Learned Man of God Mr. *John Cotton,*
lately of *New England,* upon the way of Mr. *Henden* of *Benenden* in *Kent,*
expressed in some Animadversions of his upon a Letter of Mr. *Henden's,* sometimes sent to Mr. *Elmeston.* 2. A brief and solid Exercitation concerning
the

the Coercive Power of the Magiltrate in Matters of Religion, by a Reverend and Learned Miniſter Mr. *George Petter*, lately of *Bread* in *Suſſex*. 3. Mr. *Hendern's* Animadverſions on Mr. *Elmeſton's* Epiſtle reviſed and chaſtiſed. *London*, Printed for *John Stafford*. 1656. 4to. *p.* 55.

LEAH and *RACHEL*, or the two fruitful Siſters *VIRGINIA* and *MARYLAND* their preſent Condition, impartially ſtated and related ; with a Removal of ſuch Imputations as are ſcandalouſly caſt on thoſe Coun-tries, whereby many deceived Souls choſe rather to Beg, Steal, or Rot in Priſon, and come to ſhameful Deaths, than to better their Being by going thither, wherein is plenty of all things neceſſary for Humane Subſiſtance. By *John Hammond*. *London*, Printed by *T. Mabb*. 1656. 4to. *p.* 32.

A Letter from the Fleet in *Jamaica*-Harbour, concerning our Affairs in the *Weſt-Indies* : Dated *June* 25. 1656.

A True and Exact Hiſtory of the Iſland of *BARBADOES*, Illu-ſtrated with a Map of the Iſland, as alſo the principal Trees and Plants there, ſet forth in their due Proportions and Shapes, drawn out by their ſe-veral and reſpective Scales ; together with the Ingenio that makes the Sugar, with the Plots of the ſeveral Houſes, Rooms, and other places that are uſed in the whole Proceſs of Sugar-making, *viz.* the Grinding-Room, the Boyl-ing-Room, the Filling-Room, the Curing-Houſe, Still-Houſe and Furnaces. All cut in Copper. By *RICHARD LIGON*, Gent. *London*, Printed for *Humphry Moſeley*. 1657. Fol. *p.* 122.

1657.
9 Car. 2.

The Life and Death of that deſervedly Famous Mr. *John Cotton*, the late Reverend Teacher of the Church of Chriſt at *Boſton* in *New-England*. Col-lected out of the Writings and Information of the Reverend Mr. *John Da-venport*, Paſtor of the Church at *Newhaven*, the Reverend Mr. *Samuel Whi-ting*, Paſtor of the Church at *Lynne*, the pious Widow of the Deceaſed, and others : And compiled by his unworthy Succeſſor. *Boſton, Novemb.* 6. 1657. 4to. *p.* 51.

Abel being dead yet ſpeaketh ; Or, The Life and Death of that deſervedly Famous Man of God Mr. *John Cotton*, late Teacher of the Church of Chriſt at *BOSTON* in *New-England*. By *John Norton*, Teacher of the ſame Church. *London*, Printed by *Tho. Newcomb*. 1658. 4to. *p.* 51. [Ex dono Reverendi viri *Gerſhomi Rawlins*.]

1658.
10 Car. 2.

The Pious Votary and Prudent Traveller Characterized, in a Farewell Sermon, occaſioned by the Voyage of *Nathaniel Wych*, Eſq; Preſident to the

East-Indies.   Preached in S. *Dionys* *Back-Church.* *Nov.* 14. 1652.   By
Nath. Hardy, Minister of the Word, and Preacher to that Parish.   *London,*
Printed for *John Clark,* 1658.   4to.   p. 52.

The Baptized *Turk* ; Or, a Narrative of the happy Conversion of Signior
Rigep Dandulo the only Son of a Silk-Merchant in the *Isle* of *Txio,* from the
Delusions of that great Impostor *Mahomet* unto the Christian Religion, and
of his Admission unto Baptism, by Mr. *GUNNING* at *Excester House*
Chapel, the 8th of *Novemb.* 1657. Drawn up by *THO. WARMSTRY,*
D. D.   [Dedicated to the Countess of *Dorset,* the Lord *Gorge,* and *Philip
Warwick,* Esq; Witnesses at his Baptism.]   Printed for *J. Williams,* T. *Garth-
wait* and *Henry Marsh.* 1658. 8vo. p. 150.   [*Ex Dono Rev.* Roberti Watts,
L. L. B. Coll. D. Joan. Oxon. Socij.]

*Commercium Epistolicum de Quæstionibus quibusdam Mathematicis nuper habi-
tum : Inter Nobilissimos Viros D. Gulielmum Vicecomitem* Brouncker *Anglum.* D.
Kenelmum Digby, *item Equitem Anglum.* D. Fermalium *in supremâ Tholosa-
num Curiâ Judicem Primarium.* D. Freniclum *Nobilem* Parisinum. *Una cum*
D. Joh. Wallis *Geomet. Profess.* Oxonij. D. *Franc.* a Schooten, *Math. Prof.*
Lugduni Batavorum. *Aliisq; Edidit* JOHANNES WALLIS, S. *Th.* D.
in celeberrima Oxoniensi *Academia Geometriæ Professor Savilianus.* Oxonij. *Excudebat* A. Lichfield. MDCLVIII. 4to. p. 191.

The Touch-Stone of MONY and COMMERCE ; Or, An Expe-
dient for Increase of Trade, Money and Shipping : Shewing also how the
Arrears of the Army and other Publick Debts may be forthwith satisfied, without laying more Impositions upon the People, or Burthen on Trade.   By
S. E. a Lover of his Country.   *London,* Printed at the Author's Charge, for
his Country's Good, 4to.

1659.   TRADE REVIVED ; Or, a Way proposed to Restore, Increase,
11 *Cor.* 2. Inrich, Strengthen and Preserve the Decayed and even Dying Trade of this
our *English* Nation, in its Manufactories, Coin, Shipping and Revenue ;
whereby Taxes may be lessened, if not totally taken away, to the great
Content of the People.   As also a Way shewed how the Duty of Excise
may be regulated for the Ease and Encouragement of this Nation's Commerce, both for the outward Exportation and inward Consumption of all
sorts of Commodities :   And likewise certain Ways propounded for the raising of considerable Sums of Money to maintain the Charges of the Government, &c.   Set forth by a Well-wisher to the Nation and its Prosperity.
London, Printed for *Thomas Holmwood,* for the use of the People of *England,*
and its Dominions, in the Year of our Lord 1659.   4to. p. 57.

A

A Treaty of Peace, called the *Pyrenean* Treaty, between the Crowns of *FRANCE* and *SPAIN*, Concluded and Signed by his Eminency Cardinal *Mazarin* and Don *Lewis Mendez de Haro*, Plenipotentiaries of their Most Christian and Catholick Majesties, the 7th of *November* 1659. Printed in *Paris* by his Majesty's Command, and now faithfully rendred into *English*. *London*. 4to. p. 44.

MARTINI MARTINII *Tridentini à Societate Jesu* SINICÆ. HISTORIÆ *Decas Prima*, *Res à Gentis origine ad Christum natum in extrema* Asia *sive Magno* Sinarum *Imperio gestas complexa* Amstelædami. *Apud* Joannem Blaeu, MDCLIX. 8vo. p. 413.

A Disputation concerning Church-Members and their Children, in Answer to xxj Questions : Wherein the State of such Children when Adult, together with their Duty towards the Church, and the Churches Duty toward them, is discussed by an Assembly of Divines, meeting at *Boston* in *New-England*, *June* 4th 1657. Now published by a Lover of Truth. *London*, Printed for *Samuel Tompson*, 1659. 4to. p. 31.

Of the Gospel amongst the *Indians* in *New-England*, being a Relation of the Confessions made by several *Indians* (in the presence of the Elders and Members of several Churches) in order to their Admission into Church-Fellowship. Sent over to the Corporation for Propagating the Gospel of *Jesus Christ* amongst the *Indians* in *New-England* in *London*. By Mr. *John Eliot*, one of the Labourers amongst them. In the Year of our Lord 1659, the fift Day of the fift Moneth. *London*, Printed by *John Macock*. 4to. p. 76.

The Learned Conjectures of the Reverend Mr. *John Eliot* touching the *Americans*, of new and notable Consideration ; written to Mr. *Thorowgood*, upon reading his Book, intituled *Jews in America*, or *Probabilities that the Americans be of that Race*. 4to. p. 22.   1660. 12 Car. 2.

The *Jews* in *America*, or Probabilities that those *Indians* are *Judaical* ; made more probable by some Additionals to the former Conjectures. An Accurate Discourse is premised of Mr. *John Elliot* (who first preached the Gospel to the Natives, in their own Language) touching their Origination, and his Vindication of the Planters. By *Tho. Thorowgood*, S. T. B. *Norfolciensis*, *London*, fot *Henry Brome*, 1660. 4to. Ep. Ded. to the Noble Knights, Ladies and Gentlemen of *Norfolk*, and to those especially that declared their Desires to promote the Gospel among the *Indians* in *America* by their bountiful Encouragement to Mr. *John Eliot*. Dat. *May* 26. 1660.

The

The Humble Petition and Address of the General Court sitting at Boston in New-England, unto the High and Mighty Prince *C H A R L E S* the Second, and presented unto His Most Gracious Majesty *Febr.* 11. 1660. Printed in the Year 1660. 4to. p. 8.

An Act for the Encouraging and Encreasing of Shipping and Navigation — by providing that no Goods or Commodities whatsoever shall be Imported into, or Exported out of, any Lands, Islands, Plantations, or Territories to his Majesty belonging in *Asia, Africa*, or *America*, but in such Ships or Vessels as are *English. Anno* xij *Car.* II. *Cap.* xviij (Printed Copy.)

An Act for prohibiting the Planting, Setting, or Sowing of *Tobacco* in *England* or *Ireland*, for the better maintaining and keeping up the Colonies and Plantations of this Kingdom in *America. Anno* xij *Car.* II. *Cap.* xxxiv.

The Heart of New-England Rent at the Blasphemies of the present Generation; Or, a brief Tractate concerning the Doctrine of the *Quakers* ; demonstrating the destructive Nature thereof to Religion, the Churches, and the State, with Consideration of the Remedy against it. Occasional Satisfaction to Objections, and Confutation of the contrary Truth. By *J O H N N O R T O N*, Teacher of the Church of Christ at *Boston* ; who was appointed thereunto by the Order of the General Court. *London*, Printed for *John Allen*, 1660. 8vo. p. 89. To which is added, A Letter sent from *New-England* to a Friend in *London*, by way of Defence for their Dealing with the *Quakers.*

An Examination of the Grounds or Causes, which are said to induce the Court of *Boston* in *New-England* to make that Order or Law of Banishment upon pain of Death against the *Quakers* ; As also of the Grounds and Considerations by them produced to manifest the Warrantableness and Justness, both of their making and executing the same, which they now stand deeply engaged to defend, having already thereupon put two of them to Death. As also of some further Grounds for justifying of the same, in an *Appendix* to *John Norton*'s Book (which was printed after the Book itself, yet as part thereof) whereto he is said to be appointed by the General Court. And likewise of the Arguments briefly hinted in that which is called, *A true Relation of the Proceedings against the Quakers,* &c. Whereunto somewhat is added about the Authority and Government which Christ excluded out of his Church, which occasioneth somewhat concerning the true Church Government. By: *Isaac Penington* the younger. *London*, Printed for *L. Lloyd*, &c. 1660. 4to. p. 99. [*Ex dono Rev. Viri* Gershomi Rawlins.]

New-

New-England judged not by Man's, but the Spirit of the Lord : And the
Summe sealed up of *New-England*'s Persecutions : Being a brief Relation of
the Sufferings of the People called *Quakers* in those Parts of *A M E R I C A*
from the beginning of the fifth Moneth 1656 (the time of their first Arrival
at *Boston* from *England*) to the latter end of the Tenth Moneth 1660. Wherein the cruel Whippings and Scourgings, Bonds and Imprisonments, Beatings
and Chainings, Starvings and Huntings, Fines and Confiscation of Estates,
Burning in the Hand and cutting off Ears, Orders of Sale for Bondmen and
Bondwomen, Banishment upon pain of Death, and putting to Death of those
People, are shortly touched ; with a Relation of the Manner, and some of
the other most material Proceedings ; and a Judgment thereupon. In Answer to a certain Printed Paper intituled A D E C L A R A T I O N of the
General Court of the *Massachusets* holden at *Boston* the 18. of *October* 1658.
Apologizing for the same. By *GEORGE BISHOPE*. *London*, Printed
for *Robert Wilson* in *Martins le Grand*, 1661. 4*to. p.* 198.

1661.
13 *Car.* 2.

J A M A I C A Viewed, with all the Ports, Harbours, and their several
Soundings, Towns, and Settlements thereunto belonging ; together with
the Nature of its Climate, Fruitfulness of the Soil, and its Suitableness to
English Complexions. With several other Collateral Observations and Re-
flexions upon the Island. The second Edition. By *E. H.* (i. e. *Edmund
Hickeringhill*.) *London*, for *John Williams* 1661. 8*vo. p.* 87.

An Act for the Establishing Articles and Orders for the regulating
and better Government of his Majesty's Navies, Ships of War, and Forces
by Sea. *Anno* xiij *Car*. II. *Cap.* ix.

The first Charter granted by the King to the Proprietors of *CAROLINA*,
Edward E. of *Clarendon, George* Duke of *Albemarle, William* Lord *Craven, John*
Lord Berkeley, Anthony Lord *Ashley*, Sir *George Carteret*, Sir *William Berkeley*,
and Sir *Peter Colleton*, *being excited with a laudable and pious Zeal for the Propagation of the Christian Faith, and the Enlargement of our Empire and Dominions.* Witness the King at *Westminster* the 24th day of *March*, in the Fifteenth Year of our Reign. 4*to.*

1662.
14 *Car.* 2.

The Answer of the Elders and other Messengers of the Churches assembled at *Boston* in the Year 1662, to the Questions propounded to them by Order of the Honoured General Court. I. Who are the Subjects of Baptism ?
II. Whether according to the Word of God there ought to be a Consociation
of

of Churches, and what should be the Manner of it? &c. [Printed in the History of *New-England*. Fol. *Book V. p. 62.*]

A Letter from the *Dutch* General in *CEYLON* to Mr. *Philip Baldæus* a *Dutch* Minister there, concerning the best Ways of Propagating Christianity in that Island; with an Account of several Religious Tracts translated out of the *Portuguese* into the *Malabar* Language, for the use of the Natives. *Sept.* 18. 1662. [In the Collection of Voyages Printed for Mr. *Churchill*. Fol. *Vol. III. p. 811.*]

A List of the Losses and Damages sustained by the *Dutch East-India* Company from the *English*, ab Anno 1655. ad Annum 1662 inclusive. Signed by the Commissioners at the *Hague*, *Johan de Witt*, *R. Van Wiyberg*, &c. 3 *Sheets* MSS.

1663.
15 *Car.* 2. 23. Mey 𝕽efolutie bande Ed. Mo. Heeren 𝕾taten ban Vriefland banden 𝕾tilo Cocighenomen Mitfgadeis: Deductie bande Ed. Mo. Heeren Gecommitteerde Raden bande Ed. Groot Mo. Heeren De 𝕾taten ban Hollandt ende West-Vrieflandt tegens defelbe 𝕽efolutie ban Vrieflandt. Ober de Formulieren ban Gebeden by de 𝕾taten ban Hollandt ende West-Vrieflandt op den 23 Maert diffelben Jaers geartes treat tot Leyden. Gedruckt by Cornelis vander Linden 1663. 4to.

Glorious Glimmerings of the Life, Love, Unity and pure Joy. Written in *Rome* Prison of Madmen in the Year 1660. but conserved as in Obscurity until my Arrival at *BARBADOS* in the Year 1662. From whence it is sent the second time to the Lord's Lambs. By *J. P. London*, Printed for *Robert Wilson*. 1663. 4to. *p. 15.*

A Discourse and View of *Virginia* by Sir *William Berkley* the Governour. 1663. 4to. *p. 12.*

ISAACI VOSSII *de Motu Marium & Ventorum Liber.* Hagæ Comitis. *Ex Typographia* Adriani Ulacq. *Anno MDCLXIII.* 4to. *p. 123.* [Ex dono *Awnshami Churchill* Armig.]

Systema Cosmicum Autore GALILÆO GALILÆI *Lynceo Academiæ* Pisanæ *Mathematico extraordinario, Serenissimi Magni Ducis* Hetruriæ *Philosopho & Mathematico Primario. In quo quatuor Dialogis de Duobus. Maximis Mundi Systematibus* PTOLEMAICO & COPERNICANO *utriusq; rationibus Philosophicis ac Naturalibus indefinite propositis differitur. Ex Italica lingua*

lingua Latine converfum : Accefit Appendix gemina, quâ SS. Scriptura dicta cum terræ Mobilitate conciliantur. Londini. *Proftat venale apud* Thomam Dicas, *&c.* MDCLXIII. 8vo. *p.* 704.

An Appendix to *Aftronomia Carolina*; containing, 1. A Propofition touching the Difcovery of the true *Longitude*. 2. *Ephemerides* of the true Place of the Sun for four Years, &c. By *Thomas Streete*, Student in Aftronomy and Mathematicks. *London*, Printed for *Francis Coffinet*. 1664. 4to. *p.* 32.

1664.
16 Car. 2.

Articles and Conditions, whereupon the Trading Merchants of this Kingdom of *France* do moft humbly befeech His Majefty to grant them His Declaration, and the Graces therein contained, for the Eftablifhment of a Company for the Commerce of the *Eaft-Indies*. Done and Refolved at the Affembly held by His Majefty's Gracious Permiffion at the Houfe of Mónfieur *Faverolles*, Merchant at *Paris*, Tuefday May 26. 1664. Signed *L O U I S*. On which Occafion there followeth a Difcourfe written by a Faithful Subject to His moft *Chriftian* Majefty concerning the Eftablifhment of a *French* Company for the Commerce of the *Eaft-Indies*. [Treat. touching the *Eaft-Indian* Trade. 4to. 1676.]

Extract of a Letter from the Prefident and Council in *Surat*, dated the 24th of *November* 1664. containing an Account of the injurious Proceedings of the *Dutch* to fpoil and ruin the *Englifh Trade* in thofe Parts of the *Indies*. 1 Sheet MS.

A Catalogue of the Damages for which the *Englifh* demand Reparation from the *United Netherlands*; As alfo, a Lift of the Damages; Actions and Pretences for which thofe of the *United Netherlands* demand Reparation. and Satisfaction from the *Englifh*; together with the Anfwer of the *Englifh* fubjoin'd to the feveral and refpective Parts of their Demands. *London*, Printed for *Henry Brome*, 1664. 4to. *p.* 75.

A Relation of a Difcovery lately made on the Coaft of *F L O R I D A* (from Lat. 31. to 33. Deg. 95. Min. North Lat.) by *William Hilton* Commander and Commiffioner with Capt. *Anthony Long* and *Peter Fabian* in the Ship *Adventure*, which fet fail from *Spikes-Bay*, *Aug.* 10. 1663. and was fet forth by feveral Gentlemen and Merchants of the *Ifland of Barbadoes* : Giving an Account of the Nature and Temperament of the Soil, The Manners and Difpofition of the Natives, and whatfoever is elfe remarkable therein; together with Propofals made by the Commiffioners of the Lords Proprietors. to all fuch Perfons as fhall become the firft Settlers on the Rivers, Harbours and Creeks there. *London*, Printed for *Simon Miller*, 1664. 4to. *p.* 34.

A De.

A Defence of the Answer and Arguments of the *Synod* met at BOSTON in the Year 1662. Concerning the Subject of *Baptism* and *Consociation of Churches*, against the Reply made thereto, by the Reverend Mr. *John Davenport*, Pastor of the Church at *New-Haven*, in his Treatise entituled, *Another Essay for the Investigation of the Truth*, &c. Together with an *Answer* to the *Apologetical Preface* set before that Essay. By some who were Members of the *Synod* abovementioned. *Cambridge* Printed by G. Green, &c. 1664. 4to. p. 102.

A Sermon Preached before the Right Worshipful Company of the *Levant-Merchants*, at *St. Olave's Hart-street, London*; on *Thursday Decemb.* 15. 1662. By JOHN LUKE, B. D. Fellow of *Sidney-Sussex* Colledge in *Cambridge*. *London*, Printed by R. *Daniel*, 1664. 4to.

1665.
17 Car. 2. The Travels of Sig. *Pietro della Valle* a Noble *Roman* into EAST-INDIA and *Arabia Deserta*. In which the several Countries, together with the Customs, Manners, Traffique, and Rites both Religious and Civil of those Oriental Princes and Nations are faithfully described. In Familiar Letters to his Friend Signior *Mario Schipano*. Whereunto is added a Relation of Sir *THOMAS ROE's* Voyage into the EAST-INDIES. *London*, Printed for *John Martin* and *James Allestree*, &c. 1665. Fol. p. 430. [*Ex dono* Christopheri Bateman, *Bibliopolæ* Londinensis.]

ΠΑΛΛΑΔΙΟΥ Περὶ τῶν ΤΙΝΔΙΑΣ Ἐθνῶν ἢ τῶν ΒΡΑΓΜΑΝΩΝ. Palladius *de Gentibus* Indiæ & Bragmanibus. S. Ambrosius *de Moribus* Brachmanorum. *Anonymus* de Bragmanibus. *Quorum Priorem & Postremum nunc primum in lucem protulit Ex Bibliotheca Regia* Eduardus Bisseus *Eques Auratus*, *& titulo* CLARENCII *Rex Armorum.* Londini *Excudebat* J. Roycroft, *Anno Domini.* MDCLXV. 4to. p. 103. [*Ex dono* Awnshami Churchill, *Armigeri.*]

A Copy of the Letters Patents for especial Reprisals from the King of *Great Britain*, (under the Great Seal of *England*) against the States General and their Subjects, for relief of Sir *Edmond Turner*, Kt. and *George Carew*, Esquire, upon the unjust Sufferings of *William Courten*, Esq; deceased, who in the Year 1643. by the depredation and hostile Act of one *Gailand*, Commander in Chief of two Ships belonging to the *East-India* Company of the *Netherlands*, was between *Goa* and *Mateao* in the Streights of *Malacca*, deprived, and most injuriously spoiled of a certain Ship named the *Bona Esperanza*.— Witness Our self at *Westminster* the 19th Day of *May*, in the 17th Year of Our Reign. [Printed in *Molloy, de Jure Maritimo.* 8vo. 1688. p. 32.]

Voyage

The Lords Wonders in the Deep: Being a Sermon preached at the time
of the Publique Affizes at Allbhallow in NORTHAMPTON, July 4.
1665. Being the Day appointed for Solemn Thanksgiving for the late Remarkable Victory obtained againft the Dutch by the Royal Navy, under the
Conduct of His ROYAL HIGHNESS; And publifhed at the
fpecial Inftance of His Majefty's Reverend Judges, &c. By SIMON FORD,
D. D. Chaplain to His Majefty, and Minifter there. Oxford, Printed by
W. Hall, &c. 1665. 4to.

Voyage à la CHINE des PP. I. Grueber & D'Orville, 1665 —— Excerpta ex Libris Grueberi Kirchero infcriptis, cum Effigie Reverendi Patris
Jo. Adami Schall Sac. Jefu Presbyteri, Aula Sinofartarica fupremi Concilij
Mandarini. —— Viaggio del P. Giovanni Grueber tornando per terra, da China
in Europa. 1665. —— Autres Pieces fur le Sujet du Voyage du P. Gueber.—
Epiftola ejufdem Patris Latine &c. de rebus Tartaricis & Sinicis. [Relation
de divers Voyages. IV. Partie 1672. Fol.]

Directions to be obferved by fuch as go on long Voyages, drawn up by
Mr. Hook, a Fellow of the Royal Society, and Geometry Profeffor of Gresham-
College. by Order of the faid Society. Publifhed in the Philofophical Tranf-
actions of the 5th of January, 1665-6. And Reprinted in the Preface to the
Collection of Voyages for Mr. Churchill, p. lxxiij.

Subfidium Peregrinantibus: Or, An Affiftance to a Traveller in his Con-
verfe with, 1. Hollanders. 2. Germans. 3. Venetians. 4. Italians. 5. Spaniards. 6. French. Directing him after the lateft Mode to the greateft Honour, Pleafure, Security, and Advantage in his Travels. Written to a
Princely Traveller for a Vade Mecum. By Balthazar Gabier Knt. Mafter of
the Ceremonies to King Charles the Firft. Oxford, Printed for Robert Gaf-
goigne, Anno Dom. 1665. 8vo. p. 120.

An Exact Relation of the moft execrable Attempts of John Allin committed on the Perfon of his Excellency FRANCIS Lord WILLOUGHBY
of Parham, Captain General of the Continent of Guiana, and of all the Ca-
ribby-Iflands, and our Lord Proprietor. London, Printed for Richard Lowndes,
1665. 4to. p. 12.

A brief Defcription of the Province of Carolina on the Coafts of Florida:
And more particularly of a New Plantation begun by the Englifh at Cape
Feare, on that River now by them called Charles River, the 29th of May,
1664. Wherein is fet forth the Healthfulnefs of the Air; the Fertility of

1666.
18 Car. 2.

G g
the

the Earth and Waters; and the great Pleasure and Profit which will accrue to those that shall go thither to enjoy the same. Also Directions and Advice to such as shall go thither, whether on their own Accounts, or to serve under another. Together with a most accurate Map of the whole Province. Printed at London for *Robert Horne*, 1666. 4to. p. 10.

A Character of the Province of *MARYLAND*, wherein is described in four distinct Parts, *viz.* I. The Situation and Plenty of the Province. II. The Laws, Customs and natural Demeanour of the Inhabitants. III. The worst and best Usage of a *Mary-land* Servant, opened in view. IV. The Traffique and vendable Commodities of the Country. Also a small Treatise on the Wild and Naked *Indians* (or *Susque hanoks*) of *Mary-land*, their Customs, Manners, Absurdities, and Religion: Together with a Collection of Historical Letters. By *George Alsop*. London, Printed for *Peter Dring* 1666. 8vo. p. 118.

The History of the *Caraby-Islands*, *viz.* *BARBADOES*, *St. CHRISTOPHERS*, *St. VINCENTS*, *MARTINICO*, *DOMINICO*, *BARBOUTHOS*, *MONSERRAT*, *NEVIS*, *ANTEGO*, &c. in all xxviii. In two Books; The first containing the Natural, the second the Moral History of those Islands. Illustrated with several Pieces of Sculpture, representing the most considerable Rarities therein described. With a *CARIBBIAN* Vocabulary. Rendred into *English* by *JOHN DAVIES* of *Kidwelly*. London, Printed by *J. M.* for *Thomas Dring* and *John Starkey*, 1666. Fol. p. 351.

The History of *ALGIERS* and its Slavery, with many remarkable Particularities of *AFRICK*: written by the Sieur *D'ARANDA*, sometime a Slave there. Englished by *JOHN DAVIES* of *Kidwelly*, London Printed for *John Starkey*. MDCLXVI. 8vo. p. 279.

HYDROSTATICAL PARADOXES made out by new Experiments for the most part Physical and Easie. By the Honourable *ROBERT BOYLE*, Fellow of the Royal-Society. *Oxford*, Printed by *William Hall*, for *Richard Davis*. MDCLXVI. 8vo. p. 247.

A full and perfect Account of the Sizes and Lengths of Rigging of all his Majesty's Ships and Frigats: As also Proportions of Boatswains and Carpenters, Stores of all kinds for 8 Months Sea-service on the Coast of *England*. Also a particular List of those Ships whose Names have been changed since his Majesty's blessed Return; with an Index discovering each Particular, as it was presented to his Royal Highness the Duke of *York*. By *E. H. Esq;*

As

As also Directions to all Merchants, Ship-Carpenters and others in the Building, Furnishing and Fitting out greater or lesser Vessels, according to their several Proportions. Published for the Benefit of this Kingdom. London, Printed for *Robert Miller*. 1666. Fol. p. 60.

A true Narrative of the Engagement between his Majesty's FLEET and that of *Holland*, begun *June* the *First* 1666, at Two a Clock in the Afternoon, and continuing till the *Fourth* at Ten a Clock at Night. Published by Command. *London*, Printed by *Thomas Newcomb*. 1666. Fol. p. 8.

A Report of the good Services of *William Carter* in discovering of twelve French Shallops loaded in one Night from *Rommey Marsh* in *Kent* with considerable Quantities of *Wool* : And in obtaining by his Majesty's Grace and Favour, a Party of Horse to scout about *Rommey-Marsh*, and some Frigats to cruise at Sea : And in presenting a Complaint of the National Dangers in the *Exportation* of *Wool* to the House of Commons, who thereupon made an Address to his Majesty to revoke his Licence for exporting some hundred Packs of *Wool* from *Ireland*, upon the apparent Frauds practised therein ; which his Majesty accordingly did, &c. [Abstract of Proceedings of *William Carter*. 1694. 4to. p. 1]

1667.
19 Car. 2.

Strange News from *Virginia*, being a true Relation of a great Tempest in *Virginia*, by which many People lost their Lives, great Numbers of Cattle destroyed, Houses, and in many places whole Plantations overturned, and whole Woods torn up by the Roots. As a further Addition to this Calamity, the Sea exceeded its usual Height above twelve Foot, carrying away much Corn and Tobacco, with many Cattle, forcing the Inhabitants into the Mountains for the security of their Lives. *London*, Printed for *W. Thackeray*. 1667. 4to. p. 7.

An Answer of the *Company of Royal Adventurers of* England *trading into* AFRICA to the Petition and Paper of certain Heads and Particulars thereunto relating and annexed, exhibited to the Honourable House of Commons by Sir *Paul Painter*, *Ferdinando Gorges*, *Henry Batson*, *Benjamin Skutt*, and *Thomas Knight*, on the behalf of themselves and others concerned in his Majesty's Plantations in *America*. London. 4to. p. 18.

Sir *Walter Rawleigh*'s Judicious and Select Essays and Observations upon the *first Invention of Shipping*. *Invasive War*. *The Navy Royal and Sea Service*. With his *Apologie* for his Voyage to *Guiana*. London, Printed for *A. M.* to be sold by *Robert Boulter*. 1667. 8vo.

Tractatus

Tractatus Pacis & Amicitiæ *inter Coronas Magnas* BRITANNIÆ &
HISPANIÆ *conclusus* Matriti ⅓ *die Maii, Anno Dom.* 1667. Londini,
Excusum per Assignatos Johannis Bill & Christopheri Barker, *MDCLXXVI. Cum
Privilegio.* 4to. *p.* 34.

Tractatus Pacis & Amicitiæ *tam continuata tum renovata inter Coronas* Hispaniæ & Magnæ Britanniæ, *Matriti,* 1667. *Cum licentia Consilij Status,
& Venditur in Typographia* Dominici Garsiæ Morris *Typographi Status Ecclesi-
ast. Regnorum* Castellæ & Legionis. 4°. *fol.* 24.

Articles of *Peace, Commerce* and *Alliance* between the Crowns of *Great-
Britain* and *Spain,* concluded in a Treaty at *Madrid* the 13-23 day of *May,*
in the Year of our Lord God 1667. Translated out of *Latin.* Published
by His Majesty's Command. Printed by the Assigns of *John Bill,* &c.
1667. 4to. With the Copy of a *Patent,* containing several Gracious Priviledges lately granted by the High and Mighty *Philip* the *Fourth,* King of
Spain, &c. Which are confirmed by the foregoing Treaty, and whereof
mention is made in the *Ninth* Article of the said Treaty. Published by His
Majesty's Command.

ARTICLES touching *Navigation* and *Commerce* between the most
Serene and Mighty Prince *CHARLES* II. By the Grace of God King
of *England, Scotland, France* and *Ireland,* Defender of the Faith, &c. And
the High and Mighty Lords the STATES GENERAL of the *United
Netherlands,* Concluded the 21-31 day of *July,* 1667. Published by his
Majesty's Command. Printed by the Assigns of *John Bill* and *Christopher*
Barker. 1667. 4to. *p.* 75.

His Majesty's *Declaration* concerning the Restoring of all Places, Forts, &c.
which his Subjects shall have taken or recovered from the *Dutch* after the ¼⁰
day of *May* last past. Given at *Westminster,* *July* 29th O. S. & *Aug.* 8.
N. S. 1667. *Ibid.*

ARTICLES of *Peace* and *Alliance* between the most Serene and
Mighty Prince *CHARLES* II. By the Grace of God King of *England,*
&c. And the most Serene and Mighty Prince *LEWIS* XIV. the Most
Christian King, Concluded the 21-31 day of *July,* 1667. Published by his
Majesty's Command. Printed by the Assigns of *John Bill* and *Christopher*
Barker. 4to. *p.* 46.

ARTICLES

ARTICLES of PEACE and ALLIANCE between the most Serene and Mighty Prince *CHARLES* II. by the Grace of God King of *Great-Britain*, &c. And the most Serene and Mighty Prince *Frederick* III. King of *Denmark* and *Norway* ; Concluded at *Breda* the 21-31 day of *July*, 1667. Published by His Majesty's Command. Printed in the *Savoy*, 1667. 4to. by the Assigns of *John Bill* and *Christ. Barker*.

ARTICLES of PEACE and ALLIANCE between the most Serene and Mighty Prince *Charles* II. by the Grace of God King of *England*, &c. and the High and Mighty Lords the *States General* of the *United Netherlands* ; Concluded at *Breda* the 21-31. day of *July* 1667. Published by His Majesty's Command. In the *Savoy*, 1667. 4to.

A Treaty of a League Offensive and Defensive between the most Serene and Mighty Prince *Lewis* XIV. and *Alphonso* VI. Kings of *France* and *Portugal*, against the King of *Castile*: Concluded at *Lisbon* the last of *March*, 1667. [Printed in the Memoirs of the Sieur *D'Ablancourt*. 8vo. 1703. p. 206.]

Le Flambeau Reluisant Ou proprement thresor de la Navigation, dans lequel est clairement & pleinement decouvert l'Art & la Science des Maitres de Navires *& des* Pilotes. *Et pour plus d'exercise de la* Navigation, *on y a ajouté la* Chart Quarree *composée par M.* Pierre Ruëlle. *Traduit du flamend ou François par* J. Virer, Amsterdam, 1667, 4to. p. 276. & 26.

Philosophical Transactions in October 1668. Containing an Extract of a Letter written to the Publisher from the *Bermudas* by Mr. *Richard Stafford*, concerning the Tydes there ; as also Whales, Sperma Ceti, strange Spiders-Webs, some rare Vegetables, and the Longevity of the Inhabitants. Dar. *Bermudas*, *July* 16. 1668. 4to. As likewise Observations concerning *Cochineal*: Accompanied with some Suggestions for finding out and preparing such like Substances out of other *Vegetables*, particularly out of a *Berry* growing both in the *Bermudas* and *New-England*, call'd the *Summer-Island Red-weed*.

1668. 20 Car. 2.

The *Isle* of *Pines* ; Or a late Discovery of a fourth Island in *Terra Australis Incognita*. Being a true Relation of certain *English* Persons, who in the Days of *Queen Elizabeth*, making a Voyage to the *East-India*, were cast away and wreck'd upon the Island near to the Coast of *Terra Australis Incognita*, and all drown'd except one Man and four Women, whereof one was a *Negro*. And now lately, *Anno Dom*. 1667. a *Dutch* Ship driven by foul Weather, there by chance have found their Posterity (speaking good *English*) to amount to ten or twelve thousand Persons, as they suppose, &c. Licensed *June* 27. 1668. *London*, for *Allen Banks* and *Charles Harper*, 1668. 4to. p. 9.

Disputatio Juridica de Jure Navium, *quam favente Divino Numine, Consensu & Authoritate Magnifici, Venerandæ Facultatis Juridicæ, Senatus in Illustri & Celeberrimâ Academiâ* Brandenburgicâ, *Præside Viro Nobilissimo Consultissimo atq; Excellentissimo Domino* Sam. Strykio, *J. U. D. & Novellarum Professore Publico dignissimo, publico Eruditorum Examini subjicit in Augusto Juris-Consultorum Collegio* BALTHASARUS GOTHOFREDUS. *Servesta* Anhaltinus *Author & Resp. ad Diem.* 2. Maij, *Anno Salutis reparatæ* MDCLXIIX. Francofurti ad Viadrum. *Excudit* Andreas Becmanus.

A short Addition to the Observations concerning T R A D E and Interest of Money. By the same Hand. *London*, for *Henry Mortlock*, 1668. 4to. p. 14.

An Account of the Proposals humbly presented by *William Carter* to His Majesty in Council, in order to prevent the Exportation of Wool; referr'd to the Council of Trade, with a particular Order. 20. *November*, 1668. [Abstract of the Proceedings of *Will. Carter*, 1694 4to. p. 1.]

A Curious and Exact Account of a Voyage to *Congo* in the Years 1666 and 1667. By the R. R. F. F. *Michael Angelo* of *Gattina*, and *Dennis de Carli* of *Piacenza*, Capuchins, and Apostolick Missioners into the said Kingdom of *Congo*. With some Particulars of *Brazil* and the Coasts thereof in *America*. [In the Collection of Voyages printed for Mr. *Churchill*. Vol. I. p. 613.]

A Perpetual *League of Mutual Defence* and *Alliance* between His Majesty and the *States General* of the *United Provinces* of the *Low-Countries*; together with a Confirmation of the *Articles of Commerce*, agreed upon by the Treaty at B R E D A. Published by His Majesty's Command. In the *Savoy*, by the King's Printers. 1668. 4to. p. 8.

Relation du Voyage du Sayd ou de la Thebayde *fait en* 1668. *par les* P. P. Protais *&* Charles Francois d' Orleans, *Capucins Missionaires.* [*Relation de divers Voyages Curieux.* IV. *Partie.* A Paris 1672. Fol.]

A *League of Union* agreed on at the *Hague*, *Jan.* 13-23, 1668, betwixt His *Majesty* King *Charles* II. of *England*, &c. and the *States General* of the *United Provinces* of the *Low-Countries*, for an Efficacious Mediation of Peace between the two neighbouring Crowns now in War. Published by His

Majesty's

Majesty's Command in the *Savoy*, by the Assigns of *J. Bill*, &c. 1668. 4to. p. 8.

Tractatus Pacis *inter* Carolum *II. Regem* Hispaniæ & Alphonsum *VI. Regem* Portugalliæ *factus Mediante* Carolo *II. Rege* Angliæ, &c. Lisbonæ, 13. Februarij, *Anno* 1668. And a Translation of it [published at the End of the Memoirs of the Sieur *D' Ablancourt*. 8vo. 1703.]

Articles of *Peace* between the two Crowns of *France* and *Spain*; Concluded at *Aix la Chapelle* the Second of *May*, 1668. Translated out of *French*. *London*, Printed for *William Crook*. 1668. 4to.

A Treaty of Friendship and Commerce between His Majesty of *Great Britain*, &c. and the most Serene Prince the Duke of *Savoy*; Concluded at *FLORENCE* the 19th day of *September*, 1669. Published by His Majesty's Command. *London*, by the King's Printers. 4to.

1669.
21 Car. 2.

Questions proposed to the Holy General *Congregation* of the Holy *Roman* and Vniversal *Inquisition*, by the *Missioners* in *China*; with Answers given to each of them; allowed and confirmed by a Decree of the Sacred *Congregation* of the Holy *Inquisition*, on *Wednesday*, *Novemb.* 13. 1669. [In the Collection of Voyages, Printed for Mr. *Churchill*. *Vol. I. p.* 395]

A Relation of Three EMBASSIES from His Sacred Majesty *CHARLES* II. to the Great Duke of *Muscovie*, the King of *Sweden*, and the King of *Denmark*. Performed by the Right Honourable the EARL of *CARLISLE*, in the Years 1663 and 1664. Written by an Attendant on the Embassies, and published with his Lordship's Approbation. *London*, Printed for *John Starkey*, 1669. 8vo. p. 461.

A Voyage into the *Levant*; Being a brief Relation of a Journey lately performed from *England* by the Way of *Venice* into *Dalmatia*, *Sclavonia*, *Bosnia*, *Hungary*, *Macedonia*, *Thessaly*, *Thrace*, *Rhodes*, and *Egypt* unto *Grand Cairo*. With particular Observations concerning the modern Condition of the *Turks* and other People under that Empire. By Sir *Henry Blunt*, Knight. *London*, for *William Crook*. 1669. 8vo. p. 165.

Captain *Wood's* Voyage through the Streights of *Magellane*, in company with Sir *John Narborough*; taken from his own Journal, beginning *Sept.* 26. 1669. [Printed in Capt. *Hack's* Collect. of Orig. Voyages. 1699. 8vo.]

The

The Fundamental Constitutions of *Carolina*, in Number a Hundred and Twenty, agreed upon by the *Palatine* and *Lords Proprietors*, to remain the sacred and unalterable Form and Rule of Government of *Carolina* for ever. Dat. the first day of *March*, 1669. 4to.

A Report of the *Council of Trade* to His Majesty in Council, that they find the Exportation of Wool to be of a destructive Consequence to the Trade of this Kingdom, and that the same hath grown into practise, as well by reason of the Doubtfulness of the Provisions in the Statute made in the 12th Year of His Majesty's Reign, prohibiting the Exportation of Wool, as by the Neglect and Remissness of Officers, in not putting the Laws in execution. Delivered 2. *Apr.* 1669. [Abstract of the Proceedings of *W. Carter*, 1694. 4to. p. 2.]

An Account of the Commission passed under the Great-Seal of *England* to the President and Governours of *Christ-Hospital* in *London*, for preventing the Exportation of Wool; which they declined and returned back to the King and Council, refusing to act therein, in 1669. [*Ib.*]

An Account of the Explanatory Bill for hindring the Exportation of Wool brought into the House of Lords by Sir *Orlando Bridgeman*, Lord Keeper; with a Copy of his Lordship's Letter to the Mayors of *Dover*, *Folkstone* and *Hyth*. Dat. *Aug.* 30. 1669, &c. [*Ib. p. 3.*]

USURY at *Six per Cent.* Examined and found unjustly charged by Sir *Thomas Culpepper* and *J. S.* with many Crimes and Oppressions whereof 'tis altogether innocent; wherein is shewed the Necessity of retrenching our Luxury and vain Consumption of *Foreign* Commodities imported by *English* Money: Humbly presented to the High Court of Parliament now sitting. By *Thomas Manley*, Gent. *London*, sold by *Ambrose Isted*, MDCLXIX. 4to. p. 69.

1670.   *Opus Epistolarum* PETRI MARTYRIS Anglerij Mediolanensis
22 *Car.* 2. *Protonotarij Apostolici Prioris Archiepiscopatus Granatensis, atq; à Consiliis Rerum* Indicarum Hispanicis, *tantâ curâ excusum, ut præter Styli venustatem quoq; fungi possit vice Luminis Historiæ superiorum temporum.* Cui accesserunt Epistolæ Ferdinandi de Pulgar *Coætanei* Latinæ *pariter atq;* Hispanicæ cum Tractatu Hispanico *de Viris* Castellæ *illustribus.* Editio Postrema. Amstelodami. *Typis* Elzevirianis. *Veneunt* Parisiis *apud* Fredericum Leonard *Typographum Regium.* MDCLXX. *Fol. p.* 486. 32, & 62.

A

A Letter from a Gentleman of the Lord Ambaffador HOWARD's Retinue to his Friend in LONDON, Dated at FEZ, Nov. 1. 1669. [wherein he gives a full Relation of the moft remarkable Paffages in their Voyage thither, and of the prefent State of the Countries under the Power of TAFALETTA, Emperor of Morocco; with a brief Account of the Merchandizing Commodities of Africa; as alfo the Manners and Cuftoms of the People there. Publifhed for Publick Satisfaction. London, Printed for Mofes Pitt, 1670. 4to. p. 31.

The late Travels of S. Giacomo Baratti an Italian Gentleman, into the remote Countries of the Abiffins or of Ethiopia Interior. Wherein you fhall find an exact Account of the Laws, Government, Religion, Difcipline, Cuftoms, &c. of the Chriftian People that do inhabit there, with many Obfervations which fome may improve to the advantage and increafe of Trade with them. Together with a Confirmation of this Relation drawn from the Writings of Damianus de Goes, and Jo. Scaliger, who agree with the Author in many Particulars. Tranflated by G. D. London, for Benjamin Billingfley, 1670. 8vo. p. 238.

A Relation of the Coafts of AFRICK called GUINNEE, with a Defcription of the Countreys, Manners, and Cuftoms of the Inhabitants; of the Productions of the Earth, and the Merchandife and Commodities it affords; with fome Hiftorical Obfervations upon the Coafts. Being collected in a Voyage made by the Sieur Villault Efouyer, Sieur de Bellefond, in the Years 1666, and 1667. Written in French, and faithfully Englifhed. London, for John Starkey. 1670. 8vo. p. 266.

The Adventures of Mr. T. S. an Englifh Merchant, taken Prifoner by the Turks of Algiers and carried into the Inland Countries of Africa; with a Defcription of the Kingdom of Algiers, of all the Towns and Places of Note thereabouts. Whereunto is added a Relation of the Chief Commodities of the Country, and of the Actions and Manners of the People. Written firft by the Author, and fitted for the publick View, by A. Roberts. Whereunto is annexed an Obfervation of the Tide, and how to turn a Ship out of the Straights-Mouth, the Wind being Wefterly. By Richard Norris. London, for Mofes Pitt, 1670. 8vo. p. 252.

Concerning Contraband Goods, and what fort of Goods and Merchandife are to be fo reputed, in the feveral Articles touching Navigation and Commerce in the Treaties between the King of Great-Britain and other Princes

I i and

and States ; Particularly what Goods *Contraband* with *Spain*. MS. Paper by Mr. *William Griffith*.

Articles of Alliance and Commerce between the moſt Serene and Potent Prince *CHARLES* II. By the Grace of God King of *Great-Britain*, *France* and *Ireland*, Defender of the Faith, *&c.* and the moſt Serene and Potent Prince *CHRISTIAN* V. by the Grace of God King of *Denmark*, *Norway*, &c. Concluded at *Copenhagen* the 11th day of *July*, 1670. Publiſhed by His Majeſty's Command. In the *Savoy*, &c. 4to.

1671.
23 *Car.* 2.

The Voyage of *Frederick Marten* of *Hamburga* into *Spitzburgen* and *Greenland* ; containing the Paſſages of the whole Voyage ; together with ſome Account of the Weather from the 15th of *April* to the 21. of *Auguſt*, *Anno* 1671. With a Deſcription of *Spitzburgen*, &c. [Tranſlated from the *High Dutch*, and printed in the Collect. of Voyages for Mr. *Churchill*. *Fol.* 1704. and in an Account of ſeveral Voyages of Sir *John Narborough*, &c. 8vo. 1711.]

The *Idolatry* of the *Eaſt-India* Pagans ; giving a full and true Account of the Religious Worſhip of the *Indoſthans*, the Inhabitants of *Coromandel*, the *Malabars*, and *Cyloneſes* ; with a Deſcription of their Idols and the Figures of them. [In the Collection of *Voyages* Printed for Mr. *Churchill*. *Vol.* III. 831 to *p.* 901.]

A Short Introduction to the *Malabar* Language ; with ſome Rules for attaining the Knowledge of it : Tables of Orthography in it ; and the *Lord's Prayer* and *Apoſtles Creed* in that Tongue ; With an Epiſtle concerning the *Malabars* Way of Writing, by *Philip Baldæus*. Dated at *Geervliet* 21. *July*, 1671. [In the Collection of *Travels* and *Voyages* by Mr. *Churchill*. *Fol.* *Vol.* III. *p.* 663.]

A Relation of a Journey of the Right Honourable My Lord *HENRY HOWARD* from *London* to *Vienna*, and thence to *Conſtantinople*, in the Company of his Excellency Count *Leſley*, Knight of the Order of the *Golden Fleece*, Counſellor of State to his *Imperial* Majeſty, *&c.* and Extraordinary Ambaſſador from *Leopoldus*, Emperor of *Germany*, to the Grand Signior *Sultan Mahomet Han* the Fourth. Written by *John Bunbury*, Gent. *London*, Printed for *J. Collins*, &c. 1671. 12°. *p.* 225.

The Relation of a Voyage made into *MAURITANIA* in *Africk*, by the Sieur *Roland Fr. j. . . Marſeilles*, by the *French* King's Order in the Year 1666.

1666. to *Muley Arxid*, King of *TAFILETTA*, &c. for the Eſtabliſhment of a Commerce in all the Kingdom of *FEZ* and all his other Con-
queſts: With a Letter in Anſwer to divers curious Queſtions concerning the
Religion, Manners and Cuſtoms of this Country. Alſo their Trading to
Tombutum for Gold, and divers other Particulars by Monſieur *de Charant*, who
lived fifteen Years in the Kingdom of *Fez* and *Morocco. Engliſhed* out of *French.*
London, ſold by *Moſes Pitt,* &c. 1671. 8vo. p. 119 & 71.

A Brief Narrative of the Progreſs of the Goſpel amongſt the *Indians* in
New-England in the Year 1670. Given in by the Reverend Mr. *John Eliot,*
Miniſter of the Goſpel there; in a Letter by him directed to the Right Wor-
ſhipful the Commiſſioners under His Majeſty's Great-Seal, for the Propaga-
tion of the Goſpel amongſt the poor blind Natives in thoſe United Colonies.
London, Printed for *John Allen.* 1671. 4to. p. 11.

A Journal kept by Capt. *John Narborough* from *May* 15. 1669, to *June* 10.
1671. in his Voyage to the *South-Sea,* by the Command of King *Charles* II.
And his Inſtructions for ſettling a *Commerce* in thoſe Parts. With a Deſcription of the Capes, Harbours, Rivers, Cuſtoms of the Inhabitants, and
Commodities in which they trade. *London,* 8vo. 1711.

An *Act* to prevent the Delivery up of Merchants Ships, and for the Increaſe
of good and ſerviceable *Shipping,* to the Honour of the *Engliſh* Navigation.
Anno xxij & xxiij. *Car.* II. *Cap.* xj.

An *Act* to prevent the Planting of *Tobacco* in *England,* and regulating the
Plantation Trade. *Ib. Cap.* xxvj.

Les Us & Coutumes de la Mer. I. *De la* Navigation. II. *Du* Commerce
Naval, *&* Contraites Maritimes. III. *De la* Juriſdiction *de la* Marine. *Avec
une Traité des Termes de Marine, Reglemens de la Navigation des Fleuves &
Rivieres & les nouveaux Edits, Reglemens, Arreſts & Jugemens rendus ſur le fait du*
Commerce *de la* Mer. *A* Rouen. MDCLXXI. 4to. p. 581 & 87.

A Treatiſe wherein is demonſtrated that the CHURCH and STATE
of *England* are in equal Danger with the TRADE of it. Treatiſe I. By
ROGER COKE. *London,* Printed for *Henry Brome.* 1671. With a
Second Treatiſe, containing Reaſons of the Increaſe of the *Dutch* Trade.
Wherein is demonſtrated from what Cauſes the *Dutch* govern and manage
Trade better than the *Engliſh*; whereby they have ſo far improved their
Trade

Trade above the *English*. P. 151. [*Ex dono Reverendi Viri* Lilij Butler, S. T. P.]

A Deputation given to Mr. *William Carter* by several *Woolen-Drapers* and other Dealers in the *Woolen Manufactures*, to Appear, Petition and Present before His *Majesty* and *Council*, and before the *Parliament*, their great Grievance from the Officers of the *Aulnage*, who enter their Shops, and carry away their Goods, &c.   Sign'd 14. *June* 1671, &c. [Abstract of the Proceedings of *W. Carter*. 1694. 4to. *Preface*.]

The History of the late Revolution of the Empire of the Great *MOGOL*; Together with the most considerable Passages for five Years following in that Empire.   To which is added a Letter to the Lord *Colbert* touching the Extent of *Indostan*, the Circulation of the Gold and Silver of the World to discharge it self there ; as also the Riches, Forces and Justice of the same, and the principal Cause of the Decay of the States of *Asia*, by Monf. F. *BERNIER*, Physitian of the Faculty of *Montpelier*.   *Englished* out of *French*. *London*, by *Moses Pitt*. 1671. 8vo. in 2 *Tomes*. Tom. I. *p*. 258. Tom. II. *p*. 176, & 102.

1672.   A Continuation of the Memoirs of Monsieur *BERNIER* concerning
24 *Car*. 2. the Empire of the Great *MOGOL* ; Wherein is contained, 1. An exact Description of *DEULI* and *AGRA*, the Capital Cities of the Empire of the Great *MOGOL* ; together with some Particulars making known the Court and Genius of the *Mogols* and *Indians*, &c. 2. The Emperor or *Mogol*'s Voyage to the Kingdom of *Kachemira* in the Year 1664. 3. A Letter written by the Author to M. *Chapelle* touching his Design of returning after all his Peregrinations to his Studies.   Tome III. and IV. *Englished* out of *French* by *H. O.* *London*, Printed for *Moses Pitt*. 1672. 8vo.

A Brief Advertisement to the *Merchants* and *Clothiers* concerning the *Woolen Manufactures* of *England*, &c. in the Year 1672. [Abstract of the Proceedings of *Will. Carter*. 1694. 4to. *p*. 16.]

A Letter out of *France* from one of the Duke of *Monmouth*'s Soldiers to his Friend in *London* ; Written from *Pontoise* the 1st. of *May*, 1672. *London*, Printed for *Robert Cutler*, 1672. Fol. 1 Sheet.

His Majesty King *Charles* IId's Declaration against the *States General* of the *United Provinces* of the *Low-Countries* ; Published by the Advice of His Privy Council.   Printed in the *Savoy* by the Assigns of *John Bill* and *Christopher Barker*, 167¾. Fol. *pag.* 8.

His

His Majesty's Gracious Declaration for the Encouraging the Subjects of the *United Provinces* of the *Low-Countries* to transport themselves with their Estates, and to settle in this His Majesty's Kingdom of *England*. Given at *Whitehall* the 12th of *June*, 1672. Printed in the *Savoy* by the Assigns of *John Bill* and *Christopher Barker*. 1672. In 2 Sheets. *Fol.*

A True Relation of the Engagement of His Majesty's Fleet under the Command of his Royal Highness with the *Dutch Fleet*, *May* 28. 1672. In a Letter from *Henry Savile*, Esq; on board his Royal Highness, to the *Earl of Arlington*, Principal Secretary of State. Dated from on Board the *Prince*, near the *Middle Ground*, *June* 6. 1672. With a Postscript giving an Account of the Number killed and wounded. Published by Authority, and Printed in the *Savoy* by *Thomas Newcomb*. 1672. 9 pages *Fol.*

An *Order of Privy Council*, giving Orders to the Commissioners of Prizes to release all *Dutch Ships*, Goods and Merchandizes seized in any of His Majesty's Ports before the Declaration of the War, or which voluntarily come in thither ; together with all Persons belonging to the same, and giving free Leave to all *Dutch* Merchants or others to depart the Kingdom if they think fit, without any Incumbrance or Molestation. Dated *Whitehall*, *May* 15th, 1672. Subscribed *Edw. Walker*, and Printed in the *Savoy* by the Assigns of *John Bill* and *Christopher Barker*. 1672. *Fol.* 1 Sheet.

The *most Christian Kings Declaration* of War against the States General of the *United Provinces* ; Done out of *French* according to the Copy printed at *Paris*. Published by Authority ; and Printed in the *Savoy* by *Tho. Newcomb*. 1672. *Fol.* 1 Sheet.

The Power of *Congregational* Churches Asserted and Vindicated ; in Answer to a Treatise of Mr. *J. Pages*, intituled, *The Defence of Church Government exercised in Classes and Synods*. By *JOHN DAVENPORT*, B. D. and Pastor to the Church in *Newhaven* in *New-England*. *London*, Printed in the Year 1672. 8vo. p. 179.

NEW-ENGLAND's Rarities discovered in Birds, Beasts, Fishes, Serpents and Plants of that Country : Together with the Physical and Chyrurgical Remedies, wherewith the Natives constantly use to cure their Distempers, Wounds and Sores. Also a perfect Description of an *Indian* SQUA in all her Bravery ; with a Poem, not improperly conferred upon her. Lastly, A Chronological Table of the most remarkable Passages in that Country

K k

amongst

amongst the English. Illustrated with Cutts. By JOHN JOSSELYN, Gent. London, Printed for G. Widdowes. 1672. 8vo. p. 184.

The American Physician; Or, A Treatise of the Roots, Plants, Trees, Shrubs, Fruit, Herbs, &c. growing in the English Plantations in AMERICA: Describing the Place, Time, Names, Kinds, Temperature, Vertues and Uses of them, either for Diet, Physick, &c. Whereunto is added a Discourse of the Cacao-Nut-Tree, and the Use of its Fruit; with all the Ways of making Chocolate: The like never extant before. By W. Hughes. London, for William Crook. 1672. 8vo. p. 159.

The Discoveries of John Lederer in three several Marches from VIRGINIA to the West of CAROLINA and other Parts of the Continent; begun in March, 1669, and ended in September, 1670. Together with a General Map of the whole Territory which he traversed. Collected and Translated out of Latin from his Discourse and Writings, By Sir William Talbot, Baronet. London, Printed for Samuel Heyrick. 1672. 4to. p. 27.

Relation de Divers Voyages curieux, qui n'ont point esté publiees, ou qui ont esté traduites d'Hackuyt, de Purchas, & d'autres Voyageurs Anglois, Hollandois, Portugais, Alemands, Italiens, Espagnols; & de quelques Persans, Arabes, & autres Autheurs Orientaux. Enrichies de Figures de Plantes non decrites, d'Animaux inconnus à l'Europe, & de Cartes Geographiques de Pays dont on n'a point encore donné de Cartes. Dedicees au Roy. IV. Partie. A Paris chez André Gramoisy. MDCLXXII. Fol. a ii.

Historica Relatio de Ortu & Progressu Fidei Orthodoxæ in Regno Chinensi per Missionarios Societatis Jesu ab Anno 1581. usq; ad annum 1669. Novissimè collecta ex Literis eorundem Patrum Societatis Jesu. Præcipue R. P. JOANNIS ADAMI SCHALL Coloniensis ex eadem Societate. Editio altera & aucta Geographicâ Regni Chinensis descriptione; Compendiosa Narratione de Statu Missionis Chinensis: & Prodigiis quæ in ultima Persecutione contigerunt, & Iudice. Cum Facultate Superiorum. Sumptibus JOAN. CONRADI EMMRICH Civis & Bibliopolæ. Ratisbona. Anno MDCLXXII. 8vo pag. 393.

Sinarum Scientia Politico-Moralis sive Scientia Sinicæ Liber inter CONFUCII Libros secundus à P. Prospero Intercerta Siculo Soc. Jesu è Sinensi Lingua in Latinam versa. Parisiis. MDC.LXXII. Fol. cum Confucii Vitâ Lat. Gal.

Beschre=

Beschreibung der OST-INDISCHEN Kusten MALABAR und COROMANDEL Dersabben angranthenden Konigreich und Landschaften als auch der Kaiserreichs ZEYLON Abgotterey der Ost Indischen Heyden. Amsterdam. By Johannes Janssonius van Waasberge en van Someren. *Anno* 1672. *Folio. per* Philippum Baldæum. *p.* 610. [*Ex dono* Awnshami Churchill, *Armigeri.*]

Madagascar, where the Author and his Company were massacred by the Inhabitants in 1672. Extracted from his own Journals. [In the Collection of Voyages by Mr. *Churchill.* Vol. II. p. 367]

Epistolæ Duæ, Quarum altera de Moribus ac Institutis Turcarum *agit, Altera Septem Asiæ Ecclesiarum notitiam continet. Authore* Tho. Smith, *Coll. D.* Mariæ Magdalenæ Oxon. Oxonii *Excudebat* H. Hall, &c. 1672. *8vo. p.* 171.

Philippi Cluverii. *Introductionis in Universam* Geographiam *tam veterem quam novam Libri VI. Tabulis Æneis illustrati. Accessit* P. Bertii *Breviarium Orbis Terrarum.* Amstelodami *ex* Off. Elzevir. *Anno* 1672. *8vo. p.* 388. [*Ex Dono Rev. Viri.* Geo. Baxter. *S. T. B.*]

An Act for the Encouragement of the *Greenland* and *Eastland* Trades, and for the better securing the Plantation Trade of *Newfoundland,* and other his Majesties Colonies and Plantations. *Anno* XXV. *Car.* 2. *Cap.* vii.   1673. 25 *Car.* 2.

The Travels of Father *Dominick Ferandez Navarette,* in *New-Spain* and *Mexico,* with his Voyage to the *Philippine* Islands, written by himself at his return home in the Year 1673. after he had been abroad 26 Years; being soon afterward promoted to an Archbishoprick in *Hispaniola.* [In the Collection of Voyages printed for Mr. *Churchill.* Fol. Vol. 1. p. 225.]

An Account of the Cape of *Good Hope* and the *Hottentotes,* the Natives of that Country, by *William ten Rhyne,* Native of *Daventry,* Physician in Ordinary, and a Member of the Council of Justice to the *Dutch East India Company,* with some Animadversions upon the same, by *Henry Secreta a Zevorzit.* Translated from the *Latin* Original, printed at *Schafhausen* in *Switzerland.* [Collection of Voyages for Mr. *Churchill.* Vol. 4. p. 829.]

Relations du R. P. IERONYMO LOBO *de L'Empire des ABYSSINES, des Sources du* Nil, *de la Licorne, du Palmiers, &c. imprimees la premiere fois le* II. Fevrier. 1673. [*Relation de divers Voyages Curieux.* 1672. Fol.]

The

The History of the United Provinces of *ACHAIA*. Collected in *Latin* by the Learned *Jacobus Gothofredus*, and rendred into *English*, with some Additions, by *Henry Stubbe*. *London* printed by *Andrew Clark*. 1673. 4*to*. *p*. 32.

A Relation of the Re-taking of the Island of St. *Helena* and 3 *Dutch East-India* Ships. Published by Authority, and Printed in the *Savoy* by *Thomas Newcomb*. 1673. *Fol*. 1 Sheet.

His Highness Prince *Rupert*'s Letter to the *Earl* of *Arlington*, His Majesty's Principal Secretary of State, from on Board the Royal *Charles* off the *Oster-bank*, the 29th of *May*, 1673. distant from *East-Capel* 7 Leagues at One of the Clock Afternoon, the Wind S. S. W. Published by Authority, and Printed in the *Savoy*, by *Tho. Newcomb*, in 1673. one Sheet *Fol*.

A Relation of the Engagement of His Majesty's *Fleet* with the Enemies on the 11th of *August*, 1673, as it has been represented by Letters from the several Squadrons. Published by Authority, and Printed in the *Savoy*, by *Thomas Newcomb*, in 1673. *Fol*. *p*. 12.

1674.
26 *Car.* 2.
Articuli PACIS & AMICITIÆ inter Serenissimum & Potentissimum Principem CAROLUM II. *Dei gratia* Magnæ Britanniæ, Franciæ & Hiberniæ, *Regem*, *Fidei Defensorem, &c. & Celsos ac Præpotentes Dominos* ORDINES GENERALES *Fœderatarum* Belgii *Provinciarum : Conclusi apud* Westmonasterium 9·19. *die* Februarij, *Anno Domini* 1673-4. *Excudebant Regiæ Majestatis Typographi*. 1674. 4*to*.

Articles of Peace between the most Serene and Mighty Prince *Charles* II. by the Grace of God King of *England*, &c. and the High and Mighty Lords the *States General* of the *United Netherlands* ; Concluded at *Westminster* the $\frac{9}{19}$ day of *February*, 167$\frac{3}{4}$. Published by His Majesty's Command. Printed by the Assigns of *John Bill* and *Christopher Barker*. 167$\frac{3}{4}$. 4*to*. *p*. 12.

The Prevention of *Poverty*; Or, A Discourse of the Causes of the Decay of *Trade*, Fall of *Lands*, and Want of *Money* throughout the Nation ; with certain Expedients for remedying the same, and bringing this Kingdom to an eminent Degree of Riches and Prosperity ; By saving many hundred thousand Pounds yearly, raising a full Trade and constant Employment for all sorts of People, and increasing His Majesty's Revenue, by a Method no way burthensome, thenfome, but advantagious to the Subject. By R. H. *London*, Printed for *Nathaniel Brooke*. MDCLXXIV. 4*to. p. 22.*

Doubts of the *Chinefe* Miffioners propofed *Anno* 1674. By the R. F. F. *Dominick Navarette* of the Order of Preachers, and Miffioner in *China*, to the Sacred General Congregation of the Holy *Roman* and Univerfal *Inquifition*; with the Anfwers returned to them, *Apr.* 22. 1674. [In the Collection of Voyages, Printed for Mr. *Churchill*. Fol. 1704. *Vol. I. p.* 396. *ad. p.* 421.

A New Voyage into the *Northern* Countries; Being a Defcription of the Manners, Cuftoms, Superftition, Buildings and Habits of the *Norwegians*, *Laponians*, *Kilops*, *Borandians*, *Siberians*, *Samojedes*, *Zemblans* and *Iflanders*: With Reflexions upon an Error in our Geographers about the Scituation and Extent of *Greenland* and *Nova-Zembla*. *London*, Printed for *John Starkey*. 1674. 12°. *p.* 153.

An Account of two Voyages to NEW-ENGLAND, wherein you have the Setting out of a Ship, with the Charges; the Prices of all Neceffaries for fur-nifhing a Planter and his Family at his firft coming: A Defcription of the Country, Natives and Creatures, with their Merchantil and Phyfical Ufe; the Government of the Country as it is now poffefs'd by the *Englifh*, &c. A large Chronological Table of the moft remarkable Paffages from the firft difcovering of the Continent of *America* to the Year 1673. By *John Joffelyn*, Gent. *London*, Printed for *Giles Widows*. 1674. 8*vo. p.* 279. Ep. Ded. to the Prefident and Fellows of the Royal Society

1675.
27 *Car.* 2.

The firft Principles of *NEW-ENGLAND*, concerning the Subject of Baptifm and *Communion* of *Churches*. Collected partly out of the printed Books, but chiefly out of the Original Manufcripts of the firft and chief Fathers in the *New-Englifh* Churches; With the Judgment of fundry Learned Divines of the *Congregational* Way in *England* concerning the faid Queftions. Publifhed for the Benefit of thofe who are of the Rifing Generation in *New-England*. By *Increafe Mather*, Teacher of a Church in *Bofton* in *New-England*. *Cambridge*, Printed by *Samuel Green*. 1675. 4*to. p.* 43.

A Difcourfe concerning the *Subject of Baptifm*, wherein the prefent Controverfies that are agitated in the *NEW-ENGLAND* Churches are, from Scripture and Reafon, modeftly enquired into. By *Increafe Mather*, Teacher of a Church in *Bofton* in *New-England*. *Cambridge*, Printed by *Samuel Green*. 1675. 4*to. p.* 76.

An

An Account of the Bay of *Campeachy* in the *West-Indies* and Parts adjacent, given by Mr. *William Dampier* in his Voyage thither from *Port-Royal* in *August*, 1675. [Captain *Dampier's* Voyages. *Vol. II. Part II.*]

England's Improvement. In Two Parts. In the Former is discoursed, how the Kingdom of *England* may be improved in Strength, Employment, Wealth, Trade. By encreasing the Value of Lands, the Revenues of the Crown and Church, Peace and Amity with Foreign Nations, without any Charge to the Subject. In the Latter is discoursed, how the *Navigation* of *England* may be increased, and the *Sovereignty* of the *British Seas* more secured to the *Crown* of *England*. By *Roger Coke*. *London*, for *Henry Brome*, &c. 1675. 4*to*. *p.* 115. [*Ex dono Rev. Viri* Lilij Butler, *S. T. P.*]

A *Proclamation* for the Discovery and Apprehension of Captain Don *Philip Hellen* alias *Fitz-Gerald*, who being our Natural born Subject took an *English* Merchant Ship within Musquet-shot of the Castle of *Havana*, a *Spanish* Port in the *West-Indies*, and after tortured and murdered *Timothy Stamp*, Master of the said Ship, called the *Humility of London*, and most of his Men. Given at *Whitehall* the first day of *October*, 1675. in the 27th Year of Our Reign.

A *Proclamation* for prohibiting the Importation of Commodities of *Europe* into any of his Majesty's *Plantations* in *Africa*, *Asia*, or *America*, which were not laden in *England*; and for putting all other Laws relating to the *Trade of the Plantations* in effectual Execution. Given at *Whitehall* the 24th day of *November*, 1675. in the 27th Year of our Reign.

The Present State of *NEW ENGLAND*, with respect to the *Indian* War; wherein is an Account of the true Reason thereof, (as far as can be judged by Men) together with most of the remarkable Passages that have happened from the 20th of *June*, till the 10th of *November*, 1675. Faithfully composed by a Merchant of *Boston*, and communicated to his Friend in *London*. Licensed *Dec.* 12. 1675. *London*, Printed for *Dorman Newman*. 1675. Fol. *p.* 19.

1676.
28 *Car.* 2. A Brief History of the War with the *Indians* in *New-England*, from *June* 24. 1675. (when the first *Englishman* was Murdered by the *Indians*) to *Aug.* 12. 1676. when *Philip*, alias *Metacommet* the principal Author and Beginner of the War was slain. Wherein the Grounds, Beginning, and Progress of the War is summarily express'd. Together with a serious Exhortation to the Inhabitants of that Land. By *INCREASE MATHER*, Teacher

of

of a Church of Chrift in *Bofton* in *New-England. London.* Printed for *Richard Chifwel.* 1676. 4to. *p.* 52. [*Ex dono Rev. viri* D. Gerfhomi Rawlins.]

News from *NEW-ENGLAND*; Being a true and juft Account of the prefent bloody Wars carried on betwixt the Infidels, Natives, and the *English* Chriftians and Converted *Indians* of *New-England,* declaring the many dreadful Battles fought betwixt them : As alfo the many Towns and Villages burnt by the mercilefs Heathens. And alfo the true Number of all the Chriftians flain fince the Beginning of that War, as it was fent over by a Factor of *New-England* to a Merchant in *London.* Printed for *J. Coniers,* 1676. 4to. *p.* 6.

A Continuation of the State of *NEW-ENGLAND*; being a further Account of the *Indian* War, and of the Engagement betwixt the joynt Forces of the *United English Colonies* and the *Indians,* on the 19th of *December,* 1675. With the true Number of the Slain and Wounded, and the Tranfactions of the *English* Army fince the faid Fight : With all other Paffages that have there happened from the 10th of *November,* 1675. to the 8th of *February,* 1675-6. Together with an Account of the Intended Rebellion of the *Negroes* in the *Barbadoes. London,* Printed for *Dorman Newman,* 1676. Fol. *p.* 20.

A New and Further Narrative of the State of *NEW-ENGLAND*; Being a continued Account of the Bloody *Indian War,* from *March* till *August,* 1676. Giving a perfect Relation of the feveral Devaftations, Enlargements and Tranfactions there ; As alfo the great Succeffes lately obtained againft the barbarous *Indians,* the Reducing of *King Philip,* and the Killing of one of the *Queens.* Together with a Catalogue of the Loffes in the whole fuftained on either fide fince the faid War begun, as near as can be collected. Licenfed *Octob.* 13. *London,* Printed for *Dorman Newman,* &c. 1676. Fol. *p.* 14.

A True Account of the moft confiderable Occurrences that have happen'd in the *War* between the *English* and the *Indians* in *NEW-ENGLAND,* from the *Fifth* of *May,* 1676, to the *Fourth* of *August* laft ; as alfo of the Succeffes it hath pleafed God to give the *English* againft them. As it hath been communicated by Letters to a Friend in *London.* The moft exact Account yet Printed. Licenfed *Octob.* 11th. *London,* for *Ben. Billingfley.* 1676. Fol. *p.* 6.

Several Remarkable Obfervations upon divers felect Articles in *Treaties* of Common *Alliance* and *Commerce,* concluded between Sovereign Princes and States. —— Fraud and Oppreffion detected and arraigned. — Several neceffary

sary Advertisements concerning the Improvement of *Navigation* and *Trade* : More especially the *Manufactures of England*, called the Old and New *Draperies*. — With an Epistle to the *Merchants Adventurers* of England, and all other *Merchants*, Subjects to the King of *Great-Britain*. By *George Carew* Dar. *Antwerp. Novemb.* 28. 1676. [*Ex dono Reverendi Viri* Willoughby Willey.]

A Treatise touching the *East-Indian* Trade : Or, A Discourse (turned out of *French* into *English*) concerning the Establishment of a *FRENCH COMPANY* for the *Commerce* of the *EAST-INDIES*. To which are annexed the Articles and Conditions whereupon the said COMPANY for the *Commerce* of the *East-Indies* is established. *London.* Printed for *H. B.* &c. 1676. 4to. p. 48.

ARTICLES of PEACE and COMMERCE between the most Serene and Mighty Prince *CHARLES* II. By the Grace of God King of *Great Britain*, &c. And the most Illustrious Lords, *Halil Bashaw Ibraim Dey*, Aga, Divan and Governours of the Noble City and Kingdom of *TRIPOLI* in *BARBARY*, concluded by Sir *John Narborough*, Knight, Admiral of his Majesties Fleet in the *Mediterranean* Seas, on the 5th day of *March*, old Stile, 1675-6 Published by his Majesties Command. *London.* By the King's Printer. 1676. 4to.

Feroæ & Feroa Reserata : That is, A Description of the Islands and Inhabitants of *FOEROE*, being Seventeen Islands subject to the King of *Denmark*, lying under 62 Deg. 10 Min. of North Latitude. Wherein several Secrets of Nature are brought to light, and some Antiquities hitherto kept in darkness are discovered. Written in *Danish* by *Lucas Jacobson Debes*, M. A. and Provost of the Churches there. Englished by *J. S.* [i. e. *John Sterpin*] Doctor of Physick. Illustrated with Maps. Printed for *William Iles*, &c. 1676. 8vo. p. 408. [concluding with a Learned Dissertation of *Specters, and Illusions of Satan in Feroe.*]

A Relation of a Voyage for the Discovery of a Passage by the *North-East* to *Japan* and *China* ; performed in his Majesties Ship the *Speedwell*, and *Prosperous Pink. Anno Domini* 1676. Wherein is shew'd the Reasons and Grounds of the Probability of a Passage before the Attempt ; with some good Observations made in the said Voyage, by *Captain John Wood*. [Account of Voyages. 1. Sir *John Narborough*, &c. 8vo. 1711.]

A Sup-

A Supplement to Captain *Wood's* and *Marton's North-East* Voyages. Containing some Observations and Navigations to the *North-West* of *Groenland*, and other Northern Regions. *Ibid. p.* 329.

The King's Letters Patents to his trusty and well beloved Subject *Henry Bond*, giving him full Leave, License, and Authority to print and vend his Book entituled, The LONGITUDE FOUND; Or, *A Treatise wherein is shewed and demonstrated an easy and speedy way, as well by Night as by Day to find the Longitude (having the Latitude of the Place) by the use of the Magnetick Inclinatory Needle ;* whose Pains therein has been greatly to our Satisfaction, *&c.* Given, *&c.* at *Whitehall* the 28th of *June*, in the 28th Year of our Reign, 1676. [Printed before the said Book. 4*to.* 1677.]

Two Letters concerning the *EAST-INDIA* Company. Printed in the Year 1676. 4*to. p.* 11.

An Answer to two Letters concerning the *EAST-INDIA* Company. Dat. *Bristol* 30. *June* 1676. [in Vindication of their just and honourable Measures, and their Undertakings great and successful.] Printed in the year 1676. 4*to. p.* 14.

The Happiness of a People in the Wisdom of their Rulers Directing, and in the Obedience of their Brethren Attending unto what *Israel* ought to do. Recommended in a Sermon before the Honourable Governour and Council, and the Respected Deputies of the *Massachusets* Colony in *New England.* Preached at *Boston, May* 3d. 1676. Being the day of Election there. By *William Hubbard*, Minister of *Ipswich. Boston.* Printed by *John Foster.* 1676.

Great News from the *BARBADOES*, or a true and faithful Account of the Grand Conspiracy of the *Negroes* against the *English*, and the happy Discovery of the same. With the number of those that were *burned Alive, Beheaded,* and otherwise *Executed* for their horrid Crimes. With a short Description of that *Plantation.* With Allowance. *London*, Printed for *L. Curtis.* 1676. 4*to. p.* 4.

Articles of Peace between the most Serene and Mighty Prince *CHARLES* II. 1677. by the Grace of God King of *England, Scotland, France* and *Ireland*, De- 29 *Car.* fender of the Faith, *&c.* And several *Indian* Kings and Queens, *&c.* Concluded the 29th day of *May*, 1677. *Published by his Majesty's Command. London*, Printed by *John Bill, Christopher Barker*, &c. 1677. 4*to.*

M m   The

The War in *NEW-ENGLAND* visibly ended. King *Philip* that barbarous *Indian* now Beheaded, and most of his bloody Adherents submitted to Mercy; the rest fled far up into the Country, which hath given the Inhabitants encouragement to prepare for their Settlement. Being a true and perfect Account brought in by *Caleb More*, Master of a Vessel newly arrived from *Rhode Island*. And published for general Satisfaction. Licensed *Novemb.* 4. *London*, Printed for *Francis Smith*. Fol. 1677. *p.* 5.

A Relation of the Troubles which have hapned in *NEW-ENGLAND* by reason of the *Indians* there. From the Year 1614. to the Year 1675. Wherein the frequent Conspiracies of the *Indians* to cut off the *English*, and the wonderful Providence of God, in disappointing their Devices is declared. Together with an Historical Discourse concerning the Prevalency of P R A Y E R, shewing that *New England*'s late Deliverance from the Rage of the Heathen is an eminent Answer of Prayer. By *Increase Mather*, Teacher of a Church in *Boston* in *New England*. *Boston*, Printed and sold by *John Foster*. 1677. 4to. *p.* 76. & 19. [*Ex dono Rev. Viri* Philippi Stubbs.]

The present State of *NEW-ENGLAND*, being a Narrative of the Troubles with the *Indians* in *New-England*, from the first planting thereof in the year 1607. to this present year 1677. But chiefly of the late Troubles in the two last Years, 1675, and 1676. To which is added a Discourse about the War with the *PEZUODS* in the Year 1637. By *W. Hubbard*, Minister of *Ipswich*. *London*, for *Tho. Parkhust*. 1677. 4to. 1. P. *p.* 131. 2 P. *p.* 88. Another Edition Printed at *Boston* by *John Foster*. 1677. Published by Authority.

Strange News from *VIRGINIA*. Being a full and true Account of the Life and Death of *Nathaniel Bacon*, Esq. who was the only cause and Original all the late Troubles in that Country. With a full Relation of all the Accidents which have happened in the late War there, between the *Christians* and *Indians*. *London*. Printed for *William Harris*. 1677. 4to. *p.* 8.

A List of several *Ships* belonging to *English Merchants*, taken by *French Privateers* since *December* 1673. Also a brief Account touching what Application hath been made for Redress at the Council Board, and with the Committee of Trade. *Amsterdam*, 1667. 4to. *p.* 44.

A Treaty Marine between the Most Serene and Mighty Prince C H A R L E S II. By the Grace of God King of *England*, *Scotland*, *France* and *Ireland*, Defender of the Faith, &c. And the most Serene and Mighty Prince

Prince *Lewis* the XIV the moſt *Chriſtian King.* Concluded at St. *Germains in Laye* the twenty fourth day of *February* 1676-7. Publiſhed by his Majeſty's Command. *London,* Printed by the Aſſigns of *John Bill* and *Chriſtopher Barker,* &c. 1677. 4*to. p.* 22.

Tractatus Marinus *inter Sereniſſimum & Potentiſſimum Principem* Carolum *II. Dei gratia* Angliæ, *&c. Et Sereniſſimum ac Potentiſſimum Principem* Ludovicum *XIV. Regem* Chriſtianiſſimum. *Concluſus apud* Sancti Germani *Fanum in* Layâ *decima quarta die* Februarii 1676-7. Londini-Regiæ *Majeſtati a Typis.* 1677. 4*to.*

The great Loſs and Damage to *England* by the tranſportation of WOOL to Foreign Parts. 4*to. p.* 20.

Iſrael Redux; Or, The Reſtauration of *Iſrael* exhibited in two ſhort Treatiſes: The firſt contains an Eſſay upon ſome probable Grounds, that the preſent *Tartars,* near the *Caſpian* Sea, are the Poſterity of the *Ten Tribes* of *Iſrael.* By *Giles Fletcher,* L. L. D. The ſecond a Diſſertation concerning their ancient and ſucceſſive State, with ſome Scripture Evidences of their future *Converſion,* and *Eſtabliſhment* in their own *Land.* By *S. L. London,* Printed by *S. Streater,* for *John Hancock,* &c. 1677. 8*vo. p.* 124. To which is added,
Eccleſia Gemens; Or two Diſcourſes on the mournful State of the Church, with a Proſpect of her dawning Glory. Exhibited in a View of two Scriptures, repreſenting her as a Myrtle Grove in a deep Bottom, and as a Knot of Lilies among Thorns. By *S. L.* Dat. *Apr.* 6. 1673. 8*vo. p.* 92.

Obſervations made by a Curious and Learned Perſon [Dr. *Henry Stubbs*] ſailing from *England* to the *Caribee-Iſlands*; concerning the Ruſting of *Iron* by the *Sea-Air*; the Changes of *Thames-Water* carried by *Sea*; the Variety of the Colours of the *Sea*; the Burning of the ſame; the Night-Winds in the *Indies*; The Relations of the Seaſons of the Year rectified; Obſervables about Tortoiſes; the Condition of *Engliſh* Bodies firſt coming to *Jamaica*; A way of preſerving *Ale* as far as to the ſame Iſland. [*Philoſophical Tranſactions,* Monday, *Septemb.* 23. 1667. 4*to.*

A Preface to the Four Goſpels, *&c.* of our Lord *Jeſus Chriſt,* and the *Acts of the Holy Apoſtles.* Tranſlated into the *Malayan* Tongue, by Dr. *Tho. Marſhall.* Dated *Lincoln-College* in *Oxon. Aug.* 9. 1677. Printed at *Oxford* by *H. Hall.* 1677. *p.* 14. [At the Charge of the Honourable *Robert Boyle,* Eſq;.]

An

An Abridgement of the Life and Death of *F. Gabriel Magaillans* of the Society of *Jesus* (Author of the New History of *China*) Missionary into *China*, written by *F. Lewis Buglio*, his inseparable Companion for six and thirty Years to the time of his Death at *De Kim* in 1677. [Annexed to *P. Magaillan's Hist.* of *China*. 8vo. 1668.]

The LONGITUDE Found; Or, A Treatise shewing an Easy and Speedy Way, as well by Night as by Day, to find the *Longitude*, having but the *Latitude* of the Place, and the Inclination of the *Magnetical Inclinatory Needle*. By *HENRY BOND*, Senior, Teacher of *Navigation*, and other Parts of the Mathematicks in *Storehouse*-Yard in *Ratcliffe*. Printed by the King's Majesty's Special Command. *London*, Printed by *W. Godbid*, and are to be sold by the Author *Henry Bond*. 1677. 4to. p. 65.

1678.
30 Car. 2.

The LONGITUDE not found; Or, An Answer to a Treatise written by *Henry Bond*, Senior, shewing a way to find the *Longitude* by the *Magnetical Inclinatory Needle*. Wherein is proved that the LONGITUDE is not, nor cannot be, found by the *Magnetical Inclinatory Needle*. By *Peter Blackborrow*, Gent. *London*, Printed for *Robert Harford*. 1678. 4to. p. 78.

The Antiquity of *CHINA*; Or, An Historical Essay, endeavouring a Probability that the Language of the Empire of *China* is the Primitive Language spoken through the World before the Confusion of *Babel*. Wherein the Customs and Manners of the *Chineans* are presented, and Ancient and Modern Authors consulted with: With a large Map of the Country. By *John Webb* of *Butleigh* in the County of *Somerset*, Esq; *London*, for *Obadiah Blagrave*. 1678. 8vo.

A Description of the Present State of *SAMOS, NICARIA, PATMOS* and Mount *ATHOS*. By *Joseph Georgirenes*, Archbishop of *SAMOS*, now living in *London*. Translated by one that knew the Author in *Constantinople*. *London*, by *Moses Pitt*, &c. 1678. 8vo. p. 112.

An Account of the Adventures of Captain *Cook* and his *English Bucaniers* in the Year 1678. His being taken by the *Spaniards*. The bold Exploits and Revenge of his Losses, performed by some few *Bucaniers* that were on board his Ship. [In the History of the *Bucaniers*. 1684. 4to. Part III. Chap. xj.]

State of the *Trade* between *England* and *Portugal* ; with the Particulars of the Benefits and Profits thereof, especially as to *Sugars* ; and what Consideration ought to be had to the encouraging our *English Plantations*, especially as to *Sugars* imported from *Barbadoes*.

An Act of Parliament for the Establishing Articles and Orders for the Regulating and better Government of His Majesty's Navies, Ships of War, and Forces by Sea. Anno XIII. *Car.* II. *London*, Printed by S. and B. *Griffin*, by Order of the Principal Officers and Commissioners of His Majesty's Navy. 1678. 4*to. p.* 12.

PHILOSOPHY Delineated ; Containing a Resolution of divers Knotty Questions upon sundry Philosophical Notions, *viz.* Concerning the Original of Springs, and of their irregular Ebbings and Flowings : Fresh Water Springs at the Bottom of the Sea : Motion of the Celestial Bodies about their particular Axes, *&c.* By *William Marshall*, Doctor of Physick, of the College of Physicians, *London*. *London*, Printed for *Obad. Blagrave*. 1678. 8*vo. p.* 237.

A Brief Account of the Rebellions and Bloodshed occasioned by the Antichristian Practises of the *Jesuites* and other Popish Emissaries in the Empire of *Ethiopia*. Collected out of a Manuscript History. Written in *Latin* by *JO. MICHAEL WANSLEBEN* a Learned Papist. *London*, Printed by *Jonathan Edwin*, &c. 1679. 4*to. p.* 37.

1679.
31 *Car.*

A Demonstration, how it is practicably possible to make a *Ship*, which shall be sustained by the *Air*, and may be moved either by *Sails* or *Oars* : Produced from an *Italian* Book, published by P. *Francesco Lana*, called *Prodromo*. [In Philosophical Transactions. 1679]

A Breviat of some Proposals prepared to be offered to the great Wisdom of the Nation, the King's Most Excellent Majesty, and Both Houses of Parliament, for the speedy Restoring the WOOLEN MANUFACTURE. By a Method practised in other Nations. Already Perused and Approved by those known Promoters of *England's* Weal and Safety, the most Illustrious Prince *Rupert*, and the Right Honourable the Earl of *Shaftsbury*, and since heard and encouraged by divers Members of the House of Commons, who upon perusal were pleased to declare, that the same would be of great Advantage to the NATION, *&c.* By R. *HAINES*. *London*, Printed for *Langly Curtis*. 1679. 4*to.*

N n   Certain

1680.
32 Car. 2. Certain Confiderations relating to the Royal *African* Company of *England*, in which the Original, Growth and National Advantages of the *Guiney* TRADE are Demonftrated. As alfo that the fame *Trade* cannot be carried on but by a *Company* and *Joint Stock*. Printed in the Year MDCLXXX. 4to. p. 10.

The Improvement of NAVIGATION a great Caufe of the Increafe of Knowledge. A Sermon Preached *June* 7. 1680. before the *Corporation* of TRINITY-HOUSE in *Deptford-Strand*, at the Election of their Mafter. By *Richard Holden*, Vicar of *Deptford*. Publifhed by their Appointment. *London*, Printed for *John Martyn*, at the *Bell* in St. *Paul's Church-yard*. 1680. 4to.

Wusku Wuttestamentum Nullordumun, *Jesus Christ* Nuppoquohwussuacneumun. [*i. e.* the *New Testament* of *Jesus Christ* tranflated into the *Indian* Tongue by Mr. *John Eliot*.] *Cambridge*, Printed for the Right Honourable *Corporation* in *London*, for the Propagation of the Gofpel among the *Indians* in *New-England*. 1680. 4to. With the *Pfalms* tranflated into *Indian* Metre; and a fhort *Catechifm* for the Inftruction of the *Indians*. [See the Old Teftament tranflated into the fame *Indian* Language, under the Year. 1685.]

A Confeffion of Faith Owned and Confented to by the Elders and Meffengers of the Churches affembled at *Boston* in *New-England*, May, 12. 1680. Being the fecond Seffion of that Synod. [Inferted in the *History of New-England*, by Mr. *Cotton Mather*, Fol. 1702. Book V. p. 5.]

Captain *Sharp's* Journal of his Expedition to the *Golden Island*, where he landed in *April* 1680. with defign to attack the Town of *Santa Maria*, &c. [Printed in Capt. *Hack's* Collection of Original Voyages. 8vo. 1699.]

An *Order* of the King in Council for the better Encouragement of all His Majefty's Subjects in their *Trade* to his Majefty's *Plantations*, and for the better Information of all His Majefty's Loving Subjects in thefe Matters. At the Court at *Whitehall*, the 16th of *February*, 1680. [*London. Gazette*, Numb. 1596.]

1681.
33 Car. 2. A Treatife, wherein is demonftrated; I. That the *East-India* TRADE is the moft National of all foreign Trades. II. That the Clamours, Afperfions and Objections made againft the prefent *East-India Company* are Siniter, Selfifh, or Groundlefs. III. That fince the Difcovery of the *East-Indies*, the

Domi-

Dominion of the *Sea* depends much upon the Wane or Increase of that *Trade*, and confequently the Security of the Liberty, Property, and the Proteftant Religion of this Kingdom. IV. That the Trade of the *Eaft-Indies* cannot be carried on to National Advantage in any other way than by a *General Joint Stock*. V. That the *Eaft-India* Trade is more profitable and neceffary to the Kingdom of *England*, than to any other Kingdom or Nation in *Europe*. *London*, Printed by *J. R.* for the Honourable the *Eaft India Company*. 1681. 4to. *p*. 43.

The Allegations of the *Turkey Company*, and others, againft the *Eaft-India Company*, relating to the Management of that *Trade* : Prefented to the Right Honourable the Lords of His Majefty's moft Honourable *Privy Council*, the 17th of *Auguft*, 1681. Together with the Anfwer of the faid *Eaft-India Company* thereunto, delivered in Writing the 22d Inftant, according to their Lordfhip's Order ; Upon which a Hearing was had before their Lordfhips the 24th of the faid Month. *Fol. p*. 15.

A Sermon Preached before the Right Honourable *GEORGE* Earl of *BERKELEY*, Governour, and the Company of Merchants of *England* trading into the *Levant-Seas*, at St. *PETER*'s Church in *Broadftreet*, *January* 25. 1680. By *CHARLES HICKMAN*, A. M. Student of *Chrift-Church* in *Oxon*. and Chaplain to his Excellency the Lord *Chandois*, Ambaffador to *Conftantinople*. *London*, Printed for *Henry Brome*. 1681. 4to.

An Hiftorical Relation of the Ifland *CEYLON* in the *EAST-INDIES* : Together with an Account of the Detaining in Captivity the Author, and divers other *Englifhmen* now living there ; and of the Author's miraculous Efcape. Illuftrated with Figures and a Map of the Ifland. By *ROBERT KNOX* a Captive there near twenty Years. *London*, Printed by *Richard Chifwell*. 1681. *Fol*.

A Sermon Preached before the Corporation of *TRINITY-HOUSE* in *Deptford-Strand*, *May* xxx. 1681. By *JOHN ROGERS*, A. M. Chaplain to the Right Honourable *GEORGE* Earl of *BERKELEY*. *London*. 4to. 1681.

The *HOLY INQUISITION* ; Wherein is reprefented what is the Religion of the Church of *Rome* ; And how they are dealt with that Diffent from it. *London*, Printed for *Joanna Brome*. 1681. 8vo. *p*. 250.

The

The Travels of the Sieur Mouette in the Kingdoms of FEZ and MOROCCO, during his eleven Years Captivity in those Parts, from his being taken by two Pirates of Salle in 1670, to his Redemption in 1681. With a Map of the Dominions of the King of Fez, by Talbe Rangiman, Doctor of the Alcoran. [Translated and Published in the Collection of Travels, by John Stevens. 1711. 4to. Vol. II.]

The Fundamental Constitutions of CAROLINA, and Form of Government agreed to by the Lords and Proprietors of the Province, with the Form of Subscription and Oath of Allegiance, under 110. Heads or Chapters; with Rules of Precedency 11 in Number; Witnessed the Twelfth day of January, 1681. Fol. p. 23. [Ex dono Reverendi Viri Gershomi Rawlins.]

1682.
34 Car. 2. CAROLINA; Or, A Description of the Present State of that Country, and the Natural Excellencies thereof; Viz. The Healthfulness of the Air, Pleasantness of the Place; Advantage and Usefulness of those rich Commodities there plentifully abounding, which much encrease and flourish by the Industry of the Planters that daily enlarge that Colony. Published by T. A. Gent. Clerk on board His Majesty's Ship the Richmond, sent out in the Year 1680. With particular Instructions to enquire into the State of that Country, by His Majesty's Special Command, and returned this present Year 1682. London, Printed for W. C. 1682. 4to. p. 36.

An Account of the Province of CAROLINA in America; together with an Abstract of the Patent and several other necessary and useful Particulars to such as have Thoughts of Transporting themselves thither. Published for their Information. London, Printed for Francis Smith. 1682. 4to. p. 26.

Some Account of the Province of PENSILVANIA in America, lately granted under the Great-Seal of England to William Penn, &c. Together with the Privileges and Powers necessary to the well governing thereof. Made publick for the Information of such as are or may be disposed to Transport themselves or Servants into those Parts. London, Printed and Sold by Ben. Clarke, &c. 1682. Fol.

The Frame of the Government of the Province of PENSILVANIA in America; together with certain Laws agreed upon in England by the Governour and divers Freemen of the aforesaid Province; to be further Explained and Confirmed there by the first Provincial Council and General Assembly that shall be held, if they see meet. Printed in the Year MDCLXXXII. Fol. p. 11.

A

A Brief Account of the Province of *East-Jerfoy* in *America*, publifhed by the prefent Proprietors, for Information of all fuch Perfons who are or may be inclined to fettle Themfelves, Families and Servants in that Country. *London*, Printed for *Benjamin Clark*. 1682. 4*to.* *p.* 6.

Propofals by the Proprietors of *East-Jerfoy* in *America*, for the Building of a Town on *AMBO-POINT*, and for the Difpofition of Lands in that Province: And alfo for Encouragement of Artificers and Labourers that fhall Tranfport themfelves thither out of *England*, *Scotland* and *Ireland*. *London*, Printed for *Benjamin Clarke*. 1682. 4*'c.* *p.* 6.

A Brief Account of Captain *Sharp* and other his Companions, *Bucaniers*; their Voyage from *Jamaica* unto the Province of *Darien* and the *South-Sea*; with the Robberies and Affaults they committed there for the fpace of three Years, till their Return for *England* in the Year 1682. Given by one of the *Bucaniers* who was prefent at thofe Tranfactions. [In the Hift. of *Bucaniers*. 4*to.* 1684. *Part* III. *Chap.* xij.]

The Humble Addrefs and Petition of His Majefty's Council and the Gentlemen of the Affembly for His Ifland of *Jamaica*, being met at *S*. *Jago de la Vega* the 21. day of *September*, 1682. by Order of His Excellency the Governour Sir *Thomas Lynch*. Prefented to His Majefty by the Lord Prefident and Lords of His Majefty's moft Honourable Privy Council for Governing His Majefty's Foreign Plantations. [*London Gazette*, N°. 1789.]

An *Order* of the King in *Council* to punifh and redrefs the frequent Abufes of a lewd fort of People, called *Spirits*, in feducing many of His Majefty's Subjects to go on *Ship-board*, where they have been feized and carried by force to His Majefty's Plantations in *America*.—— With a Declaration of His Majefty, that fuch Merchants, Factors, Mafters of Ships, or other Perfons that fhall ufe the Method hereafter following in the Hiring of Servants for His Majefty's Plantations, fhall not be difquieted, &c. *Whitehall*, Decemb. 13. 1682. [*London Gazette*, N°. 1782.]

Philofophical Tranfactions for *March*, 1682. Containing among other things, 3. A Relation of a Voyage made towards the *South Terra Incognita*; Extracted from the Journal of Captain *Abel Janfen Tafman*; by which not only a new Paffage by Sea to the Southward of *Nova Hollandia*, *Vandemen's Land*, &c. is difcovered, and a vaft fpace of Land and Sea incompaffed and failed round, but many confiderable and inftructive Confiderations concerning the Variation of the *Magnetical Needle* in Parts of the World almoft Antipodes

tipodes to us ; and several other curious Remarks concerning those Places and People are set forth. *London*, for *Richard Chiswell.* 1682. 4*to.*

A New History of *Ethiopia* ; Being a full and Accurate Description of the Kingdom of *Abyssinia*, vulgarly, though erroneously, called the Empire of *Prester John.* In Four Books : Wherein are contained, I. An Account of the Nature, Quality and Condition of the Country and Inhabitants, &c. II. Their Political Government, the Genealogy and Succession of their Kings, &c. III. Their Ecclesiastical Affairs, their Conversion to the Christian Religion, and the Propagation thereof, &c. IV. Their private Oeconomy, their Books and Learning, &c. Illustrated with Copper Plates. By the Learned *Job Ludolphus*, Author of the *Ethiopic Lexicon.* Made *English* by *J. P.* Gent. *London*, Printed for *Samuel Smith.* 1682. *Fol. p.* 398.

Philosophical Transactions for *February*, 1682. Containing, I. An Account of some very considerable Observations made at *Ballasore* in *India*, serving to find the Longitude of that place, and to rectifie great Errors in some modern Geographers, as to the Longitude of the *East-Indies*, communicated by Mr. *Edmund Halley.* 4*to.*

A Voyage to *Congo* and several other Countries, chiefly in *Southern-Africk.* By Father *Jerom Merolla da Sorrento*, a *Capucin*, and *Apostolick Missioner*, in the Year 1682. relating the Discovery of that Country, and first Missions to those Parts ; the Superstitions and Customs of the Blacks, &c. [In the Collection of Voyages Printed for Mr. *Churchill. Fol.* 1704. *Vol.* I. *p.* 655.]

Lex Talionis ; Or, the Law of Marque or Reprisals, fully represented in the Case of Spoils and Depredations upon the Ships, Goods and Factories of Sir *WILLIAM COURTEN* and his Partners in the *East-Indies*, *China* and *Japan.* Whereupon Letters Patents for Reprisals were granted, &c. Together with three several Proposals of the Creditors to the King, and their Answer (in a Postscript) to the Lord Chancellor's Arguments upon the *Scire Facias*, brought by Sir *Robert Sawyer*, His Majesty's Attorney-General, concerning the Letters Patents aforesaid. *London*, Printed in the Year MDCLXXXII. 4*to. p.* 28.

An Extract of Captain *John Usher's* Letter to Mr. *Edward Rudge*, Merchant in *London* : Dated from *Polose* the 20th of *June*, 1682. With Extracts out of the Consultation Books received from *Bantam*, and several Depositions there taken upon the Destruction of the *English* Factory in *BANTAM*, and the *Dutch* taking possession of it in 1682. [Printed at large in the Impartial Vindication of the *English East-India Company.* 1688. 8*vo.*]

A

A New Voyage to the *East-Indies*; Containing an Account of several of those rich Countries, and more particularly of the Kingdom of *BANTAM*,. Giving an exact Relation of the Extent of that Monarch's Dominions, the Religion, Manners and Customs of the Inhabitants, their Commerce, and the Product of the Country. And likewise a faithful Narrative of the Kingdom of *SIAM*, of the Isles of *JAPAN* and *MADAGASCAR*, &c. By Mr. *Glanius*. *London*, Printed for *H. Rodes*. 1682. 8*vo*. *p*. 183.

England's Interest; Or, The great Benefit to Trade by *Banks* or *Offices of Credit* in *London*, &c. As it hath been agreed upon by a *Committee* of *Aldermen* and *Commons* thereunto appointed by the Right Honourable the *Lord Major*, *Aldermen* and *Commons* in *Common Council* Assembled. Being a brief Account of the Management, Nature, Use and Advantages of the said *Offices*. *London*, Printed by *John Gain*, for the Office. 1682. 4*to*. *p*. 8.

Compendium Geographicum: Or, A more Exact, Plain, and Easie Introduction into all GEOGRAPHY than yet extant, after the latest Discoveries or Alterations. Very useful, especially for young Noblemen and Gentlemen, the like not Printed in *English*. By *Peregrine Clifford*, *Chamberlayne* of the *Inner Temple*, Gent. *London*, for *William Crook*. 1682. 8*vo*. *p*. 140.

A Description of *NEW-ENGLAND* in General; with a Description of the Town of *Boston* in particular. Published by *John Seller*. *London*. 1682.

A True History of the Captivity and Restoration of Mrs. *Mary Rowlandson* a Minister's Wife in *New-England*. Wherein is set forth the Cruel Usage she underwent among the *Indians* for 11 Weeks time. And how she escaped from them. Written by her own Hand for her private Use: And now made Publick at the earnest Desire of some Friends, for the benefit of the Afflicted. Whereunto is annexed a Sermon of the possibility of God's forsaking a People that have been near and dear unto him; Preached by Mr. *Joseph Rowlandson*, Husband to the said Mrs. *Rowlandson*. It being his last Sermon. Printed first in *New-England*. And Re-printed at *London*, 1682. 4*to*. *p*. 46.

An *Order* of *Council* for issuing a *Quo Warranto* against the *Charter* of the Colony of the *Massachusets* Bay in *NEW-ENGLAND*, with his Majesty's Declaration that in case the said *Corporation* of the *Massachusets* Bay, shall before Prosecution had upon the said *Quo Warranto* make a full Submission and entire

1683.
35 *Car*. 2

entire Refignation to his Royal Pleafure, He will then regulate their *Charter* in fuch manner as fhall be for his Service, and the good of that Colony: Given at *Whitehall* the 26th day of *July*, 1683. *London*, Printed by the Affignes of *John Bill* deceas'd, *&c.* 1683. *Fol.* 1 Sheet. [See more on this Subject in the Year 1688.]

A Relation of a Storm and great Deliverance at Sea in a Voyage from *NEW ENGLAND*, in a fmall Pink caled the *Adventure*, *John Balfton* Mafter, wherein Mr *Bernard Randolph* returned with his Brother Mr. *Edward Randolph*, who was fent to *New-England* with the *Quo Warranto* againft the Charter of the Colony of the *Maffachufets Bay*; who in a general Court Refolved to defend their *Charter* at Law. [Inferted in the Prefent State of the Iflands in the *Archipelago*, by *Bern. Randolph*. *Oxford* 1687. 4*to.*]

The prefent Profpect of the Famous and Fertile Ifland of *TOBAGO*, with a Defcription of the Situation, Growth, Fertility, and Manufacture of the faid Ifland. To which is added, *Propofals for the Encouragement of all thofe that are minded to fettle there.* By Captain *John Poyntz*. *London*. Printed by *George Larkin* for the Author. 1683. 4*to. p.* 47.

A Letter from *William Penn* Proprietory and Governour of *PENSYLVANIA* in *America* to the Committee of the Free *Society* of Traders of that Province refiding in *London*; containing a general Defcription of the faid Province, its Soil, Air, Water, Seafons and Produce, both Natural and Artificial, and the good Encreafe thereof. Of the Natives or Aborigines, their Language, Cuftoms, and Manners, Diet, Houfes or Wigwams, eafie way of Living. Phyfick, Burial, Religion, Sacrifices and Cantico, Feftivals, Government, and their Order in *Council* upon Treaties for Land, *&c.* Their Juftice upon Evil Doers. Of the firft Planters the *Dutch*, *&c.* and the prefent Condition and Settlement of the faid Province and Courts of Juftice, *&c.* To which is added an Account of *Philadelphia* newly laid out; its Scituation between two navigable Rivers, *Delaware* and *Skulkill*, with a Portraiture or Platform thereof, wherein the Purchafer's Lots are diftinguifhed, *&c.* And the profperous and advantagious Settlements of the Society aforefaid, within the faid City and Country, *&c.* Printed and Sold by *Andrew Sowle*, *&c.* 1683. *Fol. p.* 13.

To his moft Excellent Majefty the Humble *Addrefs* of the *Grand Jury* for the Body of the Ifland of *BARBADOS*, at a General Seffions holden for the faid Ifland on *Monday* the 2d of *April*, 1683. before the Honourable Lieutenant General *Henry Waldfond*, *&c.* with another Humble *Addrefs* of his Majefties

Majesties Council and General Assembly at Barbadoes. [London Gazette No 1824, & 1841.

The Laws of *JAMAICA* Passed by the Assembly and Confirmed by his Majesty in Council, *Feb.* 23. 1683. To which is added, A short Account of the Island and Government thereof, with an exact Map of the Island. *London,* Printed by *H. Hills,* for *Charles Harper.* 1683. *8vo.*

The Humble Address of the Council and General Assembly of *JAMAICA.* Presented to his Majesty by Sir *Charles Littleton,* Sir *Thomas Beckford,* Colonel *William Beeston,* and others, Merchants and Planters of that Island, on *Feb.* 29. 1683. [*London Gazette* No 1008.]

The Voyage of Captain *Cowley* from *England* to *America,* in *Aug.* 1683. and so round the *World,* taken from his Original Journal. [Printed in the Collection of Original Voyages by Capt. *Hacke.* 1699. *8vo.*]

The Present State of *ENGLAND, Part* III. and *Part* IV. Containing 1. An Account of the Riches, Strength, Magnificence, Natural Production, Manufactures of this Island, with an exact Catalogue of the Nobility with their Seats, *&c.* 2. The Trade and Commerce within it self, and with all Countries Traded to by the *English,* as at this day Established, and all other Matters relating to Inland and Marine Affairs. Supplying what was omitted in the two former Parts, useful for Natives and Foreigners. *London,* Printed for *William Whitwood, &c.* 1683. *8vo. p.* 362. [*Ex dono Rev. Viri* Lilij Butler, *S. T. P.*]

ENGLAND's Guide to *Industry;* or, Improvement of *Trade* for the good of all People in general. Or a Discourse of *Trade.* Being a Comparison between *England* and other Parts of *Europe.* Wherein the Encouragement of *Industry* is promoted in these Islands of *Great Britain* and *Ireland. London,* Printed for *J. Passinger* and *B. Took.* 1683. *8vo. p.* 112. [*Ex dono Rev. Viri* Lilij Butler, *S. T. P.*]

An Account of the *Commission* given to *Francis Monk* and others, for putting in Execution the Laws prohibiting the *Transportation of Wool* by Order of *Council,* dated 21st of *March,* 1682. and the *Report* from the said Commissioners. Given in the 8th of *June,* 1683. [Abstract of the Proceeding of *W. Carter.* 4to. 1694 *p* 8.]

1684.   An Account of Proposals made by the Commissioners appointed for hin-
36 Car. 2. dring the Transportation of Wool, 4th *Apr.* 1684. and transmitted to the
Commissioners of the Customs, and their Proceedings thereupon. [Abstract
of the Proceedings of *W. Carter.* 4*to.* 1694.]

The Planter's Speech to his Neighbours and Countrymen of
PENSYLVANIA, EAST and *WEST JERSEY;* and to
All Such as have Transported themselves into New-Colonies for the sake
of a quiet retired Life. To which is added the Complaints of our Supra-
Inferior-Inhabitants. *London.* 1684. 12°. *p.* 73. [*Ex dono Rev. Viri*
Gershomi Rawlins.]

The Humble *Address* of the *Chief Governour, Council* and *Representatives* of
the Island of *N E V I S* in the *West-Indies*, presented to his Majesty by Colonel *Netheway* and Captain *Jefferson*, at *Windsor*, May 3. 1684. [*London
Gazette,* N°. 1927.]

The Humble *Address* of His Majesty's *Lieutenant* and *Governour General* of
His Colony and Dominion of *VIRGINIA;* Together with the *Council* of
the same : With another Humble *Address* of the House of *Burgesses* of the
General Assembly of His Majesty's Dominion of *Virginia,* assembled at *James
City,* 16. *Apr.* 1684. [*London Gazette,* N°. 1979.]

BUCANIERS of *AMERICA;* Or, a true Account of the most
remarkable Assaults committed of late Years upon the Coasts of the *West-
Indies*, by the *Bucaniers* of *Jamaica* and *Tortuga*, both *English* and *French*.
Wherein are contained more especially the unparallel'd Exploits of Sir *Henry
Morgan*, our *English Jamaican* Hero, who sackt *Puerto Velo*, burnt *Panama*, &c.
Written originally in *Dutch*, by *John Esquemeling*, one of the *Bucaniers*, who
was present at those Tragedies, and translated into *Spanish* by *Alonso de Bonne
Maison*, M. D. &c. the Second Edition, corrected and enlarged with two
Additional Relations, *viz.* the one of Captain *Cook*, and the other of Captain
Sharp. Now faithfully render'd into *English*. *London*, Printed for *William
Crook*. 1684. 4*to.*

The Extract of a Letter from *Callicut*, dated the 5th of *May,* 1684.
Signed by Mr. *Thomas Michell*, Mr. *John Burniston*, and Mr. *Daniel Ack-
worth*, Agent and Council for the Honourable *English East-India* Companies
Affairs there ; Concerning their great Disputes there had with the *Dutch* :
With the Extract of other Letters to the same purpose. [Printed in the
Vindication of the *English East-India* Company. 1683. 8*vo*]

Collections

Collections of Travels through *TURKY* into *PERSIA* and the *EAST-INDIES*; Giving an Account of the Present State of those Countries : As also a full Relation of the five Years Wars between *Aureng Zebe* and his Brothers in their Father's Life-time, about the Succeſſion. And a Voyage made by the *Great Mogol,* *AURENGZEBE,* with his Army from *Debli* to *Lahor,* from *Lahor* to *Bember,* and from thence to the Kingdom of *Kachemire,* by the *Mogols* called the *Paradiſe of the* Indies. Together with a Relation of the Kingdom of *JAPAN* and *TUNKIN,* and of their particular Manners and Trade. To which is added, A New Deſcription of the *GRAND SEIGNIOR's SERAGLIO*; and alſo of all the Kingdoms that encompaſs the *Euxine* and *Caſpian* Seas. Being the Travels of Monſieur *TAVERNIER, BERNIER,* and other Great Men *London,* for *Moſes Pitt. MDCLXXXIV. Fol. p.* **154.**

The Voyages and Travels of *JOHN STRUYS* through *Italy, Greece Muſcovy, Tartary, Media, Perſia, Eaſt-India, Japan,* and other Countries in *Europe, Africa* and *Aſia* : Containing Remarks and Obſervations upon the Manners, Religion, Polities, Cuſtoms and Laws of the Inhabitants : And a Deſcription of their ſeveral Cities, Towns, Forts and Places of Strength ; Together with an Account of the Author's many Dangers by Shipwrack, Robbery, Slavery, Hunger, Torture, and the like. And two Narratives of the Taking of *Aſtracan* by the *Coſſacks,* ſent from Captain *D. Butler.* Illuſtrated with Copper-Plates, deſigned and taken from the Life by the Author himſelf. Done out of *Dutch* by *John Morriſon. London,* Printed for *Abel Swalle.* 1684. *4to. p.* 378.

CONO-CUNEUS; Or, the *Shipwrights Circular-Wedge* ; that is, a Body reſembling in part a *CONUS,* in part a *CUNEUS*; Geometrically conſidered. By *JOHN WALLIS,* D. D. Profeſſor of *Geometry* in the Univerſity of *Oxford,* and a Member of the *Royal-Society, London.* In a Letter to the Honourable Sir *Robert Moray,* Knight. *London,* Printed by *John Playford,* for *Richard Davis,* Bookſeller in the Univerſity of *Oxford.* 1684. *Fol. p.* 19.

An Act to encourage the Building of Ships in *England. Anno* 1. *Jac.* II. *cap.* 18.

Trade preferred before Religion, And Chriſt made to give place to Mammon ; Repreſented in a *Sermon* relating to the *Plantations.* Firſt Preached at *Weſtminſter-Abbey,* and afterwards in divers Churches in *London.* By
Morgan

1685.
1 *Jac.* 2.

Morgan Godwyn, fome time Student of *Chrift-Church* in *Oxford.* London, for *B. Tooke.* 1685. 4to. *p.* 34.

Mamuffe Wunnee tu panatam we tip Biblum God Naneefwe Nukkone Teftament Kah Wonk Wusku Teftament. Ne quosfhimmmmuk nafhpe Wuttinncumoh CHRIST *wob effeewefit* JOHN ELIOT *Nabôbteotu ontchetôt Printeneomuk.* CAMBRIDGE. *Printewoop nafhpe* Samuel Green. MDCLXXXV. 4to. [The Old Teftament tranflated into the *Indian* Tongue by Mr. *John Eliot.* And prefixed to the New Teftament which had been tranflated and printed in *New England* by the care of Mr. *Eliot,* and under the direction of the Corporation of *London,* erected for the Propagation of the Gofpel among the *Indians* in *New-England.* 1680. 4to. [which fee under the Year 1680.]

The Solemnity and Order of Proclaiming *James* King of *England, Scotland,* &c. in the Ifland of *B A R B A D O E S,* by Sir *Richard Dutton,* his Majefties Governour. And in the *L E E W A R D Iflands* by Sir *William Stapleton,* chief Governour. And in *V I R G I N I A* by the Lord *Howard* of *Effingham,* his Majefties Lieutenant and Governour General of that Colony. With the Humble Addrefs of the faid Governour and Council of *Virginia* in *May* 1685. [*London Gazette,* N° 2051.]

The Solemnity of Proclaiming his Majefty King *James* II. &c. at St. *Jago de la Vega* in *J A M A I C A,* by Colonel *Molefworth* Lieutenant Governour of that Ifland; with the Humble *Addrefs* of the faid Governour and Council of *Jamaica. Apr.* 16. 1685. With another Addrefs of the Governour and General Affembly of his Majefties Colony of *R H O D E I S L A N D* and *P R O V I D E N C E* Plantations in *N E W - E N G L A N D* in *America.* [*London Gazette.* N° 2053.]

The feveral Papers of Bufinefs that paffed between the *Englifh* Commiffioners, Inftructors for the *Englifh Eaft-India* Company, Sir *Jofeph Afhe* Baronet, Governour; Sir *Joffiah Child* Baronet, Deputy Governour; Sir *Benjamin Bathurft* and Sir *Jeremy Sambrook* Knights: And the Commiffioners Inftructors for the *Dutch Eaft-India Company,* during the Treaty managed in *French,* Sir *John Chardin* being Interpreter, in the Year 1685. [Publifh'd at large in the *Impartial Vindication of the* Englifh Eaft-India Company. 1688. 8vo.]

A Treatife of WOOL and the *Manufacture* of it: In a Letter to a Friend occafioned by a Difcourfe concerning the great Abatements of Rents, and Low Value of Lands: Wherein is fhewed how their Worth and Value may be advanced by the Improvement of the Manufacture and Price of our *Englifh Wool.* Together with the Prefentment of the *Grand Jury* of the County of

Somerfet,

Somerset, at the *General Quarter Sessions* begun at *Brewton* the Thirteenth Day of *January,* 1684. *London,* Printed for *William Crook,* 1685. 4to. *p.* 31.

A Defence of a Treatise entituled *England's Interest by the Improvement of the Manufacture of* WOOL, presented to be answered in a *Paper* entituled, *Reasons for a limited Exportation of Wool,* published *Anno* 1677. To which a Reply was then given, and is now improved, demonstrating that effectually to hinder the *Exportation of Wool* will cause the Recovery of our *Trade,* the raising the Price of *Wool,* and consequently of *Lands.* 4to. *p.* 54.

An Account of the two Sloops fitted out by his Majesty to prevent the Exportation of *Wool,* and the good Success thereof; and the Lord Treasurer's Letter to the Company of Merchant Adventurers of *England,* and other Transactions for promoting our Woollen Manufactures in the Year 1686. [Abstract of the Proceedings of *W. Carter.* 1694. 4to. *p.* 11.] `1686.` `2 Jac. 2.`

A Letter sent by the *Dutch* Governour and Council of *Palliacat* to the *English* Governour and Council of Fort St. *George,* bearing date in *August,* 1686. with the Answer of the *English* Governour and Council; with many other Papers relating to the Differences between the *English* and the *Dutch* in the *East-Indies.* [Printed at large in the *Vindication of the* English East-India Company. 1688. 8vo.]

At the Court at *Whitehall* the 26th day of *March,* 1686. Present the King's most Excellent Majesty, and the Lords of his Majesties most Honourable *Privy Council,* an *Order* to redress the frequent Abuses of a lewd sort of People called S P I R I T S, in seducing many of his Majesties Subjects to go on *Shipboard,* where they have been seized and carried by force to his Majesties *Plantations* in *America;* with a Declaration that this shall not tend to the disquieting any Merchants, Factors, Masters of Ships, or other Persons who shall use the method hereafter following, in hiring Servants for his Majesties *Plantations.* [*London Gazette* Num. 2132.]

Treaty of Peace, good Correspondence and Neutrality in *A M E R I C A* between the most Serene and Mighty Prince *J A M E S* II. By the Grace of God King of *Great Britain, France* and *Ireland,* Defender of the Faith, *&c* And the most Serene and mighty Prince *L E W I S* XIV. the most Christian King, Concluded the 6th. 16th day of *Novemb.* 1686. Published by his Majesty's Command. In the *Savoy,* Printed by *Thomas Newcomb,* &c. 1686. 4to. *p.* 19.

Articles of Peace and Commerce between the moſt Serene and Mighty Prince *JAMES* II. By the Grace of God King of *Great Britain, France* and *Ireland,* Defender of the Chriſtian Faith, *&c.* and the moſt Illuſtrious Lords the *Douletli Baſha, Aga,* and *Governours* of the famous City and Kingdom of *ALGIERS* in *Barbary* ; Ratified and Confirmed by Sir *William Soame* Baronet, His Majeſties Ambaſſador to the *Grand Seignior.* On the fifth of *April,* Old Style. 1686. Publiſhed by his Majeſties Command. Printed by *Thomas Newcomb* in the *Savoy.* 1687. 4to.

A Tutor to *Aſtronomy* and *Geography.* Or an eaſie and ſpeedy way to know the Uſe of both the GLOBES Celeſtial and Terreſtial. In Six Books, *&c.* More fully and amply than hath yet been ſet forth, either by *Gemma Friſius, Metius, Hues, Wright, Blaew,* or any Others that have taught the Uſe of the Globes. With an Appendix ſhewing the Uſe of the *Ptolomaick Sphere.* The fourth Edition corrected and enlarged. By *JOSEPH MOXON.* Whereunto is added the Ancient Poetical Stories of the Stars : Shewing the Reaſons why the ſeveral Shapes and Forms are pictured on the Cœleſtial Globe. As alſo a Diſcourſe of the Antiquity, Progreſs, and Augmentation of *Aſtronomy.* **London,** Printed by *S. Rycroft* for *Joſeph Moxon.* 1686. 4to. p.271.

Chriſtophori Cellarii Smalcaldienſis *Geographia Antiqua.* Ad veterum Hiſtoriarum, ſive à principio rerum ad Conſtantini Magni tempora deductarum faciliorem explicationem adparata. Præmiſſa eſt in omnium temporum Geographiam brevis Introductio. Cize Sumtu Jo. Bielkij, *&c.* MDCLXXXVI. 8vo. p.264.

The Preſent State of *MOREA,* called anciently *Peloponneſus,* which hath been near 200 Years under the Dominion of the *Turks,* and is now very much depopulated : Together with a Deſcription of the City of *Athens,* and the Iſlands of *Zant, Strofades* and *Serigo.* Faithfully deſcribed by *Bernard Randolph,* who reſided in thoſe Parts from 1671 to 1679. By His Majeſty's Special Licenſe. **London,** Printed for the Author. 1686. 4to. p.26.

1687.
3. Jac. 2.
An Hiſtorical and Geographical Account of the *MOREA, NEGROPONT,* and the Maritime Places, as far as *Theſſalonica.* Illuſtrated with 42 Maps of the Countries, Plains, and Draughts of the Cities, Towns and Fortifications. Written in *Italian* by *P. M. Coronelli,* Geographer to the Republick of *Venice.* Engliſhed by *R. W.* Gent. **London,** Printed for *Matthew Gillyflower,* &c. 1687. 8vo. p.230.

The

The Prefent State of the Iflands in the *A R C H I P E L A G O* or *A R C H E S* Sea of *Conftantinople*, and Gulph of *Smyrna*, with the Iflands of *Candia* and *Rhodes*. Faithfully Defcribed by *Ber. Randolph*. To which is annexed an *Index*, fhewing the *Longitude* and *Latitude* of all the Places in the New Map of *Greece*, lately publifhed by the fame Author. Printed at the *Theater* in *Oxford*. 1687. *4to. p.* 108.

By the King A *Proclamation* for the more effectual reducing and fuppreffing of *Pirates* and *Privateers* in *America*, as well on the Sea, as on the Land in great Numbers, committing frequent Robberies and Piracies, which hath occafioned a great Prejudice and Obftruction to Trade and Commerce, and given a great Scandal and Difturbance to our Government in thofe Parts. Given at *Whitehall* this 20th day of *January*, 1687. in the Third Year of Our Reign. [*London Gazette*, N°. 2315.]

The Prefent State of His Majefty's Ifles and Territories in *A M E R I C A*, *Viz. Jamaica, Barbadoes, St. Chriftophers, Nevis, Antego, St. Vincent, Dominica, New-Jerfey, Penfilvania, Monferat, Anguilla, Bermudas, Carolina, Virginia, New-England, Tobago, Newfoundland, Maryland, New-York*. With new *Maps* of every Place. Which will ferve as a conftant Diary or Calendar for the ufe of the *Englifh* Inhabitants in thofe Iflands, from the Year 1686 to 1700, *&c.* Licenfed *July* 20. 1686. *London*, Printed for *Dorman Newman*. 1687. *8vo. p.* 262. To which are added *Aftronomical Tables*.

Voyages d'un Francois *Exilè pour la Religion, avec Une Defcription de la* V I R G I N E *&* M A R I L A N *Dans l' Amerique, A la Haye.* Imprimè *pour l' Autheur.* 1687. *8vo. p.* 136. *Propofitions pour la* V I R G I N E *à* Londres *30 May, 1687. de la part des Proprietaires par* Nic. Hayward. [*Ex dono Reverendi Viri* Samuelis Blackwell, *S. T. B. Rectoris de* Brampton *in agro* Northton.]

A Relation of the Invafion and Conqueft of *F L O R I D A* by the *Spaniards*, under *Don Ferdinando de Soto*, in the Year 1538. And two Journeys of the prefent Emperour of *C H I N A* and *T A R T A R Y*, in the Years 1682 and 1683. With fome Difcoveries made by the *Spaniards* in the Ifland of *C A L I T O R N I A*, in the Year 1683. · Licenfed *June* 7th, 1686. *London*, Printed for *John Lawrence*. 1687. *8vo. p.* 272.

A Sermon Preached before the Right Honourable *G E O R G E* Earl of *B E R K E L E Y*, Governour of the Merchants of *England* trading into the *Levant* Seas, at St. *Peter's* Church in *Broadftreet*, *Jan*. 30. being *Sunday*, 1686-7.

1686-7. By *William Hayley*, M. A. Fellow of *All Souls* College in *Oxon.* and Chaplain to his Excellency Sir *William Trumbull*, Ambaffador to *Conftantinople. London*, Printed for *Sam. Smith*, &c. 1687. 4to.

A Juftification of the Directors of the *Netherlands* E A S T-I N D I A Company : As it was delivered over unto the High and Mighty Lords the *States General* of the *United Provinces*, the 22d of *July*, 1686. Upon the Subject and Complaint of Mr. *Skelton*, Envoy Extraordinary from the King of *Great-Britain*, touching the Affair of *Bantam*, and other Controverfies at *Macaffar*, and on the Coaft of *Malabar*, and at *Gamron* in the Gulf of *Perfia*. Likewife a Juftification, in Anfwer to the feveral Memorials lately given unto the *States General* by the Marquis of *Albeville*, touching *Meffepatam* and other Places in the *Indies*. Tranflated out of *Dutch* by a good Friend, for the Satisfaction of all fuch as are impartial Judges of the Matters now in difpute between the two Companies. Printed at *London* in the Year 1687. [Reprinted at the End of An Impartial Vindication of the *Englifh Eaft-India Company*. 8vo. 1688.] With the *Memorial* of the Marquis of *Albeville*, exhibited the 1ft of *Auguft*, 1687.

An Impartial Vindication of the *Englifh* E A S T-I N D I A *Company* from the unjuft and flanderous Imputations caft upon them in a Treatife intituled, *A Juftification of the Directors of the* Netherland's Eaft-India Company ; *as it was delivered over unto the High and Mighty Lords the* States General *of the* United Provinces. *Tranflated out of* Dutch, and feignéd to be printed at *London* in the Year 1687. But fuppofed to be Printed at *Amfterdam*, as well in *Englifh* as in *French* and *Dutch. London*, for *Sam. Tidmarfh*. 1688. 8vo. p. 221.

A Supplement of the Voyage round the World by Captain *William Dampier*, defcribing the Countries of *Tonquin, Achin, Malacca*, &c. their Product, Inhabitants, Mariners, Trade, Policy, &c. from the Author's Departure from *A.hin* to *Tonquin* with Captain *Weldon*, about *July*, 1688. [Voyages and Defcriptions by Captain *Dampier*, Vol. II.]

A New Hiftory of *C H I N A* containing a Defcription of the moft confiderable Particulars of that vaft Empire. Written by *Gabriel Magaillans* of the Society of Jefus Miffionary Apoftolick. Done cut of *French. London*, Printed for *Thomas Newborough*. 1688. 8vo. p. 352.

The Hiftory of the I N Q U I S I T I O N as it is exercifed at *G O A*. Written in *French* by the Ingenious Monfieur *Dellon*, who laboured 5 Years under thofe Severities, with an Account of his Deliverance. Tranflated

into

into *English* from the *French.* [By *Henry Waarten*] *London,* Printed for *James Knapton.* 1688. 4*to. p. 70.*

De Jure Maritimo & Navali; or a Treatife of Affairs *Maritime* and of *Commerce* in 3 Books, the 4th Edition. By *Charles Molloy. London,* Printed for *John Bellinger,* &c. 1688. *p.* 433.

Sir *Roger Strickland*'s Proceedings with the Squadron under his Command, upon the Preparations of the *Prince* of *Orange* in *London.* The Inftructions of King *James,* given to Sir *Roger Strickland* for intercepting the *Dutch Fleet,* at *Windfor,* 22th *Auguft,* 1688. The Strength of that Squadron. Propofals made by Sir *Roger ;* and contrary Directions fent by the King, 26. *Aug.* 1688. [In Mr. *Burchett's* Memoirs. 1703. *p. 2. &c.*]

King *James* his Inftructions to the Lord *Dartmouth* (appointed *Admiral* of the *Fleet*) for intercepting and deftroying the *Dutch Squadron*; Given at *Whiteball* 1. *Octob.* 1688. with a Lift of the Ships in our Fleet. With the Lord *Dartmouth*'s Proceedings before and after the Prince of *Orange* landed in *Torbay. Ibid. p.* 12.

By the King a *Proclamation,* Prohibiting his Majefties Subjects to Trade within the limits affigned to the *Governour and Company of Adventures of England trading into* HUDSON's BAY; except thofe of the *Company.* Given at our Court at *Whiteball* the one and thirtieth day of *March,* 1688. in the fourth Year of our Reign. [*London Gazette.* Numb. 2336]

To the King's moft Excellent Majefty, the Humble Addrefs of feveral Congregations in *NEW-ENGLAND.* Another Addrefs of his Majefties moft Loyal and Grateful Subjects the Inhabitants of his moft Ancient Colony of *NEW-PLIMOUTH,* in his Territory of *New-England.* A third Addrefs of his Majefties Governour and Council of his Majefties Dominion of *VIRGINIA.* 1688. [*London Gazette,* Numb. 2356, & 2357.]

De Succeffu Evangelii apud INDOS *in* NOVA ANGLIA *Epiftola ad Cl. Virum D.* Johannem Leufdenum *Linguæ Sanctæ in Ultrajectina Academia. Profefforem, Scripta à* Crefcentio Mathero *apud* Boftonienfes *V. D. M. necnon Collegii* Harvardini *quod eft* Cantabrigiæ *Nov-Anglorum, Rectore.* Londini. *Typis* J. G. 1688. 8*vo. p.* 13. [Tranflation of it into *English,* publifhed in Mr. *Cotton Mather's Hift. of New-England.*]

R r   *NEW*

NEW-ENGLAND Vindicated from the Unjuſt Aſperſions caſt on the Government there, by ſome late *Conſiderations* pretending to ſhew that the **CHARTERS** *in thoſe Colonies were taken from them on Account of their Deſtroying the* Manufactures *and* Navigation *of* England. [An Account of which ſee under the year 1683.] 1688. 4to. p. 8. [*Ex dono Rev.* Roberti Watts, L. L. B. Col. D. Johan. Oxon. Socii.]

A Narrative of the Miſeries of *NEW-ENGLAND*, by reaſon of an *Arbitrary Government* erected there. 1688. 4to. p. 8. [*Ex dono Reverendi* Gerſhomi Rawlins.]

1689.
1 W. & M. A Brief Relation of the State of *NEW-ENGLAND*, from the Beginning of that *Plantation* to this preſent Year 1689. In a Letter to a Perſon of Quality. Licenſed. *July* 30. 1689. *London,* for *Richard Baldwine.* 1689. 4to. p. 18.

An Account of the late *Revolution* in *NEW-ENGLAND*, together with the *Declaration* of the Gentlemen, Merchants, and Inhabitants of *BOSTON* and the Country adjacent. *April* 18. 1689. Written by Mr. *Nathaniel Byfield*, a Merchant of *Briſtol* in *New-England* to his Friends in *London.* Licenſed *June* 27. 1689. *London,* for *Richard Chiſwel.* 1689. 4to. p. 20.

The Preſent State of *NEW-ENGLAND* impartially conſidered in a a Letter to a Friend, chiefly upon this Queſtion : *For what Reaſons and to what End did we take up Arms ?* London. 4to. p. 44.

A Copy of the Fundamental Conſtitutions of *CAROLINA*, agreed on by all the Lords Proprietors, and ſigned and ſealed by them, *Apr.* 11th. 1689. the Original being ſent to *Carolina* by Major *Daniel.* 4to.

The Groans of the *Plantations*, or a True Account of their grievous and extreme Sufferings, by the heavy Impoſitions upon **SUGAR**, and other Hardſhips relating more particularly to the Iſland of *BARBADOES.* *London,* Printed by *M. Clarke.* 1689. 4to. p. 35.

The Preſent State of the *MOREA*, called anciently *Peloponneſus* : Together with a Deſcription of the City of *ATHENS*, Iſlands of *Zant,* *Strofades,* and *Serigo*: With the Maps of *Morea* and *Greece,* and ſeveral Cities. Alſo a true Proſpect of the Grand *Seraglio* or Imperial Palace of *Conſtantinople,* as it appears from *Galata* : Curiouſly engraved on Copper
Plates.

Plates. By *Bernard Randolph* The Third Edition. *London*, Printed and Sold by *Will. Watts*, *Tho. Basset*, and *Tho. Bennet*. 1689. 4*to*. *p.* 26.

The Proceedings of the Earl of *Torrington* at Sea : His Engaging the *French* at *Bantry* on the Coast of *Ireland* : His Lordship's farther Motions with the Fleet, after refitting at *Portsmouth*. 1689 [In Mr. *Burchett's* Memoirs. 1703. 8*vo*. *p.* 20. &c.]

An Account of the Proceedings of Captain *George Rook* with a Squadron on the Coast of *Ireland*, to assist the Generals of the Land Forces in the Reduction of that Kingdom, in 1689. *Ib. p.* 25.

Admiral *Russell's* Expedition with the Queen of *Spain* to the *Groyn*, in the latter end of 1689. *Ib. p.* 34.

The *Instructions* given to Vice-Admiral *Killegrew*, Knight, with a Squadron to the *Streights* ; with an Account in what manner the *Thoulon* Ships got through and joyn'd the Fleet at *Brest*. 1690. [In Mr. *Burchett's* Memoirs. 8*vo*. 1703. *p.* 37.]

1690.
2 *W.* & *M.*

The Earl of *Torrington's* Engagement with the *French Fleet* off of *Beachy* ; with an Account of what happened thereupon, in relation as well to himself, as other Matters. 1690. [*Ib. p.* 45.]

The Proceedings of the *Fleet* in the Taking of *Cork* in *Ireland*, under the joint Command of Sir *Richard Haddock*, Admiral *Killegrew*, and Sir *John Ashby*, in *September*, 1690. [*Ib. p.* 51, &c.]

An Account of Sir *Cloudesly Shovell's* Proceedings with a Squadron on the Coast of *Ireland*, in Attendance upon King *William*, in 1690. [*Ibid. p.* 58, &c.]

A Plain Relation of the late *Action at Sea* between the *English and Dutch*, and the *French* FLEETS, from *June* 22. to *July* 5th last ; With Reflections thereupon, and upon the Present State of the Nation : Together with a *Preparation for Death*, and a *Persuasive to Criminals to do Right to their Country*, and a *Specimen* of a BILL for REFORMATION of MANNERS, drawn for the Bishops, and mentioned in the following Reflections. [By Mr. *Stafford*.] *London*, Printed for *John Harris*. 1690. 4*to*. *p.* 56, — 8, —8—.

The

The late *Plot on the Fleet detected*; with the *Jacobites* Memorial to the *French* King; and an Account of those Gentlemen who invited the *French Fleet* to invade our *English* Coasts. 1690. 4*to.* *p.* 4.

An Exact and Faithful Account of the most Glorious and Signal VICTO-RY obtained by Vice-Admiral *Killegrew*, who Commands their Majesties Ships in the *Mediterranean*, over the *French Thoulon* Squadron in those Seas, who were making their way to *Brest* : Together with a particular Relation of that happy Engagement with those Ships taken, disabled or sunk, as it is transmitted hither by Authentick and Credible Hands from the Port of *Cadiz*, and confirmed by an Express over Land from Mr. *Stanhope*, their Majesties Envoy Extraordinary at the Court of *Madrid*. *London*, Printed for *L. C.* 1690. A Half Sheet, *Fol.*

A True Copy of the Original CARTEL agreed on between the *Allies* and the *French* King, for the Exchange or Ransom of Prisoners from the General or Mareschal of *France* down to the Private Sentinel. Signed *December* 29th, 1690. *London*, Printed and Sold by *J. Whitlock*. 4*to.* *p.* 14.

Philosophical Transactions for the Months of *January* and *February*, 1690-1 ; Containing among other things, A Description of the P I M I E N T A or *J A M A I C A*-P E P P E R Tree, and of the *Tree* that bears the *Cortex Winteranus*, communicated by *Hans Sloane*, M. D. and *Reg. Soc. S.* An Account of the Circulation of the Watry Vapours of the S. E. A. and of the Cause of *Springs* ; communicated to the Royal Society by *E. Halley.*

An Account publish'd, as received from *Barbadoes*, *Aug.* 26. 1690. of the late Successes of our Forces in the *Leeward Islands*, under the Command of Colonel *Codrington*, Governour Chief, and Captain General of the same. [*London Gazette*, N°. 2602.]

A Letter from the Baron *Lahontan*, dated at *Monreal* in *Canada*, *October* 2. 1690. relating to the Attempts of the *French* and *Indians* upon *New-England* and *New-York* : A fatal Embassy sent by the *French* to the *Iroquese* ; and an ill concerted Enterprize of the *English* and the *Iroquese*, in marching by Land to attack the *French* Colony at *Quebec.* [In *Lahontan's* Voyages to *North-America.* 1703. 8*vo. Vol.* I. *p.* 155.]

An Apology for the *East-India Company* ; With an Account of some large Prerogatives of the Crown of *England*, anciently exercised and allowed for in our Law, in Relation to Foreign Trade and Foreign Parts. By *W. A.* Barrister

Barrifter at Law, Author of the Firft Anfwer to the late Chief Juftice *Herbert's* Defence of the Difpenfing Power. *London*, Printed for the Author. 1690. 4*to. p.* 40.

A Letter from the Baron *Lahontan*, lately returned from *Canada*; Dated at *Rochel*, *January* 12. 1691. Being a Relation of a fecond and very impor- 1691. tant Expedition of the *Englifh* by Sea; in which is contain'd a Letter written 3 *W. & M.* by the *Englifh* Admiral [Sir *William Phipps*] to the Count of *Frontenac*; with this Governour's verbal Anfwer. As alfo an Account of the Author's Departure for *France*. [In the New Voyages of *Lahontan* ✹ *North-America.* 8*vo.* 1703. *Vol.* I. *p.* 155.]

To the King's Moft Excellent Majefty, the Humble Addrefs of divers of the Gentry, Merchants, and others, Your Majefties moft Loyal and Dutiful Subjects inhabiting in *Bofton*, *Charles-Town* and places adjacent, within Your Majefties Territory and Dominion of *NEW-ENGLAND* in *America*. With a Letter, dated *Charles-Town*, *New-England*, *Novemb.* 22. 1690. giving an Account of the unfortunate Expedition to *Quebec* in *Canada*, the Induce- ments to it, *&c.* Sign'd *L. H.* Licenfed *Apr.* 28th. 1691. 4*to. p.* 8.

The Humble Addrefs of the *Publicans* of *NEW-ENGLAND*, to which KING you pleafe; with fome REMARKS upon it. *London*, Printed in the Year 1691. 4*to. p.* 35.

The Intereft of the Nation, as it refpects all the *Sugar Plantations* Abroad, and Refining of *Sugars* at Home; truly ftated, and humbly offered to the Honourable Houfe of Commons. *London*, Printed by *B. Motte.* 1691. 4*to. p.* 11.

Philofophical Tranfactions, for the Months of *March*, *April*, *May*, and *June*, 1691. Containing among other things, *Obfervations on the making of Co-* *chineal*, according to a Relation had from an old *Spaniard* at *JAMAICA*, who had lived many Years in that part of the *Weft-Indies*, where great quan- tities of that rich Commodity are yearly made.

Philofophical Tranfactions for the Months of *July*, *Auguft* and *September* 1691; Containing among other things, the *Method the* Indians *in* VIRGINIA *and* CAROLINA ufe to drefs *Buck* and *Doe-Skins*; as it was commu- nicated to the Royal Society by the Honourable Sir *Robert Southwell*, Knt. their Prefident.

An Act of the General Assembly of the Province of *NEW-YORK* and Territories depending thereon in *America,* for the quieting and settling the Disorders that have lately happen'd within this Province, and for the establishing and securing their Majesties present Government against the like Disorders for the future. Printed in the Tryal of Col. *Nicholas Bayard.* Fol. 172.

An Account of a large and curious *Map* of the Great *Tartary,* lately published in *Holland,* by Mr. *Nicholas Wilsen,* being an Extract of a Letter from the Author thereof to the Honourable Sir *Robert Southwell,* Knight, and President of the Royal Society. [In *Philosophical Transactions* for *June,* 1691.]

A most compleat Compendium of G E O G R A P H Y General and Special; Describing all the Empires, Kingdoms and Dominions in the whole World: Shewing their Bounds, Situation, Dimensions, &c. Together with an Appendix of General Rules for making a large Geography, with the great Uses of that Science. The second Edition. By *Lawrence Eachard* of *Christ's-College* in *Cambridge.* *London,* for *Tho. Salisbury.* 1691. 8vc. p. 227.

A Discourse concerning the most seasonable Time of Felling of Timber for the building of *Ships,* and especially in regard to the Royal *Navy.* Written by advice of the Honourable *Sam. Pepys,* Esq; Secretary of the Admiralty, and presented to His late Majesty. By *Robert Plott,* L. L. D. and R. S. Soc. Now first published in 1691. [*Philosoph. Transactions,* for *Feb.* 1691.]

An Essay towards a Scheme or Model for erecting a *National E A S T-INDIA Joynt Stock,* or a *Company* more generally diffused and enlarged for the Restoring, Establishing and better Carrying on that most important Trade ; fully discoursed in a Letter to a Person of Quality. *London,* Printed for the Author. MDCXCI. Ded. to the Honourable *Committee* of Parliament appointed to bring in a Bill for settling an *East-India Company.* Dat. *London,* 12. *Jan.* 1691-2. Fol. p. 26.

An Account of the *Trade* to the *E A S T-I N D I E S* ; together with the State of the present Company, and the best Method for establishing and managing that *Trade* to the Honour and Advantage of the Nation. Written by Mr. *George White* of *London,* Merchant, at the Desire of several Members of both Houses of Parliament, and now made publick for general Information in an Affair of so great Concern to the whole Kingdom. *London,* 1691. Fol.

Fol. p. 13. [*Ex dono Reverendi* Rob. Watts, L. L. B. Coll. D. Johan. Oxon. *Socij.*]

A True and Faithful Relation of the Proceedings of the Forces of their Majesties King *William* and Queen *Mary* in their Expedition against the *French* in the *CARIBBY-ISLANDS* in the *West Indies*, under the Conduct of his Excellency *Christopher Codrington*, Captain General and Commander in Chief of the said Forces in the Years 1689 and 1690. Written by *Thos. Spencer*, Jun. Secretary to the Honourable Sir *Timothy Thornhill*, Baronet, to whose Regiment he was Muster-Master, and supplied the Place of Commissary. *London*, Printed for *Robert Clavel*. 1691. 4to. *p*. 12.

The *Proceedings* of Admiral *Russel* in Search of the *French* FLEET in the *Soundings*, and in keeping Monsieur *Du Bart* from getting out of *Dunkirk*. 1691. [In Mr. *Burchett's Memoirs*. 1703. *p*. 63.]

The *Instructions* given to Sir *Ralph Delavall*, sent with a Squadron into the *Soundings*, after the Fleet was called in. 1691. *Ib. p.* 105.

An Account of the *Expedition* to the *West-Indies* in a Squadron under Command of Captain *Lawrence Wright*, with his *Instructions* in *December*, 1689: With the Actions at Land under General *Codrington*, &c. and Return of the Squadron in 1691. *Ib. p.* 110, &c.

The Account given by Sir *John Ashby*, Vice-Admiral, and Rear-Admiral *Rooke*, to the Lords Commissioners of the *Engagement* at *Sea* between the *English*, *Dutch* and *French* FLEETS, *June* 30th, 1690. With a Journal of the FLEET since their Departure from St. *Hellens*, to their Return to the *Buoy in the Nore*, and other material Passages relating to the said *Engagement*. *London*, Printed for *Randal Taylor*. 1691. 4to. *p*. 32.

A Letter from the Baron *Lahontan* dated at *Quebeck*, *Novemb*. 10. 1691. containing an Account of the Author's Departure from *Rochel* to *Quebeck*, of his Voyage to the Mouth of the River St. *Lawrence*; of a Rencounter he had with an *English* Ship which he fought: Of the stranding of his Ship; of his Sailing thro' the River St. *Lawrence*; of the News he receiv'd that a Party of the *English* and *Iroquese* had defeated a Body of the *French* Troops. [New Voyages to *North America*. By the Baron *Lahontan*. 1703. 8vo. Vol. 1. *p*. 171.]

A Letter from the Baron *Lahontan*, dated at *Nantz*, *Octob*. 25. 1692. Containing an Account of the Taking of some *English* Vessels of Defeating a Party of *Iroquese* ; Of an *Iroquese* burnt alive, as *Quebec* ; Of another Party of these *Barbarians*, who having surprized some *Coureurs de Bois* were afterwards surprized themselves. Of the Project of an Enterprize proposed by Mons. *Frontenac* to the Author. Of the Author's Departure in a Frigat for *France*, and his stopping at *Placentia*, which was attackt by an *English Fleet* that came to take that Post. How the *English* failed in their Design, and the Author pursued his Voyage. [Voyages of the Baron *Lahontan* to *North-America*. 8vo. 1703. Vol. I. p. 175.]

The Proceedings of Admiral *Russell* in his Engaging the *French* Fleet off of Cape *Barfleur*, and burning many of the *French* Ships at *Cherbroke* and *La Hogue*. [In Mr. *Burchett*'s Memoirs. 1703. 8vo. p. 134.]

Order of Council at *Whitehall*, *Aug.* 8. 1692. for Security of the Merchant Ships intending for the *West-Indies*, and especial Protection of such as will carry a Proportion of Men, Provisions and Stores, for their Majesties Service to those Plantations. [*London Gazette*, N°. 2791.]

The *Clothiers* Complaint : Or, Reasons for passing the Bill against the *Blackwell-Hall* Factors, &c. Shewing it to be a Publick Good. Humbly offered to the Parliament. *London*, Printed for *Randal Taylor*. 1692. 4to. p. 37. With the Substance and Intent of the said Bill.

An Account of the Cause of the Change of the Variation of the *Magnetical Needle* ; with an Hypothesis of the Structure of the Internal Parts of the Earth, as it was proposed to the *Royal Society* in one of their late Meetings. By *Edm. Halley*. [Published in *Philosoph. Transactions*, *Octob.* 1692.]

Joannis Luyts, *Philosophiæ Professoris*, *Introductio ad* GEOGRAPHIAM Novam & Veterem ; *in qua necessaria hujus Scientiæ Prolegomena ; intermixto usu* Globi Terrestris, *necnon Oceani & Regionum constitutio perspicuo ordine pertractantur. Adjiciantur suis locis Oceani, Terræ, & cujusq; Regionis Tabulæ, item Chartæ* LXV Sansonis, *inter quas quædam hac forma antè ineditæ*. Trajecti ad Rhenum *ex officina* Francisci Halma, *Acad. Typogr.* M DC XCII. 4to. p. 764.

Joannis Luyts, *Philosophiæ Professoris*, ASTRONOMICA *Institutio, in qua Doctrina* Sphærica *atque* Theorica, *intermixto usu* Sphæræ Coelestis, *& varijs Chronologicis, pertractantur. Adjunctæ sunt in illustrationem Argumenti pluribus in locis Figuræ Æneæ diversæ*. Trajecti ad Rhenum *ex officina* Francisci Halma, *Acad. Typogr.* M DC XCII. 4to. p. 231. *Institutionis* Astronomici *Synopsis*. p. 55.

Septem

Septem ASIÆ *Ecclefiarum &* CONSTANTINOPOLEOS. *Authore* Thoma Smitho, *Ecclefiæ* Anglicanæ *Presbytero. Editio nova auctior & emendatior. Trajecti ad Rhenum, ex officina* Francifci Halma. cI‫ כ‬DCXCII. *8vo. p.* 126. [*Ex dono Rev. Viri* Geo. Baxter, *S. T. B.*]

An Account of the great Divifions amongft the *Quakers* in PENS'LVANIA, *&c.* As appears by their own Book here following, Printed 1692. and lately come from thence, entitled *The Plea of the Innocent againft the falfe Judgment of the Guilty.* Being a Vindication of *George Keith* and his Friends, who are joyned with him in this prefent Teftimony, from the falfe Judgment, Calumnies, falfe Information and Defamations of *Samuel Jenings, John Simcock, Thomas Lloyd* and others joyn'd with them, being in number twenty eight. Directed by way of Epiftle to Faithful Friends of Truth in *Penfilvania, Eaft* and *Weft Jerfey,* and elfewhere, as occafion requireth. *London,* by *John Guillim.* 1692. *4to. p.* 26. [*Ex dono Rev. Viri* Gerfhomi Rawlins.] [See more on this Subject under the Year 1694.]

A Short Story of the Rife, Reign and Ruin of the *Antinomians, Familifts,* and *Libertines,* that infected the Churches of NEW-ENGLAND, and how they were confuted by the Affembly of Minifters there; as alfo of the Magiftrates Proceedings in Court againft them, *&c.* Publifhed by T. W. *London,* Printed for *Tho. Parkhurft.* *4to.* 1692. *p.* 64.

An Impartial Account of the moft memorable Matters of Fact touching the fuppofed WITCHCRAFT in NEW-ENGLAND beginning at *Salem Village,* at the latter end of *February,* 1691. and foon fpreading into feveral Parts: With the Copies of Letters, Warrants, Indictments, Trials, Confeffions, *&c.* [Printed at large in *Mr.* Caleff's *More Wonders of the Invifible World. 4to.* 1700. *p.* 90.]

The Wonders of the Invifible World: Being an Account of the Tryals   1693. of feveral WITCHES lately executed in NEW-ENGLAND; and ⸂ *W. & M* of feveral remarkable Curiofities therein occurring. By COTTON MATHER. Publifhed by the fpecial Command of his Excellency the Governour of the Province of the Maffachufets-Bay in New-England. The Second Edition. 1693. *4to. p,* 62.

A further Account of the NEW-ENGLAND *Witches*; With the Obfervations of a Perfon who was upon the Place feveral days when the fufpected *Witches* were firft taken into Examination. To which are added Cafes of Confcience concerning *Witchcrafts* and *Evil Spirits* perfonating Men. Written at the Requeſt of the Miniſters of *New-England.* By *INCREASE MATHER,* Preſident of *Haward Colledge, London,* Printed for *J. Dunton.* 4to. 1693. *p.* 10 & 39.

The Reaſons given by ſeveral Perſons why they withdraw from Communion with the Church of *Salem* Village in *New-England.* 1. The diſtracting and diſturbing Tumults and Noiſes made by the Perſons under Diabolical Power and Deluſions, &c. Read to their Paſtor Mr. *Samuel Parris,* 21. *Apr.* 1693. and ſigned by them. [Printed at large in Mr. Calef's *More Wonders of the Inviſible World.* 4to. 1700. *p.* 95. &c.] With Mr. *Parris's* Acknowledgment thereupon. See more on this Subject under the Year 1695.

Certain Propoſals made by the *Preſident* and *Fellows* of *Haward College* to the Reverend Miniſters of the Goſpel, in ſeveral Churches of *NEW ENGLAND,* for obſerving and recording the more illuſtrious Diſcoveries of the *Divine Providence* in the Government of the World. Dat. *Cambridge, March* 5. 1693-4. [Printed in Mr. Calef's *More Wonders of the Inviſible World.* 4to. 1700.]

Another Brand plucked out of the Burning, or more Wonders of the Inviſible World. Written by Mr. *C. M.* relating to the Afflictions of *Margaret Rule,* pretending to ſuffer ſtrange Fits by *Witchcraft;* with the Copies of ſeveral Letters relating to Matters of Fact and Opinion hereupon. 1693. [Printed at large in Mr. Calef's *More Wonders of the Inviſible World.* 4to. 1700. *p.* 1, &c.] See more on this Subject under the Years 1694. 1696 and 1704.

Account of the late Earthquake in *Jamaica, June* 7th, 1692. Written by a Reverend Divine there to his Friend in *London.* With ſome Improvement thereof by another Hand. *London,* for *Tho. Parkhurſt.* 1693. 4to. *p.* 20.

Philoſophical Tranſactions for the Month of *December,* 1693. containing, 1. A Letter from Mr. *John Clayton,* Rector of *Crofton* at *Wakefield* in *Yorkſhire,* giving a farther Account of the Soil of *Virginia,* and planting of *Tobacco* there, with the draining of Swamps, &c. As likewiſe a Deſcription of the ſeveral Species of Birds obſerved there by himſelf; with ſeveral curious Remarks on the Heads of Fowl, &c. 4to. *Vol.* xvii.

A Continuation of Mr. *John Clayton's* Account of *Virginia;* of the Earth and Soil; [*Philoſophical Tranſactions* for the Month of *November.* 1693. 4to.]

An

An Account of Sir *Francis Wheeler's* Proceedings in an Expedition to the *West-Indies*, from *November* 1692. to his Return in *October* 1693. [*Burchett's* Memoirs. 1703. 8vo. p. 168.]

The Proceedings of the *English Fleet* this Summer under Command of Admiral *Killegrew*, Sir *Ralph Delaval*, and Sir *Cloudesly Shovel*, &c. [*Ibid. p.* 176.]

An Order of *Council* [for the Encouragement of Sea Commanders, and for better regulating the Fleet,] done at *Whitehall* 22d of *February*, 1693. 1 sheet *Fol.*

A True and Exact Account of the retaking of a Ship called the *Friends Adventure* of *Topsham* from the *French*, after she had been taken six Days; and they were upon the Coasts of *France* with it four Days, where one *Englishman* and a *Boy* set upon seven *Frenchmen*, killed *two* of them, took the other *five* Prisoners, and brought the Ship and them safe to *England*. Their Majesties Customs of the said Ship amounting to 1000*l.* and upwards. Performed and written by *ROBERT LYDE*, Mate of the same Ship. *London*, Printed for *Richard Baldwin.* 1693. 4to. *p.* 32.

England's Safety, or a Bridle to the *French* King: Proposing a sure Method for Encouraging NAVIGATION, and raising Qualified SEAMEN for the well managing their Majesties FLEET on any Occasion in a Month's Time without *Impressing*; and a competent Provision for all such as shall be Wounded in Service against the Enemy, either in their Majesties Ships of War, Privateers or Merchantmen, to encourage the better defending them: Also an insight into the Advantages which may be made by the HERRING and other FISHERIES, in respect to the breeding of *Seamen* and otherwise. Together with a Proposal for the Maintenance and Education of the Male Children of all such as shall be killed in the Service, to Qualifie them for the Sea in Order to make Officers. Also Encouragement for Commanders of Men of War, Privateers and Seamen in taking any Ship or Effects of the Enemies, and all to be done without any sensible Charge or Burthen to the Kingdom. By Capt. *GEORGE St. LO. London*, Printed for *W. Miller.* 1693. *p.* 48. [Together with an Epistle Dedicatory to both Houses of Parliament, giving an Account of the Barbarities he met with from the *French* during his being Prisoner in *France*, and the Barbarities exercised on the other *English* Prisoners, as well as *French Protestants*.]

A Journal

A Journal of the late Actions of the French at Canada, with the manner of their being repuls'd by his Excellency *Benjamin Fletcher*, their Majesties Governour of *New-York*. Impartially related by Coll. *Nicholas Reyard*, and Lieutenant Coll. *Charles Lodowick*, who attended his Excellency, during the whole Expedition. To which is added, 1. An Account of the present State and Strength of *Canada*, given by two *Dutchmen*, who have been a long time Prisoners there, and now made their Escape. 2. The Examination of a *French* Prisoner. 3. His Excellency *Benjamin Fletcher*'s Speech to the *Indians*. 4. An Address from the Corporation of *Albany* to his Excellency, returning Thanks for his Excellency's early Assistance for their Relief. Licensed. *Sept.* 11. 1693. *London*, Printed for *Richard Baldwin*. 1693. 4to. *p.* 28.

A new Discovery of *Terra Incognita Australis*, or the *Southern World*, by *James Sandeur*, a Frenchman, who being cast there by a Shipwreck, lived 35 Years in that Country, and gives a particular Description of the Manners, Customs, Religion, Laws, Studies and Wars of those Southern People; and of some Animals peculiar to that Place: with several other Rarities. These Memoirs were thought so curious, that they were kept Secret in the Closet of a then great Minister of State, and never published till now since his death. Translated from the *French* Copy Printed at *Paris* by publick Authority. *London*, Printed for *John Dunton*. 1693. 12°. *p.* 186.

A new Historical Relation of the Kingdom of *SIAM*, by Monsieur *DE LA LOUBERE*, Envoy Extraordinary from the *French* King to the King of *Siam* in the Years 1687. and 1688. Wherein a full and curious Account is given of the *Chinese* way of Arithmetick, and Mathematick Learning. In two Tomes. Illustrated with Sculptures. Done out of *French* by *A. P.* Gen. *R. S. S.* *London*, for *Tho. Horne*. MDCXCIII. *Fol. p.* 288. [P. III. Chap. XXV. Diverse Observations to be made in preaching the Gospel to the Orientals.]

A Collection of Curious Travels and Voyages. In two Volumes. The first containing Dr. *Leonhart Rawolf*'s Itinerary into the Eastern Countries, as *Syria*, *Palestine*, or the *Holy Land*, *America*, *Mesopotamia*, *Assyria*, *Chaldea*, &c. Translated from the *High Dutch* by *Nicholas Staphorst*. The second taking in many parts of *Greece*, *Asia Minor*, *Egypt*, *Arabia Felix*, and *Petræa*, *Ethiopia*, the *Red Sea*, &c. from the Observations of Mons. *Belon*, Mr. *Vernon*, Dr. *Spon*, Dr. *Smith*, Dr. *Huntingdon*, Mr. *Greaves*, *Alpinus*, *Veslingius*, *Thevenot*'s Collections and others. To which are added three Catalogues of such Trees, Shrubs and Herbs as grow in the *Levant*. By *John Ray*, Fellow of the

the Royal Society. *London*, Printed for *S. Smith*, and *B. Walford*. 1693. 8*vo*. *p*. 396. 18*d*. & 4*s*.

The Chriſtian Doctrine and Society of the People called QUAKERS, cleared from the Reproach of the late Diviſion of a few in ſome Part of *America*, as not being juſtly chargeable upon the Body of the ſaid People there or elſewhere: *London*. Printed for *Thomas Northcote*. 1693. 8*vo*. *p*. 20.

A further Account of the great Diviſions among the QUAKERS in *Penſilvania*, &c. as appears by another of their Books lately come over from thence, Intituled, *Some Reaſons and Cauſes of the late Separation* that hath come to paſs at *Philadelphia*, betwixt us, called by ſome the *Separate Meeting*, and others that meet apart from us. More particularly opened, to vindicate and clear us, and our Teſtimony in that reſpect, *viz*. That the Separation lieth at their Door, and *They*, and not *We*, are juſtly chargeable with it. With an Apology for the preſent Publication of theſe things. *London*, Printed for *J. Dunton*, &c. 1693. 4*to*. *p*. 23. [*Ex dono Reverendi Viri* Gerſhomi Rawlins.]

More Diviſions amongſt the QUAKERS, as appears by the following Books of their own writing : *Viz*. I. The Chriſtian Faith of *New England Quakers* condemned by a Meeting of *Penſilvanian Quakers*. II. The Falſe Judgment of a Yearly Meeting of *Quakers* in *Maryland*, condemned by *George Keith*, *Thomas Budd*, &c. all *Quakers*. To which is added, A Diſcovery of this Myſtery of Iniquity, by *GEORGE KEITH*. Reprinted 1693. 4*to*. *p*. 22. [*Ex dono Rev.* Gerſhomi Rawlins.]

The Chriſtian *Quaker* ; Or, *GEORGE KEITH*'s Eyes opened. Good News from *Penſilvania*. Containing a Teſtimony againſt that falſe and abſurd Opinion which ſome hold, *viz*. *That all true Believers and Saints immediately after the Bodily Death attain to all the Reſurrection they expect, and enter into the fulleſt Enjoyment of Happineſs.* And alſo, *That the Wicked immediately after Death are raiſed up to receive all the Puniſhment they are to expect.* Together with a Scriptural Account of the Reſurrection of the Dead, Day of Judgment, and *Chriſt*'s Laſt Coming and Appearance without us. Alſo where and what thoſe Heavens are into which the Man *Chriſt* is gone and entered into. By *GEORGE KEITH*. Printed in *Penſilvania*, and Reprinted in *London*. 1693. 4*to*. *p*. 12. [*Ex dono Rev. Viri* Gerſhomi Rawlins.]

U u

The

The Judgment given forth by Twenty eight *Quakers* against *George Keith* and his Friends; With Answers to the said Judgment, declaring those Twenty eight Quakers to be NO CHRISTIANS: As also an Appeal (for which several were imprisoned, &c.) by the said *George Keith*, &c. to the Yearly Meeting. *Sept.* 1692. With a full Account of the said Yearly Meeting. Signed by 70 Quakers. Licensed *Oct.* 28. 1693. Printed in *Pensilvania*. Now Reprinted at *London*. 4*to.* *p.* 22.

The Tryals of *Peter Boss*, *George Keith*, *Thomas Budd* and *William Bradford*, Quakers, for several great Misdemeanours (as was pretended by their Adversaries) before a Court of *Quakers*; At the Sessions held at *Philadelphia* in *Pensylvania* the Ninth, Tenth and Twelfth Day of *December*, 1692. Giving also an Account of the most arbitrary Proceedure of that Court. Printed in *Pensilvania*. Reprinted in *London* for *R. Baldwin*. 1693. 4*to. p.* 34.

An Essay on WOOL and WOOLEN MANUFACTURES for the Improvement of *Trade*, to the Benefit of Landlords, Feeders of Sheep, Clothiers and Merchants: In a Letter to a Member of Parliament. *London*, for *Hen. Bonwick*. 1693. 4*to.*

An Act for the Regaining, Encouraging and Setling the *Greenland* Trade, as very beneficial to this Kingdom. *Anno* iv and v *Will. Mar. Cap.* xvii.

1694
6 *W. & M.* A Discourse of the Nature, Use and Advantages of TRADE, proposing some Considerations for the Promotion and Advancement thereof. 1. By a Registry of Land. 2. Preventing the Exportation of *Coyn*. 3. Lowering the Interest of Money. 4. Inviting Foreign Families into *England*. *London*, for *Randal Taylor*. 1694. 4*to. p.* 30.

An Abstract of the Proceedings of *William Carter* against Transportation of *Wool*. Being a Plea to some Objections urged against Him. *London*, Printed for the Author. MDCXCIV. 4*to. p.* 27.

An Abstract of the *Grievances of Trade* which oppress our Poor. Humbly Offered to the Parliament. *London*, Printed in the Year 1694. 4*to. p.* 18.

Two several Letters of a Gentleman in *New-England*, endeavouring to prove the received Opinions about *Witchcraft*. With two *Answers* of *R. C.* to the same, denying those Opinions, and rather thinking them the Errors of *Pagan* and Papal *Rome*. 1694. [Printed at large in *Mr. Calef's More Wonders of the Invisible World*. 4*to.* 1700. *p.* 83.]

An

An Account of Captain *Wilmot*'s Proceedings with a Squadron to and in the *West-Indies*, with the Instructions given him in that Expedition, and Orders for the Distribution of the Prizes and Booty that should be taken in the *West-Indies*. 1694. [Inserted in Mr. *Burchet*'s Memoirs. 8vo. 1703. p. 305.]

A Letter from the Baron *Lahontan*, dated at *Viana* in *Portugal*, *January* 31. 1694. Containing an Account of the Writer's Departure from *France* for *Placentia* in *Newfoundland*. A Fleet of thirty *English* Ships came to seize upon that place, but is disappointed and sheers off. The Reasons why the *English* have bad Success in all their Enterprises beyond Sea. The Writer's Adventure with the Governour of *Placentia*, &c. [New Voyages to *North America* by the Baron *Lahontan*. 1703. 8vo. Vol. I. p. 193.]

England's Interest; or a Discipline for SEAMEN. Wherein is proposed a sure method for raising Qualified SEAMEN, for the well Manning their Majesties FLEET on all Occasions. Also a method whereby SEAMEN will be obliged mutually to relieve each other on Board the Men of War Yearly, or thereabouts; except where any Seaman by his own voluntary Consent shall be willing to stay longer. Likewise is shewed the Advantages which by these Methods will accrue to the Nation in General, and in Particular to the Merchants and Seamen; for hereby the Wages now given in Merchant Ships, will be brought lower, and every Seaman will have the liberty of chosing his own Commander after the first Year, and continuing with him if he so likes. By Captain *GEORGE St. LO. London*, Printed for *Robert Clavel*. 1694. 4to. p. 51.

A modest and true Account of the Proceedings against Mr. *ABRAHAM ANSELM*, late Secretary to the late Admirals of the Fleet, as they happened, and were brought on before the Right Honourable their Majesties Principal Secretary of State, their Majesties most Honourable Privy Council, their Majesties Council at Law; and as they were examined by the Grand Jury for the County of *Middlesex*, at the Sessions held at *Hicks's Hall*, *Sept*. 6. 1693. in a Letter to a Friend. By *JOHN PRAED. London*, Printed for *Abel Roper*, 1694. 4to. p. 30. [Consisting of many Letters, Certificates and Affidavits relating to his Traiterous Affection to K. *James*.]

A New Discourse of TRADE, wherein is Recommended several Weighty Points relating to Companies of MERCHANTS, the Act of NAVIGATION, NATURALIZATION of Strangers
And

And our WOOLEN MANUFACTURES. The BALLANCE of TRADE, and the Nature of PLANTATIONS, and their Consequences, in Relation to the Kingdom, are seriously Discussed. And some Proposals for erecting a Court of Merchants for determining Controversies, relating to Maritime Affairs, and for a Law for transferrance of Bills of Debts are humbly offered by Sir *Josiah Child*. *London*, Printed and Sold by *Sam. Crouch*, &c. 1694. 8vo. p. 238. [*Ex dono Rev. Viri Lilii Butler. S. T. P.*]

A Continuation of Mr. *John Clayton*'s Account of *Virginia* ; giving a short Description of the Beasts and Serpents thereof. [*Philosophical Transactions* for the Month of *May*. 1694 4to.]

A further Discovery of the Spirit of Falshood and Persecution in *SAM. JENNINGS* and his Party that joined with him in *PENSYLVANIA*, and some Abetters that cloak and defend him here in *England*. In Answer to his scandalous Book, called, *The State of the Case*. By *George Keith*. *London*, Printed for *R. Levis*. 1694. 4to. p. 52.

The Life and Death of the Reverend Mr. *John Eliot*, who was the first Preacher of the Gospel to the *INDIANS* in *AMERICA*. With an Account of the wonderful Success which the Gospel has amongst the Heathen in that Part of the World. And of the many strange Customs of the Pagan *Indians*. Written by *Cotton Mather*. The third Edition carefully corrected. *London*, Printed for *John Dunton*, MDCXCIV.

A brief Narrative of the Success of which the Gospel hath had among the *INDIANS* of *MARTHAS VINEYARD* (and the Places adjacent) in *NEW-ENGLAND*, with some Remarkable Curiosities, concerning the Numbers, the Customs, and the present Circumstances of the *Indians* in that *Island*. Further explaining and confirming the Account given of those Matters, by Mr. *Cotton Mather*, in the Life of the Renowned Mr. *John Eliot*. By *Matthew Mayhew*. Whereunto is added the present State of Christianity among the *Indians* in other Parts of *NEW-ENGLAND* : Expressed in the Letters of several Persons best acquainted therewithal. *Boston* in *New England*. Printed by *Bartholomew Green*, &c. 1694. 8vo. p. 55.

The History of the Church of *Malabar*, from the time of its being first discover'd by the *Portuguezes* in the Year 1501. Giving an Account of the Persecutions and violent Methods of the *Roman* Prelates, to reduce them to the Subjection of the Church of *Rome*. Together with the Synod of *Diampro* celebrated in the Year of our Lord 1599. With some Remarks upon the Faith and Doctrine of the Christians of St. *Thomas* in the *Indies* ; agreeing

with

with the Church of *England*, in opposition to that of *Rome*. Done out of *Portugueze* into *English*. By *Michael Geddes* Chancellor of the Cathedral Church of *Sarum*. *London*, for *Sam. Smith* and *B. Walford*. 1694. 8vo. p. 443.

Instructions for our truly and well-beloved *Luke Lillingston* Esqr. Collonel of one of our Regiments of Foot, which we are now sending to the *East Indies* —— [First to *Jamaica*, for the better Security thereof, and to the neighbouring Islands, in order to annoy our Enemies the *French*.] Given at our Court at *Kensington* this 23d day of *Dec.* 1694. in the sixth Year of our Reign. [Printed in Colonel *Lillingston*'s Remarks on Mr. *Burchet*'s Account. 8vo. 1704. *p.* 32.] As also a Copy of the *Instructions* given to Captain *Wilmot*, Commander in Chief by Sea; with Order for the distribution of the Prizes and Booty that should be taken in the *West-Indies*.

Articles agreed and concluded upon between *Robert Wilmot* Esqr. Commander in Chief of all the King of *Great Britain*'s Fleets and Sea-Forces in *America*, and Collonel *Luke Lillingston*, Commander in Chief of his Majesties Land Forces on the one part, and D. *Ignatio Perez Caro*, Governour of *Saint Domingo* on the other; for the Execution of an intended *Expedition* against the *French* Settlement upon the Island of *Hispaniola*. Signed and Sealed *Apr.* —— 1695. [Printed in Coll. *Lillingston*'s Remarks on Mr. *Burchet*'s Account. 8vo. 1704. *p.* 48.]

1695.
1 W. & M.

Resolutions and Orders taken at a Council of War holden in the Town of St. *Jago de la Vega*, in the Island of *Jamaica*, on *Monday* the 29th of *July*, 1695. Present, the Right Honourable Sir *William Beeston*, his Majesties Lieutenant General, *Robert Wilmot*, Commodore of his Majesties Fleet, and Collonel *Lillingston*, Commander of the Land Forces. [*Ibid.* p. 151.]

Orders at a Council held at St. *Jago de la Vega* in *Jamaica* before the Right Honourable the Governours. With Votes and Resolutions of the Assembly, on *Wednesday*, *Dec.* 4. 1695. and a Copy of the *Act* for *Quartering the King's Soldiers.* [*Ibid.* p. 160.]

A Declaration of the Elders and Messengers of the Churches met at *Salem Village*, *Apr.* 3. 1695. to consider and determine what is to be done, for the composure of the present unhappy Differences in that Place; who after solemn invocation of God in 'Christ for his Direction, do unanimously declare as followeth. [Printed at large in Mr. *Calef*'s more Wonders of the Invisible World. 4to. 1700. *p.* 59.] The Determination of the Elders. The Judgment of the Arbitrators. The Dismissing of Mr. *Parris* from his

X x   Ministry

Miniſtry at *Salem*, &c. [See more on this Subject before, under the Year 1693.]

The Preſent Proſpect of the famous and fertile Iſland of *TOBAGO* to the Southward of the Iſland of *Barbadoes*, with a Deſcription of the Scituation, Growth, Fertility, and Manufacture of the ſaid Iſland, ſetting forth how that 100 *l*. Stock in ſeven Years may be improved to 5000 *l. per Annum*; to which is added Propoſals for Encouragement of all thoſe that are minded to ſettle there. By Captain *John Poyntz*. The ſecond Edition. *London*, for the Author. 4to. p. 50.

Europe's Glory, or Peace and Plenty to the People thereof. Being a Projection or a Scheme of Reaſonable Terms for eſtabliſhing a firm and general PEACE between the Monarch of *Great Britain*, including all the *Confederate Princes*, and the *French* King. Whereby 'tis propoſed in a few Years to reimburſe and make good the paſt and preſent depending Charges of the Wars, not only to the King of *Great Britain*, the Parliament and People of *England*, but alſo to repay the States of *Holland* and the *French* King their whole Expence and Charges they have been at in and about the ſame, provided the following Methods, or the Matter and Subſtance thereof be comply'd with, undertaken and executed. All which is propoſed to be effected with one 10th. Part of one Years Charge, each of the three Governments are now Yearly at, without any further Coſt or Expence to the People of *England*, *Holland* or *France*, whereby the Trade and Commerce of all *Europe* would ſpeedily Flouriſh, the Inhabitants increaſe in Wealth, and grow to a far greater degree in Riches than ever they have done. The Revenues and Territories of *England* and *France*, with the Dominions of *Holland* would be ſeverally enlarged; and by this Undertaking each of them and their Trades ſo vaſtly extended, that a General Good would enſue to the Subjects of theſe three Governments, and to the reſt of *Europe* in a little time. By *Thomas Houghton* of *Lymeſtreet*, Gent. *London*, Printed *Anno Dom.* 1695. 4to. p. 31.

Encouragement for SEAMEN and MARINERS in two Parts; being a Propoſed Method for the more ſpeedy and effectual furniſhing their Majeſties Royal NAVY with able *Seamen* and *Mariners*, and for ſaving thoſe Immenſe Sums of Money Yearly expended in attending the SEA-PRESS, in order to prevent thoſe many Miſchiefs and Abuſes daily committed (by diſorderly *Preſs-Maſters*) both at Sea and Land, to the great Prejudice of their Majeſties, and Injury of the Subject. By *GEORGE EVERETT* Shipwright. *London*, Printed in the Year 1695. 4to. p. 24. [With an Epiſtle Dedicatory to both Houſes of Parliament.]

Humble

Humble Proposals for the Relief, Encouragement, Security and Happiness of the Loyal Courageous *SEAMEN* of *England* in their Lives and Payment, in the Service of Our most Gracious King *William*, and the Defence of these Nations, humbly presented to the Two most Honourable Houses, the Lords and Commons of *England* in *Parliament* assembled; By a Faithful Subject of His Majesty, and Servant to the Parliament and Nation, and the Seamen of *England*; in order for Safety and Security of all aforesaid. *W. HODGES.* [Dated from the *Hermitage-Bridge*, *Jan.* 14. 1695.] To which is added A Dialogue concerning the Art of *Ticket-Buying*, in a Discourse between Honesty, Poverty, Cruelty and Villany, concerning that Mystery of Iniquity, and Ruin of the Loyal *Seamen*. Dated from the *Hermitage-Bridge*, *Feb.* 20. 1695: With a Postscript, dated *Feb.* 27. 1695. Printed in the Year 1695. 4*to.* *p.* 63.

Great Britain's Groans; or an Account of the Oppression, Ruin and Destruction of the Loyal *SEAMEN* of *England* in the fatal Loss of their Pay, Health and Lives and dreadful Ruin of their Families. [With an Epistle Dedicatory to the Lords Spiritual and Temporal, and Commons in Parliament by *William Hodges*. Dated from *Hermitage-Bridge*, *Decemb.* 26. 1695.]

Considerations requiring greater Care for TRADE in *England*, and some Expedients proposed. *London*, Printed for *S. Crouch.* 4*to.* 1695. *p.* 17.

The Naked Truth, in an Essay upon TRADE: With some Proposals for bringing the Ballance on Our side, Humbly offered to the Parliament. *London*, Printed in the Year MDCXCVI. 4*to.* *p.* 18.

1696.
8 *W.* & *M.*

The Causes of Our present Calamities in reference to the TRADE of the Nation fully discovered, with the most proper Expedient to remedy the same: Whereby the *War* it self may become as certainly advantagious as a *Peace* will be destructive. Humbly Presented by *James Whiston*. Several times printed by the Author, but now Corrected and Enlarged and Reprinted by Special Command. Printed for *Edw. Poole*, Bookseller in *Cornhill.* 1696. *Fol.* *p.* 11.

A Treatise concerning the *EAST-INDIA* Trade: Being a most profitable Trade to the Kingdom, and best secured and improved by a *Company* and a *Joint-Stock*, wrote at the Instance of *Thomas Papillon*, Esq; and in his House,

and

and Printed in the Year 1680. And now Reprinted for the better Satisfaction of himself and others. MDCXCVI. 4to. p. 27.

Proposals for Settling the *E A S T - I N D I A* T R A D E [by the Establishment of a Regulated Company, whereby all the Subjects of *England* may have liberty to concern themselves therein: With some Reasons and Considerations why the *East India* Trade should not be settled in a Joint Stock exclusive.] *London*, by E. *Whitlock*. 1696. 4to. p. 22.

A Letter to a Friend concerning the *E A S T - I N D I A* T R A D E, [by way of Reply to the Companies Answers to the Reasons for a Regulated Company.] *London*, by E. *Whitlock*. 1696. 4to. p. 20.

A Printed Copy of the Charter Party, 28. *Octob.* 1696. between Capt. *William Heath* of *Mile-End* in the County of *Middlesex*, Mariner, and *Tho. Greaves* of the Parish of *Stepney*, Shipwright, Owners of the Ship called the *Amity* of the one part, and the *Governour* and *Company* of Merchants of *London*, trading into the *E A S T - I N D I E S* of the other part, &c. Fol. p. 12.

A *Proclamation* by the Honourable the Lieutenant Governour, Council and Assembly of His Majesty's Province of the *Massachusets Bay*, in a General Court assembled for appointing a *Day* of *Prayer* with Fasting— that whatever Mistakes on either hand have been fallen into, either by the Body of this People, or any Orders of Men, referring to the late Tragedy, raised among us by *Satan* and his Instruments — God would humble us — and be atoned to His Land: Given at *Boston*, *Decemb.* 17. 1696. With an Acknowledgment made by one of the Judges; and a Retractation signed by several who had served as *Jurors* on the *Tryal* of reputed W I T C H E S; justly fearing that in bringing in those Persons Guilty, they had been themselves sadly deluded and mistaken. [Printed at large in *Mr. Calef's More Wonders of the Invisible World.* 4to. 1700. Part. V.]

A Voyage of the Sieur *Le Maiste* to the *C A N A R Y* I S L A N D S, C A P E *V E R D,* S E N N E G A L and *G A M B,* under Monsieur D A N C O U R T, Director General of the *Royal African Company* [of France.] Printed at *Paris* this present Year 1695. and now faithfully done into *English*. *London*, Printed for F. *Mills* and *W. Turner.* 1696. 12°. p. 135.

Catalogus Plantarum quæ in Insulâ Jamaica *Sponte proveniunt, vel vulgò coluntur cum earundem Synonymis & locis Natalibus; adjectis aliis quibusdam quæ in Insulis* Maderæ, Barbados, Nevis & Sancti Christophori *nascuntur.*

tar. Seu Prodromi Historiæ Naturalis. JAMAICÆ. *Pars Prima. Autore* HANS SLOANE, *M. D. Coll. Med. Lond. Nec non Soc. Reg.* Lond. *Soc.* Londini, *Impensis* D. Brown *ad insigne Cygni & Bibliorum extra Portam vulgo dictam* Temple-Bar. 1696. 8*vo. p.* 232. *Cum Indice Verborum.* [*Ex Dono Authoris.*]

Mr. *Roberts* his Voyage to the *L E V A N T* ; With an Account of his Sufferings amongst the *Corsairs* ; their Villanous way of living, and his Description of the *Archipelago* Islands. Together with his Relation of Taking and Retaking of *Scio* in the Year 1696. [Printed in Capt. *Hack's* Collect. of Orig. Voyages. 8*vo.* 1699.]

The Proceedings of Our Fleet under Command of the Earl of *Orford,* upon the Expectation of a *French* Invasion, 1696, *&c.* [Memoirs of Mr. *Burchett,* 1703. 8*vo. p.* 320, *&c*]

The *Expedition* of Vice-Admiral *Nevil,* sent to the *West-Indies* to Convoy home the *Spanish Galleons* ; With an Account of what happened upon his meeting and chasing Monsieur *Ponty,* after he had plundered *Carthagena.* [*Ibid. p.* 357.] 1697. 9 *W. & M.*

An Account of the Action of Rear Admiral *Meese,* detached by Mr. *Nevill* against *Petit Guavas* ; with an Account of that Action in 1697. [*ib. p.* 367.]

The Manner of Monsieur *Ponty's* attacking and taking *Carthagena* in 1697. [*Ib. p.* 370.]

An Act for the Encrease and Encouragement of *S E A M E N,* and for Erecting an *Hospital* at *East-Greenwich* in *Kent,* to be established and endowed for the Purposes aforesaid. *Anno* VII *& VIII Guil. Cap.* xxj.

An Act for Preventing Frauds and Regulating Abuses in the *Plantation* T R A D E, or His Majesty's *American Plantations. Anno* 7, 8 *Will.* III. *Cap.* xxij.

An Act for the better Encouragement of the *Greenland* T R A D E. *Ib. Cap.* xxxiij.

A New Voyage round the World ; describing particularly the *ISTHMUS* of *America,* several Coasts and Islands in the *West-Indies,* the Isles of *Cape Verd,* the Passage by *Terra del Fuego,* the *South Sea* Coasts of *Chili, Peru,* and

Mexico ;

Mexico; the Isle of *Guam*, one of the *Ludrones Mindanao*, and other *Philippine* and *East-India* Islands near *Cambodia*, *China*, *Formosa*, *Luconia*, *Celebes*, &c. *New-Holland*, *Sumatra*, *Nicobar* Isles; the *Cape* of *Good Hope* and *Santa Hellena*, their Soil, Rivers, Harbours, Plants, Fruits, Animals, and Inhabitants, their Customs, Religion, Government, Trade, &c. By *William Dampier*. Illustrated with particular Maps and Draughts. *London*, for *James Knapton*. MDCXCVII. 8vo. *p. 550*.

A Letter from *Manille* of *June* 10th. 1697. writ by the R. F. *Paul Clain* of the Society of *Jesus* to the R. F. *Thyrsus Gonzales*, General of the same Society, upon a new Discovery made of 32 Islands to the South of the *Mariane* Islands. [In the *Missioners Letters*, 8vo. 1707. *p. 51*.]

An Account of a Voyage from *Spain* to *Paraquaria* a Province of the Western *America*; Performed by the Reverend Fathers *Anthony Seppe* and *Anthony Behme*, both *German* Jesuits. Containing a Description of all the remarkable things, and the Inhabitants, as well as of the Missionaries residing in that Country. Taken from the Letters of the said *Anth. Seppe*. Translated from the *High-Dutch* Original. Printed at *Nurenberg*. 1697. [In the Collect. of Voyages, Printed for Mr. *Churchill*. 1704. Fol. Vol. IV. *p. 635*.] With a Fragment of the Discovery of the Islands of *Solomon*. Translated from the *Spanish*.

The Life of his Excellency Sir *William Phipps*, Knt. late Captain General and Governour in Chief of the Province of the *Massachusets Bay*, *New-England*. Containing the memorable Changes undergone, and Actions performed by Him. Writ by One intimately acquainted with him, Dedicated to his Excellency the Earl of *Bellamont*, Governour of the Province of the *Massachusets*. By *Nathaniel Mather*. Apr. 27. 1697. [Inserted in the History of *New-England*. By *Cotton Mather*. Fol. 1702. Book VI. *p. 35*.]

A Postscript relating to a Book intituled *The Life of Sir* William Phips. Printed in *London*. 1697. and taken as written by Mr. *Cotton Mather*: Recounting some Mistakes in the said Book, and Miscarriages with which Sir *William* was chargeable. [Printed in *Mr Calef's More Wonders of the Invisible World*. 4to. 1700. *p.* 146, &c.] Concluding that *Innocents have suffered as Witches*.

Terribilia Dei. Remarkable Judgments of God on several sorts of Offenders, in several scores of Instances among the People of *New England*, Observed, Collected, Related, and Improved, in two Sermons at *Boston* Lecture in the
Month

Month of *July*, 1697. By *Cotton Mather*. [Printed in the Hiftory of *New-England*. 1702. *Fol.* Book VI. *p. 23.*]

Brief Remarks upon Mr. *Whifton*'s new Theory of the Earth, and upon another Gentleman's Objections againft fome Paffages in a Difcourfe of *The Exiftence and Providence of God*, relating to the COPERNICAN *Hypothefis*. By *John Edwards*. B. D. *London*, Printed for *R. Robinfon* and *J. Wyat*, 1697. *8vo. p. 48.*

The Humble *Addrefs* of the Council General of the Company of *Scotland* Trading to *Africa* and the *Indies* to the King's moft Excellent Majefty fign'd at *Edinburgh*, *June* 28. 1697. in their Name, Prefence and by their Order. By the Lord *Yefter*, their Prefident, relating to Sir *Paul Rycaut*, his Majefties Prefident at *Hamburgh*, in Conjunction with his Majefties Envoy to the Courts of *Lunenburgh*, prefenting a Memorial to the Senate of *Hamburgh*; threatning them with the height of his Majefty's Difpleafure, if they join'd with the *Scots* in any Treaty of Commerce whatfoever. Printed in [*An Enquiry into the Caufes of the Mifcarriage of the* Scots *Colony of* Darien. *8vo.* 1700. *p. 22, &c.*]

His Majefty's *Anfwer* thereto. By the Right Honourable the Earl of *Tullibardin*, &c. and Sir *James Ogilvie* Principal Secretaries of State. Signed at *Edinburgh*, *Aug.* 2. 1697. fignifying to the Company that his Majefty would take their *Reprefentation* into Confideration as foon as he fhould return to *England*; and that in the mean Time he would give Orders to his faid Envoy and *Refident* not to make ufe of his Name or Authority for obftructing them in the Profecution of their Trade with the Inhabitants of that City. [*Ibid. p. 25.*]

The Humble *Reprefentation* of the Council General, *&c.* To the Right Honourable the Lord *High Chancellour*, and Remanent Lords of his Majefty's moft Honourable *Privy Council*; with an Humble *Addrefs* to the King. Dated at *Edinburgh*, *Dec.* 22. 1697. complaining that the King's Refident at *Hamburgh*, ftill oppos'd their Trade, pretended he had never receiv'd any Orders on their Behalf. [*Ibid. p. 26, &c.*]

An *Addrefs* to his Majefty by the *Parliament* of *Scotland*, [taking Notice of a Reprefentation of the Council General of the Company Trading to *Africa* and the *Indies*, complaining of the Obftructions they have met with in the Profecution of their Trade, by a Memorial prefented to the Senate of *Hamburgh*, by his Majefty's Refidents in that City, and recommending to his Majefty the promoting the Intereft of the faid Company, and therein that

of

of the whole Kingdom] subscribed at *Edinburgh* the 5th of *August*, 1698. in the Name, Presence, and by Warrant of the Estates of Parliament. SEA-FIELD. J. P. D. P. [*Ibid. p.* 32.]

The Declaration of the Council constituted by the *Indian* and *African* Company of *Scotland*, for the Government and Direction of their Colonies and Settlements in the *Indies.* Dated from *NEW EDINBURGH* in *Caledonia,* Dec. 20. 1698. [*Ibid. p.* 67.]

The first Letter sent from the Council of *Caledonia* to the *Company Trading to* Africa, *&c.* Dated from *New Edinburgh* in *Caledonia,* D.c. 28. 1698. and Subscribed *Robert Jolley,* J. *Montgomery,* Dan. *Machay,* Rob. *Pennicook,* Rob. *Pincartone,* and *Will. Peterson.* [giving an Account of the Scituation and exceeding Fruitfulness and Pleasantness of the Country ; with an Account of what Goods and Merchandises were vendible there, and what Provisions and Stores were necessary for their Support. [*Ibid. p.* 102. *&c.*]

Discourses on the Publick REVENUES and on the TRADE of *England.* *Viz.* I. Of the use of Political *Arithmetick,* in all Considerations about the Revenues and Trade. II. On Credit, and the Means and Methods by which it may be Revived. III. On the Management of the King's Revenues. IV. Whether to Farm the Revenues may not in this Juncture be most for the Publick Service ? V. On the Publick Debts and Engagements. By the Author of the Essay on Ways and Means. *Part* I. To which is added, A Discourse upon Improving the Revenue of the State of *Athens.* Written Originally in *Greek* by *Xenophon*; and now made *English* from the Original, with some Historical Notes by another Hand. *London,* Printed for *James Knapton.* 1698. 8vo. *p.* 279. & 62.

1698. 10 Will. 3.

Remarks upon some wrong Computations and Conclusions contained in late Tract entitled *Discourses on the Publick* REVENUES and on the TRADE of *England.* In a Letter to Mr. *D. S. London,* Printed for *W. Keeblewhite.* 1698. 8vo. *p.* 47.

Some Observations upon *Discourses* lately publish'd on the PUBLICK REVENUES, and on the TRADE of *ENGLAND, London,* Printed in the Year MDCXCVIII. 4to. *p.* 16.

NAVIGATION Improv'd ; or the Art of *Rowing Ships* of all Rates in *Calms,* with a more easy, swift, and steady Motion than *Oars* can. Also a Description of the *Engine* that performs it ; and the Author's Answer to all

Mr.

Mr. *Dummer's* Objections that have been made against it. By *THOMAS SAVERY,* Gent. *London,* Printed and Sold by *James Moxon.* 1698. 4to. p. 22.

A Scheme shewing to all Owners of SHIPS, and those concerned in SHIPPING, that the Composition newly invented by Mr. *Charles Ardefoif* will by reason of the Durableness of the same, and considering the usual Charge in *Nailing, Sheathing, Clearing, Bruming, Careening, Caulking, Painting* or *Graving* the *Bottoms* of SHIPS, with filling Nails driven into the Wood in Sheathing, or the common *Graving Stuff* now in use, save three parts in four of the Expence, last as long as the usual way of *Sheathing,* and be in a better condition of Sailing, with several Certificates relating thereunto. A Broad-side *Fol.*

A Sermon Preached before the Honourable Company of Merchants Trading to the *Levant* Seas. At *St. Hellens, January* 16. being *Sunday,* 1697-8. By *EDM. CHISHULL,* M.A. Fellow of *Corpus-Christi* College in *Oxon.* and Chaplain to the Factory at *Smyrna. London,* Printed for *S. Manship.* 1698. 4to.

The *Acts* and *Negotiations,* together with the Particular *Articles* at large of the *General Peace* concluded at *Ryswick.* By the most Illustrious *Confederates* with the *French King;* to which are prefixed the *Negotiations* and *Articles* of the *Peace,* concluded at *Turin* between the same Prince and the Duke of *Savoy.* Translated from the Original, Printed at the *Hague. London,* Printed for *Robert Clavel* and *Timothy Child.* 1698. [*Ex dono Rev. Viri* Geo. Baxter, S.T.B.]

A New Account of *East-India* and *Persia,* in Eight Letters : Being Nine Years Travels ; begun 1672. and finished 1681. Containing Observations made of the *Moral, Natural* and *Artificial* Estate of those Countries : Namely of their Government, Religion, Laws, Customs. Of the Soil, Climates, Seasons, Health, Diseases. Of the Animals, Vegetables, Minerals, Jewels. Of their Housing, Cloathing, Manufactures, Trades, Commodities. And of the Coins, Weights, and Measures, used in the Principal Places of Trade in those Parts. By *John Fryer,* M.D. *Cantabrig.* and Fellow of the Royal Society. Illustrated with Maps, Figures, and Useful Tables. *London,* for R. *Chiswel.* MDCXCVIII. *Fol.*

An Account of the taking of *CARTHAGENA* by the *French* in the 1696. Containing all the Particulars of that Expedition, from their first setting out, to their Return into BREST. By *Monsieur de Pointis.*

Z z   *Decennium*

D.cennium Luctuosum.   An History of Remarkable Occurrences in the long War which *New-England* hath had with the *Indian Savages* from the Year 1698. Faithfully Composed and Improved, the second Edition. [Inserted in the History of *New-England.* 1702. Fol. *Book* VII. *p.* 57.]

Catalogus Eorum qui in Collegio Harvardino *quod est* Cantabrigiæ NOV. ANGLORUM *ab Anno* 1642. *ad Annum* 1698. *alicujus Gradûs laureâ donati sunt.* [Hist. of *New-England* by *Cotton Mather.* 1702. Fol. B. IV. *p.* 836.]

1699.
11 *Will.* 3
The CHARTER granted by their Majesties King *WILLIAM* and Queen *MARY* to the Inhabitants of the Province of the *MASSA-CHUSETS*-Bay in *NEW-ENGLAND.* Printed at *Boston* in *New-England* by *Bartholomew Green* and *John Allen.* 1699. Fol. *p.* 192.

ACTS and LAWS of his Majesty's Province of the *MASSA-CHUSETS*-Bay in *New-England.* *Boston,* Printed by *Barthol. Green* and *John Allen.* 1699. Fol. *p.* 192.

Two Plain and Practical Discourses concerning, I. *Hardness of Heart*; shewing, that some who live under the Gospel are by a Judicial Dispensation given up to that Judgment and the Signs thereof. II. *The Sin and Danger of Disobedience to the Gospel.* By *Increase Mather,* President of *Harward* College in *Cambridge,* and Preacher of the Gospel in *New-England.* *London,* Printed for *J. Robinson.* 1699. 8vo. *p.* 187.

A Voyage round the World, by Dr. *John Francis Gemelli Careri*; of which, Book III. contains an exact Journal of his Voyage from the *Philippine Islands* to *Acapulco* in *New Spain*; and by the way describing *California.* And the other Parts contain the most remarkable things he saw in *New Spain*; With his Voyage from *Havana* to *Cadiz* in 1699. Translated from the *Italian.* [Collect. of Voyages printed for Mr. *Churchill.* Fol. 1704. *Vol.* IV. *p.* 446, &c.

A Collection of Original Voyages containing, I. Capt. *Cowley's* Voyage round the Globe. II. Capt. *Sharp's* Journey over the *Isthmus* of *Darien,* and and Expedition into the *South Seas,* written by himself. III. Captain *Wood's* Voyage through the Streights of *Magellane.* IV. Mr. *Robert's* Adventures among the *Corsairs* of the *Levant* : His Account of their Way of living, Description of the *Archipelago* Islands, taking of *Scio,* &c. Illustrated with several
veral

veral Maps and Draughts. Published by Capt. *William Hacket* LONDON, Printed for *James Knapton.* 1699. 8vo.

A New Survey of the *West-Indies* : Being a Journal of three thousand and three hundred Miles within the main Land of *A M E R I C A.* By *Tho. Gage,* the only Protestant that was ever known to have traveled those Parts. Setting forth his Voyage from *Spain* to St. *John de Ulhua,* and thence to *Xalapa, Haxcalla,* the City of *Angels,* and *Mexico* : With a Description of that great City, as in former Times, and at present. Likewise his Journey thence through *Guaxaea, Chiapa, Guatemala, Vera Paz,* &c. With his Abode twelve Years about *Guatemala* ; His wonderful Conversion and Calling to his Native Country : With his Return through *Nicaragua* and *Costa-Rica* to *Nicoya, Panama, Porto Bello, Cartagena* and *Havana* : With an Account of the *Spanish* Navigation thither, their Government, Castles, Ports, Commodities, Religion, Priests and Friers, *Negro's, Mulatto's, Mestiso's, Indians,* and of their Feasts and Solemnities. With a *Grammar* or some few Rudiments of the *Indian* Tongue, called *Poconchi* or *Pocoman.* The *Fourth* Edition enlarged by the Author, with an accurate Map. *London,* Printed for *J. Nicholson,* &c. 1699. 8vo. 477. At the End is put the Addition entitled, *Some remarkable Passages relating to Archbishop* Laud, particularly of his Affection to the Church of *Rome* : Being the twenty second Chapter of *Gage's* Survey of the *West-Indies,* as it was Printed in the *Folio* Edition before the Restoration, but supprest in the *Octavo* since. *London,* Printed for *S. Popping.* 1712. 8vo. p. 19.

An Account of the first Voyages and Discoveries made by the *Spaniards* in *America* ; containing the most exact Relation hitherto published of their unparallelled Cruelties on the *Indians,* in the Destruction of above forty Millions of People. With the Propositions offered to the King of *Spain,* to prevent the further Ruin of the *West-Indies.* By Don *Bartholomew de las Casas,* Bishop of *Chiapa,* who was an Eye Witness of their Cruelties. To which is added, *The Art of Travelling* ; shewing how a Man may dispose his Travels to the best advantage. *London,* Printed by *J. Darby, &c.* MDCXCIX. 8vo. p. 248 & 40.

Apostolick Charity, its Nature and Excellence considered, in a Discourse upon *Dan.* 12. 3. Preached at St. *Paul's* at the *Ordination* of some Protestant *Missionaries* to be sent into the *Plantations.* To which is prefixed, A general View of the *English* Colonies in *America* with respect to Religion ; in order to shew what Provision is wanting for the Propagation of Christianity in those Parts. Together with Proposals for the promoting the same : And to induce such of the Clergy of this Kingdom as are Persons of Sobriety and A-
bilities

bilities to accept of a Mission. And to which is subjoyn'd *The Author's Circular Letter, lately sent to the Clergy there*. By *Thomas Bray*, D. D. *London*, Printed for *William Hawes*. 1699. 4to. p. 30.

The Humble Address of the Lords Spiritual and Temporal to His MAJESTY, in relation to the Petition of *Charles Desborow*, late Captain of His Majesty's Ship *Mary Gally*, employed in the Expedition to *Newfoundland* in the Year 1697. under the Command of Captain *John Norris*. And His Majesty's most Gracious Answer thereto. Printed for *Charles Desborow*, 1699. 4to. p. 8.

An Act to settle the Trade to *Africa* in the Royal *African* Company *England*, as beneficial and advantagious to this Kingdom, and to the *Plantations* and *Colonies* thereunto belonging. *Anno* ix & x *Guil.* III. *Cap.* xxvj.

England's Grandeur and Way to get Wealth : Or, Promotion of TRADE made easy, and Lands advanced, beneficial to particular Persons, and to the Kingdom in general : Wherein many Thousands of Indigent Poor Families may be employed : Breaches made in our TRADE by the *French*, *Portuguese*, *Genoese*, *Swedes*, *Dutch* and *Danes*, demonstrated, *Furnishing Funerals* by *Undertakers*, making *Buttons* and *Shoe-Buckles* of various sorts of *Mettal* a great Detriment to Weavers of Tape, Cotton, Ferrit and Silk Ribband, and in short to all other *Trades*, the *West-India Trade* discouraged, it being one of the noblest Branches in *Navigation*, the Prejudice of *Trade* by *Strangers* that are *Lodgers* and *Inmates* only, who by their monopolising Ways have got Estates, and then bid farewel to *England* ; the Cause of the Rent of Houses falling ; the Reason why great *Taxes* cannot easily be paid ; laying *Taxes* on the *Back* and *Belly* the best way to raise Money, which will hurt neither Rich nor Poor, provided *Navigation* and a free Circulation of *Trade* be maintained and Merchants encouraged : Reasons why we have not a more considerable *Trade* now the *War* is over : A Remedy proposed to cure this Malady. By *T. Tryon*, Merchant of *London*. Sold by *J. Harris* and G. *Conyers*. 1699. 4to. p. 26.

The State of the NAVY Considered, in relation to the VICTUALLING, particularly in the *Straits* and the *West-Indies* ; with some Thoughts on the Mismanagements of the *Admiralty* for several Years past ; and a Proposal to prevent the like for the future. Humbly offered to the Honourable House of Commons by an *English Sailor*. *London*, Printed for *A. Baldwin*. 1699. 4to. p. 16.

A

A Difcourfe concerning the *Eaft-India* TRADE : Shewing how it is unprofitable to the Kingdom of *England* : Being taken out of an *Effay on Trade*, written by Mr. *JOHN CARY*, Merchant in *Briftol*, in the Year 1695. To which are added fome Obfervations of Sir *Jof. Child* and of the Author of the *Effay on Ways and Means relating to Trade* : And alfo a Copy of the *French* King's Decree, concerning *Printed Callicoes*. *London*, Printed for *E. Baldwin*. 1699. 4*to. p. 14.*

Confiderations relating to the Bill prohibiting the Wear and Ufe of the *Eaft-India* Manufactures, humbly offered to the Lords in *Parliament* by the *Linnen-Drapers* and other Dealers in *Eaft-India* Goods, againft the faid Bill in *Febr.* 1699-1700. *Fol.* Printed Sheet.

The SEAMANS *Obligations to Gratitude and a Good Life.* A Sermon Preached in the Parifh Church of *Deptford* in *Kent*, *June* 5th, 1699. before the *Corporation* of the *Trinity Houfe*, at their Annual Meeting on *Trinity Monday*. By *GEORGE STANHOPE*, D. D. Chaplain in Ordinary to His Majefty. Publifhed at the Requeft of that Honourable Society. *London*, Printed for *R. Sare.* 1699. 4*to.*

The Compleat *Shipwright* plainly and demonftratively teaching the Proportion ufed by experienced *Shipwrights*, according to their Cuftom of Building both *Geometrically* and *Arithmetically* performed : To which are added Certain Propofitions in *Geometry*, the Ufe of a *Diagonal Scale*, to draw a Draught with the making, graduating or marking of a Bend of Moulds, and ordering of the fame ; The Extraction of the *Square Root* ; With a Table of Squares : Alfo a Way of *Rowing* of Ships, by heaving at the *Capftain*, ufeful in any Ship becalmed, with other things ufeful in that Art. The Sixth Edition, carefully corrected by *Edmund Bufhnell*, Shipwright. *London*, Printed for *Richard Mount.* M DC XC IX. 4*to. p. 56.*

Tables containing the Names of all SHIPS or MEN of WAR, with the Rates, Length, Breadth, Depth, Ton, Men, Guns, when built, where, by whom, or bought, or taken, or rebuilt ; with other Obfervations. MS. Six Sheets, *Fol.*

An Abftract of a Letter from a Perfon of Eminence and Worth in *Caledonia*, [*Viz.* Mr. *Paterfon*] to a Friend at *Bofton* in *New-England*, [acquainting him with their *Scots*-Settlement at *DARIEN*; With an Account of the Nature and Condition of the Country, and good Difpofition of the Natives towards them, and of their having written to the Prefident of *Panama* and

A a a   acquainting

acquainting him with their good and peaceable Intentions, and willingness to procure a good Understanding and Correspondence with him, &c.] Dated *Fort St. Andrews, Feb.* 18th, 1698-9. [In An Enquiry into the Causes of the Miscarriage of the *Scots* Colony at *DARIEN, &c.* 8vo. 1699. *p.* 74.

A Proclamation by the Honourable Sir *William Beeston,* Knt. Governour and Commander in Chief for his Majesty in the Island of *Jamaica,* and of the Territories and Dependencies of the same and Admiral thereof. [Representing, that whereas he had received Orders from his Majesty by Secretary *Vernon,* importing that he was not informed of the Intentions of the *Scots* in Peopling *DARIEN,* and commanding him not to afford them any Assistance, he thereby strictly charged and required them not to hold any Correspondence with the *Scots,* nor to give them any Assistance with Arms, Ammunition, Provision, or any other Means whatever.] Dated *April* 9. 1699. [*Ibid. p.* 37.]

An Enquiry into the Causes of the Miscarriage of the *Scots* Colony at *DARIEN*; Or, an Answer to a Libel, entitled, *A Defence of the* Scots *Abdicating* DARIEN: Submitted to the Consideration of the Good People of *England.* Glasgow. 1699. 8vo. *p.* 112. [*Ex dono Rev.* Rob. Watts, *L. L. B. Coll. Div.* Johan. Oxon. *Socij.*]

By the King A Proclamation against a false, scandalous and traiterous Libel, entitled, *An Enquiry into the Causes of the Miscarriages of the* Scotch *Colony at* DARIEN; Or, *an Answer to a Libel, entitled, A Defence of the* Scots *Abdicating* DARIEN. Given at Our Court at *Kensington* the Twenty ninth day of *January,* 1699. in the Eleventh Year of Our Reign. *London,* Printed by *Charles Bill,* &c. 1699.

A Memorial delivered in to King *William* by the Ambassador Extraordinary of *Spain, May* 3. 1699. against the Settlement of the *Scots* at *DARIEN* in *America.* [In Defence of the Settlement, *p.* 2.]

A Defence of the *Scots* Settlement at *DARIEN*; With an Answer to the *Spanish Memorial* against it: And Arguments to prove that it is the Interest of *England* to joyn with the *Scots,* and protect it. To which is added, A Description of that Country, and a particular Account of the *Scots* Colony. *Edinburgh,* Printed in the Year 1699. 8vo. *p.* 86.

The *Defence of the* Scots Settlement *at* Darien Answered Paragraph by Paragraph. By *Philo-Britan.* London. 1699. 8vo. *p.* 92.

A

A Defence againſt the Scots *Abdicating* DARIEN, including an *Anſwer* to the *Defence of the* Scots *Settlement* there. *Authore* Britanno *ſed* Dunenſi. Printed in the Year 1700. 8vo. *p.* 168.

A ſhort Vindication of *Phil. Scot's* Defence of the *Scots* abdicating DARIEN. Being in Anſwer to the Challenge of the Author of *The Defence* of that Settlement, to prove the *Spaniſh* Title to *Darien*, by Inheritance, Marriage, Donation, &c. With a Prefatory Reply to the falſe and ſcurrilous Aſperſions of the new Author of *The Juſt and Modeſt Vindication*, &c. And ſome Animadverſions on the material Part of it, relating to the Title of *Darien. London*, Printed in the Year 1701. 8vo. *p.* 48. [See more on this Subject under the Years 1697, 98, and 1701.]

A Trumpet Sounded out of the Wilderneſs of *America*, which may ſerve as a Warning to the Government and People of *England* to beware of QUAKERISM. Wherein is ſhewed how in PENSILVANIA, and there away, where they have the Government in their own Hands, they hire and encourage Men to *Fight*; and how they *Perſecute, Fine*, and *Impriſon*, and take away Good for Conſcience ſake. By *Daniel Leeds*. Printed by *William Bradford*, at the *Bible* in *New-York*. 1699. 8vo. *p.* 151.

A Paper to *William Penn*, at the departure of that Gentleman to his Territory for his Peruſal in PENSILVANIA. Wherein two Points are propoſed to him concerning the *Quakers* Religion, that he may receive himſelf Conviction, or render to others that are Conſcientious about them, Chriſtian Satisfaction; The one is their Belief of an *Infallible Guidance*: The other is their Diſuſe of the two Holy and Bleſſed *Sacraments*. With an occaſional Diſſertation concerning Predeſtination, or God's Decree about ſaving Man, in reference to the Doctrine of others, and not the *Quakers* only. By a Friend unknown. *London*, Printed for *H. Mortlock*. 1700. 4to. *p.* 24.

The Order of the Goſpel Profeſſed and Practiſed by the Churches of Chriſt in NEW-ENGLAND, Juſtified by the Scripture, and by the Writings of many Learned Men, both Antient and Modern Divines, in Anſwer to ſeveral Queſtions relating to Church-Diſcipline. By *Increaſe Mather*, Preſident of *Harward Colledge* in *Cambridge*, and Teacher of a Church at *Boſton* in *New-England*. Re-printed at *London*, and ſold by *A. Baldwin*. 1700. 8vo. *p.*

More Wonders *of the Inviſible World*. Or the Wonders of the Inviſible World diſplay'd in five Parts. Part I. An Account of the Sufferings of
Margaret

Margaret Rule, written by the Reverend Mr. *C. M.* II. Several Letters to the Author, &c. And his Reply relating to *Witchcraft.* III. The Differences between the Inhabitants of *Salem* Village, and Mr. *Paris*'s their Minister in *New-England.* IV. Letters of a Gentleman uninterested, endeavouring to prove the received Opinions about *Witchcraft* to be Orthodox. With short Essays to their Answers. V. A short Historical Account of Matters of Fact in that Affair. To which is added, A Postscript relating to a Book entitled, *The Life of Sir* William Phipps. Collected by *Robert Caleff*, Merchant of *Boston* in *New-England.* *London*, Printed for *Nath. Hillar.* 1700. 4°. *p.* 156.

Reasonable Religion. Or the Truth of the Christian Religion Demonstrated. The Wisdom of its Precepts Justified; and the folly of Sinning against those Precepts reprehended. With incontestable Proofs that Men who would Act Reasonably, must Live Religiously. By *Cotton Mather, D. D.* Printed at *Boston* in *New-England* by *T. Green.* 1700. 12°. *p.* 72. [*Ex dono Rev. Viri* Gershomi Rawlins]

A General Idea of the Epitomy of the Works of *Robert Boyle,* Esqr. To which are added General Heads for the Natural History of a Country (for the sake of those who go beyond Seas.) By *R. Boulton, of Brazen Nose College, Oxon.* *London*, Printed in the Year 1700. 8vo. *p.* 122.

The Acts of Dr. *Bray*'s Visitation held at *ANNAPOLIS* in *MARYLAND*, May 23, 24, 25. *Anno* 1700. *London*, Printed by *W. Downing*, &c, *Fol. p.* 17.

A Circular Letter to the Clergy of *MARYLAND*, subsequent to the late *Visitation*, written by their Affectionate Brother and Faithful Fellow Labourer, *Thomas Bray.* To which is added, *Cursus Catecheticus Americanus.* Consisting of Books more particularly fitted to the Use of the three several Classes of *Catechumens*, in order to Season the growing Generation with the Principles of Piety and Virtue: Pursuant to the Resolutions made to that Purpose the *second Day* of the *Visitation* at *Annapolis.* May 4. 1700.

The Present State of the Protestant Religion in *MARYLAND*, under the Government of *Francis Nicholson* Esqr. by Dr. *Bray*, deputed by the Lord Bishop of *London*, to be his *Commissary* in that Province. *Half Sheet.* [See more on this Subject under the Year. 1699.]

A Me-

A Memorial Reprefenting the prefent State of Religion on the Continent of *NORTH AMERICA*. By *Thomas Bray*, D. D. *London*, Printed by *William Downing* for the Author. 1700. *Fol. p.* 15. With Propofals for the Propagation of the Chriftian Religion in the feveral Provinces on the Continent of *North America*.

Propofals for the Encouragement and Promoting of Religion and Learning in the Foreign Plantations; and to induce fuch of the Clergy of this Kingdom, as are Perfons of Sobriety and Abilities, to accept the Miffion into thofe Parts —— With an Approbation of the Defign attefted, *Tho. Cantuar. Jo. Ebor. H. Lond. W. Cov.* and *Lichf. Ed. Worcefter. Sy. Elicnf. J. Norwich.*

A Letter from Dr. *Bray* to fuch as have contributed towards the Propagating Chriftian Knowledge in the *Plantations*. Printed fheet. *Fol.*

A Letter to a Miffionary Prieft by *Socrates Chriftianus* concerning the Qualifications requifite for that Service, and the ufual Performance thereof; and the Authority by which he acts in the Service he is employ'd in, and his Performance of it. Dat. 23 *Aug.* 1700. With a Poftfcript containing *Queftions Recommended to the Confideration of the Miffioners.* 4to. p. 15.

A Short Account of the feveral Kinds of Societies, fet up of late Years, for carrying on the *Reformation* of *Manners*, and for the *Propagation* of *Chriftian Knowledge*. *London*, Printed by *J. Brudenel*. 1700. *Fol. p.* 4.

An *Act* to incourage the TRADE to *Newfoundland* as beneficial to this Kingdom. in its Trade and Navigation. *Anno* x & xi. *Guil.* III. *cap.* xxv.

An Anfwer to *the Cafe* of the *Old Eaft-India* Company, as Reprefented by themfelves to the Lords Spiritual and Temporal in Parliament Affembled. *London*, Printed by *K. Aftwood*, for the Author, 1700. 4to. p. 21. [*Ex dono Reverendi Viri* Willoughby Willey.]

A Journal of a Thoufand Miles *Travel* among the *Indians* from *South* to *North Carolina*, begun in *December* 28. 1710. With a Defcription of *North Carolina*. The prefent State of it. The Natural Hiftory of the Country. An Account of the *Indians* in it. The Second Charter of King *Charles* II. granted to the Proprietors of *Carolina*. An Abftract of the Conftitution of *Carolina*. By *John Lawfon*. [Printed in Capt. *Steven*'s Collection of Voyages. 1711. 4to. *Vol.* I.]

An

An Abstract of the *Articles* in the *Treaty* concluded concerning the Succession of the Crown and Dominions of *Spain*, in *London* 21 *Febr.* 1699-1700. and in the *Hague* the 23d of *March*, 1699-1700. Printed Sheet. 1700.

1701.
23 *Will.* 3.
A new *DARIEN* Artifice laid open in a notable Inftance of Captain *Maclean's* Name, being ufed in the *Flying-Poft*, *Feb.* 11. & 13. 1710-11. to vouch *for* the *Caledonian* Company, after that Gentleman hath been Perfecuted by them thefe Thirteen Months paft, for Vouching *againft* them. Authore *Anti Darienfi.* 1701. 4to. *p.* 14. [See more on this Subject under the Years 1698-9, 1700, and 1702.]

A Sermon Preached before the Honourable Fraternity of *TRINITY-HOUSE*, at *Deptford* Church in *Kent*, on *Trinity Monday*, *June* 16. 1701. By *WILLIAM BALDWIN*, M. A. and Rector of St. *Mary Rotherhith* in *Surrey*. Publifhed at the Requeft of the Honourable Fraternity. *London*, Printed for *Walter Kettilby*. 1701. 4to.

The Unhappinefs of *England* as to its TRADE by SEA and LAND truly Stated. Alfo a lively Reprefentation of the Miferies of the Poor, the pernicious confequence of wearing Swords, and the ill Prefidents acted at the two Theaters; with effectual Means to redrefs thofe growing Evils, and feveral other remarkable Particulars. By *Charles Povey*. *London*, Printed for the Author. 1701.

The Excellency and Advantages of Religion. A Sermon preach'd for the Reformation of Manners in St. *John's* at *Nevis* in *America*. *July* 21. 1700. By *Tho. Heskith*, M. A. and Chaplain to one of his Majefty's Regiments of Foot Commanded by the Honourable *Edward Foxe* Efqr. Lieutenant General of the *Leeward Iflands*. With an Epiftle Dedicatory to the faid *Edw. Foxe*. *London*, Printed for *Tho. Speed*. 4to. 1701. *p.* 26.

PLANTATION Juftice, Shewing the Conftitution of their Courts, and what fort of Judges they have in them. By which *Merchants* may fee the Occafions of their great Loffes and Sufferings in the *PLANTATION Trade: Lawyers* may fee fuch a Model of *Juftice* as they could not have thought of; and Others may fee how thofe Parts of the World are governed. *London*, Printed for *A. Baldwin*. 1701. 4to. *p.* 12.

A Letter from a Gentleman to the Right Reverend Father in God *HENRY* Lord Bifhop of *London*, concerning the Charities collected for the Redemption of the Captives in the Empire of *Morocco*. Dated *London*, *Octob*. 17. 1701.
                                                                    B. M.

B. M. With a Tranflation out of the *Arabick* of the Emperor of *Morocco's* Declaration, concerning the Redemption of the Captives, by which he ratifies the Agreement made with his Minifters by Capt. *G. Delavall.* 4to.

Several Circular Letters to the Clergy of *MARYLAND* fubfequent to their late *Vifitation,* to enforce fuch Refolutions as were taken therein. By *Thomas Bray,* D. D. The *Firft* Letter enforcing the Duty, and by an eafie Method, accompanied with a fuitable Provifion of Books, facilitating to them the fundamental Work of *Catechifing.* Dat. *London, March* 1. 1700. With a Courfe of *Catechifing* to be obferved in the *Plantations.* The *Second* Letter relating to the great Duty of *Preaching,* more efpecially to the fupplying the Deficiency thereof, during the prefent Paucity of Minifters, by Lending or Difperfing of good Books. Dat. *London, July* 1. 1701. With the Lay-mans Library, Being a Lending Library for the ufe of the Laity. *London,* Printed by *William Downing.* 1701. Fol. *p.* 21. [See the Year 1700]

A Sermon Preached at St. *Bartholomew Exchange* on *Wednefday* the 3d of *December,* 1701, before the Honourable Company of Merchants Trading into the *Levant-Seas.* By *JOHN TISSER,* M. A. Fellow of *Merton* College, *Oxon.* and Chaplain to the Factory at *SMYRNA.* Publifhed by their Order. *London,* Printed for *Sam. Keble,* &c. MDCCII. 4to.

1702.
1 Annæ.

A Copy of the *Patent* granted by King *WILLIAM* for Incorporating a *Society for the Propagation of the Gofpel in Foreign Parts,* and that a fufficient Maintenance may be provided for an Orthodox Clergy to live amongft them, *&c.* Witnefs Our Self at *Weftminfter* the *Sixteenth* day of *June,* in the *Thirteenth* Year of Our *Reign.* Printed Sheet, by *J. Downing.* Fol.

An Abftract of the *Charter* granted to the Society for the Propagation of the Gofpel in Foreign Parts; With a fhort Account of what hath been, and what is defigned to be done by it. 1702. 1 large Sheet. Fol.

A Sermon Preach'd before the Society for the Propagation of the Gofpel in Foreign Parts. At their firft Yearly Meeting on *Friday, Febr.* 20. 1701-2. At St. *Mary le Bow.* By *Richard Willis,* D. D. Dean of *Lincoln. London,* Printed for *Matthew Wotton,* &c. 1702. 4to. *p.* 24.

Afer Baptizatus; Or, the *Negro* turned *Chriftian:* Being a Short and Plain Difcourfe fhewing, I. The Neceffity of *Inftructing* and *Baptizing Slaves* in *Englifh* Plantations. II. The Folly of that vulgar Opinion, that *Slaves* do ceafe to be *Slaves* when once Baptized. Delivered (moft of it) in a *Sermon* Preached at *Stratford le Bow* in *Middlefex, March* 15. 1701-2. By *ANTH.*
HILL,

HILL, Lecturer there, and Chaplain to His Grace the Duke of *Richmond*. *London*, Printed for *Charles Brome*. MDCCII. 8vo. p. 55.

Magnalia Christi Americana : Or, The *Ecclesiastical* History of *NEW-ENGLAND*, from its first Planting in the Year 1620, unto the Year of Our Lord 1698. In Seven Books. I. Antiquities. II. Lives of the Governours and Names of the Magistrates of *New-England*. III. The Lives of Sixty Famous Divines. IV. An Account of the University of *Cambridge* in *New England*. V. Acts and Monuments of the Faith and Order in the Churches of *New-England*. VI. A Faithful Record of many illustrious wonderful Providences. VII. The Wars of the Lord, being an History of the manifold Afflictions and Disturbances of the Churches in *New-England*. By the Reverend and Learned *Cotton Mather*, M. A. and Pastor of the *North Church* in *Boston*, *NEW-ENGLAND*. *London*, Printed for *Thomas Parkhurst*. MDCCII. Fol.

Vox Populi : Or, A Cloud of Witnesses proving the Leading QUAKERS Great Impostors by undeniable Evidence, both of the Divines of the Church of *England*, and many of the most Eminent Preachers amongst the Protestant Dissenters. Humbly submitted to Authority. By *Francis Bugg*. *London*, Printed by *R. Janeway* for the Author, &c. 1701. 8vo. p. 33.

An Account of the Illegal Prosecution and Tryal of Coll. *Nicholas Bayard* in the Province of *New-York*, for supposed High Treason in the Year 1701-2. Collected from several Memorials taken by divers Persons privately, the Commissioners having strictly prohibited the taking of the *Tryal* in open Court. Printed and Sold by *William Bradford* at the Sign of the *Bible* in *New-York*. MDCCII. Fol. p. 44.

Proposals for carrying on an Effectual War in *AMERICA* against the *French* and *Spaniards*. *London*, for *John Nutt*. 1702. 4to. p. 24.

A Printed Copy of Her Majesty's most Gracious Letter to the Parliament of *Scotland*, in Answer to their *Address*, in relation to the *Company* trading to *Africa* and the *Indies*; expressing Her Royal Regret for the great Losses and Disappointments of the said *Company* in the carrying on and prosecuting their Designs in settling of a Colony in *America*, and promising to concur in any thing that can reasonably be proposed for their Reparation and Assistance. Given at St. *James*'s the 21st. of *April*, 1702. Of Our Reign the First Year.

The

The Solemnity of *Proclaiming* Her Majesty Queen *Anne* at *Boston* in *New-England*; With the Humble *Address* of the Council and Representatives of Her Majesty's Province of the *Massachusets*-Bay in *New-England*, in General Court assembled. Presented to Her Majesty by *Constantine Phipps*, Esq; at *Windsor*, *July* 19. 1702. [*London Gazette*, N°. 3829.]

The Humble *Address* of the President and Council administring the Government of Her Majesty's Island of *Barbadoes*; together with the Principal Officers and Inhabitants thereof, now assembled in the Chief Town of the said Island, to *Proclaim* Her Majesty. Dat. *Bridge Town*, *May* 18. 1702. [*London Gazette*, N°. 3829.]

The Humble *Address* of Her Majesty's most Dutiful and Loyal Subjects the Council and Delegates of the Assembly of Her Majesty's Province of *Maryland*, presented to Her Majesty by Colonel *Blakiston*, Governour of *Maryland*, at St. *James's*, *Octob.* 13. 1702. [*London Gazette*, N°. 3829.]

The Humble *Address* of the Governour, Council, and Representatives of Her Majesty's Province of *New Hampshire* in *New-England*, convened in General Assembly, Presented to Her Majesty by *Constantine Phipps* and *William Vaughan*, Esqrs. *Octob.*25. 1702. [*London Gazette*, N°. 3857.]

Order of the Queen's most Excellent Majesty in Council at the Court at *Whitehall*, *Nov.* 18. 1702. for the Encouragement of such *Regiments* as have been or shall be sent to the *West-Indies* in Her Majesty's Service. [*London Gazette*, N°. 3864.]

An *Expedition* of a Body of *English* Men to the *Gold Mines* of *Spanish America* in 1702. With the many strange Adventures that befel them in that bold Undertaking. By *Nathaniel Davis*. [Printed at the End of *WAFER's Description* of the *Isthmus* of *America*. *London*, 1704. 8vo.]

A Copy of the Petition of *William Freeman*, Esq; in behalf of Himself and Others against Col. *Christopher Codrington*, Governour of the *Leeward Islands*, Presented to the House of Commons the 19th of *February*, 1701. With some Remarks thereon. [With Attestations of the *Colonel's* Good Conduct and Government from the Lieutenant, Governour and Members of the Council and Representatives of *Nevis*. Dated *July* 7. *A. D.* 1701.] Printed in the Year 1702. 4to. *p.* 36. [*Ex dono Rev.* Rob. Watts, *L. L. B. Coll.* Johan. Oxon. *Socij.*]

The

The Succeſſes of the *Engliſh* in *America*, by the March of Col. *Moore*, Governour of *Carolina*, and his Taking the *Spaniſh* Town of St. *Auguſtine* near the Gulph of *Florida*. And by our *Engliſh Fleet* ſailing up the River *Darien*, and marching to the *Gold Mines* at *Santa Cruz de Cana* near *Santa Maria*. [In an Account of the *South Sea Trade*. 1711. *p*. 16.]

An Account given of the Wealth of the *Pirates* in *Madagaſcar*, and of what they offered for their Pardon, by Capt. *Wheeler*, Capt. *Brent*, Dr. *Dawſon*, &c. in the Year 1703. *ib. p*. 21.

1703.
2 *Anns.*
The Preſent State of Affairs in *Carolina*. By *John Aſh*, Gent. Sent by ſeveral of the Inhabitants of that Colony, to deliver their Repreſentation thereof to, and ſeek Redreſs from the Lords Proprietors of that Province: Together with an Account of his Reception by the Honourable the Lord *Granville*, their Preſident, or Chief of the Proprietors. 26. *June*, 1703. 4*to*.

The Caſe of the Reverend Mr. *Samuel Fullwood*, Her Majeſty's Chaplain and Incumbent of the Rectory of St. *John's* in *Barbadoes*, rudely treated and aſſaulted by Col. *Holder*, as repreſented in ſeveral Letters, written *An.* 1703. 4*to*. MS.

New Voyages to *North America*; Containing an Account of the ſeveral Nations of that vaſt Continent; their Cuſtoms, Commerce, and Way of Navigation upon the Lakes and Rivers; the ſeveral Attempts of the *Engliſh* and *French* to diſpoſſeſs one another; With the Reaſons of the Miſcarriage of the former; and the various Adventures between the *French* and the *Iroqueſe* Confederates of *England*, from 1683, to 1694. A Geographical Deſcription of *Canada*, and a Natural Hiſtory of the Country, with Remarks upon their Government, and the Intereſt of the *Engliſh* and *French* in their *Commerce*. Alſo a *Dialogue* between the *Author* and a *General* of the *Savages*, giving a full View of the Religion and ſtrange Opinions of thoſe People: With an Account of the *Author's* Retreat to *Portugal* and *Denmark*, and his Remarks on thoſe Courts. To which is added, A *Dictionary* of the *Algonkine* Language which is generally ſpoke in *North America*. Illuſtrated with twenty three *Maps* and *Cuts*. Written in *French* by the *Baron LAHONTAN*, Lord Lieutenant of the *French* Colony at *Placentia* in *Newfoundland*, now in *England*. Done into *Engliſh*. In Two Volumes. A great Part of which never Printed in the Original. *London*, for *H. Bonwicke*, &c. 1703. 8*vo*.

MEMOIRS

MEMOIRS of the Sieur d' *Ablancourt* ; Containing a General History of the Court and Kingdom of *Portugal*, from the *Pyrenean* Treaty to the Year 1668. With a full Relation of all the Battles and Sieges in the War between *Spain* and *Portugal*, under the Command of the late Duke of *Schomberg*, then in the *Portugueze* Service, &c. Tranflated from the *French* Copy, Printed at *Paris*, 1701. *London*, Printed for *Ralph Smith*, &c. 1703. 8vo. *p.* 262.

A Collection of Voyages undertaken by the *Dutch Eaft-India Company* for the Improvement of *Trade and Navigation*. Containing an Account of feveral Attempts to find out the *North Eaft* Paffage, and their Difcoveries in the *Eaft-Indies*, and the *South Seas*. Together with an Hiftorical Introduction, giving an Account of the Rife, Eftablifhment, and Progrefs of that Great Body. Tranflated into *Englifh*, and illuftrated with feveral Charts. *London*, Printed for *W. Freeman*, &c. 1703. 8vo. *p.* 336.

Memoirs of Tranfactions at Sea during the War with *France* ; Beginning in 1688, and ending in 1697. Moft humbly Dedicated to his Royal Highnefs Prince *George* of *Denmark*, Lord High Admiral, &c. By *Jofiah Burchett*, Efq; Secretary to the Admiralty. *London*, 1703. 8vo. *p.* 408.

The SEAMAN's *Monitor*, wherein particular Advice is given to *Sea-faring* Men, with reference to their Behaviour before their Voyage, In it, and After it : With fome Prayers for their Ufe. By *Jofiah Woodward*, D. D. the Third Edition enlarged. *London*, Printed for *W. Hawes*. MDCCIII. 12°. *p.* 60.

A True and Exact Account of many Great Abufes committed in the *Victualling* Her Majefty's *Navy* from *February* 3. 1702-3, to *July* 1703. as appears by the Informations and Depofitions of feveral Witneffes, with the Proceedings thereupon, both at the *Admiralty-Office*, *Hicke's-Hall*, and elfewhere : For the Information of the Parliament and Publick. *London*, 1703. Fol. *p.* 14.

An Impartial Account of all the Material Tranfactions of the *Grand Fleet* and *Land Forces*, from their firft fetting out from *Spithead*, *June* the 29th. till his Grace the Duke of *Ormond's* Arrival at *Deal*, *Novemb.* 7. 1702. In which is included a particular Relation of the Expedition at *Cadiz*, and the Glorious Victory at *Vigo* : By an Officer that was prefent in thofe Actions. *London*, Printed for *R. Gibfon* and *J. Nutt*. 1703. 4°. *p.* 32.

A

A Narrative of Sir *George Rooke*'s late Voyage to the *Mediterranean*, after he had safely landed the King of *Spain*. Dated *London Sept.* 1704. 4*to.* p. 29.

Reflections on the Management of Sir *George Rooke*, Knt. Vice-Admiral of *England*, and Admiral, *&c.* in the late *Fight* in the *Mediterranean*. *London*, for *A. Baldwin*. 1704. 4*to.* p. 7.

A Review of the late *Engagement at Sea* : Being a Collection of Private *Letters*, never before Printed (one of them from Sir *Cloudesly Shovell*.) Containing the truest and most authentick Accounts : With some Remarks on the Conduct of our Admirals, particularly Sir *G. R.* *London*, for *J. Nutt*, 1704. 4*to.* p. 23.

Christ's Fidelity the only Shield against *Satan's Malignity* : Asserted in a Sermon delivered at *S A L E M* Village the 4th of *March* 1692. Being Lecture-Day there, and a Time of Publick Examination of some suspected for *WITCHCRAFT*. By *Deodat Lawson*, Minister of the Gospel. The *Second Edition* : With an *Appendix*, containing some brief Account of those amazing things which occasioned that Discourse to be delivered ; relating to the *Afflicted*, to the *Accused*, and to the *Confessing Witches*. At *Boston* in *New-England*, and in *London*. 1704. 8*vo.* p. 120.

1704.
3 *Anne.*   A New Voyage and Description of the *Isthmus* of *America* ; Giving an Account of the Author's Abode there, the Form and Make of the Country, the Coasts, Hills, Rivers, *&c.* Woods, Soil, Weather, *&c.* Trees, Fruit, Beasts, Birds, Fish, *&c.* The *Indian* Inhabitants, their Features, Complexion, *&c.* Their Manners, Customs, Employments, Marriages, Feasts, Hunting, Computation, Language, *&c.* With remarkable Occurrences in the *South Sea* and elsewhere. By *LIONEL WAFER*. The *Second* Edition. To which are added the *Natural History* of those Parts by a Fellow of the Royal Society : And *Davis*'s Expedition to the *Gold Mines*, in 1702. Illustrated with several Copper Plates. *London*, Printed for *James Knapton.* MDCCIV. 8*vo.* p. 283.

A Collection of Voyages and Travels ; Some now first Printed from Original Manuscripts ; Others translated out of Foreign Languages, and now first Published in *English*. To which are added some few that have formerly appeared in *English*, but do now for their Excellency and Scarceness deserve to be Reprinted. With a General Preface, giving an Account of the Progress of *NAVIGATION* from its first Beginning
ning

ning to the Perfection it is now in, &c. The Whole illuſtrated with a great Number of uſeful *Maps* and *Cuts*, all engraven on Copper. In Four Volumes *Fol.* for *J. Churchill.* MDCCIV.

VOL. I. Containing, I. An Account of the Empire of *China,* &c. Written in *Spaniſh* by the R. F. *Dominic Fernandez Navarette.* II. The Travels of *Martin Baumgarten* through *Egypt, Arabia,* &c. III. A Voyage to the Kingdom of *Chili* in *America* by Mr. *Henry Brawern* and Mr. *Elias Herckemann.* IV. An Account of the Iſland of *Formoſa* by *George Candidius.* V. Curious Remarks on the Empire of *Japan.* VI. An Account of a moſt dangerous Voyage performed by Capt. *John Monck* to *Hudſon's Straits.* VII. A Deſcription of *Ukraine.* VIII. A curious and exact Account of a Voyage to *Congo.* IX. Another Voyage to *Congo.* X. Sir *Thomas Roe's* Journal to the *Eaſt-Indies,* &c. p. 812.

VOL. II. Containing, I. Mr. *John Nieuhoff's* remarkable Voyages and Travels into *Brazil,* and the beſt Parts of the *Eaſt-Indies.* Tranſlated out of *Dutch.* II. The true Travels and Adventures of Capt. *John Smith* into *Europe, Aſia, Africa* and *America,* from the Year 1592 to 1629. III. Two Journals, the Firſt kept by ſeven Sailors in the Iſle of St. *Maurice* in *Greenland,* in the Years 1633 and 1634, who paſs'd the Winter, and all died in the ſaid Iſland. The Second kept by ſeven other Sailors, who in the Years 1633 and 1634. Wintered at *Spitzbergen.* Done out of *Low-Dutch.* IV. A true and ſhort Account of Forty two Perſons who periſhed by Shipwreck near *Spitzbergen* in the Year 1646. Out of *Low-Dutch.* V. An Account of *Iceland,* ſent to *Monſ. de la Mothe de Vayer* by *Monſ. La Peyrere.* Done out of *French.* VI. An Account of *Greenland* to *Monſ. de la Mothe de Vayer* by *Monſ. La Peyrere.* Done out of *French.* VII. Capt. *Thomas James's* ſtrange and dangerous Voyage in his intended Diſcovery of the *North Weſt Paſſage* into the *South Sea* in the Years 1631-2 and 1632 ; with many curious Obſervations. VIII. An Account of Two Voyages; the Firſt of *Feodor Iskowitz Backhoff,* the *Muſcovite* Envoy, into *China.* The Second of Mr. *Zachary Wagener* through a great part of the World into *China.* Tranſlated from the *High-Dutch.* IX. The Life of *Chriſtopher Columbus,* and the Hiſtory of his Diſcovery of the *Weſt-Indies.* Written by his own Son D. *Ferdinand Columbus* : Tranſlated from the *Italian.* X. *Pyramidographia* : Or, A Deſcription of the *Pyramids* in *Egypt* : By *John Greaves,* Profeſſor of *Aſtronomy* at *Oxford* : With Additions of his own. XI. A Diſcourſe of the *Roman Foot* and *Denarius,* from whence, as from Two Principles, the *Meaſures* and *Weights* uſed by the Antients may be deduced : By the ſame *John Greaves.* XII. An Account of *Cochinchina,* in 2 Parts : The Firſt treating of the Temporal State of that Kingdom : The Second, of what concerns the Spiritual. By the R. F. *Chriſtopher Borri* of the Society of *Jeſus.* Tranſlated from the *Italian.* p. 838.

VO L. III. Containing, I. An Hiſtorical Relation of the Kingdom of *Chile*, by *Alonſo de Ovalle*, of the Society of *Jeſus*, a Native of St. *Jago* in *Chile*, and Procurator at *Rome* for that Place. Tranſlated from the *Spaniſh*. II. Sir *William Monſon*'s Naval Tracts : Treating of all the Actions of the *Engliſh* by Sea under Queen *Elizabeth* and King *James* I. The Office of the *High Admiral* and his Inferior Officers, Diſcoveries and Enterprizes of the *Spaniards* and *Portugueze*; Projects and Stratagems; and of Fiſh and Fiſhe-ry. From the Original Manuſcripts. III. A true and exact Deſcription of the moſt celebrated *Eaſt-India* Coaſt of *Malabar* and *Coromandel*, and of the Iſland of *Ceylon*, with all the adjacent Countries. By *Philip Baldæus*. Tran-ſlated from the *High-Dutch*. *p.* 901.

VO L. IV. Containing, I. A Voyage round the *World* by Dr. *John Francis Gemelli Careri* ; containing the moſt remarkable things in *Turky*, *Perſia*, *India*, *China*, the *Philippine Iſlands* and *New Spain*. Tranſlated from the *Italian*. II. An Account of the *Shipwreck* of a *Dutch* Veſſel on the Coaſt of the *Iſle* of *Quelpaert*; Together with the Deſcription of the Kingdom of *Corea*. Tranſlated from the *French*. III. An Account of a Voyage from *Spain* to *Paraquaria*, performed by the R R. F F. *Anthony Sepp* and *Anthony Behme*, *German* Jeſuits and Miſſioners into thoſe Parts. Tranſlated from the *High Dutch*. IV. A Fragment concerning the Diſcovery of the Iſlands of *Solomon*. Tranſlated from the *Spaniſh*. V. The Hiſtory of the Provinces of *Paraguay*, *Tucumon*, *Rio de la Piata*, *Parana*, *Guaira*, and *Urvaica*, and ſomething of the Kingdom of *Chile* in *South America*. By *F. Nicholas del Techo*, of the Society of *Jeſus*. Tranſlated from the *Latin*. VI. *Pelham*'s Preſervation of 8 Men in *Greenland* 9 months and 12 days. VII. *Merin*'s Journey to the *Mines* in *Hungary*; with an Account of his Obſervations made there in rela-tion to them and ſubterraneous Paſſages in general. Tranſlated out of *Latin*. VIII. *Ten. Rhyne*'s Account of the *Cape of Good Hope* and the *Hotten-totes*, the barbarous Natives of that Country. IX. *Boland*'s Obſervations on the *Streights* of *Gibraltar*, and Tides and Current. *p.* 848.

[The Gift of the Honourable Col. *Francis Nicholſon*, Governour of *Nova Scotia*, and Her *Majeſty*'s General in the *Weſt-Indies*.]

An Hiſtorical and Geographical Deſcription of *FORMOSA*, an Iſland ſubject to the Emperor of *JAPAN*: Giving an Account of the Religion, Cuſtoms, Manners, *&c.* of the Inhabitants. Together with a Relation of what happened to the Author in his Travels; particularly his Conferences with the *Jeſuits*, and others in ſeveral Parts of *Europe*. Alſo the Hiſtory and Reaſons of his Converſion to Chriſtianity; with his Objections againſt it (in Defence of *Paganiſm*) and their *Anſwers*. To which is prefixed, A *Preface* in Vindication of himſelf from the Reflections of a *Jeſuit* lately come from *China*; with an Account of what paſſed between them. By *GEORGE PSAL-*

PSALMANAZAR, a Native of the said Island now in *London*. Illustrated with several Cuts. *London*, Printed for *Dan. Brown*, &c. 1704. 8vo. *p. 331.*

An Account of the *Propagation* of the Gospel in Foreign Parts. What the Society established in *England* by Royal Charter hath done since their *Incorporation*, *June* 16. 1701. in Her Majesty's Plantations, Colonies and Factories: As also what they design to do upon further Encouragement from their own Members, and other well-disposed Christians, either by Annual Subscriptions, present Benefactions, or future Legacies. Ordered at a Court held at St. *Martin's* Library, *Febr.* 4. 1703. that the Thanks of the Society be given to the Reverend Mr. *Stubs*, for preparing the said Account. *London*, Printed by *Jos. Downing*. 1704. 1 Sheet *Fol.*

Of the *Propagation* of the Gospel in Foreign *Parts*. A *Sermon* Preached at St. *Mary le Bow*, *Feb.* 18. 1703-4. Before the *Society* Incorporated for that Purpose. [Exhorting all Persons in their Stations to assist so glorious a Design.] By the Right Reverend Father in God *Gilbert* Lord Bishop of *Sarum*. *London*, Printed by *Joseph Downing*. 1704. 4to.

By the Queen. A *Proclamation* for Settling and Ascertaining the current Rates of *Foreign Coins* in Her Majesty's Colonies and Plantations in *America*. Given at Our Castle of *Windsor* the 18th day of *June*, 1704. in the Third Year of Our Reign. [*London Gazette*, N°. 4029.]

Notice given that the Right Honourable *Thomas* Lord *Fairfax* having Her Majesty's Grant for certain *Wrecks* in the *West Indies*, had appointed Sir *Edward Laurence*, Knt. *Milford Crow*, *William Russell* and *Robert Lowther*, Esqrs. *William Brown*, *John Deneu*, and *James Dolliffe* of *London*, Merchants, Trustees for managing and carrying on the Design; who were accordingly to meet, and open Books for Subscriptions, &c. *June* 21. 1704. [*London Gazette*, N°. 4029.]

A Full and Impartial History of the *Expedition* into *Spain* in the Year 1702. Extracted from the Journals and Memoirs of the *Generals*; and from which it will be easie to draw rational Conjectures, about the present Enterprize, to settle the most Serene *Charles* III. on the *Spanish* Throne. To which is added an Account of Monsieur *Chateaurenault's* Expedition, from his first sailing from *Brest* in *Sept*. 1701. to his putting into *Vigo* in *Sept.* 1702. In a Letter from Monsieur *de Gatines*, Intendant of the Navy of *France*, to a Minister of State at *Paris*; which Letter was taken at *Redondella*,

dondella, among Monſieur *Chateaurenault*'s Papers. *London*, by *Will. Davis*. 1704. 8*vo*. *p*. 172.

Reflections on Mr. *Burchet*'s *Memoirs* ; or Remarks on his Account of Captain *Wilmot*'s Expedition to the *Weſt-Indies*. By Coll. *Luke Lillingſton*, Commander in Chief of the Land Forces in that Expedition. *London*. MDCCIV. 8*vo*. *p*. 171.

An *Act* for the more effectual Preſervation of the Government of the Province of *Carolina*, by requiring all Perſons that ſhall hereafter be choſen Members of the Commons Houſe of Aſſembly, and ſit in the ſame, to take the Oaths and ſubſcribe the Declaration appointed by this Act ; and to conform to the Religious Worſhip in the Province, according to the *Church* of *England* ; and to receive the Sacrament of the *Lord's Supper* according to the Rites and Uſage of the ſaid *Church* ; Read three times, and ratified in open Aſſembly, the 6th day of *May*, 1704. 4*to*.

Another *Act* for the Eſtabliſhment of Religious Worſhip in the Province of *Carolina*, according to the *Church* of *England* ; and for the Erecting of Churches for the Publick Worſhip of God ; and alſo for the maintenance of *Miniſters*, and the building convenient Houſes for them. Read three times, and ratified in open Aſſembly, *Novemb.* 4. 1704. 4*to*.

1705.
4 *Anns.* *Party-Tyranny* ; Or, An *Occaſional Bill* in Miniature ; Being an Abridgment of the *Shorteſt Way* with the *Diſſenters*, as now practiſed in *CAROLINA*. Humbly offered to the Conſideration of both Houſes of *Parliament*. *London*, Printed in the Year 1705. 4*to. p*.

The *Repreſentation* and *Addreſs* of ſeveral of the Members of this preſent Aſſembly, returned for *Colleton* County, and other Inhabitants of this Province, to the Right Honourable *John Granville*, Eſq; and to the reſt of the true and abſolute Lords and Proprietors of the Province of *CAROLINA*. Dat. 26. *June*, 1705. 4*to*.

The Humble Addreſs of the Right Honourable the Lords Spiritual and Temporal in Parliament Aſſembled, Preſented to Her Majeſty on *Wedneſday* the 13th day of *March*, 1705. [relating to the Province of *CAROLINA*, and the *Petition* therein mentioned of *Joſeph Boon*, Merchant, on behalf of himſelf and many other Inhabitants of the Province of *Carolina*, and alſo of ſeveral Merchants of *London* trading to *Carolina* and the neighbouring Colonies of Her Majeſty in *America*.] With Her *Majeſty's* moſt Gracious Anſwer thereunto.

thereunto. *London,* Printed by *Charles Bill* and the Executrix of *Tho. New-comb.* 1705.

A *Letter* from *Mr. Edward Marston* a Minister in *CAROLINA* to a *Member* of the Society in *London* for *Propagation* of the Gospel in Foreign Parts. Dat. *Charles-Town Library* in *South Carolina,* May 3. 1705. 4to.

The Humble *Petition* of the Reverend *Mr. Edward Marston,* Minister of the Church of *England* in *Charles-Town* in *South Carolina,* to his Excellency *John* Lord *Granville,* Palatine, and the rest of the True and Absolute Lords Proprietors of *CAROLINA.* 4to.

The Case of the Reverend *Mr. Edward Marston,* Minister of the Church belonging to the *Church of England* in *Charles-Town* in *SOUTH CAROLINA* truly stated. 4to.

The History and Present State of *VIRGINIA,* in Four Parts. I. The History of the *First Settlement* of *Virginia,* and the Government thereof to the present time. II. The Natural Productions and Conveniencies of the Country, suited to Trade and Improvement. III. The Native *Indians* their Religion, Laws and Customs in War and Peace. IV. The Present State of the Country, as to the Polity of the Government, and the Improvements of the Land. By a Native and Inhabitant of the Place. *London,* Printed for *R. Parker.* MDCCV. 8vo.

An Act for Encouraging the Importation of Naval Stores from Her *Majesty's Plantations* in *America.* With a Design to render those Colonies and Plantations as useful as may be to *England.* Anno 3, 4 *Annæ Reginæ.* Cap. X.

An Essay upon the Necessity and Excellency of EDUCATION, with these Consequences ; that the Excellence of Education is best obtained by the Application of the Genius to the Dictate of Nature, that all wise Governments have preferred an *Education* necessary to their Constitution and Interest, and for this Reason *England* obliged to cultivate the Art of *Navigation.* By *Mr. Maidwell. London,* for *J. Nutt.* 1705. 8vo. p. 63. Dedicated to *Robert Harley,* Esq; Speaker to the House of Commons, and one of the Principal Secretaries of State.

A Copy of the Marquefs of *Carmarthen*'s Method for the fpeedy *Manning* Her *Majefty*'s Royal N A V Y, and for Encouraging S E A M E N. *Feb.* 12. 1705. 8*va*   *London*, for *John Humfreys.* *p.* 8.

The Cafe of Captain *Tho. Green*, Commander of the Ship *Worcefter*, and his Crew, tried and condemned for *Pyracy* and *Murther*, in the High Court of Admiralty of *Scotland.*   *London*, by *John Nutt*, &c. 1705. 4*to.* *p.* 30.

The Agreement of the Cuftoms of the *Eaft-Indians* with thofe of the *Jews*, and other ancient People : Being the firft Effay of this kind towards the explaining of feveral difficult Paffages in Scripture, and fome of the moft ancient Writers by the prefent Oriental Cuftoms. With C U T S. To which are added *Inftructions* to young Gentlemen that intend to *Travel.* *London*, Printed for *W. Davis*, &c. 1705. 8*vo.* *p.* 159. [*Ex dono Reverendi Viri* Willoughby Wiiley, *A. M.*]

A *Sermon* Preached in the Audience of the General Affembly at the Publick Lecture in *Bofton*, *Novemb.* 1. 1705. By *Ebenezer Pemberton*, M. A. Paftor of a Church in *Bofton.* Publifhed at the Defire of the Houfe of Reprefentatives ; and Printed at *Bofton* in *New-England* by B. Green. 8*vo.* *p.* 35. [See another of his Sermons under the Year 1710.]

1706.
5 *Annæ.*   A *Sermon* Preached before his Excellency the Governour, the Honourable Council and Reprefentatives of the Province of the *Maffachufets*-Bay in *New-England*, on *May* 29. 1706. Which was the Day for *Election* of Her Majefty's Council for that Province. By *John Rogers*, A. M. and Paftor of *Ipfwich.* *Bofton*, Printed by B. Green. 8*vo.* 1706. *p.* 54.

A Printed Copy of the Humble *Addrefs* of Her Majefty's Council and Reprefentatives of Her Majefty's Province of *New-Hampfhire* in N E W-E N G L A N D, convened in General Affembly, this 25th day of *July*, 1706. to the Queen's moft Excellent Majefty.

A Difcourfe putting *Chriftians* in mind to be ready to every Good Work. As it was delivered in *Bofton*, *Octob.* 20. 1706. By *Eliphalet Adams.* *Bofton* N E. Printed by B. Green. 1706. 8*vo.* *p.* 60.

A Difcourfe concerning the *Maintenance* due to thofe that Preach the *Gofpel :* In which that Queftion whether *Tythes* are by the Divine Law the Minifter's Due, is confidered, and the Negative proved. By *J. Mather*, D. D. *Bofton* N. E. Printed by B. Green. 1706. 8*vo.* *p.* 60.

An

An Account of the Fair and Impartial Proceedings of the Lords Proprietors, Governour and Council of the Colony of *SOUTH CAROLINA*, in Answer to the untrue Suggestions contained in the Petition of *Jos. Boon* and others, and of a Paper intitled, *The Case of the Church of* England *in* Carolina. *London*, Printed by *J. Brudenell*. 1706. Fol. *p.* 4.

A full and particular Account of an Invasion made by the *French* and *Spaniards* upon *SOUTH CAROLINA*; with the Disappointment and Disgrace they met with in it; contained in a Letter from *Charles-Town* in *Carolina, Septemb.* 12. 1706.

An Account of the *Society for Propagating the Gospel in Foreign Parts*, Established by the Royal Charter of King *William* III. With their Proceedings and Success. And Hopes of continual Progress under the Happy Reign of Her most Excellent Majesty Queen *Anne. London*, Printed by *Joseph Downing*. 1706. 4to. *p.* 97.

A Journal of Travels from *New-Hampshire* to *Caratuck* on the Continent of *North America*. By *George Keith*, M. A. late Missionary from the *Society for the Propagation of the Gospel in Foreign Parts*, and now Rector of *Edburton* in *Sussex. London*, for *Brab. Aylmer*. 1706. 4to. *p.* 92.

A Collection of Papers Printed by Order of the Society for the Propagation of the Gospel in Foreign Parts, *viz. The Charter, The Request*, &c. *The Qualifications of Missionaries* ; *Instructions for the Clergy* ; *Instructions for Schoolmasters* ; *Prayers for the Charity-Schools. London*, Printed by *Joseph Downing*. 1706. 4to. *p.* 45.

A Sermon Preached before the *Society for the Propagation of the Gospel in Foreign Parts* ; at the Parish Church of St. *Lawrence Jury, Febr.* 15. 1705.6. By the Right Reverend *John* Lord Bishop of *Chichester. London*, Printed for *Thomas Speed*. 1706. 4to.

Wussukwhonk. *En Christianeve asub peantamwae* INDIANOG, &c. An Epistle to the *Christian Indians*, giving them a short Account of what the *English* desire them to know and to do, in order to their Happiness. Written by an *English* Minister, at the Desire of an *English* Magistrate, who sends unto them this Token of Love. The Second Edition. *Boston*, Printed by *Bartholomew Green*. 1706. 8vo. *p.* 14.

A

A Letter of Advice to all the Worthy and Ingenious Merchants of the City of *London*, and elfewhere in *England*, *Scotland* and *Ireland* ; and alfo to all the Worthy and Ingenious Merchants of *France* and *Holland*, and the *United Provinces*, and of *Germany*, *Spain*, *Portugal*, *Denmark*, and *Sweden*, and elfewhere in *Europe*, and to all Artifts in *Aftronomy*, *Geography* and *Navigation* ; Shewing an exact, fpeedy and eafie way to know the LONGITUDE of all Places in the World where the *European* Merchants have their Agents to make Obfervations, and alfo how the LONGITUDE of Places may be better known upon Ship-board. Written by *Digby Bull*, M. A. and late Rector of *Sheldon* in *Warwickfhire*. *London*, Printed for the Author. 1706. 4to. *p*. 26.

1707.
6 *Anna*. A New Defcription of that Fertile and Pleafant Province of *CAROLINA* ; With a brief Account of its Difcovery, Settling, and the Government there-of to this time : With feveral remarkable Paffages of Divine Providence du-ring my Time. By *John Archdale*, late Governour of the fame. *London*, 1707. for *John Wyat*. 4to. *p*. 32.

Another Tongue brought in to confefs the Great Saviour of the World : Or, Some Communications of Chriftianity put into a Tongue ufed among the *Iroquefe Indians* in *America*. And put into the Hands of the *English* and the *Dutch Traders* ; to accommodate the great Intention of communicating the *Chriftian* Religion to the *Salvages*, among whom they may find any thing of this Language to be intelligible. *Bofton*, Printed by *B. Green*. 8vo. *p*. 16. in *Indian* and *English*.

Ne Kefukod Jehovah Keffehtunkup, &c. *The* Day *which the Lord hath made.* A Difcourfe concerning the Inftitution and Obfervation of the *Lord's Day.* Delivered in a Lecture at *Bofton* 4. d. 1. m. 1703. *Bofton, N. E.* Reprinted by *B. Green*. 1707. 8vo. *p*. 36. In *Indian* and *English*.

A Sermon Preached before the SOCIETY *for the Propagation of the Gofpel* in *Foreign Parts*, at the Parifh Church of St. *Mary le Bow*, *February* 21. 1706-7. By the Right Reverend *William* Lord Bifhop of St. *ASAPH*. *London*, Printed and Sold by *Joseph Downing*. 1707. 4to.

A Propofal made to the *Society for Propagation of the Gofpel*, by the Right Rev. Father in God *Thomas* Bifhop of *Man* ; defiring them to confider, whether the *Ifle of Man* would not be the propereft Place in which to educate, and out of which to make choice of fit Perfons for their *Miffions* to the *Weft-Indies*. 12. *May*, 1707. In a Sheet of Paper under the Bifhop's own Hand. MS.

A kind Caution to *Watermen*, and such as go upon the *River*. *London*, Printed and Sold by *Joseph Downing*. 1707. 12°. *p.* 12.

The State of the Church in PENSILVANIA, most humbly offered to the Venerable *Society for the Propagation of the Gospel in Foreign Parts*. By *Evan Evans*. Dat. London 18. Septemb. 1707. in *Fol.* MS.

A Printed Copy of the Humble *Address* of the Ministers of the Gospel in *NEW-ENGLAND* to the Queen's most Excellent Majesty, with all Thankfulness admiring Her Majesty's great Moderation and gracious Indulgence towards such of Her Majesty's good Subjects as *Dissent* from the *Church of England*; and Her Royal Assurance that She will *inviolably* maintain the *Toleration*: Acknowledging Her Majesty's Favour in appointing and continuing Colonel *Dudley* to be their Captain General and Governour, &c. Published in *London*, Sept. 6. 1707.

A modest Enquiry into the Grounds and Occasions of a late Pamphlet, intituled, *A Memorial of the present deplorable State of* NEW-ENGLAND. By a disinterested Hand. [Containing the *Memorial* it self, with an *Answer* to it, and several *Letters* and *Addresses* in favour of Col. *Dudley*, Governour of *New-England*.] *London*, Printed in the Year 1707. 4to. *p.* 30.

A Disquisition concerning the State of the *Souls* of *Men* (especially of *Good Men*) when separated from their *Bodies*, in which some late very remarkable Providences relating to *Apparitions* [in *New-England*] are considered. By *J. Mather*, D.D. With a *Postscript*, containing some *Letters* from *Boston*, &c. confirming the said *Relations*. *London*, Printed for T. *Parkhurst*. 1707. 8vo. *p.* 36.

An Act for Ascertaining the Rates of *Foreign Coins* in Her *Majesty's* Plantations in *America*. *Anno 6 Annæ Reginæ*, *Cap.* xxx.

An Act for the Encouragement of the *Trade to America*, *Ib.* *Cap.* xxxvii.

A Sermon Preached at St. *Bennet-Finke* Church on *Thursday October* 24th, 1707. before the Honourable Company of *Merchants* trading to the *Levant Seas*. By *Lawrence Hacket*, Chaplain to the Factory at *Constantinople*. *London*, for *Jonah Bowyer*. 1707. 4to. *p.* 32.

Edifying and Curious Letters of some *Missioners* of the *Society of Jesus*. from Foreign *Missions*. Vol. I. Printed in the Year 1707. 8vo. *p.* 258. Dedi-

cated

cated to the Jesuites of *France* by *Charles Gobien* of the Society of *Jesus*. As
I. A Letter of *F. Martin*, Missioner of the Society of *Jesus*, to *F. de Vilette*
of the same Society, dated from *Balassor* in the Kingdom of *Bengala*, the
30th of *January* 1699. II. A Letter of *F. Mauduit* to *F. le Gobien*, dated
Poleour in the *East Indies*, *Sept.* 29th, 1700. III. A Letter of Father *Dolu*
to *F. le Gobien*, dat. from *Pondicherry*, the 4th of *Octob.* 1700. IV. A Letter
of *F. Bouchet* to *F. le Gobien*, dated from *Madura*, 1. *Decemb.* 1701. V. A
Letter of *F. Diusse* to the Father *Director* of the *French Missions*, dat. *Surrat*
28. *Jan.* 1701. VI. Letter of F. *Pelisson* to Father *de la Chaize*, dated from
Canton, Decemb. 9. 1700. &c. [See the 2d Volume under the Year 1709.]

A Voyage round the *World*, containing an Account of *Captain Dampier's*
Expedition into the *South Seas*, in the Ship *St. George*, in the Years 1703
and 1704. With his various Adventures, Engagements, &c. And a particular and exact Description of several Islands in the *Atlantick* Ocean, the *Bra-
zilian* Coast, the Passage round Cape *Horn* and the Coast of *Chili*, *Peru* and
Mexico Together with the Author's Voyage from *Amapalla* on the West-
Coast of *Mexico* to *East-India*. His passing by three unknown Islands, and
through a new discovered Streight near the Coast of *New Guinea* : His Arrival
at *Amboyna* ; with a large Description of those and other *Spice Islands* ; as also
of *Batavia*, the *Cape* of *Good Hope*, &c. Their Rivers, Harbours, Plants,
Animals, Inhabitants, &c. With divers Maps, Draughts, Figures of Plants
and Animals. By *William Funnell*, Mate to Captain *Dampier*. *London*, for
James Knapton. 1707. 8vo. *p.* 300.

An Answer to Capt. *D A M P I E R*'s Vindication of his Voyage to the
South Seas in the Ship St. *George* ; With particular Observations on his unge-
nerous, false, and barbarous Usage to his Ships Crew. By *JOHN WELBE*,
Midship-man, on board Capt. *D A M P I E R*'s Ship. *London*, Printed and
Sold by *B. Bragge*, &c. 1707. 4to. *p.* 8.

1708.   The Discovery and Conquest of the *Molucco* and *Philippine* Islands ; con-
7 *Anna.* taining their History Ancient and Modern, Natural and Political : Their Description, Product, Religion, Government, Laws, Languages, Customs,
Manners, Habits, Shapes and Inclinations of the Natives. With an Account
of many other adjacent Islands, and several remarkable Voyages through the
Streights of *Magellan*, and in other Parts. Written in *Spanish* by *Bartholomew Leonardo de Angensola*, Chaplain to the Empress, and Rector of *Villa
Hermosa*. Now translated into *English* ; and illustrated with *Maps* and several *Cuts*. *London*, Printed in the Year 1708. [In Capt. *Stevens's* Collection
of Voyages. 4to. Vol. I. *p.* 1.]

A

A General Hiſtory of all VOYAGES and TRAVELS throughout the OLD and NEW VVORLD, from the firſt Ages to this preſent Time, illuſtrating both the Ancient and Modern Geography. Containing an accurate Deſcription of each Country, its Natural Hiſtory and Product, the Religion, Cuſtoms, Manners, Trade, &c. of the Inhabitants, and whatſoever is curious and remarkable in any kind. An Account of all hitherto made in the moſt remote Parts, and the great Uſefulneſs of ſuch Attempts, &c. By Monſieur DU PEREIR of the Royal Academy. Made Engliſh from the Paris Edition. Adorn'd with Cuts. London, Printed for Edmund Curll, &c. 1708. 8vo. p. 364. [Given by Mr. Samuel Pendleton of Peterborough.]

An Account of the Cruelties exerciſed by the Inquiſition in Portugal : To which is added a Relation of the Detention of Mr. Lovis Ramè in the Priſons of the Inquiſition in the Kingdom of Mexico in New Spain, in the Years 1679, 1680, 1681, 1682. and of his happy Deliverance. Written by one of the Secretaries to the Inquiſition. London, for R. Burrough and J. Baker. 1708. 8vo. p. 164.

Propoſals for Erecting Lending LIBRARIES in the Market-Towns of North and South Wales ; With Parochial ones for the Poorer Miniſters throughout that whole Dominion ; As alſo for Diſperſing ſome Devotional and Practical Books in thoſe Parts, both in the Engliſh and Welſh Tongues : Being an Attempt to Propagate Religion in thoſe Parts. Printed Half-ſheet. 1708. Fol.

Geography Anatomized : Or the Geographical Grammar ; Being a Short and Exact Analyſis of the whole Body of Modern Geography : After a New and Curious Method, &c. Collected from the beſt Authors, and Illuſtrated with divers Maps. The Fifth Edition corrected and ſomewhat enlarged. By PAT. GORDON, M. A. F. R. S. With an Appendix, comprehending a Brief Account of the European Plantations in Aſia, Africk and America : As alſo ſome Reaſonable Propoſals for the Propagation of the Bleſſed Goſpel in all Pagan Countries. London, Printed for John Nicholſon, &c. 1708. 8vo. p. 428.

A Sermon Preached at Trinity-Church in New-York in AMERICA, Auguſt 13. 1706. At the Funeral of the Right Honourable Katharine Lady Cornbury, Baroneſs Clifton of Leighton-Bromſwold, &c. Heireſs to the moſt Noble Charles Duke of Richmond and Lenox, and Wife to His Excellency Edward Lord Viſcount Cornbury, Her Majeſty's Captain General, and Governour

vernour in Chief of the Provinces of *New-York*, *New-Jersey* and Territories depending thereon in *America*, &c. By *John Sharp*, M. A. Chaplain to the Queen's Forces in the Province of *New-York*. *London*, Printed for *J. Morphex*. 1708. 8*vo. p.* 16.

The Deplorable State of *N E W - E N G L A N D* by reason of a Covetous and Treacherous *Governour* and Pusillanimous *Counsellors*; With a Vindication of the Honourable Mr. *Higginson*, Mr. *Masson*, and several other Gentlemen, from the scandalous and wicked Accusation of the *Votes*, Ordered by them to be Published in their *Boston* News-Letter. To which is added An Account of the shameful Miscarriage of the late Expedition against *Port-Royal*. *London*, Printed in the Year 1708. 4*to. p.* 39.

Corderius Americanus. An Essay upon the good Education of Children; And what may hopefully be Attempted for the Hope of the Flock. In a *Funeral Sermon* upon Mr. *Ezekiel Cheever*, the Ancient and Honourable Master of the Free-School in *Boston* : Who left off, but when Mortality took him off in *August* 1708. the *Ninety fourth* Year of his Age. With an *Elegy* and an *Epitaph* upon him, by one that was once a Scholar to him. *Boston*, Printed by *John Allen*. 1708. 8*vo. p.* 34:

The *Sot-weed Factor* Or a Voyage to *M A R Y L A N D* : A Satyr. In which is described the Laws, Government, Courts and Constitutions of the Country; and also the Buildings, Feasts, Frolicks, Entertainments, and Drunken Humours of the Inhabitants of that Part of *America*. In Burlesque Verse. By *Eben Cook*, Gent. *London*, by *B. Bragg*. 1708. 4*to. p.* 21.

The *British Empire* in *A M E R I C A*, containing the History of the Discovery, Settlement, Progress and Present State of all the *British* Colonies on the *Continent* and *Islands* of *America*: In *two* Volumes. Being an Account of the Country, Soil, Climate, Product and Trade of them, *viz.* Vol. I. *Newfoundland*, •*New-Scotland*, *New-England*, *New-York*, *New-Jersey*, *Pensilvania*, *Maryland*, *Virginia*, *Carolina*, and *Hudson's-Bay*. With curious Maps of the several Places, done from the newest Surveys By *Herman Moll*, Geographer. *London*, Printed for *John Nicholson*, &c. 1708. 8*vo. p.* 412.

The *British Empire* in *AMERICA*. The *Second* Volume. Being an Account of the Country, Soil, Climate, Product and Trade of *Barbadoes*, *St. Lucia*, *St. Vincents*, *Dominico*, *Antego*, *Monserrat*, *Nevis*, *St. Christophers*, *Barbuda*, *Anguilla*, *Jamaica*, the *Bahama*, and *Bermudas Islands*. With curious *Maps*, &c. *London*. 1708. 8*vo. p.* 382.

By

By the Queen, A *Proclamation* for the better executing an *Act of Parliament* to encourage the *Trade* to *Newfoundland*, and for better obferving the Rules and Orders in the faid *Act* for regulating the *Fifhery*, &c. Given at Our Court of *Kenfington* the 26th day of *June*, in the Seventh Year of Our Reign. [*London Gazette*, N°. 4452.]

An Account of the Trials of two Captains for their Behaviour in the late *Engagement* between Her Majefty's *Ships* under the Command of Commodore *Wager* and the *Spanifh Galleons.* At a Court-Martial held on board Her Majefty's Ship *Expedition* at *Port-Royal* in *Jamaica* the 23d of *July*, 1708. [*London Gazette*, N°. 4476.]

The *Memorial* of Capt. *Thomas Smith*, late Commander of the *Nightingale*; wherein a true State of his Cafe is delivered, with Certificates proving his Conduct and Services to this Notion : Recommended under his own Hand to the ferious Confideration of all Sober and Judicious Perfons of all Conditions. From the Prifon of *Newgate*, dated *May* 7th, 1708. *London*, Printed and Sold by *B. Bragg*. 4to. 1708. A Half-fheet.

Eben Ezer ; Or a Monument of Thankfulnefs : Being a true Account of a late miraculous Prefervation of 9 Men in a fmall Boat, which was inclofed within *Iflands of Ice* about 70 Leagues from Land, and continuing in Diftrefs 20 Days ; with the moft remarkable Paffages which happened in their Voyage from *Plymouth* to the *Newfoundland*, in the Ship called the *Langdon Frigate*, Capt. *Arthur Holdfworth* Commander ; with a Lift of the Names of thofe that furvived, and can witnefs to the Truth of this Relation. Written by *Allen Geare*, Chief Mate of the Ship, who was a Principal Sharer both in the *Mifery* and the *Mercy. London*, Printed by *Sam. Smith*. 1708. 8vo. p.8.

Captain *Kerr's* Cafe, in Anfwer to Mr. *Wood's* Allegations : [*viz*, of Complaint againft him for not allowing him a Convoy to two of his Ships in the *Weft-Indies* in the Year 1707.] A Broadfide, *Fol.* 1708.

Some Obfervations on the *Royal Hofpital* at G R E E N W I C H ; humbly offered to the Judicious Confideration of the Honourable Houfe of Commons. A Half-fheet. *Fol.* 1708.

The *Englifh* Acquifitions in G U I N E A and E A S T-I N D I A ; Containing *firft*, the feveral Forts and Caftles of the Royal *African* Company, from *Sally* in *South Barbary* to the Cape of *Good-Hope* in *Africa.* Secondly, The Forts and Factories of the Honourable *Eaft-India Company* in *Perfia*, *India*,

G g g

Sumatra,

Sumatra, China, &c.   With an Account of the Inhabitants of all thefe Countries, &c.   *London*, Printed for *Nat. Crouch*.   1708. *8vo.* *p.* 179.

A Dialogue between *Jeft* an *East-India Stock-Jobber*, and *Earnest* an Honeft *Merchant*. [Againft the *East-India Company*.] *London*. 1708. *p.* 12. 16°.

Some *Propofals* towards *Promoting the Propagation of the Gofpel in our* AMERICAN *Plantations*. Humbly offered in a Letter to *Mr. Nelfon*, a worthy Member of *the Society for Propagating the Gofpel in Foreign Parts*. To which is added a Poftfcript. *London*, Printed for G. *Sawbridge*. 1708. 4*to. p.* 30.

An Abftra&t of the Journal of *Mr. William Cordiner* a *Miffioner* of *the Society for Propagation of the Gofpel in Foreign Parts*, taken in the *Chefter* by feveral *French* Men of War, and carried Prifoner to *Breft*, with his Mother, Wife and two Children, &c. Dat. *Novemb.* 9th. 1708.   Subfcribed *William Cordiner*.   MS.

The New Gofpel of the *Jefuits* compared with the old one of *Jefus Chrift* : Or a fhort Colle&tion of fome choice *Maxims* of thefe Politick Cafuifts againft the Plain Dealing of the *Prophets* and *Apoftles*. To which is annexed the Condemnation of their Opinions by the *See* of *Rome*. By a Friend to their Perfons, but no Lover of their Principles. *London*, Printed for the Author. 1708. [Written by a Papift.]

1709.
8 *Aunz.*   A true Account of the prefent State of Chriftianity in *CHINA*, with full Satisfaction as to the Behaviour of the *Jefuits*. As alfo the *Pope*'s Determination, which has been kept fo long fecret. Containing, 1. A Letter from the Province of *Fokien* in *China*, about the End of the Year 1700. of the ill Treatment of M. *Maigrot*, Bifhop of *Conon* and *Apoftolick Vicar*. 2. The Ordinance of M. *Maigrot*, Do&tor of the Houfe and Society of *Sorbonnè*, *Apoftolick Vicar*; nominated to the Bifhoprick of *Conon*. Dat. 20. *March*, 1703. 3. The Letter of the Cardinal of *Tournon*, Patriarch of *Antioch*, fent into *China* by our Holy Father the *Pope*, with the Powers of *Legate à latere*. Written from *Lin-Chin* the 6th of *O&tober*, 1706. To my Lord the Bifhop of *Conon*, *Vicar Apoftolick* of one of the Provinces of *China*, to comfort him in the Prifon wherein he was confined by the Order of the *Emperor* at *Pekin*, under the Cuftody of the *Jefuits*. 4. *Breve SanEtiffimi Domini noftri* Clementis Papæ XI. *ad* Epifcopum Cononenfem Vicarium Apoftolicum Fokienfem *apud* Sinas, *ab eminentiffimo Cardinali* Turnonio *delatum*. Dat. Romæ *apud* S. Petrum *die* xx Junij, MDCCII. *Pont. noftri anno fecundo*. 5. A Letter
writ

writ by the said *Monf. Maigrot* to the Pope at his Return from *China*, Dated from *Galloway* in *Ireland*, *May* 4. 1708. 6. The *Decree* published in *China* by the *Cardinal de Tournon*, Patriarch of *Antioch*, Translated from a Copy in *Spanifh.* Given at *Nankin* 25. *January*, 1707. *London*, Printed for *John Morphew* 1709. 4*to. p.* 26. [See more on this Subject under the Year 1710.]

Edifying and Curious Letters of some *Miffioners* of the *Society* of *Jefus* from Foreign *Miffions.* Vol. II. Printed in the Year 1709. 8*vo. p.* 173. with an *Epiftle Ded.* to the *Jefuits* of *France*, by F. *Charles le Gobien*, of the Society of *Jefus.* Containing 1. A Letter of Father *Verzeau* of the Society of *Jefus* in *Syria* to F. *Fluriau* of the same Society. Dated from *Aleppo* the 10th of *March*, 1704. II. A Letter from the same Father *Verzeau* to R. F. *de la Chaize* of the same Society, *Confeffor* to the *King*, concerning the *Miffion* of *Syria.* Dated from *Rome*, *Dec.* 20. 1703. III. A Letter from *Monf. Hanna* a *Syrian Ecclefiaftick*, to *Monf. Abdalla* his Nephew, educated in the *Seminary* of the *Orientals* in the *College* of *Lewis the Great.* Translated from the *Arabick*, Dat. *Aleppo*, *Feb.* 14. 1702. [See the First Vol. under the Year 1707.]

A Voyage to *Æthiopia* made in the Years 1698, 1699, and 1700. Describing particularly that famous Empire; as also the Kingdoms of *DONGOLA*, *SENNAR*, Part of *ÆGYPT*, &c. With the Natural Hiftory of those Parts. By *Monf.* P O N C E T, M. D. Faithfully Translated from the *French* Original. *London*, Printed for *W. Lewis.* 1709. 12° *p.* 138.

The Seventeen Years Travels of *Peter de Chieza* through the mighty Kingdom of *Peru*, and the large Provinces of *Cartagena* and *Popayan* in *South-America*, from the City of *Panama* in the *Ifthmus*, to the Frontiers of *Chile.* Now first translated from the *Spanifh*, and illuftrated with a *Map* and feveral *Cuts. London*, Printed in the Year M DCC IX. [Publifh'd in *the Collection of Voyages.* By Capt. *John Stevens.* 1711. 4*to.* Vol. I.]

By the Queen, A *Proclamation* recalling all *Seamen* and *Mariners* into Her Service, upon a Defire that Her *Navy* be fet out to Sea with all the Expedition that is poffible. Given at Our Court at St. *James's* the 18th day of *February*, 1709-10. in the eighth Year of Our Reign.

The Piety and Bounty of the *Queen* of *Great-Britain*, with the Charitable Benevolence of Her Loving Subjects towards the Support and Settlement of the Diftreffed Proteftant *P A L A T I N E S. London*, by the Queen's Printers. M DCC IX. Fol. *p.* 67.

Decretum

Decretum *in Congregatione* Generalis Inquisitionis *coram* CLEMENTE XI. *in Causâ* Rituum *seu Ceremoniarum Sinensium*. The Decree or final Decision (which is the *fifth*) against the *Jesuits Idolatry* in *China*, made upon *Thursday* the 25th day of *September, 1710*. With a *Monitory* written by the Affeffor of the Holy Office upon Orders from his Holinefs to curb the infolent Prevarication of the *Jesuits*. Dated *Octob.* 11. 1710. 8*vo. p.* 8.

The true Sentiments of the *Jesuits* concerning fome Articles of Religion between the Emperor of *C H I N A* and the Pope of *R O M E*. In a *Letter* to the *Jesuits*, making out the Charge against them. 1. *Rebellion* to their own Church. 2. *Apostacy* to their Vow. 3. Their *Insincerities*. 4. Their *Falsifications*. *London*, Printed for *Benjamin Tooke* and *George Strahan*. 1710. 8*vo. p.* 8.

Memoirs for R O M E, concerning the State of the Christian Religion in *C H I N A*; with the Decree of his prefent Holinefs Pope *Clement* XI. concerning the Affair of the *Chinefe Worship*: And the Ordinance of my Lord *Cardinal* of *Tournon* upon the fame Subject. *Ann.* 1710. 8*vo. p.* 271.

The Sentiments of the *Jesuits* upon the Controverfies of *C H I N A*, in a *Letter* to a Gentleman. Tranflated from the *Italian* Original, Printed at *Rome* this prefent Year M DCC X. To which is prefixed *fome Modern* Reflexions upon a Book lately publifhed, Intitled *Memoires* for *Rome, &c.* Alfo the Act of Appeal of the Bifhop of *Afcalona*. *London*, Printed in the Year 1710. 8*vo.*

The Travels of the *Jesuits* in *Ethiopia*; containing, I. The Geographical Defcription of all the Kingdoms and Provinces of that Empire; the Natural and Political Hiftory; the Manners, Cuftoms and Religion of thofe People, &c. II. Travels in *Arabia Felix*, wherein many things of that Country not mentioned in other Books of this nature, are treated of; As a particular Defcription of *Aden, Moca*, and feveral other Places. III. An Account of the Kingdoms of *Cambate, Gingiro, Alaba*, and *Dancali* beyond *Ethiopia* in *Africk*, never travelled into by any but the *Jesuits*, and confequently unknown to us. Illuftrated with an exact *Map* of the Country, Delineated by thofe Fathers, as is the Draught of the true Springs and Courfe of the *Nile*, within *Ethiopia*, befides other ufeful Cuts. The Whole Collected and Hiftorically Digefted by F. *Balthazar Tellez* of the *Society* of *Jefus*, and now *firft* Tranflated into *English*. *London*, Printed for *J. Knapton*, &c. 1710. *In* Capt. *Stevens*'s Collect. of Voyages. 1711. 4*to.* Vol. II.]

The

The Divine Original and Dignity of Government Asserted, and an Advantageous Prospect of the Rulers Mortality recommended. A *Sermon*, Preached before his Excellency the *Governour* of the Honourable *Council* and *Assembly* of the Province of the *Massachusetts-Bay* in *Newfoundland*, May 31. 1710. the Day for the Election of Her Majesty's Council there. By *EBENEZER PEMBERTON*, Pastor of a Church in *Boston*, Fellow of *Harward-College* in *Cambridge*. *Boston* in N. E. Printed by B. *Green*, &c. 1710. 8*vo*. *p.* 106. [The Gift of Mr. *Jeremy Dummer*, Agent to Her *Majesty* at *London* for the said Province.]

A Journal of the *Votes* of the General Assembly of Her *Majesty's* Colony of *New-York* in *America*, *Die Veneris* 1. *Sept*. 1710. With a Copy of his Excellency's Speech.

A *Sermon* Preached at the Funeral of the Honourable Colonel *Christopher Codrington*, late General and Governour in Chief of Her *Majesty's Caribbee-Islands*; who departed this Life at his Seat in *Barbadoes* on *Good-Friday* the 7th of *April*, 1710. and was Interr'd the Day following in the Parish Church of St. *Michael*. By *William Gordon*, M. A. Rector of St. *James's* in *Barbadoes*. *London*, Printed for G. *Strahan*. MDCCX. 4*to*. *p*. 24.

A *Letter* from *SOUTH CAROLINA*, giving an Account of the Soil, Air, Product, Trade, Government, Laws, Religion, People, Military Strength, &c. of that Province. Together with the Manner and necessary Charges of Settling a *PLANTATION* there, and the Annual Profit it will produce. Written by a *Swiss* Gentleman to his Friend at *Bern*. *London*, Printed for A. *Baldwin*. 1710. 4*to*. *p*. 63.

To the Queen's most Excellent *Majesty*, the Humble *Address* of the General Council of the Islands of St. *Christopher's Nevis*, *Antegoa*, and *Montserrat*, thanking Her *Majesty* for making Colonel *Parke* their General, and praying for his longer Continuance amongst them. Dated at St. *Christopher's*, *April* 6. 1710.

Memoirs of the *British Fleets* and *Squadrons* in the *Mediterranean*, *Anno* 1708 and 1709. Wherein an Account is given of the Reduction of *Sardignia*, *Minorca*, the late Sieges of *Port Mahon*, *Alicant* and *Denia*. With Descriptions of the most frequented places touch'd by the Fleets, of the Court of *Barcelona*, their Majesties residing in it, and of our neighbouring Royal Allies their Majesties of *Portugal*. To which is annexed, A Cursory View of *Naples*, &c. By the Rev. *Mr. Nathaniel Taubman*, Chaplain in the Royal Navy. *London*, for *Arthur Collins*. 8vo. 1710. p. 194.

By the Queen, A *Proclamation*, requiring *Quarantain* to be performed by *Ships* coming from the *Baltick Sea*. Given at Our Court at *Hampton-Court* the Ninth Day of *November*, 1710. In the *Ninth* Year of Our Reign. [*London Gazette* of *Novemb*. 14. 1710.]

A Publication of several *Clauses* in two *Acts* of *Parliament* passed the last Session for preventing the *Running* of *Prohibited* and *Uncustomed Goods*, and the *Relanding* of *Goods* exported by Certificate ; as well to promote her *Majesty*'s Service, as to prevent Surprize to the Persons that may be concerned therein. [*London Gazette* of *June* 8th, 1710.]

A Speech made to Her *Majesty* by the *Four Indian* Princes of the Continent of *America*, between *New-England* and *Canada*, at a Publick Audience, by their Interpreter, *Apr*. 20. 1710. Printed in the Year 1710. Half-sheet.

A Copy of the Letter from the *E. of Sunderland*, Secretary of State, to the Lord Archbishop of *Canterbury*, inclosing a Copy of what had been given in to the Queen by the Ambassadors lately arrived from the *five Indian* Nations, to be laid before the *Society for Propagating Religion*, to consider what may be the most proper Ways of cultivating that good Disposition these *Indians* seem to be in for receiving the *Christian Faith*. Dat. *Whitehall*, 20. *April*, 1710. With a *Letter* of his Grace the Lord *Archbishop* of *Canterbury* to the *Society*, recommending this Important Affair to a *select Committee* : And the Humble *Representation* of the *Society for the Propagation of the Gospel in Foreign Parts*, to the Queen's most Excellent Majesty on that Occasion. MS. Fol. 1 Sheet.

The History and Progress of the *four Indian Kings* to the Kingdom of *England*, &c. *London*, Printed by *A. Hinde*. 1710. p. 8.

The *Four Kings* of *Canada* ; Being a succinct Account of the *Four Indian Princes* lately arrived from *North-America* : With a particular Description of their Country, their strange and remarkable Religion, Feasts, Marriages, Burials, Remedies for their Sick, Customs, Manners, Constitution, Habits, Sports, War, Peace, Policy, Hunting, Fishing, &c. *London*, Printed and Sold by *John Baker*. 1710 8vo. p. 47. [*Ex dono Rev. Viri* Philippi Stubs.]

A

A *Proposal* for *Propagating the Christian Religion*; with the Christian Judgment and Righteousness; most Humbly Offered to the Queen's most Excellent *Majesty*, who by those Ways and Means may now be the *Foundress of a New Empire*, &c. In a large Printed Sheet : Communicated to the *Society for Promoting Christian Knowledge*, in *June* 1710.

The Word of God the Fountain of Wisdom to the House of God. At which Judgment must begin, by the true Ways and Means for the future Reasons both of Church and State. Written in due time, as an *Appendix* to a Proposal most humbly offered (as Occasion requires) to the Queen's most Excellent Majesty. *London*, Printed for *John Isted*. A large Sheet, *Fol.*

The Present State of the whole World, and the Future State of *Sion* and her Converts. Written in due time, as *Appendix* II. to a Proposal most humbly offered to the Queen's most Excellent Majesty. Most humbly Dedicated to *Sion* and her Converts. *London*, Printed for *John Isted*. A large Sheet, *Fol.*

To the *Queen's* most Excellent *Majesty*, The Humble Petition of *John Praed*, Esq; a Member of Parliament; Humbly praying That Your *Majesty* would be graciously pleased to peruse (or cause to be perused) the Prints herewith most humbly presented; as they are by him prepared to promote those great *Matters* of Church and State which will highly exalt Your Nation, *&c. Printed Half-sheet.*

A Sermon Preached before *the Society for Propagation of the Gospel in Foreign Parts*; At the Parish-Church of St. *Mary le Bow*, on *Friday* the 17th of *February*, 1709-10. Being the Day of their Anniversary Meeting. By the Right Reverend Father in God *CHARLES* Lord Bishop of *NORWICH*. *London*, Printed and Sold by *Joseph Downing*. 1710. 4to.

To the *Queen's* most Excellent *Majesty*, The Humble *Address* of *the Society for the Propagation of the Gospel in Foreign Parts*; Humbly praying, That towards promoting so good a Work, Her *Majesty* would be graciously pleased to issue Her Royal Letter to the *Lords Bishops* of *London* and *Winchester*, for a Collection to be made in all Churches and Chapels within the Cities of *London* and *Westminster* and Borough of *Southwark*, and other Places within the *Weekly Bills* of *Mortality*, &c. Presented 10th of *February*, 1710. MS. *sheet.*

A

A *Letter* from a Member of *the Society for Propagating the Gospel in Foreign Parts*, to an Inhabitant of the City of *London*; giving an Account of the late *Address* from the said *Society* to the QUEEN, for causing their Designs to be recommended to the Citizens of *London*, by the Ministers of *London* and *Westminster*, and Borough of *Southwark*, in their *Sermons* on *Trinity Sunday* next, &c. 4to. p. 4.

The QUEEN's Letter to the Lord Bishop of *London*, to permit the making Collections in all Parishes within the Cities of *London* and *Westminster*, and other places within the *Weekly Bills* of *Mortality*, towards carrying on the good Design of *Propagating the Gospel in Foreign Parts*. Given at Our Court of St. *James*'s the fifth Day of *March*, 1711. In the Tenth Year of Our Reign. 4to. p. 4. The same to the Lord Bishop of *Winchester*.

A *Letter* from the Lord Bishop of *London* to his Clergy within the *Bills of Mortality*, for a careful Collection within their several Parishes for the good Work of the *Society for the Propagation of the Gospel in Foreign Parts*. 4to. p. 4.

A *Letter* from the Lord Bishop of *Winchester* to his Clergy within the *Bills of Mortality*, upon his transmitting to them the Royal Pleasure of Our Good and Gracious Queen for a charitable Collection to be made in their Parishes to help the *Society* for the *Propagation of the Gospel in Foreign Parts*. 4to. p. 4.

A *Sermon* Preached before the Society for the *Propagation of the Gospel in Foreign Parts*, at the Parish-Church of St. *Mary le Bow*, on *Friday* the 16th of *February*, 1710-11. Being the Day of their Anniversary Meeting By the Right Reverend Father in God, WILLIAM, Lord Bishop of St. *ASAPH*. To which is added, A short *Abstract* of the most material Proceedings and Occurrences in the *Society for the Propagation of the Gospel in Foreign Parts*; between *February*, 1709-10, and Ditto 1710-11. *London*, Printed and Sold by *Joseph Downing*. 4to. 1711.

The Divine Mission of Gospel Ministers, with the *Obligations upon all Pious and Rich Christians* to promote it: Set forth in a Sermon Preached before the Right Honourable the *Lord-Mayor* and *Court of Aldermen*, at the Cathedral of St. *Paul*, on *Trinity Sunday*, *May* 27. 1711. the Day appointed by Her *Majesty* for a Collection to be made in the City, &c. towards the more effectual *Propagation of the Gospel in Foreign Parts*. Humbly offered to the Venerable Society

Society Incorporated for that purpose. By *PHILIP STUBS*, Rector of St. *Mary Garlick, Hyth, London*, First Chaplain of the *Royal Hospital* for Seamen at *Greenwich*, and a Member of the *Society for Propagating the Gospel in Foreign Parts. London*, for *R.* and *J. Bonwicke.* 1711. 8vo. p. 32.

The Duty and Manner of Propagating the Gospel; shewn in a *Sermon*, Preach'd at the Parish-Church of St. *Martin Outwich*, and *Poplar-Chapel*, on *May* xxvij, 1711. being *Trinity Sunday*, on the Reading the *Queen's* and Bishop of *London's* Letters, requiring a *Collection* to be made the Week following in the several Parishes within the *Bills* of *Mortality*, for the use of the *Society for propagating the Gospel in Foreign Parts*. By *ROBERT WATTS*, L. L. B. Fellow of St. *John's College* in *Oxford*. Published at the Request of several that heard it. *London*, Printed for *J. Downing.* 1711. 8vo. p. 30.

A *Pindarique Poem*, on the *Propagation of the Gospel in Foreign Parts*. A Work of Piety so zealously recommended and promoted by Her most Gracious *Majesty. London*, Printed for the Author [*E. Settle.*] M DCC XI. With a *Dedication* to the *Queen's* most Excellent *Majesty. Fol.*

The Rich Man's Charge. A Sermon Preached at *MORDEN-COLLEGE* upon *BLACK-HEATH, September* 6. 1711. Being the Day of Annual Commemoration of Sir *JOHN MORDEN*, Baronet, Founder of the said College. By *Robert Warren*, A. M. Rector of *Charlton* in *Kent*. Published at the Request of my Lady *Morden. London*, for *Henry* and *George Mortlock.* 1711. 4to.

A *Letter* written by Dr. *Francis le Jau*, dated *South-Carolina*, Parish of St. *James's Goos-Creek, April* 5. 1711. to *John Chamberlayn, Esq;* Secretary of the Honourable and Religious Society for Propagating the Gospel : Giving an Account of the *Indian* Nations settled on the South of the Province of *Carolina*, commonly known by the Name of *Creek-Indians*; such as he could gather from several Persons that had treated with them; and chiefly by a Conversation he had in the Month of *January*, 1710-11. with Captain *John Musgrove*, who had lived for several Years among them. MS. three Sheets, *Fol.*

Propagation of the Gospel in the *East* : Being an Account of the Success of two *DANISH Missionaries* lately sent to the *East-Indies* for the Conversion of the Heathens in *MALABAR*, in several Letters to their Correspondents in *Europe*. Containing a Narrative of their Voyage to the Coast of *Coromandel*, their Settlement at *Tranquebar*, the Divinity and Philosophy of the *Malabarians*, their Language and Manners, the Impediments obstruct-

ing

ing their Conversion, the several Methods taken by these Missionaries, the wonderful Providences attending them, and the Progress they have already made. Rendered into *English* from the *High-Dutch*, and Dedicated to the most Honourable Corporation for Propagating the Gospel in Foreign Parts. The Second Edition. *London*, Printed and Sold by *J. Downing*. 8vo. p. 78. To which is prefix'd, *A Preliminary Discourse concerning the Character of a* Missionary. p. xxxij.

A further Account of the Progress made by some *Missionaries* to *Tranquebar* upon the Coast of *Coromandel*, for the Conversion of the *MALABARIANS*; Of the Methods by them taken for the effecting of this great Work; Of the Obstructions they meet with in it; And of the Proposals which they make in order to promote it. Together with some Observations relating to the *Malabarian* Philosophy and Divinity: And concerning their *Bramans*, *Pantares* and *Poets*. Part II. The Second Edition. *London*, by *J. Downing*. 1711. 8vo. p. 60. To which is annexed, A Proposal for Printing the *New-Testament* in *Portuguese*; In order to be dispersed among the Natives at *MALA-BAR* and other Parts in the *EAST-INDIES*; and also for furnishing some other Helps to the Missionaries sent thither to propagate the Gospel. 8vo. p. 4.

A Copy of Mr. *Finck's Letter*, dated at St. *Sebastian*, near the River *Janeiro* in *Brasil*, under the Tropick of *Capricorn*, dated *Octob.* 20. 1711. to a Friend and Correspondent in *London*. Translated out of the *High-Dutch*. Giving an Account of their *long* and *tedious Voyage*; Of the gross *Idolatry* and *Superstition*, and barbarous *Cruelty* of the *Inquisition* in those *Portuguese* Territories, and State of Religion in those Parts among the *Negro Slaves* and other pretended *Christians*; Of the *Expedition* of the *French* Squadron under Admiral *Trouin*, their Taking of *Santa Cruce*, or Saint *Sebastian*, with the Plunder, Redemption, &c. MS. 3 Sheets. *Fol.*

A True Account of the Voyage of the *Nottingham Galley* of *London*, *John Dean*, Commander from the River *Thames* to *New-England*, near which place She was cast away on *Boon-Island*, *Decemb.* 11. 1710. by the Captain's Obstinacy, who endeavoured to betray her to the *French*, or run her ashore; with an Account of the Falshoods in the Captain's *Narrative*: And a faithful Relation of the *Extremities* the Company was reduced to for *twenty four* Days on that desolate Rock, where they were forc'd to eat one of their Companions who died, but were at last wonderfully delivered: The whole attested upon Oath by *Christopher Langman*, Mate, *Nicholas Mellen*, Boatswain, and *George White*, Sailor, in the said Ship. *London*, Printed for S. *Popping*. 1711. 8vo. p. 36.

Abstract

Abstract of a Printed News-Paper, called *The Boston News-Letter*, from *New-England*. Published by Authority; giving an Account of the said Sufferings of the Seamen who had been Shipwreckt on *Boon-Island*. Published in the *Supplement*, *Septemb*. 10. 1711. A single Sheet, *Fol.*

Two *Addresses* from the Council and Burgesses of Her *Majesty's* Colony and Dominion of *VIRGINIA*, transmitted to *Nathaniel Blakiston*, *Esq*; by *Alexander Spotswood*, Esq; Her Majesty's Lieutenant Governour and Commander in Chief of the said Colony. Presented to Her Majesty by the Lord *Dartmouth*, in *July* 1711. A single Sheet.

The Printed Copy of an *Act* made by *Charles Gookin*, Esq; by the Queen's Royal Approbation Lieutenant Governour under *William Penn*, Esq; of the Province of *PENSILVANIA*, with the Advice and Consent of the Freemen of the said Province in General Assembly met, *directing an Affirmation to Such, who, for Conscience-sake cannot take an Oath*, as received in a Letter from *Pensilvania*, and Publish'd. *London*, *July* 3. 1711.

An *Act* of the General Assembly of the Governour, Council and Representatives of *New-England*, toward promoting the *Expedition* now on foot against *Quebec*: With the Governour's *Proclamation* of it, dated at *Boston* the 20th *July*, 1711. An Half-sheet.

Journal of an *Expedition* performed by the Forces of Our Sovereign Lady *ANNE*, by the Grace of God of *Great-Britain*, *France* and *Ireland*, QUEEN, Defender of the Faith, *&c.* under the Command of the Honourable *Francis Nicholson*, General and Commander in Chief in the Year 1710. for the Reduction of *Port-Royal* in *Nova Scotia*, or any other Place in those Parts in *America*, then in Possession of the *French*. *London*, Printed for *R. S.* and Sold by *J. Morphew*. M DCC XI. 4to. *p.* 24.
[See more on this Subject under the Year 1712.]

A New Collection of *Voyages* and *Travels* into several Parts of the World, none of them ever before Printed in *English*; Containing, 1. The Description, *&c.* of the *Molucco* and *Philippine* Islands, by *L. de Argensola*. 2. A New Account of *Carolina*, by Mr. *Lawson*. 3. The Travels of *P. de Cieza* in *Peru*. 4. The Travels of the Jesuits in *Ethiopia*. 5. The Captivity of the Sieur *Movette* in *Fez* and *Morocco*. 6. The Travels of *P. Teixera* from *India* to the *Low-Countries* by Land. 7. A Voyage to *Madagascar* by the Sieur *Cauche*. In Two Volumes. Illustrated with several *Maps* and *Cuts*. *London*, Printed for *J. Knapton*, &c. 1711. 4to.

The

The Prefent and Ancient State of *PORTUGAL*: Containing a particular Defcription of that Kingdom, its prefent and former Divifions, the Antiquity of it, the Manner of the *Cortes* or Parliament, its feveral Names, Rivers, Forts, Lakes, Baths, Minerals, Plants, and all other Product, the Religious and Military Orders of the Nobility, Prelates, Prime Families, Great Officers, Courts and Councils, the Coins, Language, Famous Writers, and other Great Men. With a Curious Account of the INQUISITION, and of all the Towns and Rivers in that Kingdom. Alfo an Account of the Towns of the Frontiers of *Spain*: With a *Map* of *Portugal* and *Spain*. Written by a Gentleman who lived feveral Years in that Country. [Mr. *John Stephens*.] *London*, Printed and Sold by *J. King*. 1711. 8vo. *p*. 310.

Some Obfervations on *Extracts* taken out of the *Report* from the Lords *Commiffioners* for *Trade* and *Plantations*, concerning the Number of *Negroes* yearly imported into the *English Plantations* and *Colonies*, &c. on Occafion of the Falfities of Private Traders to *Africa* difcovered, and the Mifchiefs thereof demonftrated. 1 Printed Sheet. *Fol.*

A *Letter* to a *Member* of *Parliament* on the Settling a Trade to the *South Sea* of *America*, dat. 3d of *May*, 1711. With *Reafons* to encourage a *Trade* from *Great-Britain* to the Countries fcituate in the *South Seas* of *America*. *London*, Printed for *J. Philips*. 1711. 4to. *p*. 14.

A True Account of the Defign and Advantages of the *South Sea Trade*: With Anfwers to all the Objections raifed againft it. A Lift of the Commodities proper for that *Trade*: And the Progrefs of the *Subfcription* towards the *South Sea Company*. *London*, Printed for *J. Morphew*. 1711. 8vo. *p*. 38. [See more on this Subject under the Year 1712.]

Confiderations on the *Trade* to *NEWFOUNDLAND*; giving Reafons for which it may be proper to petition Her *Majefty* that no Peace may be concluded with the Enemy, unlefs the *French* King will reftore to Her Crown of *Great-Britain* all *Newfoundland* and the *Iflands* that belong to it, as Her undoubted Right and Property. *London*, Printed for *Andrew Bell*. One Sheet, *Fol.* 1711.

1712.
11 *Anna.*   A *Letter* from a *Weft-India Merchant* to a Gentleman at *Tunbridge*, concerning that Part of the *French Propofals* which relates to *North America*, and particularly to *Newfoundland*. With fome Thoughts on their Offers about our *Trade* to *Spain* and the *Weft-Indies*: And an *Abftract* of the *Affiento*. *London*, Printed in the Year 1712. 8vo. *p*. 34.

The

The Cafe of Mr. *Edward Marfton,* late Minifter of the Church of St. *Philip* in *Charles-Town* in the Province of *SOUTH CAROLINA,* as reprefented by himfelf in a *Letter* to the Duke of *Beaufort,* Palatine of the Province, and other Honourable Gentlemen. Dat. from his Study againft *Trinity* Church in the *Minories,* Novemb. 15. 1712. 4*to.* p. 12.

A Short Hiftory of the *Attempts* that have been made to Convert the *Popifh* Natives of *Ireland* to the Eftablifhed Religion : With a Propofal for their Converfion. By *John Richardfon,* Rector of *Annah,* alias *B·lturke:,* in the Diocefs of *Kilmore* in *Ireland,* and Chaplain to his Grace the Duke of *Ormond,* and the Lord Bifhop of *Clogher. London,* Printed by *Jofeph Downing,* &c. 1712. 8*vo.* p. 154.

A Propofal for diftributing in *Ireland* and the *Highlands* of *Scotland* the Book of *Common-Prayer,* the *Church-Catechifm* fingle, and an *Expofition* thereof ; All of them both in *Englifh* and *Irifh,* and now ready to be diftributed. *Printed Sheet.* By Mr. *Richardfon.*

A *Letter* to A Noble Lord concerning the late *Expedition* to *CANADA* [offering Satisfaction in three Points. I. Of what Importance the Conqueft of that Country would have been to the Crown, and whether it would have anfwered the Expence of the great Armament that was made againft it. II. Whether the *Expedition* was well concerted ? And *laftly,* If the Ill Succefs of it ought wholly to be charged on *New-England,* as People here are made to believe.] *London,* Printed for *A. Baldwin.* 1712. 8*vc.* p. 26 [See more on this Subject under the Year 1711.]

RELIQUIÆ LUDOLFIANÆ. The Pious Remains of Mr. *Hev. Will. Ludolf* ; Confifting of, 1. *Meditations* upon *Retirement* from the World. II. Alfo upon divers Subjects tending to promote the inward Life of Faith, &c. III. Confiderations on the Intereft of the Church Univerfal. IV. A *Propofal* for promoting the Caufe of Religion in the *Churches* of the *Levant.* V. Reflections on the prefent State of the *Chriftian Church.* VI. A Homily of *Macarius:* To which is added his *Funeral Sermon,* Preached by *Anthony William Boehm,* Chaplain to his late Royal Highnefs Prince *George* of *Denmark. London,* Printed and Sold by *J. Downing.* 1712. 12°.

The *Lets and Impediments in Planting and Propagating the Gofpel of Chrift* ; A Sermon Preached before the *SOCIETY* for the *PROPAGATION* of the *GOSPEL* in *FOREIGN PARTS,* at their Anniverfary Meeting in the Parifh Church of St. *Mary le Bow,* on *Friday* the 15th of

February, 1711-12. With some References relating to Matters of Fact : And an Abstract of the Proceedings of the Society within the Year last past. By *WHITE KENNET*, D. D. Dean of *Peterborough*, and Chaplain in Ordinary to Her *Majesty*. *London*, Printed and Sold by *Joseph Downing*. 1712. 4to. *p.* 52.

De Missione Evangelica : *Concio habita coram Clero* Londinensi *in Ecclesia Parochiali Sancti* Ealfegi, *tertio. Id.* Maij, *Anno à Christo incarnato* M DCC XII. *A* PHILIPPO STUBBS, *A. M. Ecclesiæ Sancti* Jacobi Garlick-Hythe *intra dictam Civitatem Rectore, &* Collegij Sionensis *ibidem pro tempore Decano.* Hagæ Comitis. *Prostat venalis apud* Thom. Jonsonium. M DCC XII. 4to. *p.* 23.

The Nature and Office of Good Angels ; Set forth in a *Sermon* Preached before the Honourable Company of *Merchants* trading to the *LEVANT SEAS*, at St. *Bennet Fink* on *Sunday*, Dec. 14. 1712. By *William Crosse*, A. M. Chaplain to the Factory at *Constantinople*. *London*, Printed for *Daniel Brown*. 8vo.

An Essay on the Nature and Methods of carrying on a Trade to the *South Sea.* By *Robert Allen*, who resided some Years in the Kingdom of *PERU*. *London*, Sold by *John Baker*. 1712. 8vo. *p.* 37. [See more on this Subject under the Year 1711.]

A Cruising Voyage round the WORLD : First to the *South Seas*, thence to the *East-Indies*, and homeward by the Cape of *Good Hope*. Begun in 1708, and finished in 1711. Containing a Journal of all the remarkable Transactions ; particularly of the Taking of *Puna* and *Guiaquil*, of the *Acapulco* Ship, and other Prizes ; An Account of *Alexander Selkirk*'s living alone four Years and four Months in an Island ; And a Brief Description of several Countries in our Course noted for Trade, especially in the *South Sea*. With *Maps* of all the Coast, from the best *Spanish* Manuscript Draughts. And an Introduction relating to the *South Sea* Trade. By Captain *WOODES ROGERS*, Commander in Chief on this Expedition, with the Ships *Duke* and *Dutchess* of *Bristol*. *London*, Printed for *A. Bell, &c.* M DCC XII. 8vo. *p.* 428. With an *Appendix*, containing A Description of the Coast, Roads, Harbours, Rocks, Shoals, Islands, Capes, Watering Places, Creeks, Coves, Makings of Land, Courses and Distances from *Acapulco* in the Latitude of 17. Degr. N. to the Island of *Chiloe* in the Latitude of 44. Degr. S.

Advice

Advice from *Nevis*, dat. *Aug.* 20. 1712. of the *French Fleet* appearing off that Ifland, and their landing in two places at *Monſerrat*, carrying away about 1400 *Negroes*, with abundance of other Booty.

A Specimen of Papal and *French* Perſecution. As alſo of the Faith and Patience of the late *French* Confeſſors and Martyrs, exhibited in the cruel Sufferings, and moſt exemplary Behaviour of that eminent Confeſſor and Martyr Mr. *Lewis de Marolles*, Counſellor to the *French* King, and Receiver of the Conſignations in the Bailywick of St. *Meneholt* in *Champaigne* ; from his Condemnation to the Galleys, 1686. to his Death in the Dungeon 1692. Done newly out of *French*. To which is prefixed An Account of the Torments which the *French* Proteſtants endure aboard the Gallies. Given by an Eye-witneſs. *London*, Printed by *S. Holt*, &c. 1712. 8vo. With a Preface of the Publiſher to the Reader.

An Account of *South-Weſt Barbary* ; Containing what is moſt remarkable in the Territories of the King of *Fez* and *Morocco*. Written by a Perſon who had been a Slave there a conſiderable time, and publiſhed from his authentick Manuſcript. To which are added *Two Letters* ; One from the preſent King of *Morocco* to Col. *Kirk* ; the other to Sir *Cloudeſly Shovell* : With Sir *Cloudeſly Shovell*'s Anſwer. By *Simon Ockley*, B. D. Profeſſor of *Arabick* in the Univerſity of *Cambridge*, and Chaplain to the moſt Honourable *Robert* Earl of *Oxford* and *Mortimer*, Lord High Treaſurer of *Great-Britain*. *London*, Printed for *J. Bowyer*. 1713. 8vo. p. 152.

1713.
12 *Annæ.*

A True and Melancholly Hiſtory of the miſerable and cruel Hardſhips of the Chriſtian Slaves in *Barbary* ; with an Account of the ſeizing ſeveral Ships belonging to *England* and other Countries, and making Slaves of all on board them : As alſo the Reaſons for ſeizing the *Morocco* Ambaſſador in *England*, who is now under Confinement, and the K. of *Morocco*'s Anſwer to Her Maqeſty's Letters ; Together with a Liſt of the Squadron fitting out, to be commanded by the *Duke of Leeds*, to cruiſe on their Coaſts, and burn and deſtroy their Harbours. Particularly the unheard of Cruelties practiſed on the *Engliſh* Slaves there, ſufficient to melt the Heart of every Chriſtian Reader. Written by one who is lately return'd from that miſerable Bondage. *London*, Printed by *J. Read*. 1713. 4to. p. 12.

A True Liſt of the ſeveral Ships arrived at *LEGHORN* from *Great-Britain*, *Ireland*, and *Newfoundland*, in one Year, commencing at *Lady-Day*, 1712, to *Lady-Day*, 1713. *Printed Half-ſheets.*

A

A Letter from the Society for Promoting Christian Knowledge in London, to the English Governour and Council of Fort St. George; expressing their Endeavours and Attempts for Propagating Christianity within the British Territories in *India*, being encouraged by the Success of the *Danish* Missionaries at *Tranquebar*: Recommending this useful Design to their Patronage and Encouragement, for the Glory of God and the Good of Mankind. Dat. *London*, 2. *Febr.* 1712-13. MS. 4to. 1 Sheet.

A Copy of the Speech made by his Excellency *Rob. Hunter*, Esq, Governour of *New-York*, *New Jersey*, &c. to the *Clergy* of those Provinces met together, 27. *Febr.* 1712-13. MS.

A Copy of the Humble Address of the Clergy to His Excellency *Robert Hunter*, Esq; Captain General and Governour in Chief of the Provinces of *New-York* and *New-Jersey*, and Territories depending thereon in *America* and Vice-Admiral of the same: At *New-York*, *March* 4th, 1712-13. MS.

The Present Case of the *AFRICAN Trade* truly stated; With Reasons for the *Bill* for establishing the same now depending. *Printed Half-sheet*; in *May*, 1713.

The Case of the *National Traders* to *AFRICA*, against the *Company* contending for an Exclusive Trade by *Patent* from K. *Charles* II. in 1672. Presented to the Members of *Parliament* in *May*, 1713. *Printed Half-sheet.*

The Improvement of the *AFRICAN Trade* further Demonstrated by *Separate Traders*, in Answer to a scurrilous Paper, called *The Falsities of Private Traders Discovered.* Printed Sheet.

The Case of the *Woollen Manufacturers* of the *Western Countries*, particularly *Cornwall* and *Devon*, as it relates to the *Trade* to *AFRICA*. Humbly hoping this Honourable House will not suffer the *African* Trade to be Monopolized, &c. *Printed Half-sheet.*

The State of the *Silk* and *Woollen Manufacture*, Consider'd, in relation to a *French Trade*; Representing the Hardships we shall labour under by a *French Trade*, our *Silk Manufacture* will be lost, our *Woolen* suffer extremely, *Printed Sheet.*

The State of *Silk* and *Woollen* Manufacture considered in relation to a *French* Trade; also the Case of the *Silk-Weavers*, humbly offered to the Consideration fideration of both Houfes of Parliament. Likewife the Cafe of the Parifh of St. *Giles's Cripplegate*, before the Act for laying a Duty on *Gilt* and *Silver Wire*. *London*, Printed for *J. Baker*. 1713. 8vo. p. 23.

Tractatus Pacis & Amicitiæ *inter Sereniſſimam ac Potentiſſimam Principem* ANNAM *Dei Gratia* Magnæ Britanniæ, Franciæ, & Hiberniæ *Reginam, & Sereniſſimum ac Potentiſſimum Principem* LUDOVICUM XIV. *Dei Gratia Regem Chriſtianiſſimum, conclusus* Trajecti ad Rhenum, *die* 31. Martij, O. S. 11. Aprilis, N.S. *An.* 1713. Treaty of *Peace* and Friendſhip between the moſt Serene and moſt Potent Princeſs *ANNE*, by the Grace of God Queen of *Great-Britain, France* and *Ireland,* and the moſt Serene and moſt Potent Prince *LEWIS* the XIVth the moſt *Chriſtian King*. Concluded at *Utrecht* the 31th day of *March* O.S. 11th day of *April* N. S. 1713. By Her Majeſty's Special Command. *London*, Printed by *John Baskett*, Printer to the Queen's moſt Excellent Majeſty, &c. 1713. 4to. p. 84.

Tractatus Navigationis & Commerciorum *inter Sereniſſimam ac Potentiſſimam Principem* ANNAM, *Dei gratia* Magnæ Britanniæ, Franciæ & Hiberniæ *Reginam, & Sereniſſimum ac Potentiſſimum Principem* LUDOVICUM XIV. *Dei gratia Regem Chriſtianiſſimum. Conclusus* Trajecti ad Rhenum *die* 31. Martij O.S. 11. Aprilis N.S. *Anno* 1713. Treaty of *Navigation* and *Commerce* between the moſt Serene and moſt Potent Princeſs *ANNE* by the Grace of God Queen of *Great-Britain, France* and *Ireland,* and the moſt Serene and Potent Prince *LEWIS* the XIVth the moſt Chriſtian King. Concluded at *Utrecht* the 31. day of *March* O.S. 11. day of *April* N.S. 1713. By Her Majeſty's Special Command. *London*, By the Queen's Printers. 1713. 4to. p. 55.

The RENUNCIATION of the King of *Spain* to the Crown of *France* and of the Dukes of *Berry* and *Orleance* to the Crown of *Spain*. Together with the *Letters Patents* of his moſt Chriſtian Majeſty, dated in the Month of *December* 1700, and thoſe dated in the Month of *March* 1713, allowing of the aboveſaid *Renunciation* and revoking the ſaid *Letters Patents* of the Month of *December* 1700. *Publiſhed by Authority. London*, Printed by *Benj. Tooke*, 1713. 4to. p. 44.

The Juſtice and Validity of RENUNCIATIONS in the Opinion of the King of *France* and the *French* Nation : Being a Supplement and fit to be bound up with the *Renunciations* of the King of *Spain* to the Crown of *France*, and of the Dukes of *Berry* and *Orleance* to the Crown of *Spain*. Publiſhed by Authority. Printed by *Benj. Tooke*. 1713. 4to. p. 22.

Some further Observations on the Treaty of *Navigation* and *Commerce*, between *Great-Britain* and *France*, and on the Scheme of the *French* Trade, from 1668, to 1669. [Which Scheme is annex'd thereto, being presented on *Nov.* 29. 1674. to the Lords Commissioners for the Treaty of *Commerce* with *France*, by *Patience Ward, Thomas Papillon*, and 14 others.] *London* Printed for *J. Baker* and *T. Harrison*. 1713. 8vo. p. 16. The Second Edition.

A Letter to a Member of the Honourable House of Commons, relating to our True Interest in Trade and Commerce, by a Lover of his Country. Publish'd in the *Flying-Post*, from *Thursday, June* 4th, to *Saturday, June* 6th, 1713. In a Sheet and a Half. *Fol.*

The Eighth and Ninth Articles of the Treaty of Commerce, with relation to the Trade of *Scotland* with *France* considered; With a Postscript, shewing the Falsities of a Letter published in the *Mercator*. Printed at *Edinburgh*, and Reprinted at *London* for *J. Baker.* 1713. 8vo. p. 22.

The TRADE with *France, Italy, Spain* and *Portugal* Considered; with some Observations on the *Treaty of Commerce* between *Great-Britain* and *France. London*, Printed for *J. Baker.* MDCCXIII. 8vo. p. 23.

A Letter from a Member of the House of Commons to his Friend in the Country relating to the *Bill of Commerce*; with a true Copy of the *Bill*, and an exact *List* of all those who voted *for* and *against* Engrossing it. *London*, Printed and Sold by *J. Baker.* 1713. 8vo. p. 46.

Remarks on a scandalous Libel, entitled [*A Letter from a Member of Parliament*, &c. *relating to the* Bill of Commerce.] In which the TRADE with *France* is considered, and the Falsities and Absurdities of the *Mercator* are exposed: To which is added, A Caution to the *Freeholders* of *Great-Britain* in their Approaching Elections, and an Exact *List* of the *House of Commons* under several Distinctions. *London*, Printed for *A. Baldwin.* 1713. 8vo. p. 40.

A Collection of PETITIONS presented to the Honourable House of Commons against the TRADE with *France*, viz. 1. The Course of Exchange between *London* and *Paris* before the Revolution: Or a Demonstration that Our Bullion was then Exported upon the Ballance of our *Trade* with *France*. 2. The Case of the Manufacturers of Gilt and Silver Wire. 3. Some Reasons humbly offer'd to the Consideration of both Houses of Parliament,

liament, shewing the Necessity for making a Law this present Session of Parliament to oblige all Foreign Plain black Silks to be imported at the Port of *London*, &c. 4. An Account of the *Woollen* Manufacture made in the Province of *Languedoc* and at *Abbeville* in *Picardy*. 5. The Case of the *Woollen* Manufacturers of *Great-Britain* and the Poor they employ. 6. Particulars wherein the Bill for laying the *Trade to Africa* free and open, takes away and destroys the Property of the *African* Company and their Creditors now united by an Act passed in the last Session of *Parliament*. 7. The Case of the *Clothiers* with Reference to their several *Petitions*. Printed for *J. Baker* and *T. Harrison*. 1713. 8vo. p. 24.

A Brief Account of the Present State of the *A F R I C A N* Trade. *London*, Printed for *J. Baker*. 1713. 8vo. p. 55.

A Scheme for an Effectual Method to prevent the Exportation of WOOL. By *Richard Carter* and *Peter Ellers*. *June* 20. 1713. *London*, Sold by *J. Morphew*. 1713. 4to. p. 12.

The Importance of *D U N K I R K* Considered in Defence of the *Guardian* of *August* 7th. in a Letter to the Bailiff of *Stockbridge*. By Mr. STEELE. The Second Edition. *London*, Printed for *A. Baldwin*. 1713. 8vo. p. 4c

CADUCEUS SINICUS *modernorum Decretorum Explanatio Theologica Apostolicæ Sedis Judicio Subjecta*. *Colon Agrippin*. *Apud Balthasarem ab Egmond*. M DCC XIII. 8vo. p. 107.

Of the Truth and Excellency of the Gospel. A Sermon preach'd before the *Society for the Propagation of the Gospel in Foreign Parts* at their Anniversary Meeting in the Parish Church of St. *Mary le Bow*, on *Friday* the 20th of *February*, 1712-13. By the Right Reverend Father in God *JOHN* Lord Bishop of *E L Y*. To which is added An Abstract of the most remarkable Proceedings and Occurrences of the *Society for the Propagation of the Gospel in Foreign Parts*, from *Febr.* 15. 1711-12. to *Febr.* 20. 1712-13. 4to. p. 78.

F I N I S.

Auctarium

Auctarium Bibliothecæ Americanæ.

AN
ADDITION
Of some other
BOOKS and PAPERS

Humbly given to the SOCIETY *for Propagation of the Gospel in Foreign Parts.*

THE *BIBLE* Tranflated according to the *Ebrew* and *Greeke*, and conferred with the beſt tranſlations in divers languages. With moſt profitable Annotations upon all the hard places, and other thinges of great importance, as may appeare in the Epiſtle to the Reader. Whereunto is added the Pſalter of the common tranſlation agreeing with the booke of Common Prayer. Imprinted at *London* by *Chriſtopher Barker* Printer to the Queens Majeſtie. *Cum gratia & privilegio Regie Majeſtatis.* 1578. Folio. Together with The Booke of *Common Prayer* and Adminiſtration of the Sacramentes. [*The Gift of a Gentlewoman at* Maidſtone in Kent.] $\quad$ 1578. 19 *Eliz.*

The Advice of the Emperour *SIGISMUND* when in *England* to K. HENRY V. recommending to him the keeping of *CALICE* and *DOVER*, and the *Dominion of the Narrow Seas.* Deſcribed in *Old Engliſh Verſe* by the Author of ENGLISH POLICY IN KEEPING THE SEA. Publiſhed *A. D.* 1435. [Inſerted in the *Preface to the Golden Coaſt, or a Deſcription of* GUINNEY, *&c.* 1665. 4*to.*] $\quad$ 1435. 14 *Hen.* 6.

M m m $\qquad$ *Exemplar*

1481.
22 *Edw.* 4. An Account of the Expedition made to Guinney by Sir *JOHN TIN-TAM* and Sir *PIERCE FABIAN* in the Year 1481. With the Particulars of their Difficulties and Success therein; and of the immense Riches they gained thereby [Inserted in *the Golden Coast, or a Description* of Guinney, &c. 1665. 4to. p. 89.]

1490.
5 *Hen.* 7. *Exemplar Fœderis isti* Hafniæ *inter* HENRICUM *VII. Angliæ, &* JOANNEM *II.* Daniæ & Norwegiæ, *Reges, de* Mercandisa, Piscatura, & Navigatione, *Anno Christi* M CD XC. *Quod renovatum est anno* M D XXIII *ab* Henrico *Angliæ VIII. &* Christierno *II.* Daniæ & Norwegiæ *Regibus.* [*Ap.* Soldeni Mare Clausum. 1635. *Fol. p.* 298.]

1495.
10 *Hen.* 7. *Exemplar Tractatus* Pacis, Mutui Commercij, *sive Intercursus Navigationum. qui confirmatus est* Londini *anno* CIↃCCCCXCV. *inter* HENRICUM *VII.* Angliæ *Regem &* PHILIPPUM *Archiducem* Austriæ, Burgundiæ *&c. ex bibliotheca* Marci Zuerij Boxhornij. *Sequuntur tenores* Commissionum *ab* HENRICO *Rege concessarum dilecto & fideli Consiliario suo* Ricardo Dunelm. *Episcopo, custodi privati Sigilli,* Joanni Vicecomiti Welles, & Joanni Kendall *Priori Domus Sancti* Joannis Jerusalem *in Anglia, ad dictam Pacem tractandam & concordandam.* [*Ad finem* Marci Zuerij Boxhornij *Apologiæ pro Navigationibus* Hollandorum. 12°. 1633.]

1503.
18 *Hen.* 7. The *Navigation* and *Voyages* of *LEWES VERTOMANNUS*, Gentleman of the City of *Rome*, to the Regions of *Arabia, Egypte, Persia, Syria, Ethiopia,* and *East-India*, both within and without the river of *Ganges*, &c. in the yeare of our Lorde 1503. Conteyning many notable and straunge thinges both historicall and naturall. Translated out of Latine into Englyshe by *Richarde Eden.* [Printed in his *History of Travayle*, 4to. 1577. f. 354.]

1519.
10 *Hen.* 8. A briefe Declaration of the viage or navigation made about the world, Gathered out of a large booke written hereof by Master *ANTONI PIGAFETTA VINCENTINE* Knyght of the Rhodes, and one of the companie of that Vyage, in the which *FERDINANDO MAGALIANES*, a *Portugale* (whom some call *MAGELLANUS*) was General Captayne of the Navie, in the Yeer of our Lord 1519. [Historie of Travayle by *Rich. Eden, &c.* 4to. 1577. fol. 430.]

1522.
13 *Hen.* 8. Of the *Voyage* made by the *Spaniardes* round about the World, written by Don *PETER MARTYR* of *Angleria.* First printed in the *French* Tongue,

Tongue, and then in the *Italian*, in the yeere 1522. *Englyshed* by *R. Eden*. [History of Travayle by M. *Eden*. 4to. 1577. f. 429.]

An Account of the Debate and Stryfe between the *Spanyardes* and *Portugites*, for the Division of the *Indies*, and also for the Ilandes of *Molucca*, which some call *Maluca*, with the Sentence given by the Judges upon the Brydge of *Caya*, in the yeere 1524. Written in the *Spanish* Tongue by *FRANCISCO LOPES DE GAMARA*. [History of Travayle by M. *Eden*, &c. 4to. 1577. f. 448.]   1524. 15 *Hen.* 8.

The fyrst Booke of the *Decades of the Ocean*, written by *PETER MARTYR* of *Angleria*, Counseylour to the Kynge of *Spayne*, and Protonoratye Apostolicall to *Ascanius Sphorcia*, Vicount Cardinall, &c. With the 2d and 3d *Decades* translated into *Englyshe* by *Richard Eden*. Also an Abridgment of the 5th, 6th, 7th, and 8th *Decades*, and particularly of *Ferd. Cortesius* Conquest of *Mexico*, made by *Richarde Willes*. [Published in their History of Travayle. 4to. 1577.]   1525. 16 *Hen.* 8.
[See other Editions under the Years 1612, 1670.]

Certain Notable Things gathered by *Richard Eden* out of the Book of *GONZALUS FERDINANDUS OVIEDUS* of the *WEST-INDIES* intituled the Summarie or Abridgment of his General History of the *West-Indies*, written in the firm land of the same, in the city of *Sancta Maria Antiqua* in *Dariena*, where he dwelt and was Governour many yeares, and dedicated to the Emperours Majesty *Charles* the Fifth. [In the History of Travayle in the *West* and *East-Indies* gathered by *Richard Eden*, &c. 4to. 1577. f. 185.   1530. 21 *Hen.* 8

Rudimenta Mathematica *quæ in duos digeruntur libros, quorum prior Geometriæ tradit principia seu prima Elementa, una cum rerum & variarum figurarum dimensionibus: Posterior vero omnigenûm* Horologiorum *docet delineationes,* Autore *SEBASTIANO MUNSTERO*. Basileæ, *in officina* Henrici Petri. *Anno Christi MDLI. Mense* Martio. *Fol. p.* 242.   1551. 5 *Edw.* 6

An Account of a vast Estate got in *Guinney* by an *Englishman* an Apprentice of *London*, who ran from his Master, *May* 1. 1551. and afterwards listed himself in a *Guinney* Ship as a Chaplains Boy, and was landed at *Mina*, and afterwards became K. of *Tombuto*, and left an hundred *Millions* of Gold among 40 Children he had gotten of the *Negro Women*, as was discovered by *Tho. Gregory* of *Taunton*, and *William Pope* to whom Queen *Elizabeth* granted a Patent for 10 Years to traffick to *Guinney* from the Northernmost part of

the

the River *Nonnia* to the Southernmost part of the Rivers *Madrabunda*, and *Sierra Leona.* [Inserted in the *Golden Coast, or a Description of* Guinney, &c. 1665. 4to. p. 88.]

1552.   An *Order* and *Decree* made by certain Lords Commissioners of the *Privy*
6 Edw. 6. *Council* in a Matter touching the Information exhibited against the *Merchants* of the *Hanse* commonly called the *Merchants of the Steelyard.* Given at *Westminster* the 24th day of *February* in the sixt year of the reign of King *Edward* VI. [Printed at large in Mr. *Wheeler's Treatise of Commerce.* 1601. 4to. p. 94.]

1553.   A Relation of the two *Viages* made out of *Englande* into *Guinea* in *Affricke,*
1 Mar. at the charges of certain *Merchants Adventurers* of the Citie of *London* in the yeares of our Lord 1553 and 1554. [History of Travayle by M. *Eden.* 4to. 1577. f. 336.]

An Account of the first Voyage made from *England* to *GUINNEY* begun with Ships *August* 12. 1553. with a Description of the Country and an Account how at their Return the Keels of their Ships were overgrown with Shells of two Inches length and more as thick as they could stand, and so big that a Man might put his Finger in their Mouth ; and also that whereas they sailed thither in 7 Weeks they could not return in 20 With the Reason thereof : To which are annexed Accounts of other Voyages, and Rules for Fortifications and Settlements at the Coast of *Guinney* observed by all that Trade thither. Rules agreed on at a Meeting of the Adventurers for *Guinney.* The Merchandize, Wares and Commodities that are most desired in *Guinney.* A Note of the Heights of the most eminent Places in the *South Sea,* and Soundings on the Coast of *Guinney.* [Inserted in *the Golden Coast, or a Description of* Guinney. 1665. 4to. p. 20. &c.]

1554.   Of the *North-East Frosty Seas,* and Kingdoms lying that way, discover'd by
2 Mar. the *Viage* of that excellent young Man *RYCHARD CHAUNCELLER,* no less learned in all Mathematical Sciences, then an expert Pilotte, in the year of our Lord 1554. as declared by the Duke of *Moscovia* his Ambassador to a learned Gentleman of *Italie,* named *Galeatius Butrigarius.* And likewise of the *Viages* of that worthie old Man *SEBASTIAN CABOTE,* sometimes Governour of the *Companie* of the *Merchants* of *Cathay* in the Citie of *London.* [In the History of Travayle in the *West* and *East-Indies* gathered by *Richard Eden,* &c. 1577. 4to. f. 254.]

1561.   Certaine Extracts of the *Voyage* of Mr. *ANTHONY JENKINSON*
3 Eliz. sent as Ambassadour into *Persia* with the Queens Majesties Letters in the
yeer

Yeer 1561. [Inferted in the Hiftory of Travayles in the *Weft* and *Eaft Indies* gathered by Mr. *Eden*, &c. 4*to.* 1577. *f.* 322.]

An Account of the great Eftate got at *Guinney* by a *Dutchman* left at *Cormantin May* 3d. 1562. [Inferted in the *Golden Coaft, or a Defcription of* Guinney *&c.* 1665. 4*to. p.* 86.] Whereto is added an Account of a moft miraculous Prefervation of one *Alphonfo* a *Portuguefe* at Sea, and of his being caft on the Shore of *Guinney* and of his being prefented by the King thereof, with his Weight in *Gold*, for a C A T to kill their *Mice* and an O Y N T M E N T to kill their *Flies*, which he improved within five years to 60000 *l.* on the place and returning to *Portugal* after 15 years Traffick, becoming the *third* Man in the Kingdom. [*Ibid. p.* 87.]

1562.
4 Eliz.

P A U L I J O V I J Novocomenfis Epifcopi Nucefini, M O S C H O V I A *in qua Situs Regionis antiquis incognitus, religio gentis, mores &c. fideliffime referuntur. Caeterum oftenditur error* Strabonis, Ptolomaei, *aliorumq; Geographie Scriptorum, ubi de* Riphaeis *montibus meminere, quos bac atate nunquam effe plane compertum eft.* Bafilee *MDLXII. Ejufdem Defcriptio* Larij Lacus.

An Affertion proving that the S E A is under the Laws of *Propriety*, declared in a full Convention betwixt *Ferdinando* Emperour of *Germany*, and the Republick of *Venice* in the year 1563. [Printed in *His Majefties Propriety and Dominion of the Britifh Seas.* 1665. 8*vo. p.* 102.]

1563.
5 Eli.

The profperous Voyage of A R T H U R E D W A R D E S into *Perfia* in the year 1567. and of the favour that he found with the *Sophy*, and alfo what Conference He had with that Prince. [The Hiftory of Travayles by *Richard Eden,* &c. 4*to.* 1577. *f.* 333.]

1567.
9 Eliz.

An Account of fuch Informations as was given by Maifter *Jefery Ducate* principal Agent of the *Merchants* for the laft voyage into *Perfia* in the yeare of our Lord 1568. beginning in the dominion of the *Sophia*, at the City of *Shamack* in *Media* [In the Hiftory of Travayles by Mr. *Eden.* &c. 4*to.* 1577]

1568.
10 Eliz.

By the Queen, A *Proclamation* for the ordering of the *Exchange of Money* ufed by *Merchants* according to the Laws and Statutes of the Realme. Given at *Greenwich* the 20th of *September* 1576. in the eighteenth year of our Reign. [Printed at large in *Malyne's* Center of the Circle of Commerce. 4*to.* 1623. *p.* 122.]

1576.
18 Eliz.

M. Capt. *F U R B Y S H E R's* Paffage North Weft of *China* in *Cathayo* fituated in the Eaft fide of Great *Afy.* Of the Ifland *Giapan*, and other little

N n n

Iles

Iles in the *East Ocean*, by the Way from *Cathayo*, to the *Moluccaes*. By *RICHARD WILLES*. With an Epiftle Ded. to the right Honourable and Vertuous Lady the Lady *Anne* Counteſs of *Warwick*. And another Epiftle to the right Worſhipfull my ſingular good Miſtreſs M. *Elizabeth Moryſyn*, dated at *London* the 21. of *February* 1576. [In *the Hiſtory of Travayle gathered by* Richard Eden, &c. 4*to.* 1577. *f.* 230.]

1577.
19 *Eliz.*   The Hiſtory of Travayle in the *Weſt* and *Eaſt-Indies*, and other countrey's lying eyther way towards the Fruitfull and ryche *Moluccaes*, As *Moſcovia*, *Perſia*, *Arabia*, *Syria*, *Ægypte*, *Ethiopia*, *Guinea*, *China* in *Cathayo* and *Giapan*. With a Diſcourſe of the *Northweſt Paſſage*. Gathered in parte, and done into *Englyſhe* by *RICHARD EDEN*. Newly ſet in order, augmented and finiſhed by *RICHARDE WILLES*. Imprinted at *London* by *Richard Jugge*. 1577. *Cum privilegio*. 4*to.* *Folijs* 466. With an Epiſtle Ded. To the ryght noble and excellent Lady the Lady *Brigit* Counteſs of *Bedford* my ſingular good Lady and Myſtreſſe. dated at *London* the 4th day of *July* 1577. *Richard Willes*. Certaine Preambles here folowe, geathered by *Richard Eden* for the better underſtanding of the whole worke.

1580.
21 *Eliz.*   A Pollitique Platt for the honour of the *Prince*, the greate profite of the *publique State*, reliefe of the *poore*, preſervation of the *riche*, reformation of *Roges* and *Idle* perſones, and the wealthe of thouſandes that knowes not how to live. Written for an *Neweyeares* gift to *Englande*, and the inhabitantes thereof by *ROBERT HITCHCOK* late of *Caversfeelde* in the Countie of *Buckyngham* Gentleman. Imprinted at *London* by *Jhon Kyngſton*. 1. *Januarie*. 1580. 4*to.* *f.* iiii. [*Ex dono Rev. in Chriſto Patris* Caroli *Epiſcopi* Norwicenſis.]

1581.
22 *Eliz.*   Ephemerides *JOANNIS STADIJ* Leonnouthenſis *Mathematici ſecundum Antwerpiæ longitudinem ab anno* 1584. *uſq; ad annum* 1606. *jam recens ab auctore aucta : Adjecto quoq; Canone* Sinuum *vel* Semiſſium *rectarum in circulo ſubtenſarum eodem auctore.* Coloniæ Agrippinæ. *Apud hæredes* Arnoldi Birckmanni. *Anno* M·DLXXXI.

1582.
23 *Eliz.*   Copies of the Atteſtations given by the Citie of *Antwerp*, and by ſeveral *Merchants* of ſundry Nations therein on the behalfe of the *Engliſh Company of Merchants Adventurers* in that Citie fully teſtifying their Orderly *Trade*, and clearneſs from *Monopolies*. Dat. *Apr.* 1582. with a like Atteſtation of the Town of *Embden* in *Eaſt-Frieſland*. [Printed in Mr. *Wheeler's* Treatiſe of Commerce. 1601. 4*to.* *p.* 169, 170, &c.

Mores

Mores Leges, & Ritus omnium Gentium per JOANNEM BOEMUM AUBANUM Teutonicum, *ex multis clarissimis rerum Scriptoribus collecti.* Lugduni *apud* Joan. Tornæsium *Typogr. Regium* 1582. 12°. *Cui annectitur* Fides, Religio, Moresq; ÆTHIOPUM *sub imperio pretiosi* Joannis (*quem vulgo* Presbyterum Johannem *vocant*) *degentium, una cum enarratione Confederationis ac Amicitiæ inter ipsos* Æthiopum *imperatores & Reges* Lusitaniæ *initæ,* DAMIANO a GOES *Equite* Lusitano *autore ac interprete. Subnectitur* Deploratio LAPPIANÆ *Gentis ipso etiam* DAMIANO a GOES *autore.*
[See a Tranſlation of it in *p.* 53.]

A Diſcourſe of that which happened in the *battell* fought between the two *Navies* of *Spaine* and *Portugall* at the Iſlands of *Aʒores, Anno Dom.* 1582. Imprinted at *London* by *Thomas Purfoote*, and are to be ſold at his ſhop over againſt Saint *Sepulchres* Church without *Newgate.* 1582. · This Relation was ſent by the Lord Marques *de Sainta Cruſe* unto his Majeſtie by Sqr *PETER PONCEI* of *Lyon* his Nephew, who departed from *Villa Franca* which is in the Iſle of *Saint Michael* the fourth day of the moneth of *Auguſt* and arrived at *Liſhborne* the 24th day of the ſame, being St. *Bartholomew*'s day in the morning.

A true Copy of the Report made by three Reverend Judges, *viʒ. Sir Chriſtopher Wray* Lord Chief Juſtice, *Sir Gilbert Gerrard* Maſter of the Rolls, and *Sir Roger Manwood* Lord Chief Baron, in behalſe of the *Merchants of the Staple of Wool*, Subſcribed, 14. *May.* 1583. on occaſion of bringing in and paſſing a *Bill* for them intituled, *An Act reſtoring the Free Trade of the Merchants of the Staple for the Exportation of Cloth and all other Manufactures made of* Wool *into the parts beyond the Seas.* [Malyne's *Center of the Circle of Commerce.* 1623. 4to. *p.* 93] 1583. 24 *Eliʒ*

Elucidatio fabricæ uſuſq; ASTROLABII, JOANNE STOFFLERINO *Juſtingenſi autore. Cui perbrevis ejuſdem* ASTROLABII *declaratio a* JAC. KOEBELDIO *adjecta eſt.* Pariſijs *apud* Hieronymum de Marne, *& viduam* Gulielmi Cavellat, *ſub Pelicano monte D.* Hilarii. 1585. 8vo. *p.* 172. *& 31.* 1585. 26 *Eliʒ.*

COSMOGRAPHIA *in quatuor Libros diſtributa ſummo ordine, miriſq; facilitate ac brevitate ad magnam* PTOLOMÆI *Mathematicam conſtructionem, ad univerſamq;* Aſtrologiam *inſtituens,* FRANCISCO BAROCIO *Jacobi Filio, Patritio* Veneto *Autore. Cum Præfatione ejuſdem Autoris in qua perfecta quidem* | ASTROLOGIÆ *diviſio, &*
enarratio

enarratio Autorum Illustrium, & Voluminum ab eis conscriptorum in singulis ASTROLOGIÆ *partibus habetur:* Joannis de Sacro bosco *vero* 84 *errores, & alij permulti suorum Expositorum, & Sectatorum ostenduntur, rationibusq; redarguuntur. Præcesserunt etiam quædam Communia* Mathematica, *necnon* Arithmetica *&* Geometrica *principia. Cum Privilegio.* VENETIIS. *Ex officina* Gratiosi Perchasini *MDLXXXV.* 8vo. *p.* 348.

1586.
28 *Eliz.*
Historia INDIAE OCCIDENTALIS *tomis duobus comprehensa. Prior res ab* Hispanis *in* INDIA OCCIDENTALI *hactenus gestas, acerbam illorum in eas Gentes dominationem, insigneq; in* Gallos *ad* Floridam *insulam sævitiæ exemplum describit. Alter vero* BRASILIÆ *(quæ &* America *dicitur, rerumq; in ea observatione dignarum à nobis penitus incognita) descriptionem continet.* HIERONYMO BENZONE *Italo &* JOANNE LERIO *Burgundo, testibus oculatis autoribus. Ex eorum autem idiomate in* Latinum *sermonem* URBANI CALVETONIS *&* G. M. *studio conversi. Excudebat* Eustathius Vignon. *MDLXXXVI.* 8vo. *p.* 480.

Fabrica & usus Instrumenti ad HOROLOGIORUM *descriptionem peropportuni: Auctore* CHRISTOPHERO CLAVIO Bambergensi *Societatis Jesu.* Romæ *apud* Bartholomeum Grassium. 1586. *Permissu Superiorum. Fol. p.* 144.

1591.
33 *Eliz.*
Of the Rule, Commonwealth, or Manner of Government by the *RUSSE* EMPEROUR (commonly called the EMPEROUR of *MOSKOVIA*) with the manners and fashions of the people of that Countrey. The Contents are noted in the Table set down before the Beginning of the Booke. At *London*, Printed by *T. D.* for *Thomas Carde.* 1591. 8vo. Dedicated to the Queens most Excellent Majestie by *G. Fletcher. Fol.* 116.

1592.
34 *Eliz.*
A true Relation of the French Kinge [*viz.* HEN. IV.] his good Successe in winning from the Duke of *Parma* his Fortes and Trenches and slaying 500 of his Men, with the great Famine that is now in the sayde Duke's Campe. With other Intelligences, given by other Letters since *May* 2. 1592.

A most wonderful and rare Example, the like whereof never hapned since the Beginning of the World, of a certaine *Mountaine* in the Isle of *PALME*, which burned continually for five or six weeks together. With other both fearful and strange Sights seen in the Aire over the same place. Imprinted at *London*, by *John Wolfe* 1592. 4to.

The

The Defcription of the *Low-Countries* and of the Provinces thereof, gathered into an Epitome out of the Hiftorie of *LODOVICO GUICCHARDINI*.
Imprinted at *London* by *Peter Short* for *Thomas Chard*. 1593. 8*vo*.

1593.
35 *Eliz*.

A Difcourfe of the Ufage of the *Englifh Fugitives* by the *S P A N I A R D*.
London, Printed by *Thomas Scarlet* for *John Drawater*, and are to be Solde
at his Shop in *Pater-nofter-Row* at the Sign of the Swan. 1595. 4*to*. 10
Sheets. [*Ex dono Rev.* Roberti Watts, *L. L. B.*]

1595.
37 *Eliz*.

The Copy of a Letter from her *Majeftie* in Anfwer of a Letter received
from the *Emperour* in *High Dutch*, relating to Complaints in *Trade* made by
the *Dutch Hans Towns*. Dat. *Richmond* 8 *Novemb*. 1595. (Lat. and Engl.)
[Printed in Mr. *Wheeler*'s Treatife of Commerce. 1601. 4*to*. *p*. 116.]

Literæ Annuæ J A P O N E N S E S *Anni* 1591 *& 1592. quibus Res
Memoratu digna, quæ novis Chriftianis ibidem toto biennio acciderunt recenfentur
à* P. L U D O V I C O F R O I S *ad Reverendum Patrem Generalem Societatis Jefu confcriptæ. Nunc vero ex linguâ* Italicâ *in* Latinam *à quodam ejufdem
Societatis traductæ*. Coloniæ Agrippinæ *ap* Hen. Falchenburg CIƆ IƆXCVI.
8*vo. p.* 174. [*Ex dono Rev. E. Waddington*, S. T. P.] 1595.

1596.
38 *Eliz*.

A B R A H A M I O R T E L I I Antverpiani *Thefaurus Geographicus recognitus & auctus. In quo omnium totius terræ Regionum, Montium, Promonto-
riorum, Collium, Silvarum, Defertorum, Infularum, Portuum, Populorum,
Urbium, Oppidorum, Pagorum, Fanorum Tribuum. Item Oceani, Marium,
Fretorum, Fluviorum, Torrentium, Sinuum, Fontium, Lacuum, Paludumq; no-
mina & appellationes veteres, additis magnâ ex parte etiam recentioribus. Ex
Libris typis excufis, calamo exaratis, chartis geographicis, marmoribus vetuftis,
nummis atq; tabulis antiqui æris. Obiter multi in hoc opere auctorum loci cor-
rupti, falfi, dubij, & difcrepantes emendantur, arguuntur, enodantur, & conciliantur*. Antverpiæ *ex officina* Plantiniana. MDXCVI. *Fol*.

The *Speech* of the King of *Poland*'s Embaffadour *Paul d' Jaline* having
Audience of her Majeftie *Aug*. 4. 1597. complaining of his Mafter's Sub-
jects being debarred all *Trade* and *Traffique* in her Kingdome; and had for-
bidden Navigations and Trade into *Spaine*. With the Anfwer made on her
Majefties behalfe unto the faid Embaffage by certaine of her Highneffe Ho-
nourable Privie Counfell the *Lord Burghley*, the *Lord High Admiral* Sir *John
Fortefcue* and Sir *Robert Cecill*, at *Greenwich Aug*. 13. 1597. [Inferted in
Mr. *Wheeler*'s Treatife of Commerce 1601. 4*to*]

1597.
39 *Eliz*.

O o o

The

The *Mandate* or *Edict* of the Emperour R O D O L P H to prohibite, banish out and proscribe all *English Merchants Adventurers* together with their hurtfull dealings, traffickes and contractings. Given at *Praghe* the first day of the moneth of *August Anno* 1597. [*Ibid. p.* 80.]

The *Edict* and *Decree* of P H I L I P II. King of *Spaine* published and proclaimed by the said King touching the *Exchangings* and *Levyings* of *Monies by him made and passed with Merchants* : With a brief Discourse of the Habilities and Affaires of the said King. First translated out of *Spanish* and now out of *French* into *English* by *W. P. London*, Printed by *John Wolfe.* 1597. *4to.* [*Ex dono Rev.* Roberti Watts, *L. L. B.*]

H I E R O N Y M I O S O R I I Lusitani Silvensis in Algarbiis Episcopi, *De rebus* E M A N U E L I S Lusitaniæ *Regis*, &c. *Item* J O H. M A-T A L I I M E T E L L I Sequani I. C. *in eosdem libros Præfatio & Commentarius de reperta ab* Hispanis *&* Lucitanis *in Occidentis & Orientis* IN-D I A M *Navigatione, deq; Populorum ejus vita, moribus, ac ritibus. Ad* Ant. Augustinum *Archiepiscopum* Tarraconensem. Coloniæ *In Officina* Birckmannica *sumptibus* Arnoldi Mylij. *Anno M. D. XCVII. 8vo. Folijs* 368.

1598.
40 *Eliz.* The Queens *Commission* to the *Major* and *Sheriffs* of *London* against a *Mandate* from the R O M A N E M P E R O U R concerning the Complaints made by the Allied Towns of the *Dutch Hanses* in *Germany*, pretending Injuries in *Trade* committed against them. Witness our self at *Westminster* the 13th of *January* in the 40th Year of our Reign. [*Ibid. p.* 130]

The *Letters* of the Queen to the *Major* and *Sheriffs* of *London*, assuring them that she had required the said *Mandate* of the *Emperour* to be either revoked or suspended ; and in the mean time commanding that All the *Empercurs* Subjects and others appertaining to the *Hanse* Towns scituate in the Empire, forbear to use any manner of *Traffique* of *Merchandise* and to depart the Kingdom. Witness Our self at *Westminster* the 40th Year of Our Reign. [*Ibid. p.* 91.]

1599.
41 *Eliz.* *Exemplar Literarum* E L I Z A B E T H Æ Angliæ *Regine ad* C H R I-S T I E R N U M *IV.* Daniæ *Regem de libera* Piscatione *Subditis suis asserenda in Mari circa littora* Islandica *&* Norwegica. *dat. Cal.* Septembris, *Anno* M DXC IX. [Seldeni *Mare Clausum.* 1655. *Fol. p.* 301.]

A Copy of the *Proclamation* made by the Illustrious *Infanta* I S A B E L L A C L A R A E U G E N I A Sovereign Princess of the *Netherlands* and the Countie

Countie of *Burgundie* touching the Defence, Interdiction and Reftraint of all Communication dealing and Traffique with *HOLLAND, ZEALAND* and their Adherents. Faithfully tranflated out of the Printed Copie, printed at *Antwerpe*. Imprinted at *London* by *John Wolfe*. 1599. 4*to.* with an Advertifement at the End, that *the like* Proclamations *have been difpatched*, Mutatis Mutandis, *for* Gelderland, Flanders *and* Malines *and in French for* Artoys. [*Ex dono Rev.* Roberti Watts, L.L.B.]

A *Proclamation* of the Lords the STATES GENERAL *of the United Provinces* whereby the *Spaniards* and all their Goods are declared to be lawful Prize ; as, alfo containing a ftrict Defence or Reftraint of fending any Goods, Wares, or Merchandizes to the *Spaniards* or their Adherents Enemies to the *Netherlands*. Faithfully tranflated out of the *Dutch* Copy printed at St. *Graven Haghe* by *Aelbercht Heyndrichfon*, Printer to the General States. Imprinted at *London* by *John Wolfe*. 1599. 4to. [*Ex Dono Rev.* Roberti Watts, *L.L.B.*]

Orders Eftablifhed by the Lords the GENERAL STATES touching the muftring and well-governing of the *Companies* to prevent all Abufes therein heretofore ufed. Renewed and Concluded the 4th of *Februarie* 1599. tranflated out of the *Dutch* Copy printed at. S. *Grauen Hage* by *Aelbreght Hendrichfon*, Ordinary Printer to the General States. Imprinted at *London* by *John Wolfe* and are to be folde at his Shop in *Popes-Head-Alley* neere to the *Exchange*. 1599. 4to. [*Ex Dono Rev.* Roberti Watts, *L.L.B.*]

The Hiftorie of the Uniting of the Kingdom of *PORTUGALL* to the 1600. Crown of *CASTILE*, containing the laft warres of the *Portugalls* againft 42 Eliz. the *Moores* of *Africke*, the end of the houfe of *Portugall* and the change of that Government. The Defcription of *Portugall*, their principall Towns, Caftles, Places, Rivers, Bridges, Paffages, Forces, Weakneffes, Revenues and Expences. Of the *Eaft-Indies*, the Ifles of *Terceres* and other Dependences, with many batailes by Sea and Lande, skirmifhes, encounters, fieges and ftratagems of warre. Imprinted at *London* by *Arn. Hatfield* for *Edward Blount*. 1600. Fol. *p.* 324. Ded. to *Henry Earl of Southampton* by *Edward Blount*.

An Atteftation given by the Town of *Middleburgh* in *Zealande* in behalfe of the *Englifh Company* of MERCHANTS ADVENTURERS there refiding. dat. 7. *July* 1600. [Printed in *Mr. Wheeler's* Treatife of Commerce. 1601. 4to. *p.* 176.]

A

1601.   A Treatife of COMMERCE, wherein are fhewed the Commo-
43 Eliz. tidies arifing by a well ordered and ruled Trade, fuch as that of *the Society of
Merchants Adventurers* is proved to be.   Written principallie for the better
information of thofe who doubt of the neceffarinefs of the faid *Society* in the
State of the Realme of *England*.   By *J O H N W H E E L E R, Secretary*
to the faid *Society*.   *Middieburgh*.   By *Richard Schilders* Printer to the States
of *Z-land*.   1601.   4to.   p. 170.   Ded. to the Right Honourable Sir *Robert Cecill* Knt. dat. *Middleburgh* the fixth of *June*.   1601.   [*Ex dono Reverendi in Chrifto Patris* C A R O L I *Epifcopi* N O R W I C E N S I S.]

1604.   An *Edict* or *Proclamation* publifhed by the King, to fignify his Pleafure,
2 Jac. I. that within his Ports, Havens, Rodes, Creeks, &c. there fhall be no force,
violence, furprife or offence fuffered to be done, either from Man of Warre
to Man of Warre, or Man of Warre to Merchant, or Merchant to Merchant
of either partie.   But that All of what Nation foever, fo long as they fhall
be within thofe our Ports and Places of Jurifdiction, fhall be underftood to
be under our Protection to be ordered by courfe of juftice to be at peace
each with other.   Dat. 1 *March*. 2 *Jac. Anno* 1604.   [In Mr. *Selden's Mare
Claufum, Fol.* 1635. p. 236]

A *Report* and *Certificate* made and given in to Sir *Julius Cæsar* Knt. Judge
of the High Court of Admiralty by twelve Men well skill'd in Sea Affaires,
whofe names are hereunto fubfcribed, appointed and fworn to mark out the
bounds and limits into which the Kings Chambers, Havens, or Ports do
ftretch and extend themfelves, in a Table hereunto affixed, fhewing the
names and order of the feveral Capes and Promontories, the Bearing of them,
and their Courfe and Diftance.   Dated the 4th day of *March* in the year
1604. in the *fecond* year of the reign of *K. James*.   [In Mr. *Selden's Mare
Claufum, Fol. p.* 240.]

1607.   *Duæ Regis* Hifpaniarum [P H I L I P P I *III.*] *Literæ ad* D. Martinum Al-
5 Jac. I. fonfum de Caftro *Confiliarium fuum & fuum Proregem* I N D I Æ. *Aliæ fcriptæ*
Ulyfsiponæ *xxviii*. Novembris 1606. *Altera Madritij xxvij*. Jan. 1607. [*Ad
finem libri* Hugonis Grotij *de Mari Libero*. 1633. 12°.]

1609.   S A U L E's *Prohibition Staide* :   Or the *Apprehenfion and Examination of*
7 Jac. I. S A U L E, *And the Indictment of All that perfecute* Chrift, *with a Reproofe
of thofe that traduce the Honourable Plantation of* V I R G I N I A.   Preached
in a Sermon commanded at *Pauls Croffe*, upon *Rogation* Sunday, being the
28. of *May* 1609.   By *D A N I E L P R I C E* Chapleine in ordinarie to
the Prince, and Mafter of Artes of *Exeter Colledge* in *Oxford*.   *London*, Printed
for

for *Matthew Law*, and are to be sold in St. *Paul's* Church yard, neer unto Saint *Austins* Gate, at the Signe of the Faxe. 1609. 4*to*.

1612
10 Jac. 1.

Descriptio et delineatio Geographica Detectionis FRETI *sive* TRANSITUS AD OCCASUM *supra Terras* Americanas *in* Chinam atq; Japonam ducturi, Recens investigati ab M. HENRICO HUDSONO Anglo. *Item Narratio Serenissimo Regi* Hispaniæ facta super tractu, in quinta Orbis terrarum parte, cui AUSTRIALIÆ INCOGNITÆ nomen est, recens detecto per Capitaneum PETRUM FERDINANDEZ DE QUIR. *Una cum descriptione Terræ* SAMOIEDARUM & TINGOESIORUM in Tartaria ad ortum freti Waggats sitæ, nuperq; Imperio Moscovitarum subactæ. Amsterodami. Ex officina Hesselij Gerardi. Anno 1612. 4*to*. cum Cartis accuratis. [Ex dono Reverendi admodum Patris CAROLI Episcopi NORWICENSIS]

The *Travells* of four English Men and a Preacher into *Africa, Asia, Troy. Bythinia, Thracia*, and to the *Black Sea*: And into *Syria, Cilicia, Pysidia, Mesopotamia, Damascus, Canaan, Galile, Samaria, India, Palestine, Jerusalem, Jericho*, and to the *Red Sea*, and to sundry other places. Begunne in the yeere of Jubile 1600. and by some of them finished in the yeere 1611. the others not yet returned. Very profitable for the help of Travellers, and no lesse delightfull to all persons who take pleasure to heare of the manners, government, Religion and customes of Foraigne and Heathen Countries. At *London* Imprinted by *Felix Kyngston* for *William Aspley*. 1612. 4*to*. p. 102. The Preface by THEOPHILUS LAVENDER. The Letters sent by *Mr. WILLIAM BIDDULPH* Preacher to the Company of English *Merchants resident in* Aleppo, attested by *Mr. Jefferie Kirbie* Merchant, Mr. *Edward Abbot* Merchant, &c.

The D O V E and the S E R P E N T. In which is contained a large Description of all such Points and Principles as tend either to *Conversation* or *Negotiation. London*, Printed by T. C. for *Laurence Lisle*. 1614. 4*to*. p 92. Dedicated to the right Worthy *Sir Henry Mountagu*, Knt. Recorder of the City of *London*. Subscrib'd— Your Worship's, D. T. 1614
12 Jac. 1.

An Abridgement of the IMPERIAL SEA LAWES of the *Haunce Towns* made at *Lubeck* on *May* 23. *A. D.* 1614. [Inserted in *Gerard Malyne's* Lex Mercatoria, Fol. 1629. pag. 175.]

England's Way to win Wealth, and to employ *Ships* and *Mariners*. Or a plaine Description what greate profite it will bring unto the Commonwealth of *England* by the Erecting, Building and Adventuring of BUSSES

to

to *Sea* a FISHING. With a true Relation of the ineftimable weakh that is yearly taken out of his Majefties *Seas* by the *Hollanders*, by their great numbers of *Buffes*, *Pinkes*, and *Line-boats*. And alfo a Difcourfe of the *Sea Coaft Towns* of *England*, and the moft fit and commodious places and *Harbours* that we have for *Buffes*, and of the fmall number of our *Fifhermen*, and alfo the true valuation and whole charge of building and furnifhing of *Sea Buffes* and *Pinkes* after the *Holland* manner. By *TOBIAS GENTLEMAN Fifherman* and *Mariner*. London, Printed for *Nathaniel Butter*. 1614. 4to. [*Ex dono Rev. admodum Patris* CAROLI *Epifcopi* NORWICENSIS.]

1615.
13 *Jac.* 1.
The TRADES *Increafe*. London, Printed by *Nicholas Okes*, and are to be fold by *Walter Burre*. 1615. 4to *p.* 56. Epiftle to the Reader fign'd *J. R.* the Subject of it to recommend the Neceffitie, Facilitie, Profit, and Ufe of FISHING; and objecting the hindrance and mifchief done to it by the *Trade* to the *Eaft Indies*. [*Ex dono Reverendi admodum Patris* CAROLI *Epifcopi* NORWICENSIS.]

The DEFENCE of TRADE. In a Letter to Sir *Thomas Smith* Knight, Governour of the *EAST-INDIA* Companie. From one of that Societie. London, Printed for *John Barnes*. 1615. 4to. *p.* 50. ending— *by your Faithfull Friend and Kinfman, that wifheth well to Trade and Merchants.* DUDLY DIGGES. [*Ex dono ejufdem Reverendi Patris.*]

1620.
18 *Jac.* 1.
The Invitement to the *Golden Trade* fhewing the caufe of the firft undertaking it, and orderly Proceedings therein, particularly in a third Voyage from *Dartmouth Nov.* 4. 1620. to the River *GAMBRA* in *Afrique*; with an Epiftle Ded. to the right worfhipfull Sir *William St. John* Knight Governour of the Countries of *Ginney* and *Binney*, Sir *Allen Appefley* Knight Deputy Governour, Sir *Thomas Button* Knight, and other Adventurers for the faid Countries of *Ginney* and *Binney*. Subfcribed, *Your devoted Servant* RICHARD JOBSON. 4to. *p.* 166.

A Declaration of the State of the Colonie and Affaires of *VIRGINIA*, with the Names of the Adventurers and Summes adventured in that Action by his Majefties *Counfell* for *VIRGINIA* 22. *Junij* 1620. [giving an Account of the Advantages of fettling there, by way of Preface, then a Note of the Shipping, Men and Provifions fent to *Virginia* by the *Treafurer* and *Company* in the Yeare 1619. *viz.* 871. Perfons in the 8 Ships fent out by the *Treafurer* and *Company* and 390 by *Private Adventurers*; with an Account of the Employment they were defigned for, 50 Men whereof were by their labours to bear up the charge of bringing up 30 of the Infidels Children in true Religion and Civility; with an Account of fome particular Gifts and

and Legacies made and Patents granted for this Purpose, a Declaration of the Supplies intended to be sent to *Virginia* in the Year 1620. by Report from the Counsell for *Virginia* 18. *July* 1620. and the Names of the Adventurers with their several Sums adventured, whereof there was paid to *Sir The. Smith* the Treasurer 35693 : 1 : 5 to *Sir Baptist Hicks* 1541 : 00 : 04 and to *Sir Edward Sandys* 200 *l.* to which are added the ORDERS and Constitutions partly collected out of his Majesties *Letters Patents* and partly ordained upon mature deliberation by the *Treasurer, Counsail* and *Companie* of *VIRGINIA* for the better governing of the Actions and Affaires of the said *Companie* here in *England* residing *Anno* 1619 and 1620.] *London,* Printed by *T. S.* 1620. 4*to. p.* 11, 16, 30, 4, and 39.

NEW-ENGLANDS TRIALS declaring the successe of 26 *Ships* employed thither within these six yeares, with the benefit of that Countrey by sea and land : and how to build threescore sayle of good ships, to make a little Navie Royall. Written by Captaine *JOHN SMITH. London,* Printed by *William Jones.* 1620. 4*to.* C. 3.

Description des INDES OCCIDENTALES *&c. Amsterdam* 1620. 1622. *Fol.*

1622.
20 *Jac.* 1.

An Experimentall Discoverie of *SPANISH* Practises or the Counsell of a well wishing Souldier, for the good of his Prince and State. Wherein is manifested from known Experience both the Cruelty and Policy of the *Spaniard* to effect his own Ends.——— In a Discourse tendred to his Majestie of *Great-Britain*—— humbly advising his Majestie not to stray from the pathes of his Predecessors, who built their only Safety upon the preservation of the *Netherlands,* and abatement of the *Spaniards* Greatnes.——— and therefore to distress him in his *AMERICAN* World, to which his Majestie has a better title by the discovery of *Sebastian Cabot,* than the K. of *Spain* by that of *Christ. Columbus,* &c, Printed *Anno* 1623. 4*to.*

1623.
21 *Jac.* 1.

A Reply to the *Remonstrance* of the *Bewinthebbers or Directors of the Netherlands East-India Company* lately exhibited to the Lords *States General* in Justification of the Proceedings of their Officers at *AMBOYNA,* against the *English* there. Together with a Copy of the said *Remonstrance* translated out of *French. Lond.* 4*to.* 1625. *p.* 47 & 49. [*Ex dono Rev* Rob. Watts, *L.L.B.*]

1625.
1 *Car.* 1.

Sir *Walter Raleigh's* Ghost, or *England's* Forewarner. Discovering a Secret Consultation newly holden in the Court of *Spaine*—— laying open many treacheries intended for the subversion of *England. Utrecht,* Printed by *John Schellem.* 1626. 4*to. p.* 41.—— making *Gondomar* speake thus to *Raleigh, p.* 16.

1626.
2 *Car.* 1.

p. 16. " I dare not (for the honour of my Nation unfolde the woefull per-
" plexitie in which *Spaine* ftood, during thy Voyage, how fhe quaked to
" think of the general View which thou badft taken without impeachment
" of all the *Weft-Indies* ; but moft of all when fhe was advertifed of thy long
" and laborious paffage upon the river *Oranaque*, the diftinguifhments thou
" hadft made betwixt it and the river of *Amazons*, and the intelligences which
" thou hadft gotten for thine difcent to the great Citie of *Manoa* and King-
" dom of *Gayana*, Defigns which if they had been purfued we had not had
" at this day one foot of earth in all the *Weft-Indies*.

Refpublica five Status Regni G A L L I I Æ *diverforum Auctorum.* Lugduni
Batavorum. *Ex Officinâ* Elzeviriana. *Anno* MDCXXVI. *Cum Privilegio.*
24to *p.* 613.

1628.   The MERCHANTS *Jewel* : or a New Invention *Arithmetical*, with a
4 *Car.* 1. plenary Defcription and perfect Explanation of a moft rare and admirable
T A B L E : refolving with Speed and pleafing Facility above ten hundred
thoufand Queftions in either *Reduction*, *Practice* or the *Golden Rule*, *Forraine
Coynes*, *Meafures* and *Weights* ; as *Danifhe*, *Dutch*, *French*, *Portugall*, *Spanifh*,
are readily reduced to ours, and the price of the one found by the other.

A Catalogue of *Wares*, with their *Meafures* and *Weights* Alphabetically digefted ; Perfpicuoufly explained for the Service of the Great Tab'e. A Table
and Rule for the Maintenance of an Armie, devifed by *N. H.* [*viz. NICHO-
LAS HUNT*] of *Exon.* in *Devon.* *London,* Printed by *Auguftine Mathewes*
1628. 4·o. [*Ex dono Reverendi admodum Patris* CAROLI *Epifcopi* NOR-
WICENSIS.]

1629.   *De Regno* D A N I Æ & N O R W E G I Æ *Infulifq; adjacentibus juxtà*
5 *Car.* 1. ac de H O L S A T I A, *Ducatu* S L E S W I C E N S I & *finitimis pro-
vinciis Tractatus varij.* Lugduni Batavorum.   *Ex officina* Elzeviriana.
MDCXXIX. *Cum Privilegio.* 24to. *p.* 510.

C O N S U E T U D O vel L E X M E R C A T O R I A, or the *Antient* LAW-
MERCHANT. Divided into 3 parts : According to the effential Parts of
Traffique : Neceffarie for all *Statefmen, Judges, Magiftrates, Temporall* and *Ci-
vile Lawyers, Mint-Men, Merchants, Mariners* and all others *Negotiating* in
all places of the World by *G E R A R D M A L Y N E S*, Merchant. *London,*
Printed by *Adam Iflip* for *Nich. Bourne* at the South entrance of the *Royal
Exchange, Anno Dom.* 1629. Fol. *p.* 501. Dedicated to the King.

A

A Coppie of a Letter from an Ingineer fent out to *NEW-ENGLAND* written to a Friend in *England*, A. D. 1629. giving an Account of his landing with a fmall Company at *SALEM*, and thence going and making a Settlement at *MASSACHUSET's* Bay, and laying the Foundation of a Town, to which the Governour gave the Name of *CHARLES-TOWN*, with a pleafing Defcription of the exceeding Pleafantnefs and Fruitfulnefs of the Country, and of the Civility of the Natives. In one fheet MS. [*Ex dono Rev.* Alexandri Young, *S. T. B.*]

TURCICI IMPERII Status feu Difcurfus varij de Rebus Turcarum. Lugduni Batav. *Ex officina* Elzeviriana. *Anno MDCXXX. Cum privilegio.* 24to. *p.* 314.

Gotfriti Hegeniti *ITINERARIUM FRISIO-HOLLANDICUM & Abra. Ortelij Itinerarium* GALLO-BRABANTICUM. *In quibus quæ vifu quæ lectu digna.* Lugd. Batavorum. *Ex officina* Elzeviriana. *Anno MDCXXX. Cum privilegio.* 24to. *p.* 343.

Joh. Angelij Werdenhagen *I. C. de Rebus publicis* HANSEATICIS *Tractatus generalis. Cum privilegio.* Lugduni Batavorum. *Ex officina* Joannis Maire. *MDCXXX.* 24to. *p.* 558.

Joh. Angelij Werdenhagen *I. C. de Rebus publicis* HANSEATICIS *Tractatus generalis pars fecunda.* 24to.

Joannis Angelij Werdenhagen *de Rebus Publicis* HANSEATICIS *& eorum nobili Confœderatione Tractatus fpecialis.* Lugduni Batavorum. *Ex officina* Joannis Maire. *Anno* 1631. 24to. *p.* 750.

Joh. Angelij Werdenhagen *I. C. de Rebus publicis* HANSEATICIS *Speeialis Tractatus pars pofterior & alias quarta ad p.* 1346.

De Imperio MAGNI MOGOLIS *five* INDIÆ VERA *Commentarius ex varijs auctoribus congeftus. Cum Privilegio.* Lugduni Batavorum. *Ex officina* Elzeviriana. *Anno MDCXXXI.* 24to. *p.* 299.

De Principatibus ITALIÆ *Tractatus varij. Editio fecunda priore longe auctior.* Lugd. Bat. *Ex officina* Elzeviriana. *Anno MDCXXXI* 24to. *p.* 371.

1630.
6 *Car* 1.

1631.
7 *Car.* 1.

Petri Gyllij *de* BOSPORO THRACIO *Lib. III.* 24*to. p.* 379. *ad finem additur ejusdem Auctoris Epitaphium marmoreo lapidi inscriptum in ade Divi* Marcelli Romæ.

1632.
8 *Car.* 1.
The Prefent Eftate of *SPAYNE*, Or a true Relation of fome remarkable things touching the Court and Government of *Spayne*; with a Catalogue of all the Nobility, with their Revenues. Compofed by *JAMES WADSWORTH* Gent. late Penfioner to his Majefty of *Spayne*, and nominated his Captaine in *Flanders*. Imprinted at *London* by *A. M.* 1632. 4to *p.* 84.

P. GYLLII *de* CONSTANTINOPOLEOS *Topographia, lib. IV.* Lugduni Batavorum. *Ex officina* Elzeviriana. *Anno* 1632. 24to. *p.* 422.

Joannis Leonis AFRICANI *Defcriptio* AFRICÆ *IX. lib. abfoluta.* Lugduni Batavorum *apud* Elzevir. *Anno* 1632. 24to. *p.* 384.

Joannis Leonis AFRICANI *De* AFRICÆ *Defcriptione. Pars altera* Lugduni Batavorum. *Ex officina* Elzeviriana. MDCXXXII. 24to. *p.* 800.

1633.
9 *Car.* 1.
De LEODIENSI *Republica Auctores præcipui, Partim nunc primum editi, in quibus defcriptæ antiquitates, antiftitum Hiftoria, & alia habentur. Edidit* MARCUS ZUERIUS BOXHORNIUS. *Cum Privilegio.* Amftelodami. *Apud* Joannem Janffonium. *Anno* 1633. 24to. *p.* 516.

PERSIA *feu Regni* Perfici *Status Variaq; itinera in atq; per* Perfiam *cum aliquot Iconibus Incolarum. Cum Privilegio.* Lugd. Batav. *ex officina* Elzeviriana *Anno* MDCXXXIII. 24to. *p.* 374.

JOSIÆ SIMLERI *VALLESIÆ ALPIUM Defcriptio cum Appendice continente* 1. *Martyrium beati* Mauritij *& Sociorum ejus ex V. C. defcriptum.* 2. *Elogium* Matthæi *Cardinalis* Sedunenfis, *ex* Paulo Jovio. 3. *De* Thermis *& fontibus medicatis* Vallefianiorum *liber,* GASPARO COLLINO *Pharmacopæo Sedunenfi auctore.* Lugduni Batavorum. *Ex officina* Elzeviriana. *Anno* 1633. 24to. *p.* 377.

ARABIA *feu* Arabum *vicinarumq; Gentium Orientalium leges, ritus facri & profani, mores, inftituta & hiftoria. Accedunt præterea varia per* Arabiam
itinera

itinera in quibus multa notatu digna enarrantur. Amftelodami, *Apud* Joannem Janffonium. *Anno* 1633. 24*to. p.* 297.

L' Art de NAVIGUER de M. PIERRE De MEDINE Efpagnol *contenant toutes les Reigles, Secrets & Enfeignemens neceffaires a la bonne Navigation. Traduit de* Caftillan *en* Francois *avec augmentation & illuftration de plufieurs figures & annotations, par* NICOLAS *de* NICOLAI, *du* Dauphinè, *Geographe du tres* Chreftien Roy Henry II. *de ce nomme, & dedie a fa tres Augufte. Majefte. Nouvellement reveu corrigè & augmentè de plufieurs figures par* JEAN de SEVILLE *dit le* Soucy. *Medecin, Mathematicien, Geographe & Hydrographe du Roy. A* Rouen *chez* David Ferrand. MDCXXXIII.
[See another Edition *p.* 14.]

Refpublica Bohemiæ *a* M. PAULO STRANSKII *defcripta.*   1634.
Lugd. Batavorum. *Ex officina* Elzeviriana. *Anno* 1634. 24*to. p.* 507.   10 *Car.* 1.

TURCICI IMPERII *Status. Accedit de Regno* Algeriano *atq;* Turnetano *Commentarius.* Lugduni Batav. *Anno* 1634. *Rerum* Turcicarum *commentarius autore* JO. BAPT. MONTALBANO. HOR. MALAGUZZI *de* Turcici *Imperij magnitudine Differtatio, & varia Excerpta.* 24*to. p.* 363.

SABAUDIÆ *Refpublica & Hiftoria.* Lugd. Batav. *Ex officina* Elzeviriana. 1634. 24*to. p.* 314.

Refpublica & Status Imperij ROMANO-GERMANICI Lugduni Batavorum *ex officina* Elzeviriana. *Anno* 1634. Tom. I. 24*to. p.* 414.

Refpublica five Status Imperij ROMANO GERMANICI *Tom. II.* Lugd. Batav *ex officina* Elzevir. 1634. 24*to. p.* 382.

Tractatus de Conftitutione Imperij ROMANO GERMANICI *Auctore* JACOBO LAMPADIO I. C. Lugduni Batavorum, *ex officina* Joannis Maire. 1634. 24*to. p.* 380.

Refpublica NAMURCENSIS, HANNONIÆ, & LUTSENBURGENSIS. Amftelodami. *Apud* Joannem Janffonium. 1634. 24*to. p.* 522.

Refpublica & Status Regni HUNGARIÆ. *Ex officina* Elzeviriana. 1634. 24*to. p.* 330.

A

A moſt pleaſant Proſpect into the Garden of Natural Contemplation, to behold the natural cauſes of all kinde of *METEORS*, as well fierie and, airie, as watrie and earthlie —— By *W. FULKE* Doctor of Divinitie the ſecond Edition corrected and amended. *London*, Printed by *John Haviland*. 1634. 8*vo. Folijs* 71. [*Ex dono Rev:* R. Watts, L. L. B.]

Commentum de Terræ Motu Circulari *duobus Libris Refutatum : quorum Prior* LANSBERGI *Poſterior* CARPENTARII *Argumenta vel Nugamenta potius refellit, Operâ* ALEXANDRI ROSSEI Aberdonenſis *ed.* Londini *apud* Thomam Harperum MDCXXXIV. 4*to. p.* 62. *Cui præfigitur.* Imprimatur. Guil. Bray, *Arch. à* Cant. *Sacris Dom. una cum Epiſt. Nuncupatoriâ.* Guil. *Arch.* Cantuar. *dicatâ.*

1635.
11 *Car.* I.　Joannis Seldeni *MARE CLAUSUM, ſeu D: Dominio Maris, Libri Duo :* Primo *Mare ex jure Naturæ ſeu Gentium omnium hominum non eſſe commune, ſed* Dominij privati *ſeu* Proprietatis *capax, pariter ac Tellurem eſſe demonſtratur.* Secundo *Sereniſſimum* Magnæ Britanniæ *Regem Maris circumflui ut individuæ atq; perpetuæ Imperij* Britannici *appendicis, Dominum eſſe aſſeritur.* Londini. *Excudebat* Will. Stanesbeius, *pro* Richardo Meighen. MDCXXXV. *Fol. p.* 304. *præter* Interſerenda locis deſignatis.

An Account of the Expedition of 5 Ships fitted out to the *EAST-INDIES* by Sir *WILL. COURTEN, A. D.* 1635. [Inſerted in Strange News from the *Indies*, &c. 1650. *p.* 4 *&c.*]

1636.
12 *Car.* I.　Litteræ Annuæ Provinciæ PARAQUARIÆ *Societatis* Jeſu *ad admodum R. P.* Mutium Vitelleſcum *ejuſdem Soccietatis* Præpoſitum Generalem. *Miſſæ a R. P.* Nicolao Duran Paraquariæ *Præpoſito Provinciali. Ejus nomine ac juſſu ſcripto* P. Jacobo Ranconier *Belga ejuſdem Societatis.* ANTVERPIÆ. *Typis* Joannis Meurſi. *Anno* MDCXXXVI. 8*vo. p.* 147. [*Ex dono Rev.* Roberti Watts, L. L. B.]

1637.
13 *Car.* I.　A true *Journal* of the SALLY FLEET [ſet out by his Majeſtie againſt the *Turkiſh Pirats* and *Pirats of Sally* in *January* 1636.] with the Proceedings of the Voyage, publiſhed by *JOHN DUNTON London* Mariner, Maſter of the Admiral called the *Leopard.* [Together with a true Copie of a *Merchants* Letter [viz. *Chriſt. Willoughby's*] being an Anſwer to the *Maſters* Letter ſent aſhore about his Sonne that is Slave in *Algere.* Dated from *Salle* the 21th of *July,* 1637. and *Articles of Peace,* Accorded and Agreed upon between the High and Mighty Prince *CHARLES* by the Grace of God K of *Great-Britain, &c.* and the Right Excellent and Renowned Lord
SIDDIE

SIDDIE HANNET LAISHI, his Majeſtie of *Great-Britains* Forces beſieging NE*W* SALLE*Y* by Sea, and the Lord *Saint Siddie Hannett Laiſhi* by Land.] Whereunto is annexed a Liſt of *Salley Captives* Names [that were then redeemed, *viz.* 339.] and the places where they dwell, and a deſcription of the 3 Towns in a CARD. *London,* 1637. 4*to.*

Articles of Agreement between the *Governour and Company of Merchants of* England *trading into the* Levant *Seas,* and Sir *SACKVILE CROW* Baronet choſen to negotiate their Affaires at *Conſtantinople* ; and appointed by his Majeſty his Ambaſſador to the Grand Signior, in the Year 1638. [*Pref. to the Relat. of the Abuſes* &c. *exerciſed by Sir* Sackvile Crow. 4*to.* 1646.]

1638. 14 Car. 1.

BULLARIUM *Romanum Noviſſimum a* Clemente *VIII.uſq*; *ad* Gregorium *XV. cum vitis & Iconibus omnium Pontificum, opus* LAERT*IJ* CHERUBINI. *tertio nunc editum a D.* ANGELO MARIA CHERUBINO *qui Conſtitutiones S. D.N.* URBANI *VIII. addidit.* Romæ 1638. *fol. Ex Typogr. Rev. Cameræ Apoſtolicæ.*

Regni CHINENSIS *Deſcriptio ex varijs Auctoribus.* Lugd. Batav. *ex officina* Elzeviriana. 1639. 24*to.* p. 365. NIC. TRIGAUTIUS *de Regno* CHINÆ. *Itinerarium* BENEDICTI GOESIJ *ex* India *in* Sinarum *regnum,* &c.

1639. 15 Car. 1.

Reſpublica PORTUGALLIÆ. Lugd. Batav. *ex officina* Elzeviriana. 1641. 24*to.* p. 460.

1641. 17 Car. 1

The Petition and Remonſtrance of the *Governour* and *Company of Merchants of* London *trading to the* Eaſt-Indies, exhibited to the Right Honourable the Lords and Commons, in the High Court of Parliament aſſembled. *London,* Printed for *Nicholas Bourne.* 1641. 4*to.* p. 34.

The Treaſure of *Trafficke,* or, A Diſcourſe of FOREIGN TRADE, wherein is ſhewed the Benefit and Commodities ariſing to a Commonwealth or Kingdom by the skilful Merchant and by a well ordered Commerce and regular Traffique, dedicated to the High Court of Parliament now aſſembled. By *LEWES ROBERTS* Merchant and Captain of the City of *London.* By E. P. for *Nicholas Bourne.* 1641. 4*to.* p. 103. [*Ex dono Reverendi* Caroli *Epiſcopi* Norwicenſis.]

A Key into the *Language* of *AMERICA* ; Or an help to the Language of the *Natives* in that part of *America* called NEW-ENGLAND. Together with brief Obſervations of the Cuſtomes, Mannners, and Worſhips, &c. of the aforeſaid Natives in Peace and Warr, in Life and Death.

1643. 19 Car. 1.

On

On all which are added Spiritual Obſervations General and Particular by the Author, of chief and ſpecial uſe (upon all occaſions) to all the *Engliſh* inhabiting thoſe parts, yet pleaſant and profitable to the view of all Men. By *ROGER WILLIAMS* of *Providence* in *New-England*. *London*, Printed by *Gregory Dexter*. 1643. 8*vc*. *p*. 197. [*Ex dono Rev*. Roberti Watts, *L. L. B.*]

Secrets diſcovered; in *Englands* Complaint or Outcry againſt the High and Mighty Lords the *States General* of the *United Provinces*, for their perfidious, deceitfull, and unthankfull proceedings againſt the welfare of this *Kingdom*. Clearly laid open in a Letter tranſmitted to a Friend who is a Subject to the ſaid States of *Holland*. Wherein is declared ſeverall Acts of *State*, not onely betweene them and the Queen of *England*; but alſo betweene the ſaid States and this preſent *Parliament*, by way of Anſwer to our Parliaments ſeverall Declarations. Likewiſe a Diſcovery that notwithſtanding their firme Reſolutions and Promiſes to the repreſentative body of this Kingdome, concerning their Neutrality, have made uſe of the firſt opportunity to ſtrengthen the enemy againſt us, and ſuffered our *Queen* (not only in the time ſhe was there) to tranſport all manner of Military Ammunition and People, beſides Money, to his Majeſtie: But alſo at her departure hath given Her leave by virtue of an unlimited Licence, to transfer with Her all Her Baggage and Goods, of what kind ſoever, whether in whole, or in part, in ſuch Ships as ſhee, or Her Commiſſioner ſhall judge fitting; forbidding any to viſit or ſearch thoſe Ships under what pretence ſoever, either in, or after her departure out of thoſe Dominions; under pretence of which Licence many hundred barrels of Gun-powder, Bullets, Mortars, and ſuch like Military Inſtruments have bin fraughted away in *Newcaſtle* Ships from *Rotterdam* at *Delf-haven*, under the title of her Majeſties Baggage. Tranſlated out of a *Dutch* printed Copy into *Engliſh*, to undeceive this Kingdom. *London*, Printed for *Benjamin Allen* in *Popes-head-Alley*; Anno *Dom*. 1643. 4*to*. *p*. 30.

1646.
22 *Car*. 1. *cij*. A *Certificate* under the Hand of R. H. at *Rabagg* in the *Eaſt-Indies*, 4 *March* 1644. Atteſted upon Oath before a Maſter in *Chancery*, *Feb*. 23. 1646. [giving an Account of a Conſpiracy entred into by the *Engliſh and Dutch Eaſt-India Companies*, to deſtroy the Ships fitted out to the *Eaſt-Indies* by *WILL. COURTEN*, Eſq; [Inſerted in *Strange News from the* Indies, 1652. 4*to*. *p*. 13.] See the Year 1647.

Subtilty and Cruelty: Or a true Relation of the horrible and unparallelled Abuſes and intolerable Oppreſſions exerciſed by Sir *SACKVILE CROW* his Majeſty's Ambaſſador at *Conſtantinople* and his Agents, in ſeizing upon the Perſons and Eſtates of the *Engliſh* Nation reſident there, and at *Smyrna*.

To-

Together with the barbarous and tyrannical intentions to do the like upon their Perſons and Eſtates in all other parts of the Grand Signior's Dominions. Directly contrary to the Truſt repoſed in him, and his own *Agreement with the Merchants,* &c. *London,* Printed by *R. Cotes.* 1646. 4to. *p.* 75. [*Ex dono Rev.* Roberti Watts, *L. L. B.*]

A brief Diſcovery or Deſcription of that moſt famous Iſland of *M A D A-G A S C A R* or *St. L A W R E N C E* in *Aſia* near unto *Eaſt-India.* By *R I C H A R D B O O T H B Y* Merchant. *London,* Printed by *E. C.* for *John Hardeſty.* 1646. 4to. *p.* 72.

The New Planet no Planet. Or the E A R T H *no wandring Starr,* except in the wandring heads of *Galileans.* Here out of the principles of Divinity, Philoſophy, Aſtronomy, Reaſon and Senſe, the *E A R T H S I M M O B I L I T Y* is aſſerted, the true ſenſe of Scripture in this Point cleared, the Fathers and Philoſophers vindicated; divers Theological and Philoſophical points handled; And *Copernicus* his Opinion as erroneous, ridiculous and impious fully refuted. By *A L E X A N D E R R O S S E.* In Anſwer to a Diſcourſe that the Earth may be a Planet. *London,* Printed by *J. Young.* 1646. 4to. *p.* 118.

The Goſpel Covenant, Or the Covenant of Grace opened, &c. Preached in *Concord* in *New-England,* by *P E T E R B U L K E L E Y* ſometimes Fellow of *John's Colledge* in *Cambridge.* Publiſhed according to Order. *London,* for *Benjamin Allen.* 1646. 4to. *p.* 383.

The humble and true Atteſtation to the Right Honourable the Lords aſ- 1647. ſembled in Parliament of *T. H.* Factor concerning *Eaſt-India.* Paſſages re- 23 *Car.* lating to 5000 *l.* in Controverſie between *W I L L I A M C O U R T E N* Eſq; and *The Old* Eaſt-India *Company. Jurat.* 15. *April.* 1647. at the Lords Bar. [Inſerted in *Strange News from the* Indies. 4to. 1652. *p.* 16]

Several Queſtions of ſerious and neceſſary Conſequence propounded by the Teaching Elders unto Mr. *J O H N C O T T O N* of *Boſton* in *New-England.* With his reſpective Anſwer to each Queſtion. *London,* 1647. 4to. *p.* 10.

The A R T I C L E S and *Conditions* of the *Perpetual* P E A C E con- 1648. concluded between the moſt Potent King of *S P A I N E,* &c. on the one 24 *Car.* partie and the High and Mighty Lords the S T A T E S G E N E R A L of the *United Netherlands* on the other partie; ſubſcribed and ſealed the 13. *January,* 1648. at *Munſter.* Printed at *Rotterdam* by *Haſt van Voort-ganch,*

ganch, Printer of the Articles of Peace. 1648. and Reprinted at *London* by *Robert White*. 1648. 4to. *p.* 28.

A Defcription of the Province of *N E W - A L B I O N*, and a Direction for Adventurers with fmall Stock to get two for one and good Land freely; and for Gentlemen and all Servants, Labourers and Artificers to live plentifully; and a former Defcription reprinted of the healthiest, pleasantest and richest Planta-tion of *New-Albion* in *North Virginia*; proved by 13 Witneffes. Together with a *Letter* from Mr. *R O B E R T E V E L Y N*, that lived there many years; fhewing the particularities and excellency thereof. With a brief of the charge of victuall, and neceffaries to tranfport and buy Stock for each Planter or Labourer, there to get his Mafter 50 *l. per Ann.* or more in twelve trades, and at 10 *l.* charges only a Man. [To which is prefixed the *Order*, *Medall* and *Riban* of the *Albion Knights*, of the Converfion of 23 Kings, their Support in 3 little Plates, and an Epiftle Dedicatory to the Lord Pro-prietor, Earl Palatine of *New-Albion* and the Adventurers of the *Company of New-Albion*, 44 in number. By *B E A U C H A M P P L A N T A G E N E T* of *Belvil* in *New-Albion*, Efq; one of the Company] 1648. 4to. *pag.* 32. [*Ex dono admodum Reverendi* Caroli. *Epifcopi* Norwicenfis]

The humble *Petition* of Sir *S A C K V I L E C R O W* Prifoner in the *Tower* to the Parliament [reprefenting the Miferie he and his Family were re-duced to by 4 Years Imprifonment, and defiring to be admitted to *Baile*] with the Objections by the *Levant Company* againft it and his Anfwers to them. 1648. 4to. *p.* 8. [*Ex dono Rev.* Roberti Watts. *L. L. B.*]

Sir *S A C K V I L E C R O W*'s Cafe as it now ftands the 8. of *July* 1648. at the Intreaty and for the Satisfaction of fome of his private Friends at large. [Containing a great Number of Papers offered by the *Levant Compa-ny*, and Sir *Sackvile* to the Committee of the Navie.] Printed in the Year 1648. 4to. *p.* 68. [*Ex dono Rev.* Roberti Watts, *L. L. B.*]

1649.
Car. 2.
A *Letter* fign'd in the Name and by the Authority of the *Delegates of the Univerfity of* Oxon: *Ed. Reynolds* Vicecan. *Oxon.* " To our Reverend Bre-" thren the Minifters of the Gofpel in *England* and *Wales*, to ftir up their " minds for the promoting and propagating the Gofpel of Chrift, and for the " taking fome Chriftian Compaffion upon the Souls of barbarous *Indians*, " who fit in the fhadow and region of Death— and to contribute cheerfully " and liberally to fo glorious a Work. Dated *October* 22. 1649. MS. " Sheet.

A

A Letter of the *Vicechancellor* and *Heads of Houses* in the University of
Cambridge, to our Reverend and Dear Brethren the Ministers of *England* and
Wales, " in compliance with the just and pious Desires of a late established
" Corporation for Propagation of the Gospel in *New-England*, to put their
" helping Hands to a Work so purely Christian. Subscribed *Ant. Tuckney*
Procan. *Richard Love, Richard Minshull, Thomas Hill, John Arrowsmith, Ben-
jamin Whichcot, Thomas Young, Samuel Bolton, William Spurstowe, Da. Seaman,
William Dell, Richard Vines.* Dated *Cambridge*. Octob. 24. 1649. MS.
sheet.

1649.
1 *Car*. 2

The Relation of *Master ANTONIE MONTERINOS* translated
out of the *French* Copie sent by *Manasseh Ben Israel* of *Jews* found *in America*,
upon his own experience at *Honda* and other places, Thus attested. ' I *Ma-*
' *nasseh Ben Israel* underwritten, bear witness that this present paper hath been
' copied with the whole truth of the originall, and that the Author *Monterinos*
' is a virtuous man, and separate from all manner of worldly interests, and that
' he was swore in my presence, that all that was declared which he a truth.
' *Manasseh Ben Israel.*—— *J. Dury* received this at *London* 27. of *Novemb.* 1649.
[Inserted in *Mr. Thoroughgood's Jews* in *America*. 4to. 1650.]

An Epistolical Discourse of Mr. *JOHN DURY* to Mr. *THOROUGH-
GOOD* concerning his conjecture that the *Americans* are descended from the
Israelites. With the History of a *Portugal Jew Antonie Monteriros* attested by
Manasseh Ben Israel to the same effect. dat. St. *James*, this 27. *Jan.* 1649-50.
[Inserted in *Mr. Thoroughgood's Jews* in *America*. 4to. 1650]

Jewes in *America*: Or Probabilities that the *Americans* are of that race.
With the removal of some contrary reasonings and earnest desires for effectual
endeavours to make them Christian. Proposed by *THO. THOROUGHGOOD*,
B. D. one of the *Assembly of Divines*. *London*, Printed by *W. H.* for *Tho.
Slater*. 1650. 4to. [*Ex dono Rev.* Rob. Watts, *L. L. B.*]

1650.
2 *Car*. 2.

The Soveraignty of the BRITISH SEAS proved by Records, History, and the Municipal Lawes of this Kingdome. Written in the yeare
1633. By that Learned Knight Sir *JOHN BOROUGHS* Keeper of
the Records in the Tower of *London*. *London*, Printed for *Humphry Moseley*.
1651. 12°. *p.* 165.

1651.
3 *Car*. 2.

A Paper intituled, Some Observables concerning the *Treaty of Peace*
between *England* and *Holland* in 1654. By Mr. *COYTMORE*, Secretary to the Earl of *Warwick* when Lord Admiral.———— concluding, If

1654.
6 *Car*. 2.

S f f
Oliver

Oliver *had forbore the interrupting of the then pretended Parliament but six moneths longer,* the Dutch *Nation had been brought to such termes, as they would have presented blank papers to the State of* England, *to have subscribed to what they would have demanded.* MS. single sheet.

·1658.
0 *Car.* 2.
A true Relation of the Reasons which necessitated his Majesty of *S W E-D E N* to continue the War with *D E N M A R K.* Together with a satisfactory Answer to all those Objections which have been industriously contrived and spread abroad by the *Danish* Party and their Adherents with design to obscure the Justice of the *Swedish* Cause, and raise an ill Report upon his Majesty's Proceedings. *London,* Printed for *T. Pierrepont* at the *Sun* in *Paul's Church-Yard.* 1658. 4to. *p.* 39. [*Ex dono Rev.* Alexandri Young. S. T. B.]

1659.
11 *Car.* 2.
The whole Proceedings of the *T R E A T Y* held at *R O S K I L D* between his Majesty the King of *S W E D E N* and the King of *D E N-M A R K.* Together with the several *Mediations* from *France, England* and *Holland* for the concluding and settling the *P E A C E* between them; being the very *Original Acts and Records* themselves. Translated out of *Latine* into *English. London,* Printed by *J. M.* for *Daniel Pakeman,* and are to be sold at his Shop at the Sign of the *Rainbow* in *Fleetstreet.* 1659. 4to. *pag.* 168. [*Ex dono Rev.* Alexandri Young, S. T. B.]

1660.
12 *Car.* 2.
An *Act* to prevent Frauds and Concealments of his Majesties CUSTOMS and SUBSIDIES, *Anno* 12. *Caroli* II. *Regis.* [Inserted in a *Subsidy granted to the King of Tonnage and Poundage,* &c. 1667. *p.* 175, &c.]

The *World surveyed;* or the famous *Voyages* and *Travailes* of *V I N C E N T L E B L A N C,* or *W H I T E* of *Marseilles* who from the Age of 14 Years to 78 travelled through most parts of the World, *viz.* the *East* and *West* Indies, *Persia, Pegu,* the Kingdoms of *Fez* and *Morocco, Gunny,* and through all *Africa.* From the *Cape of Good Hope* into *Alexandria* by the Territories of *Monomotapa,* or *Prester John* and *Egypt* into the *Mediterranean Isles* and through the principal Provinces of *Europe,* containing a more exact Description of several parts of the World than hath hitherto been done by any other Authour, the whole Work enriched with many Authentick Histories. Originally written in *French* and faithfully rendred into English by *F. B.* [*viz. FRANCIS BROOKE*] Gent. *London,* Printed for *John Starkey* 1660. fol. 407. besides a Table of Contents and an Alphabetical Index.

1662.
14 *Car.* 2.
A *Treatise of Taxes and Contributions,* shewing the nature and measures of *Crown-Lands, Assessments, Customs, Poll-Money, Lotteries,* &c. with several
Dis-

Difcourfes and Digreffions concerning Wares, Exportation of Money, and Wool-free Ports, &c. Applied to the prefent State and Affaires in *Ireland.* *London*, Printed for *N. Brooke*. 1662. 4*to. p. 75.*]

VIRGINIA's Cure, or an Advifive Narrative concerning *Virginia*, difcovering the true Ground of that *Churches* Unhappinefs, and the only true Remedy, as it was prefented to the Right Rev. Father in God *GILBERT* Lord Bifhop of *London*, *Sept.* 2. 1661. now publifhed to further the Welfare of that and the like *Plantations*. By *R. G.* [fuggefting among other Propofals, *p.* 10. the Procuring an *Act of Parliament* to order a certain Number of *Fellowfhips* as they happen to be next proportionably vacant in both the *Univerfities* to bear the Name of *VIRGINIA FELLOWSHIPS,* fo long as the Needs of that Church fhall require it, and none to be admitted to them but fuch as fhall engage by Promife to hold them 7 Years and no longer, and at the Expiration of thofe 7 Years tranfport themfelves to *Virginia,* and ferve that Church in the Office of the Miniftery 7 Years more, the Church there providing for them, which being expired, they to be left to their own Liberty to return or not, and not performing the Conditions of their Admittance, then to be uncapable of any Preferment.] *London,* Printed by *W. Godbid* for *Henry Brome* at the Signe of the *Gun* in *Ivy-Lane.* 1662. 4*to. p.* 22. [*Ex dono Rev.* Roberti Watts, *L. L. B.*]

The **TRADE** and **FISHING** of *Great-Britain* difplayed with a Defcription of the Iflands of *Orkney* and *Shotland* by Capt. *JOHN SMITH,* ded. to his Majefty. *London,* Printed by *William Godbid.* 1662. 4*to* p. 16.

The Prefervation of the Kings Majefties Royal Perfon, Crown and Dignity, the Preparing of the *Fifhing Trade,* Maintenance of the *Poor,* Preferving of Peace and Safety of the Kingdomes by *W. O.* [*viz. William Okeham, Gent.*] *London,* Printed by *R. D.* 1663. 4*to. p.* 9. 1663. 15 Car. 2

A Difcourfe written by Sir *Geo. Downing* the King of *Great-Britains* Envoyeé Extraordinary to the *States* of the *United Provinces,* vindicating his Royal Mafter from the Infolences of a fcandalous Libel Printed under the Title of [*An Extract out of the Regifter of the Refolutions of the* States General *of the United Provinces upon the* Memorial *of Sir George Downing Envoyee,* &c.] and delivered by the Agent *de Heyde* for fuch to feveral publick Minifters : Whereas no fuch Refolution was ever communicated to the faid Envoyée, nor any Anfwer at all returned by their Lordfhips to the faid Memorial. Given at the *Hague* this 16th of *December* 1664. *London,* Printed by *J. M.* 1664. 4*to. p* 21. 1664. 16 Car. 2.

A

1665.   A Reply of Sir *GEO. DOWNING*, Knight and Baronet, Envoy Ex-
17 *Car.* 2. traordinary from his Majesty of *Great-Britain*, to the Remarks of the *Deputies* of the *Estates General* upon his *Memorial* of December 20th 1664. Old Stile. *London*, Printed *Anno Dom.* 1665. 4*to. p.* 104.

The Golden Coast, or a Description of *GUINNEY*. 1. In its Air and Situation. 2. In the Commodities imported thither and exported thence. 3. In their Way of Traffick, their Laws and Customes. 4. In its People Religion, War, and Peace. 5. In its Forts and Havens. 6. In 4 Rich Voyages to that Coast. 7. In its Merchandize and Commodities; together with a Relation of such persons as got wonderful Estates by their Trade thither. [With an Epistle Dedicat. to the Reader, giving among other things the Advice of the Emperour *SIGISMUND* when in *England* to King *HENRY* concerning his keeping *Calice* and *Dover*, and the *Dominion of the Narrow Seas*, related in *Old English Verse* in a Book intituled, **The English Policy in keeping the Sea**, made in the Year 1432. and suggesting the Usefulness of founding a *Lecture of Navigation* in *Gresham-Colledge* at *London*, answerable to that in the *Contraction-House* in *Sevill*, set up by *CHARLES* V. for remedying the many *Shipwrecks* his Subjects sustained in passing and repassing from *Spain* to the *West-Indies*.] Licensed according to Order. *London*, Printed for *S. Speed* at the *Rainbow* in *Fleetstreet*. 1665. 4*to. pag.* 88. [*Ex dono Rev.* Rob. Watts, *L. L. B.*]

Literæ autogr. Georgij Stephani *Principis* Moldaviæ *Illustrissimo ac Excellentissimo D mino Ablegato* Angliæ [Henrico Coventry] *Amico meo Honoratissimo*────── ' *Peto illustriss. vestram excellentiam ut explorare velit apud sacram* ' *Regiam Majestatem ut clementer acceptaret Ablegatum meum.*────── *ut ego ex cle-* ' *mentia sua Regia aliquod levamen videre possim, si non Armis tamen Intercessione* ' *& Recommendatione apud Portam Ottomannicam, ut aliquando Regionem meam* ' *ac bona mea tranquille possidere possim, &c.* 1665. MS. single Sheet.

An Original Letter of Sir *Thomas Clifford* (his Majestie of *Great-Britain*'s Envoye Extraordinary to the Crowns of *Denmark* and *Sweden*) to Mr. *Henry Coventry* his Majesties Envoye Extraordinary, Resident at *Stockholm*, from *Guttenburgh*, Dec. 29. 1665.────── complaining of a Disrespect paid to him by President *Griffinklow*, for which he ought to have a just Resentment and speedy Satisfaction.────── MS. single Sheet.

His Majesties Propriety and Dominion of the *British* Seas Asserted. Together with a true Account of the *Neatherlanders* insupportable Insolencies and Injuries they have committed, and the inestimable Benefits they have
gained

gained in their Fishing on the *English* Seas, &c. to which is added an ex-
act Map containing the Isles of *Great-Britain* and *Ireland*, with the several
Coastings, and the adjacent Parts of our Neighbours. *London*, Printed for
T. Mabb. 1665. 8vo. *p.* 176. [*Ex dono Rev.* Roberti Watts, *L. L. B.*]

1666.
18 *Car.* 2.

The *INDIAN* GRAMMAR Begun ; or, An Essay to bring the
Indian Language into Rules, for the Help of such as desire to learn the same,
for the furtherance of the Gospel among them. By *JOHN ELIOT.*
Cambridge, Printed by *Marmaduke Johnson.* 1666. 4to. *p.* 65. Epistle
Ded. to the Right Honourable *Robert Boyle*, Esq; Governour, with the rest
of the Right Honourable and Christian Corporation for the Propagation of
the Gospel unto the *Indians* in *New-England.* 1666. 4to.

Literæ Autographæ Georgij Stephani *Principis Moldaviæ inscriptæ Illustrissimo ac Excellentissimo Domino* Henrico Coventry *Sacræ Regiæ Majestatis Regis
Angliæ Ablegato Sueciæ Domino nostro Amico à* Stockholm———— *dalantur Se-
dini* 3. Febr. *Anno* 1666.——— ' *Rogamus obnixe, ut Nos certos reddere dignemini*
' *an petitum nostrum quod* Holmiæ *factum, nempe ut Sacræ Regiæ Majestati Regi*
' *Angliæ scripserit, ac Responsionem obtinuerit, illustrissima vestra Excellentia, nec*
' *ne,* &c. [Single Sheet MS.]

Literæ Sereniss. Regiæ Majestatis Magnæ Britanniæ *Legatorum,* DENZEL
Baronis HOLLES *&* HENRICI COVENTRYE *de PACE
facta & publicata inter* D. CAROLUM I. *Regem Magnæ Britanniæ &*
D. FREDERICUM III. *Daniæ,* &c. *Regem.*——— *In uberirem testi-
ficationem manus nostras his ipsis subscripsimus, & heic in oppido* BREDA,
*clangentibus tubis publicè promulgavimus die vicesimo quarto novi & decimo quarto
veteris stili mensis* Augusti. *Anno Domini millesimo sexcentesimo sexagesimo septimo.* [MS. single Sheet.]

1667.
19. *Car.* 2.

Declaratio Serenissimi Regis Angliæ *super nonnullis negotijs illustrissimo Domino Legato* Sueciæ *per illustrissimum Dominum Legatum* COVENTRY *tra-
dita.*——— *Dabam in Palatio nostro de* Whitehall *decimo die* Julij. 1667.
CAROLUS R.——— [MS. single Sheet.]

A Placaert of the STATES GENERAL for prohibiting all Acts
of Hostility within the terms limited by the Publication of the PEACE
at *Breda*, in 1667. [MS. single Sheet.]

A Narrative or Journal of the Proceedings of their Excellencies the Right
Honourable the Lord *HOLLES* and the Lord *COVENTRY* appointed
by his Majesty of *Great-Britain* to be his Ambassadours Extraordinary and Ple-

Tt t   *nipotentiaries*

nipotentiaries for the TREATY held at *Breda* with the *Ambaſſadours* of the *French King*, and the K. of *Denmark* and the States General of the *United Provinces*. By a Perſon of Quality concerned in this *Ambaſſy*. Printed in the *Savoy* by *Tho. Newcomb*, and are to be ſold by *Robert Pawlet* at the Bible in *Chancery-Lane*. 1667. 4to. *p.* 31. [*Ex dono* Thomæ Granger *Generoſi.*]

A Commiſſion of the States General of the *United Provinces* for certain other Perſons to be joyn'd with their former Plenipotentiaries the Sieurs *de Beverningk, de Huybert*, and *de Jongeſtal*, for treating and concluding a Peace with the King of *Great-Britain*, at *Breda*. *Donne a la Haye en noſtre grande Aſſemble——— le 28. Jour de Juillet l'an mille ſix cent ſoix ant ſepte.* [Single Sheet.]

𝔓𝔲𝔟𝔩𝔦𝔠𝔞𝔱𝔦𝔢 𝔳𝔞𝔫𝔡𝔢𝔫 𝔄𝔯𝔢𝔡𝔢 𝔗𝔲ſſ𝔠𝔥𝔢𝔫 𝔈𝔫𝔤𝔢𝔩𝔞𝔫𝔱 𝔢𝔫𝔡𝔢 𝔡𝔢 𝔄𝔢 𝔯𝔢𝔢𝔫𝔦𝔤𝔥𝔡𝔢 𝔑𝔬𝔡𝔢𝔯𝔩𝔞𝔫𝔡𝔢𝔫, 𝔱𝔬𝔱 𝔅𝔯𝔢𝔡𝔞, 𝔡𝔢𝔫 14. 𝔄𝔲𝔤𝔲ſ𝔱𝔦. 1667. [Single Sheet.]

Praxis Curiæ ADMIRALITATIS *Angliæ* *Auctore* FRANCISCO CLERKE, *olim Curiæ* Cantuar. *de Arcubus* London. *Procuratore*. Londini *Impenſis* Guil. Crooke. 1667. 12°. *p.* 48.

A *Subſidy* granted to the King of TONNAGE and POUNDAGE and other Sums of **Money** payable upon *Merchandize Exported* and *Imported* together with a Book of RATES agreed upon by the Honourable Houſe of Commons and hereunto annex'd. *London*, Printed by the Aſſigns of *John Bill* and *Chriſtopher Barker*, Printers to the King's moſt Excellent Majeſty. 1667. 12°. *p.* 178.

Rules and Inſtructions for the TARE of *Goods* and *Merchandize* imported into any Port of *England*. Reviſed and Publiſhed by the Farmers of his Majeſties Cuſtoms, as a Direction to all their Officers concerned therein. *London*. 1667. 12°. *p.* 14.

Philoſophical Tranſactions for *February* 1666. containing (among other things) 1. A Method for obſerving the ECLIPSES of *the* MOON, free from the common Inconveniencies, as it was left by the Learned Mr. ROOK, late *Greſham Profeſſor of Geometry*. 2. An Account of ſome *Celeſtial Obſervations* lately made in *Spain* by his Excellency the Earl of *Sandwich*, *&c*. Printed in the *Savoy*. 4to. 1667.

An

An Impartial Description of *SURINAM* upon the Continent of *Guiana* in *America* ; with a History of several strange *Beasts*, *Birds*, *Fishes*, *Serpents*, *Insects* and *Customs* of that Colony, *&c.* [Treating of 1. the *River*. 2. The *Climate* and Country in General. 3. The *Provisions*. 4. The *Birds* and *Beasts*. 5. The *Fruits*. 6. The *Commodities*. 7 The *Plantations*. 8. The *Negroes* or *Slaves*. 9. Things *Venemous* and *Hurtful*. 10. The *Indians*.] worthy the perusal of all, from the Experience of *GEORGE WARREN*. Gent. *London*, Printed by *William* Godbid for *Nathaniel Brooke*. 1667. 4.to p. 28. [*Ex dono Rev.* Rob. Watts, *L.L.B.*]

A Sermon preach'd before the Right Worshipful Company of *Merchants trading into the* LEVANT at St. *Olaves Hartstreet, London.* Tuesday, *June* 2. 1668. By *THO. SMITH*, M. A. Fellow of *Magdalen College* in *Oxford*, and Chaplain to the Right Honourable Sir *Daniel Harvey* his Majesties Ambassadour to *Constantinople*. *London*, Printed by T. *Roycroft* for S. *Mearn*, Bookbinder to the King's most Excellent Majesty. 1668. 4.to p. 51. [*Ex dono Reverendi* Alexandri Young, *S.T.B.*] *1668* *20 Car.*

DARY's Miscellanies being for the most part a brief Collection of MA-THEMATICAL THEOREMS from divers Authors upon these Subjects following. 1. The *Inscription and Circumscription* of a CIRCLE. 2. *Plain Triangles*. 3. *Spherical Triangles*. 4. The *Projection of the Sphere in Plano*. 5 *Trigonometry* and the *Centre of Gravity*. 6. *Solid Geometry* and therein *Gauging*. 7. The *Scale of Ponderosity*, alias the *Stilliard*. 8. The 4 *Compendiums* for *Quadratine Equations*. 9. *Recreative Problems*. By *MICHAEL DARY*. *London*, Printed by *W. G.* and sold by *Moses Pitt, Tho. Rookes* and *Will. Birch*. 1669. 12°. p. 46. [*Ex dono* Thomæ Granger *Generosi*] *1669* *21 Car.*

ENGLAND's Interest asserted in the Improvement of its Native Commodities, and more especially the Manufacture of WOOL, plainly shewing its *Exportation Unmanufactured* amounting unto Millions of Lots to his Majesty and Kingdom. With some brief Observations of that Worthy Author Sir *WALTER RAWLEY* touching the same. All humbly presented to his Majesty and both Houses of Parliament, by a true Lover of his Majesty and Native Country. Licented by *Roger L'estrange. London*, Printed for *Francis Smith*, and are to be sold at the *Elephant and Castle* without Temple-Bar, and by *Henry Mortlock* at the *White Hart* in *Westminster-Hall*. 1669. 4.to. p. 34–36. [*Ex dono Reverendi Admodum Patris* CAROLI, *Episcopi* NORWICENSIS.]

A

An Extract of a Letter, containing the whole Proceſs uſed in *France* for making S E A-S A L T by the S U N. Communicated to the Publiſher in *French*, by an Ingenious Doctor of Phyſick of that Nation, reſiding near the chief Place where it is practiſed. [Inſerted in the *Philoſophical Tranſactions* of *September* 20. 1669.]

1670. A *Treaty* for Compoſing of Differences, Reſtraining of Depredations and
22 *Car.* 2. Eſtabliſhing of Peace in *A M E R I C A* between the Crowns of *G R E A T-BRITAIN* and *S P A I N.* Concluded at *Madrid* the 8.-18. day of *July*, A. D. 1670. Tranſlated out of Latin and Publiſhed by his Majeſties Command. Printed in the *Savoy* by the Aſſigns of *John Bill* and *Chriſtopher Barker*. 1670. 4to. p. 11. [*Ex dono* Thomæ Granger *Generoſi*.]

1671. The Uſe and Abuſes of M O N E Y, and the Improvements of it; by two
23 *Car.* 2. Propoſitions for *Regulating* our C O I N; whereby his Majeſties Occaſions may be ſupplied with the moſt likely Way to advance a *General Trade*, Domeſtick as well as Foreign. Conſidered and Preſented to view of all that wiſh the publick Good of the Kingdom in General, and of themſelves in particular. With ſubmiſſion to better Judgments. *London*, Printed for *Allen Banks* and *Charles Harper* at the 3 *Flower de Luces* againſt St. *Dunſtans* Church, and *Geo. Marriott* under the *Kings Head Tavern* in *Fleetſtreet*. 1671. 4to. p. 31. [*Ex dono Rev.* Alexandri Young, *S. T. B.*]

Tracts written by the Honourable *R O B E R T B O Y L E* about the *Coſmical Qualities* of Things. *Coſmical* Suſpicions. The Temperature of the *Subterranean Regions*. The *Bottom of the Sea*. To which is prefix'd an Introduction to the Hiſtory of Particular *Qualities*. *Oxford*, Printed for *Ric. Davis*. 1671. 8vo. [*Ex dono Rev.* Roberti Watts, *L. L. B*]

1673. The *Grand Concern* of *E N G L A N D*, explained in ſeveral *Propoſals* of-
25 *Car.* 2. fered to the Conſideration of the *Parliament*. 1. For Payment of *Publick Debts*. 2. For Advancement and Encouragement of *Trade*. 3. For Raiſing the *Rents of Lands*, &c. By a Lover of his Country and Well-wiſher to the Proſperity both of the King and Kingdoms. *London*, Printed in the Year. 1673. 4to. p. 92.

Het. Eerſte Boeck MOSIS **Genaempt** GENESIS. **Na de oorſpronckelycke vaper heydt. ouer-geſet in de Nederduytſche ende Maleyoſtiche Tale, Ende is dit eerſte Boeck Moſis,** &c.
The firſt Book of *M O S E S* called *G E N E S I S*, according to the Original in *Low-Dutch*. Tranſlated into the *Malayan Tongue* by *D A N I E L BROWE*

BROWERIUS, Minister of the Gospel in the Congregation of Jesus Christ at *Helle-Voet-Sluys* and afterwards in the *East-Indies* by the Order of the Honourable the *Dutch East-India Company*. Printed by the Order of the *Directors of the* East-India *Company* at *Amsterdam*, by *Paulus Matthyz* in *Stoof-street*, Printer to the *East-India* Company. 1673. 4*to. p.* 104. with an Epist. Dedicatory to the Hon. the Directors of the *East-India Company* residing in *Holland* and *Zealand*. [*Ex dono* Thomæ Granger *Generosi.*]

An Explication or the DIALL set up in the King's Garden at *London, Ann.* 1669. in which very many sorts of *Dyalls* are contained ; by which besides the Hours of all Kinds diversly expressed many things also belonging to *Geography, Astrology,* and *Astronomy* are by the *Sunnes* Shadow made visible to the Eye, amongst which very many *Dialls,* especially the most curious are new Inventions hitherto divulged by none : All these Particulars are shortly yet clearly set forth for the common Good, by the Reverend Father *FRANCIS HALL* otherwise *LINE,* of the *Society of Jesus,* Professor of *Mathematicks.* Printed at *Liege* by *Guillam Henry Streel* in the Yeare of our Lord 1673. *Superiorum Permissu.* 4*to. p.* 60. [*Ex Dono Reverendi* Roberti Watts, L. L. B.]

A Discourse of the FISHERY : Briefly laying open not only the *Advantages* and *Facility* of the Undertaking, but likewise the Absolute *Necessity* of it, in order to the Well-Being both of King and People, asserted and vindicated from all material Objections, by *ROGER LESTRANGE. London,* Printed for *Henry Brome* at the *Gun* in S. *Paul's Church* at the West End. 1674. 4*to. p.* 10.

1674.
26 *Car.* 2.

A TREATY MARINE between the most Serene and Mighty Prince *CHARLES* II. By the Grace of God King of *England, Scotland, &c.* Defender of the Faith, *&c.* and the High and Mighty Lords the STATES GENERAL of the *United Netherlands* to be observed throughout all and every the Countries and Parts of the World by Sea and Land. Concluded at *London* the 1st day of *December.* 1674. S. V. publish'd by his Majesties Command. *London,* Printed by the King's Printers. 1674. 4*to. pag.* 31. [*Ex Dono Reverendi* Alexandri Young, *S. T. B.*]

The True *English Interest* ; or an Account of the Chief National Improvements, in some Political Observations, demonstrating an Infallible Advance of this Nation to Infinite Wealth and Greatness, Trade and Populacy, with Imployment and Preferment for all Persons. By *CAREW REYNEL* Esquire. *London,* Printed for *Giles Widdowes* at the *Green Dragon* in St. *Paul's*

Church-Yard, 1674. *Dec. p.* 92. [*Ex dono Reverendi Admodum Patris* CAROLI *Episcopi* NORWICENSIS.]

1676.
28 Car. 2. A Plain and Eafie Rule to *Rigg* any SHIP by the length of his *Mafts* and *Yards,* without any further trouble. *London,* Printed for *William Fifher.* 1676. 4*to. p.* 8.

1677.
29 Car. 2. The BOAT-SWAINS Art, or the Complete *Boat-Swain,* wherein is fhewed a true Proportion for the *Mafting, Yarding,* and *Rigging* of any SHIP whofe Length, Depth and Breadth is known, with Rules for the Sizes and Lengths of all forts of *Rigging* that belongs to any *Ship.* Alfo the Ufe of an *Opening Scale* to meafure the *Lengths* and *Thicknefs* of all *Mafts* and *Yards.* By *HENRY BOND,* Teacher of Navigation, Surveying and other Parts of the *Mathematicks,* near *Ratcliffe-Crofs. London,* Printed for *William Fifher,* 1677. 4*to. p.* 28.

The *EAST-INDIA* TRADE, a moft profitable Trade to the Kingdom, and beft fecured and improved in COMPANY and JOINT-STOCK. Reprefented in a Letter written upon the Occafion of two Letters lately publifhed [*viz.* in 1676.] infinuating the contrary. *London,* Printed in the Year 1677. 4*to. p.* 27.

A Treatife of WOOL and CATTLE in a Letter written to a Friend, occafioned by a Difcourfe concerning the great *Abatement of Rents* and *low Value of Lands* ; wherein is fhewed how their Worth and Value may be advanced, by the Improvement of the Manufacture of our *Englifh* WOOL, and the fpending of our CATTLE ; and it is further proved that CLOATHING and HOSPITALITY tend to the Support of the Honour, Wealth and Strength of our *Englifh* Nation. Licenfed by *Roger L'eftrange, March* 28. 1677. *London,* Printed by *J. C.* for *Will.* Crook at the *Green Dragon* without *Temple-Bar.* 1677. 4*to. p.* 33. [*Ex dono Reverendi Admodum Patris* CAROLI *Epifcopi* NORWICENSIS.]

A Difcourfe fhewing that the EXPORTATION of WOOL is Deftructive to this Kingdom ; wherein is alfo fhewed the *Abfolute Neceffity* of promoting our *Woollen Manufacture* and moderating the *Importation* of fome Commodities and Prohibiting others, with fome eafie Expedients tending thereunto by *THOMAS MANLY* Efquire. Licenfed by *Roger L'Eftrange. Mar.* 8. 1678. *London,* Printed for *Sam.* Crouch. 1677. 4*to. p.* 12. [*Ex dono Reverendi Admodum Patris* CAROLI *Epifcopi* NORWICENSIS.]

ENGLAND's Great Happiness; or a Dialogue between Content and Complaint wherein is demonstrated that a great part of our Complaints are causeless, and that we have more *Wealth* now than ever we had at any time before the Restauration of his sacred Majestie. By a real and hearty Lover of his King and Country. *London*, Printed by *J. M.* for *Edward Croft*, and are to be sold at the *Printing-Press* in *Cornhill*. 1677. 4to. p. 22. [*Ex dono Reverendi Admodum Patris* CAROLI *Episcopi* NORWICENSIS.]

Proposals to increase TRADE and to advance his Majesties REVENUE without any Hazard or Charge to any Body. By Mr. *LEWIS*. *London*, Printed for *Henry Milllon* at the Sign of the *Bible* in *Fleetstreet*. 1677. 8vo, p. 16.

Proposals for Building in every *County* a WORKING-HOUSE or HOSPITAL as the best Expedient to perfect the *Trade* and *Manufactory* of LINNEN-CLOTH. *London*, Printed by *W*. G. for R. *Harford* at the Sign of the *Angel* in *Cornhill*. 1677. 4to. p. 12. With a *Postscript* in Answer to several Objections, p. 16. [*Ex dono Rev. Admodum Patris* CAROLI *Episcopi* NORWICENSIS.]

Order of the *Lords Spiritual and Temporal* in Parliament Assembled for Addressing his Majestie from this House, that by his Majesties Royal Mediation the ENGLISH FACTORIES in *Foreign Parts* may have CHAPLAINS professing the *Protestant Religion* allowed to them. And that his Majestie will be pleased to take Order that no *Agents, Residents* or *Consuls* may be employed abroad but such as are *Protestants*. And lastly that his Majestie will be pleased to take into his special Care the Protestant Interest Abroad. *Die Jovis* 12. *Decemb.* 1678. [*Extract from the Journal of the House of Lords.*] 1678. 30 *Car.* 2.

The *Jew turned Christian* : Or the Corner Stone, wherein is an Assertion of *Christ* being the true *Messiah*. By *JOHN JACOB*, formerly a *Jew* but now turned *Christian*. *London*, Printed for *Tho. Cockerill*. 1678. Ded. to the KING, the *Archbishop* of *Cant.* the *Bishops, Deans* and *Doctors in Divinity.* 4to. p. 36.

A Letter from Captain *JOHN TOSIER*, Commander of his Majesties Ship the *Hunter* at *JAMAICA*; with a Narrative of his Embassy and Command in that Frigat, to the Captain General and Governour of *HAVANNAH* to demand his *Majesty* of *Great-Britain's* Subjects kept *Prisoners* there. The Account and Manner of their Delivery ; with a List of 1679. 31 *Car.* 2.

of their Names, and Times of Bondage ; as also the miraculous Preservation of 15 English his Majesties Subjects cast away, and remaining 18 Days in a Long Boat at Sea in a sad Condition, taken up by the said Captain John Tosier. Printed in the Year 1679. 4to. and faithfully transcribed. [*Ex dono Reverendi* Roberti Watts, *L. L. B.*]

1680.
32 *Car.* 2.

A Plea for the bringing in of I R I S H C A T T L E and keeping out of F I S H *caught by Foreigners* ; together with an Humble Address to the Honourable Members of Parliament of the Counties of *Cornwall* and *Devon* about the Advancement of T I N, F I S H E R Y, and divers *Manufactures.* By J O H N C O L L I N S, Accomptant to the *Royal Fishery Company.* London, sold by *Lengly Curtis.* 1680. 4to. *p.* 37.

The N E G R O E S and I N D I A N S *Advocate,* suing for their Admission into the CHURCH ; Or a Persuasive to the *Instructing and Baptizing* of the *Negroes* and *Indians* in our *Plantations.* Shewing that as the Compliance therewith can prejudice no Man's just Interest ; So the wilful Neglecting and Opposing of it is no less than a manifest Apostacy from the Christian Faith. To which is added a brief Account of Religion in *VIRGINIA*, as it was sometime before the late Rebellion represented in a Letter to Sir *W. B.* [Sir *William Beeston*] then Governour thereof. By M O R G A N G O D W Y N. Sometime Student of *Christ Church, Oxon. London,* Printed for the Author by *J. D.* 1680. 8vo. *p.* 174. [*Ex dono Rev.* Roberti Watts, *L. L. B.*]

A Narrative of unheard of *Popish Cruelties* towards *Protestants* beyond Seas. Or a New Account of the Bloody *Spanish Inquisition.* Published as a Caveat to Protestants. By Mr. *D U G D A L E. London,* Printed for *John Hancock.* 1680. Fol. *p.* 27.

1681.
33 *Car.* 2.

T A N G E R's Rescue, or a Relation of the late memorable Passages at *Tanger* ; giving a full and true Account of the several Skirmishes of his Majesties Forces there against the *Moors*, and particularly of that bloody Engagement with them upon the 27th of *October* last, very pleasant and satisfactory ; together with a Description of the said City, with the considerable Forts thereof ; as also a Description of the *Moors*, their Nature and Country. In Verse, by J O H N R O S S, Gent. an Eye-witness. *London,* Printed for *Hen. Hills.* 1681. 4to. *p.* 36. [*Ex dono Reverendi Admodum Patris* CAROLI *Episcopi* NORWICENSIS.]

An Account of the Arrival of 6 *Ships* belonging to the *East-India Company* from *India*, and the great Advancement of their Stock thereupon ; with an
Account

Account of the *Cham of Tartary*'s taking, thro' the help of the *Dutch* Shipping, *Onnay* and *Titnan* two great Ports in the Island of *Formosa*, where the *English* had settled Factories, which they lost thereby: Of the K. of *Bantam*'s coming over with 30 Followers in an *English Ship* to *England*. [Inserted in the *Impartial Proteſtant Mercury*, Numb. 77. from *Friday Jan.* 13. to *Tueſday Jan.* 17. 1681-2. Fol. a Half-ſheet.

LITHGOW's Nineteen Years Travels through the moſt eminent Places in the habitable World; containing an exact Deſcription of the Cuſtoms, Laws, Religion, Policies and Government of Emperours, Kings and Princes, alſo of the Countries and Cities, Trades, Rivers and Commerce in all Places through which he travelled; alſo an Account of the Tortures he ſuffer'd under the *Spaniſh Inquiſition*, by Racking and other inhumane Uſages, for his owning the Proteſtant Religion, together with his miraculous Deliverance from the Cruelties of the Papiſts, which far exceeded any of the Heathen Countries herein largely deſcribed. *London*, Printed for *John Wright* at the *Crown* on *Ludgate-hill*, and *Thomas Paſſinger* at the *Three Bibles* on *London-Bridge*. 1682. 8vo. p. 481. With ſeveral Cutts.
(margin: 1682. 34 Car. 2.)

ARTICLES of PEACE and COMMERCE between the moſt Serene and Mighty Prince *CHARLES II.* by the Grace of God, King of *Great-Britain*, *France* and *Ireland*, &c. And the moſt Illuſtrious Lords, the *Baſhaw*, *Dey*, *Aga*, and *Governours* of the famous City and Kingdom of *ALGIERS* in *Barbary*. Concluded by *ARTHUR HERBERT*, Eſquire, Admiral of his Majeſties *Fleet* in the *Mediterranean* Seas on the 10th day of *April*, Old Stile, 1682. Publiſhed by his Majeſties Command. *London*, Printed by the King's Printers. 1682. 4to. pag. 19.

The REVIVAL or Directions for a Sculpture, deſcribing the extraordinary Care and Diligence of our Nation in publiſhing the Faith among Infidels in *AMERICA*, and elſewhere, compared with other both Primitive and Modern Profeſſors of Chriſtianity. In a Figure to be placed before p. 3. of the *Negroes advocate*. *London*, Printed by *J. Darby*. 1682. Half ſheet.

A Collection of Letters for the Improvement of HUSBANDRY and TRADE. By *John Houghton*, Fellow of the *Royal Society*. The ſecond Volume. Containing, 1. A Token for Ship Boys, or *Plain Sailing* made more plain and ſhort than uſual, by *A. Martindale*. 2. Some Experiments of *Port Sea Salt* from Mr. *Cragg*, ſometime *Husband* to the *Royal Fiſhery*, &c. *London*, Printed for the Author. 1683. 4to. p. 144.
(margin: 1683. 35 Car. 2)

1684.
36 *Car.* 2.

AQUA SALSA DULCORATA. *Sive accurata novi hujus Artificij, qua-tenus tum Maris tum Portuum Incolis, utilis Descriptio. Accessit præterea Plena omnium alicujus momenti contra novum hoc Adinventum Objectionum Solutio. Necnon Approbatio* Collegij Medicorum Londinensis. *Epistola denique Honorabilis* Roberti Boylei *hac super re ad Amicum conscripta. Editio* secunda. Londini, *Excudebat* J. Gain, 1684. 8vo. *p.* 29.

Dissertatio Quæ complectitur Nova Experimenta, utilesq; Observationes circa AQUAM MARINAM. *Secundum Eorum Artem quibus Regium Diploma concessum est* DULCORATAM. *Sereniffimo Principi* CAROLO II. Magnæ Britanniæ *Regi Humillime oblata. Offerebat* NEHEMIAS GREW, M. D. & Societatis Regiæ Londinensis utriusq; Socius. Londini, *Excudebat* J. Gain, 8vo. *p.* 24.

Sea Water made Fresh ; with Queries and Answers concerning the Wholesomness and Cheapness of Water thus prepared, the Approbation of the *Colledge of Physicians,* A Letter of Mr. *Boyles* to the Learned Dr. *John Beale, &c.* 8vo. *p.* 21

New Experiments and Useful Observations concerning *Sea-Water made Fresh,* according to the Patentee's Invention. In a Discourse humbly dedicated to his Majesty the King of *Great-Britain.* By *NEHEMIAH GREW* M. D. Fellow of the *Colledge of Physitians,* and of the *Royal Society.* The Ninth Edition. *September* 29. *London,* Printed by *John Harefinch.* 1684. 8vo.

An Essay for the Recording of *Illustrious Providences,* wherein an Account is given of many Remarkable and very memorable Events which have happened in this last Age, especially in *New-England.* [Treating, 1. of remarkable *Sea Deliverances.* 2. Other remarkable *Deliverances.* 3. Remarkables about *Thunder* and *Lightning.* 4. Philosophical Meditations of *Antipathies* and *Sympathies* of the *Loadstone, Lightning* and *Thunder-storms.* 5, 6, 7. *Witches, Demons* and *Apparitions.* 8. *Amulets* to drive away *Evil Spirits.* 9. *Deaf* and *Dumb* Persons, and Methods of curing them. 10. *Tempests, Storms, Hurricanes* and *Floods.* 11. Remarkable *Judgments* especially on *Quakers* and *Drunkards.* 12. *Sudden Deaths* and *Miraculous Answers in Prayer* and *Conversions of Sinners.*] By *INCREASE MATHER,* Teacher of a Church at *Boston* in *New-England.* Printed at *Boston* in *New-England,* and are to be sold by *George Calvert* at the Sign of the *Half Moon* in *Paul's Church-Yard.* 1684. 8vo. *p.* 372. [*Ex dono Reverendi* Roberti Watts, L. L. B.]

A

A brief but full Account of the Doctrine of *TRIGONOMETRY,* both *Plain* and *Spherical.* By *JOHN CASWELL,* M. A. *London,* Printed by *John Playford* for *Richard Davis,* Bookseller in the University of *Oxford.* 1685. *Fol. p.* 17. 1685. 1 *Jan.* 2.

E. BERNARDUS de Mensuris *&* Ponderibus xaτ' ἐπιπραφὴ. *Oxoniæ e* Theatro Sheldoniano. 1685. *Fol.* Ded. to Dr. *Edward Pocock,* Regius Professor of *Hebrew* in the University of *Oxford.*

Sciothericum Telescopicum, or a New Contrivance of adapting a *Telescope* to an *Horizontal Dial,* for observing the *Moment* of *Time* by Day or Night, useful in all *Astronomical* Observations, and for regulating and adjusting curious *Pendulum Watches* and other *Time Keepers,* with proper *Tables* requisite thereto. By *WILLIAM MOLYNEUX,* Esq; Fellow of the *Royal Society,* and of that of *Dublin. Dublin,* Printed by *Andrew Crook* and *Samuel Helsham,* at the Printing House on *Ormond Key,* and are to be sold by *W. Norman* in *Damestreet,* and *S. Helsham* and *El. Dobson,* Booksellers in *Castlestreet.* 1686. *4to. p.* 54. besides large Tables. 1686. 2 *Jan.* 2.

A New and Easie Method to the Art of *DYALLING:* Containing, 1. All *Horizontal Dyals,* all *Upright Dyals, Reflecting Dyals, Dyals without Centres, Nocturnal Dyals, Upright Declining Dyals* without knowing the Declination of the Plane. 2. The most natural and easie Way of describing the *Curve Lines* of the *Sun's Declination* on any Plane. By *THOMAS STRODE,* Esq; of *Maperton* in the County of *Somerset. London,* Printed by *H. C.* for *J. Taylor* at the *Ship,* and *T. Newborough* at the *Ball* in St. *Paul's Church Yard.* 1688. *4to. p.* 66. 1688. 4 *Jan.* 2.

Logarithmotechnia, or the making of Numbers call'd *Logarithms* to 25 places from a *Geometrical Figure* with Speed, Ease and Certainty. By *EUCLID SPEIDEL,* Philomath. *London,* Printed by *Henry Clark* for the Author, and are to be sold by *Philip Lea* in *Cheapside* near *Friday-street.* 1688. *4to. p.* 15 [*Ex Dono* Thomæ Granger *Generosi.*]

A true and exact Relation of the most dreadful *Earthquake* which happened in the City of *Naples* and several other parts of that Kingdom, *June* 5. 1688 whereby about 40 Cities and Villages were either wholly ruined or extremely damnified, 8000 Persons destroyed, and about 800 wounded, of which 400 were digg'd out of the Ruins and many others miraculously preserved. Translated from the *Italian* Copy printed at *Naples* by an Eye-Witness of
those

those miserable Ruins.   *London,* Printed and are to be sold by *Randal Tayle*
near *Stationers Hall.* 1688. 4to. p. 27.

An Account of his Excellence ROGER Earl of CASTLEMAINE's
Embassy from his Sacred Majesty *JAMES* II. King of *England,* &c, to
his Holiness *INNOCENT* XI. Published formerly in the *Italian* Tongue
by Mr. *MICHAEL WRIGHT,* Chief Steward of his Excellencies House
at *Rome,* and now made *English* with several Amendments and Additions.
London, Printed by *Tho. Snowden* for the Author. 1688. Fol. p. 111.
adorned with many curious Sculptures, and dedicated to the Queen. [*Ex dono*
Thomæ Granger, *Generos.*]

1689.
W. & M.
Observations concerning the Dominion and Sovereignty of the SEAS; being an Abstract of the Marine Affairs of England. [Shewing, 1. what is meant
by the *Dominion of the Sea* ; 2. What things are incident to it, and insepara-
bly follow it.   3. What the *Salutation at Sea* by the Flag and Topsail signi-
fies.   4. The whole Matter of Fact betwixt the *Crown of* England and Foreign Princes and States, in the several Incidents of *Sea Dominion,* and occasionally treating of the *Quatuor Maria,* the *Laws of* Oleron, the *Roll in the
Tower* de Superioritate Maris, *The Fishery licensed and limited,* &c.]   By
Sir *PHILIP MEDOWS,* Knight.   Printed in the *Savoy* by *Edw. Jones*
and sold by *Sam. Lowndes* against *Exeter Change* in the *Strand,* and by *Edward
Jones* in the *Savoy.* 1689. 4to. p. 47. [*Ex Dono Reverendi* Roberti
Watts, L. L. B.]

A *Supplement* to a Treatise concerning the *EAST-INDIA* TRADE.
Printed in 1681. 4to. Wherein is demonstrated, 1. That the *East-India
Trade* is the most National of all Foreign Trades, &c. [shewing what Ships
the Company has built, what Forts they have Fortified and Garrisoned in
India, for the Security of the *Pepper Trade,* what Goods they have in their
Warehouses unsold, what Customs they have paid the King in two Years
time, and how the Inhabitants of the Island of Bombay, which were but
4000 in Number, when the Company first got Possession of it, are since increased to 50000 all subject to the Companies Laws.   Together with an
Account of the Success of their Arms against the Forces of the *Mogul,* and
the *Articles* of the Peace lately concluded between him and the Company,
&c.] 1689. 4to. p. 14.

1690.
W. & M.
An Account of what passed on *Monday the 28th of October* 1689. in the
House of Commons, and since at the *Kings Bench-Bar* at *Westminster* in relation
to the Earl of *CASTLEMAINE.* *London,* Printed for *Matthew*
                                                            Granger.

Granger. 1690. 4to. *p.* 17. [*Ex dono Reverendi* Alexandri Young, *S. T. B.*]

Late Memorable Providences relating to *Witchcrafts* and *Possessions*, clearly 1691. manifesting not only that there are *Witches*, but that Good Men (as well as 3 *W. & M.* others) may possibly have their Lives shortned by such evil Instruments of *Satan.* Written by *COTTON MATHER*, Minister of the Gospel at *Boston* in *New-England.* Recommended by the Reverend Mr. *Richard Baxter* in *London*, and by the Ministers of *Boston* and *Charlestown* in *New-England.* *London*, Printed for *Tho. Parkhurst.* 1691. 8vo. *p.* 144. [*Ex dono Rev.* Roberti Watts, *L. L. B.*]

Naval Speculations and Maritime Politicks. Being a Modest and Brief Discourse of the R O Y A L N A V Y of E N G L A N D : Of its Oeconomy and Government; and a Projection for an everlasting Seminary of *Seamen* by a *Royal Maritime Hospital.* With a Project for a *Royal Fishery.* Also necessary Measures in the present War with *France.* By *H E N R Y M A Y D M A N.* *London*, Printed by *William Bonny*, and sold by *Sam. Manship*, &c. 1691. 8vo. *p.* 348. [*Ex dono Rev.* Roberti Watts, *L. L. B.*]

A Description of the I S L E of O R K N E Y. By Master *J A M E S* 1693. *W A L L A C E*, late Minister of *Kirkwall.* Published after his Death by 5 *W. & M.* his Son. To which is added, An Essay concerning the T H U L E of the *Ancients.* *Edinburgh*, Printed by *John Reid* in the Year 1693. 12°. *p.* 94, & 36. Ded. to Sir *Rob. Sibbald.* [*Ex Dono* Thomæ Granger, *Generosi.*]

An Account of the Conversion of *T H E O D O R E J O H N*, a late Teacher among the *Jews* ; together with his *Confession of the Christian Faith*, which he deliver'd immediately before he was baptized in the presence of the *Lutheran* Congregation in the *German* Church in *Little Trinity Lane, London*, on the 23d *Sunday* after *Trinity*, being the 31th of *October*, in the Year of our Lord God, 1692. Translated out of *High Dutch* into *English.* *London*, Printed for *John Dunton* at the *Raven* in the *Poultry.* 1693. 8°. *p.* 54.

Ornaments for the Daughters of 'Zion, or the Character and Happiness of a 1694. *Virtuous Woman* in a Discourse which directs the *Female Sex* how to express the 6 *W. & M.* Fear of God in every Age and State of their Life, and obtain both Temporal and Eternal Blessedness. Written by *COTTON MATHER.* *London*, Printed for *Tho. Parkhurst* at the Bible and 3 Crowns the lower End of *Cheapside.* 1694. 12°. *p.* 144.

Septem ASIÆ Ecclesiarum & CONSTANTINOPOLEOS Notitia. Authore THOMA SMITHO Ecclesiæ Anglicanæ Presbytero. Editio nova auctior & emendatior. Trajecti ad Rhenum. Ex officina Francisci Halma, Academiæ Typographi. MDCXCIV. 8vo. p. 126. [Ex dono Rev. Viri Geo. Baxter, S. T. B.]

The *Earth* twice shaken wonderfully : Or, An Analogical Discourse of EARTHQUAKES, its natural Causes, Kinds, and manifold Effects occasioned by the last of these, which happen'd on the eighth day of *September*, 1697. at two of the Clock in the Afternoon : Divided into Philosophical Theorems, &c. By *J. D. R. French Minister.* London, Printed for the Author at *Sion Colledge.* 1693-4. 4to. p. 47.

The Path-Way to Peace and Profit : Or Truth in its Plain Dress ; wherein is methodically set forth a sure and certain Way for the more speedy and effectual building and repairing their Majesties ROYAL NAVY by such Means as may be saved more than one hundred thousand Pound *per Annum.* Together with a proposed Method for the Raising and Saving of Moneys for Monthly Payments accordingly. As also proper Rules and Methods observable toward the making a Regulation in their Majesties Yards. By GEORGE EVERETT, Shipwright. *London,* Printed for the Author. 1694. 4to. p. 23.

The Causeless Ground of Surmises, Jealousies and unjust Offences remov'd, in a full Clearing of Faithfull Friends, and a sober Vindication of my Innocency, and the Friends concerned with me, in relation to the late Religious Differences and Breaches among some of the People called QUAKERS in *AMERICA.* By GEO. KEITH. *London,* Printed for *R. Levis.* 1694. 4to. p. 16.

1695.
7 Will. 3. An *Act* for continuing several Duties granted by former Acts upon *Wine* and *Vinegar,* and upon *Tobacco* and *East-India Goods,* and other *Merchandize Imported,* for carrying on the War against *France, Anno 7, 8 Gulielmi III. Regis. London,* Printed by *Charles Bill,* &c. 1695. *Fol.*

An Account of *ROBERT CROSFIELD's* Proceedings in the *House of Lords* the last Session and this Session of Parliament : Wherein will appear the present miserable State and Condition of the Nation by the open Violating and Invading of the Law and Liberty of the Subject. Humbly presented to the Consideration of the *Lords* and *Commons* in Parliament Assembled. [Setting forth the Corruptions, &c. of the *Admiralty, Navy, Sick* and

and *Wounded* Offices, and the Grievances of *Seamen*.] Sign'd *Robert Crosfield*, *Feb*. 18. 169¾. *Fol. p.* 8.

A true Copy of the Original CARTEL agreed on betwixt the *Allies* and the *French King* for the Exchange or Ransom of *Prisoners*, from the *General* or *Mareschal of France* down to the private *Centinel*. *London*, Printed by *J. Whitlock*. 1695. 4to. *p.* 14.

An Essay on the State of *ENGLAND* in relation to its *Trade*, its *Poor*, and its *Taxes*, for carrying on the present War against *France*. By *JOHN CARY*, Merchant in *Bristol*. *Bristol*, Printed by *William Bonny* for the Author, and are to be sold in *London* by *Sam. Crouch*, at the Corner of *Popes-Head Alley* in *Cornhill*, and *Timothy Goodwin* at the *Queen's Head* near the *Temple*; also by *Thomas Wall* and *Richard Gravett* near the *Tolzey* in *Bristol*. *November*. 1695. 8vo. *pag.* 178. Ded. to the King.

An Essay on the COYN and CREDIT of *England*, as they stand with respect to its TRADE. By *JOHN CARY*, Merchant in *Bristol*. *Bristol*, Printed by *Will. Bonny* and sold by the Booksellers of *London* and *Bristol*, *October* the 22d. 1696. 8vo. *p.* 40. Ded. to the *Lords* and *Commons*.

An Essay towards the Settlement of a *National Credit* in the Kingdom of *England*, humbly presented to the two Honourable Houses of Parliament. By *JOHN CARY*, Merchant in *Bristol*. *London*, Printed by *Freeman Collins*, and are to be sold by *S. Crouch* at the Corner of *Popes-Head Alley* in *Cornhill* and *E. Whitlock* near *Stationers-Hall*. 1696. 8vo. *p.* 19.

Proposals for Raising a *Colledge* of all useful Trades and Husbandry, with Profit for the Rich, a plentiful Living for the Poor, and a good Education for Youth. Which will be Advantage to the Government by the Increase of their People and their Riches. By *JOHN BELLERS*. *London*, Printed and sold by *T. Sowle*. 1696. 4to. *p.* 28.

A *Sermon* Preached before the Honourable Company of *Merchants* trading to the *Levant Seas*, at St. *Peter Poor*, *Dec*. 15. 1695. By *HENRY MAUNDRELL*, A. M. Fellow of *Exeter-Colledge* in *Oxford*, and Chaplain to the Factory at *Aleppo*. *London*, Printed for *Dan. Brown*. 1696. 4to. *p.* 28.

England's

England's Calamities Difcovered, with the proper Remedy to reftore her ancient Grandeur and Policy. Humbly prefented by *JAMES WHISTON*. *London*, Printed for the Author. 1696. 4*to.* *p.* 40.

The Proceedings of the *Houfe of Commons* with relation to the *Scots Company trading to* Africa *and the* Indies. Extracted out of the Votes. MS. [*Ex Dono Rev.* Roberti Watts, L. L. B.]

1697.
o *Will.* 3.

The Great Honour and Advantage of the *Eaft-India Trade* to the Kingdom Afferted. Ded. to the Honourable the *Governour*, the Right Worfhipful the *Deputy Governour*, and to the Worfhipful the Committee of the Honourable the *Eaft-India Company*, by *J. C. London*, Printed by *Thomas Speed*. 1697. 8*vo.* *p.* 39.

England and *Eaft-India* Inconfiftent in their Manufactures : Being an Anfwer to a Treatife Intituled *An Effay on the* Eaft-India *Trade*. By the Author of the *Effay of Ways and Means. London*, Printed in the Year 1697. 8*vo.* *p.* 59.

1698.
10 *Will.* 3.

Some Thoughts of the Intereft of *England* : Shewing firft how the Nation may be eafed of all manner of *Taxes*. 2. How to reduce all *Exchequer Tallies*. 3. To fave the Nation all the *Intereft* the King now pays. By a Lover of Commerce. *London*, fold by E. *Whitlock*. 1697. 8*vo.* *p.* 12.

Loyalty and Fidelity Rejected and Oppreffed ; Or the Cafe of *GEORGE EVERETT*, Shipwright truly ftated. Moft humbly offered to the *Commons* of *England*, Affembled in Parliament. Wherein is briefly fet forth his zealous Endeavours for promoting the Service of the Publick ; with the Obftructions and illegal Proceedings of fome Perfons employed in the Adminiftration of Publick Affairs, &c. *London*, Printed in the Year 1698-9. 4*to.* *p.* 16.

A Vindication of the *Parliament of* England, in anfwer to a Book written by *WILLIAM MOLYNEUX* of *Dublin*, Efq; intituled, *The Cafe of* IRELAND's *being bound by Acts of Parliament in* England *Stated*. By *JOHN CARY*, Merchant in *Briftol. London*, Printed by *Freeman Collins*, and are to be Sold by *Sam. Crouch* in *Cornhill* and *Eliz. Whitlock* near *Stationers-Hall*. 1698. 8*vo.* *pag.* 127. Ded. to *John* Lord *Somers*.

The *Voyage* and Unfortunate *Adventures* of a Gentleman of *Breffe* to *Rodrigo*, *St. Maurice Ifland* and *Batavia* ; parting from *Amfterdam* the 10th of *July* 1690. and arriving back at *Flufhing* 28. *June* 1698. [Printed in the *Hiftory of the Cruelties of the* Dutch. 1712. 8*vo.* *p.* 236.]

Britannia

Britannia Nova : Or a reasonable Discourse, demonstrating how we may serve our King and Countrey : By discouraging *Prophaneness* and *Immorality* By preventing a great deal of *Robbery* and *Injustice* and *Oppression* : By relieving and employing the *disbanded Soldiers* : By supplying the *Deficience* of the *Funds* : By discharging the Nations *Debts* : By easing and advantaging the *Poor* : By doubling the Value and Rents of *Land* : By doubling the Number of our *Seamen* and *Naval Forces*, &c. *London*, Printed for *Matthew Gilliflower*. 1698. 4to. p. 68.

Ruin to Ruin, *after Misery to Misery* ; Being the Distressed and Ruined and Perishing State of the Loyal and Faithful SEAMEN of *England*, and wherein is laid down, I. Their ruined State in several Particulars. II. That it is like to be three or four Years more before they are paid, except an extraordinary Supply be raised and appropriated for them, &c. All humbly represented by a Faithful Subject to his Majestie and Servant to the Parliament and Nation *WILLIAM HODGES*. Dated from *Hermitage-Bridge*, *Jan.* 1699. *London*, Printed to give away. 1699. 4to. p. 43.

1699.
11 Will. 3.

A Letter from the *Council General* of the *Company of* SCOTLAND trading to *Africa* and the *Indies* to his Majestie, giving an Account of their Colonies arriving safe at their intended Port within a League of Golden Island or the Coast of *Darien* in *America*, and that they had given the Name of *New Edinburgh* in *Caledonia*, to their present Settlement. Dat. *Edinburgh* 31. *March*, 1699. [Printed at large in the Original Papers relating to the *Scots* Company. 1700. 8vo. p. 34.]

1700.
12 Will. 3.

The Colonies *Address* to the Kings most Excellent Majestie, assuring him, ' that ' upon their Arrival the Natives on all hands in compliance with former Agree- ' ments received and entertained them with all possible demonstrations of joy ' and satisfaction, their being no possession, nor so much as pretended possession ' for any Prince or State in *Europe* upon that whole Coast, extending ' more than one hundred Leagues together. [*Ib. p.* 40.]

Copies of the several *Proclamations* published by his Majesties Lieutenant Governours and Commanders in Chief of the Islands and Territories in *America*, forbidding any assistance to be given to the *Scots* settled at *Darien*, or any Correspondence to be held with them. [*Ib. p.* 42.] With the Companies Petition, the *King's Answer*, *Address* to the *Privy Council*, &c. [*Ibid.*]

The Original Papers and Letters relating to the *Scots Company* trading to *AFRICA* and the *INDIES* from the Memorial given in against
Z z z their

their taking Subfcriptions at *Hamburgh* by Sir *Paul Ricaut* his Majefties Refident there, to their laft *Addrefs* fent up to his Majeftie in *December* 1699. Faithfully extracted from the Companies Books. Printed *Anno* 1700 *8vo*. p. 56. [*Ex dono Rev.* Roberti Watts, *L. L. B.*]

A *Letter* to a Member of Parliament occafioned by the growing Poverty of the Nation from the Want and Decay of TRADE, and wrong Management thereof: With fome Overtures for encreafing and promoting the One, and rectifying the Other. *Edinburgh*, Printed in the Year 1700, *4to*. p. 22.

The Confeffions, Behaviour and Dying Speech of the ten PYRATES at *Execution-Dock*, on *Friday* the twelfth of *July*, 1700 Attefted by R. *Wykes* Ordinary. *London*, Printed for E. *Mallet*. [Half-fheet.]

1702.
1 *Anna.*

An Exhortation to thofe *Redeemed Slaves* who came in a folemn Proceffion to St. *Paul's Cathedral* on the 11th of *March* 1701-2. to give Thanks to God for their Deliverance out of their *Captivity* at *Machanefs*. By *W. SHERLOCK*, D. D. Dean of St. *Paul's*. *London*, Printed for *William Rogers*. 1702. *8vo*. p. 18.

The Sailors *Groans*, or a fhort but faithful Relation of many of the horrid Abufes and Oppreffions the *English Seamen* lay under the late War, none of them ever before made publick: With fome Propofals for encreafing their Pay and encouraging of them; that our *Fleet* may be always well Mann'd and in a Readinefs, and our *Seamen* well ufed that the King and Country may be well ferved, &c. By a *Sailor*. Humbly recommended to the Confideration of both Houfes of Parliament. *London*, Printed in the Year 1700. *8vo*. p. 29.

A Copy of the Petition of *WILLIAM FREEMAN*, Efq; on behalf of himfelf and others againft Col. *CHRISTOPH. CODRINGTON* Governour of the *Leeward Iflands*. Prefented to the *House of Commons* the 19th of *February*, 1701. [Containing a Complaint of their being difpoffefs'd of a great part of their Eftates in the faid Iflands, by the Colonies Mifgovernment: With fome Account of the Complaint of Mr. *Freeman* and Mr. *Mead* to his late Majefty in *Council*, and the *Proceedings* thereon.] Printed in the Year. 1702. *4to*. p. 13. [*Ex Dono Reverendi* Roberti Watts, *L. L. B.*]

A Copy of the *Articles* exhibited by Mr. *FREEMAN* to the Houfe of Commons againft Col. *CODRINGTON*, and fome Obfervations and Re-

Remarks in Anſwer to the ſame [containing the 15 Articles, and particular Anſwers to each of them, with Atteſtations of the Colonel's good Conduct and Government, from the Lieutenant Governour and Members of the Council and Repreſentatives of Nevis. Dated *July* 9th, 1701. Printed in the Year 1702. 4*to*. *p*. 36. [*Ex Dono Rev* Roberti Watts, *L. L. B.*]

News from *Penſilvania*, or a brief Narrative of ſeveral remarkable Paſſages in the Government of the QUAKERS of that Province touching their Proceedings in their pretended Court of Juſtice, their Way of Trade and Commerce, with Remarks and Obſervations upon the whole. Publiſhed by the Author of *the Pilgrims Progreſs* [viz. *Francis Bugg*.] Together with a *Poſtſcript* containing a Collection of ſeveral blaſphemous Paſſages taken out of ſome noted *Quakers* Books. *London*. 1703. *p*. 36. [*Ex dono Rev.* Rob. Watts, L. L. B.] 1703. 2 *Anna.*

ENGLAND's State Diſtempers traced from their Originals; with proper Remedies and Means to make her Vertuous and Proſperous. Humbly preſented by *JAMES WHISTON*. The Miſmanagement in TRADE diſcovered and adapt Methods to preſerve and improve it with an *Appendix*, ſhewing the Decreaſe of *Proteſtants* in *Europe*. 1704. 4*to*. *p*. 44 and 32. 1704. 3 *Anna.*

An Introductory Diſcourſe to *Catechetical Inſtruction*, ſhewing how the ſame may be made both practicable and eaſie, by being digeſted into ſuch a Method as will render it as well agreeable as profitable both to the Catechiſt and Catechumen, in a *Paſtoral Letter* to the *Clergy* of *Maryland*; enforcing the Duty, and by an eaſie Method accompanied with a ſuitable Proviſion of Books, facilitating to them the fundamental Work of *Catechiſing*; containing a Courſe of *Catechiſing* to be obſerved in the *Plantations*, conſiſting of Books more particularly fitted for the Uſe of three ſeveral Claſſes of *Catechumens* there, purſuant to the Reſolutions made to that purpoſe the 2d day of the Viſitation in *Maryland*, *May* 24. 1700. With a *Preface* to the Reverend the the *Parochial Clergy* and *Schoolmaſters* in this Kingdom. By *THOMAS BRAY*, D. D. *London*, Printed by *J. Brudenell* in *Little-Britain* for *William Hawes* at the *Roſe* in *Ludgateſtreet*. 1704. 8*vo* [*Ex dono Rev.* Roberti Watts, L. L. B]

An Addreſs to the Officers and Seamen in Her *Majeſty's* Royal Navy. By the Author of the *Seaman's Monitor*. *London*, Printed by *Joſeph Downing*. [Half-ſheet 4*to*]

Quæſita à D. MAIGROT *& Reſponſa data à* S. Congregatione Rom. Univerſalis Inquiſitionis, *& à* CLEMENTE XI. *anno* 1704 *opprobata*

de

de Cultu Christiano inter Evenenses. [*Cadterne Sinierum. Lon.* MDCCXIII. *N° 9*]

Of the Propagation of the Gospel in Foreign Parts. A Sermon preached at St. Mary le Bow, *Feb.* 16. 170$\frac{4}{5}$ before the Society Incorporated for that purpose, exhorting all Persons in their Stations to assist so glorious a Design. By the Right Reverend Father in God *JOHN* Lord Bishop of *Litchfield* and *Coventry.* To which is annexed an Abstract of the Reverend Mr. *Stubb's* Account of the Society, continued to the Year 1705. *London,* Printed by *Joseph Downing.* 1705. 4*to.* p. 32.

An Account of the Propagation of the Gospel in Foreign Parts continued to the Year of Our Lord 1705. Representing what the Society established in *England* by *Royal Charter* hath done since their Incorporation *June* 16. 1701. in her *Majesties Plantations, Colonies* and *Factories;* as also what they design to do upon further Encouragement from their own Members and other well disposed Christians, either by Annual Subscriptions, present Benefactions or future Legacies: To which is annexed the Order of the Societies Thanks of *Feb.* 4. 1703. to the *Rev.* Mr. *Stubbs* for the Pains he hath taken in preparing it. *London,* Printed by *Joseph Downing.* 1705. [1 Sheet *Fol.*]

An *Act* for the better Ordering and Governing the *Watermen* and *Lightermen* upon the River of *Thames, A* in. 4 & 5 Annæ *Reginæ. London.* By the Queens Printers. 1705. *Fol.*

An *Act* for making the River *Stower* Navigable from the Town of *Manningtree* in the County of *Essex,* to the Town *Sudbury* in the County of *Suffolk, Anno* 4 & 5 Annæ *Reginæ. London,* by the Queens Printers. 1705. *Fol.*

Epistola Dua D. B. PICTETI *Pastoris & Professoris in Theologiâ Genevæ : Una missa ad Societatem de Propagando Evangelio in Partibus Exteris altera ad* D. Johannem Chamberlaine, *ejusdem Societatis Secretarium. Dat.* Geneva, 3°. Decemb. 1706. [*At the End of the Relation de la Societé etablie pour la Propagation de l' Evangile,* &c. 1708.]

An *Abstract* of the marvellous Footsteps of *Divine Providence* in the Building of a very large *Hospital,* or rather a Spacious *Colledge* for charitable and excellent Uses: And in the maintaining of many Orphans and other poor People at *Glaucha* near *Hall* in the Dominions of the King of *Prussia* Related by the Reverend *Augustus Hermannus Franck,* Professor of Divinity and Minister of *Glaucha* aforesaid. With a *Preface* written by *Josiah Woodward,* D. D.

And

And recommended by another eminent Divine of the City of *London*. Printed for *H. Burrough*. 1706. 12°. *p.* 64. [*Ex dono Rev.* Roberti Watts, L. L. B.]

A Dialogue between a *JAPONESE* and a *FORMOSAN* about some Points of the *Religion* of the Time. By G. P———n———r. *London*, Printed for *Bernard Lintott*. 1707. 8vo. *p.* 41.

1707. 6 *Anna*.

A Narrative of the Imprisonment of two Non-Conformist Ministers, and Prosecution or Trial of One of them, for preaching a Sermon in the City of *New-York*. With a *Postscript* or Conclusion for the Information of *America*; containing Copies of these following Particulars : 1. The Act of Assembly of *New-York*, for settling a *Ministry*, and raising a Maintenance for them, only in some particular places of that Government. 2. A *Copy* of that Act of Parliament of *England* for punishing Governours of Plantations in *England* for Crimes committed by them in the Plantations. 3. A Copy of such Licenses as are granted by Lord *Cornbury* to some *Ministers*. 4. An Account of the exorbitant Charge of the Confinement and Prosecution, for preaching two *Sermons* in *New-York* Government. 5. A *Copy* of Mr. *Makemies* Certificate from a Court of *Virginia*, And of his *Letter* to the Lord *Cornbury*, dated *Boston*, *July* 28. 1707. Printed at *Boston* in *New England*, and Reprinted at *London*. 1708. 8vo. *p.* 48.

1708. 7 *Anna*.

A *Sermon* preached before *the Society for the Propagation of the Gospel in Foreign Parts* at the *Parish Church* of *St. Mary le Bow*, *Feb.* 20. 170$\frac{7}{8}$. [Representing earnestly how great the Work they were engaged in was, and how few the Labourers were.] By *WILLIAM STANLEY*, D.D. *Dean of St.* A saph. *London*, Printed by *J. Downing*. 1708. 4to. *p.* 26.

A *Token* for *Mariners*; containing many famous and wonderful Instances of God's Providence in *Sea Dangers* and *Deliverances* in mercifully preserving the Lives of his poor Creatures, when in humane probability at the point of perishing by *Shipwreck*, *Famine*, or other Accidents. Much enlarged, with the Addition of many new Relations mostly attested by the Persons themselves. Also the *Sea Man's Preacher*, being a Sermon on the right Improvement of such Mercies, and Prayers for *Sea-Men* on all occasions. *London*, Printed for *H. N.* 1708. *p.* 103, and 147. [*Ex dono Rev.* Roberti Watts, L. L. B.]

Relation de la Societe etablie pour la Propagation de l'Evangile dans les Pais Etrangers par les Lettres Patentes du Roy Guillaume III. *Ou l'on voit les Methodes & les progres de cette Societé avec l'Esperance qu'il y a de nouveaux*

A a a a   *progres*

progres fous l'heureux Regne de fa Majeftè la Reine Anne *traduite de l' Anglois & fuivie de* trois Sermons *faits fur la Converfion des Gentils & prononcez dans l' Eglife de la* Savoye *par* CLAUDE GROTESTE DE LA MOTHE *l'un de fes Miniftres.* A Rotterdam *chez* Abraham Acher. 8vo. 1708. p. 255. *Avec une Preface fur le meme fujet.* p. 80. [*Ex dono Rev.* Rob. Watts, *L.L.B.*

1709.
8 Anna.
JOH. ALPHONSI TURRETINI *Paftoris S. Theol. & Hift. Ecclefiaft. Profefforu Academiæ p. t. Rectoris,* De varijs Chriftianæ Doctrinæ Fatis, *Oratio Academica, dicta ftatis* Academiæ Genevenfis *Solemnibus xj.* Maij, *Anno* MDCCVIII. *Cui addita eft* GULIELMI NICHOLSII *Epiftola, qua juffu* Societatis de Evangelio in exteris propagando *&c.* gratias egit C.J. Alphonfo Turretino *pro Oratione de varijs* Chriftianæ Doctrinæ Fatis *ei nuncupatâ.* In Latin *and* Englifh. London, Printed for W. Taylor. 1709. 4to. p. 42. [*Ex dono Rev.* Roberti Watts, *L.L.B.*]

Lettre a un Prelat fur un Ecrit Intitulè Lettre de M. le Cardinal de Tournon, Patriarche d' Antioche, *&c.* a M. Maigrot Eveque de Conon, *An.* 1709. 8vo. p. 39.

A *Sermon* preached before *the Society for the Propagation of the Gofpel in Foreign Parts* at the *Parifh Church* of *St. Mary le Bow,* on *Friday Febr.* 18. 170⅝. [Reprefenting the Obligations that lie on all Chriftians in every Capacity to promote the *Propagation* of the *Gofpel,* and fhewing how they may in their feveral Capacities be affifting thereunto.] By *WILLIAM* Lord Bifhop of *CHESTER.* London, Printed by *Jofeph Downing* for *Ann Speed.* 1709. 4to. p. 25.

A Letter from a *Member* of the *Society for promoting Chriftian Knowledge in* London to his Friend in the Country newly chofen a *Correfponding Member* of that Society. London, Printed by *J. Downing* in *Bartholomew-Clofe* near *Weft-Smithfield.* 12°. 1709. p. 28.

A Dialogue between a *North-Britain* concerned in the FISHING TRADE. Fol. 1709. 1 Sheet.

Advertifement from the *Charitable Fund* intended to be eftablifhed in London, by voluntary Gifts and Loans of Money, to relieve and fupport poor SEAMENS Families, and other neceffitous Perfons, not otherwife provided for; by giving them Money, or lending it upon Pledges without any Intereft or Charges whatfoever, and employing fuch as want Work. Dat. *Apr.* 28. 1709. London, 1709. Half-fheet. 4to.

The

The Wonders of God in the Deep. Shewing his peculiar Providence over those that are concerned at Sea. In a *Sermon* preach'd at *Deptford* before the Rt Honourable the Corporation of the *Trinity-House* on *Trinity Monday.* 1709. Published at the Request of that Honourable Body. By R. *WELTON,* D.D. Rector of *St. Mary White Chapel. London,* Printed for *S. Manship.* 4*to. p.* 28.

The great Advantage of Navigation and Commerce to any Nation or People: Represented in a Sermon preach'd at *Deptford* before the Right Honourable the *Corporation* of the *Trinity-House* on *Trinity Monday.* 1710. Published at the Request of that Honourable Body. By R. *WELTON,* D.D. Rector of *St. Mary White-Chapel. London,* Printed for *S. Manship.* 1710. 4*to. p.* 19. 1710. 9 *Annæ.*

A Letter from an *Old Whig* in *Town* to a *Modern Whig* in the *Country* upon the late Expedition to *Canada.* Subscribed *X. Z.* dated *Octob.* 23. 1711. *London,* Printed and Sold by *J. Morphew.* 4*to. p.* 8. 1711. 10 *Annæ.*

An Answer to the Reasons against an *African Company.* Humbly submitted to the Consideration of the Patriots of *Great-Britain* in this present Parliament assembled. *London,* Printed in the Year 1711. 8*vo. p.* 31.

A Letter to a Gentleman concerning the SOUTH SEA TRADE. Printed for *J. Morphew* near *Stationers-Hall.* 1711. *Fol.* 1 Sheet.

An Account of the TRADE in INDIA [*viz.* the *East-Indies.*] Containing Rules for good Government in *Trade, Price Courants* and *Tables,* with Descriptions of *Fort St. George, Acheen, Malacca, Condore, Canton Anjengo, Muskat, Gombroon, Surat, Goa, Carwar, Telichery, Panola, Calicut,* the *Cape of Good Hope* and *St. Helena,* their Inhabitants, Customs, Religion, Government, Animals, Fruits, *&c.* To which is added, An Account of the Managements of the *Dutch* in their Affairs in *India.* By *CHARLES LOCKYER. London,* Printed for the Author, and Sold by *Samuel Crouch* at the Corner of *Popes-Head-Alley* in *Cornhill.* 1711. 8*vo. p.* 340. [*Ex dono* Thomæ Granger, *Generosi.*]

An Account of the Life, Birth, Death, *&c.* of Mr. *THOMAS MAY,* a notorious Traitor executed for being in the *French King's* Service by Sea, on *Wednesday* the 14th of *March,* 1710-11. at *Execution-Dock.* With the Manner of his Trial at a *High Court of Admiralty* on *Monday* the 19th of *February* last. As also his Dying Speech, *&c. London,* Printed by *J. Smith.* 1711. 8*vo. p.* 8.

A

A Copy of the Order of the Queen's most Excellent Majesty in Council at the Court at *Windsor* the 1st of *Octob.* 1711. that Mr. *ISTURMA* Mode such other *Chaplain* as the Right Reverend the Lord Bishop of *London* shall recommend to Her Majesty be forthwith sent to *Lyborne* in such Manner and with such Circumstances as the Reverend Mr. *Basil Kennet* was sent, and that Directions be given to Mr. *Molsworth* Her Majesties Envoy at the Court of *Florence* accordingly.

1712. The Breach of *Publick Faith* exemplified, Or the *Contract of Marriage* between
11 *Anno.* L E *W* I S XIV. of *France* and the most *Serene* I N F A N T A of *Spain*,
eldest Daughter of the Catholick King : Concluded the 7th of *Novemb.* 1659.
Together with the *French King*'s Power to *Cardinal Mazarine* to treat of the
said *Marriage*. 2. His Ratification of the said Treaty. 3. His Mandate to
the *Parliament* of *Paris*, to enregister his *Contract of Marriage*. 4. The Extract of the *Records* of Parliament. And 5. the *Solemn Oath* taken by that
Prince for the Observation of the said Contract. *London*, Printed for *A. Bald-*
win. 1712. *8vo. p. 23.*

A *Letter* from a Merchant in *Amsterdam* to a Friend in *London*, about the
South Sea Trade. *London*, Printed and Sold by *John Baker*. MDCCXII.
8vo. p. 24.

The History of the Barbarous Cruelties and Massacres committed by the
D U T C H in the *East-Indies*. 1. The Massacre of the *English* at *Amboyna*,
Batavia, *Macassar*, and the taking, burning, and destroying several *English*
Ships in the Streights of *Malacca*. 2. The Massacre of the *Orankeys* and
Nobles of *Poleroon* for a pretended Conspiracy of Massacring the *Dutch*. 3. How
the King of *Candi* being in a Confederacy with the *Dutch* made War with the
Portuguese. And 4. Some Difference happening between the Old and Young
Kings of *Bantam*, the *Dutch* under Pretence of Assisting the Young King
destroyed the Old King's Forces, &c. By R. H A L L, B. D. formerly of
Queen's-Colledge, *Oxford*. Printed and Sold by the Booksellers of *London* and
Westminster. 1712. *8vo. p. 236.* [*Ex dono Reverendi* Roberti Watts,
L. L. B.]

O NOVO TESTAMENTO *isto he, Todos os Sacrosanctos Livros e escritos*
Evangelicos e Apostolicos de Novo Concerto do Nosso Fiel Senhor Salvador e Redemp-
tor JESU CHRISTO *Traduzido em* Portuguez *pelo Padre* JOAM FERREI-
RA A D'ALMEIDA *Ministro Pregador do Sancto Evangelho com todas as Li-*
cenzas necessarias. Em Amsterdam. *Par* Joam Crellius, 1712. *i. e.* The
NEW TESTAMENT, that is all the Holy Books Evangelical and Aposto-
lical

lical Writings of the *New Teſtament* of our Lord Saviour and Redeemer JESUS CHRIST. Tranſlated into *Portugueſe* by the Father *JOHN FERREIRA A D'ALMEIDA*, Miniſter, Preacher of the Holy Goſpel, with all the neceſſary Licences. At *Amſterdam*. By *John Crellius.* 1712. *8vo. p.* 425.

A ORDEM DA SALVACAŌ ou a Doɛtrina Chriſtiana brevemente emperguntas e Repoſtas declarada e provada com Principaes Teſtemunhos da Eſcritura Sagrada, Juntamente com albūas Oracoens e Cantigas. Tranquebar *em India Oriental na Coſta de Coromandel, na Eſtampa dos* Miſſionarios *del Rey de* Dennemark. *i. e. The Order of Salvation,* or the Chriſtian Doɛtrine briefly declared and proved in Queſtions and Anſwers : With the principal Proofs from Holy Scripture : Together with ſome Prayers and Hymns. Printed at *Tranquebar* in the *Eaſt-Indies* on the Coaſt of *Cormandel* in the Printing-Houſe of the *Miſſionaries* of the K. of *Denmark.* 1712. 12°. *p.* 44.

MANUAL ou Breve Inſtruɛcatiō que ſerve por Uſo D'as CRIANCAS *que Apprendem Ler e comecam rezar nas Eſcholas Portuguezas, que ſaō em* India *Oriental ; e eſpecialemente na Coſta Dos* Malabaros *que ſe Chama* Cormandel. *Anno* 1713. *i. e.* A ſhort Inſtruɛtion which ſerves for the Uſe of the Children that learn to read, &c. in the *Portugueſe* Schools in the *Eaſt-Indies,* and particularly on the Coaſt of the *Malabarians* called *Coromandel.* 1713. 12°. *pag.* 47. 1713. 12 *Anna.*

An Abſtraɛt of the Account of the Proceedings of the INQUISITION in *PORTUGAL*. *London,* Printed for *John Baker* at the *Black-Boy* in *Pater-Noſter Row.* 1713. *8vo. p.* 8, and 35.

By the Queen, A PROCLAMATION for putting in Execution the Laws and Statutes of this Realm for the preventing the *Exportation* of *Wooll, Wooll-Fells, Woollen-Yarn, Mortlings, Shorlings, Wooll-Flocks, Fullers-Earth* and *Fulling-Clay.* Given at Our Court at *Windſor* the 18th day of *Oɛtober,* 1713. in the Twelfth Year of our Reign. *London,* Printed by *John Baskett,* Printer to the Queen's moſt Excellent Majeſty, and by the Aſſigns of *Thomas Newcomb* and *Henry Hills* deceaſed. 1713. *Fol.* On a Broad-ſide.

An Account of the Methods uſed by the *Dutch* in propagating the Goſpel in their Faɛtories in the *Eaſt-Indies,* in a Letter from *HADRIANUS RELANDUS,* Profeſſor of   in the Univerſity of *Utrecht.* Dated 3 Cal. *Maij,* 1713. Together with Claſſical Aɛts for the *Comforters of the Sick* and *Chaplains* to the *Eaſt-Indies.* Tranſlated out of *Dutch* into *Engliſh* [MS. 4*to.*]

Bbbb   *Declaratio*

APPENDIX

Declaratio & Sponsio de Juribus & Privilegiis Mercatorum Britannicorum in Regno Siciliæ facta Ultrajecti Die, 25. Februarij, O. S. & 8 Martij, N. S. Anno 17$\frac{12}{13}$. A Declaration and Engagement concerning the Rights and Privileges of the *British* Merchants in the Kingdom of *Sicily*, made at *Utrecht* the 25th of *February*, O. S. and 8th of *March*, N. S. 17$\frac{12}{13}$. By Her Majesties special Command. *London*, Printed by *John Baskett*, Printer to the Queen's most Excellent Majesty and by the Assigns of *Thomas Newcomb* and *Henry Hills* deceased. 1713. 4*to.*

Reglement Provisional du Commerce dans les Pays bas Espagnols fait a Utrecht le $\frac{15}{26}$ *Jour de Juil'et.* 1713. A Provisional Regulation of *Trade* in the *Spanish Low-Countries* made at *Utrecht* the $\frac{15}{26}$ day of *July*, 1713. By Her *Majesties Special Command. London*, Printed by *John Baskett*, Printer to the Queens most Excellent Majesty and by the Assigns of *Thomas Newcomb* and *Henry Hills* deceased. 1713. 4°. *p.* 16.

1714.
? Annæ.
Four small Tracts, *viz.* 1.[1] A brief Discourse concerning the *Unlawfulness* of the *Common-Prayer Worship*, and of the *Laying the Hand on*, and *Kissing the Book* in *Swearing.* [Supposed to be wrote by *INCREASE MATHER* of *New-England*.] 2. A brief Discourse of the *Lawfulness* of *Worshipping God* by the *Common-Prayer*; in Answer to the Objections against *Common-Prayer Worship*. By the Right Reverend *JOHN WILLIAMS*, late Lord Bishop of *Chichester*. 3. Some *Remarks* on a pretended Answer to a *Discourse concerning the Common-Prayer Worship*: With an Exhortation to the *Churches* of *New-England*, to hold fast the Profession of their Faith without wavering. By *INCREASE MATHER*, D. D. 4. A Reply to *D. MATHER'S* Remarks. By *GERSHOM RAWLINS*. *London*, Printed by *Joseph Downing*. 1714. 12*o.*

Propagation of the Gospel in the East; being a further Account of the Success of the *Danish Missionaries* sent to the *East-Indies* for the Conversion of the Heathens in *Malabar*. Extracted from the Letters of the said Missionaries, and brought down to the Beginning of the Year 1713. Part III. Wherein besides a Narrative of the Progress of the Christian Religion in those Parts, with the Helps and Impediments which hitherto have occurr'd, several Hints are inserted concerning the Religion of the *Malabarians*, their *Priests, Poets* and other *Literati*, and what may be expected from the *Printing Press* lately set up at *Tranquebar*. *London*, Printed and Sold by *J. Downing* in *Bartholomew-Close* near *West Smithfield*. 1714. 8*vo. p.* 50.

POST-

POSTSCRIPT.

Atalogus Plantarum quæ in Insulâ Jamaicâ *sponte proveniunt vel vulgò coluntur cum earundem Synomymis & locis Natalibus ; adjectis aliis quibusdam quæ in Insulis* Maderæ, Barbados, Nevis *&* Sancti Christophori *nascuntur seu Prodromi Historiæ Naturalis* Jamaicæ *Pars Prima. Autore* HANS SLOANE, *M. D. Coll. Med. Lond. Necnon. Soc. Reg. Lond. Soc.* Londini, *Impensis* Dan. Brown *ad insigne Cygni & Bibliorum extra Portam vulgo dictam* Temple-Bar 1696. 8vo. p. 232. *Cum Indice Verborum.* [*Ex Dono Authoris.*]

1696.
8 Will.

A Voyage to the Islands *Madera, Barbadoes, Nevis, St. Christophers, and Jamaica,* &c. By *H A N S S L O A N E,* M. D. London, Printed by B. M. for the Author. 1707. Fol.

1707.
6 Annæ.

La Liturgia Yrglesa o Ex Libro de Oracion Commun, &c. el Londres. 1707. 8vo. [*Ex Dono D.* Alvarado *Traductoris.*]

Compendium Historiæ Reformationis a Zuinglij *&* Lutheri *Temporibus ad nostra usq; Tempora deductæ Auctore* D. JOHAN. ANGELO BERNIERA *in* Italica *Lingua Concionatore.* Londini, *apud* Isaac Vaillant. 1707. 120. *p.* 222.

The *C A R O L I N A Calendar* for 4 Years ; beginning 1712. and ending 1716. By *J O H N N O R R I S.* Lond. 1711. [*Ex Dono Authoris.*]

1711.
10 Annæ.

Historia Collationum publicarum inter Professores Reformatos *&* Catholicos *in Academiâ* Heidelbergensi *coram illustri Auditorio habitarum & juxta cum Animadversionibus necessariis ad* R. P. MELCHIORIS KIRCHNERI. S. I. *Appendicem secundi Generis ; Edita a* Reformatis *Academiæ* Palatinæ *Professoribus Theologiæ* LUDOVICO CHRISTIANO MIEGIO & JOHANNE CHRISTIANO NIRCHMEJERO *Anno* 1711. 4to. p. 144. [*Ex dono Authorum.*]

Entretiens sur la Religion par Monsf. BASNAGE *en* 2 Tomes. A Rotterdam *chez* Abraham Acher. 1711. *pag.* 515 & 459. besides the Tables. [*Ex dono Authoris.*]

THE

AN
INDEX
OF THE
MATTERS, PERSONS and PLACES
Contain'd in the preceding
CATALOGUE.

N. B. *The* First *Number denotes the* Page, *and the* Second, *the* Article *or* Paragraph *in the* Page.

The INDEX.

A D D E R-

The INDEX.

The INDEX.

Dddd

The INDEX.

AL.

The INDEX.

The INDEX.

The INDEX.

The INDEX.

The INDEX.

The INDEX.

Ffff

and France, A. D. 1667. 250, 1, 2. Spain, A. D. 1608. 51, 3. January 13. 1648. at Munster 245, 7. Several INDIAN Kings and Queens and England, May 29. 1677. The Great MOGUL and England. 260, 4. PORTUGAL and England, Jan. 29. 1642. 87, 4. France, March 31. 1667. 121, 3. SAVOY and England, September 19. 1669. 123, 4. and France at Ryswick, A. D. 1697. 173, 4. SAXONY and the Emperor of Germany. 81, 3. SPAIN and England for restraining of Depredations and settling of Peace in America, A. D. 1670. 252, 2. France, A. D. 1598. 39, 3. Holland, January 13. 1608. 51, 3. January 13. 1648. 243, 7. SWEDEN and Denmark by the Mediation of England, France and Holland at Roskild, A. D. 1659. 246, 3. England with relation to Commerce in America, May 19. 1654. 106, 2. TRIPOLI and England, March 5. 1675-6. 128, * 3.

ARUNDEL (Thomas, Baron of Warder) an Account of a Discovery towards the Northward of Virginia by Capt. George Waymouth, A. D. 1605. employed by him.
46, 1

St. ASAPH (Bishops of) [See Beveridge and Fleetwood.]

ASCALONA (the Bishop of) his Act of Appeal, A. D. 1710.
204, 4

ASH (John) his Account of the Affairs in Carolina, A. D. 1703.
186, 3

ASHE (Sir Joseph, Baronet) an Account of his Proceedings in conjunction with several other English Commissioners, Instructors for the East-India Company, with the Commissioners Instructors for the Dutch East-India Company, A. D. 1685.
144, 5

ASHE (Simeon) an Account of his Publishing in Conjunction with Mr. William Rathband, an Account of the New Church Way in New-England, wrote by Mr. John Ball of Whitmore, A. D. 1637.
90, 4

ASHBY (Sir John) an Account of the English Fleets taking of Cork in Ireland under his and some others Command, in Septemb. 1690. 151, 7

ASHLEY (Anthony Lord Ashley) A Copy of the Charter that was granted to him and other Proprietors of Carolina, by Charles II. King of England, A. D. 1662.
113, 4
ASH-

The INDEX

ASTRO

A 2-

The INDEX.

labar

The INDEX.

The INDEX.

The INDEX.

Hhhh   BAU-

The INDEX.

The INDEX.

B L A C K-

The INDEX.

BOS-

The INDEX.

                                                                 B U G-

The INDEX.

Porto

C A M-

CAMPANELLA (*Thomas*) his Discourse concerning the *Spanish Monarchy* in *Latin*, A. D. 1653. 105, 2. In *English*, A. D. 1654. *Ibid.* 5

CAMPEACHY (the Bay of in the *West-Indies*) Captain *Dampier's* Description thereof and the Parts adjacent. 126, & 1

CANADA (in *North America*,) an Account of the *French* Voyages thither and *Plantations* there, A. D. 1564. 17, 3. By S. *Chaplaine*, 1603. 44, 6. By Monf. *de Monts*, 1603. 45, 1. The Baron *Labontan's* Account of the Attempts of the *French* and *Indians* there upon *New-England* and *New-York*, &c. A. D. 1690. 152, 6. A full Account thereof, and of the Repulse they met with : Given by Col. *Reyard* and Lieutenant Col. *Ludwick*, who attended the Governour of *New-York* during the whole Expedition : With several Matters relating thereto. 160, 1. An Account of its State and Strength given by two *Dutchmen* who had been a long time Prisoners there, A. D. 169?. *Ibid.* A Geographical Description and Natural History thereof ; with Remarks upon their Government and the Interest of the *English* and *French* there in their Commerce, and a full View of the Religion and strange Opinions of the Natives there, and of the various Adventures between the *French* and the *Iroquese* Confederates of *England* from 1683 to 1694. by the Baron *Labontan*. 186, 5. His Account of the unfortunate Expedition of the *English* and *Iroquese* in marching by Land to attack the *French* Colony at *Quebec*, A. D. 1690. 152, 6. and 153, 2. and 155, 7. Two Letters giving an Account of the Expedition made thither by the *English*, A. D. 1711. 271, 3. and 213, 4. An Account of the four Kings thereof coming into *England*, A. D. 1710. and of their Proposals to Queen *Anne*, &c. 206, 4, 5, 6, 7

CANAAN (the Land of) an Account of the Travels of four *English* Merchants of *Aleppo* with the Chaplain thither, A. D. 1600, &c. 233, 3

CANARIES (the Island of.) Sir *William Monson's* Answer to a Project of the *Hollanders* for surprising of it, A. D. 1599. 40, 3

CANDI (the King of in the *East-Indies* ;) An Account of his being in Confederacy with the *Dutch* and making War on the *Portugueses*. 272, 4

CANDIDIUS (*George*, a *Dutch* Minister in *Formosa*) his Account of the Island of *Formosa*, &c. 85, 4

CAN-

The INDEX.

CAP.

The INDEX.

CA-

The INDEX.

CAR.

it offered to the Confideration of both Houfes of Parliament. *Ibid.* 5. The Reprefentation and Addrefs of feveral of the Members of the Affembly returned for *Colleton* County, and other Inhabitants of the Province to the *Lords Proprietors* thereupon. *Ib.* 6. The humble Addrefs of the Lords Spiritual and Temporal to the Queen, with Her moft gracious Anfwer thereunto. *Ib.* 6. A Vindication of the Proceedings of the *Lords Proprietors* hereon. 195, 1. Another ACT paffed in the Affembly on *Novemb.* 4. 1704. for the Eftablifhment of Religious Worfhip there according to the Church of *England*, and for the erecting of Churches for the Publick Worfhip of God, and alfo for the Maintenance of Minifters and the Building convenient Houfes for them. 192, 4. The State of Affairs there, A. D. 1703. Given by Mr. *John Afh*, Gent. fent by feveral of the Inhabitants to deliver their Reprefentation thereof, and to feek Redrefs from the Lords Proprietors of that Province ; together with an Account of his Reception by the Lord *Granville* their Prefident, *June* 26. 1703. 186, 3. An Account of the *Indians* bordering thereon by *J. Lawfon.* 181, 8. By Dr. *Le Jau.* 209, 5. An Account of their Method of Dreffing of *Buck* and *Doe Skins.* 153, 7. An Account of the Invafion made by the *French* and *Spaniards* on *South Carolina*, A. D. 1706. with the Difappointment and Difgrace they met with in it. 195, 2

CARTAGENA (the Province of in *South America*) an Account of the 17 Years Travels of *Peter de Cieza* through it and other Provinces in *America*, &c. A. D. 1541, &c. 13, 4. The Travels of Mr. *Gage* through it. 96, 1. and 175, 2. An Account of Vice-Admiral *Nevil's* plundering it A. D. 1697. 169, 4

CARTER (*Richard*) his and anothers Scheme of an effectual Method to prevent the Exportation of Wool, *A. D.* 1713. 219, 3

CARTER (*William*) an Abftract of his Proceedings againft Tranfportation of *Wool* ; being a Plea to fome Objections urged againft him, *A. D.* 1694. 162, 6. Several remarkable Paffages extracted from thence. 119, 3. 124, 2, 3, 4. 128, 2, 5. 141, 7. 142, 1. 145, 3

CARTERET (Sir *George*) the Copy of the firft *Charter* granted by King *Charles* II. to him and feveral other Proprietors of *Carolina*, A. D. 1662. 113, 4

CARTHAGENA : See *Cartagena.*

CAS-

CA-

The INDEX.

The INDEX.

The INDEX.

CHER-

The INDEX.

CHIL-

CLAYTON (John, Rector of Crofton or Wakefield in Yorkshire) his Account of the Soil of Virginia, and planting of Tobacco there, with the draining of Swamps, &c. With a Description of the several Species of Birds, which he observed there. Published in the Philosophical Transactions of December 1693. 158, 6. His Continuation thereof, giving a short Description of the Beasts and Serpents thereof, Published in the Philosophical Transactions of May 1694. 164, 2

CLEMENT VII. Pope of Rome; Ferdinand Cortez his Account of his Transactions among the West-Indians, with an Epistle Dedicatory of Doctor Severgnanus to him A. D. 1524. 9, 1

CLEMENT VIII. Pope of Rome; His Bull, ordering that Friars shall not be made Provincials in the Indies, except they were born in or made free in those Provinces, dated March 4th. 1600. 41, 2. His Orders relating to the Arrival of the Regulars in Japan and the adjacent Islands of China and the East-Indies to preach the Gospel. Dated Dec. 12th. 1600. Ibid. 3. His Bull for approving the Order of Jesuits established in the Provinces of Peru, with the Grant of several Indulgences. Dated June 22. 1603. 44, 9

CLEMENT XI. Pope of Rome; his Bull concerning the Proceedings of the Jesuits in China delivered to the Bishop of Conon, Apostolick Vicar at Fokien in China by the Cardinal Tournon, dated June 20th 1702. 202, 6. and 204, 3. A Letter wrote to him by the said Bishop at his Return from China, dated from Galloway in Ireland, May 4th, 1708. 203, 1. An Account of his Orders to curb the insolent Prevarication of the Jesuits there. 204, 1. His Answer to the Queries of Monsr. Maigrot the aforesaid Bishop of Conon, relating to the Christian Worship among the Chineses, A. D. 1704. 267, 6

CLERKE (Col. one of the Commanders in Chief of all the Forces belonging to the English Parliament) the Original Articles of Agreement made between him and Sir John Greenvile, Governour of the Islands of St. Mary's and Agnes in Scilley on the Behalf of King Charles II. touching the Rendition of the Islands thereof; with all their Castles, &c. A. D. 1651. 120, 6

CLERKE (Francis, Dean of the Court of Arches) his Account of the Practice of the Court of Admiralty. 250, 4

CLIF-

The INDEX.

The INDEX.

The INDEX.

The INDEX.

The INDEX.

Sums

The INDEX.

R r r r

The INDEX.

CON-

The INDEX.

The INDEX.

The INDEX.

The INDEX.

The INDEX.

of his second Voyage towards the Coasts of *Spain*, A. D. 1588. and his third Voyage toward the *West-Indies*, A. D. 1589. 30, 7. An Account of his Voyage to *Spain* in Queen *Elizabeth*'s Ship the *Garland*, with 7 other Ships of his own and his Friends, *A. D.* 1591. 33, 2. An Account of his 7th Voyage towards the *Spanish West-Indies*, and his Descent on *Hispaniola*, *Jamaica*, &c. *A. D.* 1593. 34, 2. An Account of his 8th Voyage towards the Coasts of *America*, and of his engaging with *Spanish Carricks*, A. D. 1594. *Ibid.* 4. An Account of his Voyage to the Island of *Puerto Rico* to intercept the Carrick going to the *East-Indies*, as taken out of the printed Copy, published by Dr. *Layfield*, Chaplain in that Expedition, *A. D.* 1596.   37, 6

C U N N I N G H A M (*William*) his *Cosmography*, *Geography* and *Hydrography*, A. D. 1559.   16, 6

C U R O (Don *Ignatius Peris*, Governour of St. *Domingo* in the *West-Indies*) the Articles between him and *Rob. Wilmott*, Esq; and *Luke Lillingston*, Esq, the Commanders of the *English* Forces in *America* for the Execution of an Expedition against the *French Settlement* in *Hispaniola*, A. D. 1695.   165, 3

C U R T E S (*Martin*) his Art of *Navigation*, Engl. by *R. Eden*, A. D. 1572.
                                                                                    19, 3

St. C Y P R I A N his Epistle concerning the Redemption of the Brethren from Bondage of *Barbarians*. English'd. *A. D.* 1637.   82, 6

D.

D A L E (Sir *Thomas*) an Account of the State of *Virginia* under his Government. 56, 2, 5. and 57, 1, 2. An Account of his Return to *England*.   62, 4

D A L M A T I A ; an Account of Mr. *Henry Blunt*'s Travels thither. 83, 3

D A M A S C E N E (*Nicholas*) several Extracts out of his History concerning the Laws and Customs of all Nations.   53, 4

D A M A S C U S ; an Account of the Travels of 4 *English* Merchants belonging to the Factory at *Aleppo* and their Chaplain, thither, *A. D.* 1600 &c.   233, 3

The INDEX.

The INDEX.

The INDEX.

The INDEX.

The INDEX.

DOWN-

The INDEX.

D·U-

The *INDEX.*

demand Reparation from them, and they from the *English*, A.D. 1564.
115, 5. King *Charles* the Second's Declaration of *July* 29. 1667, concerning the restoring of all Places, Forts, &c. which his Subjects shall have taken or recovered from them after *May* 20th. last past. 120, 5.
See more under the Articles of *the Company of* Dutch *Merchants trading to the* East-Indies *and the States General of the United Provinces.*

E.

E ACHARD (*Lawrence*) his Compendium of *Geography.* 154, 3

The EARTH; Discourses concerning its Motion, by *P. Lansbergius*, A.D. 1630. 75, 4. By *Al. Rosse*, A. D. 1635. 240, 2. and *A. D* 1646. 24, 3, 3. An Hypothesis of the Structure of its internal Parts, proposed to the Royal Society, *A. D.* 1692. by *E. Halley.* 156, 5. Some brief Remarks on Mr. *Whiston's* new Theory thereof, &c. by *J. Edwards*, A. D. 1697. 171, 2

EARTHQUAKES; an Account of that which happened at *Naples*, &c. *June* 5. 1688. whereby about 40 Cities and Villages were either wholly ruined or extreamly damnified, 8000 Persons destroyed, and about 800 wounded. 259, 6. Of that at *Jamaica*, A. D. 1692. in a Letter from a Divine there. 158, 5. An Analogical Discourse of them, occasioned by one that happened on *Sept.* 8. 1697. 262, 2

E AST-INDIA *Company* ; See *Company of English Merchants trading to the* East-Indies.

E A S T-INDIA *Trade* , See *Trade to the* East-Indies.

E AST-INDIANS ; the Agreement of their Customs with those of the *Jews* and other ancient People, *A. D.* 1705. 194, 2

E A S T-INDIES ; an Account of the Navigation and Voyages of *Lewis Vertomannus* thither, *A. D.* 1503. 222, 4. An Account of the Debate and Strife between the *Spaniards* and *Portugals* about the Islands of *Moluccas*; and of the Sentence given by the Judges upon the Bridge of *Caya*, A D 1524. 223, 2. An Account of the first Discovery thereof by the *Portugals*, A.D. 1582. 24, 5. Instructions given by the Lords of the Council [in *England*] to *Edward Fenton*, Esq; for the Order to be observed in the Voyage, recommended to him thither, and to *Cathaya* A. D. 1582

X x x x

The INDEX.

The INDEX.

EDU.

The INDEX.

Y y y y

EPHE-

The INDEX.

The *INDEX*.

The INDEX.

The INDEX.

The INDEX

The INDEX.

FORT

The INDEX.

FORT St. GEORGE in the *East-Indies*: See *Society for promoting Christian Knowledge*.

FOSCARINUS (*Paulus Antonius*, a Carmelite Friar) his Treatise on the System of the *Pythagoreans* and *Copernicans*, concerning the *Earth* being moveable and the *Sun* fixed, and the new System of the World, wrote to F, *Seb. Fanton* the General of the *Carmelites* Order, A. D. 1615.   58, 2

FOTHERBY (*Robert*) his Voyage to *Greenland*, A. D. 1614.   57, 3

FOURNIER (*George*) his Description of the World.   99, 1

FOXE (*Edward*, Esq; Lieutenant General of the *Leeward* Islands): See *Hesketh*.

FOXE (*John*) his Sermon at the Baptizing of a *Jew* on *April* 1. 1577. 22, 1

FOXE (Capt. *Luke*) his Collection of Voyages to the *North-west Parts*, A. D. 1635.   80, 1

FOXE (*Richard*, Lord *Bishop of Durham*) The Commission of *Henry* VII. King of *England* to him and others, authorizing them to make Peace between him and *Philip*, Arch-Duke of *Austria*, A. D. 1495.   222, 3

FRAMPTON (*John*) his Account of the Commodities that are brought from the *West-Indies*, A. D. 1577. 21, 5. Another Edition enlarged, A. D. 1597.   36, 5

FRANC (*Augustin Hermannus*, Professor of Divinity at *Glaucha* near *Hall* in *Germany*) his Relation of the marvelous Footsteps of Divine Providence in the Founding and Building the *Hospital* there.   268, 7

FRANCE ; Descriptions thereof by *Anonymus*, A. D. 1627. 236, 2. *Iodocus Sincerus*, A. D. 1649. 99, 5. *Peter Heylyn*, A. D. 1656. 107, 4. A Manifesto of the Cardinal Infant of *Spain* for a War with *France* both by Sea and Land, A. D. 1635. 81, 2. A Letter from thence from one of the Duke of *Monmouth*'s Soldiers to his Friend in *London*, dated *May* 1. 1672. 128, 6. [See *New France*, *French*, and *Trade*.]

FRANCISCANS (the Order of) two *Bulls* of Pope *Clement* VIII. and *Urban* VIII. relating to several of them in the *East-Indies*. 41, 2. and 73, 4

The INDEX.

GALI-

The INDEX.

GEARE

The INDEX.

The

The I N D E X.

The INDEX.

The INDEX.

The I N D E X.

The INDEX.

H.

The INDEX.

HAMOR

The *INDEX.*

The INDEX.

E e e e e &c.

The INDEX

HE Y-

The INDEX.

The INDEX.

The INDEX.

Fffff   HOWARD

The INDEX.

The INDEX

I. J.

JACK-

The INDEX:

JAMES

The INDEX.

The INDEX.

JERL-

The INDEX:

IN-

The INDEX.

H h h h h   lation

The INDEX.

The INDEX.

ISELAND

The INDEX.

K.

KECKER-

The INDEX.

The INDEX:

The INDEX.

Kkkkk   N. S.

LINDSEY

L. O-

The INDEX.

The INDEX.

The INDEX.

M.

The INDEX.

The INDEX.

ing

MAYHEW

The INDEX.

Nnnnn   MEN-

MINES

The INDEX.

The

The INDEX.

MON-

M O N-

The INDEX.

N.

The INDEX.

NEVIS

The INDEX.

The INDEX.

The *INDEX*.

The INDEX.

The INDEX.

The INDEX.

ORDERS

The *INDEX*.

The INDEX.

The INDEX

PECHAM

The INDEX.

Ttttt   PENNIN-

The INDEX.

The INDEX.

The INDEX.

PLATE

The INDEX.

The INDEX.

The INDEX.

The INDEX.

The INDEX.

PYRAMIDS of *Egypt*. A Description thereof by *J. Greaves*. *A. D.* 1641.   85, 5

PYSIDIA. Travels thither by the Preacher, and several Gentlemen of the of the Factory of *Aleppo*. *A. D.* 1600, &c.   233, 3

Q.

QUAKERS. The Meditation of one wrote in a Prison at *Rome*. *A. D.* 1660. 114, 5. (in *Maryland*.) An Account of the false Judgment given by a Yearly Meeting of them, by *Geo. Keith*, &c. *A. D.* 1699. 161, 4. (in *New England*;) an Account of their Blasphemous Tenets and Prosecutions for them. 94, 1. 112, 4, 5. 113, 1. (in *Pensilvania*.) An Account of the Differences there, between Mr. *Keith*, Mr. *Penn*, &c. 157, 1. 161, 2, 3, 4, 5. 162, 1, 2. 164, 3. 179, 3. 262, 4. 267, 2. A Paper delivered to Mr. *Penn* on his Departure for *Pensilvania*, relating to the *Quakers* Religion. *A. D.* 1700.   179, 4

QUALITIES. An Account of the Nature of them, by *R. Boyle*. *A. D.* 1671.   252, 4

QUARANTAIN. A Proclamation by Q. *Anne*, of *Nov.* 9. 1710. enjoining all Ships coming from the *Baltick Sea* to perform it.   206, 1

QUEBEC. [See *Canada*.]

QUELPAERT (The Isles of) an Account of the *Shipwreck* of a *Dutch* Vessel on the Coast thereof.   190, 2

QUIR (*Petrus Ferdinandez de*) an Account of his Discovery of *Terra Australis Incognita*. *A. D.* 1612.   233, 2

QUO-WARRANTO's. An Order of Council, for issuing one out against the Charter of the Colony of *Massachuset's Bay* in *New England*. *A. D.* 1683. 139, 6. An Account of Mr. *Randolph's* carrying it.   140, 2

Yyyyy   RALEIGH

R.

RATH-

The INDEX.

The INDEX:

The INDEX.

The INDEX.

The INDEX.

SAL:

The INDEX.

The INDEX.

The INDEX.

The INDEX.

The INDEX.

The INDEX.

The INDEX.

The INDEX.

Orders

The INDEX

The INDEX.

The INDEX.

TAFFA

The INDEX.

TEIXERA

The INDEX.

The INDEX.

The INDEX.

The INDEX.

To

The INDEX.

The INDEX.

TUNKIN

The INDEX.

VLLE

The INDEX.

VEGA

The INDEX.

The INDEX.

The *INDEX*.

The INDEX.

W.

WADSWORTH (*James*) his Discovery of the *Spanish* Popery, and *Jesuitical* Stratagems in *Spain*. A. D. 1630. 75, 3. His Account of the Court of *Spain*. A. D. 1632. 238, 2

WAFER (*Lionel*) His Description of the *Isthmus* of *Darien*. A. D. 1704. 188, 5. An Extract from thence. 185, 6

WAGENER (*Zachary*) his Journal of his Voyages in thirty five Years, through *Europe*, *Asia*, *Africa* and *America*, beginning *June* 3. 1633. 78, 4

WAGER (Commodore) The Tryals of 2 Captains for their Misbehaviour under his Command, in a *Sea-Fight* with the *Spanish* Galleons. *A. D.* 1701. 201, 2

WALDSON (*Henry* Lieutenant-General of *Barbadoes*) The Address of the Grand Jury of *Barbadoes*, assembled before him *April* 2. 1683 140, 5.

WALES. A Scheme for erecting of Schools for those of the inferior Sort there. A. D. 1620. 66, 3. Proposals for erecting *lending Libraries* there, and dispersing Devotional Books in *English* and *Welsh* therein. *A. D.* 1708. 199, 3

WALL (Mr.) His and others Proposals for *Propagating the Gospel*, offered to a Committee of the House of Commons. A. D. 1652. 102, 5

WALLACE (*James*) his Description of the Isle of *Orpkney* ; an Essay concerning the *Thule* of the Ancients. *A. D.* 1693. 261, 4

WALLIS (*John*) his Edition of several Letters concerning the *Mathematicks*, between him and the Lord Viscount *Brouncker*, Sir *Kenelm Digby* and other Mathematicians. A. D. 1658. 110, 3. His Geometrical Discourse of the *Ship-wrights*, *Circular-wedge*. A. D. 1684. 143, 3

WALSING-

The INDEX.

The INDEX.

WELTON

The INDEX.

The INDEX.

WINGFIELD

The INDEX.

The INDEX.

X.

ZEM-

INDEX.

FINIS.
